Register in Alphabetical Order, of the Early Settlers of Kings County, Long Island, N. Y., From Its First Settlement by Europeans to 1700

REGISTER

In Alphabetical Order,

OF THE

Early Settlers of Kings County,

LONG ISLAND, N. Y.,

FROM ITS

First Settlement by Europeans to 1700;

WITH CONTRIBUTIONS TO THEIR BIOGRAPHIES AND GENEALOGIES, COMPILED FROM VARIOUS SOURCES.

By TEUNIS G. BERGEN,

Author of Bergen, Van Brunt, and Lefferts Genealogies.

NEW YORK:
S. W. GREEN'S SON, PRINTER, ELECTROTYPER AND BINDER.
1881.

PREFACE.

HAVING in my researches among the ancient and musty records and papers in possession of the old families of King's County (who have kindly favored me with the use of the same), gathered much genealogical and other information worthy of preservation and of use to future genealogists and historians, I take this method of endeavoring to effect that object, and of preserving the same for the use of the public, hoping that it will prove acceptable. To make the work more complete, the records of the state, county, towns, and churches have been carefully examined, and the name of every resident, and of landholders not resident therein found, inserted. That the work is so perfect as to contain the names of all such, the names of all their children, with correct dates in all cases, is not pretended, but an honest effort has been made to effect this object. Surnames and names of parents are in many cases enclosed in brackets.

Bay Ridge.   TEUNIS G. BERGEN.

ABBREVIATIONS USED IN THIS WORK.

A	acres.
ag	aged.
ass	assessed or assessment.
Ave	Avenue.
b	born.
bap. or bp	baptized
bd	bounded.
Bⁿ	Bronklyn.
Buͪ	Bushwick.
cal	calculation.
Cal. of Eng. Man	Calendar of English Manuscripts.
cen	census.
ch	church.
chil	children
cl	clerk.
co	county.
Col	Colonel.
Conn	Connecticut.
capt	captain.
con	conveyances.
cong	containing.
d	died.
da	dated.
dau. or da	daughter.
dec	deceased.
D. Ch	Dutch Church.
doc	documents.
Do	Dominie.
Ex	executors.
fl. or f	florens.
Flͪ	Flatbush.
Fldˢ	Flatlands.
Gᵈ	Gravesend.
Gen. Rec	Genealogical and Biographical Record.
gl	guilders.
His	history or historical.
I. or Id	Island.
Jˢ	Jamaica.
Ks. Co	King's County.
£	pounds.
$	dollars.
Lib. of Con	unless otherwise specified, refers to the books of conveyances on file in the office of the Register of King's County.
Lieut	Lieutenant.
L. I	Long Island.
m	married.
mag	magistrate.
man	manuscript.
me n	members.
mort	mortgage.
N. A	New Amsterdam.
N. L	New Lotts.
N. N	New Netherlands.
N. U	New Utrecht.
N. Y	New York.
off	office.
O. S	old style.
p	page.
Pa. or Penn	pence.
Pa. or Penn	Pennsylvania.
Philˢ	Philadelphia.
pro	proved.
R. D. Ch	Reformed Dutch Church.
rec	records or recorded.
Reg	Register.
s	son.
S	South.
S. I	Staten Island.
sec	secretary.
sh	shillings.
st	stivers.
sup	suppose.
surr	surrogate.
trans	translation
Va	Virginia
w	wife
wid	widow
y	years.

EARLY SETTLERS.

AARDSZ, RINIER, name on N. U. (New Utrecht) ass. roll of 1690. Overseer of Fl^h (Flatbush) in 1691.
Simon, see Vander Hard.

AATEN, ADRIAEN, see Arien Hendricksen Aten.
Hendrick, native, and on lists of oaths of allegiance in Fl^h of 1687. No further trace.
Thomas, native, and on lists of oaths of allegiance in Fl^h of 1687. *

AARTSE, JAN, see Middagh.

ABBE, SOLIMAN ; his wid. resided in 1659 on the S. side of the mill-house in Fl^h, as per p. 385 of Cal. of Dutch Man.

ABEL, STOFFEL JANSEN † of Bu^k (Bushwick) in 1664, as per p. 258 of Cal. of Dutch His. Man. There was a Stoffel Janse Abeel, master carpenter, in Beverwyck (Albany) in 1653, who m. Neeltje Janse, and d. after 1670, as per Pearson's Early Settlers of Albany, having children, Magdalena, b. 1653 ; Maria, b. 1656; Johanna, b. 1659; and Elizabeth.

ABELL, PIETER of G^d (Gravesend) in 1656, per Thompson's L. I. (Long Island). In 1657, John Hawse built a barn for him as per G^d town rec. (records).

---

* For oaths of allegiance of 1687 herein referred to, see a list on p, 659 of Vol. I. of documentary History of New York.
† Throughout this work the second name inserted of an individual is the name of his father, as " *Abel Stoffel Jansen*" represents Abel the son of Stoffel Jansen, or Abel Jansen, son of Stoffel Jansen. At the period of the early settlement of this country it was customary for individuals to add to their names that of their father, and omitting their surnames (many had none). On these pages the compiler has affixed to the names of individuals the names of their fathers, although in many cases not used by said individuals, for the purpose of aiding in identifying persons.

ABRAHAM or ABRAHAMSZ, ADRIAEN, see Hegeman.

Cornelis, on list of catechumens of Br^n (Brooklyn) R. D. ch. in 1662, as per said ch. rec.

Frans, of Bedford, m. 1st Nov. 3, 1680, in N. Y., Lucretia Hendricks; m. 2^d Nov. 13, 1705, in N. Y., Isabella Salamons. Took the oath of allegiance in Br^n in 1678 as a native. On Br^n ass. (assessment) roll of 1683, on cen. (census) of 1698.* Issue:—Abraham, bp. Oct. 30, 1681, in Fl^h; Anna Maria, bp. Oct. 10, 1683, in N. Y.; Jan., bp. Nov. 5, 1686, in N. Y.; Frans, bp. Oct. 9, 1706, in N. Y.; Ysabella, bp. Apl. 5, 1708, in Br^n; and Besbertje, bp. May 14, 1710, in Br^n.

Made his mark to documents.†

Hans. His name appears on a deed of freeholders of Br^n to Adrian Bennet of Jan. 2, 1696–7.

Joris, see Brinckerhoff.

John, see Lott.

William, on ass. roll of N. U. (New Utrecht) of 1693. He may be a son of Ab^m Willimse Van Westervelt.

ACEDLLAN, JAN, on deed of freeholders of Br^n to Adrian Bennet of Jan. 2, 1696–7.

ACKE, RICHARD. Oct. 6, 1660. Joan, his wife, as his attorney, sold a house and one-half an acre of land in G^d (Gravesend) to John Emans, as per town rec.

ACKERMAN or AKKERMANN, ABRAHAM, from Berlicum in the Majous or Hertegen-Bosch, a resident of Bedford, and on ass. roll of Br^n of 1683; m. May 28, 1683, in N. Y.; Altie Van Laren, or Luren, of Bedford. Ackermans reside in Bergen and Hudson counties, N. J., and in Dutchess Co., N. Y. Issue:— David, bp. May 11, 1684; Gerret, bp. May 3, 1685; Lysbeth, bp. May 19, 1689; Johannes, bp. Sep. 15, 1790; Anneken, bp. Dec. 27, 1691; and Anna Maria, bp. July 12, 1693, all bp. in N. Y.

ADAMS, see Brower.

ADLEY OR AUDLEY, EDMOND, of G^d (sup. English). Sept.

---

* The assessment rolls referred to in this work of 1675 are to be found in p. 470, and of 1683 on p. 493 of Vol. II. of the Doc. Hist. of N. Y. The census of 1698 is to be found on p. 133 of Vol. III. of said Doc. Hist.

† The marks made by individuals to documents are noted, and also copies of their signatures given in all cases which have come to the notice of the compiler.

6, 1646, he hired land of Anthony Jansen from Salee, as per His. Man. Ap¹ 21, 1651, he bought the plantation of Nathaniel Watsen in G⁴, as per town rec. Had a dau. Ann.

ADRIANSE, ANDREW, see Onderdonk.

ADRIAANSZ OR ADRIAENSEN, ABRAHAM, BENJAMIN, DENYSE, HENDRICK, ISAAC, JACOBUS, JOHN, JOSEPH, AND PETER, see Hegeman.

Arie, Adriaen, and Abraham, see Bennet.

Elbert, m. Ap¹ 18, 1689, Catalina dau. of Rem Janse Vanderbeek. Resided in N. L. (New Lotts), and a mem. of Flᵇ. R. D. ch. in 1677, in which town he took the oath of allegiance in 1687. Jan. 9, 1692–3, he bought of Aucke Janse Van Nuyse 20 morgens of land lying on the N. side of the highway in N. U. for 6,600 gl., as per p. 329 of Lib. D. of Flᵇ rec. Signed his name "*Elbert Adriaensen.*"

Jacob and Jan, see Bennet.

Jacob, (s. of Adriaen Pieterse Kinne) bp. Jan. 5, 1680 in Flᵇ and b. in Fld⁸ (Flatlands).* Mar. 22, 1695, he was apprenticed by his father to Jan Berdan to learn the weaver's trade. Finally settled in Franklin township, N. J.

Jan, a carpenter in Buᵏ in 1681, per town rec.

Joost, a miller; m. Mary Hays of Buᵏ about 1688, who after his death m. Capt. Pieter Praa of Newtown. On Buᵏ ass. roll of 1683. Issue:—Sara. A Joost Adriensen on the Delaware in 1658, as per p. 196 of Cal. of Dutch His. Man.

Martin (s. of Adn. Reyerse), b. Mar. 9, 1668; m. Sarah Remsen, dau. of Rem. Janse Vanderbeek; d. Oct. 30, 1754. Resided in Flᵇ, where he took the oath of allegiance in 1687, was known as Martin the boor or farmer, and was the ancestor of the Martense family of said town. Issue:—Rem Martense of Flᵇ, b. Dec. 12, 1695; Gerret Martense of Flᵇ, b. Dec. 24, 1698; Jannetje Martense, b. Jan. 31, 1702, m. May 18, 1720, Peter Stryker, of Flᵇ; Antje Martense, b. Nov. 5, 1705; and Adrian Martense of Flᵇ, b. Oct. 24, 1707, m. Neeltje——. Signed his name "*Martin Adriaens.*"

Willem, see Bennet.

AELBERTSEN, see Albertsen.

---

* The baptisms referred to in New Amsterdam, New York, Brooklyn, Flatbush, Flatlands, New Utrecht, Gravesend, Bushwick, and the N. J. churches, were generally administered in the Reformed Dutch churches of those localities, and taken from the records of said churches.

AELBURTUS, JAN, s. of Pieter Cæser, on Hegeman's books.[*] Made his mark in 1670 to documents. See Alburtis.

AELDERICKX, EVERT, a resident of Fl[h], Aug. 30, 1669, as per p. 173 of Lib. D. of Fl[h] rec.

AELES, JAN, borrowed Ap[r] 19, 1697, of the R. D. Ch. of N. U., 1,200 gl. as per ch. rec.

AESEN, SIMON, see De Hart.

AERNENSEN, RYN, allotted a meadow lot, Aug. 6, 1668, on the Fl[h] meadows at Canarisie, as per Fl[h] rèc. Probably the same individual as Reinier Aertse.

AERSEN or AERTSEN, AERT, DIRCK, GERRET AND JAN, (see Middagh).

AERTSE or AERSEN, CLAES, see Vechte.
Cornelis, Hendrick, Jacob, Jan, Jeremias and Rem, (see Vanderbilt).
Cornelis, sold land (sup.) in Fl[h] in 1675 to Do. Polhemius, as per p. 30 of Vol. VIII. of Dutch Man.
Huyck, see Van Rossum.
Jan, see Van Pelt.
Jan, immigrated in 1661, and took the oath of allegiance in Br[n] in 1687.
Jan from Utrecht.   Obtained a patent for land in Br[n] which was forfeited, and the premises patented Mar. 15, 1647, to Cornelius Van Tienhoven.
Petrus, see Van Pelt,
Reinier or *Reyndert,* emigrated in 1653, and took the oath of allegiance in Fl[h] in 1687; on ass. roll of Fl[h] of 1675, and held the office of Overseer of said town in 1681 and '82, as per p. 60 of Strong's Fl[h].   Signed his name " *Reynier Aertsen.*"
Reyn, on ass. roll of Br[n] in 1675.

AGASURES, HENDRICK, on Fl[h] ass. roll of 1683.

ALBERTSE, ALBERTSZ or ALBERTSEN, see Terhune and Voorhies.
Nicholas, of Fl[h], made his mark to documents in 1689. There was a Nicholas Albertsen, who was sentenced in 1658 for deserting his ship and betrothed bride after publication of bans, to have his head shaved, flogged, ears bored, and to work two years with the negroes, as per p. 195 of Cal. of Dutch His. Man.

---

[*] Hegeman's books, refer to the account books of Ad[n] Hegeman, the emigrant, as auctioneer &c., in hands of John Lefferts of Fl[h].

Renate, paid 2 gl. minister's salary in Fl^h in 1680, as per town rec.

Rut or *Rutgert*, m. Josina Verhagen, and had no issue. Jan. 13, 1689–90, he and his wife executed a joint will or nuptial agreement, by which it was provided that the survivor should have the use of their joint estates during life. If after his death she again marries, then she to give 50 gl. each to the two children of whom he is godfather, to wit, Albert Janse, s. of Jan Cornelise Boomgaert of Hackensack, and Albert Gerritse, s. of Gerrit Stoffelse of Yellow Hoek, N. U.: if she d. first, then he to give to her children, Jacobus Cornelise, Elizabeth Cornelise, and Cornelia Cornelise Van Oosten, the first 210 gl., and the others 200 gl. each, as per p. 146 of Lib. A of Fl^h rec. As a carpenter with Jan Aukuse (Van Nuyse), in 1678, contracted to do the carpenters' work on a parsonage house for Do. Van Zuuren in Fl^h for 1000 gl. wampum value (the building to be 46 ft. in length, 21 ft. in width, with 11 bents). with the constable and overseers of said town, as per p. 43 of Lib. AA of Fl^h rec. His name appears on the ass. roll of Fl^h of 1675, on list of ch. mem. of 1677, and cen. of 1698. Sold his house and lot in the village of Fl^h Aug. 22, 1679, to Catharine Cronenborgh, as per p. 54 of Lib. AA of Fl^h rec., and his will is dated Oct. 24, 1700, and recorded on p. 247 of Lib. A of said rec. He signed his name " *Rut Aelbertsen*."

The cost of the parsonage of which Aucke Janse Van Nuyse and Jan Suebringh appear to have had charge, as per p. 67 of Lib. AA of Fl^h rec. was as follows:

Paid to the (saw) miller at "Sicmeecky" for boards and "schade" (damages)	fl505
Nails to Mr Philips	430
Blacksmith work to Hendrick Ryke (Suydam)	340
Glazing or to the glazier	200
For 10,000 brick of Titus (Sirachs) at fl30	300
" 4,000 " by ourselves " fl25	100
" 4,000 " " A. Brouwer " fl25	100
" Masons' labor bill	400
" " Offerlieden" (assistance)	150
" " Kost gelt" (refreshments)	24
" the diggers	40
" frame timber and squaring the same, with 50 casks of lime and 2,000 shingles	800
" 3,000 shingles at fl60	180
" the kitchen	200
" Beer and wine	200
" the carpenters	1,250
" Cartage of 20 loads from "Sicmeecky"	160
" " " 8 " by Adam Brouwer	32
" " " 12 " " De Vries	24
" " " 100 " of field stone	150
Total cost	fl5,585

ALBURTUS, PIETER CÆSER, an Italian and native of Venice; m. Aug. 24, 1642, in N. A. Judith Janse Meynje, dau. of Jan Manje from Amsterdam. Resided at first in N. A. Obtained, June 17, 1643, a patent for a plantation of 24 morgens and 420 rods at the Wallabout, of which he sold in 1651 a part to Samuel Menjer; the remainder of which after his death was sold to Jan Damen. Issue:—Jan of Newtown, bp. Aug. 30, 1643, m. Elizbeth, dau. of John Scudder; Marler or Marles, bp. May 7, 1645; Aert of Newtown, bp. Ap^l 14, 1647; Marie or Margretie, bp. June 27, 1649, m. John P. Bant; Francyntje, bp. Ap^l 2, 1651, m. John Allen; and Willem, bp. Mar. 31, 1652, all bp. in N. A. (New Amsterdam).

In 1695 Jan and Willem Alburtus appointed Peter Cocke their attorney to sell their Wallabout farm of 100 A. (acres), as per p. 65 of Lib. 2 of con. His descendants reside principally in Queens Co., and N. J., some of whom use " Burtis" for their surname. Jan Alburtus made his mark to documents.

Reynier, defendant in a suit of Pieter Jansen, Jan. 13, 1662, as per Lib. B. of Fl^h court rec.

ALLDRIDG, WILLIAM (sup. English), sold, Mar. 20, 1651, to John Thomas his house and lot in G^d for 380 lbs. of merchantable tobacco, as per town rec. Signed his name "*William Alldridg.*"

AMACK, TEUNIS JANSE, emigrated in 1673, and took the oath of allegiance in Fld^s in 1687; m. (sup.) Eyke   ; on ass. rolls of Fld^s of 1683 and '93. Removed to N. J., (sup.) to have been a mem. of the D. ch. of Marlboro in 1723, his descendants residing in that vicinity. Issue:—Jan, m. Mary, dau. of Andrew Johnson, whose will is da. Jan. 23, 1709, pro. June 21, 1721, having children, Jonatye, Andrew, and Teunis, who m. Lena or Helena Laan.

Thomas Janse, on ass. roll of and buried in Fld^s in 1693, per ch. rec.

AMELAND, DERCK JANSE, a juryman in 1699, per court rec.

AMERMAN, ALBERT (DIRCKSE), on ass. roll of Fld^s of 1693 and cen. of 1698. Removed to Monmouth Co., N. J., and in 1713 was a mem. of the R. D. ch. of Freehold; m. Geertje   . Issue:—Jannetje, bp. May 29, 1705, in Br^n; and Paulus, bp. June 13, 1712, at Freehold.

Derick, Janse, emigrated in 1650 and settled in Fld^s; m. Aeltje Paulus Vander Beeck. Mem. of R. D. ch. of Fld^s and deacon in 1682, and elder in 1703; took the oath of

allegiance in said town in 1687, on ass. roll of 1693 and cen.
of 1698. In 1689 was appointed ensign of militia of Fld^e
by Gov. Leisler, and in 1690 capt.* Will da. Sep. 20, 1709,
pro. Feb. 1, 1723, rec. p. 438 Lib. 9, N. Y. surr. off. Issue:—
Catharine or Cantie Derckse, bp. Ap^l 2, 1677, (sup.) m.
Hendrick Gulick; Anke or Annetje Derckse, bp. Oct. 30,
1681, in Fl^h; Isaac Derckse of Fld^e, bp. Sep. 2, 1683, in Fl^h,
m. Grietje Wyckoff; Gerbrecht Derckse, bp. Ap^l 3, 1685, in
Fldⁿ; Paulus Derckse; Jacobus Derckse; Aeltje Derckse, m.
Auke Van Nuyse of N. U.; Jan Derckse; Albert Derckse;
and Marike Derckse. Signed his name "*Derck Jansen
Amerman.*"

Jacobus Derckse of Fld^e, m. Nov. 1, 1712, Magdaleentje
Janse. Was a deacon in the D. ch. of Fld^e in 1720, '22, '25,
'26, '27, and 29. No trace of issue.

Jan Derckse of Fld^e, b. 1674; m. 1st Maria Wyckoff; m.
2^d Sara   . ; d. May 2, 1757. Will da. Ap^l 1st, 1747,
pro. Aug. 9, 1758, rec. p. 78, Lib. 21, N. Y. surr. off. Issue:—
Sara, bp. May 29, 1705, in Brⁿ, (sup.) m. Aug. 5, 1727, Peter
Wyckoff of Fld^e; Derick of Fld^e, m. Margaret Polhemius;
Jan, Junr, of Fld^e, m. Jan. 13, 1748, Lammetje Stryker;
Petrus of Fld^e, b. May 29, 1716, m. Nov. 3, 1753, Willemtje
Schenck; and Nicholas. His descendants are scattered, and
few if any are left in Fld^e. The farm of Petrus Amerman
is now (1879) owned by Jeremiah Ryder.

Isaac Derckse of Fld^e, bp. Sep. 2, 1683; m. May 9, 1718,
Grietje Wyckoff. Deacon in Fldⁿ R. D. ch. in 1716 and '18.
No trace of his descendants.

Paulus Derckse of Fld^e, m. Dec. 1, 1699, Cornelia Emans
of G^d. In 1699 a mem. of Fld^e R. D. ch. Appears to have
resided in G^d in 1700, at which date he sold land there to
Cor^e Van Cleef as per G^d rec. Suppose he finally settled
in Monmouth Co., N. J. No trace of his descendants.
Signed his name "*Pooulues Amernmen.*"

ANDERS, JAN, paid 9 gl. 8 st. minister's salary in Fl^h in
1680, per town rec.

ANDRIESEN OR ANDRIESZ, ANDRIES. See Onderdonk.
Andries, Abraham and Anthony, see Emans, and see Andries
Janse.
Arent, m. Magdalena Jans; also m., Nov. 8, 1695, in N. Y.,
Helena Adrians from Achterkol. On ass. roll of Bu^k of

---

* For military and civil appointments or commissions from 1685 to
1700, see Calendar of English Manuscripts. edited by E. B. O'Callaghan,
Albany, 1866.

1693, and cen. of 1698. Paid towards the minister's salary in Fl^h in 1681.

Arie, on ass. roll of Fl^h of 1675. (Probably an Onderdonk.)

Benjamin, see Emans.

David, occupied a plantation on the East River and Norman's Kil (Williamsburg), patented May 15, 1647, to John Forbes, as per p. 46 and 375 of Cal. of Dutch His. Man.

Derck of Bu^k, m. July 11, 1695, in N. Y., Femmetje Lorek, or Leek, of said city, a resident of Bu^k at date of m. On ass. roll of Bu^k of 1693 and cen. of 1698. There was a Dirk Andriese in Albany in 1661.

Jacobus and Jan, see Emmans.

Jan, on ass. roll of Fl^h of 1693, and cen. of 1698. Paid towards the clergyman's salary in 1681. Signed his name " *Jan Anderiese*" in 1701.

Jurian (s. of Andries Janse Jurianse), on ass. roll of Br^n of 1693 and cen. of 1698. Land conveyed to him in Br^n in 1695, by Annetje Para, wid. of Jan Evertse Bout, as per Vol. I., p. 99, of Stiles's His. of Br^n.

Lammert or Lambert, m. Lea ——. On ass. roll of Br^n of 1693, and cen. of 1698. Was probably a son of Andrew Janse Jurianse of Br^n, and his lands were N. of the Mill creek, adjoining those of Jan Evertse Bout. Made his mark to documents.

Martin, on ass. roll of Fl^h of 1693 and cen. of 1698.

ANOLEY, EDMUN, (sup.) English, agreed, Mar. 6, 1651, with Nathaniel Watson for the purchase of his house and lot in G^d for 100 gl., as per town rec. Probably intended for Edmond Adley.

ANTHONYS, CHRISTIAN, of N. U., b. 1622. His name appears on an affidavit relating to "Capt. Schott's" (Scott's) raid in 1664 in Kings Co., as per Vol. II., p. 180, of Doc. of Col. His. There was a Christian Anthony who m. Engeltje Jacobs, and had issue:—Anthony, bp. Apl. 4, 1659, and Ytie, bp. Jan. 25, 1662, in N. A. Made his mark to documents.

ANTHONIZE, AERT. See Middagh.

ANTOINE, CHARLES, of Bu^k, m. Katrina Baaly. Sick in bed, Aug. 1, 1687, and made his will, as per p. 82 of Vol. I. of Con.

APPLEBY OR APPELBURY, THOMAS of G^d (sup.) English, made his mark to documents in 1651. Genl Washington occupied the house of Joseph Appleby near White Plains in Westchester Co. in 1781.

William of G^d, m. Nov. 24, 1680, Deborah Janse Buys, of said town, as per town rec. Issue : Abagail, bp. Feb. 26, 1682 ; and Jannetje, bp. Sep. 23, 1683, at Br^n.

APPLEGATE, ARES, of G^d, in 1679, (sup.) English. Signed his name "*Ares Appellgate.*" An "Arien Appell" took the oath of allegiance to the English in 1664, as per p. 74 of Vol. iii. of Doc. of Col. His.

Bartholomew of G^d, m. Oct., 1650, at G^d, Hannah Patricke. On list of inhabitants of said town of 1650. Aug. 10, 1667, he bought of Nathan Whitman plantation lot N° 12, in G^d, as per town rec. From an entry on the G^d rec. of Nov. 6, 1671, setting forth that "whereas the Governour was pleased to order Wm Wilkins to pay ten pounds towards the release of Hanna Apelgate and her child, this sheweth that Thos Whitlock received of Mr Delavall five pounds of the aforesaid som$ǫne, of the wch the said Thomas delivered five pounds to the constable and overseers of Gravesend in red cloth," etc., it may be inferred that she was in the hands of the Indians, and that the money and red cloth were used for her ransom, Mar. 8, 1674, as per p. 694 of Doc. of Col. His. of N. Y., the Gov. Genl., Antony Colve, and his council, on petition, granted leave to " Bartholomew Appelgadt, Thomas Appelgadt, and Richard Sadler " to purchase from the Indians a tract of land about two "leagues on this side of Middle Towne, near the Neversings, fit for a settlement of 6 or 8 families," on condition that after the purchase a patent be taken out, and the settlements be made within two years on pain of forfeiture. In April John Bowne and Richard Hartshorne, and others, gave notice that the land granted was within the bounds of their patent.* See pp. 694 and 706 of Vol. II. of Doc. of Col. His. of N. Y. Signed his name "*Bartholmel Aplegate.*"

---

* The patentees of the large tract including Monmouth Co., N. J., as per p. 45 of Whithead's East N. J., were "Wm Goulding, Saml Spicer, Richd Gibbins, Richd Stout, James Grover, John Bowne, John Tilton, Nathl Sylvester, Wm Reape, Walter Clarke, Nich^s Davis, and Obediah Holmes;" and their associates, as per the Rev. G. C. Schenck, were: John Throckmorton, Peter Easson, Thomas Winterton, Richard Lippincott, Emmanuel Wooley, Wm Shaddock, Ed. Wharton, Richd Borden, Wm James, Robt Carr, Thos Potten, Geo. Webb, John Coggshall, Wm Codingten, Thos Clifton, Henry Bull, Saml Hollman, Nich^s Browne, Richd Richardsen, Chris^r Almy, Jonathan Holmes, John Cooke, Geo. Chate, Marke Lucee, Stephen Arnold, Ed. Smith, Wm Shabberly, Roger Ellis & son, Eliakim Wardell, Edward Tart, Ed. Pattison, Bar-

John, on lists of residents of G^d of 1650, as per town rec., and in 1656, as per Thompson's L. I. In 1661 a John Applegate, was charged with smuggling in N. A., as per p. 228 of Cal. of Dutch His. Man. In 1663 there was a John Applegate among the freeholders of Oysterbay. In 1696 Avis or Aevis, his wife, of Fairfield, Conn., as his attorney, sold land in G^d to Joseph Goulding, as per p. 112 of Lib. 2 of Con., and as per G^d rec. Signed his name "*John Applegate.*"

Thomas, in N. A. as early as 1641, bought John Ruckman's patent in G^d, Nov. 12, 1646, as per G^d rec. Jan. 1, 1651, he was sentenced to have his tongue bored through with a red-hot iron, and to publicly acknowledge his transgression in charging the Director - General with bribery. After making a public acknowledgment he was pardoned. There was a Thomas Appelgate among the patentees of Flushing of 1645.

The Appelgates left G^d, and settled in Monmouth and Middlesex counties, N. J. Signed his name "*Thomas Appelgate.*"

ARBUTHNOT, DAVID, of G^d in 1656 (sup. English), as per Thompson's L. I.

ARENDES, ARENT, paid 2 gl. 9 st. clergyman's salary in Fl^b in 1680, as per town rec.

ARENDSZ. See Vechten.

ARENTS OR ARENTSEN, KLAES, bought, Jan. 5, 1665, O. S., of Hendrick Jansen Oesterstroem, a house and lot on the W. side of the road in Fl^b, lying to the S. of the other land

---

tholomew West, Robt West, Thos Whislord, John Horabin, Ja^s Bowne, John Willson, John Bushmann, John Townsend, Henry Tippitts, Tobiah Handson, John Haunce, Francis Brindley, Walter Wall, Job Almey, Joseph Coleman, Wm Bowne, John Smith, John Bowne, Ed. Thurston, Jn. Allen & Robt Taylor, John Jenkins, Rochery Gant, Nathl Thompkins, Benjamin Speere, Jos^h Bryce, Geo. Mount, Ben. Bordin, Richd Sissell, Dan. Gould & Jos. Cogshall, Gerard Bourre, Gideon Fairborne, Robt Hazard, Jos^h Wood, Thos Hart, John Tomson, Ed. Cole, Robt Storey, Wm Gifford, James Leonard, Thos Dungon, John Homdell, Marmaduke Ward, Richd Moore, Ralph Goldsmith, and James Ashton. A majority of the above individuals, it is supposed, did not become actual settlers, but the descendants of many of them are yet to be found residing within the boundary of the patent. This patent was granted by Gov. Nicolls, Apr^l 8, 1665; it led to the settlement of Middletown and Shrewsbury, was disallowed by the Duke of York, but subsequently Gov. Carteret and council compromised with the claimants, who received individual grants for their lands, as per pp. 46 and 74 of said Whithead's " E. N. J."

of said Klaes, as per p. 13 of Lib. D. of Fl^h rec.   There was a Claes Arentse Toers in Bergen, N. J., as early as 1664 (of which place in 1674 he was schout), whose descendants reside in that locality, and who may have been this Klaes; or it is possible that this Klaes may be Claes Arents Vechte. A Claes Arentse and Lammetje Hendricks had a s. Arent bp. Mar. 2, 1662, in N. A.

Huyck, of Fld^a in 1668, per town rec.

Kyn, owned a village plot in Fl^h in 1681, as per p. 92 of Lib. A of Fl^h rec.

Leendert, of Fld^a in 1688, per Col. Man.   Issue:—Albert Leendertse; Arent Leendertse; Affie Leendertse; Cornelia Leendertse; and Maritie Leendertse, as per Fl^h town rec. July 16, 1674, Albert Leendertse de Grau, widower, m. Marretje Hendricks. If this is the above Albert, their family name is De Grau.

Reinier, Reyndert, or Reyn, m. 1st Annetje Hermans; m. 2^d, in 1666, Jannetje Aukes (Van Nuyse). Mar. 28, 1670, he bought of Ab^m Jorise (Brinckerhoff) a farm of 25 morgens, with meadows and plain land, in Fl^h on the W. side of the road between the farm of Do. Megapolensus and that of Jan Snedeker. Name on ass. roll of Fl^h of 1683, cen. of 1698, and a deacon in Fl^h ch. in 1682. Issue:—Tryntje, m. Ap^l 20, 1689, Nich^s Thomasse Van Dyck; and Aerenout by 1st wife; Auke Reiniesse; Barbara, bp. Dec. 26, 1679, at Fl^h; Adriaentje, bp. Mar. 12, 1682, at Br^n; Geertruy, bp. June 27, 1684; and Theunis, bp. Mar. 29, 1696, at Br^n. By his ante-nuptual agreement of Ap^l 28, 1666, with Jannetje Aukes, it appears that at that date he had but one child, Aerenout, living, as per Fl^h rec. Signed his name "*Reynier Arents.*"

Ryk, allotted woodland in N. L. in 1701, as per p. 66 of Lib. B of Fl^h rec.

ARIAENSE OR ARIAENSEN, ANDRIES.   See Onderdonk.

Jan, on ass. rolls of Bu^k of 1675 and '76. A Jan Ariaensen and Styntje Jans had children, Magdalena and Maria, twins, bp. May 23, 1673, in N. Y.

Aric, Jacob, Jan, and William, see Bennet.

ASHLEY, GEORGE, capt. (English), bought, Oct. 30, 1651, of John Morrill his two plantations in G^d, as per town rec.

ASKE OR ASQUE, JAN (sup. English), contracted in 1660 to build dams in G^d, as per p. 217 of Cal. of Dutch His. Man. Jan. 5, 1670, he bought a house and lot in G^d of Thos. Delavall, as per G^d rec.

ASUERUS HENDRICK, m. *Marretje Jans.* A tavern keeper in 1661, in N. A., fined for illegally selling liquors, as per p. 226 of Cal. of Dutch Man. On ass. roll of Fld[s] of 1675. Issue:—Hendrick, bp. May 31, 1678; and Lysbeth, bp. May 11, 1680.

AST OR ASTE, RICHARD, (English), b. 1604; m. *Joan* ——. Transported in 1634 from London to Va., as per p. 37 of Hotten's lists of emigrants. Leased, Ap[l] 2, 1660, of Nich[s] Stillwell 12 A. of the plantation Stillwell bought of Anthony Jansen from Salee, lying on the E. end of said plantation, as per G[d] rec. Oct. 6, 1660, his w. as his attorney sold half an acre of land with buildings in G[d] to John Emans, as per G[d] rec. Made his mark to documents.

ATEN ADRIAEN, HENDRICKSE, m. *Elizabeth,* wid. of Gysbert Lubbertse. Bought, Mar. 27, 1680, of Jan Strycker a house plot in Fl[h], as per p. 39 of Lib. A of Fl[h] rec. Took the oath of allegiance in Fl[h] in 1687. With his w. made a joint will, Mar. 20, 1696, rec. p. 224 of Lib. A of Fl[h] rec. Issue:— Marritie. Signed his name "*Arien Hendrickson Aten.*"
Jan or Yan, allotted woodland in N. L. in 1701, as per p. 67 of Lib. B of Fl[h] rec. Some of his and Adriaen's descendants reside in Somerset Co., N. J. Signed his name "*Yan Aten.*"

AUCKERS, STOFFEL, bought a wagon of Jan Tomasse Van Dyck, of N. U., in 1695, as per town rec.

AUDLEY, see Adley.

AUGER, NICHOLAS, m. Sep. 14, 1684, at Fld[s], Maria Quelek of Br[n], as per ch. rec.

AUCKES, AUKE, or AUKERSZ, see Van Nuyse.

AULDRIDGE, WILL, (sup. English), owned a meadow lot in G[d] in 1650, as per town rec.

BACKER, ANDRIES, of Bu[k] in 1662, per p. 332 of Vol. II. of Stiles's Br[n].
Claes Janse, see Nicholas Janse.
Gerret Hendrick. Mar. 1, 1660, with others, made application for leave to form a village in the vicinity of the Wallabout, as per Col. Doc.
Henry, of Bu[k], where he owned land in 1662, as p. 332 of Vol. II. of Stiles's Br[n].

Hendrick Willemse, owned land in Br^n in 1661, as per p. 155 of Vol. II. of Thompson's L. I. He was a baker in N. A. in 1658, in which year he made a contract to bake for the government, as per Dutch Man.; and in 1674 owned a house and land in Willemstadt, in the colony of Renselaerwyck. Backers reside in Dutchess Co.

Jacob, allotted a plantation in N. U. among the first settlers in 1657, which in 1660 was forfeited in consequence of being unoccupied, and patented to Nicasius De Sille. This plot appears to have been located adjoining the patent of Anthony Jansen from Salee. There was a Jacob Backer from Amsterdam, b. 1631, a trader in N. A., as early as 1655, supposed to have emigrated in 1653, who m. Oct. 30, 1655, Margaret Stuyvesant, had several children bp. in N. A., and afterwards became a bankrupt, deserting his w., as per p. 265 of Lib. I of Con. Also a Jacob Backer who m. Dec. 6, 1670, per G^d rec., Barbara Gysberts of N. U. A Jacob Backer took the oath of allegiance to the English in 1664. Signed his name "*Jacob Backer.*"

Nicholas, on ass. roll of Br^n in 1675, for 18 morgens of land. "Claes Jansen" and Andries Jurianse, heirs of Jan Evertse Bout, sold in 1673 a house and lot to Capt. Nicolls for 3000 fl. wampum, as per p. 672 of Vol. II. of Doc. of Col. His. He took the oath of allegiance to the English in 1664, as a resident of N. Y.* Suppose this Nicholas to be the Nicholas Janse, baker, who m. July 23, 1670, Marretje Gerrets. Issue:—Johannes, bp. Oct. 27, 1652, in N. A.

BAERDAEN, YAN, supposed to have plied his trade as weaver in Fld$^•$ in 1699, for in that year Adriaen Kenne apprenticed his son, Jacob Adriaense, to him to learn said trade. A Jan Berden, and "Eva Van Siggalen" his w., of Hackensack, N. J., in 1700. Signed his name " *Yan Baerdaen.*"

BAES, CLAES MELLES, see Claes Melles Van Baes.

Wein, or Ariaen, paid 5 gl. 12 st. clergyman's salary in Fl^h in 1680, as per town rec.

B'AEWNTSSE, CORNELIS, sold a horse in 1695 to Symon Hansen (Van Noortstrand) of Fl^h, as per town rec.

BAILEY, THOMAS, see Bayles.

---

* For list of oaths of allegiance to the English by residents of the city of N. Y., see p. 24 of Vol. II. of Doc. of Col. His. of N. Y.

BAKER, JOHN, (sup. English,) owned land in G⁴ in 1644, as per Stoothoff papers.* His wid. in 1700 had lot N° 22 assigned to her in the meadow penny lots. The penny lots of salt meadows in G⁴ in the "Long Fly and the Cedar Neck, Hugh Gerretsen's and Hog Point," were laid out by Peter Cortelyou May 25, 1700, into 30 lots. The following is a list of the persons to whom were assigned the "Long Fly and Cedar Neck" lots:

Capt. N. Stillwell...Nos. 1, 2, 3, 4		Stoffel Romeyn............No. 18
Elyas Hubbard................	5	Cor⁴ Van Cleef................	19
Steven Coerte..........	6	Jochem Gulick................	20
Joseph Golder................	7	Reinier Van Sicklen..........	21
Barent Juriansen.............	8	Wid. Baker................ ...	22
Capt. Stillwell................	9	Symon Romeyn.......... ...	23
Barent Juriansen.............	10	Wyntje Stryker................	24
J. Griggs.....................	11	James Hubbard................	25
Sam¹ Gerretsen...............	12	Reinier Van Sicklen..........	26
John Simonsen...	13	Symon Romeyn................	27
J. Poling, for Emans..........	14	Samuel Hubbard..............	28
J. Griggs.....................	15	Wᵐ Williamson................	29
J. Poling.....................	16	John Griggs..................	30
Steven Coerte..............	17		

He also owned salt meadows in Fld⁸ in 1697, as per deed of Alexʳ Sympson to Albert Coerten (Voorhies) on p. 137 of Lib. 2 of Con.

Henrich Welmsen, bought land in Buᵏ of Joost Casperse Feb. 28, 1667, per Buᵏ rec. (See Hendrick Willemse.)

, BAL, BARENT JANSE, m. Nov. 22, 1652, in N. A., *Anneken Pieters Soogemackelyck;* d. prior to 1660. He and Hendrick Dircksen leased Rem Jansen Vanderbeek's patent at the Wallabout Aug. 31, 1651, for 4 years, as per p. 55 of Cal. of Dutch Man. In 1657 he was assessed in Gowanus for Do. Polhemius's salary, as per Vol. I. p. 134 of Stiles's Brⁿ. Made his mark to documents.

Thomas, on an account of expenses incurred for repairs of Flʰ ch. in 1665 he was paid 12 gl., as per Flʰ town rec.

BALDEN, GEORGE, (sup. English,) bought Aug. 25, 1655, of Mary Whitlock, attorney of John Whitlock, a parcel of land with buildings in G⁴, as per town rec. Made his mark to documents.

BALE, VINCENT, emigrated in 1683, and took the oath of allegiance in Buᵏ in 1687.

---

* The Stoothoff papers referred to are the account-books of Elbert Elbertse and Gerret Stoothoff of Flatlands, who at an early date appear to have kept a country store, which books and papers are in the possession of the compiler.

BALTES, JAN CLAESEN, defendant in a suit by Jacob Huyges Aug. 27, 1659, as per Lib. B of Fl^h court rec.

BALTUS, BARENT, m. *Eeggeyn Poulus.* Apl. 7, 1660, Tymen Van Vleck, as attorney for his children (he being dec.), was plaintiff in a suit against his wid., who m. Isaac Classen, as per p. 21 of Lib. B of Fl^h court rec.

BALYON or BALJON, PIETER, see Billou and Bellew.

BARBIER, CLAUDE, and Anthony Jeroe sold Jan. 7, 1653, to Jacob Steendam land on the W. side of Mespat Kils in Bu^k, as per p. 376 of Cal. of Dutch Man.
Jacob France and Pieter Lamothe cultivated land together in Bu^k in 1662, per town rec.

BARCHSTOEL, PHILIP, and others petitioned Mar. 1, 1660, for liberty to form a village in the vicinity of the Wallabout.

BARDULPH, CORNELIS, a commissioner of Fl^h in 1680, as per p. 60 of Strong's Fl^h. Referred to on p. 48 of Furman's Br^n.

BARENDS, BARENTS, BARENTSE, or BARENDSZ, ANDRIES, m. Jan. 24, 1666, *Grietje Cregiers.* On muster-roll of Bu^k militia of 1663. An Andries Barentsen, a soldier in N. A., had a wife, Macheltje Martens, who was assisted in 1651 to join her husband, as per p. 76 of Cal. of Dutch Man. ·
Baltus, of Fl^h in 1663, as per p. 256 of Cal of Dutch Man.; on ass. roll of Fl^h of 1675.
Barent or *Barend,* m. May 16, 1684, Catharine, dau. of Jan Gerretse Van Markken of Fl^h. 'On ass. roll of Fl^h of 1675.
Cornelis and Kornelia Hendriks had a s. Hendrick bp. Nov. 2, 1680, and a s. Jontse bp. the same day in Br^n. (See Barent Johnson, and Van Wyck.)
Beg, of Br^n ferry July 27, 1647, per His. Man.
Bruyn, wounded in 1656, as per p. 191 of Cal. of Dutch Man. His heirs obtained Oct. 4, 1658, a patent for a house and garden-plot near the burying-ground of the R. D. ch. in Br^n, as per p. 385 of Cal. of Dutch Man.
Ceaser, on muster-roll of Bu^k militia in 1663, per town rec.
Claes and *Jan,* see Bloom.
Claes, on ass. roll of Fl^h of 1663. Bought wood lot No. 37 in New Lotts, Dec. 27, 1677, of Minnie Johannis, as per p. 17 of Lib. AA of Fl^h rec.

Claes, took the oath of allegiance in Br^n in 1687 as a native, of which place he was a mag. in 1688, as per Furman's notes of Br^n.

Cornelis, see Van Wyck and Van der Wyck.

Cornelis, m. Kornelia Hendricks. On ass. roll of Fl^h of 1683. Issue:—Hendrick and Jontse, bp. Nov. 2, 1680, in Kings Co. Signed his name "*Cornelis Barens*" in Fl^h in 1663.

Frans Pastoor. A Frans Barentsen was in Albany as early as 1651, as per p. 55 of Cal. of Dutch Man., who in Aug. 1654 was a commissary, and for several years a magistrate of the place. Aug. 6, 1663, he bought of "Aelbert Kuÿnen" a farm with plain and meadow land in Fl^h on the W. side of the highway, as per p. 141 of Lib. D of Fl^h rec. His name appears on the patent of said town of 1667, as per p. 23 of Strong's Fl^h. There was a Frans Barentsen and Delia Bringman his w. who had a s. Benjamin bp. Jan. 7, 1663, in N. A. ; and a Frans Barentsen who owned property on the Delaware and was dead in 1678, as per p. 354 of Cal. of Dutch Man. Signed his name "*Frans Barents Pastoor*."

Hendrick (Smit), a mag. of Bu^k in 1673; on ass. roll of said town of 1673, and on ass. roll of G^d of 1676. Chosen constable of Bu^k in 1666.

Jan, see Van Driest, Bloom, and Johnson.

Jan, on ass. roll of Fld^s of 1675; m. Marretje Symonse (sup.) Van Aersdalen prior to 1684. Issue:—Rachel, bp. Sept. 18, 1681.

Joost and *Joostje*, see Barent Jansen.

Johannes, on ass. roll of Fl^h of 1675, and mem. of Fl^h R. D. Ch. in 1677. Made his mark to documents in 1700.

Lambert, m. Sept. 26, 1660, Lena Dirks of Br^n.

Pastoor Frans, see Frans Barents.

Smit Hendrickse, on ass. roll of Bu^k of 1683.

William. June 23, 1642, Burger Joris leased to William Barentsen and Robert Edens his land and stock on L. I., as per p. 19 of Cal. of Dutch Man. In 1680 his name appears on the account-books of Elbert Elbertse Stoothoff.

BARENS or BARNSZ, JAN, on ass. roll of Fl^h of 1675.

Cornelis, see Cornelis Barends.

BARKELO, BARKALOO, BARKULO, BORCKELLOO or VAN BARKELOO.

Coenrad Willemse, bp. Dec. 5, 1680; d. 1754; (sup.) m. a da. of *Jacob Laen* of Monmouth Co., N. J. Settled on the

Raritan near Six Mile Run. Issue:—Mary, bp. Apl. 25, 1711; (sup.) Coenrad, m. Sara ——; and Daniel.

Daniel Willemse of Fld⁵, m. May 4, 1700, Lysbeth Gerretse. Probably removed to N. Y. Issue:—Jacomyntie, bp. Mar. 25, 1701, m. Abᵐ Ten Eyck; Elizabeth, bp. Nov. 17, 1702; and Marretje, bp. Mar. 1, 1705—all bp. in N. Y.

Dirk Willemse, b. in Fld⁵; on ass. roll of Fld⁵ of 1676; m. Sept. 17, 1709, Jannetje Van Aersdalen of Fld⁵; d. in 1744. Settled near Freehold, N. J., and mem. of Freehold R. D. ch. in 1711. Issue:—Aelke or Aeltie, bp. Oct. 30, 1710, m. Jan Wyckoff of N. J.; Elisabet, bp. May 11, 1712, m. Ryck Suydam; William of upper Freehold, bp. Jan. 16, 1715, m. Nov. 24, 1736, Anitie or Aeltie Willemse; Cornelius, bp. Nov. 17, 1717, m. Nov. 10, 1743, Jannetje Amack; Daniel of Freehold, bp. Jan. 1, 1721, m. Oct. 17, 1744, Antje Luyster; Helena, bp. Dec. 22, 1723, m. Isaac Voorhies; Jannetie, bp. Jan. 1, 1727, m. Isaac Sutphen; Maria or Mary, bp. Oct. 5, 1732, m. 1ˢᵗ Abᵐ Sutphen, m. 2ᵈ Anthony Hulsart—all bp. in N. J.

Harman Janse (Van Barkalo), m. Willemtje Eldringh, and d. prior to 1672. Emigrated with his brother Willem Janse in 1662. He bought a house and lot in N. U. Feb. 17, 1667, of Johannes Gowenburgh, as per p. 233 of Vol. 3 of deeds in office of Secʸ of State in Albany. Issue:—Hans Harmanse; and Jannetje Harmanse, who m. Hendrick Janse Van Dyck. Made his mark to documents.

Hans Harmanse, (sup.) emigrated in 1662 in the ship Trouw with w. and 2 children; m. 2ᵈ, May 12, 1672, Willemtje Wanderse or Waermerse; d. Oct. 26, 1700, in N. J. Bought a farm in N. U. Oct. 30, 1677, of Hendrick Matthyse Smack, to which he probably removed; also bought Apl. 6, 1669, of Balthazer de Vos the patent of Albert Albertse (Terhune) of 24 morgens in N. U., as per town rec. In 1690 he bought the plantation of Adriaen Willemse Bennet in said town. His name appears on the ass. roll of N. U. of 1675, and he held the office of overseer of said town in 1677, '80, and '81. In 1681 he appears to have removed to Constables Hoek on the Kils in N. J., where he d. See p. 75 of Winfield's Hudson Co. Land Titles. Issue:— Antje or Annetje, m. Claes Vreeland of N. J.; Tryntje, m. Peter Van Buskerk of N. J.; and Hartman, m. Apl. 1, 1697, Maria Cortelyou—all of N. J. Signed his name "*Hans Harmensen.*"

Jan (Willemse), took the oath of allegiance in Gᵈ in 1687 as a native. No further trace.

Willem Janse, emigrated from Borculo in the earldom of Zutphen and province of Gelderland as early as 1657, residing first in N. A., afterwards in Fld², on the ass. rolls of which town his name appears in 1676 and '83, and probably finally removed to G⁴. He m. (probably a 2⁴ w.) about 1666 Lysbet or Elizabeth Jans wid. of Christoffel Jans, and was by occupation a butcher. Jan. 5, 1664, he bought of the heirs of Loras Pieterse for 640 gl. a parcel of land and buildings in G⁴, as per town rec. After residing in this country some years, he appears to have visited his fatherland, and in 1662 returned accompanied by Harmen Jansen van Barckelo and family, and Adriana Hendricks van Barckelo, as per p. 298 of Cal. of N. Y. His. Dutch Man. Issue: —Jannetje Willemse, b. in N. A., m. May 18, 1679, Jan Barentse Van Driest; Cornelia Willemse; Jan Willemse; Willem Willemse; Dirk Willemse of Freehold, N. J., m. Sept. 17, 1709, Jannetje Van Aersdalen; Daniel Willemse, m. May 4, 1700, Lysbeth Gerrets; Coenrad Willemse, bp. Dec. 5, 1680, at Fld², and settled on the Raritan; ard Elizabeth Willemse, m. Jacob Lane of Monmouth Co., N. J. He signed his name " *Wyllem Jansen Van Borckelloo.*"

Willem Willemse of N. U., the ancestor of the Kings Co. branch of the family, m. Maria da. of Jaques Cortelyou the surveyor, took the oath of allegiance in Fld² in 1687, appears to have resided in G⁴ about 1696 and '98, and afterwards removed to N. U. on the property his wife inherited from her father, on the cen. of which town he appears in 1698, and where he was assessed in 1706 for 90 A. Issue:— Jaques of N. J.; Wilmitien, (sup.) m. Jan Nevius; Harmanus, m. about 1730 Sarah Terhune; Helen, m. Michael Blouw of N. J.; and (sup.) Anna, m. May 27, 1719, Pieter Luyster of Fl². Made his mark " W B " to documents.

BARKER, THOMAS, of N. L., on ass. roll of Fl² of 1683. In 1686 a suit was brought against him by the Consistory of the R. D. ch. of Fl² for 17 gl. 10 st. due for salary of Do. Van Zuuren, as per p. 252 of Lib. C of Fl² rec.

BARKES,——, bought Mar. 15, 1683-4, of Floris Willemse, 60 A. of land on the end of the New Lotts of Fl² adjoining J² (Jamaica), as per p. 160 of Lib. C of Fl² rec.

BARNES, CORNELIUS, owned land in Fl² in 1696, as per p. 94 of Lib. 2 of Con. He and John Okie had a caveat issued Nov. 20, 1684, in behalf of Fl² against any patent being granted to Br² unless an agreement was produced between the towns, as per p. 132 of Cal. of English Man. This Cor² Barnes may be Cor² Barentse Van der Wyck.

John, on ass. roll of G^d of 1683; probably intended for John Barentse Van Driest.

William, of G^d in 1656, per Thompson's L. I.

BARRE or BARRY, see Berry.

BARTELT, BARTELSZ, or BERTELFS, HERMEN, a tavern-keeper in Fl^h July 19, 1655, as per p. 231 of Cal. of Dutch Man., in which place he owned a lot. Oct. 3, 1661, he bought of Jan Cornelise Klyn, 20 morgens in Fl^h on the E. side of the road and abutting on Corlaers flats, with plain land and salt meadows, as per p. 83 of Lib. B of Fl^h rec. Apl. 16, 1665, he was appointed a fence-viewer of said town, and Apl. 21, 1667, on the division of the meadows at Canarisie, obtained a lot. Signed his name "*Hermen Bartelt.*"

BAS, HERMAN HENDRICKSZEN, of Br^n, m. Jan. 10, 1682, in N. Y., Anna Wynhert of Amsterdam, both residents of N. Y. at date of m.

BASHER, JACOB, m. June 6, 1670, *Berber Gisbert*, both of N. U. (by Justice Ja^s Hubbard of G^d). Quære: Is not this Jacob Bastiaense?

BASTIAENSE, JACOB, emigrated from Heicop in South Holland May 19, 1661. On ass. rolls of N. U. of 1675 and '76, and on an agreement relating to the division of the common lands of Jan. 31, 1671-2. Made his mark "I B" to documents.

Reynier, see Van Giesen.

BAUDE, THOMAS, a Frenchman, on ass. roll of Bu^k of 1693 and cen. of 1698.

BAXTER, GEORGE, m. *Alice ——*. Was English Secretary of N. N. in 1642 and '47, in which latter year he was appointed ensign, as per p. 111 of Cal. of Dutch Man. July 6, 1643, he obtained a patent for 25 morgens "in the rear of Dirck the Norman (Williamsburgh, L. I.)," as per p. 367 of said Cal. Was among the early settlers of G^d and allotted a plantation-lot there in 1646, of which place he was a mag. in 1650, '51, and '53. Jan. 21, 1647, he and his associates obtained a patent for Canarisie, L. I., on condition of settling 20 families there within 3 years, as per p. 372 of Cal. of Dutch Man., which failed. Styled Lieut. on Gov. Kieft's patent of G^d of 1647. His East River plantation he probably sold; for May 15, 1647, it was patented to

John Forbus with other lands, as per p. 375 of said Cal
From the following entry on the G^d rec. he appears at one
period to have owned what is known as Pennoyer's patent
—Nov. 1, 1665, George Baxter sold to John Tilton of G^d
" a piece of land purchased of Robert Penyer, as also
further confirmed unto me by Mon^r Pieter Stuyvesant, late
Governour," etc. In 1655 he raised the standard of rebellion in G^d against the government, which failed, was
imprisoned, absconded, and finally removed to Nevis in
the West Indies. Signed his name " *Geo. Baxter.*"

Thomas of G^d (probably a s. of George), m. July 1678 Ann or
Annatie Stillwell. A Thomas Baxter was accused of piracy
Nov. 24, 1653, as per p. 142 of Vol. V. of Dutch Man. But
this was probably another person. Bought Jan. 14, 1652,
of his father a house and plantation in G^d, which he sold
May 14, 1652, to Wm Halliott or Hallet. Signed his name
" *Thomas Backster.*"

BAVARD, CATHARINE, bought May 1, 1688, of Jan Spiegelaer a house-lot in the village of Fl^h between the lot belonging to the church and that of John Pietersen, as per Fl^h rec.

Balthazar, of the city of N. Y., with others, as guardians
of Jacob Loockerman, conveyed Mar. 19, 1674, to Roelof
Martense Schenck a bouwery of 200 A. in Fld^s, as per p.
28 of Cal. of Eng. Man.

BAYLES or BAYLIS, THOMAS, of G^d, (sup.) English, m.
Elizabeth ——; owned lots Nos. 16 and 17 in the N. woods
of G^d in 1684, and lots Nos. 8 and 15 in G^d Neck in 1688, as
per G^d rec. Feb. 11, 1688-9, he sold his house and garden-
plot in the village of G^d to Isaac Haselbury and Richard
Gregory of G^d, as per p. 87 of Lib. 2 of Con. Jan. 21, 1690,
a suit was brought against his wid. by Jan Hansen (Van
Noostrand). She m. Mar. 17, 1689-90, Isaac Haselbury, a
third husband, as per G^d rec., having previous to her marriage with Bayles m. Ralph Cardell, who by a deed of gift
gave her his whole estate. There was a John Baylis at J^a
as early as 1660, at which locality and its vicinity numerous
persons of that name reside. Signed his name " *Thomas
Bayles.*"

BAYLEY, JONATHAN, (sup.) English, on ass. roll of G^d of
1683.

BEACH, RICHARD, was sued for debt May 4, 1669, in the
court of sessions by John Rateo, as per G^d rec.

BEBOU, JAN, and Metje Beekman had a da. Marytje bp. Aug. 21, 1691, at Br".

•

BEEKMAN, ABRAHAM (s. of Gerardus), b. in Fl[h]; m. Sept. 11, 1708, *Lucretia De Kay.* Settled in N. J.

Adrian (s. of Gerardus), bp. Aug. 23, 1682, in Fl[h]; m. Abagail Lispenard about 1705.

Christopher (s. of Gerardus), bp. Jan. 16, 1681; m. Jan. 28, 1704, Maria de La Noy; d. May 1724. Left Fl[h] and settled at Six Mile Run in Somerset Co., N. J. Issue:—Cornelia, bp. May 1, 1704; Gerardus, bp. Aug. 6, 1707. Cornelia, bp. May 6, 1709; Magdalena, bp. Nov. 14, 1711; Adrian, bp. Nov. 22, 1713; Magdalena, bp. May 2, 1716 (most of the above bp. in N. Y.); Abraham; Christopher; Maria or Mary; Catharine, m. Ab[m] Lott Suydam; and Emeline, also m. Ab[m] Lott Suydam.

Cornelius, emigrated from Bremen; settled in N. U. in 1657; m. May 31, 1665, in N. A., Mariken Cornelise wid. of Hans Christiaensen. Will da. Feb. 22, pro. Mar. 9, 1668-9, rec. p. 75, Lib. 1, N. Y. surr. off. Issue:—a da. Mattie, a minor in 1669, who m. 1st Cornelis Van Deseree; m. 2[d], Nov. 5, 1690, Michael Henninck; and m. 3[d], Aug. 9, 1691, John Bibut, Babon, or Bebou.

Gerardus Willemse (s. of Wilhelmus of N. Y., who emigrated from Hesselt in Overyssel in 1647), bp. Aug. 17, 1653, in N. A.; m. Aug. 29, 1677, Magdalena Abeel of Albany, b. 1662; d. 1723. He and his w. made a joint will probably at date of marriage, which was often done, as per p. 166 of Lib. C of Fl[h] rec. Settled in Fl[h], and was col. of militia and justice of the peace in 1685; took the oath of allegiance there in 1687 as a native; was a mem. of the Colonial Assembly from Kings Co. in 1698 and '99; mem. of the Colonial Council and its president, and acting Governor in 1709 and '10. Issue:—Christopher of N. J., bp. Jan. 16, 1681, in Fld[s], m. Jan. 28, 1704, Marie De Lanoy; Adrian, bp. Aug. 27, 1682, in Fld[s], m. Sept. 11, 1708, Lucretia De Kay; Willem or Wilhelmus, bp. Aug. 10, 1684, in Br[n]; John; Catharine, bp. June 2, 1689, in Fl[h], m. Charles La Roux; Gerardus of N. J.; Abraham of N. J.; Henry of N. J.; Cornelia, m. Mar. 1, 1724, Rich[d] Van Dam; Marytie, m. Aug. 26, 1726, Jacob Walton; and Martin. Signed his name *"Gerardus Beakman"* in 1684.

Gerardus (s. of Gerardus), b. in Fl[h]; m. Oct. 12, 1718, in N. Y., Anna Mary Van Horn, and joined the R. D. ch. of that city Aug. 19, 1718; finally settled on the Raritan, N. J. Issue:—Gerardus, bp. July 29, 1719; Elizabeth, bp. Dec. 10, 1720; John; Christopher of Harlington, b. 1724;

Gerardus of Six Mile Run, b. 1725; Abraham of Griggs-town, bp. July 20, 1729, m. May 3, 1776, Ann Voorhies; Mary, m. Thomas Skillman; Ann, m. Jacob Voorhies; Catharine, m. 1ˢᵗ Vanderbilt, m. 2ᵈ Johnson; Magdalena, m. John Van Dyck; and Cornelia, m. Abᵐ Stryker. Signed his name "*Gerard: Beekman*" in 1720.

Henry (s. of Gerardus), settled in N. J. as early as 1715. Died single, and will pro. Jan. 15, 1770. A Henry Beek-man, s. of William the emigrant, obtained of Queen Anne a patent for a large tract of land on the Hudson River in Dutchess Co. Signed his name "*Henry Beekman.*"

Jacobus (Willemse), bp. Aug. 21, 1658, in N. A.; m. Eliza-beth De Peyster; d. 1727. Settled in Flʰ, and will da. Dec. 21, 1722, pro. Nov. 30, 1727, rec. p. 102, Lib. 10, N. Y. surr. off. Issue:—Anetie; Gerardus, (sup.) m. Oct. 28, 1745, Ann Van Horne; Johannes, bp. Nov. 13, 1720, in N. U.; and Jacobus. Signed his name "*Jacobus Beekman*" in 1720.

John (s. of Gerardus) of Flʰ. He finally settled in the city of N. Y., where his chil. were bp. Issue:—Catharine, bp. July 17, 1698; Rachel, bp. July 18, 1708; Catharine, bp. Oct. 18, 1719; and Johannis, bp. Nov. 16, 1720.

Martin (s. of Gerardus) of Flʰ, m. June 21, 1724, Eliza-beth a granddau. of Resolvert Waldron. Settled in N. J. Issue:—Henry, b. Mar. 24, 1729, m. Phebe Bloomfield; Samuel, b. 1729, m. Dec. 5, 1765, Elizabeth Waldren; Anna, b. June 28, 1734, m. Nov. 12, 1766, John Walthon; Elizabeth, b. Aug. 30, 1735, m. Francis Brazier; John, b. Nov. 5, 1741; and (sup.) Areaentje.

Willem or *Wilhelmus* (s. of Gerardus), bp. Aug. 10, 1684, in Brⁿ; (sup.) m. Dec. 8, 1715, Elizabeth De Peyster. Joined the R. D. ch. of N. Y. Apl. 21, 1720, to which place he probably removed from Flʰ. Was one of the pur-chasers of the Harlington tract in N. J. Issue:—Johannis, bp. Nov. 20, 1720; Jacobus, bp. Dec. 30, 1722, in N. U. Signed his name "*Wᵐ Beekman*" in 1720.

BEET, WILLIAM, sold Aug. 6, 1654, to Thoˢ Spicer plan-tation-lot No. 20 in Gᵈ, as per town rec.

BEETS, see Bescher.

BEL, WILLIAM, (sup.) English, bought Feb. 3, 1654, of Robᵗ Stoll of Boston in New England, plantation-lot No. 21 in Gᵈ, through John Tilton as his agent. Signed his name "*Willyeam Bel*" in 1650.

BELLEW or BELOU, PETER, of Gᵈ, charged at the court of sessions, June 15, 1670, with assault by Ann Stillwill.

He m. Francyn de Bon. Issue:—Pieter, bp. June 6, 1668, in N. Y. (Probably same as Pieter Billiou.)

BENNEM, BENNUM, BENHAM, or BENUM, JAN or JOHN, (an Englishman,) m. Neltye ——; on ass. roll of 1693 and cen. of 1698. Issue:—Antie, bp. Oct. 23, 1698; Joosje, bp. Sept. 8, 1700, in Br^n, and probably other children. Made his mark to documents.

Enum or *Evert*, among the early settlers of G^d, where he obtained Dec. 20, 1648, a plantation-lot, as per town rec. Also obtained Aug. 30, 1660, a patent for 28 morgens in Fld^s, now owned by the heirs of George Van Nuyse. Made his mark to documents.

Joris (English), on ass. roll of N. U. of 1693.

BENNET, ARIE or ADRIAEN WILLEMSE (s. of Willem Adriaensz), English, b. 1637; m. Dec. 3, 1662, *Annanietje* or *Angenietje Jans*, da. of Jan Tomasse Van Dyck of N. U. Settled at first in N. U., of the R. D. ch. of which place he was a member and deacon in 1677, and constable of said town in 1676. In addition to a farm in the village, he owned in 1677 lots Nos. 6, 7, 8, 9, and 10, fronting on the Bay and extending back to the present Third Ave., at Yellow Hoek, now Bay Ridge, cong. about 150 A., and covering the whole block between Bay Ridge Ave. and Van Brunt's Lane, with the exception of lot No. 5 of 30 A. In 1675 he and his associates of N. U. petitioned Gov. Colve for a grant of land on S. I., as per p. 643 of Vol. II. of Doc. of Col. His. of N. Y. Jan. 26, 1681-2, he sold his Bay Ridge premises to Denyse Theunise, the ancestor of the Denyse family. He sold his N. U. house and lot on the same date to Hans Harmense (Van Barkeloo), and his farm in 1681 to Carl Janse Van Dyck, and removed back to Gowanus, buying Jan. 14, 1681, of his mother, for 12,000 gl. in good merchantable wheat, what was lately known as the Schemerhorn farm at Gowanus. Took the oath of allegiance in 1687 at Gowanus as a native. On ass. roll of Br^n of 1683, Dongan's patent of 1686, a commissioner in 1687, and on cen. of 1698. Issue :— Jan Adriaense; Tryntje Adriaense, b. 1664, m. Nov. 12, 1685, Cornelis Rutgersz Van Brunt; Arie Adriaense; Jacob Adriaense; Cornelis Adriaense; Isaac Adriaense; Abraham Adriaense; Antje Adriaense, m. Jacob Sutphen of Freehold, N. J.; Marike or Maria Adriaense, m. Jacob Van Dorn of Freehold; Agnietje or Aneinetje Adriaense, bp. Sept. 3, 1682, in Br^n; and Engel Adriaense, bp. July 26, 1685, in N. Y. Made his mark to documents.

Arie or *Adriaen Adriaense* of Gowanus (s. of Adriaen

Willemse and Ananietje or Agnietje Bennet), m. Barbara or
Barbetje ——, and settled in Somerset Co., N. J. In 1711
he was an elder in Six Mile Run R. D. ch. Issue :—(sup.)
William; (sup.) Geertruy, m. Apl. 6, 1718, Teunis Van Pelt of
N. J.; (sup.) John, m. Eyke Van Mater; Cornelis, bp. May
19, 1700, in Br^n; Metalynke, bp. June 7, 1711; Metaanke, bp.
Feb. 10, 1712 ; Katrinke, bp. May 9, 1714 ; and Isaac, bp.
Apl. 14, 1717—the 5 last named bp. at Freehold, N. J.
Made his mark to documents.

Adriaen or *Ariaen* (s. of Jan Ariaense and Femmetje),
bp. June 7, 1697 ; (sup.) m. Maria da. of Tunis Lanen Van
Pelt; m. 2^d Grietje ——. Resided at Gowanus. Issue :—
Grietje, bp. Apl. 21, 1723, in N. U., (sup.) m. Jacob Barger or
Bergen of S. I.

Abram Adriaense (s. of Adriaen Willemse), bp. Mar. 20,
1680 ; m. Dec. 25, 1702, Jannetje Folckers. Conveyed Jan.
2, 1708, to Jacob Bennett of N. U. the Schemerhorn farm
at Gowanus, and removed to New Brunswick, N. J. Was
an elder in the Six Mile Run R. D. ch. in 1711. Issue :—
Adriaen, bp. Oct. 7, 1703, (sup.) m. Sofia Brownswell ;
Folkert, bp. Aug. 7, 1705; Abram, bp. Aug. 17, 1707, (sup.)
m. Jannetje Suydam ; Sara, bp. Oct. 23, 1711, m. John
Wagenaar—all bp. at Br^n; and (sup.) Jacob and William.
Made his mark "A B " to documents.

Christian Willemse (s. of Willem Adriaense the emigrant),
bp. Jan. 6, 1641, in N. A.; d. young.

Christian Willemse (s. of Willem Adriaense the emigrant),
bp. Mar. 30, 1642, in N. A. No further trace.

Hendrick (s. of Wm Willemse'), of Gowanus in 1726.
Suppose he m. Jannetje Kouwenhoven and settled in Monmouth Co., N. J.

Isaac Ariaense (s. of Adriaen Willemse), of Gowanus in
1698 and 1700 ; m. Lena, Helena, or Magdalena ——.
Issue :—Arie, bp. Aug. 7, 1698; Isaac, bp. June 9, 1700,
(sup.) m. Elizabeth Corson; William, bp. Apl. 18, 1704,
(sup.) m. Lena Pietersen; and Jacob, bp. Nov. 17, 1706,
(sup.) m. Dorcas Haugewout—all bp. in Br^n. He and his
chil. settled in Bucks Co., Penn.

Jacob Ariaense (s. of Adriaen Willemse), m. Barbara da.
of Jacob Ferdon of N. U. Suppose bought of his brother
Abram the Schemerhorn farm. Issue :—Angenietje, bp.
Sept. 8, 1700, in Br^n, m. Jan Scouten; Femmetje, bp. Sept.
18, 1709; (sup.) Jacob, m. Annatie —— ; (sup.) Grietje or
Margaret, m. Jacob Bergen of S. I. ; and William or Wilhelmus of Gowanus, m. Anatie ——.

Jacob Willemse (s. of Willem Willemse and Geertruy), m.
May 4, 1692, in N. Y., Neeltje Beekman of Albany. Took the

oath of allegiance in Br^n in 1687 as a native. Issue:—
William, bp. Apl. 16, 1693; and Martin, bp. Nov. 10, 1695.

Jan Ariaense (s. of Adriaen Willemse), b. in N. U.; m.
Jan. 6, 1696, Femmetje da. of Jeronemus Rapalie. On ass.
roll of Br^n of 1693. Will da. Mar. 30, 1722, rec. p. 30, Lib.
14, N. Y. surr. off. Issue:—Ariaen or Adriaen, bp. June 7,
1697, in Br^n; Joris, bp. Aug. 28, 1698; Jeromus or Hieronemus, bp. Apl. 1, 1700, in Br^n, m. Neeltje ——; Annetje;
Phebe; Johannes, m. Sarah da. of Peter Luyster; Catharine; and Angenietje, m. Apl. 22, 1737, (sup.) Rem Vanderbeek.

Jan Willemse (s. of Willem Willemse and Geertruy), bp.
Jan. 3, 1663; m. 1st Aeltje or Aefie Hendrickse; m. 2^d, July
2, 1690, in N. Y., Altje Wynants of the Wallabout, (sup.)
da. of Wynant Pieterse Van Eck; d. after 1739. Took the
oath of allegiance in 1687 in Br^n as a native, and a mem.
of the R. D. ch. of Br^n in 1677, residing at the time at
Gowanus. A Jan Bennet, who may have been this Jan,
bought land in 1683 on the Raritan in N. J. From the Fl^h
town rec. he appears to have resided at New Lotts in said
town from about 1707 to 1723. Issue:—Jan (Janse), bp.
Mar. 29, 1696, in Br^n, m. Anna ——; Geertruy, bp. Jan 9,
1697; and (sup.) Aeltye, m. Peter Haughewout of S. I.
Made his mark "I B" to documents.

Jan Janse (s. of Jan Willemse and Altie Wynants), bp.
Mar. 29, 1696; m. Anna ——. Resided on a farm at Gowanus, and is the ancestor of the N. U. Bennets. Will da.
Mar. 8, 1743, pro. Mar. 8, 1744, rec. p. 183 of Lib. 15, N. Y.
surr. off. Issue:—William, (sup.) m. Sarah Sherman; Jacob,
(sup.) m. June 28, 1747, Elizabeth Conselyea; John, (sup.)
m. Aug. 19, 1746, Anne Remsen; Wynant of Gowanus, m.
Geertje da. of Jacobus Emàns; Gertrude, (sup.) m. May
26, 1743, Jacob Boerum; Anna; Mary, (sup.) m. Dec. 9,
1752, Cor^s Vandervoort; Eve; and Aeltje, (sup.) m. May 19,
1746, Cor^s Schwout.

Johannes (s. of Wm Willemse^s), of Gowanus in 1726. No
further trace.

William Adriaense, an Englishman, and cooper by trade,
and the ancestor of the early Bennet family of Kings Co.,
was in this country prior to 1636, for in that year he and
Jaques Bentyn purchased of the Indians 930 A. at Gowanus,
of which, Dec. 26, 1639, he appears to have bought Bentyn's interest. He m. Mary Badye (sometimes written
Mary Thomas) da. of Aeltien Breckanue (w. of Willem
Bredenbent) by a former husband, and wid. of Jacob Verdon or Ferdon. After Bennet's death Mary m. 3^d Paulus
Vanderbeek. Willem Adriaense d. prior to 1644, and Mary

his wid. was living as late as Jan. 1697; and Sept. 9, 1644, as wid. of Wm Adriaense Bennet, obtained a patent from Gov. Kieft covering at least the farms late of Ab^m Schemerhorn and Garret Bergen at Gowanus. Issue:—Arie or Adriaen Willemse, b. 1639; Willem Willemse[1]; Christian Willemse, bp. Jan. 6, 1641, in N. A., and d. an infant; Sara, bp. Nov. 10, 1641, in N. A.; Christian Willemse, bp. Mar. 30, 1642, in N. A.; and Marretje, Maria, or Mary Willemse, bp. May 9, 1644, in N. A. Made his mark "W" to documents.

Willem Willemse 1st (s. of Willem Ariaense the emigrant), m. Apl. 9, 1660, Geertruyt Van Mullen, Mulhem, or Mulheym of Meurs, who was a mem. of the D. ch. of N. A. prior to 1660 (she may have been a da. of Jacob Verdon, of which there is some evidence); d. prior to 1686. Resided at Gowanus and owned the late Cor^s W. Bennet and Geo. Bennet or Joseph Dean farms, and is the ancestor of the N. U. Bennets. In 1661 he joined the R. D. ch. in Br^n, and on the ass. rolls of said town of 1675, '76, and '83. Issue:— Maria Willems, bp. Nov. 10, 1661, in N. A., m. Jacobus Verhulst; Jan Willems, bp. Jan. 7, 1663, in Br^n; Willem Willemse[2]; and Jacob Willemse.

Willem Willemse 2^d (s. of Willem Willemse[1] and Geertruy) of Gowanus, m. Dec. 15, 1686, in N. Y., Adriaentje Vandewater of N. Y. Owned and occupied what was lately known as the Garret Bergen farm at Gowanus, where he took the oath of allegiance in 1687 as a native. Issue:—Geertruy or Grietje, bp. Nov. 15, 1689; Greete or Vytie, bp. Nov. 15, 1690, m. Apl. 26, 1718, Teunis Van Pelt of N. U.; William Willemse[3] of Gowanus; Ariaentie, bp. May 30, 1695, m. Wm Cowenhoven of Monmouth Co., N. J.; Hendrick of Gowanus, (sup.) m. Jannetje Cowenhoven); Marike; and Johannis of Gowanus. Made his mark "W" to documents in 1697.

Willem Willemse 3^d (s. of Willem Willemse[2] and Adriaentje) of Gowanus, m. June 14, 1717, Maria Van Dyck of Br^n. Resided on and owned the Garret Bergen farm at Gowanus, and at one period resided in Penn. Issue:—(sup.) William, d. Nov. 8, 1776; and Nicholas, bp. July 16, 1721, of whom no further trace.

William or *Wilhelmus Jacobse* (s. of Jacob Ariaense) of Gowanus, m. Annatie ——; d. about 1759. Suppose resided on and owned the late Albert C. Van Brunt farm at Gowanus. Will da. Dec. 21, 1755, pro. Apl. 12, 1759, rec. p. 400, Lib. 21, N. Y. surr. off. Issue:—Jacob, bp. Jan. 16, 1732; Johannes; Wilhelmus; Anthony, m. July 23, 1768, Mary Hyer; Rachel, (sup.) m. Jacobus Emans; Angenietje; Cor-

nelis, m. Jan. 1772 Dorothy Voorhies; Abraham of Gowanus, b. Feb. 21, 1748, m. Jan. 17, 1768, Catharine da. of Peter
Hyer; and Margrietje, b. Sept. 4, 1749.

BENS, WILLIAM, hired land in Fld* in 1700, as per ch. rec.

BENSEN, DERCK (s. of Derk Bensen or Bensingh and Cata-
line Berg of Albany), b. 1650; m. *Thysie* or *Tytje Claesen*, who
d. about 1732; he d. about June 1717. Resided at first at
Albany, and a mem. of the R. D. ch. of that place; removed
to Claverick, from thence to the city of N. Y., and then to
Br², where he resided in 1707, as per p. 206 of Bergen
Genealogy. Issue:—Tryntje, m. 1ˢᵗ John Van de Meulen, 2ᵈ
John Kelly; Eva, bp. July 3, 1686, d. young; Rachel, b.
Apl. 13, 1689, m. Hans Machielse Bergen, d. 1752; Eva, bp.
Mar. 19, 1693, in N. Y., m. May 4, 1717, Anthony Duane;
Derick, bp. July 5, 1696, in N. Y., d. 1729, single; and Thy-
sie, bp. Sept. 13, 1699, m. James Henderson.

BENTYN or BENTIN, JACQUES, and Willem Arianse Bennet, both Englishmen, purchased in 1636 of the Indians
936 A. at Gowanus, of which, Dec. 26, 1639, Bentyn appears
to have sold his interest to Bennet for 350 gl., as per p. 12
of Cal. of Dutch Man. Was schout fiscaal* of N. A. in
1636, one of the 12 men in 1641, and a mem. of the Council
in 1633, '36, '37, and '42. Went to Holland prior to July
13, 1648, as per p. 118 of Cal. of Dutch Man. Signed his
name "*JacquesBentin.*"

BERCKHOVEN, see Brower.

BERDAN, see Baerdaen.

BERBACKE, STOFFEL JURIANSE, bought Aug. 8, 1671, of
Tomas Lammerse and Tunis Jansen Coevers, 19 morgens in
Flʰ, as per p. 96 of Lib. C of Flʰ rec.

BERGEN, FREDERICK (Jacobse), bp. Nov. 27, 1681; m. *Ger-
rytje* da. of Gerret Vechte; d. prior to 1762. Left L. I. and
settled on a farm on S. I. In 1715 he was a private in
Capt. David Aersen's company of Br², in 1738 a lieut. of
militia on S. I. and a deacon in the R. D. ch. of said island.
In 1752 he appears to have joined the R. D. ch. of New
Brunswick, to which locality he probably removed. Issue:
—Jacob of Somerset Co., N. J., bp. July 19, 1719, in Br²,

---

* Schout is sheriff, and Fiscaal an office similar to that of attorney-
general.

m. Margaret Lane, d. 1781; Gerritie, bp. Apl. 29, 1722, m.
John Van Dyck; Henry or Hendrick of Somerset Co., N. J.,
bp. Sept. 26, 1725, on S. I.; and Elsje, bp. Mar. 12, 1732, m.
Koenraet Ten Eyck Jun'.

Hans Hansen, the ancestor of the Bergen family, was a
native of Bergen in Norway, a ship-carpenter by trade, who
removed from thence to Holland. From Holland he emigrated in 1633 to N. A., where he took up his residence
working at his trade and at one period cultivating a tobacco plantation, and in 1639 m. *Sarah* da. of Joris Jansen
Rapalie, b. June 9, 1625, at Albany, and reputed to be the
first white female child of European parentage born in the
colony. About 1643 removed to his plantation of 400 A.
at the Wallabout, for which he obtained a patent on the
30th of March, 1647, and d. about 1654. Issue:—Anneken,
bp. July 12, 1640, m. 1ˢᵗ, Jan. 17, 1661, Jan Clercq of Brazil,
m. 2ᵈ, Oct. 8, 1662, Derck Janse Hooglandt of Flᵇ; Breckje,
bp. July 27, 1642, m. Aert Anthonize Middagh; Jan, bp.
Apl. 17, 1644; Michael, bp. Nov. 4, 1646; Joris, bp. July 18,
1649; Marretje, bp. Oct. 8, 1651, m. Jacob Ruthzen; Jaeob,
bp. Sept. 21, 1653; and Catalyn, bp. Nov. 30, 1653—all bp.
in N. A. Made his mark "H" to documents.

Hans (*Jacobse*) of Brⁿ, bp. May 12, 1678 ; m. Dec. 14, 1707,
Sarah da. of Jeronimous Rapalie; d. prior to Mar. 1749.
In 1741 was involved in a lawsuit with Israel Horsefield
in relation to ownership and boundaries of their lands, for
the particulars of which see Bergen Genealogy. Issue :—
Jacob of Brⁿ, bp. Dec. 12, 1708, in Brⁿ, m. Antie ——— ;
Antie or Annetje, bp. Mar. 12, 1710, m. Gerret Cowenhoven ;
Elsje, m. Rem Remsen of Brⁿ ; Catelyna, m. Michael Ber-
gen of Brⁿ (s. of Hans Michaelse) ; and Sara, m. Sept. 20,
1750, Johannes Wandell of Albany.

Hans (Jorise), bp. Aug. 31, 1684, in N. U.; m. Aug. 16,
1711, Sytie da. of Evert Van Wickelen of N. L. ; d. in 1726.
Resided at first in Brⁿ, but in his latter days removed to
Hempstead, where he d. At one period owned a grist-mill
within the boundaries of the present Navy Yard, since
known as Remsen's Mill. Issue :—George, b. Oct. 9, 1712,
m. 1ˢᵗ, June 3, 1738, Grietje Du Mont, m. 2ᵈ, Sept. 14, 1744,
Maria ——— ; and Evert, b. 1717, m. Jane da. of Denyse
Hegeman, d. Nov. 17, 1776, whose descendants reside
mainly in N. J.

Hans (*Michaelse*), bp. Mar. 11, 1689, m. *Rachel* da. of
Derick Bensing or Benson ; d. in 1731. He and w. joined
the R. D. ch. of N. Y. in 1723. Store and livery-stable
keeper most of his life at Brⁿ ferry, where he owned considerable property and also carried on a bakery. In 1742

was supervisor of Br^n. Will da. Jan. 18, 1731, pro. June 20, 1732. Issue :—Annetje, bp. Mar. 12, 1710, d. young ; Tiesje, b. June 9, 1711, d. young ; Meighiel, b. Dec. 20, 1712, m. Catelyna da. of Hanse Jacobse Bergen, d. prior to Aug. 1783; Femmetje, b. July 29, 1715, m. Apl. 18, 1745, Sylvester Marius Groen, d. Oct. 31, 1793; Derick, b. Feb. 28, 1718, m. 1749 Deborah Cortelyou, d. Nov. 19, 1759; Hans, b. July 12, 1721, m. Catryntje da. of Simon De Hart, d. Apl. 28, 1786; and Tunis, b. Oct. 15, 1730, m. Apl. 1760 Johanna or Annatie Stoothoff, d. May 2, 1807. Signed his name "*Hans Bergen.*"

Jacob Hansen, bp. Sep. 21, 1653; m. July 8, 1677, Elsje Fredericks da. of Frederick Lubbertsen of Br^n; d. after 1738. Resided on and owned a plantation in S. Br^n comprising a part of his father-in-law's patent. In 1715 was supervisor of Br^n. Issue :—Hans, bp. May 12, 1678, in Br^n; Frederick, bp. Nov. 27, 1681, in Fl^h; Jacob, bp. Jan. 20, 1684, in Br^n; Sara, bp. Aug. 5, 1688, in Fl^h; Catryna, m. Johannes Slegt or Sleght ; Marretje, m. Gysbert Boogert Junr; Breckje, m. John Croesen; Elsje, m. Hendrick Croesen; and Cornelia, m. Derick Croesen. Signed his name "*Jacob Hanse.*"

Jacob (Jacobse), bp. Jan. 20, 1684; m. Margaret, Maritje, or Maria Croesen. Resided on S. I., where in 1738 he held the office of lieut. of militia, and was a deacon in the R. D. ch. Issue :—Elsje, bp. July 29, 1722, m. Nov. 9, 1747, Johannes Van Wagene of S. I.; Cornelia, bp. Jan. 1, 1728-9, m. John Swain or Sweem of S. I.; Jacob, bp. Sept. 30, 1730, m. Gretie or Margaret Bennet; and Cornelis, bp. Sept. 4, 1737. His descendants reside mainly on S. I. and write their surname *Barger*.

Jan Hansen, bp. Apl. 17, 1644; m. Jannetje da. of Teunis Nyssen (Denyse); d. after 1715. Obtained a patent in 1664 for 20 morgens or 40 A. at Bedford in Br^n, on which he appears to have resided, and which in 1697 he sold to Lucas Coeverts, having previously removed to J^a. In 1677 he hails from Bedford and in 1679 from J^a, where he owned and cultivated a farm, and from him are descended the Queens Co. Bergens. Issue:—Hans, bp. Feb. 14, 1677; Teunis, bp. Apl. 20, 1679; Adriaentje, bp. Dec. 11, 1681, at Br^n, m. Jan or Johannes Gerretse; Marretje, bp. Mar. 29, 1685, at Br^n, (sup.) m. Johannes Eldertse; Sarah, m. Jacob Hebbelem; (sup.) Peter; and (sup.) Catalyn. Signed his name "*Yan Hansen.*"

Joris or *George Hansen*, bp. July 18, 1649; m. Aug. 11, 1678, Sara da. of Jan Strycker of Fl^h; d. after 1736. Was a carpenter by trade, took the oath of allegiance in Br^n in 1687, was a commissioner of Br^n from 1690 to 1699. In

3

1698 bought a farm of nearly 40 A. (formerly of Gerret Wolfersen Van Couwenhoven) in Brⁿ E. of Smith St. and N. of
the Mill Creek. In 1703, '4, and '5, was supervisor of Brⁿ.
Apl. 10, 1697, a resolution was passed at a town meeting in
Brⁿ to divide the common lands, the holders of a house and
lot to have only a half share. For laying out and dividing
they appointed Capt. Henry Filkin, Jacob Van Deventer,
Daniel Rapalie, Joris Hansen (Bergen), John Dorland, and
Cor^s Van Duyn, as per p. 133 of Lib. 2 of Con. Issue:—
Lammetje, bp. Dec. 26, 1679, m. Joris Remsen of Haver-
straw; Sara, bp. Mar. 13, 1681; Aaltje, bp. Oct. 15, 1682,
m. Aug. 17, 1707, Rem Remsen, d. about 1724; Hans, bp.
Aug. 31, 1684; Jannetje, bp. May 27, 1688, m. Jan. 21, 1711,
Hendrick Vroom of Brⁿ; Annetje, bp. Mar. 9, 1689-90, m.
Mar. 12, 1720, Arnout Abrahams; Jan, bp. May 17, 1694;
Breckje, bp. May 24, 1696; Joris; and Catharine, m. Sept.
21, 1726, Peter Ewetse of Brⁿ and N. Y. Signed his name
" *Jores Hansen.*"

Michael Hansen, bp. Nov. 4, 1646; m. Femmetje da. of
Teunis Nyssen (Denyse); d. after Jan. 22, 1731. With his
brother Jan and others applied Mar. 18, 1662, for land at
Bedford, and obtained a patent for 20 morgens in that
locality May 15, 1664, on which he probably at one period
resided. Mar. 2, 1674, he bought, of Albert Cornelysen
Wantenaer, Huych Aerts Van Rossem's patent of 29 morgens
in the vicinity of Powers St. in the present city of Brⁿ, and
which in a confirmatory patent to Cornelysen was made to
cover 90 morgens, to which plantation he removed. His
name appears as one of the patentees of Brⁿ on Gov. Dongan's patent of May 13, 1686. Took the oath of allegiance
in Brⁿ in 1687 as a native; commissioned Oct. 22, 1688, as
capt. of militia; and appointed justice of the peace by
Gov. Bellamont Oct. 11, 1698. In 1701 he bought 466 A.
of land on the Raritan, N. J. Issue:—Sara, bp. June 2,
1678, m. Feb. 17, 1722, Jan Strycker of Fl^h; Teunis, bp. May
16, 1680, d. young; Hans, bp. May 11, 1689; Femmetje, m.
Jan. 6, 1695, Jan Cornelisse Vanderveer; and Mary. Signed
his name " *Migguel Hansen.*"

BERRIEN or BERRYEN, CORNELIS JANSE, m. 1st *Jannetje* da·
of Jan Strycker of Fl^h; m. 2^d *Hendrickje Verplancken*. Settled
in Fl^h, and Feb. 6, 1670-71, was allotted in pursuance of the
patent of said town a farm of 23 morgens lying between
the farm of Cornelis Barendse Van der Wyck and that of
Jan Janse Van Ditmarsen, and in addition salt meadows
and plain land, as per p. 16 of Lib. A of Fl^h rec. His name
appears on Fl^h ass. roll of 1675, on Gov. Andross' patent of

the New Lotts of Fl[h] of 1677, as a mem. of the R. D. ch. of Fl[h] of 1677, and a deacon in 1679. Issue:—Jan Cornelise; Jacob Cornelise, bp. Aug. 17, 1678, in Br[n]; Claus Cornelise, bp. Mar. 13, 1681, in Fl[h]; Catharine, m. Jeremiah Remsen; Cornelis Cornelise, bp. July 15, 1683, in N. U.; Pieter Cornelise; and Agnes or Angenietje, who m. Joris Rapalje. Signed his name "*Cornelis Berrien*" in 1684.

Jan Cornelise, sold May 7, 1707, to Evert Van Wikkelen lots Nos. 46 and 47 in the N. L. of Fl[h], as per p. 78 of Lib A of Fl[h] rec. Signed his name in 1687 "*Jan Berrien.*" The Berriens left Kings Co. some years ago and are principally to be found in the city of N. Y. and in N. J.

BERRY, CORNELIS, on ass. roll of Br[n] of 1675.

Samuel, m. Mar. 31, 1690, Katharine Martense Ryersen. On ass. roll of Br[n] of 1693 and cen. of 1698. Issue:—Deborah, bp. July 28, 1691, in Br[n]; Johanna, bp. Dec. 22, 1695, in N. Y.; and Samuel Jun[r], b. Apl. 1697.

Samuel Jun[r], b. Apl. 1697; m. June 10, 1744, Jemima or Jackamyntie da. of Wouter Teunise Van Pelt; d. Jan. 17, 1769. Issue:—Walter of Gowanus, b. 1755, m. Dec. 29, 1777, Rachel da. of Derick Bergen, d. Sept. 21, 1818 (gored to death by a bull); Jemima, b. Jan. 7, 1762. The Berrys of N. Y. and N. J. are mainly descendants of Capt. John Berry, an early settler in Bergen Co., N. J.

BERTELFS, HERMEN, see Bartelt.

BESCHER or BEETS, THOMAS, an Englishman, obtained Nov. 28, 1639, a patent for a tobacco plantation supposed to be located at Gowanus, which by a deed of May 17, 1639, he conveyed to Cornelis Lambertse (Cool), as per p. 7 of Cal. of Dutch Man., and for which Lambertse obtained a patent Apl. 5, 1642. This deed bears date prior to Bescher's patent, land at that period being often occupied and rights disposed of prior to dates of patents. In Bescher's deed his lands are bounded on the N. by those of "Claes Cornelise Smit," and in Gov. Kieft's patent to Cool they are bounded on the N. by land of "Jan Pietersen." This patent appears to include the farms late of Peter and John Wyckoff, Henry Story, and Winant Bennet on Butts' map of Br[n]. See pp. 33 and 34 of Book GG of Patents in off. of Sec. of State, and pp. 354 and 356 of Brooklyn Manual of 1863. Apl. 27, 1641, a marriage-contract was made between Nanne wid. of Thomas Beets and Thomas Smith, as per p. 15 of Cal. of Dutch Man.

BETTS, RICHARD, an early settler of Newtown, who emigrated in 1648, m. Joanna ——, settling at first in New · England, and in 1675 claimed a tract in N. L. by virtue of an Indian deed of 1663, which claim was disputed. He finally, probably under this claim, obtained a plantation on the boundary-line between Kings and Queens counties, on the main road from Br^n to J^a, afterwards owned by John I. Snediker and the dwelling-house converted into a tavern or hotel, famous in its day for the entertainment of sleighing parties and travellers. From 1656 to 1674 he was most of the time a mag. of Middleburgh or Newtown—in 1673 holding his appointment from Gov. Colve—and in 1679 high sheriff of Yorkshire. Issue:—Richard; Thomas, m. Mary da. of Danl Whitehead; Joanna; Mary; Martha; Elizabeth; and Sara. Signed his name "*Richard Betts.*"

BIBON, JACOB, a Frenchman, on ass. roll of Bu^k of 1693 and cen. of 1698.
Jan, a weaver, on ass. roll of Br^n of 1693, and charged in that year with defacing the king's arms, as per rec. of the court of sessions.

BIBOUT, JOHN, m. *Nelke* ——. Bought Oct. 23, 1696, of Thomas and Jasper Smith a 2 A. house-plot · and 40 A. farm at Bedford, as per p. 106 of Lib. 2 of Con. Probably Jan Bibou and John Bibout are the same persons.

BICKER, GERRET, obtained Feb. 25, 1658, a patent for 25 morgens at "Midwout" (Fl^h). Issue:—Victor, bp. Nov. 10, 1652, in N. A.

BIER, ALBERTIEN, paid 2 gl. clergyman's salary in Fl^h in 1680, as per town rec.

BILLICO, PIETER, on Hegeman's books of 1670. Probably same as Pieter Billou.

BILLOU, BALYOU, or BALJOU, PIETER, a Frenchman, who with other recently arrived immigrants applied Aug. 22, 1663, for land on S. I., as per p. 227 of Cal. of Dutch Man. Bought Sept. 12, 1670, of Cornelis Van Ruyven a farm on the E. side of the road in Fl^h, lying between the farms of Jan Hansen (Van Noostrand) and Ad^n Lammertse, with plain and salt meadow land, as per p. 87 of Lib. C of Fl^h rec. June 5, 1674, he also bought of Cor^s Van Ruyven 26 morgens with plain and meadow land in Fl^h, between land of Do. Johannes Megapolensis and that of Teunis Nyssen (Denyse), patented by Director Stuyvesant to Evert Duyckingh Van Borchem, as per p. 37 of Lib. A of Fl^h rec. See Pieter Bellew.

BLAGGE, SAMUEL, of Hartford, an Englishman. Apl. 23, 1694, *Mary* his wife, as his attorney, sold to Richard Stillwell of G^d all her husband's interest in a house-lot in G^d late of Henry Bowne, as per G^d rec.

BLANDIN, dealer in dry-goods, as per Stoothoff's books of 1678.

BLANK or BLANCK, JURRIE, JURRIAN, or JURYEN, a trader on the Schuylkill as early as 1645; m. Nov. 25, 1673, in Fl^h, *Hester Paulus Vander Beek* of Gowanus, who joined the D. R. ch. of N. Y. in 1674. Mem. of the R. D. ch. of Br^n in 1676, residing at the time on the premises occupied by Mary Badye, late the Ab^m Schemerhorn farm at Gowanus; on ass. rolls of Br^n of 1675 and '83; and took the oath of allegiance to the English in N. Y. in 1664. There was a Jeurian Blanck and Tryntje Claes his w., mem. of the D. ch. of N. A. prior to 1660. Issue:—Casparus, bp. Apl. 22, 1677, in N. Y.; Jan, bp. Aug. 17, 1679, in Br^n; Jurian, bp. Apl. 4, 1681, in N. Y.; Paulus, bp. June 24, 1683, in Br^n; and Abraham, bp. Apl. 30, 1694, in Br^n. Signed his name "*Juryen Blanck.*"
Simon, m. Wyntje Ariaens or Arents. Mem. of R. D. ch. of N. A. in 1672, and entered on the ch. rec. as removed to Br^n. Issue:—Wyntje, bp. Apl. 1, 1668; Annetje, bp. June 8, 1672; and Jeremias, bp. Feb. 18, 1673—all in N. A.

BLAUW, FREDERICK, of Br^n, m. 1st *Lena* ——; m. 2^d Abigail ——. Issue:—Jurgen, bp. Feb. 27, 1708, in Br^n; Frederick, bp. July 23, 1723; and Frederick, bp. Apl. 7, 1728. Made his mark to documents.
Harmen Jansen of Groningen. His name appears on early G^d documents.
Jan of Gowanus, m. Marytje ——. Issue:—Michael, bp. Apl. 18, 1704, in Br^n, (sup.) m. Helen da. of Willem Willemse Barkeloo, and settled in N. J. There was a Gerrit Dircksen Blauw in N. N. in 1643, as per p. 195 of Vol. 1 of Doc. of Col. His.

BLINCKERHOFF, see Brinckerhoff.

BLOM or BLOOM, BARENT JANSEN, the ancestor of the Blooms of Kings Co. Date of his emigration not ascertained. In 1665 he was killed with a knife, in a quarrel, by

Albert Cornelysen Wantenaer in self-defence, for which
Cornelysen, June 5, 1665, was convicted of manslaughter,
but pardoned by the Governor on the same day. Issue:—
Claes Barentse and Jan Barentse.

Barent (s. of Claes Barentse), m. Femmetje ——, and settled in Flushing. In 1710 he paid 6 sh. towards the support
of Grace Ch., J[a], as per p. 37 of Onderdonk's His. of said ch.
Will da. Aug. 29, 1726, pro. Mar. 29, 1735, rec. p. 307, Lib.
12, N. Y. surr. off.; a codicil da. Apl. 3, 1733, in which he
refers to Fl[h] lands. Issue:—Elizabeth, bp. May 3, 1719, in
N. U., m. Andries Andriessen of Bedford; Barbara, bp.
July 7, 1723, in N. U., m. David Springsteen; Garret; John
of Fl[h], m. Sarah da. of Cor[s] Van Voorhees; Abraham;
George; and Isaac. Made his mark "B I B" to documents.

Claes Barentse. A Claes Barentse emigrated from
Dortrecht in the Netherlands Sept. 2, 1662, who may have
been this Claes. He m. Apl. 26, 1685, Elizabeth Paulus
wid. of Paulus Vandervoort of Bedford, Br[n]. Took the oath
of allegiance in Br[n] in 1687, and on cen. of said town of
1698. Resided in Fl[h] in 1675, and on ass. roll of said town
of said year. Bought Dec. 4, 1684, of Cor[s] Barentse Van
der Wyck lot No. 20 in the N. L. of Fl[h], as per p. 177 of
Lib. C of Fl[h] rec. Issue:—Jannetje, bp. Feb. 11, 1694, in
Br[n], m. Oct. 7, 1716, Jacob Lefferts of Bedford; and (sup.)
Barent, m. Femmetje ——. Made his mark to documents.

Jan or *John Barentse*, b. in this country, and took the oath
of allegiance in Fl[h] in 1687; m. Marretje ——; d. prior to
1703. Bought Feb. 15, 1677-8, of Bartel Claesen a house
and lot in Fl[h], as per p. 23 of Lib. AA of Fl[h] rec. Also
bought Feb. 5, 1680-1, of Ab[m] Douts his farm, No. 20, in
the new allotments of Fl[h] (New Lotts), lying between the
farms of Gerret Lubbertse and his own farm, as per p. 149
of Lib. AA of Fl[h] rec. Issue:—Barent Janse of Flushing;
Simon Janse of J[a]; and Joris or George Janse of Fl[h].
He made his mark "I B" to documents. There are families of Bloms in Somerset Co., N. J., and also in Dutchess
Co., N. Y.

George or *Joris* of Fl[h] (s. of Claes Barentse), m. Jannetje
——. Constable of Fl[h] in 1723 and '24. Will da. Oct. 6,
1736, pro. May 7, 1737, rec. p. 76, Lib. 13, N. Y. surr. off., in
which he devises his real estate to Abraham s. of his brother
Simon. No issue. Signed his name "*Joris Blom*" in 1714.

Simon (s. of Jan Barentse), m. June 3, 1703, Geertje Janse.
Left Fl[h] and settled in J[a]. Will da. Jan. 11, 1721, pro. Jan.
7, 1723, rec. p. 354, Lib. 9, N. Y. surr. off. Issue:—John, bp.
Feb. 3, 1706, in Br[n], m. Sarah; Isaac of J[a], blacksmith, m.

Phebe; Barent or Bernardus of Newtown; Ann; Abraham; Jacob, (sup.) m. Gertrude Santford; George of Fl^h; Mary; and Eve. Made his mark "S" to documents in 1716.

Bobin or Bobine, James, bought Apl. 28, 1693, Moll's or Kip's patent in Bu^k or Williamsburgh. He is referred to in Gov. Cornbury's charter of the city of N. Y. of 1708.

Bode, Thomas, of Br^n, m. Sept. 29, 1692, *Maria Cats* (Van Cott) of Bu^k.

Boerden, on Stoothoff's books in 1680.

Boerhol, Willem Janse, of Fld^s, m. Mar. 29, 1690, Ariaentje Herbersz of the same place.

Boerum or Van Boerum, Charles or Karel, (s. of Jacob Willemse,) of Fl^h, m. *Rebecca* da. of Gerrit Snediker; d. 1763. On cen. of 1738, and an owner of slaves in 1755. Will da. May 1, 1762, pro. May 6, 1763, rec. p. 19, Lib. 24, N. Y. surr. off. Issue:—Elsie, bp. Dec. 25, 1721, in N. U., m. Apl. 18, 1747, Leffert Lefferts of Fl^h; Jacob, (sup.) m. May 26, 1743, Gertrude da. of John Bennet of Gowanus; Gerrit of Fl^h, m. Marretje Van Dyck wid. of Johannes Rapalje; and Abraham, bp. Apl. 7, 1728, in N. U.

Hendrick (Van Boerum) Willemse, emigrated from Amsterdam in 1649 with his father; b. 1642; m. about 1663 Maria Ariaens. On ass. rolls of Fl^h of 1675 and '76, and on cen. of 1698, residing in N. L.; took the oath of allegiance in Fl^h in 1687, and a patentee on Gov. Dongan's patent of Fl^h of 1685. May 27, 1679, he bought of his father a farm in Fl^h adjoining on the S. side said Hendrick's land, and on the N. side that of the wid. of Ad^n Hegeman, dec., with meadows
• at Canarisie and lot No. 16 in the new lotts of said town, as per p. 59 of Lib. AA of Fl^h rec. Issue:—Hendrick, b. about 1665; Arie or Adriaen of Freehold, N. J. (New Jersey,) b. 1666, m. Sarah Smock; Louise, bp. Oct. 24, 1680, in Fl^h; and Hendrick, bp. July 22, 1683, in Fl^h. Made his mark to documents.

Jacob Willemse (s. of Willem Jacobse) of N. L., emigrated with his father in 1649; m. June 15, 1684, Geertruyd De Beavois from Leiden; d. prior to 1698. Made a joint will da. July 2, 1687, and rec. on p. 90 of Lib. A of Fl^h rec. Mem. of Fl^h R. D. ch. in 1677, on ass. roll of 1675, and took the oath of allegiance in said town in 1687. Mar. 27, 1679, he bought of his father lots Nos. 15 and 16 in the new division (New Lotts) of Fl[h], with 4 lots of meadows, as per p. 61 of Lib. AA of Fl[h] rec. Issue:—Johannis of Hempstead; William of Fl[h], m. Rachel ——; Charles or Karel of Fl[h], m. Rebecca da. of Gerret Snedeker; and Jacob, m. Magdalen ——. Signed his name "*Jacop Van Boerum.*"

Johannes (s. of Jacob Willemse and Geertruyd) of Hempstead, m. May 28, 1715, Femmetje Cornel. Will da. May 21, 1737, pro. Mar. 7, 1742, rec. p. 27, Lib. 15, N. Y. surr. off. Issue:—Jacob; Cornelius; Johannis; Joynachy; and Familie. Signed his name "*Johannes Boeram*" in 1713.

Willem Jacobse, b. 1617; m. Geertje Hendrickse; d. prior to 1698. Emigrated with his sons in 1649 from Amsterdam and settled in N. L., Fl[h]. Feb. 7, 1670-1, he was allotted, in pursuance of the patent of Fl[h], 25 morgens in said town between the lands of Jan Hansen (Van Noostrand) and those of Adr[n] Hegeman, with plain land and salt meadows in addition, as per p. 16 of Lib. A of Fl[h] rec. He was a mag. of said town in 1657, '62, and '63, on ass. roll of 1675, and took the oath of allegiance there in 1687. Issue:— Hendrick Willemse; Jacob Willemse; Geertruy Willemse, (sup.) m. Francis du Puis; and Hillegont Willemse. Signed his name "*Willem Jacobse Van Boerum.*"

William (s. of Jacob Willemse and Geertruyd) of Fl[h]; m. Rachel ——. On cen. of Fl[h] of 1738. Will da. Oct. 2, 1766, pro. Nov. 14, 1768, rec. p. 326, Lib. 26, N. Y. surr. off. Issue:—John, b. about 1717, (sup.) m. Catrina Remsen; Marretje, bp. Sept. 17, 1719; William of Br[n], m. Apl. 19, 1755, Gertrude da. of Nicholas Wyckoff; Simon of Br[n], b. Feb. 29, 1724, m. Sept. 30, 1748, Maria da. of Martin Roelofse Schenck; and Geertruyd, bp. June 17, 1728, (sup.) m. Abraham Bloom, d. Mar. 11, 1813.

BOGART or BOGAERT, ADRIAN TUNISEN, (sup. s. of Teunis Gysbertse,) m. 1st *Susanna Hamilton;* m. 2[d], Sept. 14, 1685, in N. Y., *Belitje Post* wid. of Arie Juriaansz Lantsman, both of the city of N. Y., to which place he probably removed from Br[n].

Cornelis (Gysbertse), m. 1732 —— da. of Nicholas Volckersen. Of Br[n] in 1711, and in 1732 resided on the Raritan, N. J. Will da. Apl. 5, 1732, pro. July 27, 1732, rec. p. 357, Lib. 11, N. Y. surr. off. Appoints his father Gysbert, father-in-law Nicholas Volckersen, and brothers-in-law Ab[m] Schenck and Volkert Volckersen, executors. Issue:—Gysbert, m. Antie Lott, d. 1778; Neeltje, (sup.) m. Isaac Brower; . Jannetje; Nicholas, bp. Sept. 30, 1730, m. Apl. 21, 1752, Catharine Broadhurst; and (sup.) Catharine, b. Aug. 21, 1739, m. 1759 Johannes Stoothoff, d. Jan. 26, 1826.

Cornelis (Tunisen, sup. s. of Teunis Gysbertse), settled on the Raritan in N. J., and had a son Johannes bp. Apl. 25, 1711.

Gysbert (*Tunisen*), bp. Dec. 6, 1668, in N. Y.; m. Apl. 16, 1689, Jannetje Symonse Van Aersdalen, a wid. Took the oath of allegiance in Br^n in 1687 as a native; on ass. roll of Br^a of 1693 and cen. of 1698; mag. of Br^n in 1663, '64, '67, and '73, and of Bu^k in 1707. There was a Gysbert Tunisen a mag. of Fld^s in 1660, who may have been this Gysbert. Issue:—Cornelis Gysbertse, who m. a dau. of Nicholas Volkertse; Sara Gysbertse, bp. Aug. 1690, m. Apl. 20, 1717, Ab^m Schenck; Tunis Gysbertse of S. I., m. Oct. 20, 1711, Catharine da. of Jos^h Hegeman, d. 1767; Gysbert Gysbertse; Symon Gysbertse of S. I., m. Margaritje Ten Eyck; Petronella; and Maria. Signed his name "*Gysbert Boogart.*"

Nicholas, secretary of Bu^k May 8, 1666, per town rec. Probably a brother of Tunis Gysbertse.

Tunis Gisbertse, the common ancestor of the Kings Co. Bogarts, emigrated in 1652 from Heikop in the province of Utrecht; m. 1st Sarah da. of Joris Jansen Rapalie and wid. of Hans Hansen Bergen; m. 2^d, Nov. 11, 1687, in N. Y., Grietje or Geertje Jans wid. of Derick Dey. At the date of this marriage he was a resident of the Walabocht. Mag. of Br^n in 1663, '67, and '73; a representative of said town in the Hempstead convention of 1665; and on Gov. Nicolls' patent of Br^n of 1667. Apl. 5, 1667, Bogaert obtained a confirmatory patent in his own name (instead of the heirs of Hans Hansen) of Hans Hansen Bergen's patent of 200 morgen at the Walabocht. Issue:—Aertje Tunisen, bp. Aug. 19, 1655, m. Oct. 24, 1677, Theodorus Polhemius; Catalyntje Tunisen, bp. Dec. 16, 1657, m. Nov. 16, 1679, Jan Teunisen Denyse; Neeltje Tunisen, bp. Feb. 22, 1660, and d. young; Aaltje Tunisen, bp. Nov. 13, 1661, m. Dec. 11, 1681, Charles Claasz of Harsimus, N. J.; Antje or Annetje Tunisen, bp. Aug. 23, 1665, m. Joris Abrahamse Brinckerhoff; Neeltje Tunisen, bp. Aug. 20, 1665, (all bp. in N. A. or N. Y.,) m. Aug. 22, 1687, Cornelis Teunisen Denyse; Gisbert Tunisen, bp. Dec. 6, 1668; (sup.) Adriaen Tunisen; (sup.) Grietje Tunisen; and (sup.) Cornelis Tunisen of the Raritan. Signed his name "*Tenis Gisbertse Bogaert.*"

Tunis (s. of Gysbert Tunisen and Jannetje), m. Oct. 20, 1711, Catharine da. of Joseph Hegeman. Resided most of his life on S. I., but d. in 1767 in Br^n. Will da. June 2, 1767, pro. Apl. 27, 1768, rec. p. 210, Lib. 26, N. Y. surr. off., in which he devises his Br^n farm to his sons Adriaen and Cornelis. Issue:—Isaac, bp. Nov. 2, 1718, on S. I., m. Nov. 12, 1742, Sarah da. of Danl Rapalje; Gysbert, m. Annetje

Rapalje; Adriaen, bp. Dec. 18, 1720, on S. I., m. Magdalena Schenck; Abraham, bp. Apl. 21, 1723, on S. I.; Maria, bp. Mar. 28, 1725, on S. I., m. Evert Suydam; Cornelis, bp. Mar. 2, 1729, on S. I.; Jannetje; Antje; and Tunis, who d. prior to 1767.

BOISBILLAND, JOHN, took the oath of allegiance in G^d in 1687 as a native.

BOMAN, HENRY, granted a piece of land in G^d Mar. 3, 1678, as per G^d rec.

BOMMEL, JAN HENDRICKS, m. Aug. 13, 1662, in Br^n, *Annetje Abrahamsz* of Br^n.

BOOMGAERT, BONGAERT, or BONGART, CORNELIS JANSE, of Fl^h, m. *Geesje Willemse*, and d. prior to 1684. In 1661 he sold to Pieter Jansen, shoemaker, a house and village plot in Fl^h, as per p. 47 of Lib. B of Fl^h rec. His name appears on Gov. Nicolls' patent of Fl^h of 1677, as per p. 201 of Vol. 2 of Thompson's L. I., in which town he resided as late as 1683. His descendants write their surname *Bogert*, and reside principally in Bergen and Hudson counties, and in their vicinity, in N. J. Issue:—Weyntje Cornelis, m. Dec. 1673 Gerret Strycker of Fl^h; Jan Cornelise of Hackensack, N. J.; Klaasje Cornelise, m. Hendrick Jorise Brinckerhoff; (sup.) Roelof Cornelise of Hackensack in 1694, m. Oct. 1695 Geertruy Breynant or Bryant; (sup.) Marretje Cornelise, m. Mar. 1693 Jacob Stegge; and Pieter Cornelise of Hackensack, m. Hendrikje Arents. Had a s. buried in Fl^h in 1664. Made his mark to documents.

Claes Janszen of Bedford (a resident of Haerlem at the date of his marriage), m. June 28, 1695, in N. Y., Belitje Van Schayck of said city. He was undoubtedly a brother of Cornelise Janse.

Jan Cornelise, m. Angenietje Strycker. Conveyed Nov. 10, 1694, to Rem Remsen 30 A. in N. L. lying on the J^a road, as per p. 17 of Lib. 2 of Con. Removed to Hackensack, and mem. of the R. D. ch. of that place in 1686. Issue:—Roelof Jansen; Lammetje, bp. Oct. 14, 1677, m. Jan Claesen Romeyn of N. J.; Claes Janse of Bedford and Haerlem; Jan Janse; Gessie Janse, m. Roelof Lubbertse Westervelt; and Cornelis Janse, bp. Nov. 17, 1684. Made his mark to documents.

John Lowen and Cornelia his w., of N. Y., conveyed 40 A. in Bedford, Br^n, Nov. 25, 1695, to Thomas Lambertse, as per p. 51 of Lib. 2 of Con.

Roeloff Jansen (oldest s. of Jan Cornelise), conveyed Mar. 13, 1692-3, to Gerret Strycker of Fld⁸ a lot of land in Fl^h lying between the lands of Joseph Hegeman and Leffert Pieterse, as per p. 175 of Lib. A of Fl^h rec. Made his mark to documents.

BORDET or BOUDET, JAN, of Fld⁸, m. May 20, 1693, *Eva Van Sicklen* of the same place.

BORKELOO, see Barkeloo.

BORSIN or BORSJE, JAN PETERSEN, see Van Amsterdam.

BOSCH, JANTER, m. June 10, 1663, in Br^n, *Rachel Farmelie.* *Lambert Janse,* from Ootmarsen in the province of Overyssel, m. Jan. 1, 1663, at Br^n, Sarah de Planken wid. of Pieter Monfort.

BOTSER, JAN, on muster-roll of Bu^k militia of 1663, per town rec.

BOUDI, THOMAS, and *Mary* had a da. Corteina bp. Sept. 12, 1697, in Br^n.

BOUMAN, CORNELIS JORISZ, on ass. roll of Br^n of 1693 and cen. of 1698.

BOUNER, JORIS, on ass. roll of N. U. of 1676.

BOUT, JAN EVERTSEN, emigrated in 1634, in the service of the West Indian Company, from Barrevelt or Barneweld in the province of Gelderland; b. in 1603; m. 1st *Tryntje Symons De Wit;* m. 2^d *Annetje Pieters,* who after his death m. 2^d Andries Janse Jurianse, and m. 3^d Jan Janse Staats of Gowanus; d. in 1670. Was a farmer about 1638 at Pavonia (Jersey City) in N. J., and Indian interpreter in 1645. In 1643 he was one of the Eight Men representing the people, and in 1645 of the Council. Obtained a patent July 6, 1645, for 28 morgens at Gowanus Kil. Name on Nichols' patent of Br^n of 1667, and a representative of Br^n in the Hempstead convention of 1665, and a mem. of the R. D. ch. of Br^n in 1660. Obtained a patent Mar. 17, 1662, for 58 morgens at Fl^h, which he sold Mar. 23, 1669, to Pieter Giliamse Cornel, as per p. 50 of Lib. C of Fl^h rec. Was a mag. of Br^n in 1646, '53, and '54. His will was presented for proof to the court in Br^n Sept. 17, 1661, as per p. 127 of Lib. 1 of Con. Signed his name "*Jan Evertsen Bout.*"

Bowman, Henry, of G^d, (sup.) English, m. *Mary* da. of John Tilton. In 1678 the court of sessions confirmed to his use a piece of land in G^d given to him by the inhabitants, as per court rec. In 1679 he was a domestic cattle-trader at the South, as per p. 132 of Vol. 1 of Memoirs of L. I. His. Society. Signed his name *"Henry Bowman."*

Bowne, Andrew, of the city of N. Y. and of N. J., d. about 1707, his will being da. May 16, 1707, and letters of administration granted in N. J. on his estate Nov. 19, 1716, to Obedyah Bowne. Oct. 25, 1687, he sold to "Josta Rutt" (Joest Rutgersz Van Brunt) the moiety of a parcel of meadows in G^d formerly of Wm Bredenbent, as per G^d rec. In 1691 he sold 15 A. in G^d which formerly belonged to his father, Wm Bowne. In 1692 he was a member of the Council of East New Jersey, as per p. 155 of Rec. of Gov. and Council. In 1698 he was president of the court of sessions of Middletown, N. J., and Oct. 15 of the same year, hailing from Monmouth Co., he conveyed to Samuel Garretsen and Mary Remmertsen (mother of Samuel) of G^d several parcels of land in G^d, as per p. 193 of Lib. 2 of Con., all formerly of his father, Wm Bowne. In 1699 he was Deputy Gov. of East New Jersey, in 1701 Gov., in 1702 a member of the Council of Gov. Cornbury, and in 1705 a justice of the supreme court of East New Jersey. Issue:—(sup.) Obedyah, who m. Elizabeth. Signed his name *"Andrew Bowne."*

James (s. of William) of G^d and N. J., m. Nov. 26, 1665, Mary Stoute of the same place. Apl. 20, 1670, he sold to Saml Holmes 7 A. "lying at a certain neck called *Cellersneck*, betwixt Sander Lennordser and the highway," as per G^d town rec. He was among the inhabitants of G^d who purchased a tract of land at Middletown, Monmouth Co., N. J., as per p. 24 of Vol. IV. of the Genealogical Rec., to which place he removed, and in 1680 was town-clerk, as per p. 91 of Cal. of Eng. Man. Signed his name *"James Bowne."*

John (s. of William), m. Lydia ——; d. prior to May 29, 1684, as per p. 107 of Rec. of Gov. and Council of E. N. J. (East New Jersey). Came to G^d with his father, and allotted a plantation in said town Sept. 20, 1647, as per G^d rec. Sept. 10, 1660, he bought plantation-lot No. 24 in G^d of Henry Mody. Represented G^d in the Hempstead convention of 1665. Was one of the patentees of Middletown, N. J., as per p. 73 of Vol. 1 of Raum's N. J., where he appears to have resided as early as 1667, and where he took the oath of allegiance in 1668. Was elected to the Provincial Assembly in 1680, as per p. 87 of Cal. of Eng. Man., and 1682 was speaker, as per p. 107, and was appointed justice of the peace for Monmouth Co.

in 1683, as per p. 36 of Rec. of Gov. and Council of E. N. J., and also held other important offices. Issue:—John, b. Apl. 1, 1664; Obedya, b. July 18, 1666; Deborah, b. Jan. 26, 1668; Sarah, b. Nov. 27, 1669, m. Richard Salter; and Catharine. Signed his name "*John Bowne*."

John (s. of John and Lydia), b. Apl. 1, 1664, in G^d; m. Frances ——. Left G^d with his father and settled at Middletown, N. J. In 1684 he petitioned the Gov. and Council for a warrant of survey for 500 A. his deceased father, John Bowne, was entitled to as a patentee of the Neversinks, as per p. 107 of the Rec. of the Gov. and Council of E. N. J., which he obtained Mar. 10, 1685, and which he sold in 1693 to the Schencks. In 1704 he was elected a mem. of the Provincial Assembly of N. J., as per p. 41 of the Journal of the House of Representatives of said State. His will is da. Sept. 14, 1714, pro. Feb. 15, 1715, and from its provisions infer he had no children.

Obedya (s. of John and Lydia), b. July 18, 1666, in G^d; m. —— ——. Left G^d with his father and settled on a tract of 632 A. in Pleasant Valley, Monmouth Co., N. J. In 1703 he was elected a mem. of the Provincial Assembly of N. J., as per p. 41 of the Journal of the House of Representatives of said State. By his will, da. in 1725, he devised his lands to his chil. Issue:—John, Cornelius, Obedya, Thomas, Sarah, Anne, and Lydia.

William, among the first settlers of G^d, where he was allotted a plantation-lot Nov. 18, 1656, as per G^d rec., and of which town he was a mag. in 1651, '55, '56, '57, '61, and '62. He and his sons came to G^d with Lady Mody, and with them and others of said town obtained a patent in 1665 for a large tract at Middletown, N. J., to which he and his sons removed, and in which State they are principally to be found. In 1677 letters of administration were granted to John Bowne of Middletown on the estate of his father William, "heretofore of Gravesend" and late of Middletown. See pp. 24, 25, and 26 of Vol. IV. of the Genealogical Rec. Issue:—John, James, and Andrew. Signed his name " *Wili Bowne.*" *

BOYCE, CORNELIS, (sup. English,) on ass. roll of G^d of 1683. In 1785 Cornelis Boyce, one of his descendants, sold his house and lot in the village of G^d to John Emans, as

---

* The compiler is indebted to the Rev. G. C. Schenck of Marlboro, N. J., for information relating to the Amacks, Bownes, Golders, Holmes, Longstreets, Luysters, Smacks, Stouts, Ver Kerks, and Verweys of N. J.

per G⁴ rec. There was a Jacobus Boyce residing in G⁴ in 1769.

BRAGAW, see Broucard.

BRASSER, BRASIER, or BRESSE, GERRET HENDRICKSE, of Fl^h, m. June 16, 1689, in N. Y., *Catharine Hardenbrook* wid. of Hendrick Arentsen, and took the oath of allegiance in Fl^h in 1687 as a native. This may be the same person as Harry or Henry Breser.

BRAUM, JAN, m. Jan. 24, 1663, in Br^n, *Maria Hendricks.*

BREDENBENT, WILLEM, from Ceulen or Cologne, m. Sept. 4, 1644, *Aeltien Brackhanye* wid. of Cor.ª Lambertse Cool. Was deputy schout fiscaal in 1638 of N. A., and a mag. (schepen*) of Br^n in 1654, '56, '57, '58, '60, '63, and '64. Owned a farm in G⁴ in 1654, per Col. Man. Resided on Cool's patent in Gowanus in 1657, and in 1660 mem. of the R. D. ch. of Br^n. He and his w. made a joint will June 22, 1670, in which after their death they devised their property to Marrike (Mary) Tomas Baddie da. of Altien by a former husband, as per p. 81 of Lib. C of Fl^h rec. Signed his name " *Willem Bredenbent*," and she made her mark "A B."

BREETS, see Bries.

BRESER or BRASIER, HARRY or HENRY, m. Sept. 9, 1644, *Susanna* da. of Thomas Spicer of G⁴. Obtained a patent for a plantation in Br^n adjoining Claes Dircksen the ferryman's, Aug. 3, 1651, as per Col. Man. Apl. 5, 1659, bought of James Surtell half an acre taken from plantation-lot No. 28 in G⁴, with a house thereon, as per town rec. Issue:—Mary, bp. Sept. 29, 1645; Willem, bp. Nov. 18, 1646; Rebecca, bp. Apl. 26, 1648; Breser, bp. Feb. 9, 1653; Machtelt, bp. Nov. 21, 1655; Marthan or Martha, bp. May 20, 1657; Sara, bp. Dec. 14, 1659; Henry, bp. July 29, 1663, m. Aug. 5, 1685, in N. Y., Maryken Jorise Van Alst of Mispats Kil; Isaac, bp. May 16, 1666, m. May 17, 1690, in N. Y., Altje Colevelt; Abraham, bp. Nov. 25, 1668, m. Oct. 18, 1690, in N. Y., Lysbet Schouten —all bp. in N. A. or N. Y. Made his mark to documents.

GERRIT HENDRICKZEN of Fld^s, m. June 16, 1689, in N. Y., Catharine Hardenbroeck wid. of Hendrick Arentszen of N. Y.

---

* A magistrate with powers similar to those of a justice and sheriff.

BREVOORT (VAN), HENDRICK JANSE, b. 1630; resided in 1659 in Bu^k on a plantation of David Jochems, since (1695) of John Meserole Senr, as per Bu^k town rec. Of the city of N. Y. in 1695, as per p. 68 of Vol. 2 of Con. June 8, 1690, he made a deposition concerning a riot in the city of N. Y. in which the life of Gov. Leisler was endangered, as per p. 740 of Vol. II. of Doc. His. of N. Y. A Hendrick Brevoort m. 1st, Aug. 26, 1699, Maryken Cowenhoven, and m. 2^d, Oct. 6, 1705, Jacomyntje Bokke, as per N. Y. D. ch. rec., and had several chil. bp. in said ch.

John Hendrickse, b. 1644; resided in Bu^k in 1659 with Hendrick Janse Brevoort on David Jochem's plantation in Bu^k. Of the city of N. Y. in 1695. A John Brevoort constable of Haerlem in 1690, as per p. 195 of Cal. of Eng. Man.

BREYLEY, PETER, hired Oct. 20, 1639, Thos Bescher's plantation at Gowanus.

BRICKER, GERRET, conveyed Feb. 28, 1658, to Edward Griffins 25 morgens of land in Fl^h, as per p. 377 of Cal. of Dutch Man. Believe this should be Gerrit Strycker.

BRIDGES, CHARLES, (English,) of G^d in 1656, per Thompson's L. I. Owned a 15 A. lot in said town in 1674, and allotted land in said town in 1674, as per G^d rec. In 1678 had a dispute with James Hubbard about a piece of meadows sold to Sarah his wife by Saml Leynersen in G^d.

BRIES or BREETS, FOLKERT HENDRICKSZ, of Br^n, m. 1st, Apl. 1, 1680, *Neeltje Janss* wid. of Gerret Dirckse Croegier; m. 2^d *Elizabeth Poulis*. On ass. roll of Br^n of 1693 and cen. of 1698. Appointed ensign of Br^n militia in 1698. His farm was located on the N.E. side of the Port road, or road leading from Fl^h to Brower's, since Denton's and Freecke's mills, which he sold Oct. 20, 1701, to Everardus or Gerardus and Nicholas Brower, as per pp. 264 and 266 of Lib. 2 of Con. There was a Hendrick Bries shoemaker in Albany in 1666, as per Pierson's Early Rec. of Albany. Issue:—Gerbrants, bp. Nov. 15, 1697; Neeltje, bp. Dec. 25, 1698; and Wyntje, bp. June 8, 1701. A Hendrick Bries settled near New Brunswick, N. J., prior to 1699, as per p. 35 of Messler's Somerset Co. Made his mark to documents.

Jurrian Hendrickse and Angenietje his w., of Br^n, sold May 7, 1695, to Thomas Knight for £32 a plot adjoining land of Joris Hansen (Bergen) in the vicinity of the old R. D. ch. in Br^n, as per p. 59 of Vol. 2 of Con. On ass. roll of Br^n of 1693.

Suybrech, a juryman on a coroner's inquest on a corpse on the shore between the houses of Symon Aesen (De Hart) and Elyas Symonse (De Hart) at Gowanus, May 12, 1698, as per Van Sicklen papers. (Heirs of Coert Van Sicklen of G^d.)

BRIGGS, JOHN, of G^d, on ass. roll of 1683. John Briggs, ag. 40, was transported in 1635 to New England, as per p. 108 of Hotten's list of emigrants.

John Junr, on ass. roll of G^d in 1683. The family appears to have removed to E. N. J., where their descendants reside. There was a *John Briggs* who obtained a patent for 500 A. on the Delaware in 1676.

BRIMES, BRIMASEN, BRIMSAY, BRISSAY, or BRISEN, EVERT HENDRICKSE, of Fld^s, and others, convey Apl. 7, 1692, to Gerret Coerten Voorhies 26 A. in Fl^h, as per p. 136 of Lib. 2 of Con. *Gerret Hendrickse, Herman Hendrickse, Hendrick, Rutt, Walter*, and *William*, all of Fl^h, joined in the above conveyance.

BRINCKERHOFF, ABRAHAM JORISE, of Fld^s, b. at Flushing or Vlissingen in the province of Zeeland in 1632; m. May 1660 Aeltie da. of Jan Strycker of Fl^h; d. 1714. Obtained Apl. 13, 1661, a patent for 32 morgens at Fl^h, as per p. 165 of Lib A of Fl^h rec. A mag. of Fld^s in 1673, on ass. roll of said town of 1675, and with his wife mem. of Fld^s R. D. ch. in 1670 and '77, and deacon in 1672. Issue:—Joris Abramse of Fld^s and Flushing; Susanna Abramse, m. June 13, 1686, Martin Roelofse Schenck of Fld^s; Ida Abramse, m. May 17, 1687, Jan Monfort of J^a; Dirk Abramse of Flushing, b. Mar. 16, 1677; Jan Abramse of Flushing; Sarah Abramse, m. 1st Jacob Rapelje, m. 2^d Nicholas Berrien; (sup.) Margaret Abramse, m. Theodorus Van Wyck; Lammetje Abramse, m. Johannes Cornel; Cornelis Abramse; and Gerret Abramse of Flushing, bp. Oct. 23, 1681. Signed his name "*Abraham Joorise.*"

Cornelis (Abramse), removed to Flushing; m. May 24, 1708, Aegtje da. of Hartman Vreeland of Bergen, N. J., as per p. 446 of Winfield's Hudson Co.

Dirk (Abramse), b. Mar. 16, 1677; m. 1st, 1700, Altie da. of Jan Gerretse Couwenhoven; m. 2^d —— Hendrickse; d. Apl. 26, 1748. Removed from Fl^h and settled in Flushing. Issue:—Abraham of Fishkill, Dutchess Co., b. about 1700, m. Femmetje Remsen Vanderbeeck; John of Dutchess Co., b. 1701, m. Jane da. of Johannes Van Voorhies, d. 1785; Joris of N. Y., b. 1705, d. 1768; Jacob of Dutchess Co., b. 1714, m. Elizabeth

Lent, d. 1758; Isaac of Dutchess Co., b. Jan. 12, 1714, m. Feb. 28, 1737, Sarah Rapalje, d. Apl. 22, 1770; Diana, m. Isaac Brinckerhoff; Aeltie, m. Wm Hoogland; and Susanna, m. Cor^s Luyster. The Brinckerhoffs bought in 1721 a tract of 1700 A. in Dutchess Co., as per p. 184 of Smith's His. of said co.

Gerret (Abramse), bp. Oct. 23, 1681. Settled in Flushing.

Hendrick (Jorise), m. Clasie Cornelise Boomgaert or Bougaert of "Middlewout" (Fl^h). Name on Indian deed of Fl^h of 1670, and on ass. roll of 1675. Mem. of the Hempstead Assembly of 1665 from Fl^h, and a mag. of said town in 1662, '63, and '73. Removed from Fl^h to the eastern branch of the Hackensack River in N. J., where he bought land June 17, 1685. His descendants in N. J. sometimes write their name Blinckerhoff. Issue:—Susanna, bp. Jan. 16, 1661, m. Roelof Van der Linde of Hackensack; Cornelis, m. Aegie Vreeland, and resided at Hackensack; Derick of Hackensack, m. Margaret Siba Banta; and Jacobus of Hackensack, bp. Mar. 29, 1685, m. Angenietje Banta.

Jan (Abramse), m. Catrina, and settled at Flushing. Issue: —John, b. Mar. 15, 1703, m. 1^m Maratie Ryder, m. 2^d Ann da. of Ab^m Lent; and Aaltje, bp. Aug. 24, 1707.

Joris (Abramse), b. Mar. 1, 1664; m. Annetje Tunise Bogaert; d. Mar. 27, 1729. Mem. of Fld^g R. D. ch. in 1677, and removed to Flushing. Issue:—Sarah, b. Dec. 18, 1691, m. Rem Adrianse; Susanna, b. Mar. 4, 1693; Abraham, b. Dec. 10, 1694, d. May 6, 1762; Teunis of Dutch Kils, b. Mar. 29, 1697, m. Nov. 24, 1721, Elizabeth Ryder, d. June 16, 1784; Isaac, b. Apl. 26, 1699, m. Diana da. of Dirck Brinckerhoff; Altie or Aletta, b. Apl. 13, 1704, m. Nov. 30, 1727, Cornelius Rapalje of Hell Gate, d. Jan. 22, 1790; Joris, bp. May 29, 1705, (sup.) m. Maria Van Dyck; Neeltje, b. July 22, 1706, (sup.) m. Adrian Martense; Hendrick of Flushing, b. Jan. 2, 1709, m. Lametie da. of Danl Rapalje, d. 1777; and Anna, b. Oct. 4, 1712, m. May 14, 1731, Ab^m Rapalje of Newtown.

Joris Dircksen, the ancestor of the Brinckerhoff family, emigrated from Vlissingen in the Netherlands in 1638 with his wife Susanna Dubbles, settled in Br^n, where he obtained Mar. 23, 1646, a grant for a tract of 18 morgens of land, and d. Jan. 16, 1661. He was a mag. of Br^n from 1654 to 1660, was connected with the R. D. ch. of Br^n at its organization, and an elder at the time of his death. After his death his Br^n grant appears to have been sold by "Classie Boomgaert, Abraham Jorisen, and Willem Gerretse Van Cowenhoven, heirs of Susanna Dubbles," to Henry Sleght, as per p. 100 of Lib. 1 of Con. Issue:—Derick Jorise; Hendrick Jorise; Abraham Jorise; and Altie Jorise, who m. 1st —— Matthews, and m. 2^d Willem Gerretse Van Cowenhoven.

4

BRITTAN, NATHANIELL, (English,) m. in 1660 *Anna* da. of Nicholas Stillwell; d. in 1683 on S. I. Resided at one period in a house on the Anthony Jansen from Salee patent, which he built when these premises were owned by his father-in-law, probably cultivating a part of the same. De Bruynne, on the purchase of the patent from Stillwell, was required to satisfy Brittan for his house and outbuildings, which appear to have been located on the N.W. side of the plantation, and on the portion De Bruynne sold to Jan Janse Ver Ryn. In 1660 Brittan bought of Hendrick Cornelise his plantation in Fld' of 25 morgens, as per p. 15½ of Lib. B of Fl^h rec. Apl. 3, 1664, he bought of Albert Albertse (Terhune) his N. U. farm, with the meadows thereunto appertaining, which purchase he applied to the court to declare void or to have a deduction made of £100, in consequence of the loss of the meadows by the convention at Hempstead of 1665 (convened after the conquest of the colony by the English) deciding that the meadows in question belonged to G^d. After considerable litigation the court decided that a deduction of 500 gl. wampum value should be made, as per p. 496 of Valentine's Manual of 1852. In 1664 he obtained a patent for a tract of 144 A. on S. I., on which he finally settled. In 1665 he was licensed to keep a tap-house (tavern) in the city of N. Y. By the Stoothoff books it appears that at one period he was a dry-goods dealer. Issue:—William, of S. I. in 1701, b. 1661; Nathaniel, of S. I. in 1701, b. 1663; Sarah, b. 1664; Rachel, b. 1665; Joseph, b. 1667; Rebecca, b. 1668, m. Mar. 1695 Abram Cole; Benjamin, of S. I. in.1701,b. 1669; Jan, b. 1670; Abagail, b. 1671; Daniel, b. 1674; Abagail; and Nicholas, bp. Sept. 17, 1680, m. Frances ——. Signed his name "*Nathaniell Brittan*" in 1660.

BROUCARD, BROULAET, BOURGON, or BRAGAW, BROUCARD, a French Huguenot who emigrated to this country from Manheim in the Palatinate of the Rhine with his w. *Catharine Le Febre* in 1675. In 1684 he bought and resided on a farm in Bu^k, which he sold in 1688 and removed to Newtown. Previous to this he appears to have resided at Bedford, as per Do. Van Zuuren's lists of R. D. ch. mem. of 1677, on which he is entered as removed from Bedford to Fl^h. Issue:—Maria, m. Myndert Wiltse; Jane, m. Hans Coevert; Catalina; Isaac, bp. Aug. 7, 1676, m. Heyltie ——; John, m. Sarah ——, and settled at Three Mile Run, N. J.; Jacob, settled on the Raritan; Peter, m. Catharine and settled on the Raritan; and Abraham, m. Marytie or Maria ——, and settled on the Raritan. The N. J. branch of the family write their surname Broka or Brockaer. Made his mark to documents.

BROUGHMAN, JOHN, of·G^d in 1656, per Thompson's L. I.

BROULERT or BROUCHART, BOURGON, emigrated in 1675, and on ass. roll of Br^n of 1676 and '89. This may be Broucard Bragaw.

BROUSE or BROWSE, EDWARD, (sup. English,) among the first settlers of G^d in 1646, where he obtained a planter's lot. Mag. of said town in 1655, '56, and '58; acting town clerk in 1656 and '57, and owned plantation-lot No. 24. His will is da. Aug. 28, 1658, pro. Nov. 4, 1658, and rec. on the town rec. of G^d. Devises his whole estate to the Lady Debora Mody, Wm Bowne, late of G^d, and Marke Luter of Rhode Island, with the provision that if his brother John Browse and his 3 sons, late of Bath in Old England, should come here, or either of them, then he desired his property to be given to them. Signed his name "*Edward Browse.*"

BROUWER or BROWER, ADAM, sometimes written Adam Brouwer Berckhoven or Kerckhoven, emigrated in 1642 from Ceulon or Cologne; m. May 19, 1645, in N. A., *Madalena Jacobs Verdon;* d. about 1698. Resided in Br^n and occupied the old mill late of John C. Frecke. Feb. 7, 1647, he obtained a patent for a lot in N. A., where he probably resided prior to his removal to Br^n. Mem. of Br^n R. D. ch. in 1677, on ass. rolls of said town of 1675 and '83, and cen. of 1698. Aug. 20, 1667, Jan Cornelise Buys and Derick Jansen (Hoogland), on inquiry, declared under oath that Jan Evertse Bout, in the house of Jan Damen, tavern-keeper, stated to them that he had not given unto Adam Brouwer the "place and meadow whereon the mill is grounded," but that he had given "the place whereon the mill is grounded, and the corne and the meadow," unto the children of Adam Brouwer, as per p. 179 of Lib. 2 of Con. Made a will Jan. 22, 1691-2. Issue:—Peter Adams; Jacobus Adams; Aelje Adams of Gowanus, m. Apl. 30, 1682, Josias Jansz Drats; Mathys Adams, b. 1649; William Adams, b. 1651; Mary, Maria, or Marretje Adams, b. 1653; Helena or Magdalena Adams, bp. Oct. 30, 1660, m. Aug. 5, 1693, Willem Hendricksen of England, a resident of Mispat Kil; Adam Adams, b. 1662; Abraham Adams; Eytie or Sophia Adams, m. 1st Evert Hendricksen, m. 2^d, Feb. 20, 1692, Matys Cornelisen; Ann Adams, (sup.) m. William Hilton; Sarah Adams, m. 1st, July 13, 1684, Teunis Janse of Flushing, m. 2^d, Sept. 23, 1692, Tomas Knight of Br^n; Nicholas Adams, b. 1672; (sup.) Daniel Adams, b. 1678; and Rachel

Adams, m. June 5, 1698, in N. Y.,.Pieter Hendricksen of Vrieslandt. Made his mark "Ⓑ" to documents.

Abraham (Adams, sometimes written Abraham Adams Bercho or Berckhoven), m. Feb. 6, 1692, Cornelia Halsyn of Bu^k. Took the oath of allegiance in Br^n in 1687, resided in Bu^k in 1698, and in Br^n in 1714. Issue:—Elizabeth, bp. June 11, 1695, in N. Y., m. Jacob Bennet of S. I.; Magdalena, bp. Mar. 21, 1697; Marytje, bp. Mar. 12, 1699, (sup.) m. Aug. 4, 1718, Henry Lyon; Abraham of Br^n Mills, bp. Dec. 15, 1706, m. Sarah Kimber; and Jeury. Made his mark "Ⓑ" to documents.

Adam (Adams), bp. May 18, 1662, in Br^n; m. 1st, May 18, 1690, Marritje Hendricksen; m. 2^d Angenietje ——. Took the oath of allegiance in Br^n in 1687. Styled Adam Adams Kerckhoven on the records. Issue:—Madaleentje, bp. Apl. 2, 1692, in Br^n; Marytje, bp. May 4, 1695, in Br^n; and Hendrick, bp. Jan. 15, 1699. Made his mark "Ⓑ" to documents.

Adolphus (s. of Willem Adams and Elizabeth Simpson) of Br^n, bp. Aug. 10, 1684; m. (sup.) Jannetje Verdon. Issue:— Yannetje, bp. June 18, 1719, in Br^n; (sup.) Jeremiah, whose will is da. Sept. 18, 1754, in which he devises his Br^n property among his 3 sons, Abraham, William (now dec.), and Adolphus. It is probable he also had sons Abraham, Jeremiah, and Garret.

Daniel, bp. May 7, 1678, in N. Y. The ch. rec. state that he is a s. of Adam Brouwer and Aeltje Vanderbeek. No other account of Adam Brouwer the emigrant of 1642 marrying this woman. It may be some other Adam.

Derck (not a s. of Adam), m. Oct. 6, 1694, in Fld^s, Hannah Deas. Of G^d in 1694, at which date he bought land on Gisbert's I., as per town rec.

Everardus (Jacobse), bp. Dec. 8, 1689; (sup.) m. Nov. 30, 1738, Cornelia De La Noy. Appears to have removed to N. Y., the R. D. ch. of which place he joined May 22, 1739, on certificate. Issue:—Peternella, bp. Dec. 21, 1740, in N. U., and d. an infant; Peternella, bp. July 10, 1743, in N. Y.; Jannetje, bp. May 8, 1746, in N. Y.; Maria, bp Mar. 4, 1747, in N. Y.; Jacob, bp. Apl. 24, 1751, in N. Y.; Abraham, bp. Nov. 9, 1752, in N. Y.; and Abraham, bp. June 31, 1755, in N. Y.

Jacob or *Jacobus (Adams)* of Gowanus, m. June 29, 1682, at Br^n, Annetje da of. Wm Bogardus and Wyntje Sybrants, and grandda. of the Rev. Everardus Bogardus and Annetje Jans of Trinity Ch. memory. Took the oath of allegiance in Br^n in 1687; on ass. roll of said town of 1676 and cen. of 1698. Issue:—Jacob of Br^n, bp. Nov. 30, 1684; William, bp. May 8, 1687, in Br^n, (sup.) m. May 29, 1719, Maria Hennian—no account of his descendants; Sybrant, m. Antie ——, d. previous to May 1737; Everardus, bp. Dec. 8, 1689; Elizabeth, bp. Nov. 15, 1694, (sup.) m. May 16, 1715, John Parcel; Adam, bp. Mar. 29, 1696; Hillegont, bp. Dec. 27, 1697; (sup.) Wyntje, bp. Mar. 8, 1701, m. Richard Pettit; (sup.) Magdalena, bp. Mar. 8, 1704; and (sup.) Nicholas. Made his mark to documents.

Jacob (s. of Jacob and Annetje) of Brⁿ, bp. May 30, 1684; m. Oct. 1, 1709, Petronella da. of Jan De La Montague. Issue:—Jacob, bp. Sept. 24, 1710, in Brⁿ, (sup.) m. Maria Delanoy; Johannis, bp. Mar. 19, 1712, in N. Y., m. Oct. 9, 1734, Susan da. of Paulus Druljet; Abraham, bp. Feb. 6, 1717, in N. Y., m. June 10, 1743, Aafje Van Gelder; Antie, bp. Mar. 13, 1720, in N. Y.; Adam, bp. Feb. 14, 1722, in N. Y.; Antje, bp. Mar. 30, 1726, in N. Y.; and Cornelis of Dutchess Co., bp. Nov. 9, 1730, in N. Y., m. Mary Asker.

Johannes or *John* of Fld^s, blacksmith (not a s. of Adam), emigrated in 1657; m. Jannetje ——. Resided at first in N. A. He and w. mem. of the R. D. ch. of Fld^s in 1677, where he took the oath of allegiance in 1687; on ass. roll of Fld^s of 1683 and cen. of 1698. June 10, 1688, he paid for a grave for his wife in said town. July 26, 1693, Johannes Brouwer of G^d (sup. to be the Johannes of Fld^s) sold Stoffel Langestraat his house and garden-spot in G^d which he bought of John Gulick, and also lot No. 27 on Gisbert's I., which he bought of Hendrick Van Pelt of N. U. Issue:—Jannetje Jans of Fld^s, m 1st, June 11, 1677, Teunis Jans of Denmark, m. 2^d, (sup.) Oct. 24, 1713, Jan Gerretsz of J^a; Johannes Janse of Fld^s; Lucretia Jansz of Fld^s, m. Mar. 17, 1716, Johannes Luyster of Newtown; and Aris Jansz of Fld^s in 1704. There was a Jan Jansen Brouwer a member of Director Minuit's Council in N. A. as early as 1630, as per p. 43 of Vol. 1 of Doc. of Col. His. of N. Y. The following children of a Jan Brouwer and Jannetje Jansz, who possibly may be children of this Jan, were bp. in N. A., viz.:—Jan, bp. May 26, 1658; Pieter, bp. Oct. 20, 1660; Hendricus, bp. Nov. 14, 1663; and Hendrick, bp. Jan. 14, 1665. Signed his name *"Johannes Brouwers"* in 1693.

Johannes Janse (s. of Johannes of Fld^s), of Fld^s in 1683, '87, '88, and 1707, m. Sept. 2, 1683, at Fld^s, Sarah Willems of Fld^s. Issue:—Matthys, bp. Oct. 20, 1711; and Elizabeth, bp. Oct. 25, 1713.

Johannes (s. of Pieter Adamse) of Fld^s, bp. Mar. 21, 1685, in N. Y.; m. Apl. 1708 Antie or Anatie da. of Hendrick Mandaville. Resided at one period at New Harlem. Removed to Hackensack, N. J. Issue:—Maratie, bp. 1714, m. Apl. 1743 Cornelis Talman; Petrus, bp. 1717; Hendrick, bp. 1719; Lea, bp. 1724; and Lea, bp. 1727.

Matthys (*Adams*), bp. May 30, 1649, in N. Y.; m. Jan. 26, 1673, Marretje Pieters Wyckoff of New Amersfoort (Fld²). Both of Brⁿ ferry and mem. of the R. D. ch. of Brⁿ in 1677 and '85. On ass. roll of Brⁿ of 1675. Issue:—Peter, bp. Apl. 22, 1676, (sup.) m. Nov. 18, 1721, Elizabeth Quackenbosch; Hendrick of the Raritan, bp. Dec. 6, 1679, m. Elizabeth ——; William, bp. Feb. 26, 1682; Aaltje, bp. Sept. 28, 1684; Marretje, bp. Nov. 21, 1686; Annetje, bp. Oct. 20, 1689; (all in N. Y.;) Magdalen; and Willemtje, bp. Mar. 14, 1693. Made his mark to documents.

Nicholas (*Adams Berckhoven*), bp. Apl. 16, 1672; m. Sept. 15, 1692, Jannetje Calsier or Coljer of Buᵏ. On ass. roll of Brⁿ of 1683 and cen. of Buᵏ of 1698, to which place he appears to have removed. In May 1719 he and his w. joined the R. D. ch. of N. Y., and are entered as of Fordham. Issue:—Adam, bp. Oct. 15, 1693; Lysbet, bp. June 18, 1699; Jurje, bp. Mar. 30, 1701, (sup.) m. Sept. 15, 1720, Elizabeth Homes; Cornelis, bp. Apl. 18, 1705, m. Aug. 21, 1736, Hester Bodin, and had 6 children bp. in N. Y.; and Nicholas of Dutchess Co., bp. Mar. 16, 1707.

Peter (Adams), bp. Sept. 23, 1646, in N. A.; m. 1ˢᵗ Peternella Uldricks or Claine; m. 2ᵈ Geertruyd Jans; m. 3ᵈ, Feb. 15, 1687, Annetje Jansen of Fld². Resided in Fld², and in 1677 mem. of the R. D. ch. of that place. In 1679 he was bound over to answer at the Gᵈ sessions for an assault on Gerret Croesen, as per p. 80 of Cal. of Eng. Man. In 1687 he took the oath of allegiance as a native and resident of Brⁿ. Issue:—Abraham Pieterse of Hackensack, N. J., m. 1ˢᵗ, Mar. 1700, Lea Jansen De Merce; m. 2ᵈ Elizabeth Ackerman; Johannis Pieterse of Fld² and Hackensack; (sup.) Adolphus Pieterse, m. Jannetje Verden or Ferden; Magdalena, m. Oct. 1697 Wᵐ Stegge of Barbadoes Neck, N. J.; (sup.) Huldrick of Schenectady, m. 1ˢᵗ, Nov. 1698, Hester de Vouw of New Haerlem, m. 2ᵈ, Jan. 10, 1711, Ariaentje Pieters; (sup.) Adriaentje, m. Apl. 1708 Hendrick Claesen; Vroutje, bp. May 16, 1682, m. Aug. 1701 Jan Janse Jeraleman; Cornelia, bp. Mar. 13, 1692; Jacob Pieterse, bp. Nov. 13, 1694, (sup.) m. Marikee —— and settled on the Raritan; Hans Pieterse, bp. Oct. 30, 1695, m. 1ˢᵗ (sup.) Madeline ——, m. 2ᵈ Nelke Golden, and settled in E. N. J.; (sup.) Antie, m. Nov. 1726 Wᵐ Ennis or Annis; (sup.) Maritien, m. Mar. 1738 Peter Herdenay; and (sup.) Petrus Pieterse, m. Diana de Groot. Made his mark "P B" to documents.

Peter (s. of Johannes and Jannetje of Fld²), bought Apl. 22, ——, of his father his lands in Fld² and the tools of his blacksmith-shop, as per p. 243 of Lib. 2 of Con. Made his mark "P B" to documents in 1698.

Willem (Adams), bp. Mar. 5, 1651, in N. A.; m. 1ˢᵗ Aeltje or Elsje ——; m. 2ᵈ Elizabeth or Lysbeth Simpson; m. 3ᵈ Marte ——. Of Gowanus in 1677, and mem. of Brⁿ R. D. ch.; on ass. roll of Brⁿ of 1676 and cen. of 1698. There was a William Brouwer (not a s. of Adam) who in 1655 owned property in N. A., was in Beverwyck in 1657, and was buried Aug. 3, 1663, as per p. 27 of Pearson's Early Settlers of Albany. Issue:—Magdalena (by 1ˢᵗ w.), bp. Sept. 14 1679; Lysbeth (by 2ᵈ w.), bp. Oct. 12, 1681; Adolphus, bp. Aug. 10, 1684; Johannes, bp. Sept. 18, 1687; Catharine, bp. Oct. 5, 1690, in N. Y.; Jannetje (by 3ᵈ w.), bp. Jan. 18, 1702; Samuel, bp. Aug. 25, 1706; (sup.) Margarite; Maria, bp. (sup.) May 1, 1709; Annetje, bp. (sup.) July 30, 1710; and Lucretia, bp. (sup.) Aug. 31, 1712.

BROUGHMAN, JAN, of Gᵈ in 1656, per Thompson's L. I.

BROWNE, WILLIAM, (sup. English,) a mag. of Gᵈ in 1651, as per p. 156 of Vol. II. of N. Y. Doc. of Col. His.

BROWNING, MARGARET, of Gᵈ, m. July 18, 1666, Danell Estall of Middletown, N. J.

BROWSE, see Brouse.

BRUIN, REUF, of Fldˢ in 1700, per town rec. Probably same as Rutger Bruyne.

BRUINNEN or BRUMAN, JAN WARIVERT, on Stoothoff's books of 1677.

BRUMMAGA, see Cammega.

BRUYENBURGH, JAN HANSEN, emigrated in 1639, and took the oath of allegiance in Buᵏ in 1687. Probably this is Jan Hansen (Van Noortstrand), an owner of Buyennesburg; hence the name.

BRUYNE, BRUYNSEN, or BRUNOS, RUTGER, from Gelderland, m. Mar. 15, 1684, *Geertruyd Jansz.* Mem. of R. D. ch. of Fldˢ in 1677, on ass. roll of the same place of 1683 and cen. of 1698. Made his mark to documents.
William (alias *Stommetie*), bought Sept. 28, 1685, of Jacob Stryker and Rutger Bruyne meadow-lot No. 39 in the Flᵇ meadows at Canarisie, as per p. 3 of Lib. A of Flᵇ rec. On ass. roll of Fldˢ of 1693 and cen. of 1698.

BRUYNS (DE BRUYN), JOHN HENDRICK, a merchant of the city of N. Y., and an Indian trader, bought Mar. 20, 1685-6, of John Griggs Junr two 15 A. lots, No. 1 and 16, in G^d, as per town rec.

BUYR, EGBORSEN, see Buys.

BUYS or BUYSE, ADAM (JANSE), of Fl^h, bp. Dec. 11, 1684.
Cornelis, on cen. of G^d of 1698, and on a deed of 1711. Signed his name "*Cornelys Buyse.*"
Cornelis (*Janse*) of Fl^h, bp. Dec. 14, 1684.
Egborsen, paid 3 gl. 12 st., minister's salary, in Fl^h in 1680, as per Fl^h town rec.
Hendrick (*Janse*), bp. Mar. 15, 1654.
Lubbert (*Janse*), bp. Feb. 2, 1655.
Jacob (*Janse*), m. Nov. 22, 1690, Marretje Joris Jorisz. Owned lands in Bedford in 1695, as per deed of Thomas Lambertse to M. Cornelisz, on p. 129 of Lib. 3 of Con., and on cen. of Brⁿ of 1698. There was a Jacobus Buys residing near New Brunswick, N. J., in 1696. Issue:—Jan, bp. Oct. 18, 1691; Joris, bp. Mar. 4, 1694; and Femmetje, bp. Apl. 10, 1698.
Jan of the Wallabout, mem. of the R. D. ch. of Brⁿ in 1677; on ass. roll of said town of 1683 and cen. of 1698. A John Buys and Susanna his wife, of Brⁿ, conveyed in 1694 lands to Jurian Bries, as per p. 5 of Lib. 2 of Con.
Jan Cornelise, known as Jan the soldier, emigrated in 1648; m. 1st Ida or Eybe Lubbertse; m. 2^d, Aug. 24, 1663, Femmetje Jans wid. of Teunis Nyssen (Denyse), who was buried Dec. 13, 1666, in Fl^h ch.; m. 3^d Machteld Gerrets; m. 4th, prior to Nov. 29, 1686, Willemtje Tyssen wid. of Roeleph Willemse, on which date they made a joint will or ante-nuptial contract, as per p. 203 of Lib. 1 of Con. In 1654 he obtained a grant for 25 morgens in Bergen, N. J., as per p. 380 of Cal. of Dutch Man. Resided at the Wallabout and mem. of the R. D. ch. of Brⁿ in 1677, and on ass. rolls of said town of 1675 and '76. Obtained a patent in 1662 from Gov. Stuyvesant for 28 morgens in Fl^h lying between the farms of Cor^s Janse Boomgart and that of Adrⁿ Hegeman, and also for plain land and salt meadows, as per p. 31 of Lib. A of Fl^h rec. He is occasionally entered on the records as Jan the soldier. Nov. 29, 1663, Cornelis Janse (Vanderveer) of Fl^h petitioned the Director-Gen. and Council for pardon for having accidentally killed "John Damon's" son, aged 8 years, which, with the consent of several residents of Fl^h and of "Jan Cornelis Buys" of Fl^h, father of the deceased, and of "Jan Aertsen van der Bilt,

Tys Lubbertsen, Gerrit Lubbertsen, relatives of Jan Cornelis Buys," forgiveness of the same. was granted, as per pp. 255 and 256 of Cal. of Dutch Man. Conclude the "John Damon" in the above to be an error, and should have been, or was intended for, Buys. Issue:—Hendrick,. bp. Mar. 15, 1654; Lubbert, bp. Feb. 2, 1655—both in N. Y.; Diesverien or Debora, m. Nov. 24, 1680, Willem Appelby; Jacob Janse of Fl^h; (by 2^d w.) Cornelis, bp. Apl. 2, 1677; John, bp. June 30, 1678; Margrietje, bp. Oct. 2, 1679; Hendrickjen; Tryntien; (by 3^d w.) Cornelis, bp Dec. 14, 1684; Adam (twin), bp. Dec. 14, 1684; (by 4th w.) Hillelje; and Thys. Made his mark to documents. Some of his descendants reside in Somerset Co., N. J. An Abram and John Buys were freeholders of Dutchess Co. at its organization in 1714, as per p. 100 of Smith's His. of said co.

Lubbert (Janse), bp. Feb. 2, 1655.

Pieter (Jacobse), resided in N. A. in 1653, and among first settlers of N. U. in 1657, residing there in 1660.

Thys or *Matthys (Janse),* m. Lysbet. Issue:—Jan, bp. July 7, 1700, m. Neeltje; and Willemtje, bp. Oct. 26, 1702 —both in Br^n.

BYBON or BYBOUT, JOHN, of Bedford prior to 1700. Collector of Br^n in 1701, as per p. 64 of Furman's Notes of Br^n.

BYCKER, GERRET, sold Feb. 28, 1653, to Edward Griffens 25 morgens in Fl^h adjoining No. 9, the Parson's land, as per O'Callaghan's Man. Trans. of Dutch Col. Man.

BYCKRYL, CHAREL, on muster-roll of Bu^k militia of 1663, per town rec.

BYOSE, LOWYS, m. Anneken Juriaansz. Issue:—Lowys, bp. Oct. 9, 1661, at Br^n.

CAERLSE, JAN, on ass. roll of Br^a of 1676.

CAESAR or CESAR, PIETER, the Italian. See Alburtus.

CAMMEGA, KAMMEGA, or BRUMMAGA, HENDRICK JANSE, emigrated in 1679; m. 1st *Anna Maria Vervele;* m. 2^d, Feb. 1717, *Margaret Mattyse* wid. of Nicholas de Vouw. On ass. rolls of N. U. of 1683 and '93, at which place he took the oath of allegiance in 1687. From N. U. removed to Hackensack, N. J. Issue:—Anna, bp. Oct. 3, 1686, at Fl^h; Angenietje, bp. May 3, 1688, at Fl[b]; Abraham; and Johannes —all of Hackensack.

CANNON, JOHN. By a receipt in the hands of Mr. De Mott of J[s] it appears that May 13, 1763, Evert Byvanck received for the heirs of John Cannon £1 10 sh. 9 p. for 3 years' rent of two thirty-ninths of Pine and Coney islands. Byvanck was a merchant and ship-owner in N. Y. A Jan Canon had several children bp. in N. Y. between 1703 and '20.

CAPITONY, MATTHIAS or MATTHAAS, bought Dec. 2, 1653, of Ralph Cardell plantation-lot No. 13 in G[d], as per town rec. Signed his name "*Matthaas, Capitony.*"

CAPPOENS, CHRISTINA, and others applied Mar. 1, 1660, for leave to form a village in the vicinity of the Wallabout, as per p. 13 of Vol. 1 of Stiles's Br[n].

CARDELL or CARDAEL, RALPH, (sup.) English, m. *Elizabeth* ——; d. prior to Mar. 1689. Oct. 3, 1639, he and Christoffel Lawrens undertook a tobacco plantation of 3 morgens at Gowanus, as per p. 207 of Vol. 1 of O'Callaghan's Man. Trans. of Dutch Man. Accompanied Lady Mody, and among the first settlers of G[d]. Dec. 2, 1653, sold to Matthias Capito plantation-lot No. 13, and Mar. 23, 1663, bought of Jan Jansen Ver Ryn plantation-lot No. 9 in said town. Feb. 22, 1696, Isaac Haselberry and Elizabeth his wife, heirs and executors of Ralph Cardell late of G[d], dec., conveyed to Reynier Van Sickelen for £420 a lot of 20 A. in G[d] Neck, as per town rec. His will is da. June 10, 1684, and after his death his wid. m. Thomas Bayles. Made his mark to documents.

Thomas, of Fld[s] or G[d] in 1705, as per Stoothoff papers. Signed his name " *Thomas Cardale.*"

CARLSZ, CAREL, on muster-roll, of Bu[k] militia of 1663, as per town rec.

Jacobus, see De Bevoise.

Joost of N. U., m. Stryntje Jans. A Joost Carelszen took the oath of allegiance to the English in N. Y. in 1664. Issue:—Marrytje or Maria, bp. Aug. 15, 1660, m. June 12, 1678, Jacobus De Bevoise; Saertje, bp. Jan. 5, 1663; Jannetje, bp. Nov. 16, 1664; and Cornelis, bp. Oct. 13, 1666—all bp. in N. Y.

CARNELMSEN, MATTHYS, bought Nov. 20, 1695, of Thomas Lambertse land in Bedford, as per p. 129 of Lib. 3 of Con.

CARSTEN or CARSTENSEN, CLAES, the Norman, a soldier in the service of the West India Company, sometimes called Van Sant, obtained Sept. 5, 1645, a patent for 29 morgens on the East River and Noorman's Kil (Williamsburgh), which premises he sold to John Forbes, to whom they were patented May 17, 1647, as per p. 20 of Vol. 1 of Dutch Man. He m. Apl. 15, 1646, Helletje Hendricks, joined the D. ch. in N. A. Jan. 1, 1663, and took up 50 morgens in the vicinity of Constable's Hook, Bergen, N. J., as per p. 50 of Winfield's Land Titles of Hudson Co. Signed his name " *Claes Carstensen.*"
John and *Peter*, see Corsen.

CARTENSE, CARSONSEN, or CARSTENS, JAN, of G^d, (sup.) m. *Mary Johnson.* Bought land in G^d in 1681, and also he and his son Peter bought May 25, 1685, of Wm. Goulding as attorney of Thos Coddington, two garden-spots with buildings in G^d, as per town rec. On ass. roll of G^d of 1683, and took the oath of allegiance in said town in 1687 as a native. Issue:—Peter and John. Made his mark "I" to documents.
Peter, bought Mar. 2, 1687-8, of his brother, John Carstensen, a parcel of land and meadows in G^d, as per town rec.

CARTESE, JAN, on ass. roll of Bu^k of 1676.

CASAUE, JACOBUS MONSEU, one of the soldiers from Kings Co. sent in 1689 to Albany, as per p. 216 of Vol. II of Doc. His. of N. Y. Suppose this to have been Jacob Cashow.

CASPARSE, JAMES, hired a farm in 1666 in Bu^k of Clare Voorure wid. of Ryck Lydecker, as per Bu^k rec.
Caspar, Johannes, and *Joost,* see Springsteen.
Melle, on muster-roll of Bu^k of 1663, as per town rec.

CASPARTSZ, MELCHERT, (sup.) of Fl^h, m. *Geertruyd Bartholds.* Issue:—Catharine, bp. May 12, 1678; Jeuriaans, bp. Apl. 17, 1681; Lysbeth, bp. Nov. 30, 1683—all bp. in Fld^s; and Isaac, bp. Apl. 12, 1687, in N. Y.

CASPER, CASPEL, and CARPARSE, see Springsteen.

CASSHOW or CASSOU, JACOB, b. in N. Y.; m. Sept. 28, 1695, *Ann Maria Rapalje* da. of Tunis, and is the ancestor of the L. I. Casshows. Issue:—Antje, bp. June 18, 1699; Johan-

nes, bp. Sept. 21, 1701; (sup.) Jacob, who m. Lena Stockholm; and Annetje, bp. Mar. 21, 1708—all in Br^n. Made his
mark to documents.

CATJOUW, JAN, a Frenchman, among the first settlers of
Bu^k, per Thompson's L. I., of which town he was a mag. in
1662, and in that year returned to Holland.

CERGHE, JAN GOUWEN, of Fl^h in 1668, as written by
himself.

CESAR or CAESAR, PIETER, the Italian, see Alburtus.

CHANDLER or CHAUNDLER, SAMUEL, (sup. English,) obtained Sept. 9, 1649, a plantation-lot in G^d, per town rec.
Sept. 16 of said year it was ordered "by ye generall consent of ye inhabbittents (of Gravesend) y^t every man shall
give him selfe of a ladder of 20 foote or about by newe
yeare day next uppon the forfitture of 2 gilders 10 st. a
week for all that time hee is without after ye time expires."

CHOCK or CHOCKE, PETER, of Maspeth Kils, bought in
1694 of Danl Phillips of Newtown a parcel of fresh meadows in N. L. which Phillips bought Jan. 19, 1694, of
Derick Janse Hoogland, as per p. 30 of Lib. 2 of Con. He
was the agent of the Alburtus family for selling their
Wallabout farm, as per p. 68 of Lib. 2 of Con.

CHRISTIAENCE, JACOB, took the oath of allegiance in N. U.
in 1687 as a native.

CHRISTOFFEL, GERRET, m. *Lysbeth Cornelis*. Issue:—Albert,
bp. Mar. 13, 1681, in Fl^h.
Hans or *Jannes*, m. Tryntje Barents. Leased in 1663, for
6 years, Fl^h ch. lands for 200 gl. wampum value per annum.
On ass. roll of Fl^h of 1675. Issue:—Barent, bp. June 6,
1680, in Fl^h. Made his mark to documents.
Johannes, see Schaers.
Johannis, bought Feb. 18, 1664, of "Joncker Balthazer
Vosch" 21 morgens with plain and meadow land in Fl^h, as
per p. 153 of Lib. B of Fl^h rec. Was also allowed Mar.
29, 1670, a farm of 27 morgens in Fl^h, by virtue of the town
patent, lying between the farms of "Wm Gilyemsen and
that of Jan Van de Belt," with plain and meadow land, as
per p. 9 of Lib. A of Fl^h rec. This Johannes is probably
the Hans or Jannes above inserted. Signed his name
"*Johannis Crisstoffel.*"

Pitter (*Pieter*), a pauper buried by the R. D. ch. of N. U. in 1689.

CIMMER, JORIS, m. *Mary* ——. Issue:—Marya, Katrina, and Elizabeth, all bp. Oct. 19, 1695, in Brⁿ.

CINOM, JAN, from Leiden in South Holland, m. Aug. 3, 1662, at Brⁿ, *Grietje Snedinx* from Amsterdam.

CLAAS, CLAASZ, CLAASEN, CLAESEN, or KLAESEN, BARENT, a mag. of Flᵇ in 1680, as per p. 60 of Strong's Flᵇ and as per Lib. A of Flᵇ rec. This may be intended for Barthold or Bartel Claesen.

Bartel or *Barthold* (Van Ruynen, or from Ruynen, a manor in South Holland), commonly written Bartel Claesen, m. Hildegonde ——. Was taxed 10 fl., clergyman's salary, Feb. 7, 1657, as Jan Eversen's (Bout) farmer, per p. 136 of Vol. 1 of Stiles's Brⁿ. Sept. 13, 1659, he bought of Glandy La Metre his bouwery on the W. side of the road in Flᵇ, as per p. 59 of Lib. A of Flᵇ rec., to which he probably removed, his name appearing frequently from said date to 1681 on said rec. Dec. 22, 1669, he bought of Frans Barentse Pastoor a farm on the W. side of 'the road in Flᵇ of 22 morgens, which he sold in 1678 to Corˢ Janse Berrien. Feb. 2, 1670, he was allotted 22 morgens on the W. side of the road in pursuance of the provisions of the patent of Flᵇ. Mar. 29, 1677, Gov. Andross granted to him and Lowys Janse 171 A. lying next to the Paerdegat, bounded by the limits of Fldᵉ, and N. E. by the flats or plains. Feb. 4, 1681, he bought of Stoffel Probasco 19 morgens on the E. side of the road in Flᵇ, which Probasco bought June 2, 1676, of Lysbet Janse (wid. of Jan Claesz) and Auke Janse her husband (said Jan Claesz having been allotted the same in pursuance of Flᵇ patent), which farm he sold Oct. 15, 1681, to Jan Auke Van Nuyse. See p. 59 of Lib. C; pp. 4, 14, and 45 of Lib. A; p. 281 of Lib. D; and p. 122 of Lib. AA of Flᵇ rec. Bartel's name appears on the ass. rolls of Flᵇ of 1675 and '76; mem. of D. ch. in 1677, and elder in 1680; constable in 1670 and '75, as per Strong's Flᵇ; overseer in 1677, as per p. 18 of Cal. of Land Papers, also in 1682; and mag. in 1681. Oct. 5, 1681, for 5000 gl. wampum he bought of Corˢ Steenwyck a farm in Bergen, N. J., as per p. 69 of Winfield's Hudson Co. Land Titles, to which he probably removed. Issue:—Hendrick, bp. Mar. 8, 1654, in N. A. Signed his name "*Baertelt Claes.*"

Claes, see Smidt.

Cornelis, see Wyckoff.

Gerbrant, m. Aug. 25, 1674, Marretje da. of Claes Pietersen Cos. Resided in Br^n in 1691, but afterwards, or perhaps previously, resided in Bergen, N. J., as per p. 520 of Winfield's Hudson Co., where an account of his family is given. Issue:—Pieter, bp. Apl. 21, 1675; Claes, bp. Aug. 18, 1677; Herpert, bp. Nov. 26, 1679—all in N. Y.; Myndert, bp. Feb. 26, 1682, in Br^n; Neeltje, bp. Oct. 1, 1684, in N. Y.; Metje, bp. Feb. 3, 1687, in N. Y.; Meyndert, bp. June 29, 1691, in Br^n; Marretje, bp. Nov. 1, 1693, in N. U.; and Gerbrant, bp. Aug. 9, 1696, in N. U.

Gerret, m. Marretje Ariaensen; mem. of R. D. ch. of Fl^h in 1677. Issue:—Klaes, bp. May 4, 1695. There was a Gerret Claes, son of Claes Gerretse and Adriaentje Lollenokx, b. about 1660, as per p. 40 of Lib. D of Fl^h rec.

Harpert, defendant in a suit of which Nathaniel Brednel (Brittan) was plaintiff, Feb. 11, 1661, as per Lib. B of Fl^h court rec.

Hendrick, emigrated in 1654, settled in Br^n, where with others, May 26, 1663, petitioned for leave to form a concentration (village) back of the Wallabout, as per p. 12 of Vol. 1 of Stiles's Br^n. Of Bedford in 1685, and mem. of R. D. ch. of Br^n, at which place he took the oath of allegiance in 1687. Apl. 16, 1689, he sold Casper Janse a lot at Bedford, as per p. 143 of Lib. 1 of Con., and in 1690 he was a commissioner of Br^n. Feb. 8, 1665, a Hendrick Claesen from Amsterdam paid a marriage-fee to Fl^h ch. A Hendrick Claesen and Paryntie Michaels had a da. Catryntie bp. Dec. 8, 1675, in N. Y. Some of the above items may refer to Hendrick Claesen Van Vechten.

Isaac, sold Apl. 1, 1666, to Adriaen Van Laer two double building-plots in Fl^h, as per p. 58 of Lib. D of Fl^h rec. Apl. 21, 1667, he obtained, on the division of the Fl^h salt meadows at Canarisie, a meadow lot. Made his mark to documents.

Jan of Bu^k, see Zieuw.

Jan of Fl^h, cooper, m. Lysbeth Jans wid. of Christoffel Schaets; he was buried Sept. 17, 1661, in Fl^h ch. Jan. 14, 1670–1, "Leysbeth Jans wid. and heir of Jan Claesz, dec.," was allotted, as one of the patentees of Fl^h, a farm of 19 morgens lying between the farm of Jan Strycker and that of Derck Janse Vander Vliet, with plain and meadow land, as per p. 14 of Lib. A of Fl^h rec. Issue:—Claes Jansen, Lysbeth Jansen, and Christoffel Jansen. After his death his wid. Lysbeth m. Aucke Janse Van Nuyse.

Jannetje of Fl^h, midwife, sold July 1, 1680, her house and lot in Fl^h, adjoining the school-lot and abutting in the rear against the mill-lot, to Aucke Janse Van Nuyse for 800 gl., as per p. 129 of Lib. AA of Fl^h rec.

Loy Charles Deniso, on Gov. Dongan's patent of Bu^k of 1678.

Melle of N. Y. and Wm Goulding of G^d sold Oct. 29, 1679, to Klaes Jansen of G^d a house, garden, and orchard in said town, as per G^d rec.

Nicholas, see Wyckoff.

Pieter and Grietje Cornelis had a s. Jan bp. Apl. 22, 1663, in Br^n.

Pieter, see Wyckoff and Van Hasmyes.

Simon, from Groningen, on ass. roll of Br^n of 1675 and 1684. Also a Simon Claesen on ass. roll of Fl^h of 1675.

Simon (sup. Van Huyse), from Groningen—and this may be the above Simon—m. 1st, Aug. 7, 1655, Annetje Lodewyck, who d. prior to July 8, 1682; m. 2^d, June 30, 1686, Tryntje Gerrets. Resided in Br^n. Will da. July 8, 1684, rec. p. 5, Lib. 1 (copy) of Con. Issue:—Grietje, bp. July 29, 1657; Engeltie, bp. Sept. 15, 1658, in N. A.; Janneke, bp. Dec. 5, 1660; Claes, bp. Nov. 27, 1661; Lysbeth, bp. May 22, 1664; Peter; Lodowyck, bp. Apl. 25, 1666, in N. Y.; Jan, bp. Jan. 12, 1671; Margriet, b. Jan. 14, 1674—all bp. in Br^n except those set forth as bp. in N. A. and N. Y.

William of Fld^s and Gowanus, m. Oct. 9, 1681, Elsje Gerretsz Kroezen. Issue:—Gerret, bp. Aug. 27, 1682. A Wm Klassen settled near New Brunswick, N. J., prior to 1699, as per p. 35 of Messler's Somerset Co.

CLARK, ROBERT, (sup.) English, agreed July 16, 1650, to purchase John Applegate's plantation in G^d, as per town rec., which he sold Aug. 20, 1652, to Thomas Baxter. Signed his name " *Robert Clark.*"

CLAY or CLEY, HUMPHREY or OUFIE, on ass. roll of Bu^k of 1676 and '93, patent of 1687, and cen. of 1698. Came to Bu^k as early as 1667, where he obtained a patent for a plantion. He m. 1st Katharine ——; m. 2^d Sarah wid. of James Christie of Newtown.

CLAER or CLAES, TUNISE, of Br^n ferry; his name on deed of Filkins to Coe of Jan. 8, 1697, of Kings Co. reg. off. Apl. 15, 1694, he and his wife Anneke, late wid. of John Sprong of Ulster Co., sold to Jacob Rutgersz of the same county a lot at Br^n ferry, as per p. 15 of Lib. 2 of Con.

CLEMENT, JAN, emigrated in 1665, m. *Maria Bocquet* or *Bokee*. May 29, 1674, he bought of Luykes Meyer a bouwery at Yellow Hoek, N. U., formerly in possession of Pieter Jacobse, for 1700 gl., as per p. 107 of Lib. C of Fl^h rec. On ass. rolls of N. U of 1675, '76, and '83, and in 1687 took the oath of allegiance in said town. Was a mason by trade; at one period resided in Fld⁴. Issue:—Jannetje, bp. Aug. 26, 1676, in Br"; Pieter, bp. July 31, 1681, in N. U.; Johannis, bp. Apl. 26, 1685, in Fld⁴; and Annetje, bp. Dec. 8, 1687, in Fl". There was a Jean Clement, a pauper, who joined the D. ch. of N. U. in 1680. Made his mark to documents.

CLERCK or CLERCQ, JAN, from Brazil, m. July 17, 1661, *Anneken Hansen Bergen;* d. Nov. 15, 1661. Mem. of R. D. ch. of Br" in 1660. No account of issue.

CLEYN, JAN CORNELISSEN, bought May 15, 1660, of Lowis Jansen a building-plot in Fl" on the N. side of Cleyn's land, as per p. 232 of Lib. B of Fl" rec. Sold Oct. 3, 1661, to Herman Bartelfs a farm in Fl" of 20 morgens, with plain land and meadows, as per p. 83 of Lib. B of Fl" rec. Signed his name "*Jan Cornelissen Cleyn.*"

CLINCH, PIETER CORNELISE, sold his house and lot in Fld⁴ to Elbert Elbertse Stoothoff.

CLOCK or CLOCQ, PELGROM, emigrated in 1656. Oct. 26, 1663, he was employed by the mag. of Fl" and the consistory of the R. D. ch. of said town as schoolmaster, court messenger, and precentor of the ch. (as per. p. 145 of Lib. B of Fl" rec.), at a salary of 200 gl. per annum, 50 of which to be paid by the consistory. In addition to other perquisites, he was to receive, for teaching A B C, 2 gl.; spelling, 2 gl. 10 st.; reading, 3 gl.; and writing, 5 gl., from each scholar. If Adriaen Hegeman was the first schoolmaster of Fl", as per Strong's history of said town, (of which the compiler on a careful examination of the rec. of said town failed to discover a particle of evidence,) Reinier Bastiaensen Van Giesen was clearly the second, and Pelgrom Clocq the third. He appears to have resided in Bu" in 1687. Signed his name "*P. Clocq.*"

CLOMP or CLOMB, HUYBERT, see Lambert Huybertsen Mol.

CLOUDS, SAMUEL. He and Pieter Cortelyou, with consent of the major part of the inhabitants of Br", in pursuance of an agreement made at a town meeting held at Bedford on the 12th of April, 1697, surveyed and laid out the common woodlands of said town into lots.

CLOUGH, CLUFF, or CLOF, RICHARD, and his associates obtained Jan. 21, 1647, a patent for Canarisie on condition of having 20 families settled on the same within 3 years, which in consequence of non-fulfilment became void. Sold Jan. 24, 1655, to Thoª Hall a plantation in G^d, as per town rec. Signed his name "*Rich. Clough.*"

CLUMPTON, WILLIAM, (sup.) English, of G^d in 1676, per town rec.

CLUNS or CLUNEN, HUPERT or HERKERT, (alias Jacobus Van Dalen,) m. Feb. 25, 1662, *Jannetje Willems* at Brⁿ. Leased Aug. 28, 1655, Gov. Stuyvesant's bouwery and stock at Amersfoort (Fldª), as per Col. Man.

COCK, JOCHEM GERRETSEN, obtained May 27, 1656, a patent for one morgen in Brⁿ on the highway W. of the burying-ground of the R. D. ch.

COCKCOEVER, COQUEUERT, or COQUER, ALEXANDER, a Frenchman, who emigrated in 1657; drum-major of militia of Bu^k in 1663, as per town rec., and obtained a plantation in said town in the same year, as per Col. Man. Took the oath of allegiance in Bu^k in 1687, his name appearing on the patent of said town in the same year. Apl. 23, 1665, "Alexander Kockes" (sup. to be the same Alexander) paid a marriage-fee to Fl^h ch., as per town rec. Signed his name "*Alexander Cokcover.*"

COCKUIT, JOOST, emigrated in 1660, and took the oath of allegiance in Bu^k in 1687. On ass. rolls of Bu^k of 1675, '83, and '93, and patent of 1687. Lieut. in 1673 and capt. of militia in 1686, per Col. Man.

CODUINGTON, THOMAS, (sup.) English. In May 1685 Wm Goulding, as his attorney, sold to John and Peter Carsonsan two garden-spots with buildings, and also to Henry Matice his interest in the common woodlands of G^d, as per town rec. In 1686 he resided on the Raritan in E. N. J., and in 1698 was a member of the Legislature of that locality, as per p. 212 of the Rec. of the Gov. and Council of E. N. J. Signed his name "*Tho: Coduington.*"

COE, JOHN, from the town of Garscone or Gans Coone, Essex, England. June 8, 1697, Henry Filkins of Fl^h con-

5

veyed to him land in Brⁿ, as per p. 143 of Lib. 2 of Con. A
Robert Coe of Hempstead in 1641, and a Benjamin Coe of
J^a in 1683.

COËNESEN, JAN, paid 2 gl. 15 st., minister's salary, in Fl^h
in 1680, as per town rec.

COERTE or COERTEN, see Voorhies.
Harmen, b. 1610; emigrated from Voorthuyzen in Gelderland in Feb. 1659, with w. and 5 chil., and settled in N. U.
Jan. 15, 1664, he with others made an affidavit before the
notary Pilgrom Clock relating to Capt. John Scott's raid
on the Dutch towns on L. I., especially on N. U., as per p.
480 of Vol. II. of Doc. of Col. His. of N. Y. Made his mark
to documents.
Jan, on ass. roll of Fl^h of 1676.
Myndert, see Koerten.

COESAER, ANTHONY, on Brⁿ ass. roll of 1693.

COEVERS or COVERT, HANS or JAN (TEUNISZ), m. *Jannetje
Boka (Bragaw)*. Of Bu^k in 1677 and '85, and mem. of R. D.
ch. of Brⁿ.' Took the oath of allegiance in Brⁿ in 1687
as a native. Resided on the Raritan in N. J. in 1705. Is-
sue:—Ariaentje, bp. Aug. 3, 1690, in Brⁿ; Teunis, bp. Apl.
16, 1693, in N. Y.; Bragon of the Raritan, bp. Mar. 29, 1696,
in Brⁿ, m. Dec. 1, 1723, Anna Slover; Maria, bp. Aug. 6,
1705, in N. J.; and Barbara, bp. Oct. 26, 1709. Signed his
name "*Yan Teunisse Coevert.*"
Johannes (Teunisse), m. Jannetje ——, and settled near
New Brunswick, N. J., prior to 1699, as per p. 35 of Messler's Somerset Co.; see also p. 21 of the Rev. Mr. Corwin's
His. Discourse. Took the oath of allegiance in Brⁿ in 1687
as a native. Issue:—Teunis, bp. Apl. 11, 1693, in N. Y.
Lucas (Teunise), emigrated in 1653; m. Aug. 27, 1682,
Barbara Sprung of Fl^h. Mem. of R. D. ch. of Brⁿ in 1677,
and took the oath of allegiance in said town in 1687, resid-
ing at Bedford. Resided at Mad Nan's Neck in Queens
Co. in 1697, and at Three Mile Run in N. J. in 1703. Issue:
—Abraham, bp. May 27, 1683; Isaac, bp. May 27, 1683;
and Lucas, bp. Apl. 9, 1699, (all in Brⁿ,) m. Femmetje ——,
and resided on the Raritan, N. J. Signed his name "*Luces
Teunissen.*"
Mauritss (Teunise) of Bedford, bp. Aug. 6, 1663, m. Apl.
1, 1690, Anne Fonteyn wid. of Jacob Jansen of Bu^k. Took
the oath of allegiance in Brⁿ in 1687 as a native; mem. of

R. D. ch. of Br^n in 1677, and resided in Bu^k in 1697. Issue:
—Theunis Mauritsz of Monmouth Co., N. J., bp. Mar. 29,
1691, m. Antie Fonteyn; Charles Mauritsz, bp. Apl. 16,
1693; Mauritsz, bp. Jan. 16, 1696—all in N. Y.; and Sara, bp.
Dec. 27, 1697, in Br^n.

Teunis, Janse, emigrated in 1651 from Heemstede in North
Holland; m. Barbara Lucas or Jans; resided at first in N. A.
and finally settled at Bedford in Br^n, at which place he
toók the oath of allegiance in 1687. Mem of the R. D. ch.
of N. A. prior to 1660; mem. of the R. D. ch of Br^n in 1660,
'77, and '85, and d. prior to 1700. Issue:—Hans Teunise;
Marretje Teunise, m. Nov. 24, 1682, Jean Messerole Junr
of Bu^k; Lucas Teunise; Mauritsz Teunise; Aeltje Teunise,
m. May 18, 1679, in N. Y., Wm Pos or Post of N. Y.; Sarah
Teunise, m. Apl. 7, 1680, in N. Y., Arent Fredericksen of
N. Y.; Annetje Teunise, bp. Aug. 28, 1661, m. Apl. 16,
1687, Garret Sprong; Jannetje Teunise, (sup.) m. Titus
Syrachs De Vries; Aaggica or Eechtje Teunise, m. Derk
Paulus of J^a; and Johannes Teunise, m. Jannetje ——,
and settled on the Raritan.

COLEURT or COLEVELT, FOUWERENS or LAWRENCE, m. *Sara
Walderum* or *Waldron.* Issue:—Altie, bp. Mar.· 6, 1670, in
Br^n, m. June 9, 1690, Isaacq Breser of N. Y., both residents
of the latter place at date of marriage; and Cornelis, bp.
Sept. 18, 1680, in N. Y.

COLJER or COLYER, CORNELIS, of Br^n in 1699.
Jeurriaen, on ass. roll of Bu^k of 1693 and cen. of 1698.
Jochem, m. Marritje ——. Issue:—Jeurriaen, bp. Oct. 27,
1697, in Br^n; Helena, bp. July 2, 1699, in N. Y.; Jan, bp.
Jan. 1, 1703, in N. Y.; and Elizabeth, bp. Aug. 25, 1706, in
N. Y.

COMAYK, ALBERT, of Fld^s in 1666, as per town rec.

COMLITS, JAN, a mag. of Br^n in 1661, as per Thompson's
L. I.

COMTON, WILLIAM, (sup. English,) b. 1622; a freeholder
of G^d in 1656 and '70, per Thompson's L. I., and constable
in 1677. Bought Nov. 24, 1657, of Nich^s Stillwell plantation-lot No. 29 in G^d, as per town rec. Was one of the
purchasers (12 men and 24 associates) of Middletown, N. J.,
of the Indians in 1667. Signed his name *"Weillum Comton."*

CONALIN, JAN, defendant in a suit of Cornelis Wandel of Jan. 21, 1660, as per Lib. B of Fl[h] court rec.

CONCES, JEAN, a Frenchman, on cen. of Fld[s] of 1698.

CONICK or CONINGH, ALBERT, and *Tryntje Janse* his w., joined the R. D. ch. of Br[n] in 1664. An Aldert Coninck (probably the same person) took the oath of allegiance to the English in N. Y. in 1664. Signed his name "*Albert Coningh.*"

CONSELYEA or CONSELJE, JAN or JEAN DE, a Huguenot who emigrated in 1662, joined the R. D. ch. of N. A. Apl. 1, 1663, and settled in Bu[k], where he took the oath of allegiance in 1687. He m. *Fytje* or *Eytje Schuts.* Issue:—Lysbeth, bp. May 2, 1677, in N. Y.; Anneken, bp. June 27, 1686, in N. Y.; and Pieter, bp. Nov. 25, 1688, in Br[n]. His descendants resided in Bu[k], Queens Co., and in E. N. J.

Peter of Bu[k]; bp. Nov. 25, 1688; m. ——. Issue:—(sup.) Sara, bp. Oct. 23, 1717, in N. Y.

COOK or COOKE, JOHN, English; a plantation granted to him Mar. 16, 1650, in G[d], as per rec. of said town, of which place he was a mag. in 1656, '59, '61, and '62. May 29, 1660, he bought of John Applegate plantation-lot No. 12 in G[d]. Apl. 17, 1680, *Sarah Cooke* of G[d], in pursuance of the will of John Cooke her dec. husband, and as his executrix, "order and empower my loving son Obadiah Holmes of Staten Island, for me and in my behalf," to sell lands, etc., as per G[d] rec. Signed his name "*John Cooke.*"
Laurens Cornelise and Margaretta his wife, of Bu[k], mortgaged their lands, cong. 104 A., to Stephanus Van Cortland of N. Y. Jan. 17, 1693, as per p. 252 of Con. His name on Dongan's patent of Bu[k].

COOL, CORNELIS LAMBERTSEN, m. *Altien Brackhonge*, who after his death m. Willem Bredenbent. Bought May 17, 1639, of Thomas Bescher or Beets a plantation in Gowanus (for which he obtained a patent Apl. 5, 1642), to which he removed, having previously resided in N. A. This patent, as near as can be ascertained, covered the farms designated on Butts's map of Br[n] as of Peter Wyckoff, John Wyckoff, Henry Story, and Winant Bennet. Issue:—Altie Cornelis, who m. 1st Gerret Wolferse Van Cowenhoven, and m. 2[d] Elbert Elbertse Stoothoff; Peterje Cornelis, who m. Claes Jansen Van Purmerent, alias Jan Pottagie; and Lambert

Cornelise. See pp. 251 and 252 of Bergen Genealogy. Made his mark to documents.

· COOPAL or COPALL, JAN, constable of Bu^k, ordered by the court of sessions in 1670 to give an account of his chattels.

CORBESBY, GABRIEL, of Gowanus, m. June 15, 1657, *Teuntje* or *Tryntje Straetsman*, wid., who d. Oct. 9, 1662, per Br^n R. D. ch. rec. Issue:—David, bp. Mar. 28, 1659, in N. A.

CORLAER, see Van Curler.

CORNELISSE or CORNELISSEN, ARIE, m. Feb. 17, 1662, *Rebecca Idens.* Mem. of R. D. ch. of N. Y. in May 1673. On ass. roll of Bu^k of 1675. Issue:—Idens, bp. Nov. 28, 1665; Grietje, bp. Nov. 6, 1667; Cornelia, bp. Jan. 9, 1670; Lysbeth, bp. Dec. 10, 1671; Cornelis, bp. Mar. 18, 1674; Jacob, bp. Apl. 6, 1676; and Dina, bp. Apl. 10, 1678—all bp. in N. Y.

Abraham, see Van Brunt.
Albert, see Wantenaer.
Arie, see Vogel.
Barent, m. Anna Barentsen. Issue:—Cornelis, bp. Aug. 28, 1698.
Casper, on ass. roll of Br^n off. 1676. Paid a marriage-fee of 5 florens and 10 st. to Fl^h R. D. ch. Nov. 2, 1664, as per ch. rec. There was a Casper Cornelisen and Neeltje Jans who had a da. Saertje bp. Feb. 27, 1667, and a da. Sara bp. Sept. 3, 1681, both in N. Y.
Claes, a witness on will of Swantje Jans in 1692, per Col. Doc.
Claes (*Van Katt*), on ass. roll of Bu^k of 1676.
Claes, owned land in Br^n Feb. 17, 1646, as per Pieter Cornelissen's patent.
Claes, see Klaes, Mentelaer, Mitelaer, Van Brunt, Van Cott, and Van Schouw.
Claes of Fld^s, b. 1597; made an affidavit in 1664 in relation to Capt. Scott's raid on the Dutch towns on L. I. in 1664, as per p. 482 of Vol. II. of Doc. of Col. His. Made his mark to documents.
Cornelis, see Van Brunt and Van Duyn.
Cornelis of Kings Co., ag. 22, deposes in relation to the burning of Jochem Pietersen's house by the Indians in 1644, per p. 67 of Furman's Antiquities of L. I.
Derick, on ass. roll of Br^n in 1676.
Derick, see Hoogland.

Gerret, see Van Duyn and Van Nukerk.

Guilliam, see Cornel.

Hendrick, of Fld[a] in 1680. Sept. 1, 1672, Minne Johannes sold to "Hendryck Cornelisse" a house-plot in Fl[h], as per p. 19 of Lib. A of Fl[h] rec. In 1660 he sold his bouwery in Fld[a] to Nathaniel Brittan, as per p. 15½ of Lib. B of Fl[h] rec. Made his mark to documents.

Hendrick, see Sleght and Wyckoff.

Jacob, see Wyckoff.

Jan, see Buys, Cleyn, Damen, Van Rotterdam, Van Tessel, and Zieuw.

Jan, owned land in Bu[k] in 1662, as per town rec.

Jan, a carpenter in Fld[a] in 1672, as per Col. Doc. Signed his name "*Jan Cornelis*" in 1689.

Jan Buis, on ass. roll of Bu[k] in 1675.

John, see Wyckoff.

Klaes or *Claes*, of Fld[a] in 1664 and '74; b. 1597. In 1664 made an affidavit relating to Capt. Scott's raid. Made his mark to documents.

Lourens or *Louis*, on ass. roll of Fld[a] of 1676, and on that of Fl[h] of 1683. Feb. 2, 1677-8, or Dec. 29, 1687, "Laurens Cornelise, farmer, of N. Aarnhem in the jurisdiction of Bushwick" (Mispat Kil), bought of Stoffel Janse, carpenter, 2 lots of woodland, Nos. 32 and 33, in the new lotts of Fl[h] for 3000 gl., bought by said Stoffel of Minne Johannes, as per. p. 93 of Lib. A and p. 20 of Lib. AA of Fl[h] rec. There was a Laurens Cornelise and Margaret Barents who had issue:—Cornelis, bp. Mar. 29, 1677; Grietje, bp. Dec. 21, 1678; and Marritje, bp. June 22, 1687—all bp. in N. Y. Signed his name "*Lourens Cornelsen.*"

Loycan, on ass. roll of Bu[k] of 1683.

Matthys, emigrated in 1663; m. Feb. 20, 1692, Eytie or Sophia Adams Brouwer. Took the oath of allegiance in Br[n] in 1687, where he owned property; on ass. roll of N. U. of 1693 and cen. of Br[n] of 1698. Issue:—Cornelis, bp. May 4, 1695, in Br[n].

Matthys, from Jutland; of Fl[h] in 1702, per Col. Man.; may be the above Matthys.

Motlick, on deed of freeholders of Br[n] to Adrian Bennet of Jan. 2, 1696-7.

Nicholas, see Van Brunt and Wyckoff.

Pieter, (sup.) b. 1607; obtained Feb. 8, 1646, a patent for 27 morgens in Br[n] adjoining land of Cornelis Dircksen, ferryman. Bought land in Br[n] Mar. 22, 1650, of Lodewick Jongh; a mag. of Br[n] in 1654, per Col. Man., and took the oath of allegiance there in 1687. Signed his name "*Pieter Corrnelissen.*"

Pieter, of N. U. in 1682, as per Stoothoff's books.

Pieter, see Clinch, Luyster, Vanderveer, and Wyckoff.

Simon, see Wyckoff.

Teunis, bought July 3, 1647, of Wolfert Gerretse (Van Couwenhoven) 52 morgens of land on the N. end of the plains in Fld⁴, as per p. 363 of Vol. 2 of O'Callaghan's Man. Trans. of Col. Man.

Theunis, of Brⁿ in 1663, where with others he petitioned for liberty to form a new village near their salt meadows on Jᵃ Bay, as per p. 120 of Vol. 1 of Stiles's Brⁿ.

William, obtained a patent Feb. 19, 1646, of Gov. Kieft for 25 morgens at the "bight of Marrakkewick" (the Wallabout) in Brⁿ, as per p. 370 of Cal. of Dutch Man.

CORNEL or CORNELL, CORNELIS (s. of Pieter Guilliamse and Margrietje), b. 1681; m. *Jannetje* (sup.) *Hegeman*. Supervisor of Flʰ in 1717 and '18, as per Strong's Flʰ. Allotted wood-lots Nos. 25 and 45 in the 1ˢᵗ division, and 27 and 28 in the 2ᵈ division of Flʰ wood-lots, in 1701. Left Flʰ and settled in Northampton, Bucks Co., Penn., as per p. 360 of Davis's Bucks Co. Issue:—Johannes, bp. Sept. 21, 1718, and Adriaen, bp. Nov. 19, 1721, both in N. U. Signed his name "*Cornelis Cornel.*"

Cornelis Willemse (s. of Willem Guljamse and Margareta), resided in Flʰ on a farm conveyed to him Mar. 4, 1701-2, by his mother and the heirs of his father in pursuance of his father's will, located on the W. side of the highway, S. of the land of Leffert Pieterse, and N. of that of Adrian Ryerse and Marten Adrianse, with 2 lots of salt meadows, as per p. 12 of Lib. B of Flʰ rec. A Cornelis Cornel, supposed to be this Cornelis, chosen with 7 others, Sept. 12, 1757, by the congregation of Flʰ to call, in unison with the other towns of the county, as an assistant or colleague of Do. Van Sinderen, Do. Casparus Vreymoet, and if he could not be obtained, Barent Vrooman, preacher at Schenectady, or any other preacher the congregation might approve of, as per book of minutes of Flʰ town accounts, meetings, etc. No account of his issue. Signed his name "*Cornelis Cornel*" in 1720.

Gelyam or *Guilliame Cornelise*, the common ancestor of the Flʰ and Kings Co. families of Cornell, emigrated to this country at an early period (was probably a Huguenot), settled at Flʰ, and d. prior to July 1666. Aug. 9, 1658, he procured from Director Stuyvesant a patent for a plantation in Midwout (Flatbush), as per p. 591 of Vol. 2 of O'Callaghan's N. Y. In 1661 he and his s. "Pieter Geliamse" bought of Jan Evertse Bout a bouwery in Fl[h] on the W. side of the highway, 600 rods in length and 48 rods and 8 ft. in width, cong. 48 morgens and 480 rods; also two pieces of salt meadows of 5 morgens; two pieces of plain land of 5 morgens; 2 house or building plots on the W. side of the highway, of 16 rods in length and 12 rods in breadth, with the houses and barns thereon; and also 2 black draw-oxen, 3 milk-cows, a wagon, plough, iron chain, and a cramp-iron to hold saw-teeth when filing—all for the sum of 4500 gl., as per p. 73 of Lib. B of Fl[h] rec. Issue:—Pieter Gilliamsen; Willem Gillemse; (sup.) Cornelis; Jacob; and Maria. The surname of his descendants for more than a century was pronounced Cornale, with the accent on the *e* (from Cornelise son of Cornelis), and but lately changed to Cornell. What Guilliame's proper surname was (if he had any) has not been ascertained, but from his name it is evident he was a Frenchman. His descendants reside in Bucks Co., Penn., E. N. J., and in Kings Co.

Gilgam or *Guilliame* (s. of Pieter and Margrietje), b. 1679; m. Nov. 4, 1714, Cornelia Van Nortwyck dau. of Simon and Folckertje Van Nortwyck of Blanckenberg in the Netherlands. A resident of Fl[h], at which place he resided as late as 1723, after which, inferring from all of his children having been bp. in N. U., he probably resided in N. U., but finally with some of his children, as per p. 360 of Davis's Bucks Co., settled in Bucks Co. in Penn., where he has numerous descendants. In 1708 he bought of Gysber Janse, weaver, a house and lot in Fl[h] on the street in the rear of the " Keck" (stocks or pillory), and also his building-plot with house, kitchen, barn, and one half of the well located on the Cow street, so called, as per pp. 58 and 59 of Lib. B of Fl[h] rec. Issue:—Jacobus, bp. Oct. 2, 1720, m. Margrietje——; Wilhelmus, bp. July 29, 1722, and (sup.) an elder in the R. D. ch. of Bucks Co., Penn., in 1765; Giljam, bp. Oct. 23, 1724, m. May 23, 1750, Margaret Schenck of Fld[s]; Johannes, bp. June 16, 1727, m. May 23, 1750, Maria Loth or Lott of Newtown (this Johannes probably remained in Fl[h], where his s. Isaac, who m. Hannah da. of Simon Cortelyou of N. U., at one period resided, from whom is descended the Br[a] branch of the family); Simon, bp. July 13, 1729; and Abraham, bp. Oct. 10. 1731—all in N. U. Signed his name " *Gilgam Cornel* " in 1720.

Johannes Willemson (s. of Willem Guljamse and Margareta), (sup.) m. Altie Courten Voorhies. Supposed Mar. 4, 1701, to have resided in N. L. on a farm conveyed to him by the heirs of his father in pursuance of the provisions in his will, as per p. 13 of Lib. B of Fl[h] rec. No certain account of his issue. Signed his name "*Johannes Willemson*" in 1702.

Peter Willemse (s. of William Gillemse and Margreta), resided in Fl[h], and from thence probably removed to J[a], Queens Co., on a farm adjoining land of Jan Aukes (Van Nuyse), conveyed to him Mar. 4, 1701-2, by the heirs of his father, as per p. 14 of Lib. B of Fl[h] rec. No account of his issue.

Peter (s. of Pieter and Margrietje), m. Catharine Laning. Left Fl[h] and settled in Northampton, Bucks Co., Penn., as per p. 360 of Davis's Bucks Co. Issue:—Johannes, bp. Nov. 17, 1700, in Br[n]; and Thys, bp. Mar. 25, 1722, in N. U. Probably other children.

Pieter Guilliamse or *Williamse* (oldest s. of Gelyam Cornelise) of Fl[h]—commonly so written, without the addition of Cornelise, Cornele, or Cornell—m. in 1675 Margarietje Verscheur (in the marriage record "Vernelle"), and resided in Fl[h]. In 1661 he and his father bought of Jan Evertse Bout a bouwery of 48 morgens and 480 rods, with building-plots, plain and meadow land, in Fl[h]. Feb. 2, 1670, he was allotted, in pursuance of the patent of Fl[h], a double lot in said town lying between the lands of Adriaen Reyerse and those of Hendrick Joorise (Brinckerhoff), cong. 48 morgens and 39 rods, with plain and meadow land, as per p. 5 of Lib. A of Fl[h] rec. Apl. 14, 1668, as heir of his father, he sold to Lowys Jansen about 27 morgens and 330 rods of the patent of upwards of 48 morgens granted to his father Aug. 9, 1658, with salt meadows and plain land, as per p. 36 of Lib. C of Fl[h] rec. His name appears on ass. rolls of Fl[h] of 1675 and '83, on Fl[h] patent of 1685, and as a mem. of the R. D. ch. of Fl[h] in 1677; and his will is da. May 23, 1689, and rec. on p. 141 of Lib. A of Fl[h] rec. July 17, 1666, he paid 40 gl. for burying his father and mother in Fl[h] ch. Oct. 8, 1686 (as Pierre Guilleaum), he was commissioned a lieut. of militia of the Fl[h] company, as per p. 148 of Cal. of Eng. Man. Issue:—Guilliame, b. 1679; Cornelis; Jacob, b. 1683; Maria, b. 1686; and Pieter. Signed his name "*Pieter Wuellemsen.*"

William Guljamse (s. of Gelyam Cornelise) of Fl[h], m. Margarita da. of Do. Polhemius; d. prior to 1702. Was allotted, in pursuance of the patent of Fl[h], a bouwery in said town lying between the lands of Johannis Christoffelse and those of Hendrick Joorise, cong. 26 morgens, with plain and meadow land, as per p. 8 of Lib. A of Fl[h] rec. His name appears on the ass. rolls of Fl[h] of 1675 and '83, on Gov. Andross's patent of N. L. of 1677, as a mag. of the town from 1659 to 1664, and as a mem. of the R. D. ch. of

Fl[h] in 1677. Issue:—Johannes Willemse; Peter Willemse; Marike or Maria Willemse, m. Jacobus Aucke Van Nuyse; Catharine Willemse, m. Aug. 27, 1690, Johannes Fonteyn; Cornelis Willemse; Rachel Willemse, (sup.) to have d. single; and Sarah Willemse, m. Albert Coerten Voorhees, and d. in 1736. Signed his name "*Willem Guljamse.*"

CORNIL, THOMAS, (soldier.) In 1644 Thomas Maby attempted to kill him on the flats at Amersfoort (Fld[s]), as per Col. Man.

CORNISH, JOHN, of Fld[s]. His will is da. Dec. 19, 1651, in which he bequeaths all his property to Samuel London s. of Ambrose London, and to Ann da. of Edmond Audley of Fld[s], as per G[d] town rec. Made his mark to documents.
Thomas, one of the first settlers of G[d] in 1646, in which year he was allotted a plantation-lot, as per town rec. A planter's lot as fixed by the town regulations consisted of 20 morgens or 40 A., with sufficient salt meadows to keep 6 head of cattle.

CORNWELL, THOMAS, on list of inhabitants of G[d] in 1650, per town rec. Prior to 1656 owned plantation-lot No. 18 in said town. In 1648 leased for 3 years the cleared land on Lady Mody's plantation. He d. prior to 1650. His wid., Elizabeth, about Jan. 1651 m. John Morriee, at which date by the marriage papers his surviving children were:—Elizabeth, about 7 years old (bp. Jan. 12, 1644, in N. U., Samuel, about 5; Johanna, about 3; and Marah, about 1½, as per G[d] rec.

CORSON or CARSTEN, JOHN, of G[d], owned lot No. 3 on G[d] Neck in 1688. Apl. 22, 1693, sold to his brother Peter of G[d] his share in a certain lot in the Neck, as per town rec.
Peter of G[d], m. Deborah ———. Oct. 23, 1693, he sold Ab[m] Emans his dwelling-house and building-plot in G[d] which he bought of Tho[s] Coddington, as per town rec. Sept. 25, 1694, Peter Corson of Cape May, N. J., sold his interest in 2 allotments on Gisbert's I., Nos. 8 and 12, which he and his brother John Corson had bought of W[m] Goulding, to Cornelis Williamse and Derck Brower of G[d], as per town rec. Signed his name "*Peter Corsen.*"
Peter, *Cornelis*, and *Hendrick*. See Vroom.

CORTELYOU or CORTELJAU, CORNELIS (JAQUESZ), of N.U., b. about 1662; m. *Neeltje Volckers* of Bu[k]; d. about 1690.

Took the oath of allegiance in N. U. in 1687 as a native. Neeltje after his death m. 2^d, Sept. 15, 1692, Johannis Vander Grift of N. U. Issue:—Annetje, bp. Sept. 9, 1688, in Fl^h, and m. Mar. 29, 1711, Isaac Liquier of Bu^k.

Jacques 1st, emigrated from Utrecht in the Netherlands to this country about 1652, as private tutor of the children of Cornelis Van Werckhoven, and was a surveyor. He m. Neeltje Van Duyn, sister of Gerret Cornelisse, and resided at first in N. A.; d. about 1693. Owned and occupied the Nayack tract in N. U., for which he obtained a patent from Gov. Nicolls. Was Surveyor-Gen. of the colony in 1657; made, as supposed, the first map of the city of N. Y.; on patents of N. U. of 1668 and '86, of which town he was the founder; a representative of said town in the Hempstead convention of 1665; and vendue-master for the county in 1672. Oct. 20, 1685, he was appointed justice of the peace as per p. 141 of Cal. of Eng. Man. On the laying out the village of N. U. in 1657 he was allotted plantation No. 10, cong. 30 morgens, which he sold Jan. 6, 1665, to Hendrick Mattyse Smack. In addition to his Kings Co. lands, he appears to have been interested in a tract of some 12,000 morgens at Aquackanonk on the Passaic, purchased by himself and associates of the Indians. (See p. 118 of the Rec. of the Gov. and Council of E. N. J.) Issue:—Jacques 2^d, b. about 1662; Pieter, b. about 1664; Cornelis; Helena; Maria; and Willem. Signed his name "*Ja. Corteljau.*"

Jacques 2^d, b. about 1662; m. 1st, Oct. 4, 1685, Marretje Hendricks Smack; m. 2^d, Jan. 1706, Altie I. Boerman; d. in 1726. Owned and cultivated part of his father's tract in N. U., where he took the oath of allegiance in 1687 as a native, and of which town he was capt. of militia in 1693. Will da. Mar. 4, 1726. Issue:—Meeltje or Aeltje, b. Nov. 30, 1691, d. young; Geertje, b. Nov. 18, 1693, m. Hendrick Van Lieuwen; Helena, b. Nov. 29, 1695; Jacques, b. Sept. 26, 1697, d. young; Hendrick, b. Sept. 10, 1699, d. young; Neeltje, b. July 18, 1703; Marya, b. Nov. 16, 1706; Jacques of N. U., b. Sept. 25, 1707, m. Mary or Marretje ——; Hendrick of N. J., b. Apl. 18, 1711, m. 1st, Aug. 3, 1731, Antie da. of Albert Coerte Voorhies, m. 2^d, Aug. 19, 1742, Catrina ——; Dyna, b. Mar. 1, 1715; and Frederick, b. Nov. 22, 1716. Signed his name "*Jaques Cortelyou.*"

Jaques (s. of Peter and Diewertje), b. about 1698; m. Apl. 25, 1718, Jacomintie Van Pelt; d. Oct. 10, 1757. Farmer in N. U. Issue:—Deborah, b. Nov. 29, 1720, m. Derick Bergen of Gowanus; Peter, b. Oct. 3, 1722; and Nelthe, b. Mar. 6, 1726.

Peter (s. of Pieter and Diewertje), b. Sept. 26, 1699; m.

Feb. 24, 1710, Neeltje Van Pelt of N. U.; d. in 1764. No trace of his issue.

Pieter (Jaquesz), b. about 1664; m. prior to Nov. 15, 1694, Diewertje De Wit; d. Apl. 10, 1757. Was a surveyor, and owned and cultivated a part of his father's tract in N. U., taking the oath of allegiance in said town in 1687 as a native. With others of Kings. Co., about 1710, bought the Harlington tract in Somerset Co., N. J. Issue:—Neeltje, bp. Nov. 15, 1694, in Br^n, d. young; Jaques, b. about 1698; Peter, b. Sept. 25, 1699; Cornelis, b. Aug. 17, 1701, and settled on S. I.; Helena, b. Sept. 21, 1703; Willem, b. Sept. 27, 1705; Maria, b. Aug. 10. 1707, d. young; Dorotea or Deborah, b. Nov. 20, 1719; and Neeltje, b. Mar. 20, 1712, m. Sept. 29, 1745, Barent Johnson. Signed his name *"Pieter Corteljou."*

Willem (Jaquesz) of N. U., of which place he took the oath of allegiance in 1687 as a native. No further trace.

COSSART, JAQUES, on ass. rolls of Bu^k of 1675 and '83. There were Kosaerts residing on the Raritan in 1733. This may be Jacques Cousard. There was a Jacob Cossar who took the oath of allegiance to the English in N. Y. in 1664.

COSSEAU, see Cousard.

COSIN, JOB. He with others of G^d, Oct. 1655, notified the Director-Gen. and Council of their danger from the savages, as per Col. Man.

COURTEN, HARMEN, emigrated from Voorhuysen in Gelderland in Feb. 1659 with w. and 5 chil., and settled in N. U.

Myndert, see Korten.

Steven, see Voorhies.

COUSARD or COSSEAU, JACQUES or JACOB, a Frenchman, of Br^n, m. *Lydia Willems* of Bu^k. Took the oath of allegiance to the English in N. Y. in 1664; on ass. roll of Br^n in 1693 and cen. of 1698. There was a Jacques Cousseau and Magdalena du Tullier his w., mem. of the R. D. ch. of N. A. prior to 1660. Issue:—Jacques, bp. Apl. 11, 1668, and David, bp. June 18, 1671, both in N. Y.

COVERT, see Coevert.

COWENHOVEN, COUWENHOVEN, KOUWENHOVEN, or VAN COUWENHOVEN, ALBERT WILLEMSE (s. of William Gerretse), b. Dec. 7, 1676; m. Oct.2, 1701, *Neeltje* da. of Roelof Martense Schenck. Removed to the vicinity of Freehold, N. J., as early as 1709. Issue:—William of N. J., m. Elizabeth ——.

Cornelis Pieterse (s. of Pieter Wolfertse), supposed to have settled in N. J., and had a s. Peter of Galloway, near Cape May, in said State.

Cornelis Willemse (s. of William Gerretse), b. Nov. 20, 1672; m. Sept. 8, 1700, Margrietje R. Schenck; d. Mar. 17, 1736. Removed to N. J. and resided in 1707 at Middletown, Monmouth Co. Issue:—William of Carraway, bp. Sept. 8, 1700, in Br^n, (sup.) m. Mar. 17, 1744, Anna Hendricksen; Roeloff of Middletown, m. Sarah Voorhies; Alkge, m. Wm Van Doorn; Neltie, bp. May 29, 1705, in Br^n; Leah; Mary or Maria, bp. Dec. 24, 1710; Rachel, bp. Nov. 2, 1712; Yacomyntchy, bp. Nov. 28, 1717; Catrina, bp. June 1720 at Marlboro, m. Dec. 22, 1743, Danl Hendricksen of Middletown; Margaret; Sarah; Yannetje; and Anna.

Gerret Janse (s. of Jan Gerretse) of Br^n, m. 1st Lysbet ——; m. 2^d Aeltie ——; d. about 1712; will da. Apl. 16, 1711, and pro. Nov. 3, 1712. On ass. roll of Br^n of 1693 and cen. of 1698. Issue:—Jackomyntie, bp. Jan. 15, 1699, in Br^n, d. young; Jackomyntie, bp. Mar. 2, 1701, in Br^n, m. Sept. or Oct. 1720 Elbert Luyster; Aeltie, bp. Mar. 2, 1701, in Br^n, m. Jacob Cozine—all the above by 1st w.; John of Bu^k, m. Maria or Mary Cozine, d. about 1761; William, supposed to have settled at Three Mile Run, N. J.; and Adriaentje. Made his mark " K " to documents in 1697.

Gerret Willemse (s. of Willem Gerretse), b. Jan. 4, 1662; m. Aeltie ——; took the oath of allegiance in Fld^s in 1687 as a native; mem. of R. D. ch. of Fld^s in 1677. Apl. 27, 1701, he bought of his step-mother Jannetje Monfort and the other heirs of Pieter Monfort, Pieter's farm at the Wallabout, to which he probably removed. He also appears to have owned lands in Bu^k in 1704, as per rec. of said town. No further trace. Signed his name " *Gerret Counover*" in 1702.

Gerret Wolfertse, emigrated with his father in 1631 and resided in Fld^s; b. 1610; m. Altie da. of Cornelis Lambertse Cool of Gowanus; d. about 1645. Bought July 26, 1638, of Andrus Hudde 50 morgens of land at " Achtervelt" in Fld^s. He was one of the 8 men representing the people who, Nov. 3, 1643, memorialized the States-General for relief in consequence of their forlorn and defenceless condition, as per p. 139 of Vol. I. of Doc. of Col. His. of N. Y. Mar. 11, 1647, a patent was issued in his name (dated after his death) for 19 morgens of land in Br^n on the valley of

Gowanus Kil, between the lands of Jacob Stoffelsen and
those of Frederick Lubbertsen. Issue:—Willem Gerretse,
b. 1636; Jan Gerretse, b. 1639; Neeltje Gerretse, bp. Sept.
20, 1641, in N. A., m. 1660 Roelof Martense Schenck of Fld²,
d. about 1672; and Mary or Marretje Gerretse, bp. Apl. 10,
1644, in N. A., m. prior to 1666 Coert Stevense Van Voorhies. Made his mark to documents.

Jacob Wolfertse, emigrated with his father; m. 1ˢᵗ Hester
Jansen; m. 2ᵈ, Sept. 26, 1655, Magdaleentje Jacobuse Bysen;
d. about 1670, and was the oldest s. of Wolfert of Rensse-
laerswyck in 1641. Settled in N. A., residing on High
(Pearl) St., where he carried on a brewery. Obtained
July 6, 1643, a patent for 10 morgens near the ferry in Brⁿ.
Owned a bouwery in Gᵈ, which was ordered to be sold Aug.
19, 1656, to pay his debts. Sept. 24, 1664, licensed by Gov.
Nicolls to trade in his sloop to Albany and with the Indians.
Was one of the 9 men representing the New Netherlands
in 1647, '49, and '50, and in 1666 a mem. of the R. D. ch. of
N. Y. Letters of administration granted on his estate Apl.
21, 1670, to Van Brugh and Leendertse. Issue:—Neeltje,
bp. Sept. 25, 1639, m. Jan. 6, 1662, Cornelis Pluvier; John
or Johannes of N. Y., bp. Mar. 29, 1641, m. Apl. 11, 1664,
Saartje Frans of Haerlem; Lysbeth, bp. Sept. 6, 1643, m.
Samˡ Gerretsen; Aeltye, bp. Aug. 27, 1645, m. July 7, 1669,
Bernardus Hassing or Hassins; and Petronelletje, bp. May
10, 1648, (all bp. in N. A.,) m. Isaac Van Vleck. Signed
his name "*Jacob Van Kouwenhoven.*"

Jacob (s. of John or Johannes and Saartje Frans), bp. Nov.
30, 1664; m. July 7, 1685, at Newtown, by Justice Morgan
Jones, Anna Remerson, both residents of Gᵈ, as per town
rec. Joined the R. D. ch. of N. Y. May 27, 1717, on certificate. Issue:—Johannes Jacobse, bp. Aug. 16, 1685, in
Flʰ, d. young; Johannes Jacobse, bp. Mar. 8, 1696, in N. Y.;
and probably other children.

Jacob Willemse (s. of William Gerretse), b. Jan. 29, 1679; m.
Nov. 12, 1705, Sarah da. of Roelof Martense Schenck;
d. Dec. 1, 1744. Removed to the vicinity of Freehold,
N. J., as early as 1709. Issue:—Peter, b. May, 1720, m.
Catharine da. of Roelof Schenck; Matthias, m. Willemtje
Conover; Daniel, m. Ann Hendricksen; Gerret, m. Oct.
12, 1744, Nelly Schenck; Ruluf; and William—all of
N. J.

Jan³Gerretse (s. of Gerret Wolfertse), farmer, b. 1639; m.
Geradientje da. of Nicasius De Sille. Mem. of R. D. ch. of
Brⁿ in 1677 and '85, and resided at Brⁿ ferry. On the settlement of his father's estate, he was allowed more than his
brother on account of his being lame. In 1665 he was

licensed to trade to Albany. Issue:—Gerret Janse; Aaltje
Janse, bp. Apl. 18, 1678, m. Derick Abramse Brinckerhoff;
Nicasius Janse of Br[n], b. June 30, 1681; Cornelia Janse, m.
Sept. 25, 1691, Gerret A. Middagh of Br[n]; Nelly Janse, m.
July 27, 1694, Jores Rapalje; and (sup.) Willemtje Janse, m.
Feb. 8, 1685, Hendrick Emans of N. J. Signed his name
"*Jan Gerretsen Van Couwenhoven.*"

   John or *Johannes Jacobse* (s. of Jacob Wolfertse), b. May
29, 1641; m. Apl. 11, 1664, Saartje Frans of Haerlem. Resided in High St. in N. Y., and was a member of Gov. Leisler's Council in 1689, and also of the Court of Exchequer,
as per p. 683 of Calendar of Dutch His. Doc. Will da. Jan.
16, 1690; pro. Apl. 13, 1693; rec. p. 275, Lib. 4, N. Y. surr.
off. Issue:—Jacob, bp. Nov. 30, 1664, m. July 7, 1685, at
Newtown, by Justice Morgan Jones, Anna Remerson of G[d],
as per G[d] rec.; Francois, bp. Oct. 10, 1666, m. 1st, Nov. 3,
1709, Catharine Oliver, m. 2[d], Nov. 12, 1739, Mary Brouwer;
Hester, bp. Aug. 12, 1669, m. Feb. 1688 Johannes Martier of
N.Y.; Lysbeth, bp. Mar. 22, 1671, m. Nov. 19, 1690, Ab[m]
Messeur or Messier of N. Y.; Jacomyntje, bp. Mar. 25, 1673,
m. Apl. 20, 1694, Wessel Pietersen (Van Norden) of N. Y.;
Johannes, bp. Apl. 14, 1677, m. May 8, 1708, Rachel Bensen;
Maria, bp. Apl. 2, 1679, m. Apl. 21, 1699, Hendrick Brevoort;
Catelyntje, bp. Jan. 20, 1682; and Peter, bp. Dec. 1, 1683,
(all bp. in N. Y.,) m. Aug. 9, 1707, Wyntje Ten Eyck. Signed
his name "*Johannes Van Cowenhoven*" in 1662.

   John Willemse (s. of Willem Gerretse and grandson of
Gerret Wolfertse), b. Apl. 6, 1681; (sup.) m. about 1704
Coba or Jacoba Vanderveer; d. 1756. Removed from Br[n]
to N. J. prior to 1709. Issue:—William of Penn's Neck, m.
Sophia Lane, d. about 1765; Tryntje or Trynke, bp. Oct.
30, 1709, d. young; Trynke, bp. Apl. 6, 1712, and emigrated
to Kentucky; (sup.) Elias; Cornelis of Penn's Neck, bp. Apl.
6, 1712, emigrated to Kentucky; Peter of Penn's Neck, bp.
Dec. 5, 1714, m. Rebecca da. of Judge Jonathan Combs, and
emigrated to Kentucky and thence to Illinois; Jan, bp. Apl.
12, 1719, at Marlboro, d. after 1756; Jacob of Penn's Neck,
emigrated to Kentucky; and Dominicus of Penn's Neck,
m. Mary Updike, d. prior to 1788.

   Nicasius Janse (s. of Jan Gerretse and Gerdientje or Geradina) of Br[n], b. June 30 (or July 8), 1681; m. Elsie ——;
d. Sept. 16, 1749. Will da. May 15, 1746, pro. Oct. 14, 1749.
Issue:—Geradina, bp. Aug. 7, 1705, in Br[n], m. Symon Van
Wickelen; John of Br[n], b. Dec. 2, 1707, m. Cath[e] Remsen, d.
May 1, 1778; Gerret of N. U. (the ancestor of the present
family of Cowenhovens in said town), m. 1st Sarah ——, m.
2[d] Antie Bergen, d. Nov. 17, 1783; and Peter of the Raritan,

N. J., m. (sup.) Elizabeth da. of Joost Debevoise of the Wallabout. Signed his name "*Nicalus Couwenhoven.*"

Peter (s. of Wm Gerretse), b. Feb. 12, 1671; m. Patience
da. of Elias Daws, and settled in Monmouth Co., N. J.; d.
about 1754 or '55. Mem of R. D. ch. of Freehold in 1709,
and elder in 1711 and '21. Will da. Mar. 15, 1743; pro. Apl.
21, 1751; rec. p. 259, Lib. F, in off. of Sec. of State of N. J.
Issue:—Johanna, bp. Oct. 20, 1695, in Brⁿ; William of Eng-
lishtown, N. J., m. Annetje —— (by another account Marytje ——), d. 1777; Mary or Marike, b. 1700, m. Oct. 10,
1725, Koert Gerretse Schenck; Hannah, m. Antonides;
Jane, m. —— Williamson; Nelke, bp. Jan. 22, 1710, in N. J.;
Peter Junr, bp. Apl. 6, 1712, in N. J., m. Dec. 17, 1735, Leah
da. of Jan Roelofse Schenck, d. 1774; Elias of Middletown,
m. 1729 Willempie Wall, d. 1750; Aeltje, m. Willem Willemse of N. J.; and Ann, m. —— Longstreet—all of N. J.
Signed his name " *Pieter Couwenhoven.*"

Pieter Wolfertse, emigrated with his father; a boy in 1630;
m. 1st, Dec. 2, 1640, Hester Symons Daws of Amsterdam,
wid. of Jacques de Vernus; m. 2^d, Nov. 22, 1655, Aeltje Si-
brants. Was a brewer in N. A., residing on Pearl St., and
schopen in 1650, '54, '58, '59, '60, and '61, and a mem. of the
R. D. ch. of that place. In 1655 he was Surveyor-Gen. of
the colony, and from 1655 to 1660 Orphan Master. After
the conquest in 1664 he removed to his farm at Elizabeth-
town, N. J., and on the reconquest in 1673 he moved back
to the city. In 1663, as a lieut., he was engaged in the Indian war at Esopus. Issue:—Altie (natural adopted dau.);
Hester, m. Feb. 22, 1688, Johannes Martier of N. Y.; (sup.)
Cornelis; Petrus, bp. Feb. 27, 1669, m. Mary ——, his descendants residing in Gloucester Co., N. J.: will da. Sept. 9,
1700, pro. Mar. 4, 1704. Signed his name "*Pieter Wolfersen*" and "*Pieter Couwenhoven.*"

Willem Gerretse (s. of Gerret Willemse and Altie), b. 1636;
m. 1st, 1660, Altie da. of Joris Dircksen Brinckerhoff; m. 2^d,
Feb. 12, 1665, Jannetje da. of Pieter Monfoort. Resided at
first in Brⁿ, of which place he was a mag. in 1661, '62, and
'64, and a deacon of the R. D. ch. in 1663. From thence
he appears to have removed to Fld^s, his name appearing on
the patent of said town of 1667; on its ass. rolls of 1675, '83,
and '93; elder of its R. D. ch. in 1677; and taking the oath
of allegiance there in 1687. Nov. 1, 1709, he sold his Fld^s
farm to his s. William (see Lib. 5, p. 30, of Con.), and (sup.)
in 1727 he removed to Monmouth Co., N. J. Issue:—Gerret
Willemse, b. Jan. 4, 1662; Aeltje Willemse, b. Dec. 14, 1665,
m. Mar. 16, 1687, Cornelis Symonse Van Aersdalen of Fld^s,
d. prior to 1691; Neeltje Willemse, b. Feb. 7, 1669, m. John

Pieterse Wyckoff of Freehold, N. J.; Pieter Willemse of N. J., b. Feb. 12, 1671; Cornelis Willemse of N. J., b. Nov. 20, 1672; Sarah Willemse, b. Dec. 20, 1674, m. about 1692 John R. Schenck of N. J., d. Jan. 31, 1761; Albert Willemse of N. J., b. Dec. 7, 1676; Jacob Willemse of N. J., b. Jan. 29, 1679; John Willemse of N. J., b. Apl. 9, 1681; Annatie Willemse, b. Apl. 13 or 22, 1683, (sup.) m. 1ˢᵗ Aert Willemsen, m. 2ᵈ (sup.) Johannes Antonides, both of Monmouth Co., N. J.; William Willemse of Fldˢ, b. Mar. 7, 1686; (sup.) Joris Willemse; and Jacomina Willemse, b. Dec. 28, 1689, m. June 5, 1709, Elbert Williamsen of Monmouth Co., N. J. Signed his name "*Willem Gerretsen*" and "*Willem G. Couwenhoven.*"

Willem Willemse (s. of Wᵐ Gerretse) of Fldˢ, b. Mar. 7, 1686; m. June 5, 1709, Annetie da. of Lucas Stevense Voorhies; d. Jan. 19, 1769. Will da. Dec. 10, 1757; pro. Mar. 13, 1769; rec. p. 534, Lib. 26, N. Y. surr. off. Issue:—William, b. Mar. 10, 1710, d. young; Cataline, b. July 27, 1711, d. young; William of N. J., b. Jan. 22, 1713, m. Margrietje Schenck; Jannetje, b. Oct. 6, 1714, m. Nov. 1737 Gerret Schenck of N. J.; Luke of N. J., b. June 3, 1716; Aeltie, b. Mar. 21, 1718, m. Corˢ Voorhies; Annetje, b. Mar. 21, 1720, d. young; Catalyna, b. Apl. 1, 1722, m. Albert Schenck; Neeltje, b. Mar. 6, 1724; Gerret of Fldˢ, b. Nov. 11, 1726, m. May 7, 1748, Antie Lefferts, d. Sept. 23, 1777, and is the ancestor of the Fldˢ family of Kouwenhovens; Sara, b. July 23, 1728, d. young; and Jacoba, bp. Oct. 27, 1734, d. young. Signed his name "*Willem Kouwenhoven.*"

Wolfert 'Gerretse, the common ancestor of the family, m. Neeltje ——; d. after 1660; emigrated with his family in 1630 from Amersfoort in the province of Utrecht in the Netherlands; was employed at first, as early as 1630, as superintendent of farms by the Patroon at Rensellaerswick, afterwards cultivated a farm on Manhattan Island, and in June 1637, .with Andrus Hudde, purchased of the Indians the westernmost of the 3 flats in Fldˢ and Flᵇ, called Kaskuteur or Kaskateuw, patented to them by Director Van Twiller June 16, 1637. Aug. 2, 1639, Hudde conveyed to him his interest in a house, barn, barrack, and garden on Long Island, called "Achtervelt." Sept. 16, 1641, Hudde conveyed to him 68 morgens of plain land and 55½ morgens of woodland in the same locality (Fldˢ). Wolfert may possibly have removed to N. A. prior to his death: his name appears in 1657 on the list of small burghers of that place. Issue:—Gerret Wolfertse, b. 1610; Jacob Wolfertse; and Pieter Wolfertse. Made his mark to documents.

CRANEN, THOMAS, (English,) blacksmith. On ass. roll of
6

G^d of 1693 and cen. of 1698. Mar. 29, 1698, he hired a house and lot in G^d for 2 years of Daniel Lake, as per G^d rec. Signed his name "*Thomas Cranen.*"

CRAVEN, THOMAS. The sum of 47 gl. was subscribed by residents of Bu^k Aug. 23, 1662, to ransom his s. Jacob, a prisoner among the Turks, as per Bu^k rec.

CREVER or CREVEN, HENDRICK JANSE, among first settlers of Bu^k in 1661, as per p. 156 of Vol. II. of Thompson's L. I.

CRISTOFFEL, HANS, on ass. roll of Fl^h of 1676.

CRISTOFFELSEN, PIETER, buried as a pauper by the R. D. ch. of N. U. prior to 1700.

CROENENBERGH, CATHARINE, w. of *Jan Theunisse*, bought Aug. 22, 1679, of Rutgert Albertse a house and lot in Fl^h, as per p. 54 of Lib. AA of Fl^h rec.

CROESEN or CROUSEN, GERRET DIRCKSEN, from Wynso-hoort, Wynschoten, or Nim Schoten in Groningen, m. Oct. 30, 1661, *Neeltje Jans* (who m. 2^d Volkert Hendrickse Bries or Breets); d. Mar. 7, 1680. Mem. of the R. D. ch. of Br^a in 1661. Owned land in Br^a between that of Jacob Brouwer and that of Volkert Hendrickse Bries, and on ass. rolls of Br^n of 1675 and '76. In 1677 he obtained a patent for 160 A. on S. I., to which he removed. Issue:—Dirck Gerretse of S. I., bp. July 16, 1662, m. May 4, 1684, Elizabeth Kregier, settled in Bucks Co., Penn.; Annetje Gerretse, bp. Dec. 9, 1677; Elsie Gerretsz, m. Oct. 9, 1681, Wm Klaasz of Fld^a; Hendrick Gerretse of S. I.; Cornelius Gerretse, m. Helena Van Tuyl; Gerret Gerretse; and Jan Gerretse—all of S. I.

CROM or CROOM, FLORIS, see Krom.

CRYSALL, J., on deed of freeholders of Br^n of Jan. 2, 1696-7, to Adriaen Bennet, to perfect his title to his Gowanus farm.

CURLER, JACOB, see Van Curler.
James, of G^d in 1656, per Thompson's L. I.

CUYNEN, ALBERT, see Kuynen.

CUYPER, DERICK JANSEN, leased July 12, 1655, the farm of Cor⁸ Van Ruyven at Midwoud (Flʰ), as per Col. Man. Apl. 13, 1667, sold to Jan Jansen Fyn a house and lot between the school-lot .and that of Jan Strycker in Flʰ, as per p. 18 of Lib. C of Flʰ rec.

DAEMELSE, TEUNIS, plaintiff in a suit against Pieter Janse, Mar. 31, 1662, as per Lib. B of Flʰ court rec.

DAM, JAN TEUNISE, of Flʰ. In his will, da. Mar. 25, 1695, on p. 207 of Lib. A of Flʰ rec., he names his dec. wife's da. Magdalena Vonck, and Magdalena's child, Alida Vonck, to whom he devises his house, orchard, and lot on the E. side of the highway in Flʰ, which lot he bought Jan. 27, 1689-90, of Rut Albertsen, as per p. 149 of said Lib. Signed his name "*Jan Thunissen Dam.*"

DAMEN, CORNELIS JANSE, cooper, mem. of R. D. ch. of Brⁿ in 1677. Had brothers Jan Janse and Willem Janse, as per p. 435 of Vol. 1. of O'Callaghan's New Netherlands.
Jan Buys, mem. of R. D. ch. of Brⁿ in 1677.
Jan Cornelise, the common ancestor of the family, emigrated from Bunnik, a village on the Ryn in Utrecht, in 1650, and m. Fytie or Sophia Martens. The name is probably derived from "Demen," a hamlet in North Brabant, where he probably at one period resided. He bought Apl. 29, 1655, of Cor⁸ Van Tienhoven a house and land in Brⁿ adjoining Jan Dirksen's, in which he kept tavern in 1677, and which he sold in 1693 to Gerret Couwenhoven, as per p. 243 of Lib. 1 of Con. Bought Aug. 21, 1663, of Cor⁸ Hendrickse Van Eens a farm of 26 morgens, with buildings, plain and meadow land, on the W. side of the road in Flʰ, as per p. 143 of Lib B of Flʰ rec., which farm he sold Aug. 10, 1664, to Claes Melles Baes, as per p. 7 of Lib. D of said rec. Mem. of the R. D. ch. of Brⁿ in 1677, hailing from the Wallabocht; on patent of Brⁿ of 1677, and took the oath of allegiance there in 1687. In 1674 (at which date he appears by the deed to have been a resident of Norman's Kil) he bought of Claes Claessen (Smit) of N. U. a farm at "Kyckuyt," as per p. 11 of Lib. C of Flʰ rec. In 1686 he bought the main portion of the farm of Pieter Ceser Alburtis at the Wallabocht. Jan. 19, 1703-4, a Jan Damen voted at a town meeting in Flʰ, and also Aug. 12, 1704, as per Flʰ rec. With his w. made a joint will, da. Sept. 1, 1680; pro. June 20, 1707; and rec. p. 257 of Lib. 7, N. Y. surr. off. Issue:—Neeltje Janse, m. Michael Pietersz Palmenter of Dutchess Co., and had 7 children bp.; Lysbeth Janse, m.

Dec. 14, 1679, in N. Y., Jan Casier from Martinico, a resident of S. I., and had 2 children bp.; Marta Janse, bp. July 24, 1661, in Brⁿ, m. Dec. 11, 1681, John Remsen of Fl^h, and had 4 children bp.; Cornelis Janse, bp. Feb. 11, 1663, in Brⁿ; Cornelia Janse, m. Aug. 6, 1686, in N. Y., Pieter Uziel of Dutchess Co., and had 8 children bp.; Aeltie Janse, m. Oct. 29, 1695, Samuel Phillips of New England; Sophia Janse, bp. Aug. 19, 1674, in Brⁿ, d. young; Elizabeth Janse, ' bp. Sept. 20, 1676, m. (sup.) in 1700 Lucas Schemerhorn, who settled on the Raritan, and had 3 children bp. in N. Y.; Jan Janse, bp. Aug. 28, 1678; Sophia Janse, bp. Aug. 8, 1680; Celetje or Celia Janse, bp. Oct. 7, 1683, in N. U., m. 1st Frans Koning, m. 2^d, in 1707, Frans Laru (LeRoy), and had 7 children bp. at Kingston and Poughkeepsie; Geesje, bp. Nov. 1, 1685; and Russia, m. Peter Van Aken, and had 7 children bp. at Kingston. He made his mark to documents in 1674 as of Norman's Kil. There was a Jan Janse Damen, a trader, shipowner, and owner of lands, in N. A. from 1632 to 1650, about which date he died; also a John Klasen Damen in 1642, and a Thomas Damen in 1644.

DANIELS, GUSTAVUS, m. *Annetje Loons*. Obtained a patent Mar. 21, 1659, for a lot in Fl^h on the S. side of the mill-house,·per Col. Man. Issue:—Margrietje, bp. Nov. 6, 1658, in N. A.

Pieter, emigrated in 1677, and took the oath of allegiance in Brⁿ in 1687.

DARMENTIER, see Parmentier.

DARSETT, JOHN, allotted land on Gisbert's I., G^d, Jan. 5, 1670, for Wm Bowne, per G^d rec.

DARVELL, JAN, of N. Y., bought in 1686 of Jan Van Cleef about 14 morgens in N. U., as per p. 31 of Lib. 1 of Con.

DAVID, JOOST, name on Gov. Dongan's patent of Bu^k of 1687.

DAVIS, DAVIDSON, or DAVISON, ELIAS, on ass. roll of G^d of 1683.

Willem, emigrated in 1653. He m. Jan. 1664 Helena Ardszen Middagh; d. prior to 1695. Mem. of R. D. ch. of Fl^h, and deacon in 1673. On ass. rolls of Fld^s of 1675 and '83; mag. in 1679, and took the oath of allegiance in said town in 1687. In 1679 he paid 75 gl. per morgen for 18 morgens on the little flats. Issue:—Helena, bp. Feb. 3,

1678, in Fld⁹; Aard, bp. Jan. 20, 1682, in Flʰ; and Laurens, bp. June 15, 1684, in Brⁿ. Signed his name " *Willem David-sen.*"

DAWS, ELIAS, allotted a plot on the Neck meadows of Gᵈ in 1672, as per town rec.; on ass. roll of said town of 1683. Issue:—Rebecca, b. 1672; Patience, b. 1674, m. Peter Couwenhoven of N. J.; Annetje, b. 1676—all bp. in Fld⁹; and Maria, m. Jan Karsten.

DE BACKER, HENDRICK, (or the baker,) on Stoothoff's books of 1677. There was a Hendrick de Backer in N. A. in 1654.
Jan, grocer, as per Stoothoff's books of 1680.

DE BAENE, JOOST, emigrated in 1683; m. *Elizabeth Drabbe;* clerk of Buᵏ in 1684, per town rec.; schoolmaster and clerk of N. U. about 1686, losing his position for a while in consequence of his opposition to Gov. Leisler; took the oath of allegiance in N. U. in 1687; and on ass. roll of N. U. of 1693 and cen. of 1698. Removed from N. U. to Hackensack, N. J., as early as 1709, in which locality his descendants abound. Issue:—Matie, m. Nov. 1705 David Samuelse De Maree; Christiaen of Hackensack, bp. May 15, 1687, m. Jan. 1709 Judith Samuelse De Maree; Mayke, bp. May 4, 1690, at Flʰ; Karel or Charles, of Hackensack, m. Jannetje Pieterse Haring; Christyne, b. 1695; Jacobus of Hackensack, m. Antie Kennet or Kenning; and (sup.) Margrietje or Maria, m. June 1728 Theodorus Romain. Signed his name "*Joost De Baene.*"

DE BEAUVOIS or BEVOISE, CAREL, the common ancestor of the family, emigrated from Leiden in South Holland Feb. 17, 1659, with w. *Sophia Van Lodensteyn* and 3 children. Resided at first in N. A., and afterwards as schoolmaster in Brⁿ, where he took the oath of allegiance in 1687. Issue:—Jacobus; Gertrude, b. in Leiden, m. June 15, 1684, Jacob Williams Van Boerum; Catharine, b. in Leiden, m. Sept. 7, 1684, Jacob Hendrickse Harte; and Cornelia, bp. Mar. 3, 1659, in N. A., m. May 25, 1682, Gerret Gerretse Durland of Brⁿ. Signed his name "*Carel De Beauvois.*"
Jacobus (Carelsz), emigrated with his father; m. June 22, 1678, in N. Y., Maria da. of Joost Carelsz of N. Y. Mem. of the D. ch. of Brⁿ in 1677; on ass. roll of said town of 1693 and cen. of 1698. Issue:—Carel, bp. Apl. 20, 1679, in Brⁿ, d. young; Carel, bp. Aug. 1, 1680, at Flʰ; Joost, bp. Mar. 27, 1683, in N. Y.; Jacobus 2ᵈ, bp. Mar. 14, 1686, in

N. Y.; Johannes, bp. Mar. 7, 1689, in N. Y.; Johanna, bp. May 25, 1690, in Br^n, d. young; Catharine, bp. July 23, 1693, in Br^n; and (sup.) Johanna, bp. Sept. 27, 1704, in N. Y. Signed his name "*Jacobus Beavois.*"

Jacobus 2^d of Bedford, bp. Mar. 14, 1686: m. July 23, 1715, Sarah da. of Jores Remsen; d. 1767. His father-in-law conveyed to him 14 A. on Br^n heights, which he devised by his will to his s. George. Will da. June 2, 1767; pro. Apl. 27, 1768; rec. p. 210, Lib. 26, N. Y. surr. off. Issue:—Jacobus 3^d of Br^n, m. Sofia ——, d. 1751; George of Br^n, bp. Mar. 20, 1720, in N. U., m. Oct. 18, 1746, Sarah Betts; d. May 1, 1783. Signed his name "*Jacobus Debeavos.*"

Joost (Carlsz), bp. Mar. 27, 1683; m. July 19, 1707, Mary da. of Jores Remsen; d. 1773. Resided at the Wallabout, and conveyed a Br^n farm to his son-in-law John or Johannes Johnson. Will da. May 1, 1765, pro. Apl. 7, 1773; rec. p. 319, Lib. 28, N. Y. surr. off. Issue:—Jacobus of the Wallabout, m. 1736 Maria Gerretsen, d. about 1786; Phebe or Femmetje, m. John Johnson of Br^n; Mary, m. —— ——; Anna, b. Oct. 20, 1720, m. 1742 Johannes Wyckoff of Fld^s; Elizabeth or Libetie, m. Peter Cowenhoven; and Sophia, m. Albert Nostrand. Made his mark to documents.

DE BOOR, JAN, (or the farmer,) m. *Geertruyd Barents.* On Stoothoff's books of 1680. Issue:—Maria, bp. Sept. 18, 1661, in Br^n.

DE BOUR, CARSTEN, of G^d. On Stoothoff's books of 1676.

DE BRUYNNE, FRANCOYS, b. 1629, emigrated from Amsterdam about 1647, and at first settled in N. A., where he was a mem. of the D. ch. prior to 1660. He m. 1st, Aug. 17, 1657, in N. A., *Catharine* da. of Casper Varleth; m. 2^d *Anna de Sille.* . Bought property and engaged in mercantile business in N. A. Dec. 15, 1663, he entered into an agreement with Nicholas Stillwell, in pursuance of which, Aug. 24, 1664, was conveyed to him Anthony Jansen from Salee's patent of 100 morgens, known as Turk's plantation, lying on the bay partly in G^d and partly in N. U., to which he removed. His dwelling-house appears to have been located in N. U., for he was a mag. of said town in 1663 and '64, and a patentee in 1668. In 1673 he was clerk or secretary of the 5 Dutch towns, and Jan. 1, 1674, was appointed auctioneer. June 4, 1665, (Apl. 19, per G^d rec.,) he sold a portion of his purchase, adjoining the old Bath Lane and the main road from N. U. to G^d, to Jan Jansen Ver Ryn. Dec. 10, 1675, through Anne his wife as attorney, he conveyed the remainder of his purchase, now called Bruyennsburg, to Barent Jansen and Jan Hansen (Van Noostrand) of Bu^k. About 1676 he returned to Holland, his wife returning at a later date with his 10 chil. Of his issue the following were bp. in N. A.:— Casparus, bp. Sept. 14, 1659; Agatha, bp. Jan. 26, 1661; and Jacob, bp. Mar. 5, 1662. Signed his name "*Francoys D. Bruynne.*"

DE CAMP, LAURENS JANSE, emigrated in 1664, and took the oath of allegiance in N. U. in 1687. There was a Hendrik de Kamp, born in N. U. and removed to S. I., who m. Apl. 17, 1704, in N. Y., Maria de Lamars from the Bowery, who was probably a s. of Laurens Janse.

DE CLERCK, JAN, assessed in 1657 at the Wallabout 6 gl. towards Do. Polhemius's salary. Probably the same person as *Jan La Clerck.*

DE CLEY, see De Klyn.

DE CLEYN, JAN CORNELISE, bought May 15, 1660, a village building-plot of Lowys Jansen in Fl^h, as per p. 23½ of Lib. B. of Fl^h rec.

DE CONSELLIE, see Conselyea.

DE COPSEERDT, HENDRICK, assessed Feb. 7, 1657, at the Wallabout for Do. Polhemius's salary, as per p. 134 of Vol. 1 of Stiles's Br^n.

DE DRAYER, HENDRICK, a grand-juryman at court of sessions in 1699.

DEEN or DEN, LOUWUS, on Stoothoff's books of 1678.

DE EYCKE, ANTHONI, m. *Anna Bokee.* Issue:—Gerret, bp. June 28, 1683; and Anne, bp. Apl. 19, 1686, in Br^n. (See Anthoni Den Ryck.)

DE FOREEST, HANCK or HENDRICK, on petition of May, 1664, for a canal through the meadows between Red Hoek and the mainland, as per p. 18 of Vol. 1 of Stiles's Br^n, and a grand-juryman of the court of sessions of 1698. A canal or ditch was afterwards dug through these meadows, making a short cut from Gowanus Cove to the city of N. Y.

Hendrick or *Hendricus*, on ass. roll of Bu^k of 1693, cen. of 1698, and a justice of the peace of the county in 1699, as per rec. of the court of sessions. This Hendrick and the above Hanck may be the same person, and a s. of Isaac the emigrant.

Isaac (s. of Hendrick), a Huguenot and liquor-dealer, emigrated in 1635, settling at first in N. A., where he held positions in the revenue department. He m. June 9, 1641, Sarah du Trieux, and d. about 1695. Dec. 1, 1655, he obtained a patent for 27 morgens in Fl[h], to which he probably removed. He also obtained a patent for a tract in Bergen, N. J., in 1664, in which year he took the oath of allegiance to the English in N. Y. Issue:—Jesson, bp. Nov. 9, 1642; Susanna, bp. Jan. 22, 1645; Gerret, bp. May 21, 1646; Gerret, bp. June 10, 1647; Marie, bp. Jan. 10, 1649; Michiel, bp. Jan. 10, 1649; Jan, bp. Mar. 27, 1650; Philip, bp. July 28, 1652; Isaac, bp. Apl. 25, 1655; Hendrick, bp. Sept. 9, 1657; David, bp. Aug. 1, 1660; David, bp. Dec. 19, 1663; Maria, bp. July 7, 1666; and David, bp. Sept. 7, 1669—all bp. in N. A. and N. Y. The De Foreests are probably descendants of Hendrick De Foreest from Utrecht, an early settler of N. A., who d. in 1638. Signed his name "*Isaac De Foreest.*"

De Fransman (Frenchman), Nicholas, assessed in 1657 at the Wallabout 6 gl. towards Do. Polhemius's salary.

De Gewe, Machill, bought May 3, 1698, of Alex[r] Cockyeer for £200 a parcel of meadows in Bu[k], as per p. 170 of Lib. 2 of Con.

De Graef, Jan Andersen, of Br[n] in 1660. Signed his name "*Jan Andersen Degraef.*" There was a Cornelis de Graeff, Baron of South Pulabroeck in the Netherlands, in 1658, as per p. 56 of Vol. II. of Doc. of Col. His.

De Grau, De Grauw, or De Grouw, Arent Leendertsen, probably from Grouw, a village in Friesland, m. 1st *Gysbertje Hermans*, and both mem. of the D. ch. in N. Y. in 1672; m. 2[d], in N. Y., July 16, 1679, *Marritje Hendricks* wid. of Wouter Gerritzen, as per Fl[h] town rec. Issue:—Hendrick, bp. Mar. 19, 1684, in N. Y. There was a Walther De Grauw in N. Y. who m. Mary De Lanoir June 5, 1726.

De Grooet, Dirck Jansen, probably from Groet in North Holland, m. 1st *Wybrug Jans;* m. 2[d], Aug. 8, 1677, in N. Y., *Rachel Detru* or *Rosella du Trieux*, wid. of Hendrick Van Bommel; m. 3[d] *Rachel Philips.* He bought Nov. 10, 1679, of Wm Jacobse Van Boerum a house and lot in Fl^h for 700 gl., as per p. 65 of Lib. AA of Fl^h rec. Issue:—Jan (sup. of Hackensack), bp. Mar. 27, 1678, in N. Y.; Grietje, bp. Feb. 8, 1679, in N. Y., both by 2^d wife; Abraham (by 3^d wife), bp. Apl. 3, 1682, in N. Y. There was a "Jacob and a Gerret de Groote" on the Raritan in 1721. Signed his name "*Dirck Janse de Grooet.*"

DE GROOT, STATS, on ass roll of Bu^k of 1675.

DE HAEN, JAN, on ass. roll of Fl^h of 1693 and cen. of 1698.

DE HAERT, BELTHAZER, of N. Y., probably from the village of Haart in Gelderland, bought Aug. 24, 1668, of Robt Story 27 morgens on the W. side of the road in Fl^h, as sold to Story by John Jeffers, as per p. 39 of Lib. C of Fl^h rec. De Haert sold this farm to Derick Janse Hoogland, and had several children bp. in N. Y. Signed his name "*Belthazer de Haert.*"

Jacobus of N. Y., owned land in Bu^k near that of Joost Kasparse, referred to in deed of Gerret Stoothoff to Barent Egbertse, on p. 45 of Lib. AA of Fl^h rec.

DE HAES, JAN, see Haes.

DE HART or TER HART, ELYAS (SIMONSE), bp. Mar. 21, 1677; m. *Katie Laen* (who may have been a Van Pelt). Resided at first in a house on his father's farm, located on the bay S.W. of his father's residence. Afterwards left Gowanus and settled in Monmouth Co., N. J. Issue:—Symon, bp. Jan. 29, 1703; Jannetje, bp. May 2, 1705; Elias, bp. Sept. 18, 1709; Arty, bp. Oct. 23, 1711; Katalintje, bp. Feb. 7, 1716; and a child bp. in 1718, and one bp. in 1721, names not given, one probably being Gisbert, who settled on the Raritan—all bp. in N. J.

Simon Aesen, emigrated in 1664; m. 1st Geertje Cornelissen; m. 2^d, June 19, 1691, Annetje Andrieas Willjard wid. of Wm Huycken of Gowanus. Bought Mar. 2, 1664, of Thomas Fransen a plantation at Gowanus of about 300 A., comprising the farms late of Simon and John S. Bergen, his descendants, of which, probably under an agreement of sale, he appears to have been in possession at an earlier date. For these premises on which he resided he obtained a patent from Gov. Fletcher, Nov. 2, 1696. Took the oath of allegiance in Br^n in 1687, of which town he was one of the trustees or overseers from 1680 to '83, and a commissioner in 1688. Issue:—Simon; Elyas, bp. Mar. 21, 1677; Annetje, bp. July 6, 1687, (sup.) m. John Heyer of Monmouth Co., N. J.; (sup.) Catharine, m. Cor⁴ Johnsen of N. J.; (sup.) Cornelis; and (sup.) Dorothea or Donette, m. Jacob Heinne. Signed his name "*Simon Aesen.*"

Simon Junʳ of Gowanus, m. Angenietje da. of Jan Janse Van Dyck; d. in 1745. Occupied and owned his father's farm. In his will, da. July 13, 1744, pro. Nov. 27, 1745, rec. p. 478 of Lib. 15 of N. Y. surr. off., he devised his farm to his s. Simon. Issue:—Simon of Gowanus, m. Catharina or Tryntje da. of Roelof Schenck; Geertje, m. 1ˢᵗ, Corᵃ Sandford, m. 2ᵈ, July 11, 1745, Jores Remsen; Teuntje, m. Jacobus Lott of Brⁿ; Jannetje, m. 1ˢᵗ Peter Brower, m. 2ᵈ, Dec. 28, 1744, Peter Remsen; Annanetje or Angenietje, b. Jan. 4, 1722, m. Jan. 8, 1743, Peter Cortelyou of N. U.; Tryntje, bp. Aug. 14, 1726, at N. U., m. Johannes or John Bergen of Gowanus; and Mayke, bp. May 18, 1729.

DE HEEST, PIETER LAMBERTSZ, from Amsterdam, m. Sept. 16, 1663, at Brⁿ, *Sytie Dircks* wid. of Jan Martyn. Issue:— Sara, bp. Feb. 17, 1664, at Brⁿ.

DE HOUTSAGER (woodsawyer), JAN, was sued Oct. 7, 1661, by Lowys Jansen, as per Lib. B of Flʰ court rec.

DE JONGH or JONGHE, JAN (or young Jan, or Jan Junʳ), sold May 22, 1655, to Jan Hendricksen, 25 morgens at Flʰ, as per O'Callaghan's Man. Trans. of Dutch Man. Mar. 9, 1662, sold to "Albert Kuyne" 22 morgens with plain and meadow land in Flʰ, as per deed of said Kuyne to Frans Barentse Pastoor, on p. 24 of Lib. D of Flʰ rec. May 9, 1662, Gov Stuyvesant granted him a patent for a farm in Flʰ, as per p. 89 of Lib. A of Flʰ rec.

DE KAMP, HENDRICK, see De Camp.

DE KEY, CORNELIS, in 1679 owned land on the little flats in Fldᵗ, per Stoothoff papers.

Jacob Tuenissen, on Stoothoff's books of 1682. A Jacobus De Kay, grocer, on Stoothoff's books of 1696.

Teunis, on Stoothoff's books of 1685. Signed his name "*Theunis De Key.*" A Theunis De Key, b. in N. Y., who m. May 26, 1680, Helena Van Brugge, had 9 chil. bp. in N. Y. from 1681 to 1695, as per p. 759 of Valentine's Manual of 1863. Signed his name "*Theunis De Key.*"

DE KLYN or DE CLEY, BAENST or BARENT, plaintiff in a

suit against Gerret Cornelise of June 13, 1662, as per Lib. B of Fl[h] rec.

Leendert Huygen, from Buuren in Gelderland, m. Apl. 25, 1683, in N. Y., Madaleentje Wolsum wid. of Cornelis Vanderveen, and (sup.) resided at one period in Br[n]. Issue:— David, bp. May 24, 1684; Elizabeth, bp. Mar. 29, 1688; Johannes, bp. Feb. 4, 1694; Magdalena, bp. Jan. 26, 1696—all bp in N. Y.; and Catharine, bp. Nov. 29, 1698, in Br[n].

DE LAFORSE or DE LA FORGE, ADRIAEN, m. *Jannetje Loyse.* On ass. roll of Bu[k] of 1675. Issue:—Pieter, bp. Oct. 11, 1689, in Br[n].

DELAVALL, JOHN, m. May 31, 1686, *Hannah* da. of Thomas Loyd, as. per p. 31 of Vol. III. of the Genealogical Record. July 10, 1694, Hannah his wid., of Pa., for £164 conveyed to John Lake a house and 40 A. of land on Hogg's Neck in G[d], bounded by land of Sam[l] Holmes and that of Isaac Gooding, as per p. 6 of Vol. 2 of Con. He sailed for England, in the ship Blossom, Oct. 14, 1678. Signed his name "*John Delavall.*"

Thomas, of G[d] in 1656, per Thompson's L. I. Mar. 21, 1666-7, he bought of James Grover plantation-lot No. 6 in G[d], as per town rec. There was a Thomas De Laval, a trader, who came to N. Y. in 1664, owned property in Albany, obtained a patent for Randall's Island from the English after the conquest of the colony in 1664, was mayor of N. Y. in 1670 and '76, and d. in 1682. His s. John was his executor, and his da. Frances m. James Carteret, one of the proprietors of N. J. Signed his name "*Tho. D. Lavall.*"

DE MANDEVILLE, GILLIS or JILLIS, m. *Altie* or *Elsie Pieters.* Suppose he resided in Kings Co. Issue:—Hendrick Gillis, b. in Gelderland, m. July 18, 1680, Annetje Pieters Scholl of Heemstede; Gerretje Gillis, m. Sept. 4, 1681, Wyert Eppens of Ester Burum; Aeltje Gillis, m. Laurense Janse; Jan Gillis; and Tryntje Gillis, m. Cornelis Jansz Vanderveer of Fl[h].

Jan Gillis, dog-killer, m. 1st Maria Van Hoboken; m. 2[d] Aeltje Pieters. Nov. 15, 1680, Adriaen Hendrickse sued him in the local court of Fl[h] for 57 gl. claimed for weaving linen, as per town rec. Prior to 1660 he and Maria his w. were mem. of the D. ch. in N. A.

DE MENTELAER, CLAES, assessed Feb. 7, 1657, for Do. Polhemius's salary in Br[n], as per O'Callaghan's Man. Trans. of Col. Rec.

DE METZELAER, JOHN, (or the mason,) m. *Maria* ——. Issue:—John, bp. Feb. 20, 1685, in Fl[h].

DE MEYER, ANTOON, on muster-roll of Bu[k] militia of 1663, per town rec.

Francis or *Francisco*, among first settlers of Bu[k], per Thompson's L. I., in 1661, and on muster-roll of 1663.

Lucas or *Mayerse*, boatman, on ass. rolls of N. U. of 1675 and '76. May 29, 1674, he sold a farm in N. U. to Jan Clement for 1700 gl. Deacon of N. U. R. D. ch. in 1672 and '75, constable in 1677, and in the same year owned the plantation patented to Cor[s] Beekman in said town. In 1683 sold a plot to Hendrick Mattyse Smack, as per town rec. Made his mark " M " to documents.

Nicholaes of N. Y., bought land in 1670 of Jan Van Cleef in N. U., which in 1694 was sold to Hendrick Matthyse Smack. He m. Lydia Van Dyck, and had 6 chil. bp. in N. A., as per p. 761 of Valentine's Manual of 1863. Signed his name " *Nicolaes D Meyers.*"

DE MOF or MUFFE, GERRET, owned land in N. U. in 1661 adjoining that of W[m] Willemse Van Engen, as per deed of Willemse to Rutgert Joesten (Van Brunt) on N. U. rec. Apl. 18, 1653, he bought of Peter Sympson a part of his plantation in G[d], as per town rec.

DE NOORMAN, ALBERT, (or the Northman,) owned land in Bu[k] at an early date. Possibly this may be Albert Andriessen Bradt "de Noorman," for an account of whom see p. 433 of Vol. I. of O'Callaghan's N. N.

Louwerens, was plaintiff in a suit against Jan Tuenese Sept. 29, 1660, as per Lib. B of Fl[h] court rec.

DE NYCK, TOBIAS, m. *Elizabeth* ——. Issue:—Aeltye, bp. Apl. 20, 1694, in Br[n].

DE NYSE, see Van Duyn.

DE NYSE (or NYSSEN), CORNELIS TEUNISE, a minor in 1667, m. 1st, Aug. 27, 1687, *Neeltje* da. of Teunis Gysbertse Bogaert; m. 2[d] *Rebecca* ——. Settled about 1683 on the Raritan in the vicinity of Somerville, N. J., and a mem. of the R. D. ch. of that locality in 1710 and '23. His children adopted " Tunisen" as their surname, which has been continued by his descendants, who are numerous in Somerset Co., N. J. In 1703 he was a member of the Assembly of N. J. Issue:— Tunis Tunisen, bp. Apl. 22, 1688, in N. Y., m. Adriaentje

——; Ab^m Tunisen, bp. Mar. 8, 1699, in N. J., d. young;
Ab^m Tunisen, bp. Sept. 26, 1700; Jan Tunisen, bp. Apl. 20,
1704, m. Aeltje Schenck; Sara Tunisen, bp. Apl. 3, 1706;
Denyse Tunisen, bp. Apl. 28, 1708, m. Saertje ——; and
Neeltje Tunisen, bp. May 23, 1718.

Denyse [2] or *Dionys Tuenessen*, bp. Apl. 16, 1654; m. 1st, Oct.
22, 1682, Elizabeth da. of the Rev. Theodorus Johannes
Polhemius of Fl^h; m. 2^d, Aug. 12, 1685, Helena da. of
Jacques Cortelyou and wid. of Claes or Nich^s Van Brunt
of N. U.; d. prior to 1707. Was a master carpenter, and
bought land in 1687 in Fl^h, where he then resided and took
the oath of allegiance, his name appearing on the patent of
said town in 1685. After his second marriage he removed
to the lands of his wife on the Nayack tract in the vicinity
of the Narrows, and also owned lands at Yellow Hoek.
Owned lands on S. I., where he appears to have resided a
portion of his time and held the office of justice of the
peace. Dec. 30, 1701, as of S. I., he signed a petition of the
anti-Leislerian faction. Bought lands at Millstone, N. J.,
in 1701, and assessed for 80 A. in N. U. in 1706. After his
death his wid. m. Hendrick Hendricksen. His descendants
adopted *Denyse* as their surname. Issue:—Jaques; Theunis,
bp. Apl. 24, 1687, and d. young; Neeltje, bp. Sept. 22, 1689,
m. Jacob Vanderbilt of S. I.; Tunis, bp. Apl. 2, 1692;
Femmetje, m. —— Gerretsen of Six Mile Run, N. J.; Cornelis, bp. Apl. 26, 1696; and Helena, b. 1700, m. Mar. 9,
1717, Frederick Van Leeuwen or Liew of J^a, who settled
at Three Mile Run, N. J., d. Mar. 6, 1784. Signed his name
"*Denys Tuenessen.*"

Jan Teunise, bp. Apl. 12, 1654; m. Nov. 16, 1679, Cataline
da. of Tunis Gysbertse Bogaert. Resided at the Wallabout,
taking the oath of allegiance in Brⁿ in 1687. Removed to
the Raritan, N. J., where his descendants, the same as those
of his brother Cornelis, adopted Tunisen as their family
name, dropping that of Denyse. In 1704 he was a member
of the Assembly of N. J. May 22, 1723, Cornelius Ewetse
and Mary his wife, of Kings Co., conveyed to "*Jan Tunise
Van Middleswart*" of N. J. a house and lot at Brⁿ ferry, as
per p. 26 of Lib. 5 of Con. The "*Van Middleswart*" in this
tends to confirm the conclusion that the "*Van Middles-
warts*" of N. J. are descendants of *Teunis Nyssen* or *Denyse*.
Issue:—Femmetje, bp. Aug. 5, 1680, at Fl^h; Teunis, bp.
July 16, 1682, at Fld^s, m. Adriaentje ——; Sarah, bp. Feb.
1, 1685, at Brⁿ; and Abraham, bp. Sept. 19, 1699, in N. J.
—all residents of N. J. and using Tunisen as their surname.

Jaques (s. of Denyse Tuenessen), m. Reymeriga Simonsen;

d. July 1739. Resided on the homestead at the Narrows, N. U. Will da. July 21, 1739; pro. July 31, 1739; rec. p. 284, Lib. 13, N. Y. surr. off. Issue:—Denyse of the Narrows, N. U., b. Apl. 5, 1726, m. 1ˢᵗ, May 18, 1743, Teuntje da. of Rutgert Van Brunt of N. U., m. 2ᵈ Elizabeth (sup.) da. of Jacob Bennet of Gowanus, d. Sept. 21, 1806; Isaac of Gᵈ, b. Oct. 18, 1728, m. 1ˢᵗ, Sept. 23, 1748, Cornelia da. of Elias Hubbard, m. 2ᵈ Seytie da. of John Voorhies, d. Aug. 27, 1799; Helena, b. Oct. 27, 1732, m. Gerret Rapalje; Antie, bp. Dec. 24, 1732, in N. U.; and Jaques of N. U., b. Nov. 28, 1735, m. Jacoba da. of Jacobus Emmans, d. Jan. 28, 1812. Signed his name "*Jaques Denys.*"

(Sup.) *Joris Teunise*, m. Femmetje ——, suppose he settled on the Raritan, and his descendants adopted the name of Van Middleswaert or Van Middlewout (or from Midwout) as their surname. On the Somerville rec. he is known as "Joris Van Middelswart;" of this, however, there has not been seen positive proof. Issue:—Neeltje Van Middleswart, bp. July 31, 1717; and Filip Van Middleswart, bp. Aug. 12, 1720—both bp. in N. J.

Teunis[1](*Nyssen*), the common ancestor of the family, emigrated as early as 1638 from Binninck or Bunnik in the province of Utrecht, residing at first in N. A. and on a farm on Manhattan I. He m. Phebea Felix of England, known as Femmetje Jans, wid. of Hendrick the Boor and da. of Jan Seales of N. A. Femmetje after his death m. 2ᵈ Jan Cornelise Buys. From Manhattan I. he removed to Gowanus, where he owned and resided on a farm in the vicinity of that of the Brouwers. In 1655 he bought a farm in Flᵇ. In 1658 and '61 he was a mag. of Brⁿ, and in 1660 a mem. of the R. D. ch. of said place. Issue:—Jannetje Teunise, bp. Dec. 22, 1641, m. Jan Hansen Bergen; Marretje Teunise, bp. Apl. 3, 1644, m. Derick Janse Woertman; Aertje Tunise; Annetje Teunise, bp. Feb. 18, 1646, m. Hieronemus Rapalje; Elsje Teunise, bp. May 10, 1648, m. Dec. 1669 Gerret Snediker; Femmetje Teunise, bp. Apl. 3, 1650, m. Michael Hansen Bergen; Denys or Dionys Teunise, bp. Apl. 16, 1654; Jan Teunise, bp. Apl. 12, 1654—all bp. in N. A.; Cornelis Teunise; (sup.) Teunis Teunise; (sup.) James Teunise of the Raritan; and (sup.) Joris Teunise.

Teunis Teunise, m 1ˢᵗ Geertje or Geesje Hendricks; m. 2ᵈ Susanna ——. Supposed settled on the Raritan, N. J., and known there as Teunis Van Middlewout (Teunis from Middlewout, Midwout, or Flatbush).

DEN RYCK, ANTHONI, bought Oct. 7, 1679, of Thomas Tiercksen a lot of woodland in N. U. in the part last laid out, known as No. 4, for 500 gl., as per p. 64 of Lib. AA of Fl[h] rec. Probably same as Anthoni De Eycke.

De Potter, Cornelis, of Br[n], m. *Swantje Jans*, who after his death joined the D. ch in N. A., and m. Apl. 4, 1669, Pieter Delancy; d. prior to Oct. 1660. Bought Aug. 29, 1651, Herry Brezer's plantation; Jan. 4, 1652, land of Jan Haes; and Dec. 3, 1652, over 2 morgens of Cor[s] Hoogland, ferryman—all in Br[n]. In 1654 he was a mag. of Fld[s], where he then resided. Issue:—Adriaentje Cornelise, m. Jan Aardsz Middagh; (sup.) Elizabeth, m. Isaac Bedlo; (sup.) Zwantje, m. Jan Teunise of the ferry; and (sup.) David, on list of catechumens of the R. D. ch. of Br[n] of 1662.

David, a mag. of Fld[s] in 1654.

De Puy, see Du Puy.

De Raedemaker, Gerret, see Gerret Cornelise Van Duyn.

De Rivier, Abraham, (or from the river,) mem. of R. D. ch. of Br[n] in 1677, entered as removed to S. I.

Derckse, see Dirckse.

Dercks, Teunise, was sued at the sessions in 1670 by Francois De Bruynne of N. U. for leaving his service before the termination of his engagement.

De Roal, Gelyam, buried in Fl[h] ch. Jan. 23, 1665, as per Fl[h] rec.

De Sabede, Peter, owned land in Fl[h], as per p. 31 of Lib. A of Fl[h] rec.

Deschamps, Isaac, of N. Y., sold May 17, 1680, a house and lot of 2 A., and also a farm of 40 A., at Bedford to Thomas Smith. Mar. 20, 1694-5, he sold land in Bedford to Thomas Smith of J[s]. See pp. 47 and 49 of Lib. 2 of Con.

De Schoostenveger, Jan, (chimney-sweeper,) assessed at the Wallabout 4 gl. in 1657 towards Do. Polhemius's salary.

De Seen, De Zeuw, or De Seeuw, (the Zeelander,) Cornelis Janse, of N.L., emigrated in 1660; m. *Geertje Kolfs* of
Bu^k. Bought Oct. 1673 of Lubbert Lubbertse for 4000 gl.
a farm in Fl^h, as per p. 109 of Lib. C of Fl^h rec., and Mar. 2,
1674, of Titus (Syrachs) De Vries 8 morgens of cultivated
land in said town, as per p. 18 of Fl^h rec. On ass. roll of Fl^h
of 1675, and a mag. of said town in 1673,'79, and '81, and took
the oath of allegiance there in 1687. Issue:—David, b.
1682; and Jane, b. 1689. Signed his name "*Cornelis Janse
de Seen.*"

Pieter Jansen, d. in Fld^s in 1697, per town rec.

De Seu, Cornelis, of Fl^h in 1676, as per Stoothoff's
books, and probably intended for Cor^s Janse De Seen.

De Sevre, Salamon, m. *Annetje La Clayn.* Issue:—Isaac,
bp. Apl. 1, 1659, in Fl^h.

De Sille, Nicasius (s. of Laurens), of Arnhem in Gelderland, emigrated in 1653; m. 1st, in the Netherlands, ——
——; m. 2^d, May 26, 1655, *Tryntje Cregiers* or *Crougers* from
the Hague, from whom he separated in consequence of
incompatibility of temper. Was first counsellor from 1653
to '57; schout fiscal of N. A. in 1656-7; schout fiscal of
N. U. in 1660, where he was allotted a plantation in 1657,
and where he obtained Dec. 28, 1660, a patent for 25 morgens. Resided during the latter part of his life in a stone
house with a tile roof on his farm in the village of N. U.,
which house was demolished some 20 years ago. Issue, all
by his 1st wife:—Laurence De Sille, who m. a da. of Martin
Cregier, in 1657 was a clerk in the secretary's office, took the
oath of allegiance to the English in 1664, and in 1662 returned to the Hague in the Netherlands; Gerdientje, m. Jan
Gerretse Van Couwenhoven of Brⁿ ferry; and Anna, m.
Hendrick Kip Junr. Signed his name "*Nicasius de Sille.*"

De Snyder, Derck, (Derck the tailor.) His name appears
on Gov. Andross's patent of N. L., or the new lotts of Fl^h.

De Sousou, Jannetje, of Brⁿ, a resident of Haerlem at
date of marriage, m. Aug. 25, 1695, Conradus Hendricksen
Boeg of N. Y.

De Swede, Jan, (Jan the Swede,) on ass. roll of Brⁿ of 1676.

De Syeli., Auke, paid 2 gl. 9 st., minister's salary, in Fl^h
in 1680, as per town rec.

De Tarck, Abram, see Du Toiet.

De Toiet or Tooy, see Du Toiet.

Devenport, capt., a dealer in dry-goods in 1676, as per Stoothoff's books.

De Voor, David, was sued Aug. 18, 1660, by Glandy La Metre, as per Lib. B of Fl^h court rec.

De Vos, see Vosch.

De Vries, Jan Jacob, (probably from Vries, a village in Drenthe,) bought a lot at Br^n ferry, referred to in patent to Pieter Jansen Meet of July 8, 1667. A Jan De Vries m. Dec. 10, 1679, in N. Y., Adriaentje Dircks, and had children bp. in N. Y., as per p. 762 of Valentine's Manual of 1863.

Titus Syrachs, emigrated to this country at an early date; m. Jannetje Teunis (sup.) da. of Teunis Janse Coeverts. Resided in Fl^h, and part owner of a horse-mill in N. U. in 1660; lieut. of foot company of Fl^h in 1673, and d. in 1688. Apl. 12, 1669, he sold to Cor^s Barentse Slecht a house and lot in Fl^h, as per p. 53 of Lib. C of Fl^h rec. At one period censured for improper conduct, and fined £25. In 1677 he and his wife were mem. of the R. D. ch. of Fl^h. Issue:— Tryntje, bp. Dec. 23, 1663; Teunis Titus, who settled in Mansfield, N. J.; Syrach or Sjak Titus, bp. Dec. 28, 1679, in Br^n; Jannetje Titus, bp. Mar. 1682 in N. U.; Francis Titus; and (sup.) Arays Titus. His descendants use Titus as their surname, and he is the ancestor of the Dutch family of Titus or Tetus, as per p. 133 of Riker's Newtown. Made his mark to documents.

De Wael, Pieter, on Stoothoff papers of 1678.

De Wal, Gelyam, (probably from the river Waal in the Netherlands,) buried in Fl^h ch. Jan. 23, 1666, per Fl^h rec.

De Wall, Jeronimus, allotted a plot in N. U. in 1667, which he sold to Anthony Du Chene, as per town rec.

De Wit, Witt, or Widt, Pieter Jansen, emigrated in 1652 and settled in Bu^k, of which town he was a mag. in 1661, '62, and '65; on ass. rolls of 1675 and '83; cen. of 1698; and took the oath of allegiance in said town in 1687. There was a Jan De Wit, miller, of N. A. in 1661. Issue:—Maria,

7

bp. Dec. 25, 1652; and Catharine, bp. May 17, 1654, in N. A. Signed his name "*Pieter Janse Wit.*"

Volkert. His name appears on patent of Bu^k of 1687. No further trace.

DE WOLF, ABEL, of G^d in 1662, per Col. Man.

Derick, of G^d in 1662. Claimed possession of Gisbert's I. in G^d under title of Gisbert Opdyck, but ousted by the town. Allowed in 1662 to make salt on Coney I.

DEYUET, SYMON. His name appears on Stoothoff's books of 1683.

DE ZEUW, CORNELIS JANSE, see De Seen.

DIDO, ABRAHAM, of Bu^k; d. about 1700.

DIRCKSEN or DIRCKSZ, ALBERT, see Amerman.
Cornelis, see Hoogland.
Evert, see Van Nef and Van Ness.
Foulear of Br^n, complaint made against at the sessions of 1678 by Wouter Gisbertsen for hindering him in the use of a highway either to the village of Bu^k or woods, as per court rec.
Gerret and *Hendrick,* see Vander Vliet.
Hendrick, and Barent Jansen Bal leased Aug. 31, 1651, Rem Jansen Vanderbeek's patent at the Wallabout for 4 years. Mem. of the R. D. ch. of Fl^h in 1677. Had a da. Marritje bp. July 2, 1653, in N. A. Made his mark to documents.
Isaac and *Jacobus,* see Amerman.
Jacob, on ass. rolls of Bu^k of 1676 and '83 and patent of 1687; also on protest against payment of Do. Polhemius's salary, as per p. 132 of Vol. 1 of Stiles's Br^n.
Jan, see Amerman, Hoogland, Vander Vliet, and Woertman.
Joris or *George* of Br^n, see Brinckerhoff.
Paulus, emigrated in 1651; m. 1st Jannetje Janse; m. 2^d Geertje Willemse. On ass. rolls of Br^n of 1675, '76, and '83; mem. of R. D. ch. of Br^n in 1677, residing at Bedford, and entered as removed to Ja.; and took the oath of allegiance in Br^n in 1687. With others in 1663 petitioned to form a new concentration (village) back of the Wallabout, as per p. 120 of Vol. 1 of Stiles's Br^n. Issue:—Geertruyd, bp. Sept. 2, 1654, in N. A.; Paulus; and Lysbeth. Made his mark to documents.
Paulus, see Amerman.

Stoffel, took the oath of allegiance in Fld⁸ in 1687 as a native.

Tunis, see Woertman.

Volkert, *Volkherd*, or *Folkert*, m. Annetje Philips of Brⁿ, and settled in Buᵏ. On muster-roll of Buᵏ of 1663; ass. rolls of 1675 and '83; mag. in 1673; mem of Do. Van Zuuren's ch. in 1677; on patent of 1687; and took the oath of allegiance in said town in 1687 as a native. In 1686 commissioned lieut. of militia, as per p. 147 of Cal. of Eng. Man. Issue:—Rachel, bp. Nov. 11, 1683; and Rebecca, bp. Mar. 24, 1686, in N. Y. Made his mark to documents.

William, see Hoogland.

DIRCKSS, TIERCS, of Brⁿ in 1663, with others petitioned for leave to form a new village, and for salt meadows, as per p. 120 of Vol. 1 of Stiles's Brⁿ.

DIRECKIEN, the weaver, of Kings Co. in 1678, per Stoothoff's books.

DITMARS or VAN DITMARSEN, DOUWE JANSEN, of Flʰ in 1688, bp. June 9, 1642; m. Sept. 22, 1687, *Cath*ᵉ *Lott*.

Douwe Jansen Junʳ, resided at first in Flʰ, and finally settled in Jᵃ, where he d. about 1755. Issue, as per Riker's Newtown:—John; Peter; Dow, m. Aeltje ——, and settled on the Raritan; Abraham of Jᵃ, m. June 18, 1725, Bregie da. of Abᵐ Remsen; and Adriana, m. Wᵐ Van Duyne of Newtown. (It is possible that this is an error, and that the above are the chil. of Douwe Jansen and Cathᵉ Lott, who were m. in 1687.)

Jan Jansen, the common ancestor of the family, emigrated from Ditmarsen in the duchy of Holstein, and was sometimes called "Jan Jansen platneus" or flat-nose, as per Riker's Newtown. He m. Aeltje Douws or Douwesen, and d. prior to 1650. Obtained a patent Mar. 23, 1647, for 24 morgens on Manhattan I. In 1647 occupied a farm at Dutch Kils, Queens Co. No positive evidence of his having resided in Kings Co. Issue:—Jan Junʳ of Flʰ; Dow; and Reynier.

Jan Jansen Junʳ, b. about 1643; m. Adriana ——; settled in Flʰ, of which place he was a mem. of the R. D. ch. in 1677, and where he took the oath of allegiance in 1687, and where in 1676 he kept a tavern. From a map on file in the off. of the Sec. of State at Albany, made by "Ja. Cortelyan," without date and filed Aug. 8, 1681, of 6 farms in Flʰ, it appears that "John Ditmarsen" owned "a double lot" on the W. side of the main road or "highway to the ferry,"

nearly adjoining the Fld[a] boundary and S. of the land of
"Klyn Dirk" (Dirk Janse Hoogland), "Broad before 56
rods 7 foot" (about 692 ft. 7 in. English measure) "after
64 rods 5 foot (about 788 ft. 8in.), long 600 Rod "(about 7350
ft.), cong. about 60 morgens. Apl. 24, 1681, "Jan Janse
Ditmarsen" bought of Gerret Lubbertsen a farm in Fl[h] on
the W. side of the highway, S. of Hendrick Janse Oesterstroem, N. of the Fld[a] boundary, stretching W.S.W. 600
rods, broad 27 rods and 5 ft., cong. 27 morgens and 300
rods, as patented by Gov. Stuyvesant May 17, 1662, with
meadows, as per p. 49 of Lib A of Fl[h] rec. This purchase
covers a portion of the land on the above-referred-to map
of Cortelyan, which land remained in the Ditmars family
until about 1825, when Maj. John Ditmars's share (the owner
of a part of the same) was sold to David Johnson, since
which it has been sold in parcels, and on it is located the
main portion of Greenfield or Parkville. Issue:—Dow of
J[a]; Laurens of Fl[h], bp. Apl. 25, 1680, at Fl[h]; Johannes of
Fl[h]; (sup.) Rebecca, who m. Pieter Staats of Gowanus; and
(sup.) Jane, who m. Daniel Remsen of Fl[h]. Signed his
name "*Jan Jansen Van Ditmarsen.*"

Johannes (s. of Jan Janse and Adriaentje), m. Jannetje
Remsen and resided in Fl[h]. Bought Apl. 27, 1719, of Dow
Ditmars the Flatbush farm of his grandfather Jan Janse.
Issue:—Jan, bp. Aug. 31, 1718, (sup.) m. Femmetje da. of
Roeluf Voorhees, d. 1756; Marretje, b. Jan. 8, 1723, m.
Engelbert Lott, d. Apl. 1797; Johannes, bp. May 23, 1725,
in N. U., m. Apl. 20, 1748, (sup.) Rebecca Staats; Annetje,
bp. Mar. 26, 1727, in N. U., m. Leffert Lefferts of Bu[k];
Abraham, bp. Nov. 26, 1731, in N. U.; and (sup.) Jannetje,
m. about 1770 Pieter Staats. Signed his name "*Johannis
Ditmars*" in 1707.

Laurens of Fl[h], bp. Apl. 25, 1680; m. Oct. 29, 1701, Eliza-
beth Hegeman; d. July 25, 1769. Constable of Fl[h] in 1727
and '28. Issue:—Ariaentje, b. May or Aug. 23, 1703, m.
May 10, 1720, Albert Voorhees, d. Apl. 14, 1721; Joseph, b.
Mar. 25, 1704, m. Oct. 3, 1730, Altje Van Brunt, d. Mar. 22,
1732; Femmetje, b. May 23, 1707, m. Sept. 29, 1723, Elyas
Hubbard; and Yannetje, b. Oct. 2, 1708, m. Oct. 12, 1734,
Jacobus Ryder of G[d], d. Aug. 21, 1781.

Reynier or *Reyndert Janse* of Fl[h], m. Lysbeth Van Rare-
stein. On ass. roll of Fld[a] of 1675, and an elder of the R. D.
ch. of that place in 1682. Bought Mar. 8, 1666, of Hendrick
Jansen Oesterstroem or Van Oesterstroem a bouwery in
Fl[h] on the W. side of the highway, on the S. side of Pieter
Lodt, and on the N. side of Gerret Lubbertse, with a house-
plot, as per p. 56 of Lib. B of Fl[h] rec. This appears to cover

the farm of Henry S. Ditmars and part of the farm of John Ditmars, and which was probably purchased of Reynier Janse by Jan Janse his brother. Issue:—Geertje, bp. July 31, 1681, and Louis, bp. Nov. 11, 1683.

DITTON, JOHN, owned land in Brⁿ adjoining Breser's patent in 1645, as per said patent.

DOCKENS, WYLLEM, paid 3 gl. 14 st., minister's salary, in Flʰ in 1664, per minutes of town meetings, etc., of Flʰ.

DOMAN, ——, serjeant, made a contract Nov. 22, 1646, with Jan Teunissen, schout of Brⁿ, to build a house for him at the ferry, as per p. 35 of Calendar of Dutch Man.

DONVER, JOHANNES, on Stoothoff books of 1700.

DOOR, EMME, on muster-roll of Buᵏ militia in 1663, per town rec.

DORLAND or DORLANDT, GERRET. Was probably in this country, but no certain account. Issue:—Jan Gerretse; Gerret Gerretse; and Styntje Gerretse, who m. Dec. 20, 1683, Gerret Strycker.

Gerret Gerretse of Brⁿ ferry, b. 1656; m. 1ˢᵗ, May 25, 1682, Cornelia Debevois; m. 2ᵈ, prior to 1685, Geertruyd Aukes (Van Nuyse). Of the Wallabout in 1677 and mem. of the R. D. ch. of Brⁿ; took the oath of allegiance in 1687 in Flʰ as a native, and on ass. roll of said town in 1693. Mortgaged June 5, 1689, for £160 to Pieter Jacobse Marius of N. Y. 60 A. at N. L. Issue:—Gerret Junʳ; Karel, bp. Mar. 22, 1685, in Flʰ; and Cornelis, bp. Mar. 29, 1696, in Brⁿ.

Gerret Junʳ, m. Marretien —— and settled near New Brunswick, N. J., prior to 1699, as per Dr. Messler's Somerset Co. Issue:—Harmtje, bp. May 30, 1695, in Brⁿ; Annatje, bp. Nov. 14, 1704, in Brⁿ; Maria, bp. Oct. 30, 1706; Lisebet, bp. Oct. 26, 1709; Geertje, bp. Aug. 6, 1712; and William, bp. Aug, 10, 1725—all in N. J.

Jan Gerretse, emigrated in 1652, and settled at Bedford as early as 1657; m. Anna Remsen. On ass. rolls of Brⁿ of 1675 and '83 and cen. of 1698; took the oath of allegiance there in 1687, and elder in the R. D. ch. in 1711. Issue:—Maritje, bp. Apl. 11, 1672, m. Apl. 25, 1690, Lucas Seubring; Geertje, bp. Aug. 19, 1674, m. Aug. 2, 1695, Abᵐ Pietersen of Flʰ; Elsje, bp. May 22, 1678; Jan, bp. Mar. 20, 1681, (sup.) m. May 20, 1690, Jannetje Janse Schenck. Made his mark to documents.

Debevoise by another; Metpenechee, Magdalen, or Lanche, m. Jacob Boerum; Abraham of N. Y., bp. Apl. 10, 1720, m. Mar. 1, 1744, Maria Roosevelt; Catryntje b. Oct. 6, 1720, m. May 16, 1746, Joost Monfoort, d. Sept. 29, 1799; Johannes of Bu^k and N. Y., m. Neeltje da. of William Kouwenhoven; Elizabeth, bp. July 12, 1724, (sup.) d. young; and Anche, m. 1753 —— Van Cleef.

Charles (*Joosten*), farmer, of Bu^k, m. 1st Cornelia da. of Johannes Schenck; m. 2^d Mary or Maria Roberson; d. about 1753. Will da. Dec. 4, 1751; pro. Sept. 1, 1753; rec. p. 358, Lib. 18, N. Y. surr. off. Issue:—Joost of J^a; Helena, m. —— Van Zant; Johannes of N. Y., m. Apl. 30, 1748, Antje Voorhies of G^d; Cornelia, m. June 11, 1757, Frans Titus; Charles or Charel of Oyster Bay, m. Dec. 16, 1748, Antie Fryn; Elizabeth, (sup.) m. Joost Van Brunt; Tunis of Bu^k, m. May 18, 1753, Anna Rapalje; Derick of N. Y., m. June 1, 1754, Elizabeth Titus; and Abraham of Rondout, Dutchess Co., m. Sarah Van Wyck, d. 1764.

Christiaan (*Pieterse*), bp. Apl. 17, 1681. No further trace.

Jacob (*Joosten*), bp. Nov. 21, 1686; m. 1708 Catrina Polhemius; d. 1758. Resided at first in Bu^k and afterwards in Br^n. His Bu^k farm of 100 A. was sold Apl. 15, 1758, by his executors. Issue:—Joost of J^a South, farmer and millwright, b. 1709, m. 1st Willemtje Terhune, (names of his 2^d and 3^d wives not ascertained,) m. 4th Charity ——, d. 1775; Daniel of J^a, d. 1759; Johannes of N. Y., m. Oct. 29, 1763, Sara ——; Jacob of N. Y. and Bu^k, m. Mar. 21, 1747, Sara Van Noortstrant, d. 1784; Abraham of N. Y., merchant, bp. Feb. 16, 1724, m. Nov. 3, 1763, Elizabeth Low; Cornelius of Bu^k; Hendrick; and Magdalena, m. Cor^a Wyckoff of N. J. Signed his name "*Jacob Durye*."

Joost, the common ancestor of the family, emigrated about 1675 from Manheim in the Palatinate of the Rijn; m. Magdalena La Febre. Settled at first in N. U., where he owned a farm which he sold Oct. 5, 1681, for 3200 gl. and a new wagon to Gerret Cornelisen Van Duyn, as per p. 148 of Lib. AA of Fl^h rec. Left N. U. and settled on the disputed lands between Newtown and Bu^k, where he d. about 1727. On ass. rolls of Bu^k of 1683 and '93 and cen. of 1698, taking the oath of allegiance there in 1687. Issue:—Joost; Peter; Jacob; Abraham; Charles; Jaques, bp. July 13, 1679, at Fl^h; Antonette, bp. Dec. 11, 1681, m. —— Luqueer; Magdalena, bp. Oct 19, 1687, in N. Y., d. 1705; Cornelis of Bu^k; Simon, bp. Nov. 26, 1693, in Br^n; and Philip. Made his mark to documents.

Joost (*Joosten*) of Bu^k, m. Apl. 17, 1681, Lena or Helena ——; d. 1727. Issue:—Magdelientje, bp. May 29, 1705, in

Br^n, m. Dec. 31, 1743, Gerret Van Sant of Newtown; Joost (sup.) of Six Mile Run, N. J., (sup.) m. Antje Terhune; Hendrick, bp. Nov. 23, 1718; and Folkert of N. Y., m. Geartey da. of Nicholas Vechte of Gowanus, d. 1752.

Philip ^{2}(*Joosten*), m. Aug. 14, 1714, Belje Goverts. No further trace.

Simon ^{2}(*Joosten*), bp. Nov. 26, 1693, in Br^n; m. May 20, 1715, Annetje Sprung. Resided in Bu^k, and a farmer. Issue:—Simon of Bu^k, m. Dec. 17, 1758, Jane Vandervort.

Du Toict, Du Toit, or Du Torck, Abraham, (French,) soldier, m. *Jannetje Jeronemus Bocquet.* Resided at first in N. Y., of which place he was a mem. of the R. D. ch. in 1667 and '74. Obtained a tract in N. U. which he sold May 29, 1674, to Anthony Du Ceene or Seen, as per town rec. and as per p. 116 of Lib. C of Fl^h rec., at which date he appears to have resided in said last-named town. Feb. 5, 1680-81, he sold to Jan Barentse Blom his bouwery in the new division (N. L.) of Fl^h, cong. 80 A., for 1000 gl., as per p. 150 of Lib. AA of Fl^h rec. He and his w. are entered on the R. D. ch. rec. of Fl^h as residents of N. L., removed to Bergen, N. J. His name appears on the ass. roll of Bu^k of 1693 and cen. of 1698. Issue:—Catharine, bp. June 2, 1678, in Br^n; and Hester, bp. Apl. 4, 1680, in N. U. Signed his name *"Abraham du Toict."*

Dutten, Jan, his land in Br^n referred to on Breser's patent of Sept. 4, 1645.

Du Wien, Joost, m. *Magdalena* ——. Both mem. of R. D. ch. of N. U. in 1677 and '85, and entered as removed to Newtown.

Duyckhuys, Jan Teunissen, see Van Dyckhuysen.

Duyckingh, Evert, from Borken or Borkel in North Braband, glazier, m. Sept. 9, 1645, in N. A., *Hendrickje Simons* from Noordthorn. Owned land in Fl^h in 1654, as per O'Callaghan's Man. Trans. of Dutch Man. Obtained a patent under the name of "Evert Duyckingh Van Borchen" for 24 morgens in Fl^h, lying between the lands of Johannes Megapolensis and those of Teunis Nissen (Denyse), with salt meadows and plain land, which he sold Sept. 6, 1658, to Cor^s Van Ruyven, as per p. 37 of Lib. A of Fl^h rec. Also owned property in N. A. near the Fort, and in 1664 took the oath of allegiance to the English. Issue:— Relitje, bp. June 30, 1647; Jannecken, bp. July 25, 1649;

Evert, bp. Oct. 30, 1650; Symontje, bp. May 12, 1652; Aeltje, bp. Mar. 26, 1656; Marie, bp. Mar. 31, 1659; and Gerret, bp. Apl. 11, 1660—all in N. A.

DUYTS or DUITS, JAN LAURENSE or LAURENTSZEN, of N. U., was probably a s. of Laurens Duytsen, bp. Mar. 23, 1642 in N. A., m. 1st *Jannetje Jeuriaens;* m. 2d, Sept. 27, 1673, in N. Y., *Neeltje Adriaens* from Breda, both at the time residents of Mispat's Kil (she m. after his death Hendrick Thomasse Van Dyck); d. about 1679. There was a "Lourens Duyts" who July 1, 1639, with Pieter Andriesen leased a plantation of Joris Bronck on the mainland opposite Manhattan I., as per p. 9 of Calendar of Dutch Man., who may have been this Jan Laurentszen. Oct. 30, 1677, "Jan Laurense Duits" bought of Luykes Meyerse 2 half-lots of land, Nos. 13 and 14, in N. U. lying at the "fonteyn" (Yellow Hoek), adjoining land of "Rutger Joesten" (Van Brunt), on which there was a good dwelling-house and barn, as per town rec. June 14, 1679-80, Hans Harmense (Van Barkeler) and Lourens Haff, guardians of the children of Jan Laurentszen, bound his son Louris or Louranse, aged 9 years, to Jan Janse Van Dyck for 6 years to do all kinds of labor, and at the end of the term to be furnished with a Sunday suit of clothes and three good shirts. Issue:— Annetje Janse; and Louris or Laurens Janse, bp. June 4, 1671, in N. Y.

Hans Laurentszen, of N. U. in 1679, brother of Jan. Made his mark to documents.

EBELL, PETER, in N. A. as early as 1647; m. *Claertje Hendrickse.* Bought May 21, 1655, of Isaac Greveraet plantation-lot No. 27 in G^d. Feb. 3, 1657, obtained a patent for a plantation near Fort Casmar on the Delaware. Mar. 7, 1659, he sold plantation-lot No. 27 in G^d to Jan Jansen Ver Ryn, as per G^d rec. In 1664 he took the oath of allegiance to the English in N. Y. Issue:—Elsje, bp Oct. 16, 1650, in N. A. Made his mark to documents.

ECKER, JACOB, of Fl^h, a resident on Frederick Philips's land, m. June 4, 1693, in N. Y., *Magdaleentie Vonck* of Southampton, at date of m. of Haverstraw.

Wolfert of Fld^s, a resident on Frederick Philips's land (Philips Manor), m. Dec. 21, 1692, in N. Y., Marritje Siebouts of the Poor Bouwery. Issue:—Steven, bp. June 21, 1693; and Marritje, bp. July 29, 1696, both in N. Y.

EDSELL, EDSALL, ETSAL, or ELSAL, SAMUEL, from "Ridding

in Bawrychier" (Redding in Berkshire), England, hatter, m. 1st, May 29, 1665, in N. Y., *Jannetje Wessels* of Arnhem in Gelderland; m. 2^d, Aug. 27, 1689, in Fl^h, *Jannetje Stevens* wid. of Cor^s Jansen Beory of Newtown. In 1657 he was admitted a small burgher in N. A., and in 1664 took the oath of allegiance in N. Y. to the English. In 1664 he owned and resided on a farm at Constable's Hoek, Bergen, N. J., as per p. 137 of Vol. 1 of Raum's N. J., to which place he probably removed from Newtown. In 1668 he was a member of the Council of Gov. Carteret; in 1677 he was taxed in N. Y., and in 1687 a justice of the peace in Queens Co. Oct. 1, 1690, he was commissioned a justice of the peace of Kings Co., as per. Col. Man. Issue:—Annetje, bp. July 12, 1656; Judith, bp. May 15, 1658; Johannes, bp. Sept. 12, 1660—all in N. A.; Ann; Julia; and Richard. (See p. 72 of Winfield's Hudson Co.) Signed his name "*Samuel Edsall.*"

EGBERTSE, BARENT HUYBERTSE, m. *Aechtje Alberts.* On ass. roll of Brⁿ of 1675. Bought Aug. 1, 1678, of Garret Stoothoff for 6000 gl. 25 morgens of woodland in Brⁿ called the "Kruypel Bosch," bounded on the N. side by land of Joost Kasparse, and on the S. by that of Jacobus de Heart, as per p. 45 of Vol. AA of Fl^h rec. There was a Barent Egbertse (probably a s. of Egbert Teunise Metselaer) who m. Aug. 26, 1704, Maria De Garmeau at Albany, as per Pearson's First Settlers of Albany. Issue:—Tryntje, bp. Aug. 18, 1658, in N. A. Signed his name "*Barent Egberssen.*"

Sander of the Wallabout, and mem. of the R. D. ch. of Brⁿ in 1677; m. Apl. 2, 1682, Elsje Pieters (Staats) of N. U., both residents of Gowanus at date of marriage; d. Oct. 7, 1680, at S. I. Issue:—Annetje, bp. May 27, 1683.

EIGO, JOHANNES, on ass. rolls of N. U. of 1693 and cen. of 1698.

Paulus, on ass. roll of N. U. of 1693 and cen. of 1698.

ELBERSEN, JOHN, m. *Mary Hendricksen.* Issue:—Egbertje, bp. July 3, 1698, in Fld^s. Signed his name "*John Elbersen*" in 1715.

ELBERTSEN, ELBERT, and GERRET, see Stoothoff.

Gysbert, on Hegeman's auction-books of 1670 and '71. There was a Gysbert Elbertsen who m. Willemtje Claes, and had 10 children bp. in N. A. and N. Y., as per p. 766 of Valentine's Manual of 1863. Made his mark to documents.

ELDERT, HENRY or HENDRICK, of J* (s. of Eldert Lucasse
Voorhies), bp. Mar. 4, 1691; m. 1ˢᵗ, Nov. 18, 1710, *Grietje
Wyckoff* of Fld*; m. 2ᵈ *Tryntje* ——. Will da. Feb. 6, 1759;
pro. Dec. 22, 1768; rec. p. 446 of Lib. 26, N. Y. surr. off.
Issue:—Grietje, bp. May 11, 1722, m. John Stephens; Johan-
nes of N. L., m. Femmetje ——; Eldert; Styntje, m. John
Munny; Margaret, m. Nov. 29, 1761, Godfrey Heyn; Ann,
m. Hendrick Emmans; and Mary or Maria, m. Rem Van
Cleef. Signed his name "*Hendrick Elders.*"

Johannes (s. of Eldert Lucasse Voorhies), bp. Dec. 26,
1681, at Flʰ; (sup.) m. Marretje Bergen and settled at Foster's Meadows in Queens Co. Issue:—Johannes; Grace;
and Cresia, bp. Apl. 14, 1707. Signed his name "*Johannes
Eldert.*"

Lucas of J* (s. of Eldert Lucasse Voorhies), bp. Dec. 25,
1677, in Fld*; m. —— ——; his descendants assumed the
surname of Eldert. Will da. Aug. 6, 1752; pro. Oct. 18, 1756.
Issue:—Eldert, (sup.) m. Jannetje Nostrand; Grace, m.
George Bates; Jane, m. Joseph Barnet; and (sup.) Samuel.

ELLICE, JAMES, one of the first settlers of Gᵈ in 1646, and
allotted a plantation-lot in 1648, per town rec.

ELLIS or ELIAS, JOSEPH, m Mar. 10, 1681, in Fld*, Elizabeth Damerill. Issue:—Anna, bp. Oct. 3, 1682, in N. Y.

ELTYGE or ELTEN, JAN, of Drenthe in the Netherlands,
was paid 25 gl. for carpenter's work on Flʰ ch. Bought
Nov. 27, 1663, of Derick Jansen, cooper, a farm and building-
plot in Flʰ on the E. side of the main road, as per p. 150 of
Lib. B of Flʰ rec. From Flʰ he removed to Kingston. In
1679 he declared under oath that he was a son of Roeloffe
Elten and Stryker Lebring, and made declarations as to
his identity, as per p. 80 of Cal. of Eng. Man. Signed his
name "*Jan Eltyge.*"

ELTYNOCK or EELTYNOCK, JAN, owned a building-plot in
Flʰ June 12, 1665, as per a suit with Derick Jansen rec. on
p. 35 of Lib. D of Flʰ rec. He is probably the same person
as the above "Jan Eltyge."

EMANS, EMMANS, or IMANS, ABRAHAM (Andriese), settled
in Freehold, N. J.; m. 1ˢᵗ, Oct. 20, 1693, *Rebecca* da. of Mich*
Stillwell of Gᵈ; m. 2ᵈ, Aug. 17, 1702, *Margaret Williamson*, a
wid. On cen. of Gᵈ of 1698. Of Freehold Nov. 25, 1715, on
which date he conveyed to his s. John 205 A. in said place.
Issue:—Cornelius, m. Cornelia Holsaert; John of N. J.; Nich-

olas; Benjamin, m. Rachel Fenton; Abraham, m. Annatie Luyster; Maria, bp. Jan. 20, 1707, at Freehold; Daniel, bp. Apl. 11, 1714, at Freehold, m. Aelje Hulsaert; and Katryna, m. Ab^m Bidull—all being of N. J. Signed his name "*Abraham Emans.*"

Abraham (s. of John and Sara), m. Abagail (sup.) Stillwell. Settled at Freehold, N. J., as early as 1715. Will da. Jan. 1734; pro. Apl. 19, 1742; rec. p. 236, Lib. 14, N. Y. surr. off. Issue:—Stillwell; Isaac; and Thomas.

Andries, an Englishman, the ancestor of the Emmans family of Kings Co. and N. J., emigrated from Leiden in the Netherlands, in the ship Saint Jean Baptist, May 9, 1661, and settled in G^d. Aug. 21, 1661, he with 12 others petitioned the authorities for land on S. I. Issue:—John of G^d; Hendrick of N. J.; Abraham of N. J.; Jacobus of G^d; and Andries Junr of G^d.

Andries Junr of G^d and N. U., b. 1677; m. Nov. 24, 1693, Rebecca Van Cleef of G^d. Bought July 20, 1708, of Stoffel Romeyn a farm in N. U., to which he removed. On ass. roll of G^d of 1693 and cen. of 1698. Will da. Sept. 1, 1728; pro. Jan. 6, 1729; rec. p. 34, Lib. 10, N. Y. surr. off. Issue:—Hendrick, d. young; Johannes; Andries of N. U.; Benjamin of N. J., m. Sarah (or Antie) Snediker; Jacobus of N. U., m. Jannetje da. of Wm Kouwenhoven; Hendrick of Somerset Co., N. J., m. Sara da. of Roelof Verkerk of N. U.; Antie, bp. Apl. 26, 1696, d. young; Ann, m. 1st John Verkerk, m. 2^d Jacob Rapalje of Br^n; Sara, m. Teunis Polhemius of Orange Co.; and Rebecca. Signed his name "*Andries Emans.*"

Andries (s. of Andries Junr) of N. U., m. Femmetje Dorlant; d. about 1760. Will da. Dec. 28, 1759. Jan. 25, 1742-3, he bought of Saml Groenendyck a farm of 84 A. in N. U. (late the farm of J. A. Emmans, his great grandson), to which he removed. Issue:—Rebecca, bp. Apl. 3, 1729, m. Hendrick Suydam of Bedford, d. Oct. 25, 1797; Rem, d. young; Annatie, bp. Jan. 12, 1732, d. young; Andries, bp. Apl. 2, 1735, d. young, of small-pox; Johannes of N. U., the grandfather of J. A. Emmans, m. Maria Wyckoff, d. Jan. 8, 1780, inherited his father's farm; Sara, b. 1740, (sup.) m. July 27, 1764, Hendrick Wyckoff, d. July 22, 1820; and Maria, b. Sept. 2, 1752. Signed his name "*Andries Emans.*"

Anthony (s. of John and Sara), d. prior to May 6, 1699. Nov. 15, 1678, his father bound him for 2 years to Hendrick Rycke (Suydam) of Fl^h to learn the blacksmith's trade, as per p. 32 of Lib. AA of Fl^h rec.

Benjamin (s. of Andries and Rebecca), m. Sarah or Antie Snediker. Left G^d and settled on a farm at Rocky Hill, Somerset Co., N. J. Issue:—Catryna, bp. Apl. 2, 1735 ; Isaac, bp. Feb. 19, 1738, d. young ; and Isaac, bp. Mar. 6, 1739. Signed his name " *Benjamen Emans.*"

Hendrick (Andriese) of G^d and N. J., m. Feb. 8, 1685, Willemtje Jans of Fld^s; d. prior to May 6, 1699. May 19, 1685, he bought of Stoffel Jansen (Romeyn) a house and two garden-plots in G^d. Removed to Middlebush, Somerset Co., N. J., as early as 1703. Made his mark " H " to documents.

Jacobus (Andriese) of G^d. No trace.

Jacobus (s. of John and Sara) of G^d, m. May 10, 1700, Geertje or Grietje Romeyn ; d. prior to Apl. 17, 1749. Issue:— Cornelius of G^d, m. May 13, 1749, Eva Voorhies, d. May 19, 1792; Abraham of G^d, bp. Oct. 5, 1718, m. Nov. 5, 1740, Sarah Schenck, (sup.) d. Nov. 21, 1810; (sup.) Jacobus, d. 1816 without issue ; Cornelia ; and Geertie. Signed his name "*Jacobus Emans*" in 1748.

Jacobus (s. of Andries and Rebecca) of N. U., m. Jannetje da. of Wm Kouwenhoven ; d. 1735. Owned and cultivated the farm in N. U. which his father bought of Stoffel Romeyn, now (1880) of John E. Lott. Issue:—Jacoba, b. Oct. 7, 1733, m. Jaques Denyse, d. Feb. 14, 1825. Signed his name "*Jacobus Emans*" in 1704.

Jan Junr (s. of John and Sara) of G^d, m. 1st, Mar. 4, 1701, (sup.) Angelica Van Cleef ; m. 2^d Nelthe —— ; d. Feb. 1724. Will da. Feb. —, 1723; pro. Feb. 13, 1734; rec. p. 449, Lib. 9, N. Y. surr. off. Issue:—John ; Ester ; Sarah, (sup.) m. Benjamin Stymets ; Neeltie ; Samy ; Thomas ; and Johanna. Signed his name "*John Emans.*"

Johannes (s. of Andries and Rebecca) of G^d and N. U., m. Nov. 12, 1702, Neeltje Cranen by G^d rec., Neeltie Van Cleef by another account. Signed his name "*Johannes Emans.*"

John or *Jan* Senr (s. of Andries the emigrant), master cooper, of G^d, m. 1st Sarah da. of Anthony Jansen from Salee or Vaes; m. 2^d, Nov. 17, 1702, Neeltje Cranen ; d. prior to 1715. Mag. of G^d in 1673, '74, and '76, and in 1691 town-clerk. On ass. rolls of said town of 1693 and cen. of 1698, on which he is entered as of English extraction, from which it is inferred that his father, although hailing from Leiden, was among those Englishmen who left their native land and came to Holland to enjoy religious liberty and avoid persecution. Issue:—John Junr; Anthony ; Andries of G^d, who probably settled in N. J.; Abraham ; Jacobus ; Sarah, m. Oct. 14, 1696, Joseph Morgen of Freehold ; and Cornelia, m. Dec. 1, 1699, Paulus Amerman (sup.) of Monmouth Co., N. J. Signed his name "*John Emans*" and sometimes "*Jan Emans.*"

ENDE, PETER, of G^d In 1655 among those who notified

the Director-Gen. and Council of the danger they were liable
to on account of the Indians.

ENGELBERTSE, see Lott.

ERDERS, WYLEM, paid 2 gl. 9 st., clergyman's salary, in 1690
in Fl^h, as per town rec.

EVANS, ANDREW, on ass. roll of Br^n of 1693.
Randolph or *Randel*, m. Martha or Margaret Young. On
ass. roll of Br^n of 1683; a commissioner of Br^n in 1684, as per
Furman's Notes. Owned a lot in Br^n adjoining that of Thomas
White. Margaret his wid. sold Sept. 20, 1697, a piece of land
in Br^n to Ann w. of John Smith of the same place, as per p.
145 of Lib. 2 of Con. Issue:—Elizabeth, bp. Feb. 17, 1684, in
Br^n; and William, bp. Dec. 25, 1684, in Br^n.

EVERD, MICAH, purchased a planter's lot in G^d in 1647 of
Searjeant Ja^s Hubbard, as per town rec.

EVERENDEN, ROBERT, (English,) m. *Ann* ——. On cen. of
Br^n of 1698 as of the ferry. In 1699 his wife petitioned the
court of sessions to prevent his abandoning her.

EVERTSE, EVERT, obtained a patent May 11, 1647, for 49
morgens of land in the rear of "Jacous Bentyn's" land on
Long Island (Br^n). Where was this?

EVERTSEN, ARENT, molenaar or miller, m. *Susanna
Hendricks De Boog*. In 1661 he received various amounts as
comforter of the sick in the colony on the Delaware, as per p.
181 of Vol. II. of Doc. of Col. His. of N. Y. Oct. 20, 1677,
sold to Balthazer Vosch Junr a farm of 18 morgens in Fl^h,
abutting against Corlaers flats or plains, on the E. side of the
road, as per p. 23 of Lib. C of Fl^h rec. Aug. 27, 1667, owned
land in Kings Co., as per p. 179 of Lib. 2 of Con. Issue:—
Neeltje, bp. June 28, 1645; Evert, bp. Sept. 19, 1661; and
Catharina, bp. Mar. 21, 1674—all in N. A. A Sarah Molenaar
of Bu^k, probably his da., m. June 1703, in N. Y., Hendrick Play
of said city. Signed his name at times "*Arent molenaer*" and
occasionally "*A Evertsz.*" Perhaps Arent is a descendant of
Cornelius Evertsen, the celebrated Dutch admiral of Zeeland,
who was surnamed "Keesie the Devil."
Conrad, owned land in Br^n in 1660, per Col. Rec.
Jan, see Bout.
Volkherd, obtained a patent Mar. 11, 1647, for 2½ or 3 mor-

gens on L. I., (sup.) at Gowanus. Made his mark to documents.

EWOUTSE, EUWETSE, or EWETSE, CORNELIS, from Beets in North Holland. Suppose he came over with the squadron which conquered and retook the colony of New Netherlands from the English in 1673. Commissioned master-gunner Aug. 12, 1673, and placed in command of a vessel known as the "snow *Zeehont*" (Sea-dog), which made prizes of Massachusetts vessels, as per p. 726 of Vol. II. of Doc. of Col. His. Suppose he resided at Br^n ferry. Issue:—Jan ; Cornelis Junr ; Ewout ; Elizabeth, m. Samson Lasay ; and Petronella, m. Gerret Martense.

Cornelis Junr, m. Mary or Maria Polhemius. Resided at first at Br^n ferry, selling his house and lot in 1723 to Jan Teunise Van Middeswout, and in 1743 became a freeman of the city of N. Y., to which place he removed. Nov. 19, 1738, he and his w. joined the D. ch. of N. Y. on certificate from L. I. Issue:— Joris, bp. Aug. 22, 1736, in N. Y.

Ewout, m. Apl. 24, 1715, Sarah Tiebout of N. Y., ; d. prior to May 1740. Resided at first in Br^n, where he sold his house and lot in 1716 to Cor^s Ewetse, as per p. 26 of Lib. 5 of Con., and in 1717 became a freeman of the city of N. Y., to which place he probably removed. Issue:—Johannes of N. Y., carpenter, bp. Feb. 8, 1716, (sup) m. June 16, 1741, Ruth Luvois; and Maria, bp. Nov. 10, 1717, in N. Y., m. Johannes Van Gelder.

Jan, m. July 16, 1686, Elizabeth Plevier. Was a pot-baker, residing at Br^n ferry, where he sold his land, Jan. 28, 1726, to John Barbarie, as per p. 38 of Lib. 5 of Con. From the records of the court of sessions of 1700 he appears at that date to have been a liquor-dealer. In 1746 he became a freeman of N. Y., to which place he probably removed. Issue:— Anneken, bp. Oct. 16, 1689; Johannes, bp. Jan. 6, 1695 ; Elizabeth, bp. Nov. 17, 1697; Pieternella, bp. Dec. 28, 1701 ; and Petrus, b. Apl. 3, 1703, m. Sept. 21, 1726, Catharine da. of Joris Hansen Bergen—all bp. in N. Y. Signed his name "*Jan Euwetse.*"

FARCKS, TOMAS, on ass. roll of N. U. of 1683.

FARDON, FERDON, VERDON, VERDONCK, or VARDON, JACOB (s. of Thomas 2^d), m. May 17, 1678, in N. Y., *Femmetje Jans Willems* of Meppel in the province of Drenthe, a resident of Fld^s at date of marriage, of which place they were both mem. of the R. D. ch. Bought Feb. 27, 1693-4, as per town rec., of Lawrense Janse a farm in N. U. Lane, to which he probably removed, being at that date a resident of the town. On ass. roll of N. U. of 1693 and cen. of 1698. Issue:—Barbara, bp. Mar. 28, 1680, m. Jacob Adriaense Bennet of Gowanus; Willem Jacobse, bp. Apl. 23, 1682, m. Elizabeth ——; Thomas Jacobse, bp. Sept. 23, 1683; Maria, bp. June 11, 1685; Jacob Jacobse; Jannetje; Femmetje; and Dirckien. Signed his name "*Jacob Fardon.*"

Jacob Jacobse, m. Apl. 8, 1720, (sup.) Marretje or Maria Flierboom. A Jacob Verdon was constable of Br" in 1701 and 1705. Issue:—Thomas, bp. Aug. 3, 1735.

Thomas, m. Mary Badye da. of Altie Brackhoengie (wid. of W" Bredenbend) by a former husband. Mary, after the death of Thomas, m. 2ᵈ W" Ariaense Bennet, and 3ᵈ Paulus Vanderbeek. A mag. of Brⁿ in 1661, '62, '63, and '64, where he took the oath of allegiance in 1687. Suppose he resided on and owned the farm at Gowanus late of Anthony Hulst and since of Henry Story and Winant Bennet. Issue:—Thomas Junʳ.

Thomas Junʳ, m. 1ˢᵗ, June 1, 1659, Jannetje Claes; m. 2ᵈ, Apl. 26, 1695, Ytie or Elsje Juriaens wid. of Teunis ten Eyck, as per N. Y. D. ch. rec. From an entry on the records of the R. D. ch. of Brⁿ, he and his wife Annetje being mem. of said ch. in 1677, it may be inferred that she was his second wife, and that Ytie was his third. Took the oath of allegiance in Brⁿ in 1687 as a native, being at the time a resident of Gowanus, owning and occupying the homestead of his father. Previous to this, in 1658, he appears to have resided in Buᵏ. Was constable of Brⁿ in 1684, as per Furman's Notes of Brⁿ. In 1718 he resided in N. U., and was a deacon in the R. D. ch. of said town. Issue:—Jacob. Made his mark to documents.

William Jacobse, bp. Apl. 23, 1682, in Flᵇ; m. Elizabeth ——. Resided in N. U., and in 1700, on the erection of a church in said town, was allotted 3 men's and 3 women's places. In 1726 he was a deacon and in 1733 an elder in said ch. Issue:—Jacob, bp. July 19, 1709. Signed his name "*Willem Fardon.*"

FARRINGTON, THOMAS, of Gᵈ, let Oct. 26, 1669, to W" Goulder of the same place 3 cows, etc. Sept. 8, 1669, he sold John Emans plantation-lot No. 28 of said town, all as per town rec. Made his mark to documents.

FASTER, WILLEM, in 1681 on Stoothoff's books.

FELLE, SYMON, m. *Ann Vincent.* Plaintiff in a suit against Glandy La Metre Nov. 11, 1660, as per Lib. B of Flᵇ court rec. Issue:—Magdaleen, bp. June 3, 1660, in N. A.

8

FERDINANSE, see Van Sicklen.

FERDON, see Fardon.

FERMENSEN, HENDRICK, of Fld* in 1673, as per ch. rec.

FERMENSY, DERICK, of Fld* in 1671, as per ch rec.

FILKIN, HENRY, of Fl^h, m. *Catryna* ——; d. about Oct. 23, 1713. Member of Assembly for Kings Co. 1693 to 1696; justice of the peace 1693; on cen. of Fl^h of 1698 as of English descent; clerk of Kings Co. 1704 to 1714. Oct. 9, 1689, bought a lot of John Smith at Br^a ferry, as per p. 188 of Lib. 1 of Con. Sept. 10, 1685, he petitioned for license to purchase a small neck of 500 A. at Mattinock, Oyster Bay, L. I., and in 1686 to take up a parcel of vacant land in Newtown, as per pp. 132 and 154 of Vol. II. of Land Papers. In 1697 obtained a patent for about 22,000 A. in Dutchess Co. Will da. Sept. 22, 1713; pro. Apl. 20, 1714; and rec. p. 273, Lib. 8, N. Y. surr. off. Issue:—Jane; Henry Junr, m. 1st, Nov. 27, 1709, Elizabeth Smith and settled in Dutchess Co.; Magdalena, bp. Oct. 31, 1697, d. young; Abram, m. Jan. 28, 1729, Poryntje Tiebout; Isaac; Francis of N. Y., m. Catharine da. of Col. Leonard (Helen his da. m. John Vanderbilt of N. Y. and Fl^h); Cornelius, of Br^a in 1738; Katharine, m. June 16, 1727, Court Van Voorhies of Dutchess Co.; Jacob; Johannes; and Ante, m. Francis Hegeman. Signed his name "*Henry Filkin*"; his wife made her mark " K" to documents.

FISERCK, EDWARD, m. *Janne Schabuels;* d. about 1645; settled on a tract on the East River in Br^a, which was patented Apl. 2, 1647, to John Haes, who m. his wid. Issue:—Jenne, bp. Feb. 24, 1641, in N. A.

FOLCKERTSEN, HENDRICK, of Br^a ferry, b. 1634; m. *Geertje Claes*. In 1664 made an affidavit relating to the raid of Capt. Scott on the Dutch towns of L. I., as per p. 482 of Vol. II. of Doc. of Col. His. Issue:—Jurian, bp. Dec. 5, 1660, in Br^a. Signed his name "*Hendrick Folckertsen*."

FOLKERT, CLAES, m. *Neeltje* ——; of Br^a in 1699, as per a deed on p. 195 of Lib. 2 of Con. Issue:—Anna, bp. Oct. 7, 1703, in Br^a; and Neeltje, bp. July 31, 1709.
Derick, a grand-juryman at the court of sessions in 1692. uly 17, 1689, loaned money to Jacob Dircksen, as per p. 168 of Lib. 1 of Con. Signed his name "*Derck Folckerse*."
Johannes, m. Angenietje ——. A Johannes Folkertse set-

tled near New Brunswick, N. J., prior to 1699, as per p. 35 of Dr. Messler's Somerset Co. Issue:—Folkert, bp. May 30, 1708, in Br*.

Nicholas, owned lands in Bu^k in 1704, as per deed of Ab^m Bogert to Gisbert Bogert of Mar. 27, 1788, on Bu^k town rec.

FOLLEMAN, BARENT, see Fulleman.

FONTEYN or FONTEIN, CHAREL or CHARLES, m. 1st *Catharine de Balie; m.* 2^d, Aug. 21, 1691, *Mary Van Lientie* or *Magdalena Reinierse.* Was among the first settlers of Bu^k in 1661, a mag. in 1663, and on ass. rolls of said town of 1675 and '83. In 1689 he was among the soldiers sent to Albany, as per p. 216 of Vol. II. of Doc. His. of N. Y. There was a Charles Fonteyn on the Raritan in N. J. about 1685, and a James Fonteyn in 1707. Issue:—Magdalena, bp. Oct. 26, 1659, in N. A.; Annetje or Anneken, bp. July 16, 1662, m. Sept. 9, 1685, in N. Y., Jacob Janszen of said city; Lidia, bp. Feb. 2, 1664; Katryna, bp. Mar. 29, 1696; Rinier of N. J., bp. Oct. 15, 1699; and Hendrick, bp. Nov. 15, 1710, at Six Mile Run, N. J.

Jacques of Bu^k, m. May 20, 1689, in N. Y., Anna Webbers, and took the oath of allegiance in Bu^k in 1687 as a native. A Jacques Fonteyn settled near New Brunswick, N. J., prior to 1699, as per p. 35 of Messler's Somerset Co. Issue:— Catharina, bp. Feb. 8, 1691; Carel, bp. Apl. 24, 1692; Johannes, bp. Oct. 31, 1694; Johannes, bp. Apl. 26, 1696; Geertje, bp. Jan. 29, 1699; Wolfert, bp. Aug. 25, 1700; Geertje, bp. Dec. 5, 1701; Catharina, bp. Mar. 18, 1705; Annetje, bp. Apl. 28, 1706; Catharine, bp. Oct. 31, 1708; and Jaques, bp. Apl. 8, 1711—all in N. Y.

Johannes, m. 1st, Mar. 23, 1689, Reymerighis Symonse (Van Nostrand); m. 2^d, Jan. 1, 1690, Catrina Willemse (Cornell) of Fl^h. Took the oath of allegiance in Bu^k in 1687 as a native, in which town he resided. Issue:—Karel, bp. Sept. 22, 1689, in Fl^h (a Karel Fonteyn, on ass. roll of Franklin, N. J., in 1735); and Margrietje, b. 1697.

FORBUS, JOHN, of N. A. as early as 1638, obtained in 1647 a patent for 65 morgens on the East River and Norman's Kil (now in Williamsburgh.) This plantation he probably purchased of Claes Carstensen, to whom in 1644 he gave a note for 150 gl. of purchase-money, balance due on a plantation on L. I., as per p. 26 of Calendar of N. Y. His. Dutch Man. In 1685 a John Forbes took up about 400 A. on the Raritan about 20 miles above Amboy, as per p. 14 of Corwin's His. Discourse.

FORCE, MATTHEW. Apl. 5, 1666, a suit was brought against him in the court of sessions in G^d by Ralph Cardell for trespass, as per. G^d rec. At the sessions of 1669 he was tried for receiving stolen goods. June 3, 1671, while a resident of G^d, he entered into an agreement with John Grissell of Maspeth, on behalf of Grissell's daughter in-law Hanna Banan, who was to serve Force two and one half years, in consideration of which at its termination Force was to furnish her with two suits of "comely and decent clothes," and a heifer with calf, or one with a calf by her side, as per G^d rec. Made his mark to documents.

FOREST, ABRAM, allotted Apl. 21, 1667, a meadow-lot at Canarisie, as per Fl^h rec.
Hendrick, allotted Apl. 21, 1667, a meadow-lot at Canarisie, as per Fl^h rec.

FORREST, see De Forrest.

FOSTER, WILLIAM, (English,) probably capt. of the ship Concord from New England to London in 1678, m. *Ann* ———. Chosen one of the overseers of G^d in 1680, per town rec., in which year he let his G^d lands to Wm Stillwell. Mar. 1, 1681-2, Wm Foster of J^a sold to Obadiah Wilkins of G^d the title, etc., of his wife Ann in plantation-lot No. 13 with the buildings in G^d, as per town rec. His name appears on Gov. Dongan's patent of J^a of 1686, where he appears to have finally settled. Made his mark to documents.

FOUNNITON or FOUNTAIN, AARON. He and Edward Buttye hired May 1, 1674, of Ralph Cardell all his land in G^d for 5 years with the crops thereon, to be cultivated on shares, consisting of 7 skipples of wheat, 14½ of peas, and 12 of oats sown thereon, with 3 good working horses for the first year and 2 for the rest of the time; also to be furnished with 3 breeding mares of 4 years old, and 4 cows this present year and 5 the rest of the time; and further they are to have a *wrought-iron plough,* chains, and all tackling belonging thereto and necessary for their use in husbandry, both of ploughing, sowing, mowing, and clearing of land. Made his mark "A" to documents.

FOUPIER or FOOKIE, AMADER. His name appears on the list of those liable to pay for the clergyman's salary in 1665, and on ass. roll of 1675 and '76 of Bu^k.

FRANCIS, JOSEPH, of Bedford June 1, 1695, per Col. Rec.

FRANCISCUS, PIETER, of N. U., m. *Susanna Dey.* Took the oath of allegiance in N. U. in 1687 as a native. Issue:— Lysbet, bp. Sept. 9, 1688, in Fl[b]; and Fransyntie, bp. in 1694 at Hackensack, to which place he probably removed.

FRANS or FRANSEN, JOOST, (or Joost the Frenchman,) from Amsterdam, emigrated in 1654; m. 1st, about 1666, *Geertruy Aukes Van Nuyse;* m. 2[d], Jan. 30, 1692, in Fl[b], *Annatie Joris Rapalie* wid. of Martin Ryerson. Took the oath of allegiance in Br[n] in 1687, and assessed in said town in 1675 and '83 for 18 morgens of land. He with others of Br[n], May 26, 1663, petitioned to be allowed to make a new concentration (village) at the Wallabout, as per p. 120 of Vol. I. of Stiles's Br[n].

Tommes or *Thomas* (or Thomas the Frenchman,) from Denmark, m. June 16, 1677, *Jannetje Brouwers* of Amsterdam, a resident of Fld[s]. Obtained a patent May 25, 1668, for a tract of land at Gowanus. Leased Feb. 7, 1667, to Pieter Jansen Van Noort Brook a plantation at Gowanus adjoining that of Paulus Vander Beek, which probably covered his patent, and was afterwards the farm of Simon De Hart and late the farms of Simon and John S. Bergen. For a more full account of this lease, see the article or account of Van Noort Brook. The land covered by his patent was included in the Bennet and Benton purchase, from whom he probably bought the same. There was a Thomas Fransen (not the above Thomas) of the city of N. A. or N. Y., a carman, who married three wives and had 13 children bp. between 1658 and 1697, as per p. 769 of Valentine's Manual of 1863. A Thomas Fransen and Elsje Jans his wife were mem. of the D. ch. of N. A. in 1663. He made his mark to documents.

FREDERICKSE, AREND, m. 1st, Apl. 7, 1680, in N. Y., *Sarah Teunise Coevert;* m. 2[d], Aug. 29, 1690, in N. Y., *Hester Daniels.* Issue:—Frederick, bp. Jan. 29, 1681; Theunis, bp. Nov. 15, 1682; Theunis, bp. Nov. 26, 1684; Willem, bp. Jan. 9, 1687; Cornelis, bp. Mar. 1, 1689; Anneken, bp. Sept. 13, 1691; Margareta, bp. Sept. 24, 1693; and Elizabeth, bp. Dec. 8, 1695—all in N. Y.

Gerret, on ass. roll of Br[n] in 1675.

Jan, on a coroner's jury on an inquest on a body found on the shore between Red Hoek and Bompje's Hoek, held May 9, 1698. Made his mark to documents.

Jean or *Jan,* see Van Lieuwen.

FREES, HENDRICUS, had a dau. Maria bp. Mar. 29, 1696, in Br[n].

FREMENSEN, HENDRICK, of Fld² in 1673, as per ch. rec.

FULLEMAN, BARNY or BARENT, cooper, keeper of jail and court-house in Flᵇ in 1696, per court rec.

FURMAN, JOHN.   Apl. 1, 1649, he agreed to take charge of the calves of the people of Gᵈ for 3 months for 60 gl. in money, tobacco, or corn, and some bitters if desired, as per p. 176 of Vol. II. of Thompson's L. I.   There was a John Furman among the patentees of Newtown in 1686.   For a further account of the family, see p. 309 of Riker's Newtown.

FYN, JAN JANSE, bought a house and lot of Corsten Janse in Flᵇ Jan. 22, 1666, as per p. 51 of Lib. D of Flᵇ rec.; also bought a house and lot in said town Aug. 13, 1666, of Derick Janse, "cuyper," as per p. 18 of Lib. C; and Mar. 27, 1677, he conveyed to Stoffel Probasco his wood-lot in N. L., as per p. 13 of Lib. AA of said rec.   On ass. roll of Flᵇ of 1675, and one of the patentees of Newtown in 1686.   Made his mark to documents in 1698.   A John Fynn emigrated in 1635 to Sᵗ Christopher's, as per Hotten's Emigrants.

GABREY or GABRIE, CHARLES, bought Jan. 22, 1654, the land patented to Willem Cornelisse in Brᵃ, Cornelisse having absconded from the country, as per p. 82 of Vol. I. of Stiles's Brᵃ.   Charles Gabry was a merchant in Amsterdam about 1652, as per p. 469 of Vol. I. of Doc. of His. Man.
Timotheus, of Gᵈ June 13, 1661, as per Col. Man.; bought May 8, 1666, land in Buᵏ of Jan Hendricks Steelman, as per town rec.   Was Secretary of N. A. in 1657, auctioneer in 1661 and '62, schepen in 1660 and '64, and d. in 1680.   In 1664 took the oath of allegiance in N. Y. to the English. In 1674 he applied to Gov. Colve and his Council for redress in consequence of the late English government having annulled a judgment pronounced in his favor by Gov. Stuyvesant against "Jan Jansen Veryn," contrary to the concluded capitulation, as per p. 705 of Vol. II. Doc. of Col. His. of N. Y.   Signed his name "*Timotheus Gabry*" in 1660.

GANCEL, JAN, m. *Judith* ——.   Schoolmaster of Flᵇ from 1711 to 1717.   Issue:—Maria, bp. May 9, 1698, in Brᵃ. Signed his name "*Jan Gancel.*"

GANGELOFFE, CLAES, see Villet.

GANNER, YAN, on Stoothoff's books in 1700.

GARRETSE, see Gerretse.

GEISSE, WOUTER, on ass. roll of Br^n of 1675.

GELGEMES, FREDERICK, on list of those who paid for the minister's salary in Fl^h in 1680.

GERAERDY, JOHN, sold Mar. 6, 1655, to Isaac Grevenraat a house and lot in G^d, as per town rec. Signed his name "*John Gerardy.*"

GERBRANTSE or GERREBRANT, PETER, b. 1675; on ass. roll of Br^n of 1683 and '95, and cen. of 1698. The Gerrebrant family are the descendants of Gerrebrant Claesen, and are found in Bergen and Hudson counties, N. J. See p. 48 of Winfield's Land Titles of Hudson Co.

GERBRITSE, JAN, a commissioner of Br^n in 1690, as per p. 64 of Furman's Br^n. This is probably an error of Furman's, and should have been "Jan Gerretse" (Dorlandt), hereinafter referred to.

GERLET, GILLIAM, of Bu^k, one of the soldiers sent to Albany in 1698, as per p. 215 of Col. His. of N. Y.

GERRETSE, GERRETSEN, or GARRETSE, ABRAHAM. See Van Duyn.

Barent (Vlasbeck), from Zwolle in Overÿssel, m. 1st, May 11, 1658, in N. A., Grietje Dirks or Dircx, wid. of Jan Nagel; m. 2^d Marretje Hendricks. Was among the early settlers of Bu^k in 1661; mag. in 1664; on ass. roll of 1693; and on cen. of said town of 1698. Issue:—Margariet, bp. Dec. 4, 1659, in N. A.; Johannis, bp. July 20, 1664, in Br^n; (by 2^d wife) Mayken, bp. May 16, 1677; and Mayken, bp. Nov. 20, 1680, in N. Y.

Claes of Fl^h, wheelwright, m. Adriaenien Lollenox, who after his death m. Jan Jansen; buried Dec. 9, 1665, in Fl^h ch. Bought Nov. 4, 1664, of Johannes Christoffelse 21 morgens of land in Fl^h, as per p. 10 of Lib. D of Fl^h rec. Aug. 29, 1665, (on the second m. of his wid.,) Jentein Jeppes and Bartelt Claesen (Van Kuynen) were chosen guardians of his s. Gerret Claesen, as per p. 40 of Lib. D of Fl^h rec. Issue:—Gerret Claesen, b. 1660.

Cornelis, mem. of N. U. D. ch. in 1677.

Cornelis, Denyse, and *Dirk,* see Van Duyn.

Dirk of Kings Co., made a deposition in 1644 relating to

the burning of Jochem Pietersen's house by the Indians, as per p. 68 of Furman's Antiquities of L. I.

Gerret, see Dorland, Van Duyn, Voorhies, and Wyckoff.

Gerret, laborer, of Fl^h in 1672, per ch. rec. A Gerret Gerretse and Geesje his wife made an affidavit Oct. 26, 1696, before Justice Joseph Hegeman, setting forth that Jan Willemse van Geeschen was the only survivor of Wilhelmus van Geeschen, as per p. 227 of Lib. A of Fl^h rec.

Gerret, on petition for a canal at Red Hoek, Br^n, in 1664, as per p. 68 of Vol. 1 of Stiles's Br^n.

Hans, see Van Noostrand.

Harmen, on ass. roll of N. U. of 1675 and cen. of 1698.

Hugh, owned land on the borders of G^d adjoining Fld^a, prior to 1645, as per Col. Man. and p. 172 of Vol. II. of Thompson's L. I.

Jacob, see Haes or Haas.

Jacob or *Jabeq*, on ass. roll of N. U. of 1675, and in 1677 was allotted a farm on N. U. Lane, which he sold to Gysbert Tyson (Van Pelt) and Thys Jansen. Feb. 10, 1674, he and Zeegert Gerretse obtained a patent for 72 morgens on the E. side of the Fresh Kil on S. I., as per Col. Rec. In 1689 he was appointed a justice of the peace for Richmond Co. The Gerretsens of S. I. are probably descendants of this Jacob and his brothers Zeegert and Jan. A "Jacobus Garrytsen" signed his name to documents in G^d in 1730.

Jan (sup. brother of the above Jacob), obtained a patent Jan. 16, 1662, for 24 morgens in N. U. of Gov. Stuyvesant, and a confirmatory one for the same about 1680 of Gov. Andross, as per p. 164 of Vol. 1 of Land Papers in off. of Sec. of State at Albany. On ass. roll of N. U. in 1675. Nov. 1, 1675, there was made a draught of a patent to Jan Garretsen for land on Long Neck on S. I., as per p. 7 of Calendar of Land Papers. There was a Jan Gerritszen from Workum in Friesland who m. Dec. 4, 1660, in N. A., Grietje Theunis of N. A.

Jan of Bredenhiesen, on petition of May 1664 for a canal at Red Hoek, Br^n, as per p. 68 of Vol. 1 of Stiles's Br^n.

Jan and Annetje Remsen his w., of Bedford, mem. of the R. D. ch. of Br^n in 1677. Apl. 6, 1677, he bought of Aucke Janse (Van Nuyse) meadow-lot No. 18 in Fl^h, as per p. 22 of Lib. B of Fl^h rec. He and Thomas Lambertse made a statement Aug. 7, 1683, relating to the death of John Smith of Bedford, as per p. 17 of Lib. 1 of Con. in Kings Co. reg. off.

Jan or *John*, see Van Nostrand, Couwenhoven, Dorlandt, Van Marcken, and Van Noostrand.

Johannes of G^d, m. —— ——. Will da. Dec. 17, 1765; pro.

Jan. 7, 1766; rec. p. 232, Lib. 25, N. Y. surr. off. Issue:—Samuel; and Ida.

Lambert or *Lubbert*, m. Susanna dau. of Charles Morgan. Hired Dec. 4, 1650, of James Hubbard, for 3 years, 15 A. of upland and meadows, excepting and reserving the meadow on which the mill stands. This mill, every vestige of which has long ago disappeared, was located on what is known on the old maps as Hubbart's Creek, a little N. of its junction with Coney Island Creek. Sold a house and land in G^d prior to 1691 to John Stillwell, and in 1693 appears to have resided on S. I., all as per G^d rec. Made his mark to documents.

Matthew, owned land on the borders of G^d prior to 1670, and referred to in patents of that date.

Peter, see Van Noostrand. A Peter Gerritt, of Fld^s in 1690, concerned in 1690 in settling the estate of Hans Hansen Van Noostrand.

Rem, s. of Gerrit Remmersen and Mary or Maria, of G^d, where he took the oath of allegiance in 1687 as a native. Resided at Cape May, N. J., in 1696. Signed his name " *Rem Gerretsen*."

Samuel (a s. of Gerret and Mary Remmersen, or Gerret s. of Rem of G^d), m. Ida Barends. On ass. roll of G^d of 1693, cen. of 1698, and deeds of the same dates, as per pp. 175, 177, 182, and 183 of Lib. 2 of Con.; also clerk of the board of supervisors in 1703, and mem. of the colonial legislature from 1716 to 1737. Believe him to be the ancestor of the G^d family of Gerretsens, who owned a farm and the tide-mill in said town located on the Strome Kil, the boundary between G^d and Fld^s, known as Gerretsen's mill; and also of the late J. Fletcher Gerretsen and Judge Saml Gerretsen of Br^n and Thos Gerretsen of Fld^s. Issue:—Ferdinandus, bp. Apl. 25, 1696, and other children. Signed his name " *Samuel Gerretsen*."

Seger, see Zeegert.

Stoffel, took the oath of allegiance in N. U. in 1687 as a native. On ass. roll of said town of 1693.

Wessel, appointed one of the pilots on an expedition to the South River (Delaware) in 1655, on muster-roll of Bu^k militia in 1663, as per town rec., and also assessed there for the clergyman's salary in 1666.

Willem, see Couwenhoven.

Zeegert or *Seger*, from N. Albany; m. Jan. 28, 1677, in N. A., Jannetje Thyssen of N. Albany. Feb. 10, 1674, he and Jacob Gerretse obtained a patent for 72 morgens on S. I. Name on ass. roll of N. U. of 1676. In 1689 appointed ensign by Gov. Leisler in Richmond Co. May 2, 1722, he sold his woodland in N. U. to Cor^s Van Brunt. Made his mark to documents.

GERRYEDTS or GERRYS, CLAES, wheelwright, bought Nov. 4, 1664, of Johannes Christoffelse, 21 morgens of land in Fl^h, on the W. side of the road, as per p. 10 of Lib. D of Fl^h rec. He was buried in Fl^h ch. Mar. 13, 1665, as per same rec. Probably he is the same person hereinbefore described as Claes Gerretse, Signed his name "*Claes Gerryedts.*"

GERTSEN, BARNET, of Bu^k in 1665, as per town rec.

GHAUDY, THOMAS, m. May 14, 1694, *Rebecca Daws*, as per G^d rec.

GIBS or GIBBS, RICHARD or RISSIERT, of Br^n, m. *Sarah* ———, Mar. 25, 1656, he applied for a grant for half an acre of vacant land adjoining his other lands, as per p. 157 of Vol. II. of Land Papers. On ass. roll of Br^n of 1683, and of the ferry in 1695, as per Col. Man. A caveat filed against the patent for his Br^n lands, as per p. 143 of Cal. of Eng. Man. Issue:—Isaac, m. Oct. 26, 1696, at Flushing, Hanna da. of John Dickinson of Oyster Bay, as per p. 99 of Vol. IV. of Genealogical Rec. There is a Gibbs graveyard at Bensalem, Bucks Co., Pa., as per p. 146 of Vol. III. of said Gen. Rec.

William, felt-maker, of Br^n ferry in 1695; m. Sara ———. See p. 77 of Lib. 2 of Con.

GIBBINS or GIBBINE, RICHARD, of G^d in 1650 and '56; schout or sheriff in 1651 and '53, as per p. 131 of Cal. of N. Y. His. Dutch Man. One of the patentees or purchasers of Middletown, N. J., in 1669, as per p. 73 of Vol. I. of Raum's N. J. Signed his name "*Richard Gibbine.*" A Richard Gibson, aged 25, was transported to Barbadoes in 1635, as per Hotten's Emigrants.

GIBSON RICHARD, of G^d in 1656, per Thompson's L. I. Probably same as Richard Gibs.

GILLIAMSE or GUILLIAMSE, see Cornel.

GILLIS, see De Mandeville.

GILLISE, or GILLESEN, JAN, on ass. roll of 1675 of both Br^n and Fl^h. Oct. 15, 1686, in possession of a house-plot in Fl^h, as per p. 76 of Lib. B of Fl^h rec. Signed his name "*Jan Gillis*" in 1661.

GISBERTSE, see Guysbertse.

Godius or Goediris, Isaak, and *Geertruy Jansen* had a s. Jan bp. May 20, 1690, in Fl[k].

Golder, Goulder, or Goulding, Joseph, of G[d] in 1664 (sup. English); m. *Neltje* or *Ellinor Claes* (Smit). On cen. of 1698, and probably removed to Monmouth Co., N. J., where his s. Joseph in 1704 purchased a farm near the village of Middletown, and in 1709, with his w. Anneke Daws, was a mem. of the Freehold R. D. ch. Issue:—Joseph, b. 1675 (m. 1st Anneke Daws, by whom 5 children, (sup.) m. 2[d] Adrianke Laan, by whom 2 children); William, b. 1677; Nicholas, b. 1679; and Anne, b. 1682, as per G[d] rec. Signed his name "*Joseph Gollding*," and his s. Joseph made his mark to documents.

Nicholas, of G[d] in 1679.

William of G[d], m. 1st Ann ——; m. 2[d], Apl., 1676 Margaret Lake of G[d]; m. 3[d], June 19, 1689, Deborah dau. of John Quimby of Westchester Co. Owned land in N. A., where he probably at first resided. Was a patentee of G[d] in 1645, per Thompson's L. I., in which town he bought Mar. 14, 1649, of Ambrose Londen a plantation, and also Jan. 1, 1661, of Jan Smith, his son-in-law, another, as per town rec. Town-clerk of G[d] in 1662, ensign in 1665 and '73, mag. in 1679, and on ass. roll of 1683. Jan. 21, 1692-3, he sold his G[d] property to Gerret Strycker, making on the record of the sale his mark "W," and his wife also making her mark. Apl. 8, 1665, W[m] Goulding, Sam[l] Spicer, and others of his neighbors petitioned for a tract of land at the Neversinks (Monmouth Co., N. J.), as per Vol. 1. of Land Papers. Suppose he and his neighbors obtained land at Middletown and Shrewsbury in said county, which interest it appears he sold to Richard Hartshorne, as per Vol. 1. of Land Papers. A W[m] Golden was transported to Va. in 1635, as per p. 124 of Hotten's Emigrants. Issue:—Sarah, b. 1676; Mary, b. 1678; William, b. 1679: John, b. 1681; Hester, b. 1683; and Samuel, b. 1686. Signed his name "*Will[m] Goulding*."

Yacum or *Jacob*, of G[d] in 1679.

Golers, Josias, and *Neeltje Klaas* had a s. Nicholas bp. Mar. 28, 1680, in N. U.

Gooding, Isaac, (sup. English,) m. *Gertruye* ——. Owned land on Hogg's Neck in G[d] in 1692, as per deed of Delavall to Lake on p. 6 of Vol. 2 of Con., in which town he appears to have resided. Also owned a lot on Gisbert's I. in 1694 between that of Pieter Corson and the wid. Lake, as per Gᵈ rec. Signed his name "*Isaac Gooding*."

GOODYEAR, THOMAS, of Gᵈ in 1650, per town rec.

GOULDING, see Golder.

GOUNENBERGH, JAN or JOHANNES, sold Feb. 17, 1667, to Harman Van Borkeloo for 1325 gl. his house and garden-plot in N. U., as per p. 233 of Lib. 3 of deeds in off. of Sec. of State at Albany. In 1664 he appears to have owned land in Flʰ, as per deed of Balthazer Vosch to Johannes Christoffelse on p. 153 of Lib. B of Flʰ rec. May 10, 1667, he bought of Balthazer Vosch a farm in Flʰ of 23 morgens, with plain and meadow land, on the W. side of the road, as per p. 19 of Lib. C of Flʰ rec., which he sold Mar. 1, 1668, to Cornelis Jansen Van Aelckman, as per p. 33 of said Lib. C. Signed his name "*Jan Gounenbergh.*"

GOYCLIFFE, YACUM, on ass. roll of Gᵈ of 1683, of which town he was elected an overseer in 1680. Suppose he and Jochem Gulick to be the same person.

GRAHAM, JAN, owned land in Buᵏ in 1687, as per town rec.

GREEDYE, see Gridy.

GREGORY, RICHARD, (sup. English,) weaver, m. *Catharine* ——. He and Isaac Haselbury bought Feb. 11, 1688–9, of Thomas Bayley his house and garden in Gᵈ, as per p. 87 of Lib. 2 of Con. Nov. 21, 1691, he bought of John Stillwell a house and land in Gᵈ, as per town rec. Made his mark " R " to documents.

GREVENRAED, ISAAC, from Amsterdam, m. 1ˢᵗ, Mar. 24, 1652, in N. A., *Lysbet Jurians* of the same place, where they were both mem. of the D. ch.; m. 2ᵈ, June 2, 1663, in N. A., *Marretje Jans* from Amsterdam. May 21, 1655, he sold through Elbert Elbertse Stoothoff as his attorney, plantation-lot No. 27 in Gᵈ to Peter Ebal, as per p. 59 of Cal. N. Y. His. Dutch Man. In 1664 he took the oath of allegiance in N. Y. to the English. In 1673 he was appointed by Gov. Colve schout of Swaenenburgh, Hurley, and Marbletown. Issue:—Hendricus, bp. Aug. 4, 1657; Andries, bp. July 15, 1659, m. July 2, 1684, Anna Van Brug;

Hendrick, bp. June 28, 1662; Lysbeth, bp. Feb. 27, 1664;. Abraham, bp. Mar. 22, 1665; Lysbeth, bp. May 22, 1666;. Lysbeth, bp. Dec. 11, 1667; Anna Elizabeth, bp. June 9, 1669; Margaret, bp. July 11, 1670; and Johannes, bp. Aug. 28, 1678—all bp. in N. A. and N. Y. Signed. his name "*Isaack Grevenraed.*"

Jan, of G^d May 21, 1658, per Col. Man.

GREVER, HENDRICK, on muster-roll of Bu^k militia in 1663..

GRICKSEN, HENDRICK, of Lymme, obtained a patent Oct. 1, 1652, for land E. of Joris Rapalie's valley, as per p. 128. of Cal. of Dutch Man.

GRIDY, GREEDY, or GREEDYE, THOMAS, from Devonshire, England, b. 1586; m. *Maria Roberts* or *Robertsen* wid. of John Seals of N. A.; was among the first settlers of G^d in 1646, and allotted a plantation-lot, but publicly whipped and banished in the same year for theft, as per p. 103 of Cal. of His. Dutch Man. He appears, however, afterwards to have been allowed to return and obtain or hold property, which he sold May 26, 1653, to David Provoost, as per town rec. In 1656 he was again banished for 12 years, as per p. 161 of Cal. of Dutch Man. For a further account of him see p. 99 of the second edition of the Bergen Geneal-ogy. His will is da. Oct. 10, 1658, pro. Nov. 4 of the same year, and rec. on the G^d town rec. In it he makes John and Peter Tilton his heirs, from which it may be inferred he left no male children. Made his mark " T " to documents.

GRIFFIN or GRIFFING, EDWARD, of N. A. and Fl^h. He appears to have emigrated as a servant of Capt. Clever or Clebers of Va., and was claimed Aug. 27, 1640, by the Gov. of Maryland as a runaway, as per p. 73 of Cal. of Dutch Man.. Feb. 28, 1653, he bought of "Gerrit Bricker" 25 morgens of land in Fl^h. This land he sold July 28, 1653, to "Bartel Loot and Peter Loot" (Lott), describing it as "on the west. side of the road near the Flat bush, next the ministers land N° 9, as conveyed to the grantor by Gerrit Strycker:" the above "Bricker" should be "Strycker." See pp. 377 and 378 of Cal. of His. Dutch Man. He appears also to have owned land in G^d, selling Apl. 5, 1661, to Richard Stout. plantation-lot No. 26 in said town, as per G^d rec. Dec. 14, 1678, he sailed for England in the ship Blossom, and after-wards returned. There was an Edward Griffen, capt. of the ship Barbadoes Merchant, in 1679, and an Edward.

Griffen, owning 30 A. and 3 slaves of the parish of St Andrews in Barbadoes, in 1680, as per Hotten's Emigrants. In 1686 he made an application in behalf of his s. John Griffin relating to the common lands of Flushing, as per p. 157 of Vol. II. of Land Papers. For John Griffin's children see p. 96 of Vol. IV. of Gen. Rec. Made his mark to documents.

GRIGG or GRIGS Senr, (probably a s. of George Griggs, who emigrated from Lavenden, Newport, in England, to New England about 1635, as per p. 44 of Hotten's Emigrants), m. *Elizabeth* ——. Settled in G^d, where he was allotted land as early as 1672. Sold Sept. 13, 1695, to his s. John 8 A. of land on the E. side of G^d, on a neck known as Ambrose Island, as per p. 73 of Lib. 2 of Con. His name appears on the cen. of 1698. Issue:—John Junr; Daniel; Thomas; Benjamin; and Samuel—most of whom settled in N. J. Made his mark to documents. His s. Daniel signed his name "Daniell Griggs" in 1710. His descendants abound in N. J.

John Junr of G^d, m. 1st Anna dau. of Willem Willemse and Mayke Pieterse Wyckoff; m. 2^d, 1684, Martha dau. of Obadiah Wilkins. Sold Aug. 28, 1697, a plot of 20 A. in G^d to Jochem Gulick for £60, as per p. 194 of Lib. 2 of Con. Was constable of G^d in 1701. His name and that of his mother or step-mother Elizabeth appears on the cen. of 1738, and he is entered as the owner of 2 slaves in 1755. Issue:—(sup.) Maria, who m. John Van Dyke of N. U. Signed his name "*John Griggs Jun*."

GRISSILL, JOHN, made his mark to documents in G^d in 1671.

GROENENDYCK, PIETER, made a complaint against Justus Whitfield (Wentworth) Feb. 12, 1674, before the burgomaster's and schepen's court in N. A. for an assault committed by said Wentworth upon him on the same day that justice was executed on the three soldiers on the Flatt near the mill (Flatlands), and the tearing his clothes from his body, as per p. 443 of Valentine's Manual of 1851. Peter Groenendyck had issue bp. in N. Y.:—Cornelis, July 9, 1673; Johannes, Mar. 24, 1675; Maritie, Apl. 14, 1677; Pieter, Apl. 28, 1680; Abraham, May 12, 1682; and Petrus, b. Aug. 16, 1685.

Samuel of Fl^s and of the South River (Delaware), m. 1st, Oct. 24, 1713, Sara Probasco of N. L.; m. 2^d Mary or Mayke Ver Kerk wid. of Nicholas Van Brunt. Jan. 25, 1742-3, he sold to Andries Emans a farm of 84 A. in N. U. Signed his name "*Samuel Groenendyck*" in 1719.

GROOTMAN, WILLIAM, and *Margaret* had a dau. Margaret bp. at Fl[h] Aug. 28, 1698.

GROVER, JAMES, (English,) among the first settlers of G[d], per town rec., where he was granted Nov. 12, 1646, a plantation-lot. He with Baxter and Hubbard raised the standard of rebellion in G[d] in 1655, proclaiming Cromwell as Lord Protector, but failed in their effort. Mar. 21, 1666-7, he sold to Thomas Delavall plantation-lot No. 6 in G[d], as per town rec., and finally removed to N. J., where in 1669 he was one of the patentees or purchasers of Middletown, as per p. 73 of Vol. I. of Raum's N. J., and in 1683 appointed a justice of the peace for Middletown. Signed his name "*James Grover.*"

GUCKSEN, HENDRICK, a delegate from Fl[h] to the Hempstead Assembly of 1665, per Strong's Fl[h] and the N. Y. civil list.

GUILLIAMSE, see Cornell.
Jan, defendant in a suit by Albert Kuyn and Jan Cornelise Dec. 17, 1659, as per Lib. A of Fl[h] rec. A "Jan Gylyams" was buried in Fl[h] ch. Dec. 12, 1662.

GULICK or GULLYCK, HENDRICK or HENRY, of G[d], bought Nov. 15, 1698, of Jacobus Kiersted and George Rapalie a 24 and also a 4 A. lot in G[d], as per town rec. Oct. 17, 1700, he bought wood-lot No. 12 in the North woods of Thomas Stillwell, as per same rec.
Jochem, emigrated in 1653; m. Magdalena or Jacomyntje dau. of Teunis Van Pelt. Of G[d] in 1656, per Thompson's L. I.; on patent of said town of 1670, ass. roll of 1693, and cen. of 1698, taking the oath of allegiance there in 1687. Hired land of Ann Wilkins in G[d] in 1676. In 1689 he was appointed ensign for G[d], as per p. 191 of Cal. of Eng. Man. June 8, 1691, Charles Marshall of S. I. brought a suit against him in the court of sessions in G[d] for a half share of the profits of a whaling voyage which he made with said Jochem, as per town rec. Suppose he removed to E. N. J., where all his children appear to have settled. Issue:— Samuel, b. 1685; Jochem, b. 1687; and Pieter, b. 1689. Signed his name "*Jochem Guyllyck;*" his son Peter signed his name "*Peter Gulick.*"

GUSTAVUS, DANIEL, obtained Mar. 21, 1659, a patent for a lot in Fl^h.

GUTIE, DANIEL, a house-carpenter, assessed 6 gl. in 1677, as of the ferry, towards Do. Polhemius's salary, as per O'Callaghan's Man. Trans. of Col. Man.

GUYSBERTSE or GISBERTSE, JABECK, on ass. roll of Bu^k of 1675.

Jacob, on muster-roll of Bu^k militia of 1663, per town rec.

Jan, mem. of N. U. R. D. ch. at its organization in 1677, and died shortly thereafter.

Jan, on ass. roll of Fl^h of 1675. Suppose he removed to N. J., for Sept. 21, 1717, " John Gysbertse of Neversings in the township of Croswiks in the Jersies," in consideration " of the good will and affection for my brother Harman Gisbertse " of Fl^h, conveyed to him a house, barn, orchard, and garden in Fl^h, bounded in front on the N. side by the highway, E. to Simon Hansen, S. to the minister's house, and W. to John Welden's land, as per p. 3 of Lib. 5 of Con.

Jan, see Van Meteren.

Long, on Gov. Dongan's patent of Bu^k of 1687.

Lubbert, of Fl^h in 1696. Made his mark to documents. Obtained a patent in 1654 for 50 morgens on the North River in N. J., as per p. 381 of Cal. of Dutch His. Man.

Teunis, see Bogaert.

Wouter, see Verscheur.

Wouter, from Hilversum in North Holland, and a resident of Br^n, m. Dec. 14, 1679, Lysbeth Jans Van Goude wid. of Frans Bloodgood of Flushing. Both mem. of the R. D. ch. of Br^n in 1679, and entered as removed to Flushing. In 1686 a Wouter Guysbertse among the patentees of Newtown. In 1679 he complained to the court of sessions that he was hindered by Foulaer Dirricksen from the use of a highway to the woods and to the village, and desired Justice Betts to view the same and cause a sufficient highway to be laid out. There was a Wouter Gysbertsen who m. Dorothea Jochems or Kelders, and had several children bp. in N. Y. between 1666 and 1677, and a Wouter Gysberts of Bu^k who paid a marriage-fee of 6 gl. to Fl^h ch. in 1666. See Wouter Gysbertse Ver Scheur.

HADDAM, HEDDAM, or HATTUM, DERICK, m. *Annetje Tileman Van der Meyer;* d. about 1678. His wid. m. 2^d, Sept. 25, 1679, Hendrick Tyssen Lanen Van Pelt of Gowanus. He owned the farm in Gowanus, since of the Van Pelts, which said Henry Tyssen occupied during the minority of his daughter and heir. This farm he bought of Simon Aesen De Hart. Issue:—Gertie, b. 1676.

HACKWAERT, ROELANT, made a deposition Jan. 27, 1643, respecting some pits of Indian corn at Mareckkawick (Brooklyn), as per p. 84 of Cal. of Dutch Man. Issue:—Willem, bp. Aug. 31, 1642; and Jan, bp. Dec. 14, 1643—both in N. A.

HAECKS, SIMON, emigrated in 1671, and took the oath of allegiance in Bu^k in 1687. On ass. rolls of said town of 1675, '76, and '83, and a mag. in 1679, as per town rec.

HAEL, JOSEPH, on ass. roll of Bu^k of 1675.

HAES or HAAS, JACOB GERRETSE, m. *Styntje Crousen* or *Crosseren*, and had a s. Johannes bp. June 27, 1680, at N. U.
Jan, m. 1st Elsie Smith; m. 2^d, Mar. 12, 1645, in N. A., Janne Schabuels wid. of Edward Fiskock. Obtained Apl. 2, 1647, a patent for 38 morgens of land in Br^n on the East River, adjoining land of Frederick Lubbertse.

HAEY, HARMEN or HERMEN. June 5, 1671, he bought of Ryndert Janse Van Ditmarsen a building-plot in Fl^h, as per p. 105 of Lib. A of Fl^h rec. May 3, 1687, he cultivated the land of the wid. of Rem Janse, as per p. 87 of Lib. A of Fl^h rec. Signed his name "*Harmen Haey.*"

HAFF or HAF, JURIE, m. Apl. 17, 1707, *Ann Catharine Sleght.* Resided at one period at N. U., and finally removed to Flushing.
Lourens Jurianse, m. Cunira Pieterse. Bought Oct. 6, 1679, of Cornelis Berrian a house and lot in Fl^h as formerly in use by Hans Christoffelse, as per p. 85 of Lib. AA of Fl^h rec. Sold Sept. 29, 1680, to "Denyse Theunissen" for 1000 gl. his house and lot at Yellow Hoek (Bay Ridge), N. U., lying on the N. side of land of Arian Willemse Bennet and on the S. side of that of Swaen Janse, free negro, as per p. 132 of Lib. AA of Fl^h rec. Bought Jan. 11, 1681, of Denyse Theunissen of Fl^h a house and garden in G^d late in the occupation of Wm Scott, he being at the time a resident of G^d, as per G^d rec., his name appearing on the ass. roll of said town of 1683. Issue:—Jurian, bp. May 18, 1679; Teunis, bp. July 24, 1681; Styntje, bp. Aug. 5, 1683—all at Fld^s; Maria, bp. June 15, 1685, at Fl^h; Jacob, bp. Sept. 18, 1689,

9

.at Br[n]; and Laurens or Lawrence of N. J., bp. Apl. 20, 1699. Signed his name *"Lourens Haff."*

HAFFTE, HAFTE, or HAFFTEN, JACOB HENDRIXS, emigrated in 1664, and took the oath of allegiance in Fl[h] in 1687. Sold Apl. 22, 1689, to "Jacob Hendrixs Van Zuitdam" (the ancestor of the Suydam family) the house and lot on which he (Hafte) resided, located on the W. side of the highway in Fl[h], as per p. 140 of Lib. A of Fl[h] rec. Made his mark to documents.

HAFTE, JAN HENDRICK, made his mark "I H" to documents in Fl[h] in 1692.

HAFTER, PIETER, m. *Deborah Bus;* they both joined the R. D. ch. of N. U. in 1677, and had a dau. Christine bp. Dec. 20, 1685.

HAGELL or HAGEL, JURIAN or VRIAN, (s. of John Hage,) .b. Sept. 28, 1653, in N. A.; resided in Bu[k], and fined Oct. .20, 1693, by the court of sessions for using seditious language at a military training in Fld[s].

HAINELLE, MICHIL, m. *Hendrica Strockels,* and d. in 1685. He appears to have resided at first in N. A., of the D. ch. of which locality he and his wife were mem., and entered on the ch. rec. in 1665 as removed to Br[n]. Apl. 3, 1666, he bought of Michael Tadens the patent of Claes Jansen Van Naerden of about 21 A., located on the East River in Br[n], between the patent of Frederick Lubbertse and that of Jan Mange, to which he appears to have removed. His name and that of his wife appear on Do. Van Zuuren's list of D. ch. mem. of 1677, hailing from the Walabocht, of which church he was an elder in 1680. He was clerk of the five Dutch towns from 1674 to '80, and constable of Br[n] ·in 1669 and '70. Oct. 18, 1667, his name appears as one of the patentees on Gov. Nichols' patent of Br[n]; and May 14, 1670, as one of the grantors on the deed purchasing from the Indians their claims to the lands in and about Bedford, .as per p. 159 of Vol. I. of Stiles's Br[n]. June 28, 1673, he petitioned to be appointed register of horses exported from L. L at Br[n] ferry, as per p. 37 of Cal. of Eng. Man. The Rev. Dr. Strong in his History of Fl[h] erroneously makes him schoolmaster of said town. Mar. 2, 1684-5, Jan Theunisse (Van Dyckhuys), and Pieter Hendricksen, carpenters, at the request of Hendrica his wid., deposed that at the time they were building a windmill in Br[n] for Michil

Hainelle he was sickly, and while lying before the fire in his house, but of full understanding, he requested of them that in case of his death they should be helpful to his widow and encourage her in the building and completion of the mill; and further, that after his death it was his will that his widow should remain in full possession of the whole of his estate until remarriage, on which occurrence she should part with the one half of the same to his children, and that he d. shortly after this took place. June 17, 1695, Hendrica Strockels wid. of Michil Hainelle, as his administrator, and John Hainelle his son, conveyed to Dirk Janse Woertman a plantation on the East River, the premises Michil bought of Tadens, as per p. 53 of Lib. 2 of Con. Hendrica his wid. m. 2^d, Oct. 21, 1685, Jan Pieterse Mackelick widower of Styntje Jans. Issue:—Michil, bp. May 14, 1674, in Br^n; Jan or Johannes, bp. Dec. 27, 1676, in N. Y.; and Thomas, bp. June 26, 1679. Signed his name "*Michil Hainelle.*"

HAKES, SIMON, on Dongan's patent of Bu^k of 1687.

HALL, THOMAS, (English.) Was in the employ of George Holmes in 1637, when he with 12 or 13 persons from Connecticut made an effort to form a settlement on the Delaware, but failing, were taken prisoners by the Dutch and carried to New Amsterdam on the "Manhattans," where most of them settled.[*] There were several Thomas Halls, who emigrated to Va. at an early date. Nov. 17, 1641, Thomas Hall of Gloucester, England, m. Anne Mitfort of Bristol, wid. of Wm Cuyck of N. A., where he resided, and who was probably this Thomas. In 1643 he was one of the eight men representing the people who memorialized the States-General on the subject of their defenceless and forlorn condition. On Lady Mody attempting to form a settlement in G^d in 1643, he followed her there. Jan. 5, 1655, he bought a parcel of land in said town of Richard Cloughs, as per town rec. In 1664 he took the oath of allegiance to the English in N. Y. Signed his name "*Thomas Hall.*"

HALLETT, WILLIAM, bought May 14, 1652, of Thomas Baxter the house and plantation Baxter bought of his father. Sold Dec. 25, 1655, through Richard Clough to Nich^a Stillwell plantation-lot No. 40 with the buildings

---

[*] Hazard's Annals of Penn., p. 40. Gen. Rec., Vol. IV. p. 127. Vol. I. p. 431 of Doc. of Col. His. of N. Y.

thereon, in G^d, all as per town rec. According to Riker's Newtown, in which there is a full account of the family, he was b. in Dorsetshire, England; emigrated at first to Greenwich, Connecticut, and from thence to Newtown, L. I., settling on what is known as Hallet's Cove, where he lived to the age of 90 years, leaving sons William and Samuel. See pp. 177, 178, etc., of Cal. of Dutch His. Man. Signed his name "*William Hallett.*"

HALLES, ROBERT, on Hegeman's books of 1670. Made his mark to documents.

HALSINGH, B., see Haszingh.

HANOUT, B., town-clerk of Bu^k in 1663.

HANSEN or HANSZ, GERRET, HANS, and SIMON, see Van Vostrand.
Hans, see Hans Hansen Bergen.
Hendrick, of N. U. in 1693.
Jacob, Jan, Joris, and *Michael,* see Bergen.
Jan and Marretje his w., mem. of R. D. ch. of N. U. in 1677. See Jan Hansen Van Nostrand.
Joost, m. Elsje Jacobs, and had a s. Jacob bp. Apl. 1698 in Fl^h.
William of N. U., bought May 10, 1690, of John Griggs Senr and John Griggs Junr of G^d, plantation No. 37 with the buildings thereon in said town, also other lands and lot No. 9 on Gisbert's I., as per G^d rec. Signed his name " *Willem Hansen.*"

HARDENBROOK, PETER, mem. of R. D. ch. of N. U. in 1682, residing at Yellow Hoek.

HARDY, THOMAS, on deed given by the freeholders of Br^n of Jan. 2, 1696-7, to perfect Adriaen Bennet's title to his Gowanus farm.

HARMAN, TOMAS DYE, paid 7 gl. 15 st. in 1663 towards the minister's salary in Fl^h, as per town rec.

HARMAN, HARMANSEN, or HARMANSZ, CORNELIS, see Vogel.
Hans, see Barkeloo.
Hendrick, made his mark to documents in Fld^s in 1661.
Jan (sup. Van Putten), master-tailor, on ass. roll of Fl^h of 1675. July 9, 1695, he sold to Lambert Sickles of Fl^h

for £14, a garden-plot and orchard in Fl^h, as per p. 62 of Lib. 2 of Con. By a will on p. 219 of Lib. A of Fl^h rec., which was afterwards annulled, he appears to have had a s. Hendrick Janse, a dau. Jaapjes (which dau. had a child Annetje Janse), and a dau. Sophias, who had a s. Harmen Gisbertse and others. A Myndert Harmense bought Aug. 30, 1699, of Peter Schuyler a tract of land on the Hudson River near Poughkeepsie, as per p. 334 of Smith's Dutchess Co.

Thomas Dye, paid Jan. 10, 1665, a marriage-fee of 7 gl. 15 st. to Fl^h ch., as per town rec.

HARNEY, RICHARD, of G^d, charged at the court of sessions of June 16, 1669, with a misdemeanor.

HARRILL or HARRELLIS, JAN, one of the overseers of Br^n in 1678, as per Furman's Notes and rec. of court of sessions.

HARVEY, MATTHIAS, one of the justices of Kings Co. Oct. 1, 1690, as per Col. Man.

HASE, JOHN, and Christian Jacobsen had a dispute about work which was settled by the court of sessions in G^d June 4, 1663, as per G^d rec.

HASELLBERY, ISAAC, of G^d, weaver, (English,) b. 1649; m. Mar. 17, 1689-90, *Elizabeth Bayles* of G^d. He and R. Gregory bought in 1689 the house and lot of Thomas Bayles in said town. Dec. 22, 1697, he sold land to Reinier Van Sickelen. Apl. 8, 1690, he sold lot No. 34 on Gisbert's I. to John Emans. Name on ass. roll of 1693 and cen. of 1698. Signed his name "*Isaac Haselbery*."

HASZINGH, HASSINGH, or HALSSINGH, BERNARDUS, m. July 7, 1669, in N. Y., *Aeltje* da. of Jacob Wolfertse Van Couwenhoven. He and his w. mem. of Fl^h R. D. ch. in 1677, and entered on the rec. as removed. Apl. 20, 1680, he agreed to buy of Jan Gerretse Van Marcken a house and 2 ordinary building-lots in Fl^h for 1200 gl., as per p. 119 of Lib. AA of Fl^h rec. Issue:—Bernardus or Wernardus of Fl^h, bp. Aug. 27, 1670, m. July 7, 1689, Aaltje Van Cowenhoven; Jacob, bp. Sept. 22, 1672; Hester, bp. Dec. 19, 1674; Heyltje, bp. Feb. 7, 1677; Johannes, bp. Nov. 14, 1678; Pieter, bp. Dec. 24, 1679; Lysbet, bp. Jan. 17, 1685—all bp. in N. Y.; and Gerret of Fl^h, m. June 6, 1707, in N. Y., Engeltie Burger of N. Y. Signed his name "*Bernardus Hassingh*."

HATAWAY, JOHN, of Fld[s], sold Mar. 21, 1650, to Thomas Cornwell of G[d] a yoke of oxen, etc. Was sued in 1646 for slandering John Underhill's da., as per p. 106 of Cal. of Dutch Man. Signed his name *"John Hataway."*

HATTUM, see Haddam.

HAWKINS, RICHARD, (sup. English,) of the city of N. Y., mariner, bought Aug. 2, 1693, of Thomas Lyndell his interest in the farm of Jan Janse Staats of Br[n], as per p. 79 of Lib. 2 of Con. A Richard Hawkins, ag. 15, emigrated to New England in 1635, as per p. 59 of Hotten's Emigrants.

HAWSE or HAWES, JOHN, a carpenter, bought in 1653 W[m] Musgrave's plantation in G[d]; also Jan. 5, 1658, of John Vaughen plantation-lot No. 18 in G[d], formerly of Thomas Cornewell; Feb. 20, 1662, he sold Jan Emans 8 A.—all as per G[d] rec. Made his mark " I. H." to documents.

HAY or HAYS, JACOB, bought Sept. 9, 1653, of Dirck Volkertse his patent of 25 morgens on the East River and Noorman's Kil in Bu[k]. He m. *Christina Cappoens*, who after his death m. David Jochems. Issue:—Maria.

HAYES, JAN, sold June 3, 1653, to Daniel Whiteheade a lot at Br[n] ferry, as per p. 378 of Cal. of Dutch Man.

HEDEMAN, EBEHART or EVERT, of the earldom of Schouwenburg, one of the first settlers of Bu[k] in 1660; a mag. in 1664 and '65; sergeant of militia in 1663; secretary of the town in 1666, '67, and '68; and on ass. roll of 1675. He m. Apl. 20, 1657, in N. A., *Elsje Reuvenkomp* from Marken in North Holland.

HEENRY, JACOB, owned salt meadows in G[d] in 1694, as per town rec.

HEGBERTSE, BARENT (probably same as Barent Huybertse Egbertsz), on ass. roll of Br[n] of 1675.

HEGEMAN, ABRAHAM, of Fl[h], where he took the oath of allegiance as a native in 1687; m. Aug. 30, 1690, *Geertruy Jans* of New Albany. Mem. of D. ch. of Fl[h] in 1687. Will da. Jan. 10, 1715, and on file in the N. Y. surr. off. Issue:—

Adriaen of Fl[h]; Jan; and Catharine. Signed his name "*Abram Hegeman.*"

Adriaen, the common ancestor of the family, emigrated about 1650 or '51 from Amsterdam; m. Catharine ——; d. Apl. 1672. About 1653 he resided in N. A., and Apl. 25, 1661, he obtained a patent for 50 morgens, with plain and meadow land in addition, in Fl[h], to which he removed. This patent is entered Feb. 2, 1670, on p. 2 of Lib. A of Fl[r] rec. as a double lot on the E. side of the road, to the N. of land of Willem Jacobse (Van Boerum), and to the S. of that of Jan Seubringh, stretching W., a little southerly; broad 50 rods and 1 ft.; in length 600 rods; containing 50 morgens and 60 rods: 2 pieces of salt meadows, the one No. 12, broad 8 rods, containing 2 morgens; the other No. 4, broad 12 rods, cong. 3 morgens, stretching from the woods southerly to the sea: and 2 pieces of plain land, Nos. 24 and 25, broad taken together 48 rods 4 ft., stretching southerly from the road to the woods, cong. 5 morgens. Of this patent his heirs, Aug. 26, 1693, after his death conveyed, as per p. 200 of Lib. A of Fl[h] rec. (on which page the patent is entered) a piece of 37½ rods broad and 600 rods in length, cong. 37½ morgens, to his s. Abraham. He also appears to have obtained a patent for another plantation of 24 morgens in Fl[h]. He was a mag. of Fl[h] in 1654, '55, '56, '57, '58, '60, and '63; schout fiscaal of the five Dutch towns in 1661; secretary of Fl[h] and Fld[s], 1659 to 1661; of Fl[h], Fld[s], Br[n], and N. U., 1662 to 1665; secretary of Fl[h] in 1671; and auctioneer. Apl. 29, 1688, Catharine his wid. joined the R. D. ch. of N. Y., to which place she appears to have removed. Issue:—Joseph; Hendricus; Jacobus, bp. Mar. 9, 1653, in N. A.; Abraham; Denyse; Isaac; Benjamin; Elizabeth, who m. Apl. 12, 1684, Tobias Ten Eyck; and John. Signed his name "*Adriaen Hegeman.*"

Adriaen (s. of Abraham) of Fl[h], m. Adriaentje ——. County-clerk from 1726 to 1750; Will da. Sept. 1, 1770; pro. Apl. 16, 1772; rec. on p. 280 of Lib. 28, N. Y. surr. off. Issue:—Abraham of Hunterdon Co., N. J.; Petrus of Fl[h]; Geertruy; Adriaen of Fl[h]; and Rem. Signed his name "*Adrian Hegeman.*"

Adriaen (s. of Hendrick and Ariaentje), bp. Mar. 14, 1686, in N. Y.; m. May 1, 1713, Marytje Vandervliet of Fl[h]; d. 1755. Will pro. May 1, 1755. Removed from Fl[h] to J[a], and also resided in Hempstead. Issue:—Hendrick of Hempstead, b. 1714; Benjamin, b. 1716, (sup.) m. Helena Polhemus; Aeltie, b. 1718; Marragriete, b. 1719; Peter, b. 1722. Barentje, b. 1724; Jan of Hempstead, b. 1728; and Thomas, b. 1734.

Adriaen (s. of Isaac) of Fl[h], bp. Sept. 9, 1688; m. Dec. 3, 1714, Martha Vanderbeek. Issue:—Adrian, bp. Dec. 4, 1720, d. young; Adrian of Fl[h], bp. Sept. 9, 1722, (sup.) m. Oct. 3, 1747, Sietje Stryker; Rem of Fl[h], bp. May 9, 1725, (sup.) m. Nov. 10, 1743, Sarah Berrian; Geertruy, bp. Feb. 4, 1728, d. young; Geertruy, bp. Jan. 26, 1729; and (sup.) Peter, who m. Antje Hoogland.

Adriaen (s. of Joseph) of N. L., b. Oct. 29, 1680; m. Marytje ——; d. 1737. At one period he resided at Br[n] ferry. Issue:—Joseph of Cedar Swamp, Queens Co., b. June 29, 1710, m. May 17, 1735, Sarah Martense or Vanderbilt, d. Feb. 5, 1793. Signed his name *"Adriaen Hegeman."*

Benjamen (Adriaense) of Fl[h], espoused Apl. 9, 1688, Lavennettie or Barentje Jansen of New Albany. Mem. of the D. ch. of Fl[h] in 1677, resided in N. Y. in 1685, on ass. roll of Fl[h] of 1693 and cen. of 1698, and supervisor of said town in 1710. Issue:—Catharine, bp. Feb. 12, 1696, in N. Y., m. 1st Hendrick Vonk, m. 2[d], July 30, 1735, Aucke Lefferts; and Alida, bp. Oct. 26, 1702. Signed his name *"Benjamen Hegeman."*

Denys (Adriaense) of Fl[h]; m. Lucretia ——; d. prior to 1710. In 1673 a private in Capt. Stemnek's company of New Orange (New York); in 1675 a resident of the city of N. Y. and mem. of the R. D. ch. of that place; in 1691 sent by Gov. Sloughter to Pemaquid to treat with the Indians, taken prisoner by the French under Castin, sent to Quebec, thence to France and imprisoned there 3 years; and on ass. roll of Fl[h] of 1693 and cen. of 1698. Issue:— Jacobus of the Raritan, m. Jannetje ——; Adriaen of Br[n] ferry, m. Sarah ——; Dallius, of the Raritan as early as 1703, m. Geertruy ——; Joseph Denyse of Fl[h], b. in Canada, m. June 4, 1714, Alida Andreisz; and Denyse of the Raritan, bp. 1703 at J[a], m. Mary or Maria——, d. 1748. Signed his name *"Denys Hegeman."*

Elbert (Josephse) of Oostwoud or N. L., b. 1687; m. Apl. 30, 1710, Marytje Rapalje; d. Oct. 22, 1777, in his 91st year. The N. Y. Gazette of Nov. 10, 1777, says "he was no less remarkable for his Piety than his Benevolence, and exhibited to us in a remarkable instance of his Attention to the divine Laws of his Creator, having read the Bible through no less than Three Hundred and Sixty-five Times." Issue:— (sup.) Catharine, b. Nov. 11, 1691, m. Nov. 15, 1709, Ab[m] Lott, d. Nov. 19, 1741; Jacobus of Manhasset, b. Feb. 12, 1711, m. Gertruyt Onderdonk, d. Dec. 20, 1747; and (sup.) Daniel of Manhasset, b. Dec. 22, 1712, m. Apl. 6, 1734, Catharine Onderdonk, d. Mar. 12, 1786. Signed his name *"Elbert Hegeman."*

Frans (Josephse) of N. L. and J[a], m. Oct. 29, 1709, Antie Ruard. No further trace.

Hendrick, s. of Jacobus (Adriaense). No further trace.

Hendricus (Adriaense), emigrated with his father; b. in Amsterdam; m. Apl. 12 or 26, 1685, Ariaentje Bloodgood, and at the time a resident of N. L. In 1677 was a mem. of the R. D. ch. of Fl[h], and took the oath of allegiance in Fl[h] in 1687. In 1691 he bought land of W[m] Whitt in J[a], as per p. 241 of Lib. A of Con. in off. of clerk of Queens Co. About 1710 with others bought the Harlington tract in Somerset Co., N. J. Issue:—Adriaen of J[a], bp. Mar. 14. 1686, in N. Y.; Joost; Jacobus; Phebe; (sup.) Catharine, m. Sept. 8, 1716, Jan Van Pelt of N. U.; and (sup.) Joseph. Signed his name *"Hendrikus Hegeman."*

Isaac (Adriaense) of Fl[h], m. Feb. 15, 1687, Marytje Roelofse Schenck; d. in 1700. Took the oath of allegiance in Fl[h] in 1687 as a native; mem. of R. D. ch. of Fl[h] in 1685; on ass. roll of 1693 and cen. of 1698; and ensign of Fl[h] company of militia in 1686, as per p. 148 of Cal. of English Man. Issue:—Adriaen of Fl[h], bp. Dec. 9, 1688, m. Dec. 3, 1714, Martha Vanderbeek; (sup.) Jan, m. Geertruyd ——; and Elizabeth or Libertje, m. Feb. 16, 1717, (sup.) Barend Stryker. Signed his name *"Isaack Hegeman."*

Jacobus (Adriaense) of Fl[h], emigrated to this country with his father; m. Oct. 14, 1683, Jannetje Ariens of Fl[h]. Mem. of R. D. ch. of Fl[h] in 1677; took the oath of allegiance in said town in 1687; on ass. roll of 1693 and cen. of 1698. Issue:—Hendrick; and Adriaen, bp. July 27, 1684, in Fl[h].

Jan (Isaacse), m. Geertruyd ——. No further trace.

John (Adriaense, sup. s. of Adriaen and Catharine) of Fl[h], m. Mar. 22, 1650, Marretje Clock. Issue:—(sup.) Marcus, bp. Jan. 19, 1653, in N. Y. A John Hegeman m. Feb. 12, 1692, Femmetje Titus, both of Fl[h].

Joseph (Adriaense) of N. L., emigrated from Amsterdam with his father; m. Oct. 21, 1677, Femmetje Rems or Remsen of New Albany; d. about 1725. Resided in Fl[h] as early as 1658, where he owned a farm of 40½ morgens; in 1677 mem. of D. ch of said town, and in 1690 an elder; took the oath of allegiance in Fl[h] in 1687; appointed Cornet of Horse in 1689; in 1690 opposed the Leislerian faction; and on cen. of 1698. In 1710 with others bought the Harlington tract in Somerset Co., N. J.

The following is a list of the owners of the New Lotts of "Midwout" as made Apl. 2, 1680, by Joseph Hegeman and Stoffel Probasco, overseers of said town, by order of Gov. Andros:

Floris Willemse (Krom)....	2 lots.	Cornelis Boomgaert........	1 lot.
Minne Johannis..........	3 "	Rem Remse..............	1 "
Dirck Janse Hooglant.....	1 "	School lot..............	1 "
Hendrick Strycker........	1 "	Pieter Gillamse (Cornell)....	2 "
Jan Snediker.............	1 "	Willem Gillamse (Cornell)...	2 "
Dirck Janse Van der Vliet..	1 "	Syman Hanse (Van Nostrand)	2 "
Pieter Lot..............	1 "	Cornelis de Zeeuw........	2 "
Gerret Lubbertse..........	1 "	Catharine Hegeman........	2 "
Jan Subringh.............	1 "	Adriaen Reyerse..........	1 "
Catharine Polhemius......	2 "	Gerret Snediker..........	1 "
Willem Jacobse (Van Boerum)......	2 "	Titus Sirachs............	1 "
		Aris Janse Van de Bilt......	2 "
Jan Strycker.............	2 "	Leffert Pieterse..........	1 "
Jacob Hendrickse (Suydam)	1 "	Stoffel Probasco..........	2 "
Cornelis Barentse (Van Wyck)........	1 "	Catharine Hegeman........	2 "
Jan Ditmars.............	2 "	Cornelis Berrien...	2 "

Altogether 47 lots.

Issue:—Jannetje, b. Oct. 24, 1678; (sup.) Elbert of N. L.; (sup.) Catharine, m. Oct. 20, 1711, Tunis Bogaert of S. I.; (sup.) Peter of Oyster Bay; Adriaen of N. L.; Elizabeth, b. Nov. 2, 1682, m. Oct. 29, 1701, Lourens Ditmars; Rem of Fl^h, bp. Feb. 8, 1685; (sup.) Neeltje, m. Sept. 8, 1716, Court Van Voorhees; Joseph; Francis of N. L.; and (sup.) Frans. Signed his name "*Joseph Hegeman.*"

Joseph (s. of Joseph and Femmetje), bp. Aug. 2, 1687; m. 1st, May 1, 1712, Adriaentje Van Wyck, both of Fl^h at date of marriage; m. 2^d, Feb. 6, 1714, Sarah dau. of Jan Dirckse Vander Vliet; d. 1741. Resided at one period at Gowanus, owning the farm late of Theodorus Bergen and adjoining land, which he sold May 10, 1734, to Cornelius Santford, and (sup.) then removed to J^a. In 1716 a Joseph Hegeman mem. of Assembly for Kings Co. Issue:— Ariaentje, bp. 1716; John, bp. 1716; Hendrick, bp. 1717 in J^a; Joseph, bp. 1719; Cornelis, bp. 1722; Elizabeth, bp. 1723; Sarah, bp. 1725; Rem, bp. Sept. 25, 1726, m. Dec. 3, 1748, Metje Suydam; and Maria, bp. 1736. Signed his name "*Joseph Hegeman.*"

Peter (sup. a s. of Adriaen), schout fiscaal of Br^n in 1656, '59, and '60, and on patent of Fl^h of 1685, per Thompson's L. I.

Peter (sup. s. of Joseph and Femmetje) of Oyster Bay, m. 1st —— ——; m. 2^d, Dec. 13, 1746, Anna or Magdalena Hoogland; d. about 1770. Issue:—Andrew of Oyster Bay; Adriaen; Joost; Jacobus; and Gertrude.

Rem (Josephse) of Fl^h, bp. Feb. 8, 1685; m. May 6, 1715, Peternella Van Wicklen of N. L. Was a freeholder of Br^n in 1724. Will da. May 19, 1759; pro. Apl. 6, 1767, and rec. in N. Y. surr. off. Issue:—Metje, bp. Nov. 2, 1718, m. Adrian

Cornell of Bucks Co., Pa.; Evert of Fl^h, b. Jan. 30, 1720, m. Nov. 17, 1750, Seytje Suydam, d. Oct. —, 1779; Femmetje, bp. Apl. 25, 1725, m. John Suydam of Newtown; and Rem, bp. Aug. 11, 1728, (sup.) m. ——, 1748, Grietje Benham. Signed his name *"Rem Hegeman."*

HEIMANS, JOSEPH, paid clergyman's salary in Fl^h in 1681, as per town rec.

Kornelis, paid clergyman's salary in Fl^h in 1681, as per town rec.

HELLAKERS, JACOB, see Swart.

William, of Fld^a in 1689, as per Fld^a ch. rec.; m. Apl. 2, 1682, in N. Y., Tryntje Boelen of the same place, of which they were both residents at date of marriage. Issue:— Bayken, bp. Jan. 24, 1685; Dina, bp. Mar. 13, 1687; Tryntje, bp. Mar. 31, 1689; Bayken, bp. Oct. 25, 1691; and Hendrick, bp. Mar. 11, 1694—all in N. Y. Signed his name *"Willem Hellakers."*

HENDRICKS or HENDRICKSEN, ADAM, see Vrooman.

Abraham, see Sleght and Suydam.

Aeltje of Bu^k, m. June 16, 1693, Isaac Van Tilburg of Fordham, both of city of N. Y. at date of marriage, as per N. Y. D. ch. rec.

Albert, emigrated in 1662, and took the oath of allegiance in Bu^k in 1687, where he settled, his name appearing on the patent of said town of the same year. He m. 1st Lyntje Dircke Seerjeans; m. 2^d Grietje Kroegers. On ass. rolls of Bu^k of 1676, '83, and '93, and cen. of 1698. Issue by 2^d w.:— Johannis, bp. Jan. 4, 1685.

Ariaen or *Adriaen*, see Hendrick Janse.

Arie or *Adryaen*. Constable of Fl^h in 1665. Mar. 28, 1677, there is a reference on p. 15 of Calendar of Land Papers to a patent to him of land in N. L. On ass. rolls of Fl^h of 1675, '83, and '93, and on cen. of 1698. He m. Lysbeth Thomas or Aten, who by a former m. had a s. Lubbert Gysbertse. Will da. Mar. 20, 1696, and rec. on p. 224 of Lib. A of Fl^h rec. Issue:—Martie or Marytie, bp. Mar. 31, 1678, in Br^n; and Paul, bp. Nov. 14, 1680, in N. U. Signed his name *"Adryaen Hendrycksen."*

Barent, see Sleght.

Bruno of Fld^a, m. Apl. 27, 1682, Elizabeth Jans of Esopus. Mem. of R. D. ch. of Fld^a in 1677.

Cornelis, see Sleght.

Court, see Hendrick Janse.

David, an Englishman, m. Oct. 22, 1681, Helena dau. of Adam Brouwer of Gowanus, the emigrant, b. in 1660.

Ephraim, emigrated in 1664, and took the oath of allegiance in Brⁿ in 1687.

Evert or *Everd*, m. Sophia Adams Brouwer. On ass. rolls of Brⁿ of 1675 and '83. Issue:—Jacobus, bp. June 2, 1678, in Brⁿ; Aaltje, bp. Aug. 1, 1680, in Flʰ; Jannetje, bp. Nov. 30, 1684, in Brⁿ; and Sarah, bp. Mar. 9, 1690, in Brⁿ. An Evert Hendricksen, a Fin, was banished from Altona in 1663, as per p. 346 of Cal. of Dutch His. Man.

Folkert, see Bries or Breets.

Frans, made his mark to documents in Flʰ in 1670.

Gerret of Fldˢ. Mem. of R. D. ch. of Fldˢ in 1677, and name on church-books in 1689 and '91. Signed his name "*Gerret Hendryckn.*"

Gerret m. Anne Johannis, and had a s. Hendrick bp. Sept. 24, 1662, in Brⁿ.

Gerret, mem. of R. D. ch. of Flʰ in 1677.

Gerret, see Backer.

Harman, m. 1ˢᵗ Elizabeth ——; m. 2ᵈ Margaret Sodder. In 1663 he and others of Brⁿ asked liberty to found a new village, and for salt meadows between the 3ᵈ and 4ᵗʰ kils near the new lotts of Flʰ, as per p. 120 of Vol. I. of Stiles's Brⁿ. On ass. roll of Fldˢ of 1675, and in 1677 entered as a mem. of the R. D. ch. of Flʰ, residing in N. L., and removed to Hempstead. Issue by 2ᵈ wife:—Hendrick, bp. in 1679 in N. Y.; and Cornelia, bp. July 8, 1681, in Flʰ.

Hendrick of N. U., m. Helena dau. of Jacques Cortelyou the emigrant, wid. successively of Claes or Nicholas Van Brunt and Denyse Teunisse (Denyse). Resided for a period on the lands at Nyack, N. U., which Helena inherited from her father. Apl. 18, 1718, he bought of Abᵐ Emans of Freehold, N. J., for £350 a farm of 250 A. in Monmouth Co., as per p. 289 of Lib. E of Con. in Monmouth Co. clerk's off. He also bought other lands in that vicinity, as per the rec. of said clerk's off., to which he probably removed. In 1706 he appears to have resided in Middletown in said county. Oct 9, 1738, letters of administration on his estate were granted to his s. Hendrick of Middletown. Issue:—Hendrick; and Geesje, who m. Nicholas Van Brunt of N. U. and N. J. Made his mark "H H" to documents.

Hendrick, (English,) m. Dec. 10, 1683, Helena Brown of Gᵈ. Name on ass. roll of Brⁿ of 1693 and cen. of 1698.

Jacob, see Suydam.

Jacob of N. U., m. 1ˢᵗ (prior to July 12, 1677, as per p. 350 of Lib. D of Flʰ rec., at which date they made a joint will on which his surname is *Kee*) Geesje Bartels dau. of Bartel Claesen; m. 2[d], Sept. 7, 1684, Catharine Beavois from Leiden.   Aug. 29, 1684 (prior to his 2[d] marriage), Bartel Claesen and Engelbert Lott were appointed guardians of the minor children by his first marriage, as per p. 173 of Lib. C of Fl[h] rec., on which their names are given.   On ass. roll of N. U. of 1693, and a church-master of said town in 1695. Issue:—Hillegonde, b. 1673; Hendrickje, b. 1675; Bartelt, b. 1677; Hendrick and Catalyntje, twins, bp. Apl. 18, 1679, at N. U.; Cornelis; and (by 2[d] wife) Karel, bp. June 13, 1685, at Fl[h]. Made his mark "I H" to documents.

Jacob of Fl[h], bought the farm of 23 morgens, with plain and meadow land appertaining thereto, which was allotted Feb. 7, 1670-1, to Cornelis Janse Berrien, as per p. 16 of Lib. B of Fl[h] rec. Was allotted wood-lot No. 17 in N. L., as per deed of Feb. 15, 1677-8, of Bartel Claesen to J. B. Blom on p. 23 of Lib. AA of Fl[h] rec. Probably Jacob Hendrickse Haften and this Jacob are the same person. Made his mark "I" to documents.

Jan of Bu[k], of which place he was one of the first settlers in 1661, and a mag. in 1663. He m. Gretie Barents. Issue:—Barent Janse, bp. Sept. 21, 1663, in Br[n]. This may be Jan Hendrickse Pulman.

Jan, see Bommel and Van Gunst.

Johanna of Bu[k], m. July 2, 1692, in N. Y., Laurens Van Hoeck of N. Y., where both resided at date of marriage.

Johannes, see Lott, Sleght, Smack, and Vandewater.

John. Apl. 6, 1696, he and others conveyed 54 A. in Fl[h] to Cornelius Luyster, as per p. 118 of Lib. 29 of Con.

Jeurriaen, m. 1st Cornelia Beauvois. Entered on Do. Van Zuuren's ch. rec. as of the Wallabout, and a mem. of his ch. in 1677; m. 2[d] Ariaentje Barens. Issue:—Fytie, bp. Nov. 13, 1687; and Jannetje, bp. Dec. 8. 1689—both in Br[n].

Jurian, see Vander Breets.

Lambert of Gowanus, mem. of Br[n] R. D. ch. in 1677. A Lambert Hendricksen Van Campen took the oath of allegiance in N. Y. in 1664.

Leonard and *Mattys*, see Smack.

Mindert, on Stoothoff's books of 1676.

Pieter, see Hendrick Janse.

Pieter of Fl[h], with others conveyed Apl. 7, 1692, 26 A. in Fl[h] to Gerret Coerten (Voorhies) of Fld[s], as per p. 136 of Lib. 2 of Con.

Pieter, m. Catharine Jansz. Mem. of Fld[s] R. D. ch. in 1677, and on ass. rolls of said town of 1675 and '83. In 1678 and '80 he was a dealer in whalebone, as per Stoothoff's books. Issue:—Jan, bp. Sept. 30, 1680, in Fl[h]; Hendrick, bp. July 23, 1682, in N. U.; and Adam, bp. Apl. 20, 1684, in N. U.

Pieter from Friesland in the Netherlands, m. June 5, 1698, in N. Y., Rachel Berckhoven (Brower) dau. of Adam Brower of Gowanus, both residents of N. Y. at date of m. Made his mark to documents in 1698.

Pieter, a carpenter, who assisted in building a windmill in Br[a] about 1684 for Michil Hainelle, as per p. 24 of Lib. 1 of Con.

Ryck, see Suydam.

Volckert, see Breets.

Walter, see Hendrick Janse.

Willem, took the oath of allegiance in Fl[h] in 1687 as a native.

William from Mispat Kil, m. Aug. 5, 1693, at the Highlands, Magdalena dau. of Adam Brower of Gowanus, both residents of the Highlands at date of marriage, as per N. Y. D. ch. rec.

HENDS, BOMAN, allotted land on Gisbert's I. in G[d] about 1670, per G[d] rec.

HENSZ, VOLKERT, of Fld[s], entered on lists of mem. of the R. D. ch. of that place as removed.

HERMANSE, see Vogel.

Gerret of 1663, m. Elizabeth Gerrets. A Gerrit Hermans on the Delaware in 1660.

Hendrick or *Herremensen*, m. Egbertje Jans, and d. prior to 1677. Resided in Fld[s] in 1674, as per ch. rec. of said town. Apl. 3, 1683, Egbertje his wid. sold land in Fld[s], as per town rec., on the deed of which his name is written "Herremensen Henderyck." Issue, as per p. 224 of Lib. C of Fl[h] rec.:—Herman Hendrickse; Styntje Hendrickse, who m. Eldert Lucasse Voorhies; Jannetje Hendrickse, who m. Loutweyns Mattyse; John Hendrickse; and Annetje Hendrickse, minors in 1681.

Jan, a tailor, of Fl[h] in 1666, per p. 63 of Lib. D of Fl[h] rec. In 1660 paid tuition-money to —— Van Giesen, as per p. 44 of Lib. B of Fl[h] rec. Signed his name "*Jan Hermanse*" in 1695.

Martin, see Hoffman.

HERRECKS, AERTEN, paid minister's salary in Fl[h] in 1680, as per town rec.

HERRY ——, a Frenchman, among the first settlers of

Bu[k]. There was a Johannes Herry of Albany who m. Apl. 26, 1700, in N. Y., Jannetje Missepadt from Zeelandt.

HESELANT, JAN, rented land in Fl[h] in 1700, as per ch. rec.

HESSELSE, PETER, in N. U. as early as 1659; m. *Elisabeth Gerrets.* From N. U. he removed to Bergen, N. J., and finally settled in the vicinity of Hackensack. In 1686 and '88 he was elected a deputy to the General Assembly of E. N. J., as per p. 119 of Rec. of Gov. and Council. Issue:— Hessel, bp. July 21, 1668, in N. Y.; Metje, bp. Oct 12, 1670, in N. Y.; William of Hackensack; Elsje, bp. May 1, 1675, in N. Y.; Neeltje; Marretje, bp. Oct. 8, 1677, in Bergen; Johannes, bp. ——, 1680; Ragel or Rachel, bp. Sept. 14, 1682, in Bergen; Peter of Hackensack; Ariaentje, bp. Apl. 6, 1685, in Bergen; Jannetje, bp. Oct. 3, 1687, in Bergen; and Vrouwtje, bp. Oct. 5, 1691, in Bergen.

HEY or HEEY, HARMEN, see Haey.

HEYNANT, CHARLES, of Bedford, obtained a patent Dec. 3, 1677, for 6 A. of woodland adjoining his other lands at that locality.

HIBON, JAN, a tailor, m. 1st *Anneken Claes Duurkoop;* m. 2[d], June 4, 1688, in N. Y., *Gertruyt Breedstede.* He and his w. Anneken mem. of the D. ch. of N. A. prior to 1660, and entered on the ch. rec. as removed to Br[n] and thence to Virginia. Resided at Br[n] ferry in 1660, where his w. obtained Mar. 19, 1664, a patent for a lot, as per p. 28 of Cal. of Eng. Man., and a mem. of the D. ch. of that place. Issue:—Maria or Mary, m. June 9, 1680, in N. Y., Jillis Provoost, both residents of N. Y. at date of m.; and Gerty, who m. Cornelis Van Tienhoven. There was a Jan Hibon, a cadet, discharged from the service of the West India Company in 1658, as per p. 197 of Cal. of Dutch Man.
Claes, with others in 1663 asked leave to form a new village, as per p. 37 of Vol. X. of N. Y. Col. Man.

HILLEBRANTS,'TOMIS and TEUNIS, see Van Dyckhuys.

HILTON, WILLIAM, of Br[n], (sup.) m. *Rachel Adamse Brouwer.* Made his mark to documents in 1698.

HOCK, THOMAS, of Br[n] ferry, per deed of W[m] Morris to

the corporation of the city of N. Y. of Oct. 12, 1694, as per p. 23 of Furman's Brⁿ.

HOFFMAN, MARTEN HERMANZEN, saddler, of Revel, m. 1st, Apl. 22, 1663, at Brⁿ, *Lysbeth Hermans* (of Ootmarsum, a town in Overyssel), by Brⁿ D. ch. rec.—Mar. 31, 1663, by N. A. D. ch. rec.; m. 2^d, May 16, 1664, *Emmerentje De Witts* from "Edent in Emberlandt." Resided in N. A. and in Albany.

HOLLIS, ROBERT, granted Jan. 4, 1668, exclusive privilege of selling liquor in Brⁿ, as per p. 157 of Vol. I. of Stiles's Brⁿ. Obtained a patent July 18, 1669, for 13 morgens in Brⁿ. Made his mark "R H" to documents.

HOLMES, HOMS, or HULMES, GEORGE, (English,) bought Mar. 14, 1649, the lot of Ambrose London in G^d of Wm Golder, as per G^d rec. There was a Joris Holmes in N. A. who had several children bp. in the R. D. ch. of that place, and who was inspector of tobacco in 1653. Made his mark to documents. A George Holmes (probably the above George) with 12 or 13 persons, besides his hired man Thomas Hall, all English from Connecticut, undertook in 1635 to make a settlement in the Dutch territory on the Delaware, making an attack on Fort Nassau which failed, they being made prisoners by the Dutch and carried to Manhattan, as per p. 40 of Hazard's Annals of Pa. (see also p. 127 of Vol. IV. of the Genealogical Record), where most of them remained and settled. He probably with other English settlers at N. A. followed Lady Mody to G^d. There was a Joris Homs of N. Y. who m. Aug. 22, 1695, in N. Y., Anneken Kaljiers of N. Albany, both residents of Bu^k at date of marriage.

Joseph of G^d (s. of Samuel and Ales Stillwell), b. Mar. 17, 1672; m. 1st Annake Daws; m. 2^d (sup.) Adriaentje Laan. Served as a juror in the court of sessions of Kings Co. in 1695; and sold Feb. 7, 1695-6, with consent of his mother Ales or Alse and of his w. Anna, to his uncle Nicholas Stillwell of G^d his lands in said town, as per p. 86 of Lib. 2 of Con. Bought in 1704 a farm near the village of Middletown, N. J., to which he removed. Issue (as per Rev. G. C. Schenck):—Elias, b. 1704, m. Mar. 1730 Ariaentje Aersen; Patience, b. Sept. 28, 1712; Sarah, b. Mar. 27, 1715, m. Johannes Tyse; Wilhelmus, b. Aug. 24, 1718; Joseph, b. Aug. 1726; and Antie, b. Aug. 22, 1731. Made his mark to documents.

Samuel of G^d (s. of Rev. Obadiah Holmes), b. 1642; m.

Oct. 26, 1665, Ales or Abagail dau. of Nicholas Stillwell the emigrant; d. prior to 1684. May 3, 1665, he bought of John Ruckman plantation-lot No. 22 in G^d; owned 1½ lots on Gisbert's I. in 1670, as per G^d rec.; lieut. of militia in 1673, and a mag. in 1674. His will is da. Apl. 28, 1679; presented to the court of sessions in 1679 for proof; and rec. on p. 351 of Lib. 1 of N. Y. surr. off. His children settled in Monmouth Co., N. J., where they have numerous descendants. Issue:—Samuel, b. Feb. 12, 1668; Ann, b. Dec. 30, 1670, m. May 22, 1691, Gedaen Jacobus Kierste of N. Y.; Joseph, b. Mar. 17, 1672; Catharine, b. June 15, 1675 —all as per G^d rec.; and Mary, as per will. Signed his name *"Samuell Hulms."*

HOLSART, see Hulsart.

HOLWELL, JOHN, surveyed May 22, 1689, a disputed line between land of Dirk Janse Hoogland and Pieter Lott in Fl^h, as per p. 174 of Vol. I. of Con.

HOOGLAND, CHRISTOFFEL or CHRISTOPHER (s. of Christopher of Haerlem), bp. Nov. 24, 1669, in N. Y.; m. *Neeltje Voorhies.* On ass. roll of Br^n of 1693 and cen. of 1698. Resided in Fl^h in 1706 and N. U. in 1737. His father emigrated from Haerlem, settled in N. A., where he m. June 23, 1661, Catharine Cregiers of Amsterdam; d. about 1684 or '86 (his will being dated Mar. 12, 1676, and rec. on p. 83 of Lib. 3 in off. of surr. of N. Y.), having children, Dirk, Lysbeth, Marten, Christopher, Francis, Jacob, Deynoot, and Harmen. *Christopher* and *Neeltje* had issue:—Christopher of Millstone, N. J., bp. Jan. 14, 1728; Harmanus, bp. May 29, 1732; Sara, bp. Dec. 8, 1734; Adriaentje, bp. Sept. 19, 1736; Harman, bp. Sept. 29, 1739; John of Millstone; and Martinus. Signed his name *"Christoffel Hoogland."*

Cornelis Dircksen, b. 1599. Kept goats for their milk in 1638 for Wouter Van Twiller, as per p. 2 of Cal. of Dutch His. Man. Sold cows to Tunis Nyssen (Denyse) in 1643, as per p. 25 of do. Was ferry-master at Br^n in 1652, when he sold a lot with house and barn, on the shore of L. I. near the ferry, to Cornelis de Potter, as per p. 55 of do. Dec. 12, 1645, he obtained a patent for upwards of 12 morgens on L. I. next to Harry Breser's land in Br^n, as per p. 370 of do. Dec 3, 1652, sold Cornelis de Potter upwards of 2 morgens of land with buildings in Br^n, as per p. 376 of do. Oct. 15, 1653, while ferryman, he bought of "Daniel Whytheade" a house and lot at the ferry, which lot Whytheade bought June 2, 1653, of Jan Hayes, as per pp. 378 and 379 of do. Signed his name "*Cornelis Dierckse.*"

Cornelis Janse, m. Aeltje Ariaans wid. of Jacob Dircksen Vogel. Issue:—Dirck Cornelise.

Dirck Cornelise of Br[n], m. Lysbeth or Elizabeth Jorise Rapalie. Obtained a patent for 12 morgens in Br[n] Dec. 22, 1645, and a patent for 17 morgens at the ferry Jan. 24, 1647. Feb. 10, 1660, he sold to W[m] Goulder plantation-lot No. 3 in G[d], as per town rec. Resided on S. I. in 1689. A Derrick Cornelissen bought a tract of the Indians at Chesquakes, N. J. Issue:—Johannes, bp. Nov. 7, 1666; Joris, bp. Feb. 19, 1668; Marretje, bp. July 13, 1673; Marretje, bp. July 29, 1687; and (sup.) Sara, bp. Sept. 28, 1692, (sup.) m. Abraham Lefferts—all bp. in N. Y. Signed his name "*Dirck Cornellissen Hoochlandt.*"

Dirck Janse, from Maarssenveen in the province of Utrecht, b. 1635; emigrated in 1657; m. 1st, Oct. 8, 1662, Annetje Hansen Bergen (or Annetje Feddens) wid. of Jan Clercq; m. 2[d], prior to 1689, Elizabeth ——. On ass. roll of Br[n] of 1675, and ferryman. On ass. rolls of Fl[h] of 1676 and '83 and patent of 1685, as per Thompson's L. I. Took the oath of allegiance in Fl[h] in 1687. Apl. 29, 1689, he sold 20 morgens at Bedford to Derick Cornelissen Hoogland of S. I., as per p. 145 of Lib. I. of Con. From a map on file in the office of the Sec. of State at Albany, made by "Ja. Cortelyan, sworn surveyor," filed Aug. 8, 1681, it appears that "Klyn Dirk," who was probably Dirk Janse Hoogland, owned a farm of 2 lots in Fl[h] on the W. side of the "highway to the ferry," S. of "Pieter Lott's" and N. of "John Ditmarsen's," about 622 ft. in width and 7241 ft. English in length, cong. upwards of 52 morgens, covering the farms as lately held by Henry S. Ditmars and of John Ditmars in his own right, or what they inherited from Abraham Ditmars their father. In 1677 there was a dispute between him and Pieter Lott about the boundary between their farms, which was finally settled by arbitration, as per pp. 39 and 53 of Lib. AA of Fl[h] rec. Issue:—Annetje Dirkse, bp. 1663; Joris Dirkse; Lysbeth Dirkse, bp. May 16, 1677, in N. Y.; (sup.) Arie Dirkse, who m. in 1694 in N. Y. Anne Byvanck; Willem Dirkse; Sara Dirkse, bp. Aug. 7, 1681; (sup.) Jan Dirkse; and Neeltje Dirkse, bp. June 11, 1686. Made his mark to documents.

Jan Dirkse, took the oath of allegiance in Fl[h] in 1687 as a native. A Jan Dircksen m. Aug. 4, 1686, in N. Y., Catelina Cloppers. Made his mark to documents.

Johannis of Br[n] (s. of Dirk Cornelise), bp. Nov. 7, 1666, in N. Y., m. May 30, 1686, on S. I., Annetje Duycking wid. of

Pieter Van de Water, both residents of N. Y. at date of marriage, as per N. Y. D. ch. rec.

. *Joris Dirkse*, took the oath of allegiance in Fl^h in 1687 as a native. He m. Apl. 5, 1689, Catryntje Daemelse Righant of Br^n.

Willem Dirkse, took the oath of allegiance in Fl^h in 1687 as a native. June 9, 1702, he conveyed to Leffert Pieterse a lot of woodland in Fl^h lying under the Long Hill adjoining woodland of said Leffert, as per p. 17 of Lib. B of Fl^h rec. Issue:—Dirk, b. 1698, d. 1766, m. Mary Stot of N. Y., and settled at Southampton, Bucks Co., Pa., and is the ancestor of the Hooglands of that locality; and (sup.) Elizabeth and Marytje.

HOOK, LOURENS, on ass. roll of Bu^k of 1693 and cen. of 1698.

HOOK, HUYBERT JANSE, see Stoock.

HOONIS, GYSBERT, among the first settlers of Bu^k of 1661, per Thompson's L. I.

HORN ——, a fisherman, who settled at an early day at the point in Canarisie where the present public landing is located and the railroad terminates; said point being designated on the early maps as "Vischer's Hoek," or Fisherman's Point.

HORNZEEUES, JAN, owned land in Bu^k at an early date.

HOUSEMAN, CHARLES, on ass. roll of Bu^k of 1675. There are Housemans residing in the vicinity of Hackensack, N. J., at which place Abram Houseman of Bu^k m. Nov. 1701 Gerrebrecht Terhune.

HRAPHAGEN, WILLEM, see Willem Jansen Traphagen.

HUBBARD, ELIAS (s. of James the emigrant), b. Apl. 11, 1673; m. Dec. 15, 1699, Jannetje wid. of Jan Barentse Van Driest. Resided in G^d and a farmer. No trace of his descendants. Signed his name "*Elias Hubbard.*"

Elias (s. of Samuel), m. Sept. 29, 1723, Femmetje dau. of Lourans Ditmars of Fl^h; d. Dec. 1, 1731. Issue:—Ariaentje, b. Apl. 7, 1731, m. Adriaen Voorhies of Fl^h, and d. July 23, 1810; and Cornelia (twin with Ariaentje), b. Apl. 7, 1731,

m. Sept. 23, 1748, Isaac Denyse. Signed his name "*Elias Hubbard Juner.*"

James, the common ancestor of the Kings Co. and N. J. Hubbards, emigrated from Langham in the county of Rutland, England. Came to G^d with Lady Mody and others, who left New England to enjoy their peculiar religious views, where they settled about 1643; m. 1st Martha ——; m. 2^d, Dec. 31, 1664, Elizabeth Bailies or Baylis. Mag. of G^d in 1645, '51, '53, '63, and '64; and schout fiscaal of G^d in 1650. On Gov. Kieft's patent of G^d of 1645, having a plantation-lot granted in 1646: With Baxter and Grover rebelled, in 1655, against the Dutch authorities, who had sheltered and protected them, for which he was imprisoned. Was a representative of G^d in the Hempstead convention of 1665. Had a tract of 176 A. surveyed for him at the head of the Fresh Kil on S. I., as per p. 206 of Vol. I. of Land Papers. Issue:— James, b. Dec. 10, 1665; Rebecca, b. Apl. 28, 1667; Elizabeth, b. June 3, 1669; John, b. Mar. 20, 1670; Elias, b. Apl. 11, 1673; (sup.) Hannah, who m. Myndert Johnson; and Samuel, b. May 3, 1676. Signed his name "*J^s Hubbard.*"

The following curious entry is copied from Lib. 3 of G^d rec.: " The record of mee James Hubbard: To Certifie mine or any other of his brethren William: John: Henry & Margret wth him selve ye youngest of leaven sonns & Dafters: yet butt five known of here, of our father Henry Hubbard & our mother Margrett: of ye Towne of Langham: in ye Countye of Ruttland yeaman: stands upon ye record of ye regester To be ye 123: Generation: As I have receved by letters in ye yeare 1669: & my Chilldren wth ye Rest of my Bretherens chilldren are ye 124: Generation: wch I James Hubbard of Gravesend on ye wester end of long Ile land desired To have Recorded on ye Townes Regester of Gravesend: for his Chilldren To add & to have.Respect unto: for there better knowledge of There Relations in ye parts of Urope ye land of England in Cass of There Travells To Those parts."

Allowing 30 years for a generation, this would carry the genealogy of the family back over 4000 years, or to about the time of Noah's flood. If there is any foundation for the 123 generations, the inference would be that the ancestors of the Hubbard's were Jews, for they alone through the Bible trace from Noah to the days of our Saviour, and are the only race who could be supposed to make a pretence of tracing from that period to the present time. There was a James Hubbard, ag. 27, who emigrated from London to St Christopher's in 1635, as per p. 80 of Hotten's Emigrants.

James (s. of James), b. Dec. 10, 1665; m. Rachel ——; d.

1723. On cen. of G^d of 1698, which town he left and settled at Middletown, Monmouth Co., N. J., where he bought land of —— Stout, and where he died, his will being da. Jan. 30, 1718-19; pro. Jan. 16, 1723-4; and rec. in Lib A, p. 284, off. of Sec. of State of N. J. Issue:—James (an imbecile), b. 1686, d. 1764, leaving no issue; and Mary, b. about 1689, m. John Wall of Middletown, N. J., who had children, Williampie, Rachel, and Mary Wall.

John (s. of James the emigrant), b. Mar. 20, 1670. Resided in G^d in 1695. No trace of his descendants.

Samuel of G^d (s. of James the emigrant), b. May 3, 1676; m. —— ——. Issue:—James, b. June 18, 1706, m. Sept. 1729 Allye or Aaltje Ryder, b. June 8, 1712. The (sup.) will of James is da. Apl. 13, 1798, and pro. Jan. 11, 1799; he resided in G^d, and had children:—Johanna, b. Aug. 30, 1730, and d. young; Bernardus, b. Feb. 1, 1732, m. Nov. 18, 1756, Neeltje Lake; Elizabeth, b. 1733 and d. young; Adriaentje, b. 1735 and d. young; Areantje, b. Dec. 7, 1736, and (sup.) m. Jacobus Lake; Phebe, b. 1739 and d. young; Samuel, b. Apl. 25, 1742, m. 1st Catryna ——, m. 2^d, Mar. 26, 1774, Ann Emans (from Samuel and Bernardus are descended the G^d branch of the family); Jacobus of N. J., b. May 23, 1744, m. Nov. 17, 1765, Rebecca Swart, and is the ancestor of the Monmouth Co. branch of the family; Elias of Fld^s, b. Feb. 13, 1746, d. Dec. 31, 1832, m. Margaret Lake, and is the ancestor of the Fld^s branch of the family; Johanna, b. July 28, 1748; Stephen of G^d, b. May 28, 1752, m. Maria Ryder; and James, bp. Mar. 25, 1764, d. Nov. 23, 1798. Signed his name *"Samwell Hubbard."*

HUBERTSEN, ADRIAEN, obtained a patent Dec. 12, 1653, for a lot at Br^n ferry, as per p. 588 of Vol. II. of O'Callaghan's New Netherlands. Was of Rensselaerswyck in 1648.

HUDDEN, ANDRES, m. Geertie ——; d. Nov. 4, 1663, at Appoqinimy, on his way to Maryland. Emigrated in 1629, and was one of the burgomasters of N. A., holding various public offices during most of his life. July 2, 1638, he and Wolfert Gerretse Van Couwenhoven obtained a patent for the westernmost of the 3 flats in Fld^s. He also obtained a patent for 37 morgens in Br^n. Issue:—Aeltje, bp. Mar. 18, 1640; Hendrick, bp. Sept. 28, 1642; Hendrick, bp. Jan. 13, 1644; and Rutgert, bp. June 26, 1660—all bp. in N: A. Signed his name *"Andres Hudden."*

HUDDLESTON, WILLIAM, m. Sara ——. Bought the main part of the Pieter Cesar's patent at the Walabocht Aug. 8,

1695, as per p. 70 of Lib. 2 of Con. There was a Wm Huddleston, clerk of Orange Co., in 1703, as per p. 43 of Ruttenberg's Orange Co.

HUETT, RANDELL, had a plantation granted to him Mar. 5, 1650, in G^d, as per G^d rec.

HUIKEN, see Huycken.

HUISMAN, GERRET CORNELISE, a resident of Fl^h, acknowledged May 3, 1663, in the presence of the magistrates of said town that he was indebted to Huick Barentse de Klyn of N. A. in the sum of 493 gl. 15 st., as per p. 132 of Lib. B of Fl^h court rec. Made his mark to documents.

HULET, WILLIAM, on ass. roll of Fld^a of 1676.

HULSARDT, HOLSAERT, HULST, or HOLST, ANTHONY, probably from "Hulst," a town in Zeeland, a (sup.) s. of Johannes of Fld^a. Aug. 27, 1710, he was paid by the D. ch. of N. U. 108 gl. for his services, probably as precentor. Of N. U. in 1719. Signed his name *"Anthony Holsaert."*

Benjamin (sup. s. of Johannes), m. Annetje Luyster, and settled at Marlborough, Monmouth Co., N. J., where he had several children bp. Signed his name *"Benjamin Holsaert."*

Johannes, emigrated from Sluys in Flanders in 1684, and settled in Fld^a; m. 1st Johanna Havens; m. 2^d, Oct. 11, 1686, Debby Blake. Supposed issue:—Anthony; Benjamin; Cornelis; and Gerardus, bp. Sept. 5, 1685. Signed his name *"Yohannes Holsaerdt."*

Tomas, a pauper, who d. in 1692, as per Fld^a R. D. ch. rec.

HUNT, RALPH, (sup.) English, of G^d in 1674, as per town rec. Made his mark to documents. A Ralph Hunt, ag. 22, was transported to Va. in 1635, as per p. 115 of Hotten's Emigrants.

HUTCHINSEN, WILLEM, leased land in Bu^k July 2, 1643, of Ab^m Rycken, as per p. 23 of Cal. of Dutch Man.

HUYBERSE, ADRIAEN, m. 1st *Judith Roberts;* m. 2^d, May 3, 1663, *Thysie Gerrets*, wid. Obtained Dec. 12, 1663, a patent for a lot at Brⁿ ferry; also Nov. 14, 1654, a patent for 22½ morgens at Mespat, and Jan. 26, 1664, a patent for 24 morgens at Mespat, as per pp. 381 and 387 of Cal. of Dutch His. Man. Issue:—Huybert, bp. Sept. 15, 1652; Ariaentje, bp. Aug. 20, 1660; Geertje, bp. Feb. 18, 1663; and Frank, bp. Feb. 3, 1664—all in N. A. Signed his name *"Adriaen Huyberse."*

Barent, see Egbertse.

Lambert, see Lambert Huybertsen Moll.

HUYCKEN or HEOCKEN, WILLEM, tailor, of Gowanus, emigrated in 1663; m. *Annetje Andrieas Willjard*, who after his death m. 2[d] Simon Aesen De Hart. Mem. of R. D. ch. of Br[n] in 1677, and of R. D. ch. of Fld[t] in 1675, where he then resided; and took the oath of allegiance in Br[n] in 1687. Bought one half of Cornelis Lambertse Cool's patent at Gowanus of Paulus Vanderbeek, he selling the other one half to Cornelis Gerretse Van Duyn. (The Huycken part was afterwards owned by Anthony Hulst, and the Van Duyn part by Peter Wyckoff.) This patent passed from Cool to Bredenbent, and from the latter to Vanderbeek. Issue:—Jacob, bp. Dec. 29, 1666, in N. Y.; Jannetje, bp. Jan. 28, 1683, in Br[n]; Margaret, bp. July 29, 1688, in Br[n]; Marretje, m. Denyse Gerretse Van Duyn; Machtel or Matilda, m. Cor[s] Gerretse Van Duyn; Annetje; Geertruy; Catharine; and Elizabeth. Signed his name *"Wyellem Heocken."*

HUYGES, JACOB, plaintiff in a suit against Hendrick Mattysen (Smack), Aug. 27, 1659, as per Lib. B of Fl[h] rec.

HUYLE, DIRK, a justice of the peace of Kings Co. in 1693, as per p. 28 of Vol. IV. of N. Y. Doc. of Col. His.

HUYSBERTSEN, LAMBERT, see Moll. ·

HUYSEN, DERICK. He and Rynier Bastiaensen Van Giesen bought Mar. 31, 1661, of Tuenis Hillebrants a house, barn, and lot in the village of Fl[h] on the S. side of the church, as per p. 58 of Lib. B of Fl[h] rec.

HYBON, see Hibon.

HYMEN, HAMEN, on Stoothoff's books of 1695.

IDENS, IDENSEN, IDESSE, or YDESSE, TEUNIS (VAN HUYNN), b. 1639; m. *Jannetje Thyssen Van Pelt.* Owned and occupied a village plot in N. U. in 1661, and also lands at Haerlem in 1690, and in 1680 joined the R. D. ch. in N. Y. He paid a marriage-fee to Fl[h] ch. in 1664. Issue:—Ide, bp. Feb. 11, 1674; Joost, bp. June 27, 1677; Dina, bp. Jan. 22, 1679; Saertje, bp. May 14, 1681; Catalyntje, bp. Sept. 6, 1685; and Catalyntje, bp. Nov. 28, 1686—all bp. in N. Y.

ISAACS or ISAACZEN, ARENT, m. 1st *Geertie Everts;* m. 2d *Styntje Laurens.* He and his w. Geertie mem. of the D. ch. of N. A. prior to 1660; in 1664 he took the oath of allegiance in N. Y. to the English, and on ass. roll of Brn of 1676. Issue:—Vroutje, b. 1657; Catharine, b. 1666; Vroutje, bp. Nov. 17, 1672; Maria, bp. July 3, 1675—all bp. in N. A. and N. Y.; and Roelof, bp. Sept. 30, 1677, in Brn.

Jan, see Hegeman.

JACOBSE or JACOBSEN, see Van Nuyse and Vandewater.
Aechtje of Fld, m. Oct. 31, 1677, at N. Y., Johannes Thomaszen from Amsterdam.
Barent, m. Marretje dau. of Leendert Arendsen, as per Flh ch. rec., where at one period he appears to have resided. Issue:—Aeltje, bp. Sept. 20, 1640; Dievertje, bp. Feb. 1, 1642; Appolonia, bp. Jan. 29, 1645; Leendert, bp. Dec. 1, 1647; Tryntje, bp. Dec. 22, 1647; Theunis, bp. Aug. 17, 1653; Pieter, bp. Aug. 29, 1657; and Arent, bp. Oct. 9, 1660—all bp. in N. A.
Bartel, and Helena Doulis had a s. Jacob bp. Oct. 5, 1685, in Brn.
Bartelt, b. 1677, a s. of Jacob Hendrickse and Geesje of Flh.
Christian, see Wolfe.
Claes, see Larzelear.
Cornelis, see Stille and Vandewater.
Cornelis, on ass. roll of Flh of 1675 and town rec. of 1666. Signed his name "*Cornelis Jacobse.*"
Frederick, see Bergen.
George, of Brn ferry in 1692, per a deed on p. 108 of Lib. I. of Con.
Hans, see Bergen.
Harman, on ass. roll of Brn of 1693.
Hendrick, see Brinckerhoff.
Hendrick, b. about 1680, a s. of Jacob Hendrickse and Geesje of Flh.
Jacob, see Bergen and Jacob Jorise.
Jan, and Evertje Bogaert had a s. Jacob bp. Oct. 8, 1662, in Brn.
Jan from Nortwyck, m. Jan. 27, 1680, Margaret dau. of Gerret Janse Snediker.
Jan, among the first settlers of N. U. in 1657, and allotted a plantation, but no evidence of his having occupied it.
John, see Couwenhoven.
Johannes, see Vander Grift.
Joris from Amsterdam, b. 1626; m. Tryntje Claesen. Resided at the ferry; made an affidavit in 1664 relating to

Capt. Scott's raid; on ass. rolls of Br^n of 1675 and '83; on Br^n patents of 1667 and '77, as per Thompson's L. I. Bought a house and lot at the ferry May 7, 1660, of Cornelis Dirksen Hoogland, which he obtained of John Haas, as per p. 6 of Vol. I. of Land Papers and per p. 81 of Vol. I. of Con. Mem. of the R. D. ch. of Br^n in 1677. Issue:—Jacob Jorise of Fld^{a} and Bedford, bp. May 20, 1652; Aefje Jorise, bp. June 12, 1661; Marretje Jorise; Harman Jorise of the ferry, bp. Oct. 21, 1666; Cornelis Jorise of the ferry; Agatha Jorise; and Willem Jorise. Made his mark to documents.

Nicholas, see Vander Grift.

Pieter, owned a lot in Fl^h prior to 1680, as per p. 44 of Lib. A of Fl^h rec.

Pieter, on Bu^k ass. roll of 1683.

Pieter, allotted a plot or farm in N. U. in 1657 which he sold to Lucas Mayerse, as per town rec. and as per p. 117 of Lib. C of Fl^h rec. On ass. roll of N. U. of 1676, and owned a farm on N. U. Lane in 1681. A Pieter Jacobsen obtained Dec. 5, 1679, a patent for 35 A. on Manhattan I. A Pieter Jacobsen, from Uitdam in North Holland, m. Oct. 20, 1689, Rebecca Jans of Bruynenburg (in N. U.), as per p. 121 of Vol X. of the Genealogical Record.

Pieter, see Buys and Noortbrook.

Robert, a patentee of N. U. in 1668, per Thompson's L. I.

Thomas, s. of Lysbeth Thomas of Bedford, 1695.

Tileman, see Vander Hard.

Tyleman, on ass. roll of N. U. of 1683.

Wilhelmus, see Bennet.

William, see Boerum and Van Nuyse.

Willem, on ass. roll of Bu^k of 1675.

JAMES, CRAZY, supported by the R. D. ch. of N. U. in 1679, etc., as a pauper.

JANEVIER, WILLEM, of Bu^k in 1663, as per p. 335 of Vol. II. of Stiles's Br^n.

JANNBEUS, on application for a canal at Red Hoek, Br^a, in 1664, as per p. 68 of Vol. I. of Stiles's Br^n.

JANSE or JANSEN, ABRAHAM, carpenter, of Bu^k Jan. 28, 1664, per Col. Man. Permission granted him Feb. 7, 1664, to build a mill at Mespath Kils. See p. 259 of Cal. of Dutch His. Man. Charged for payment of his share of the salary of the clergyman in Bu^k in 1666, as per town rec. An Ab^m Janse paid Apl. 4, 1665, 8 gl. towards the clergyman's salary in Fl^h, as per town rec. Aug. 10, 1659, an Abraham Jansen, from "Zuydtland" in the land of Brielle, South Holland, m. in N. A. Tryntje Kip from Amsterdam. An Ab^m Janzen took the oath of allegiance to the English in N. Y. in 1664.

Abraham (a mulatto) of Br^n, with others summoned Mar. 26, 1658, to appear before the council for abusing Sheriff Tonneman while collecting Do. Polhemius's salary, and fined 12 gl. ($4.80), his excuse of not understanding the Dutch being viewed as frivolous, as per pp. 193 and 194 of Cal. of Dutch His. Man.

Abraham, see Luqueer, Van Dyck, Ver Kerk, and Ver Rhyn.

Ackeus or *Agyas*, see Van Dyck.

Adam, see Buys.

Aert, see Van Pelt and Ver Kerk.

Albert, see Terhune and Van Heemst.

Amstelhoop Jan. Catharine Cronenbergh and Richard Paynten bought Aug. 27, 1679, of Rutgert Albertse his house, orchard, etc., in Fl^h for 3000 gl., in which purchase he appears to have been interested, as per p. 54 of Lib. AA of Fl^h rec. Apl. 12, 1683, he bought of R. Albertse a house and lot in Fl^h, as per p. 29 of Lib. D of Fl^h rec. Made his mark to documents.

Andries or *Andrew*, cooper, m. Grietje ——. On ass. roll of Fl^h of 1693 and cen. of 1698. Bought Feb. 1, 1693-4, a house and lot in Fl^h, as per p. 191 of Lib. A of Fl^h rec. In his will, da. Jan. 7, 1712-13, and rec. Apl. 8, 1718, on p. 83 of Lib. B of Fl^h rec., he names his dau. Hilitie Andriese w. of Peter Van Norstrand, and on p. 84 his dau. Jannetje Andriese w. of Hendrick Van Voorhees. Had also a dau. Alida and s. Lucas. Signed his name *"Andries Jansen."*

Andries of N. U., m. Jan. 25, 1690, Hendrickje or Hanna Mynders dau. of Myndert Korten of N. U. On ass. roll of N. U. of 1693, cen. of 1698 and 1704, and constable in 1695. He finally removed to Middletown, Monmouth Co., N. J. Issue:—Corten or Korten Andries. Signed his name *"Andres Jansen."*

Andries, m. Geertje Andriessen, and had a s. Jan bp. May 5, 1695, in Br^n.

Anthony from Salee, Vaes or Fez, emigrated at an early date to N. A., where he resided from 1633 to '39, owning a town lot and a bouwery. He m. 1st Grietje Reiniers; m. 2^d, in 1670, Metje Gravenraet, and d. about 1676 intestate. In Apl. 1639 he and his wife were banished from N. A. in consequence of their being slanderous and troublesome persons. He, however, appears to have managed to remain in the town until Aug. 3, 1639, when on petition he was granted by the Director-Gen. or Gov. Kieft 100 morgens on the W.

end of L. I., lying within the present bounds of N. U. and G^d, to which he removed, and for which the patent was dated May 27, 1643. Feb. 9, 1660, he sold his patent to Nicholas Stillwell for 1600 gl. and the fee of plantation-lot No. 29 in G^d, with the buildings and improvements thereon, which plantation-lot Anthony sold Dec. 1669 to Fernandus Van Sickelen, his son-in-law. After this he appears to have removed back to N. A., where he died. Anthony's patent during this period was known as " Turk's plantation," from his being designated as " Turk" on some of the old records. Stillwell sold said patent Feb. 28, 1664, to Francois de Bruynne, after whom it was called Bruynnsberg. June 4, 1665, De Bruynne sold a part of the patent located on the main road from the village of N. U. to G^d, and on the old Bath road or lane, to Jan Janse Ver Ryne. Dec. 10, 1678, he sold the remainder, through Anna his wife as his attorney, to Barent Joosten and Jan Hansen (Van Noortstrand). June 1, 1696, Jan Hansen of N. U. sold to Barent Joosten his one half of " Turk's plantation," containing 100 A., as per p. 98 of Lib. 2 of Con., and on the same date Joosten and Hansen conveyed the one half of said plantation to Gerret Coerten (Voorhies), as per p. 99 of said Lib. 2. Oct. 9, 1699, Gerret Coerten of N. U., as per p. 203 of said Lib., sold to Albert Coerten his s. one half of said plantation, and Feb. 12, 1702-3, Barent Joosten of N. U. sold to said Albert Coerten his one half of the same, as per p. 261 of said Lib. 2, thus · making Albert the sole owner of the whole of the patent, except the part sold to Ver Ryne. May 9, 1747, Albert Coerten conveyed to his son Coert Voorhies, and Oct. 5, 1756, Coert conveyed to his sons Coert and Barnardus said premises. In 1879, in levelling the sand-dunes on the upland on the edge of the bay a little S.E. of the buildings of Mr. Gunther at Locust Grove, which dunes had been blown up from the beach, and which had been gradually extending back with the abrasion of. the shore or coast, the remains of two separate pieces of stone wall about 2 ft. high and 1 ft. wide, made mainly of unbroken field-stones laid in clay mortar, with a clay floor between them, were exhumed. These remains were covered with from 4 to 10 ft. of sand, and are probably those of the barn or other farm buildings of Anthony Jansen, it being customary in the early settlement of this country to construct their threshing-floors of clay, of which specimens existed and were in use in this country in the younger days of the author, their roofs being made of thatched straw instead of shingles, as at present. Issue by 1st wife:—Annica, who m. Thomas Southard of G^d; Cornelia, who m. William Johnson of N. Y.; Sara, who m.

John Emans of G^d; and Eva, b. 1641, who m. Ferdinandus Van Sickelen of Fld^s. Made his mark "A I" to documents.

Anthony, see Westbrook.

Arens, paid minister's salary in Fl^h in 1681, per town rec. There was an Arent Janse, master carpenter, in 1641, in the service of the West India Company, and an Arent Janse, "moesman" (porridgeman), who signed the petition to the Director-Gen. and Council in 1664 advising surrender to the English to avoid useless bloodshed, as per p. 249 of Vol. II. of Doc. of Col. His.

Aris, see Vanderbilt.

Auke or *Ouke*, see Van Nuys.

Barent, took the oath of allegiance in Fl^h in 1687 as a native, where he paid a marriage-fee May 3, 1665.

Barent, b. 1608; m. Wylemyntie Pieters, and of Br^n in 1651 and '70, per Col. Man., at which place he bought Manje's patent Jan. 29, 1652. In 1664 he made an affidavit relating to Capt. Scott's raid on the Dutch towns on L. I. Oct. 31, 1671, Aucke Janse (Van Nuyse) and Symon Hansen (Van Nortstrand) accounted as his administrators. Aug. 25, 1674, Jan Barentse, Aucke Janse, and Symon Hansen, as guardians of the children of Barent Janse, dec. (procured by Wylemyntie Pieters, dec., residing in "Midwout"), sold a farm to Derick Janse Woertman, as per p. 107 of Lib. A of Fl^h rec. Issue:— Jan Barendsz; Claes Barendsz; Engel Barendsz; and Tytje Barendsz, as per Fl^h rec. Made his mark "B I" to documents.

Barent of Br^n, killed with a knife about 1665 by Albert Cornelise Wantanaer in self-defence, and dying of the wound the same day, as per p. 103 of the Bergen Genealogy. Suppose this to be Barent Janse Blom. Made his mark to documents.

Barent of Bu^k, sold Feb. 17, 1697-8, land to Peter Willemse of the same place, as per p. 158 of Lib. 2 of Con.

Barent, m. Annetien ——. May 3, 1661, Derick Janse, cooper, sold to Annetien wid. of Barent Janse, dec., a bouwery at Gowanus between Teunis Nyssen's (Denyse) and Jan Pieterse's (Staats), in size as per patent, as per p. 69 of Lib. B of Fl^h rec.

Barent of G^d. Apl. 16, 1680, his name appears among the freeholders of G^d, who conveyed some 5 A. of land to "Jacobus Ouke" (Van Nuyse), as per G^d rec. Made his mark to documents.

Barent, see Bal, Blom, and Ver Kerk.

Benjamen and *Cornelis*, see Van Cleef.

Bernardes of Yellow Hoek, N. U., m. Jannetie ——. As-

sessed for 48 A. in 1706. Will da. Mar. 10, 1715-16; pro.
July 7, 1719; executors, Claes and Hendrick Van Dyck. Issue:—Jan. Signed his name *"Bernardes Janse."*

Carel or *Charles*, see Van Dyke.

Carsen, Caersten, or *Kaersten,* bought Jan. 21, 1666, of Dirck
Jansen ("cuyper," or cooper) a farm in Fl^h on the S. side
of that of Arent Moelenaer, as per p. 47 of Lib. D of Fl^h rec.
Allotted Aug. 6, 1668, on the division of the Fl^h meadows at
Canarisie, a lot. His mother was buried in Fl^h ch'. Nov. 5,
1665. He appears to have resided in G^d in 1677. Jan. 10,
1695-6, he sold, as attorney of his son Peter, 2 lots of meadows
in G^d to John Lake; and in 1697 he sold his house and lot
in G^d, which he had bought of Michael Spicer, to Jacobus
Emans, as per G^d rec. A Carsten Janssen obtained a patent
from Gov. Stuyvesant Oct. 25, 1653, for a lot in Albany, as
per Pearson's Albany rec. Issue:—Jan Carsen; and Peter
Carsen or Carsonsenn. Signed his name *" Carsen Jansen."*

Casper, m. Fransyntie ——. On ass. roll of Br^n of 1683,
and in 1687 took the oath of allegiance in the same place
as a native. Bought Apl. 16, 1689, of Hendrick Claasen a
lot in Bedford, as per p. 143 of Lib. 1 of Con. Indicted at
the sessions of Nov. 1692 for an assault, as per court rec.

Caspert, on ass. roll of Bu^k of 1675.

Christian, owned land in the village of Fl^h in 1670, as per
p. 10 of Lib A of Fl^h rec.

Christoffel, carpenter, m. Lysbeth Jans. On ass. roll of
Fl^h of 1675, and mem. of R. D. ch. of Fl^h in 1677. Feb. 20,
1678-9, he sold to Louris Cornelise of Mespath Kil 2 lots of
woodland in the new lots of Fl^h, Nos. 32 and 33, purchased of
Minne Johannis for 3000 gl., as per p. 20 of Lib. AA of Fl^h
rec., and sold by said Louris Jan. 7, 1679-80, to Cornelis Janse
de Seeuw, as per p. 89 of said Lib. Dec. 29, 1687, styling
himself farmer of G^d, he again appears to have conveyed
the same premises to " Laarens Cornelise" of New Aarnhem
in Bu^k, as per Lib. A of Fl^h rec., from which it may be inferred they had been reconveyed to him. In 1681 he appears to have resided in Fld^s. Issue:—Johannes Christoffelse. Signed his name *"Stoffel Janse."*

Claes, see Van Naerden, Van Purmerent, and Romeyn.

Claes, on ass. roll of G^d of 1683. Probably Klaes Jansen
Romeyn. Signed his name *"Klaes Jansen."*

Claes, a s. of Jan Claesen and Lysbeth Jans, said Jan dy-
ing and Lysbeth marrying Auke Janse Van Nuyse prior to
Dec. 16, 1666, as per p. 85 of Lib. D of Fl^h rec. A Claes
Janszen took the oath of allegiance in N. Y. in 1664 to the
English.

John Emans of G^d; and Eva, b. 1641.   ...tent for land
Van Sickelen of Fld^s. Made his   : 1638. Signed
ments.

Anthony, see Westbrook.   ...n Aleck, Vander-
Arens, paid minister's salary in   ...d De Seen.
There was an Arent Janse, ma...
service of the West India C...   h. in 1662.
"moesman" (porridgeman), .   Col. Man.
Director-Gen. and Council
the English to avoid usele...
II. of Doc. of Col. His.   . Cuyper, Hoogland, Mid-
Aris, see Vanderbilt.   Vliet, and Woertman.
Auke or *Ouke*, see V   :3, 1661, to Annetien Pieter-
Barent, took the oa...   . farm at Gowanus between the
tive, where he paid ...   ...se) and that of Jan Pieterse
Barent, b. 1608: n   ...9, 1661, he bought of Engelbert
and '70, per Col. M   ...de of the road in Fl^h, with plain
tent Jan. 29, 165   ...ging thereto, as per p. 52 of Lib.
Capt. Scott's r...   ..., he was allotted a building-plot at
Aucke Janse (...age of Fl^h, in pursuance of the patent
strand) acc...   ...of Lib. A of Fl^h rec. Signed his
Barentse, A
the childr...   : .700.
Pieters. ...   ., 1632. In 1663 Dirck Jansen of the
Janse W   ...arged by authorities for 1 lb. powder, as
Jan Ba   ...l. of Doc. of Col. His. of N. Y. Feb. 19,
Baren   ...of the ferry made an affidavit relating to
mer...   ...gainst the Dutch towns of L. I., as per p.
/'   ... In 1683 his name appears on the ass. roll
C   ...s name "*Dirck Jansen*."
:'   ...Medemblik, North Holland, shipwright, sold
    ...uildings in Fl^h to Cornelis Van Ruyven, as
    Vol. III. of O'Callaghan's Man. Trans. of Col.
    ...his name "*Deirck Janse*" in 1670.
    ...om Bergen, m. 1st, June 28, 1664, Gesstje Pieters;
    ...17, 1685, Elizabeth Simons Van Uythuysen of

    ...see Ditmars.
    ...on the list of those who paid the clergyman's salary
    ...o8o and '81.
    ...mem. of R. D. ch. of Fl^h in 1677.
    ...see Van Meckelen and Van Wickelen.
    ..., carpenter, owned lands in Fl^h in 1660, as per deed of
    ...and to Coerten on p. 37 of Lib. B of Fl^h rec. In 1661
    ...was a suit pending between him and Govert Loockermans
    ...a lot in Fld^s, as per p. 228 of Cal. of Dutch Man.
    ...w, see Van Hoochten.

Garret and Geertje Reyniers his w., mem. of Fl^h R. D. ch. ·'77, entered on the record as moved.

·ret Dierckse, of Fl^h in 1660. Made his mark to docu- ·.

Gerret, see Cowenhoven, Dorland, and Snedeker.

Gillis or *Jillis*, on ass. roll of N. U. in 1675, and of Fl^h in 1675 and '76.

Gisbert or *Gysbert*, weaver, m. Sophia or Feytien Van Putten dau. of Jan Hermansen. On ass. roll of Fl^h of 1675 and cen. of 1698. Jan. 23, 1679-80, he bought of Cornelis Berrien his house and lot in Fl^h, as per p. 99 of Lib. AA of Fl^h rec. July 16, 1695, he sold a house and orchard in Fl^h to John Hermanse, as per p. 63 of Lib. 2 of Con. Issue:—Heyltje Gysbertse, bp. May 12, 1678, in Fl^h; Geertruyt Gysbertse, bp. Nov. 14, 1680, in N. U.; Martha Gysbertse, bp. May 27, 1683, in Fl^h; and Harman Gysbertse. Made his mark to documents.

Gisbert, on ass. roll of Br^n of 1693.

Hans, see Van Nostrand.

Hans, emigrated in 1640, took the oath of allegiance in Fld^s in 1687, and sold land in Fld^s to Lucas Stevense (Voorhees), as per deed of Garret Stoothoff and others of Feb. 3, 1696-7, on p. 114 of Lib. 2 of Con.

Hanse of Br^n, accused July 22, 1647, of appropriating or raiding on the maize (Indian corn) belonging to the Indians in this county, as per p. 111 of Cal. of Dutch Man.

Harman, see Barkeloo and Blauw.

Hartman Antoni. Oct. 27, 1661, Aerseltien Dircks of Fort Orange, as attorney of Hartman, sold to Gerret Cornelise 18 morgens in Fl^h on the E. side of the road, as per p. 87 of Lib. B of Fl^h rec.

Hendrick, m. Elizabeth Lake, and suppose he resided in G^d. Issue:—Phebe, bp. Apl. 6, 1677; Phebe, bp. Mar. 30, 1683; Maria, bp. Mar. 30, 1683; and Court, bp. Dec. 25, 1696.

Hendrick, m. Geurtien Hendricks, and had a dau. Aertje Hendrickse bp. June 11, 1677, in Br^n. Mem. of R. D. ch. of Br^n in 1677.

Hendrick, m. Marretje or Maria Jans. On ass. roll of Br^n of 1693, on that of Bu^k of 1693 and cen. of 1698. Issue:—Cornelia Hendricks, bp. Feb. 1, 1685, in Fld^s; Marretje Hendricks, bp. July 29, 1688, in Br^n; Arien Hendricks, bp. Jan. 12, 1690, in Br^n; Susanna Hendricks, bp. Aug. 6, 1692; Wouter Hendricks, bp. Nov. 14, 1694; and Annetje Hendricks, bp. July 10, 1698, in Br^n.

Hendrick (sup.) of Br^n, m. Hester Cartoys. Issue:—Anneke bp. July 10, 1688; Annetje, bp. —— 1693; Anna Maria, bp. Dec. 10, 1695; Femmetje, bp. Apl. 25, 1696; and Geertje, bp. Apl. 11, 1700.

· *Claes* (" ruyter," or horseman), obtained a patent for land in Br^n Sept. 30, 1645. Of Rensselaerwyck in 1638. Signed his name "*Claes Janse.*"

Cornelis, see Berrian, Boomgart, Loy, Van Aleck, Vanderveer, Van Deventer, Ver Kerk, Zieuw, and De Seen.

Cornelis, on ass. roll of Bu^k of 1675.

Cornelis, a catechumen of Br^n R. D. ch. in 1662.

Cornelis, of G^d Feb. 5, 1656, as per Col. Man.

Creyn, see Van Mater.

Daniel, see Lake.

Derick, see Amerman, Ameland, Cuyper, Hoogland, Middagh, Sutphen, Van Dyck, Van Vliet, and Woertman.

Derick, cooper, conveyed May 23, 1661, to Annetien Pietersen wid. of Barent Janse, dec., a farm at Gowanus between the farms of Teunis Nyssen (Denyse) and that of Jan Pieterse (Staats), as per Fl^h rec. Feb. 19, 1661, he bought of Engelbert Steenhuys a farm on the E. side of the road in Fl^h, with plain land and salt meadows belonging thereto, as per p. 52 of Lib. B of Fl^h rec. May 30, 1670, he was allotted a building-plot at " Rustenburgh" in the village of Fl^h, in pursuance of the patent of the town, as per p. 10 of Lib. A of Fl^h rec. Signed his name "*Deirck Jansen.*"

Derrick, of N. U. in 1700.

Derrick or *Dirck*, b. 1632. In 1663 Dirck Jansen of the " Walebocht " was charged by authorities for 1 lb. powder, as per p. 464 of Vol. II. of Doc. of Col. His. of N. Y. Feb. 19, 1664, Dirck Jansen of the ferry made an affidavit relating to Capt. Scott's raid against the Dutch towns of L. I., as per p. 482 of said Vol. II. In 1683 his name appears on the ass. roll of Br^n. Signed his name "*Dirck Jansen.*"

Dirk, from Medemblik, North Holland, shipwright, sold his farm and buildings in Fl^h to Cornelis Van Ruyven, as per p. 344 of Vol. III. of O'Callaghan's Man. Trans. of Col. Man. Signed his name "*Deirck Janse*" in 1670.

Ditmars from Bergen, m. 1st, June 28, 1664, Gesstje Pieters; m. 2^d, Mar. 17, 1685, Elizabeth Simons Van Uythuysen of Br^n.

Douwe, see Ditmars.

Egbert, on the list of those who paid the clergyman's salary in Fl^h in 1680 and '81.

Everd, mem. of R. D. ch. of Fl^h in 1677.

Evert, see Van Meckelen and Van Wickelen.

Frans, carpenter, owned lands in Fl^h in 1660, as per deed of Hoogland to Coerten on p. 37 of Lib. B of Fl^h rec. In 1661 there was a suit pending between him and Govert Loockermans about a lot in Fld', as per p. 228 of Cal. of Dutch Man.

Frans, see Van Hoochten.

Garret and Geertje Reyniers his w., mem. of Fl[h] R. D. ch. in 1677, entered on the record as moved.

Gerret Dierckse, of Fl[h] in 1660. Made his mark to documents.

Gerret, see Cowenhoven, Dorland, and Snedeker.

Gillis or *Jillis*, on ass. roll of N. U. in 1675, and of Fl[h] in 1675 and '76.

Gisbert or *Gysbert*, weaver, m. Sophia or Feytien Van Putten dau. of Jan Hermansen. On ass. roll of Fl[h] of 1675 and cen. of 1698. Jan. 23, 1679-80, he bought of Cornelis Berrien his house and lot in Fl[h], as per p. 99 of Lib. AA of Fl[h] rec. July 16, 1695, he sold a house and orchard in Fl[h] to John Hermanse, as per p. 63 of Lib. 2 of Con. Issue:—Heyltje Gysbertse, bp. May 12, 1678, in Fl[h]; Geertruyt Gysbertse, bp. Nov. 14, 1680, in N. U.; Martha Gysbertse, bp. May 27, 1683, in Fl[h]; and Harman Gysbertse. Made his mark to documents.

Gisbert, on ass. roll of Br[n] of 1693.

Hans, see Van Nostrand.

Hans, emigrated in 1640, took the oath of allegiance in Fld[e] in 1687, and sold land in Fld[e] to Lucas Stevense (Voorhees), as per deed of Garret Stoothoff and others of Feb. 3, 1696-7, on p. 114 of Lib. 2 of Con.

Hanse of Br[n], accused July 22, 1647, of appropriating or raiding on the maize (Indian corn) belonging to the Indians in this county, as per p. 111 of Cal. of Dutch Man.

Harman, see Barkeloo and Blauw.

Hartman Antoni. Oct. 27, 1661, Aerseltien Dircks of Fort Orange, as attorney of Hartman, sold to Gerret Cornelise 18 morgens in Fl[h] on the E. side of the road, as per p. 87 of Lib. B of Fl[h] rec.

Hendrick, m. Elizabeth Lake, and suppose he resided in G[d]. Issue:—Phebe, bp. Apl. 6, 1677; Phebe, bp. Mar. 30, 1683; Maria, bp. Mar. 30, 1683; and Court, bp. Dec. 25, 1696.

Hendrick, m. Geurtien Hendricks, and had a dau. Aertje Hendrickse bp. June 11, 1677, in Br[n]. Mem. of R. D. ch. of Br[n] in 1677.

Hendrick, m. Marretje or Maria Jans. On ass. roll of Br[n] of 1693, on that of Bu[k] of 1693 and cen. of 1698. Issue:—Cornelia Hendricks, bp. Feb. 1, 1685, in Fld[e]; Marretje Hendricks, bp. July 29, 1688, in Br[n]; Arien Hendricks, bp. Jan. 12, 1690, in Br[n]; Susanna Hendricks, bp. Aug. 6, 1692; Wouter Hendricks, bp. Nov. 14, 1694; and Annetje Hendricks, bp. July 10, 1698, in Br[n].

Hendrick (sup.) of Br[n], m. Hester Cartoys. Issue:—Anneke bp. July 10, 1688; Annetje, bp. —— 1693; Anna Maria, bp. Dec. 10, 1695; Femmetje, bp. Apl. 25, 1696; and Geertje, bp. Apl. 11, 1700.

Hendrick, b. in Fld[a] and a resident of Br[n]; m. Jan. 21, 1688, Hester Hidelte of N. Y. Name on ass. roll of Br[n] of 1683. Issue:—Geertje Hendricks, bp. Aug. 11, 1700, in Br[n].

Hendrick. A Hendrick Jansen leased land at the Wallabout Aug. 31, 1651, as per Col. Man. A Hendrick Janse's name among those who, May 26, 1663, requested leave to form a hamlet in the rear of the "Walebocht," as per p. 107 of Vol. X. of Col. Man. And a Hendrick Janse, a journeyman, at a coroner's inquest on a body on the beach at Gowanus between Symon Aesen (De Hart's) and Elyas Symonse (De Hart's), May 12, 1698.

Hendrick, m. Hendrickje Meinders (sup.) wid. of Andries Jansen, dau. of Meindert Korten. Issue:—Meindert, bp. Apl. 25, 1696, in Br[n].

Hendrick, m. Geertje Andriessen, and had a dau. Jannetje Hendricks bp. Oct. 15, 1698, in Br[n].

Hendrick, m. Geertje Verkerk. Mem. of R. D. ch. of N. U. in 1682; on ass. roll of said town of 1693; and of N. Y. in 1704. Made his mark " H I " to documents.

Hendrick, was allotted Sept. 12, 1670, in pursuance of the patent of Fl[h], a farm in said town, between the lands of Gerret Lubbertse and those of Jan Cornelise Boomgart, of 29 morgens, with plain land and salt meadows, as per p. 11 of Lib. A of Fl[h] rec. In 1687 he took the oath of allegiance in Fl[h] as a native. Made his mark to documents.

Hendrick of N. U., m. Mary (sup.) Korten. Allotted 6 women's and 6 men's places in the new R. D. ch. of N. U. in 1700, of which he was a deacon in 1711. Bought Oct. 20, 1724, of Benjamen Steymets a farm of 76¾ A. in N. U. on the E. side of De Bruynne's or Bath Lane, now of the heirs of Maria w. of Egbert Benson. His w. Maria Korten inherited from her father Meyndert Korten his farm on the S.E. side of said Bath Lane. Issue:—Meyndert; Jan; Hendrick Jun[r]; Peter of N. J.; Court; Mary or Maria; and Jannetje.

Hendrick, see Cammega, Creven, Buys, Oesteroem, Van Erurde, Van Dyck, Ver Kerk, and Van Pelt.

Herbert, paid 2 gl. 9 st. towards the preacher's salary in Fl[h] in 1681.

Hubert, see Stook.

Huybert. Aug. 8, 1644, Huybert Jansen, with others, was found guilty of cutting Peter Wolpherson (Van Couenhoven's) wainscot with their cutlasses, for which he was sentenced to ride the wooden horse for 3 hours, as per p. 90 of Cal. of Dutch Man. Feb. 15, 1656, a judgment was obtained against him by Cornelia Johnson for slander in the court of G[d], as per p. 160 of do. There was a Huybert Janse in Albany in 1667, whose surname was De Vroome.

Isaac, see Van Nuyse.

Isbrant, see Van Cleef.

Jabecq, on ass. roll of Fld[a] of 1675.

Jacob, see Vanderbilt.

Jacob of Bu[k], where he took the oath of allegiance in 1687 as a native; m. Anna Fonteyn; d. 1690. On ass roll of Bu[k] of 1675 and '93, and patent of 1687. Issue:—Annetje Jacobse, bp. Aug. 1, 1686, in Br[n]; and Katharine Jacobse.

Jacobus, see Emans and Nagel.

Jan, see Bennet, Ditmars, Fyn, Kuyper, Lake, Nagel, Staats, Syn, Vanderbilt, Van Dyck, Van Pelt, Vander Vliet, Ver Kerk, Van Nuyse, and Ver Rhyn.

Jan from Hamburgh, resided in Fl[h]; m. Apl. 26, 1681, Harmtje Jans wid. of Jurian Jansz, also of Fl[h].

Jan, an overseer of Fl[h] and mem. of R. D. ch. of said town in 1677. Jan Janse sold Feb. 24, 1678-9, to Cornelis Janse Vanderveer his farm in Fl[h], S. of the farm of the grantee, for 2600 gl., as per town rec. A Jan Jansen paid Aug. 6, 1665, a marriage-fee of 6 gl. to Fl[h] ch., who may have been Jan Jansen Fyn.

Jan, of G[d] July 6, 1646, per Col. Man. A "Jon Jonson" was m. Nov. 2, 1676, in G[d], to Hester W. Goulding by Justice Hubbard, as per town rec.

Jan (sup.) of Bu[k], m. Anneke Pieters (Praa) and had issue:— Jan Janse, bp. Mar. 16, 1684; Neeltje Janse, bp. Nov. 17, 1687; Anneke Janse, bp. Sept. 9, 1688, in Fl[h]; and Aaltje Janse, bp. Oct. 30, 1692, in Br[n].

Jan, emigrated in 1651, and on ass. roll of Bu[k] of 1675. This may be the Jan who m. Anneke Pieters.

Jan, on patent of Br[n] of 1667 and ass. rolls of 1676 and '83. A Jan, known as "Big Jan," on ass. roll of Br[n] of 1675.

Jan, on ass. roll of Fld[a] of 1683.

Jeffer, on petition for a canal across the meadows at Red Hoek, as per p. 68 of Vol. 1 of Stiles's Br[n].

Jemis, owned land in Fld[a] in 1696-7, as per deed on p. 126 of Lib. 2 of Con.

Jillis or *Yelis*, on ass. roll of Fld[a] of 1676. Signed his name "*Yelis Jansen*." A Jellis Jansen in N. A. in 1649.

Johannes, m. Neeltje Johannis. Issue:—Catryntje, bp. Apl. 9, 1694, in Br[n]. .

Johannes, cooper, bought May 27, 1704, of Aaron Van Nordstrant (both of Fl[h]) 2 house-plots in the village of Fl[h], with buildings and improvements, on the S. side of the road leading to "East Midwout," as per p. 31 of Lib. B of Fl[h] rec. Sold June 16, 1711, to John Van Dyck, Anthony Van Pelt, and Joost Van Brunt of N. U., for £75, "for the use of themselves and for all the freeholders and inhabitants

11 .

of New Uytrecht abovesaid that now pay to the salary of
Mr. Freeman," the one-fourth part of the house and. lot in
Fl[h] bounded N. by Isaac de Peyster, S. and E. by Ryck
Hendricksen (Suydam), and W. by the highway, cong. 1 A.
These premises appear to have been bought for a parsonage
by the congregations of Fl[h], Fld[s], N. U., and Br[n]. Signed
his name "*Johannis Jansen.*"

Johannes of N. U., m. Mar. 31, 1686, in N. Y., Maria Van
Giesen of Fl[h].

Johannis, (sup.) m. Albertje Barens. On ass. roll of Br[n]
of 1693 and cen. of 1698. Issue:—Jannetje, bp. Mar. 13,
1692, in Br[n].

Jores, paid 2 gl. 9 st., minister's salary, in Fl[h] in 1680.

Josias, see Drets.

Jurian, see Nagel.

Karsten of G[d], see Carson Johnsen.

Klaes, see Romeyn.

Kryn, see Van Meteren.

Lambert, see Dorland and Van Dyck.

Lambert, emigrated in 1665, and took the oath of allegiance in N. U. in 1687.

Lambert of Fl[h], m. Feb. 23, 1688, Annetje Jans. On ass.
roll of Fl[h] of 1675, at which place he took the oath of
allegiance in 1687 as a native. There was a "Lambert
Jonson," m. June 30, 1673, by Justice Hubbard in G[d] to
Sara Baene, as per G[d] rec. Made his mark to documents.

Laurens, see De Camp and Duyts.

Laurens, owned land in Fl[h] previous to 1661, at which
date he was dead, as per p. 109 of Lib. A of Fl[h] rec. A
"Lowes Jansen" paid 3 gl. towards the minister's salary in
1680, as per Fl[h] town rec.

Laurens or *Louris*, of N. U., a s. of Jan Laurens Duyts, m.
1st Aaltje Gillis (De Mandeville), and both mem. of the
R. D. ch. of said town in 1677; m. 2[d] Hendrickje Jacobus.
Name on the ass. rolls of said town of 1675, '76, '83, and '93,
and on the patent of 1686. Assessed for 66 A. in 1708, and
took the oath of allegiance in N. U. in 1687 as a native.
Feb. 27, 1692-3, he sold a farm in N. U. to Jacob Farden.
Issue:—Johannes Laurensz, bp. Feb. 2, 1679, in Fld[s];
Styntje Laurensz, bp. Jan. 16, 1681, in Fld[s]; Aegidius
Laurensz, bp. Apl. 8, 1683, in N. U.; and Wererchie or
Werarichiel Laurensz, bp. June 5, 1687, in Fl[h], (by 2[d] wife):
Jannetje Laurensz, b. ——, 1697; and (sup.) Gesie Laurensz.
Signed his name "*Lourens Jansen.*"

Leffer, on petition of May 1664 for the making of a canal
through the meadows between Red Hoek and the main-

land of Br⁰, as per p. 68 of Vol. I. of Stiles's Br⁰. Made his mark to documents.

Lowys or *Louis*, farmer, m. Aeltje Douwes; mem. of the R. D. ch. of Fl^h in 1677; on ass. rolls of said town of 1675 and '83. Allotted 3 building-lots in the village, as per p. 12 of Lib. A of Fl^h rec. Mar. 29, 1677, Gov. Andros granted to him and Bartel Claessen a patent for 170 A. adjoining Paerdegat on the boundary of Fld', and bounded N.E. by the flats or plains, as per p. 281 of Lib. D of Fl^h rec. This patent appears to cover a part, and perhaps the whole, of the farms late of Gerret and John C. Vanderveer. Made his mark to documents.

Lubbert, see Buys.

Marten. June 2, 1654, judgment on appeal from the decision of the court of "Midwout" affirmed in the suit of Martin Jansen *vs.* Thomas Spicer, as per p. 138 of Cal. of Dutch Man.

Martin, see Van Breuckelen.

Mattheus, on ass. roll of Bu^k of 1676.

Matthys or *Thys*, of Fld' in 1682, as per ch. rec. He paid a marriage-fee in Fld' in 1664. A Matys Jansz obtained a patent for 50 morgens on Manhattan I. in 1646, as per p. 371 of Cal. of Dutch Man.

Matthys, see Buys, Van Dyck, and Van Pelt.

Neltje, on ass. roll of Bu^k of 1675.

Nicholas, baker; his farm in Br⁰ sold Sept. 13, 1698, to Joris Hansen Bergen by Marretje Gerretsen his wid. He resided in the city of N. Y. See p. 120 of the Bergen Genealogy and p. 50 of Winfield's Land Titles of Hudson Co., N. J., for further information.

Nieuw Amsterhoop, see Jan Amstelhoop.

Okie, see Van Nuyse.

Paulus, see Vanderveer.

Pieter, see Buys, Lay, Lozier, Luqueer, Meet, Noert Brook, Noorman, De Witt, Staats, Van Deventer, Van Dyck Van Pelt, and Zieuw.

Pieter, m. Marretje Jans. Among the first settlers of N. U. in 1657, and on ass. roll of 1693. Issue:—Jacobus Pieterse, bp. June 27, 1680, in N. U.

Pieter, residing on Lagebergh's land, and assessed at the Wallabout for Do. Polhemius's salary 6 gl. in 1657, as per O'Callaghan's Man. Trans. of Col. Man.

Pieter, m. Femmetje Hermans, and d. previous to Oct. 1662. Oct. 15, 1662, his wid. (m. to Pieter Jacobse Van Nortwyck), requested of the mag. of Fl^h to appoint guardians for her children by Pieter Janse, viz. Leffert Pieterse and Pieter Pieterse, upon which "Jan Suebern and Pieter Lodt" were appointed, as per p. 108 of Lib. B of Fl^h rec. The above Leffert Pieterse is the ancestor of the Leffert family of Kings Co., N. J., and Pa.

Pieter. A Pieter Janse, shoemaker, bought a house and lot of Cornelis Janse Bongert or Boomgert in Fl^h in 1661, as per p. 47 of Lib. B of Fl^h rec. Quære: Is not this the Pieter Janse the father of Leffert Pieterse and Pieter Pieterse? A Pieter Jansen of N. L. was a mem. of the R. D. ch. of Fl^h in 1677, and took the oath of allegiance in 1687, who was probably the above Pieter. Signed his name "*Peter Janse.*"

Pieter of G^d. His trunk was seized Nov. 10, 1654, by the sheriff of G^d, as per Col. Man.

Pieter of Kings Co., made a deposition in relation to the burning of Jochem Pietersen's house by the Indians in 1644, as per Furman's Antiquities of L. I.

Pieter, on the patent of Br^n of 1677, as per Thompson's L. I. This may be Pieter Jansen Staats.

Pieter, coroner of Kings Co., as per rec. of the court of sessions of 1698.

Pieter, sup. to have emigrated in 1642. Mortgaged Nov. 27, 1649, to John Forbus a plantation on the East River (Williamsburgh) previously occupied by Claes Carstensen and others, as per p. 34 of Vol. 1 of Col. Man. A Pieter Jansen a mag. of Br^n in 1678.

Pieter from the Manhattans, m. Annetje Jans from Amsterdam, and joined the R. D. ch. of Br^n in 1660.

Pieter. Suits were brought against him by Hendrick Hermensen, Jan Van Cleef, Nicholas De Meyer, and Jan Cornelisse Van Tessel in 1668, and by Symen Hansen (Van Nordstrand) in 1669, as per pp. 108, 144, 153, and 154 of Lib. D of Fl^h rec.

Pieterguil, emigrated in 1642, and took the oath of allegiance in Fl^h in 1687.

Qurin or *Kryn,* see Van Mater.

Rem, see Vanderbeek and Vanderbilt.

Reyn or *Reyndert,* of Fl^h in 1660, as per town rec. Apl. 8, 1643, he leased to John Lock and Jan Pietersen a plantation on L. I., as per p. 21 of Cal. of Dutch Man. Mar. 8, 1666, he bought of Hendrick Jansen Oesteroem a farm in Fl^h on the W. side of the highway, and on the N. side of that of Gerret Lubbertse, as per p. 56 of Lib. D of Fl^h rec. Made his mark to documents.

Rinier, see Ditmars.

Roelof; see Terhune and Ver Kerk.

Roeloff, on Hegeman's books, who signed his name "*Roe-*

loff Janse" in 1670. There was a Roelof Janse in Rensselaers-wyck in 1631, on Manhattan I. in 1646; and a Roelof Janse, butcher, a patentee for 25 morgens at Mespath in 1654, as per p. 382 of Cal. of Dutch Man.

Rutgert of Fl[h], bought Feb. 29, 1656, a cow of Lieut. N. Stillwell, as per p. 161 of Cal. of Dutch Man.   July 1, 1661, he was plaintiff in a suit against Jan Cornelise, as per Lib. B of Fl[h] rec.

Ruth, a s. of Jan Wouterse, b. 1670; was bound by his father July 12, 1678, to serve Lourens Jurianse for 8 years, at the end of which period Lourens to furnish him with a good Sunday and a good every-day suit with good under-garments, and also a milk-cow, as per p. 30 of Lib. AA of Fl[h] rec.

Sara of Gowanus, m. Mar. 17, 1686, in N. Y., John Berry widower of Maria Thomas, both of N. Y. at date of marriage.

Stoffel, see Abel and Romeyn.

Stoffel, on Fl[h] ass. roll of 1676.   Jan. 7, 1679-80, Stoffel Janse, carpenter, of Fld[t], bought of Cornelis Janse de Seeuw lots 32 and 33 of woodland in N. L., as per p. 89 of Lib. AA of Fl[h] rec., which he sold in Feb. of the same year to Louis Cornelise of Mespath.   This may be Stoffel Jansen Romeyn.   Signed his name *"Stoffel Jansen."*

Symen, see Romeyn and Van Aersdalen.

Swaen, see Van Luanè.

Swantje, wid. of Cor[s] De Potter.   Will da. Mar, 3. 1676; rec. p. 208 of Lib. 1 of Con.

Teunis, see Amack, Coevert, and Van Pelt.

Teunis of Br[n], cultivated part of Frederick Lubbertse's land in Br[n] in 1657, as per p. 134 of Vol. 1 of Stiles's Br[n], where he was assessed for Do. Polhemius's salary.   On ass. rolls of said town of 1676 and '83, and a mag. in 1661 and '62, and of Bedford in 1677.   This Teunis may be Teunis Janse Coevers.   Signed his name " *Teunis Janssen.*"

Theophilus, on G[d] rec.   Intended for Stoffel Jansen.

Thomas, see Amack and Van Dyck.

Thyman, ship-carpenter, had a dispute Jan. 11, 1643, with Joris Jansen Rapalie about the land of Rapalie the latter cultivated, as per p. 85 of Cal. of Dutch Man.

Thys or *Matthys*, see Buys, Van Pelt, and Van Dyck.

Thys, among the early settlers of N. U., who may be the Matthys Jansen from Leiden who m. Lysbeth Elswaerts, June 9, 1675, in N. Y.

Tierck and others applièd in 1663 for leave to settle a village, and for salt meadows, as per p. 120 of Vol. 1 of Stiles's Br[n].

Willem or *William*, see Barkeloo, Traphagen, and Van Nuyse.

William or *Wyllem*, of G^d in 1666, shoemaker. Jan Van Cleef acknowledged in Aug. 1665 to be indebted to him 350 gl., as per G^d rec. Signed his name "*Wyllem Jansen.*"

Williamguil, emigrated in 1640, and took the oath of allegiance in Fl^h in 1687.

Wouter of Fl^h. Signed his name "*Wouter Jansoen*" in 1689.

Zwaen, see Van Luane.

Janselert, Peter, on Dongan's patent of Bu^k of 1687.

Jeffers, Capt. John, bought Nov. 20, 1677, of Claes Milles Baes a farm on the W. side of the road in Fl^h between the farms of "Peter Lodt" and Jan Roeloffsen, of 26 morgens with plain and meadow land, the same premises which Baes bought Nov. 17, 1677, of Van Ens, as per p. 27 of Lib. C of Fl^h rec. Dec. 5, 1677, Jeffers conveyed this property to Robert Story, signing his name "*John Jeffers.*"

Jentien, appointed Aug. 29, 1665, a guardian of Gerret s. of Claes Gerretse and Adryaentje Lollenox by the mag. of Fl^h, as per p. 40 of Lib. D of Fl^h rec. This may be Capt. John Jeffers.

Jelleon, Yan or Jan, on Stoothoff's books of 1678. In 1681 the consistory of the R. D. ch. of Fl^h sued him for salary of Do. Van Zuuren, as per p. 253 of Lib. C of Fl^h rec. A Hans Jelisen was skipper of the ship Union in 1645, as per p. 32 of Cal. of Dutch Man.

Jenes, Niclaes, on muster-roll of Bu^k militia of 1663, as per town rec.

Jeroe, Anthony, and Claude Raber sold Jan. 7, 1653, to Jacob Steendam a tract on the W. side of Mespath's Kil in Bu^k, as per p. 376 of Cal. of Dutch Man.

Jewell, George, (sup. English,) sold Jan. 22, 1652, to Enum Benum his house and plantation in G^d. Mar. 3, 1656, he bought of Wm Provoost, as attorney of his father David Provoost, plantation-lot No. 26 in G^d, which he sold Dec. 11, 1656, to Richard Gibbins, as per G^d rec. Made his mark to documents.

Jillekes, Henry, alloted Mar. 22, 1701, a meadow-lot on the division of Fld^s meadows, as per town rec.

JILLIS, see De Mandeville.

JOCHEMS, JANNEKEN, of Fl[b], m. Oct. 17, 1683, in N. Y, *Johannes Gerretszen*, both of said city at date of marriage.

JOCHIMSEN or JOCHEM, DAVID, from Amsterdam, m. Aug. 5, 1659, in N. A., *Christina Cappeens* wid. of Jacob Hey, and d. prior to 1695. In Apl. 1660 he joined the D. ch. of N. A. Owned a plantation in Bu[k] in 1659, since of John Messerole Jun[r], and a mag. of said town in 1664. Of N. U. in 1675 or '76.

Anneken of Fl[b], removed to Philips Manor, where she m. June 4, 1693, Johannes Minne from Friesland, now of Haverstraw, as per N. Y. D. ch. rec. Johannes Minne was probably a s. of Minne Johannes, b. in Friesland prior to his father's emigration.

JOCHUM, ANTHONI, from Saumur in France, on ass. roll of Bu[k] in 1684.

JOESTEN, see Joosten.

JOHANNES, MYNNE, (or MINNE JOHANNES MINEOLA,) emigrated from Friesland in the Netherlands in Sept. 1663 with w., 4 chil., and wife's sister. He m. 1st *Rensje Feddans* or *Feddes*, in the fatherland; m. 2[d], Apl. 1, 1689, *Madalena Rixe* or *Hendrixe* of Fl[b], wid. of Cornelis Vonk, who after his death m. in 1693 Agyas Van Dyck. He appears to have resided in N. L. in 1675, his name appearing in that year as of that locality on the ass. roll of Fl[b]. On patent of N. L. of 1677, and mem. of the R. D. ch. of Fl[b] in said year; constable of Fl[b] in 1676, '77, and '79, as per p. 64 of Strong's Fl[b]. Bought at an auction Jan. 5, 1675, of Claes Claesen Smit a house and lot in the village of N. U., which he sold Dec. 17, 1677, to Jan Verkerk, as per N. U. town rec. Feb. 3, 1680, he sold his N. L. farm to W[m] Morris. Previous to his marriage to Madalena he removed to Haverstraw. May 4, 1684, he petitioned for license to buy 3000 A. behind his farm at Haverstraw, as per p. 45 of Vol. II. of Land Papers. Mar. 12, 1685 he was commissioned as high sheriff of Orange Co., as per p. 143 of Cal. of English Man. Issue:—Jannetje Minnes, who m. Jan. 26, 1689, Lucas Stevense Voorhees; Albert Minnes, whose name appears on Gov. Andros's patent of N. L.; Grietje Minnes of Haverstraw, late of Fld[t], m. Jan. 20, 1686, at Bergen, N. J., Harmen Douwenszen Taelman of Tappen, as per N. Y. D. ch. rec. No account of his fourth child. Signed his name *"Mynne Johannes."*

Johnson or Jansen, Andrias, constable of Fl[h] in 1697, per court rec.

Barent (s. of Jan Barentse Van Driest), bp. Dec. 18, 1681; m. Maria da. of Nicholas Stillwell Jun[r], and was a farmer in G[d]. Issue:—Jan Barentse of J[a]; Claes Barentse of N. J.; (sup.) Catharine Barentse, who m. Dan[l] Stillwell; Barent Barentse of G[d]; and William Barentse of G[d], b. July 4, 1718. Signed his name "*Barent Jansen.*"

Claes, of G[d] in 1694, per Stoothoff papers. Elected an overseer of said town in 1681, per G[d] rec.

Cornelis, on Gov. Dongan's patent of Bu[k] of 1687.

Cornelis of G[d] (s. of Jan Barentse Van Driest), bp. Jan. 29, 1684. No further trace.

Hendrick of Br[n], m. Mary da. of Nicholas Stillwell Jun[r], who was b. in 1683 in G[d].

Jan or *John* (sup. s. of Jan Barentse Van Driest), m. 1st to (sup.) Marretje ——; m. 2[d] (sup.) Jannetje Joris. A John Johnson about this period resided in G[d], as per Thompson's L. I., who was probably this John. Issue:—Johannes, bp. (sup.) Jan. 18, 1715; Barent, bp. (sup.) July 27, 1721; Jores, bp. (sup.) May 12, 1722; Maria or Marytie, bp. Dec. 19, 1737; Catharine, bp. Dec. 30, 1739; and Elizabeth, bp. Nov. 21, 1747: the last 3 by the second wife.

Jan, see Ver Rhyn.

John, of G[d] in 1656, per Thompson's L. I., and Sept. 1, 1659, per Col. Man.

Lambert, constable of Br[n] in 1671, per Furman's Br[n] (probably Lambert Janse Dorland). The signature of "Lambert Jansen" appears on Lib. AA of Fl[h] rec. in 1680, and also that of "*Lammert Jansen*" on same book and date.

Lambert, m. June 30, 1673, Sarah Barne, per G[d] rec.

Lawrence or *Lowraie* of G[d], sold Aug. 22, 1653, to Water Wall land and buildings in G[d], as per town rec. Of G[d] in 1656, per Thompson's L. I.

Maudlinn of the Manhattans, bought Nov. 19, 1652, of "Enum Benum" his house and plantation in G[d], per town rec.

Pieter, appointed coroner of Kings Co. in 1685, as per p. 141 of Cal. of Eng. Man., and lieut. of horse in 1690, per Col. His.

Pieter, on Gov. Dongan's patent of Br[n] of 1686, as per p. 345 of Vol. II of Stiles's Br[n], who was probably the coroner above referred to.

Stoffel, see Romeyn.

Theophilus, on G[d] rec., intended for Stoffel. See Romeyn.

William (s. of Jan Barentse Van Driest) of G[d], was sued at the sessions of 1670, by Ralph Cardell for debt. Was a merchant in N. Y., and finally returned to his brother's house in G^d, where he d. single, as per Riker's Newtown. Signed his name "*William Johnson*" in 1666.

JONES, JOSELL, assaulted by Casper Jansen in 1692, per court rec.

Thomas of Br^n. His will is da. June 1, 1684, as per p. 20 of Lib. 1 of Con.

JONGE, AUEGUERYE, bought Jan. 21, 1681, of Dirck Janse Van Sutphen his farm in "Midwout" and meadows, as per p. 155 of Lib. AA of Fl^h rec.

JONGES, JAN JANSEND, of Fld^s, name appears on a complaint to the court of sessions against Fl^h for encroachments on the Canarisie meadows. Signed his name "*Jan Jansend Jonges.*"

JONGH, HANS, and Daniel Steger obtained Aug. 20, 1657, a patent for a lot near the Br^n ferry. A "Hans Jong" resided on the Raritan in 1725.

Jan de, see Van Gunst.

Lodewyck, bought Dec. 10, 1651, Andries Hudde's patent for a plantation in Br^n, per Minutes of the Governor and Council.

JOORES, see Jores.

JOORITH, HARMEN, on a deed of the freeholders of Br^n of Jan. 2, 1696-7, to Adriaen Willemse Bennet. Made his mark "H" to documents.

JOOSTEN, BARENT, from "Witmont in Emberland," "ridder" (horseman or knight), emigrated in 1652, settling in Bu^k in 1661, of which place he was a mag. in 1663 and '64. Apl. 6, 1675, he and Jan Hansen (Van Nordstrant) bought, of Francois de Bruynne, Anthony Jansen from Salee's patent in G^d and N. U. of 100 morgens, which they sold Dec. 11, 1693, to Albert Coerten (Van Voorhees) for 38,750 gl. wampum value, or about $15,340—a large sum for that period. On ass. rolls of N. U. of 1675, '83, and '93; constable in 1683, '86, and '87; on Dongan's patent of 1686; on cen. of 1698; and took the oath of allegiance in said town in 1687. He m. Dec. 7, 1658, *Cytie, Seytie,* or *Eytie Laurens* of L. I., and had issue:—Annetie, bp. Nov. 2, 1659, in N. A; Joostje Barents, bp. Dec. 26, 1661, in Br^n; Joost Barents, bp. Jan. 7, 1663, in Br^n; and Geertruyt Barents, bp. May 11, 1664, in Br^n. Made his mark "B. J." to documents.

Abraham, Joost, Philip, and *Simon,* see Duryee.

Cornelis, constable of Fl[h] in 1681.

Frans of Bruges, m. Geertruy Auke Van Nuys. Issue:—Magdalen, bp. Nov. 2, 1679, at Fl[h].

Jacob, town-clerk of the 5 Dutch towns from 1670 to '73. Schoolmaster of Fl[h] and precentor of the ch. from 1671 to '73, as per p. 109 of Strong's Fl[h]. His term commenced Nov. 1, 1670, O. S., as per p. 207 of Lib. D. of Fl[h] rec. A Jacob Joesten took the oath of allegiance to the English in N. Y. in 1664. Signed his name *"Jacob Joesten."*

Rutgert, see Van Brunt.

Saertje of Bedford, m. Feb. 15, 1699, in N. Y., Michael Van der Koeck from Zeeland, as per N. Y. D. ch. rec.

Simon from "Meerbeecke," m. Apl. 18, 1649, in N. A., Annetje Boelens from Amsterdam. Both mem. of the R. D. ch. of Br[n] in 1660. He succeeded Cornelis Dircksen Hoogland as ferry-master at Br[n] ferry; was court messenger in N. A. in 1656, and in 1657 in Br[n]. Issue:—Joost, bp. Nov. 26, 1651; and Catharine, bp. Aug. 23, 1654, in N. A.

Tunis, allotted a plantation among the first settlers of N. U. in 1657; but having no further account of him, and his failing to improve the same, it was forfeited.

JORISE or JORISEN, see Brinckerhoff.

Abraham, took the oath of allegiance in Br[n] in 1687 as a native.

Bruyn, on Stoothoff and Hegeman's books of 1670.

Cornelis of the ferry, sold land to Thomas Lambertse Apl. 22, 1695, as per p. 55 of Lib. 2 of Con.

Daniel, see Rapalie.

Gysbert, on Stoothoff books of 1678.

Harmen, took the oath of allegiance in Br[n] in 1687 as a native.

Hendrick, see Brinckerhoff.

Jacob (s. of Jores Jacobsen), m. May 27, 1677, Lysbeth Thomas da. of Thomas Lambertse of Bedford. Resided at Bedford, and was a mem. of the R. D. ch. of Br[n] in 1685, where he took the oath of allegiance in 1687 as a native. On ass. rolls of Br[n] of 1675 and '83. Bought Feb. 8, 1688-9, of W[m] Joorise 20 morgens at Bedford, as per p. 148 of Lib. 1 of Con. Will da. Feb. 19, 1691-2; rec. Lib. 1, p. 108 (copy) of Con. Issue:—Jores Jacobse, bp. Feb. 17, 1678, in Fld[s]; Thomas Jacobse, bp. July 25, 1680, in N. U.; Joris Jacobse, bp. Apl. 23, 1682, in Fl[h]; Jacob Jacobse, bp. Nov. 30, 1683, in Br[n]; Andreas Jacobse; Tryntje Jacobse; Harman Jacobse; and Jannetje Jacobse.

Jan, on Bu[k] ass. roll of 1675. A Jan Jorise m. Maria

Fredericks; said Maria m. 2[d], Oct. 24, 1663, Symen Hansen Van Noorstrand.

Jan and *Jeronemus*, see Rapalie.

Kleyn or *Heyn Drick* of Fl[h], supposed to be intended for Dirck Joorese Brinckerhoff. Signed his name "*Heyn'Drick Jooressen.*"

Marcus of Br[n], m. Dec. 17, 1662, Lysbeth Nachtegal. Issue:—Jannetje, bp. Dec. 11, 1663, in Br[n].

Symon, of Fl[h] in 1680, per ch. rec.

Willem of Bedford (s. of Joris Jacobse), m. Hendrickje Johannes or Willems. Mem. of R. D. ch. of Br[n] in 1685 ; on ass. roll of Br[n] of 1683; and resided in Richmond Co. in 1689. Issue:—Elsje Willemse, bp. Oct. 14 or 24, 1677, in Fl[h]; Joris Willemse, bp. May 6, 1683, in Fl[h]; Eytie Willemse, bp. Oct. 28, 1688, in Br[n]; and Nelkje Willemse, bp. Mar. 4, 1694, in Br[n].

JORNEY, WEYNART, from Manheim, joined Br[n] R. D. ch. Oct. 28, 1663.

JOSEPHS, ADRIAEN, FRANCIS, ELBERT, JOSEPH, PETER, and REM, see Hegeman.

JOURNAY, MAILLARD, occupied land in Bedford in 1694, as per p. 49 of Vol. 2 of Con.

JUER or JAER, MICHAE, owned land in G[d] in 1648, per town rec. Mar. 5, 1648, he agreed to build a house for Ambrose London, 22 ft. by 12, for 40 gl.; London furnishing the main part of the materials, as per said rec.

JURIANSE, ANDRIES JANSE, m. *Annetje Pieters* wid. of Jan Evertse Bout, and Apl. 1, 1688, was in possession of Bout's patent of Br[n] lands. On ass. roll of 1675; constable of Br[n] in the same year; and deacon in 1678. Signed his name "*Andries Juriansen.*"

Barent or *Barne*, emigrated in 1658; mag. of G[d] in 1673 and '79; took the oath of allegiance there in 1687; and on ass. roll of 1683. Purchased in 1672 the farm in the village of G[d] late of Anthony Jansen from Salee (not Turk's plantation). Signed his name "*Barent Jurjansen.*"

Christoffel, see Probasco.

Jacobus, see Nagel.

Laurence, see Haf.

Laurens of Brazil, m. July 5, 1676, in N. A., Kenira Pieters from Amersfoort. Mem. of the R. D. ch. of N. U. in 1677 and '79, residing at Yellow Hoek, and entered on the ch. rec. as removed. His name afterwards appears as a mem. of the R. D. ch. of Fl^h and a resident of N. L. He was a brother-in-law of Jan Woutersz.

Phillippus, see Nagel.

KAAR, JAMES, of G^d, m. *Johanna* ——. Chosen pound-master of G^d in 1692. Accused May 9, 1693, of murder, as per court rec. Oct. 9, 1693, he bought of John Stillwell a garden-spot with the buildings thereon in G^d, as per town rec. Made his mark to documents.

KAFTER, PIETER, and *Debora Bras* had a dau. Christina bp. May 27, 1685.

KAMMEGA or KAMMINGA, HENDRICK JANSE, see Cammega.

KANNENS, SIMON, was sued by Carston Jansen in the court of sessions in G^d for one year's wages, as per G^d rec.

KAPEN, WILLIAM, on Stoothoff's books of 1680.

KARLESZ, see Carlesz.

KARSTEN, JAN, m. *Maria Eliase Daws*. Issue:—Andries, bp. Jan. 23, 1681, in N. U.

KASPARSE, JOHANNES, on Fl^h ass. roll of 1675.
Joost, see Casparse.

KATS, CLAES CORNELISE, see Van Cott.

KEE, JACOB HENDRICKSE, see Jacob or Jabecq Hendrickse.

KENGER, CORNELIS, paid 8 gl. 12 st., minister's salary, in Fl^h in 1681, as per Fl^h rec.

KENNE, ADERYAEN PIETERSE, emigrated in 1660; m. *Willemtje Pieterse Wyckoff;* mem. of R. D. ch. of Fld* in 1666, where he took the oath of allegiance in 1687; on ass. roll of said town in 1693 and cen. of 1698. Issue:—Jacob, bp. Dec. 5, 1680, and settled on the Raritan; Jan, bp. July 22, 1683; and Lourens, bp. May 2, 1686. Signed his name "*Aderyaen Kenne.*" There was a Peter Kinne at North Branch, Somerset Co., N. J., in 1710, who may have been a s. of this Aderyaen Pieterse.

KERTEN, GERRET, of N. U., who signed his name "*Geret Kerten*" prior to 1700.

KEY, JACOB TEUNISEN, on petition for a canal between Red Hoek and the mainland of Brⁿ of May 1664, as per p. 68 of Vol. 1 of Stiles's Brⁿ.
Harman, m. Tryntje Jans. On ass. rolls of Fl^h of 1675 and '83. Issue:—Emmetje Harmanse, bp. July 13, 1679.

KEYER, AEREYEN, paid 5 gl. 5 st., minister's salary, in Fl^h in 1680.

KICKHAM, THOMAS, had a dau. Marytje bp. Jan. 29, 1691, in Brⁿ.

KIERSE, KIERSEN, or KIERSTEDE, JAN or HANS, emigrated in 1660, and probably resided at first in Fld^s with Stephen Coerte (Van Voorhies), his father-in-law and the ancestor of the Voorhies family, whose dau. *Hendrickjen Stephense* he married. Mem. of R. D. ch. of Fld^s in 1666. Nov. 15, 1680, he bought a farm of 48 morgens in N. U. of Hans Harmense Van Barkeloo, as per p. 137 of Lib. AA of Fl^h rec.; resided in N. U. as early as 1678, of which place he was a mem. of the ch. in 1679; on ass. roll of 1683; on Dongan's patent of 1686; and took the oath of allegiance in 1687. He conveyed Apl. 5, 1700, his N. U. farm to Garret Coerte Voorhies, as per p. 271 of Lib. 2 of Con., having previously removed back to Fld^s, where his name appears on the cen. of 1698. His N. U. farm was probably the one lately owned by John A. Emmans, dec. Made his mark to documents. There was another Hans Kierstede, a surgeon, in N. A. as early as 1638.

KIERSTE, GIDEON JACOBS, m. May 22, 1691, *Anna Homer* of G^d.
Lucas, on Stoothoff books of 1683 and '88.

KIERSTED, JACOBUS, m. *Anna* ——. Was a surgeon or physician in 1691, as per R. D. ch. rec. of Fld^s. May 2, 1692, Jacobus Kierstede of Fld^s exchanged lands with Nicholas Stillwell of G^d, as per G^d rec. Apl. 5, 1698, Jacobus Kierstede and Joris Rapple, both of N. Y., sold a 15 A. lot, No. 17, in G^d to Capt. John Van Dykhuysen of Fld^s, as per same rec. Issue:—Maria; Sara; Samuel; Jacobus; Daniel; Marretje; and Lucas—all bp. between 1693 and 1719 in N. Y., and supposed to be his children. Signed his name "*Jacobus Kiersted*."

KINBEAR, JORIS, b. in England; m. May 26, 1685, in Brᵃ, *Maria* wid. of Joseph Fenton, b. in London, England.

KINNE, see Kenne.

KIP, ANNA, had a hop-garden in the village of Flʰ, as per deed of Adriaen Hendrickse to Gerardus Beekman, surgeon, da. Sept. 14, 1678, on p. 31 of Vol. AA of Flʰ town rec. She bound her s. Nicasius, ag. 14 years, for 6 years from May 1, 1678, to Jan Montange to learn the cooper's trade; Montange to board the apprentice, find his washing and mending, to give him 8 st. every Sunday for spending money, send him to evening-school, and at the end of his term give him a Sunday and every-day suit of clothes, as per p. 145 of Lib. AA of Flʰ rec.

Hendrick or *Hendricus*. Jan. 16, 1666, he and Bartel Claesen (Van Ruynen) bought of Jan Leeck 15 morgens, with plain and meadow land, in Flʰ, as per p. 1 of Lib. C of Flʰ rec. Mar. 15, 1670-71, he bought of Jan Cornelise Van Tessel a building-lot in Flʰ, as per p. 104 of Lib A of Flʰ rec. His name appears on ass. roll of 1693 and cen. of 1698 of Flʰ. Hendrick Kipp the eldest took the oath of allegiance in N. Y. in 1664. Signed his name "*Hendrick Kipp*."

Hendrick Junʳ. His name appears among the residents of Flʰ discharging Do. Polhemius, and also on other papers. Was on the Delaware in 1662. Signed his name "*Hendrick Kip Jun*," and in 1720 "*Hendricus Kip*."

Jacobus, obtained Feb. 25, 1667, a patent for a lot in Buᵏ; name on patent of said town of 1667, and Apl. 6, 1667, obtained a patent for land at Brᵃ ferry. This Jacob is probably the Jacob Hendrickse Kip, b. May 6, 1631, in Amsterdam, referred to on p. 70 of Vol. VIII. of the N. Y. Genealogical Record, who m. Feb. 14, 1654, Maria de la Montangie of Amsterdam. A Jacob Kipp took the oath of allegiance to the English in 1664. Jacob and Maria had issue:—Johannes, b. 1655; Jacobus, b. 1656; Abraham, b. 1658; Jesse, b. 1660; Rachel, b. 1664; Maryken, b. 1666; Hendrick, b. 1669; Benjamin, b. 1678; and Salomen, b. 1682 —all bp. in N. Y. Signed his name "*Jacobus Kip*."

KLAAS or KLAASZ, HENDRICK, of Bedford, m. *Jannetje* —— Issue:—Pieter, bp. Aug. 7, 1681, in Flʰ.

Barthold, see Bartel Claesen.

Cornelis, see Van Hasmyes.

William of Fldᵃ, m. Oct. 9, 1691, Elsie Gerretsz, and both residents of Gowanus at date of marriage.

KLEMENT, JAN, see Clement.

KLEY, OUFRE, see Clay.

KLEYN, JAN CORNELISE, see Cleyn.

KLINCKENBERG, WILLEM, took the oath of allegiance in N. U. in 1687 as a native.

KLOCK, PILGRIM, see Clock.
Minster, farmer, on Stoothoff's books of 1678.

KLOMP, see Lambert Huybertse Moll.

KLYNCK, PIETER, of Fld⁸ in 1695, where he paid in said year to the church for a grave and use of the pall.

KNIGHT, JOHN, (sup. English,) bought Dec. 2, 1685, of Hendrick Thomasse Van Dyck 12 morgens at the fountain of the Yellow Hoek in N. U., adjoining land of Rutger Joesten (Van Brunt), as per town rec. Was clerk of Kings Co. from 1684 to '87, and Dec. 23, 1684, appointed one of the clerks of the court of chancery, as per p. 134 of Cal. of Eng. Man. The bay or river at Yellow Hoek in some old deeds is described as the "fountain." In 1638 a John Knight, carpenter, emigrated from England to New England, as per p. 299 of Hotten's Emigrants.
Thomas, (English,) m. Sarah Adamse Brouwer. On ass. roll of Brⁿ of 1698. Bought May 7, 1695, of Jurian Hendrickse Bries for £32 a house and lot on the main road in the village of Brⁿ not far from the church, where he and his wife kept tavern, as per p. 57 of Lib. 2 of Con. A Thomas Knight appears on the list of soldiers engaged in the expedition against Canada in 1689, as per p. 214 of Vol. II. of Doc. His. of N. Y.

KOCKES, ALEXANDER, paid 6 gl. to Flʰ ch. in 1665.

KOCKUYT, JOOST, see Cockuyt.

KOECK or KOOK, LAURENS, emigrated in 1661, and took the oath of allegiance in Brⁿ in 1687. He m. about 1690 *Margriet Barens*.

KOEGER, CALIB, on Stoothoff's books in 1691.

KOENICK, see Coenick.

KOKER, MINSTER, on Stoothoff's books of 1677 and '80.

KOKER or KOOK, TOMAS, on Stoothoff's books of 1680 and '83.

KOLESEN, HENDRICK, on Stoothoff's books of 1677 and '78.

KOLF, JACOB, from Leiden, m. June 1, 1684, *Jannetje Johannes* of Brⁿ.

KONGER, CORNELIS, paid 8 gl. 12 st., minister's salary, in Flʰ in 1681, as per town rec.

KOROM, JAN, on ass. roll of Buᵏ of 1676.

KORSEN, JAN, on ass. roll of Buᵏ of 1676. See Corsen.

KORTEN, MYNDERT, (sometimes written Coerten,) from Arnhem in Gelderland, a soldier and shoemaker, who emigrated about 1660; m. Jan. 9, 1660, *Maria Pieters, Pia*, or *Pea*, of N. A.; d. in 1706. In 1661 he with 12 others petitioned for land on S. I. Resided at first in Flushing, and about 1676 or '79 bought of Jan Janse Ver Ryn a part of the Robert Pennoyer and of the Anthony Jansen from Salee patents located on the main road leading from the village of N. U. to Gᵈ, and on De Bruynne's Lane or the old Bath road, to which he removed and on which he continued to reside until his death. No vestige or remains of his dwelling-house or tradition of its location has been found. Was a mem. of the R. D. ch. of N. U. in 1677 and '78; a mag. of said town in 1680, '82, and '83; on Dongan's patent of 1686; high sheriff of Kings Co. in 1689, as per p. 186 of Cal. of Eng. Man.; mem. of Assembly in 1698; and a mem. of Gov. Leisler's Council, for his adherence to whose cause he was convicted of treason, and came near losing his life. Issue:— Pieter, bp. Jan. 16, 1661, d. young; Hanna, who m. Jan. 25, 1690, Andries Jansen; Wyntje or Winta, bp. July 18, 1666, in N. Y., m. June 20, 1680, Isaac Le Febre; Myndert, (sup.) d. young; Hendrickje, bp. Jan. 16, 1670, in N. Y., m. Hendrick Jansen; Maria, bp. Oct. 25, 1673; Court, bp. May 14, 1682, d. young; and Abraham, who also probably d. young. By his will, da. Oct. 25, 1704, he devised to his dau. Hanna a farm in Middletown, Monmouth Co., N. J., and to his dau. Maria his N. U. farm. Signed his name *"Myndert Korten."*

Harmen, see Coerten.

KOUWENHOVEN, see Couwenhoven.

KROESEN, see Croesen.

KROM, FLORIS WILLEMSE, of N. L., m. 1ˢᵗ *Catalintie Ariens* dau. of Adriaen Lambertse; m. 2ᵈ, Sept. 1699, *Grietje Van Houte* at Hackensack. His name appears on Gov. Andros's patent of .N. L. of 1677. Mar. 15, 1683-4, he sold to —— Barkes a piece of land cong. 60 A. in the end of the N. L. adjoining Jˢ, as per p. 160 of Lib. C of Flʰ rec. From the deed it is inferred he m. a dau. of Adriaen Lammerse of Bedford. There was a Floris Willemse Crom commissioned as high sheriff of Orange Co. Feb. 29, 1690, as per p. 104 of Cal. of Dutch Man. June 24, 1703, Flores Crom in behalf of himself and others of Haverstraw, Orange Co., petitioned for a confirmatory patent of the town; Apl. 13, 1686, 158 A. were surveyed for Gisbert Crom at Maple, Ulster Co., N. Y. There was a Willem Krom on the Raritan, N. J., as early as 1718, and a Hendrick Willemszen Krom, a mem. of the D. ch., in N. Y. in 1679. Issue:—Willemtje, bp. May 3, 1685, in N. Y.; (sup.) Gisbert; Willem; and probably others. Signed his name *"Floris Willemse Krom."*

KUENINCK, ALBERT, a pauper in 1686, as per Flʰ ch. rec.

KUIPER or COOPER, see Derick Janse and Johannes Janse.

KUNNE, see Kenne.

KUYNEN, ALBERT, sold Aug. 8, 1663, to Frans Barentse a farm in Flʰ on the W. side of the highway, with plain and salt meadow land, as per p. 141 of Lib. B of Flʰ rec. An Albert Keuninck took the oath of allegiance to the English in N. Y. in 1664. Owned land in Flʰ in 1670 in the locality known as "Rustenburch," adjoining the village plot of Derick Janse, cooper, as per p. 10 of Lib. A of Flʰ rec. Made his mark "A" to documents.

KUYPER, CLAES, on Stoothoff's books of 1678.
Claes Jansen, see Van Purmarent.
Jan Jansen, on ass. roll of Buᵏ of 1675.

LA ALOOT, JACOB, of Brⁿ; his name appears on the patent of May 16, 1668, of land to Charles Fonteyn.

LAAN, see Lane.
12

LA CLERK, LE CLERK or DE CLERK, JEAN or JAN, owned
land at the Wallabout. Mar. 6, 1660, he and others petitioned for leave to plant a village at the Wallabout, as per
La Chain's Notarial Register and Col. Man. He was from
Brazil; m. Jan. 17, 1661, *Annetje Hansen Bergen,* and d. Nov.
15, 1661, as per p. 80 of Bergen Genealogy.

LAEN, JOHN. Overseer of a farm at Bedford, per deed of
Thomas Lambertse and others to Lysbeth Thomas of May
10, 1695, as per p. 53 of Lib. 2 of Con.

LA FEBRE, LE FEBRE, or LE FEVRE, ISAAC, emigrated in
1683, and took the oath of allegiance in Bu[k] in 1687. He
m. 1st *Jannetje Bonderick;* m. 2[d], June 23, 1689, *Wyntje* dau.
of Myndert Korten of N. U His children appear to have
settled in E. N. J. There was a Myndert Le Febre in
Somerset Co. in 1716. Issue:—Myndert, bp. Mar. 16, 1690,
at Fl[h].

Myndert, bp. Mar. 16, 1690; m. Nov. 2, 1714, in N. Y.,
Catharine Van Blaricum. Resided in N. U., and Jan. 30,
1710-11, was licensed by Joseph Hegeman and Peter Cortel-
you, two of his Majesty's justices of the peace, to "keep a
Tavern and Common Alehouse or tippling house at
Newutrecht aforesaid in the house where he now dwelleth."
Suppose he left N. U. and settled in Monmouth or Somer-
set Co., N. J.

Peter. A resident of N. A. in 1658, where on petition he
was allowed to sell "liquors or waters of a peculiar virtue"
in large or small bottles in his own house, as per p. 132 of
Cal. of Dutch Man. He appears to have owned a farm at
the Walabocht, which being subject to a mortgage, he was
summoned in 1659 to discharge, as per p. 326 of said Cal.
There was a Peter Le Febre in Somerset Co., N. J., in 1705,
who had a dau. Jantien bp. in that year.

LA FORGE or LA FORSE, ADRIAEN, emigrated in 1652, and
took the oath of allegiance in Bu[k] in 1687; m. *Jannetje Jans.*
On ass. roll of Bu[k] of 1683. Issue:—Maria and Aaltje, both
bp. May 27, 1685, in Br[n].

LAGEBERGH, ——, owned land in Br[n] in 1657, as per p. 134
of Stiles's Br[n]. See Peter Jansen.

LAHERC, FRANCOYS, his land referred to in patent of Gov.
Stuyvesant to Cornelis Janse Berrien of Mar. 12, 1661, for
26 morgens in Fl[h], as per p. 25 of Lib. A of Fl[h] rec.

LAKE, LEEK, or LEUCK, ABRAHAM (s. of Daniel), of G^d. Made his mark to documents in 1691.

Daniel of G^d, m. Alse or Allee ——. Name on ass. roll of G^d of 1683; in 1684 hired land in G^d of Jan Barentse Van Driest, and bought land in said town in the same year, as per town rec. July 12, 1694, he bought land in G^d of John Lake, formerly of Stout, as per Lib. 2 of Con. In 1689 he was appointed lieut. for G^d. He appears to have finally removed to S. I., from which locality, Dec. 21, 1696, he conveyed meadow-land located in G^d to Reinier Van Sicklen, as per G^d rec. Dec. 30, 1701, as a resident of S. I., with others he petitioned the king to overthrow the power of the followers of the martyred Gov. Leisler. Supposed issue:—John; Abraham; Elizabeth; Thomas; and Ann. Made his mark to documents.

Daniel (*Janse*) of G^d, English, b. Mar. 10, 1696; m. " Elizabeth Sutvin;" d. Apl. 10, 1776. Issue:—Daniel of G^d, b. July 27, 1730; Derick of G^d, who m. Maria Voorhies; Neetje or Nelthe, who m. Bernardus Hubbard; Maria or Mary, bp. June 10, 1733, in N. U., who m. Stephen Voorhies; Abraham, bp. Sept. 5, 1735, in N. U.; (sup.) Margaret, bp. Feb. 22, 1739; Helena, bp. Aug. 31, 1740, in N. U.; Jacobus of G^d; (sup.) Geertje, who m. Johannes Van Sicklen; John of G^d; Sarah, who m. —— Johnson; Ellen, who m. —— Bennem; and Elizabeth.

Jan Senr of G^d, the common ancestor of the family, and of G^d as early as 1656, as per Thompson's L. I.; farmer; m. Ann dau. of Thomas Spicer of G^d; d. prior to Aug. 14, 1696. Was a witness on the Indian deed of Bergen's Island in Fld[•] in 1652. Sept. 20, 1661, he sold to Tys Lubbertse a parcel of land of 15½ morgens, a village plot, a plot of plain land, and 3 morgens of salt-meadows in Fl^h, as per p. 91 of Lib. B of Fl^h rec. He also sold in 1666 a farm in Fl^h to Bartel Claesen as per p. 1 of Lib. C of Fl^h rec. His name appears on the ass. roll of G^d of 1683. Issue:—Metje, bp. May 20, 1652, in N. A.; Jan Junr; and probably others. Made his mark for his signature, and on deeds in which he was concerned his name is written "*Jan Leek*" and "*John Leeck*."

Jan Junr of G^d, m. Neeltje Claessen. On ass. roll of G^d of 1683, and capt. of militia in 1700, as per p. 809 of Vol. IV. of Doc. of Col. His. In 1694 he bought of Hannah wid. of John Delavall of Penn., for £164, a house and 40 A. of land on Hogg's Neck in G^d, as per p. 6 of Vol. 2 of Con. May 6, 1696, a plot of 85 A. at Smoking Point on S. I., with 9 A. at the mouth of the Fresh Kil, was surveyed for "John Lake and Joakim Gulick," as per p. 233 of Vol. II. of Land Papers. There was a John Lake of Fld[•] who

bought Nov. 21, 1670, of James Hubbard of G^d a horse, as
per G^d rec. Issue:—Jan Janse of G^d, bp. Apl. 16, 1688, in
Fl^h; and Daniel Janse of G^d, bp. Apl. 25, 1696. Made his
mark to documents. ˙

Jan Janse of G^d, bp. Apl. 16, 1688. No further trace.

LA MAISTRE, LE MAISTRE, or LA METER, GLANDE or
CLAUDE, m. *Hester Du Bois;* conveyed Sept. 13, 1659, to
" Baertelt Claesen " (Van Ruynen) his bouwery on the W.
side of the highway in Fl^h, as per p. 13½ of Lib. B of Fl^h
rec. July 31, 1662, he sold to Joncker Balthazer Vosch
(Balthazer Vosch Junr) a farm of 21 morgens in Fl^h, as per
p. 105 of Lib. B of Fl^h rec. Oct. 12, 1665, he and w. joined
the D. ch. of N. Y. Issue:—(sup.) Johannes, bp. Mar. 6,
1653, in N. A. Signed his name *"Glande Le Maistre."*

LAMBERTSZ or LAMBERTSEN, ADRIAEN, on Gov. Andros's
patent of N. L. of 1677, and on ass. roll of Fl^h of 1675.
Owned 60 A. in N. L. adjoining J^a. Issue:—Catalina.
Made his mark to documents.

Cornelis, see Cool.

Hendrick, took the oath of allegiance in Br^n in 1687. He
may be one of the sons of Lambert Huybertsen Moll.

Jacob of Kings Co., ag. 20, deposes in 1644 in relation to
the burning of Jochem Pietersen's house by the Indians, as
per p. 68 of Furman's Antiquities of L. I.

Jan, m. Harentje Williams; both of Fl^h ch. in 1677.

Jan, m. Gerretje Reiniers. Mem. of Fld^a ch. in 1677,
entered on the record as removed.

Peter, among first settlers of Bu^k in 1661, per Thompson's
L. I.

Peter, see De Hart.

Peter, and others of Br^n, in 1663 applied for liberty to
form a village, and for salt-meadows, as per p. 120 of Vol.
1 of Stiles's Br^n. A catechumen of Br^n ch. in 1662.

Ryer, see Moll.

Thomas, carpenter, emigrated from Naarden in North
Holland in 1651; m. Nov. 27, 1654, in N. A., Jannetje Jans
or Jurians, wid. Resided at first in N. A. May 26, 1663,
he with others, as per p. 117 of Vol. X of Col. Man., setting
forth that they had obtained a piece of land in the rear of
the Wallabout and back of Marcus plantation, which they
had commenced to improve, asked leave to build a hamlet
there. This was probably the commencement of the village
of Bedford. Feb. 18, 1666, he obtained a patent for 20
morgens at Bedford (probably on the land referred to in
the rear of the Wallabout), on which he settled. Was con-

stable of Br^n in 1672, as per p. 7 of Cal. of Eng. Man.; a mag. of Br^n in 1673 and '79; name on the patent of 1677; elder in the R. D. ch. of Br^n in 1678; on ass. rolls of 1675, '76, and '83; on cen. of 1698; and took the oath of allegiance in Br^n in 1687. In 1689 he was appointed lieut. of the militia of Br^n. A Thomas Lambertse's name appears on the patent of J^a, as per p. 85 of the Bergen Genealogy and p. 11 of the Lefferts Genealogy. Issue:—Lysbeth or Elizabeth Thomas, bp. Apl. 26, 1656, who m. Jacob Jorise; and Lambert Thomas, bp. May 26, 1658, of whom no further trace—both bp. in N. A. Signed his name *"Thomas Lambertsen."*

LAMOTHE, PETER, among the first settlers of Bu^k in 1661. By an inventory of his property, made Oct. 31, 1662, it appears that he and Jacob France Barbier cultivated lands together, as per Bu^k rec.

LANE, LAAN, LAEN, or LANEN, ADRIAEN, GYSBERT THYSEN, JACOB THYSEN, JAN THYSEN, and TEUNIS JANSE, (see Van Pelt). It is probable that many if not all of the Lanes or Laans of Monmouth Co., N. J., are of the same stock or family as the Van Pelts, using Lane, Laan, or Laen as their surname instead of Van Pelt, and that they are the descendants of Gysbert Thysz Van Pelt Lanen and Jacob Thysz Van Pelt Lanen.

Symon, of G^d in 1657, as per town rec. Signed his name *"Symon Lane,"* Clericus.

LANELL, THOMAS, allotted land on Gisbert's I., G^d, Jan. 5, 1670, as per G^d rec.

LANGESTRAAT, ADRIAEN, bp. Sept. 16, 1677; d. 1728; m. *Christina Janse.* On ass. roll of Fld^s of 1693 and cen. of 1698; also owned land in G^d; deacon of Freehold R. D. ch. in 1721, to which place he had removed. In 1723, an Adriaen Langestraet and Christina Janse his w., mem. of Freehold R. D. ch. Issue, all bp. at Marlboro:—Christine or Katharine, bp. Nov. 27, 1709, m. Aug. 24, 1741, Wm Williamsen of the Raritan; Jan, bp. Jan. 13, 1712, m. Dec. 17, 1746, Antje Cowenhoven; Dirck of Princeton, b. about 1713, m. about 1749 Margaret Schenck wid. of Wm Cowenhoven; Nelly, b. about 1715; Winnifred, b. about 1718; Maria, b. about 1721, m. Dec. 5, 1742, Dirck Sutphen; Arianche, b. about 1723; and Stoffel, b. about 1726, m. Nov. 28, 1753, Nelly Schenck, as per Rev. G. C. Schenck.

Derick Stoffelsz, emigrated in 1657, m. 1st Catharina Van

Lieuwen; m. 2ᵈ, prior to Feb. 13, 1690, Johanna **Havens** wid. of Johannis Holsaert. Mem. of Fldˢ D. ch. in 1677, took the oath of allegiance there in 1687; on ass. roll of said town of 1693 and cen. of 1698. In ante-nuptial agreement with his 2ᵈ w. on the Gᵈ rec. of Feb. 13, 1690, reference is made to his s. Stoffel Dircksen. At an early period, as per Rev. G. C. Schenck, he bought land at Shrewsbury, N. J., which he devised by will to his s. Richard. Issue:— Stoffel Dircksen; Claasje Dircksen, b. about 1672, m. Abraham Lott of Jˢ; Adrian, bp. Sept. 16, 1677; Richard of Shrewsbury, b. about 1680; (sup.) Johannis; and Samuel, (sup.) m. Barbara Antonides. Signed his name "*Dirck Stoffels.*"

(Sup.) *Jan* or *Johannis Dircksen*, b. 1629. Appointed Apl. 28, 1666, by the mag. of Flʰ one of the guardians of Aernout Reynders s. of Reyndert Arensen and Annetien Hermans, said Annetien being dec. and said Aernout having married Annetien Aukens, as per p. 61 of Lib. D of Flʰ rec. Allowed to follow the occupation of carman by the court in N. A. in 1674,' as per p. 494 of Valentine's Manual of 1855. June 8, 1690, he made an affidavit relating to the troubles in N. Y. during Gov. Leisler's administration, as per p. 741 of Vol. III. of Doc. of Col. His.

Stoffel Dircksen of Fldˢ and N. J., m. Mayke Laanen dau. of Gysbrecht Tuysz Lanen Van Pelt of N. U. Deacon of Fldˢ D. ch. in 1698. Removed to the Neversinks in Monmouth Co., N. J., where his descendants abound. In his will, da. Dec. 1, 1739, pro. Mar. 1, 1741, he calls himself Theophilus, an improper change for Stoffel or Christopher. The will of Mayke his w. is da. Apl. 8, 1752, and pro. Mar. 13, 1753. These wills name as their children, Jonica, Catharine, Mary, Sarah, Maria, Ann, and Gisbert. Issue:—Dirck, bp. Apl. 25, 1696, in Brⁿ, m. Jane or Jonica, probably d. at date of his father's will; Jonica or Jane; Catharine, (sup.) m. Jan Sutphen of N. J.; Mary or Maria, bp. May 6, 1702, m. 1ˢᵗ Wᵐ Hendricksen of N. J., m. 2ᵈ (sup.) Dirck Sutphen; Sarah, b. about 1705; Gisbert, b. about 1707, m. Rachel Schenck, d. 1758; Aurie, bp. Nov. 6, 1710, m. May 6, 1754, Lydia Hull; Stoffel, bp. Dec. 25, 1713, resided at Upper Freehold, m. Dec. 16, 1743, Abagail Wooley, d. 1784; Moica, bp. Mar. 6, 1716, m. (sup.) Johannes Leek; and Ann, b. about 1718. Signed his name "*Stoffel Langstrat.*"

, LAORILLE, JACOB, on ass. roll of Buᵏ of 1676.

LARENSEN, JAN, of Gᵈ, exchanged lands with Nichˢ Stillwell Jan. 31, 1688-9, as per Gᵈ rec.

LARZELERE or LA RESIELIERE, CLAES JACOBSE, of N. L., m. *Mary* or *Maria Granger* or *Gransen;* d. prior to 1699; both mem. of Fl^h ch. in 1677, and on ass. roll of Fl^h of 1683. Bought May 7, 1682, of Catharine Van Werven wid. of Do. Polhemius 2 lots of woodland, Nos. 13 and 14, lying in the new division (N. L.) of Fl^h, between the lots of Jan Sebringh and of Willem Jacobse (Van Boerum). Mar. 22, 1688-9, Mary his wid. sold to Garret Garretse Dorlant 2 lots in the new lots of Fl^h, on the 3^d kill, conveyed to him by Theodorus Polhemius Mar. 4, 1679-80, cong. each 30 A., as per p. 160 of Lib. 1 of Con. Clute, in his History of S. I., says Jacob Larzelere bought land there in 1686. Issue:—Magdalena, bp. Jan. 5, 1679; Maria, bp. June 12, 1681; and Claes or Nicholas. Made his mark "J L" to documents.

Claes or *Nicholas,* of N. L. in 1688. The Larzelere family appear to have removed to S. I., where Nicholas bought land in 1693, was at one time sheriff of the county, and had several children, some of whom or their descendants settled in Bucks Co., Pa., and some now reside in this county.

LAURENS, CHRISTOFFEL, see Lawrence.

LAURENSE or LAURENTSZ, see Louwerense.
Hans and *Jan,* see Duyts or Duits.

LAURENTSEN, COSYN, with others made an affidavit, July 6, 1664, as to the circumstances attending the killing of a man near the house of Gerrit Wolfertsen (Cowenhoven) on the flats or plains in Fld^s, as per p. 89 of Cal. of Dutch Man.

Jan or *John,* held land in Bedford prior to 1700, as per deed of Lamberts to Vanderhove on p. 694 of Lib. 9 of Con. He m. Marritje Vonk. Issue:—Cornelis, bp. Apl. 25, 1696.

LAUS, JOHN, of G^d in 1656, per Thompson's L. I.

LAVALL, CAPT., a merchant, on Stoothoff's books of 1682. His old ketch, sunk in Westchester Creek, was confiscated in 1673, as per p. 603 of Vol. II. of Doc. of Col. His. of N. Y. Had a dau. Margaret.

LAW, LYMAN, of G^d in 1656, per Thompson's L. I.

LAWRENCE, CHRISTOFFEL, and Raef Cardell undertook

Oct. 3, 1639, a tobacco plantation of 3 morgens adjoining that of William Adriansen (Bennet) at Gowanus. Adriansen to furnish the necessary palisades (fence), and the necessary food from the 1ˢᵗ of March until one month after the tobacco is housed, for which they were to pay Adriansen 350 lbs. of tobacco and to build the necessary tobacco-house, as per O'Callaghan's Trans. of Dutch Man. and p. 11 of Cal. of Dutch Man. July 3, 1643, he obtained a patent for 20 morgens, 400 rods of land adjoining E. the Indian maize-land, on the bay of the North River, as per p. 367 of said Cal.

William, d. about 1680; bought Sept. 2, 1660, of John Thomas parcel or plantation-lot No. 4 in Gᵈ, as per town rec., which he sold Sept. 9, 1663, to Richard Stillwell. Settled in Hempstead; see p. 12 of Vol. X. of Gen. Rec. Made his mark "W. L." to documents. A Wᵐ Lawrence, ag. 12, was transported to New England, as per p. 45 of Hotten's Emigrants.

LAY, PIETER JANSEN, on ass. roll of Buᵏ of 1683.

LAYFORCE, ADRIAN, on Gov. Dongan's patent of Buᵏ of 1687.

LEACOCK, ROBERT, bought a house and lot at the ferry in Brⁿ in 1680 of Jan Aertse Middagh, as per deed on p. 77 of Lib. 2 of Con.

LEBLIANTHE, JOHN, owned one half of lot No. 14 in Gᵈ Neck in 1688, as per town rec.

LECHINIER or LESCUIER, JEAN, see Luquier or Lesquier.

LE CLER or CLERK, see La Clerk.

LEDGE, ACKNOW, of S. I., sold June 14, 1696, his title to a house, orchard, and garden in Gᵈ to Hendrick Ricke (Suydam) of Flʰ, as per Gᵈ rec.

LEE, ESCUYER, among the early settlers of Brⁿ, per Thompson's L. I. Sept. 22, 1693, a Mary Lescuye of Buᵏ m. in N. Y. Jan Swenhoven of "Rochel."

James, (sup.) English, of Gᵈ in 1676, per Thompson's L. I.

Joseph, complained Jan. 20, 1683, to the court of sessions against Theodorus Polhemius for levying on money in the hands of Auke Jansen (Van Nuyse), as per court rec. Was deputy sheriff in 1682, as per p. 162 of Lib. A of Fl^h rec. Signed his name "*Joseph Lee.*"

LEENDERTSE, see Vander Grift and Arentse.
Albert, of Fld^a in 1668, per town rec.
Arent, of Fld^a in 1688, per town rec.

LEENDERTSEN, JACOB, see Vandegrift.

LEENSEN or LENNORDSEN, ALEXANDER or SANDER, bought Sept. 10, 1652, of Capt. Brian Newton his plantation with the improvements thereon in G^d. Owned land in said town in 1670 at Seller's Neck, between land of James Bowne and the highway, as per G^d rec. Signed his name "*Alexander Leensen.*"

LEERS, GERRET, see Serdts.

LE FEBRE, see La Febre.

LEFFERTS, ABRAHAM, (s. of Leffert Pieterse,) b. Sept. 1, 1692, in Fl^h; m. *Sarah Hoogland.* Settled in the city of N. Y. and engaged in mercantile business. Issue:—Elizabeth, bp. Aug. 1, 1714; Abraham, bp. Sept. 25, 1715, d. young; Leffert, bp. Dec. 18, 1716, probably d. young; Dirck of N. Y., bp. Apl. 26, 1719—all bp. in N. Y.; Catharine, m. Peter Luyster of Oyster Bay; and Elizabeth, bp. Oct. 21, 1724, m. Peter Clopper of N. Y. Signed his name "*Abraham Lefferts.*"

Auke (s. of Leffert Pieterse), b. Apl. 4, 1678; m. 1st, May 29, 1703, Marytje Ten Eyck of N. Y.; m. 2^d, July 30, 1735, Catharine dau. of Benjamin Hegeman of Fl^h, wid. of —— Vonk. At first a farmer in Fl^h, and prior to 1709 removed to the vicinity of Middletown, Monmouth Co.,N. J. Issue:—Abagail, b. Mar. 15, 1708, m. Cyrenus Van Mater of N. J.; Leffert of N. J., bp. Oct. 4, 1711; Aelke or Nelke, bp. Nov. 22, 1713, m. Okey Wyckoff of N. J.; Anne; Benjamin of N. J.; Mary; and Peter of N. J., whose descendants compose the N. J. branch of the family, and generally write their surname "*Leffertson.*"

Isaac (s. of Leffert Pieterse), b. June 15, 1688; m. Harmpie ——; d. Oct. 18, 1746. Resided in Fl^h, a farmer, of which town in 1726 and '27 he was constable. Issue:— Leffert of Fl^h, b. Feb. 20, 1723; Hendrick of J^a, b. July 5, 1725; Isaac of J^a, bp. Aug. 16, 1730, at N. U.; and Harmpje;

m. Hendrick Suydam of Hallet's Cove. Signed his name
"*Isaac Leffertze.*"

Jacob or *Jacobus* (s. of Leffert Pieterse), b. June 9, 1686;
m. Oct. 7, 1716, Jannetje dau. of Claes or Nicholas Barentse
Blom; d. Sept. 3, 1768. Was a farmer in Bedford, and his
name is sometimes written "Isaac Hagewoutt." Will da.
May 11, 1768; pro. Dec. 9, 1768; rec. p. 460, Lib. 26, N. Y.
surr. off. Issue:—Abagail, b. Oct. 1, 1717, m. Lambert
Suydam; Nicholas of Bu^k, b. Apl. 6, 1719; Elizabeth or
Eliza, b. Mar. 8, 1721, m. Hendrick Fine; Aeltje or Neltye,
b. Nov. 3, 1723, m. Jacobus Vanderbilt; Leffert of Bedford,
b. Mar. 14, 1727; Jannetje, b. June 25, 1729, m. Jeronemus
Rapalje; Jacobus of N. Y., b. Nov. 26, 1731; and Barent of
Bedford, b. Nov. 2, 1736. Signed his name "*Jacobus Lef-
fertsz.*"

Jan (s. of Leffert Pieterse), b. Jan. 14, 1684; m. Margrietje
——. Issue:—Margrietje. No further trace.

Leffert (*Leffert Pieterse*) from Haughwout or Hauwert in
North Holland, whose children sometimes used Hagewout
or Haughwout as the family name, emigrated with his
parents in 1660; m. Abagail da. of Auke Janse Van
Nuyse, commonly known as Auke Janse; and d. July 19,
1748. Settled, on a farm in Fl^h, where he was assessed in
1675, his name appearing on the patent for the land in N.
L. of 1677, and where he took the oath of allegiance in
1687. In 1700 he bought a farm in Bedford, on which his
s. Jacobus settled. From an entry on p. 108 of Lib. B of
Fl^h town rec. of Oct. 15, 1662, it appears that the father of
Leffert Pieterse was Pieter Janse, and his mother Femmetje
Hermens, who after the death of her husband m. 2^d Pieter
Jacobse Van Noortbrook; that, on her second marriage, at
her request "Jan Seuberen and Pieter Lodt," both old
schepenen, were appointed guardians of Leffert Pieterse
and Pieter Pieterse, her children by her first husband, and
minors. At a town meeting in Fl^h on the 21st of March,
1695-6, it was unanimously resolved " that for the time of six
following years from the date hereof, noe men shall cutt off or
fell any young trees within the limits or bounds of our towne
of fflatbush for the use off firewood or burning brick, smith's
coals, or brewing, or such like, upon the penalty off two
pieces of eight the first default, and the second double, and
further are chosen by the towne people three men, to wit,
Jan Van Ditmarse, Stoffel Probasco, and *Leffert Pieterse*, to
run over and stake the meadows, and according so that
every one shall be bound to dig his part of ditches over his
lott to the breadth of two ffeet and a half, in depth two
spades. As also on the outside each his part of fences, and

that before the sixth day of Aprill next with good or sufficient fence, upon the penalty of two pieces of eight."

"Joseph Hegeman,

"May 12, 1696."   Stoffel Probasco."

The above law is confirmed by the court of sessions. See
p. 97 of Lib. 2 of Con.

Issue:—Altien, b. June 2, 1676, and d. single; Auke, b.
Apl. 4, 1678; Pieter, b. May 18, 1680; Rachel, b. Jan. 17,
1682, and m. Jan Waldron; Jan, bp. Jan. 14, 1684; Jacobus,
b. June 9, 1686; Isaac, b. June 15, 1688; Abraham, b. Sept.
1, 1692; Madalina, b. Aug. 20, 1694, m. Garret Martense;
Ann or Antien, b. Mar. 1, 1696, d. single; Abagail, b. Aug.
14, 1698, d. young; Leffert, b. May 22, 1701; and Benjamin,
b. May 2, 1704. Signed his name "*Leffert Pietersen.*"

Pieter (s. of Leffert Pieterse), b. May 18, 1680; m. Eyte or
Ida da. of Hendrick Suydam of Fl[h]; d. Mar. 13, 1774. Occu-
pied his father's farm in Fl[h], of which town he was super-
visor in 1626 and '27. Issue:—Leffert, who settled in Bucks
Co., Pa., and is the ancestor of the Pennsylvania branch of
the family; Jan, b. Mar. 16, 1719; Seytie, b. Jan. 8, 1721, m.
W[m] Johnson of G[d]; Adriaentje, m. Ab[m] Voorhees of Fld[s];
Antje, b. May 12, 1728, m. Gerret Kouwenhoven of Fld[s];
Jacobus, b. May 9, 1730; Geertje, b. July 11, 1731; and Aba-
gail, b. Sept. 12, 1735, m. (sup.) Jacobus Van Deventer of
Fl[h]. Signed his name "*Pieter Leffertsz.*"

LEFFERTSEN, BARENT. His name appears on the petition
of May, 1664, for a canal at Red Hoek, as per p. 68 of Vol.
1 of Stiles's Br[n]. Made his mark to documents.

Jan. His name appears on the above-referred-to petition
of 1664. Made his mark to documents.

LEHEY, WILLIAM, agreed Dec. 10, 1675, with John Lake to
build him a house, 26 by 16 ft., in G[d], as per G[d] rec.
Signed his name "*Will. nol Lehey.*"

LE MAISTRE, see La Maistre.

LEMMERT, ANTHONY, servant of Anthony Jansen from
Salee of N. U., as per Col. Rec.

LENARD or LENARDSEN, JACOB. June 7, 1669, he brought a
suit against John Griggs in the court of sessions at G[d] for
debt, as per G[d] rec.

LEOOME or LOONE, ANTHONY, (Spaniard,) made an agreement Feb. 14, 1651, with the inhabitants of G[d] to attend

their cattle as herder for 8 months; he to go out with the herd in the morning and bring them back at such time towards night as might be required, for which he was to receive 280 Carolus guilders, as per G[d] rec.

LEQUIER, see Luquier.

LETELIER, BARNET GANITZEE, a mag. of Bu[k] in 1664 and '65.
Jan, see Tilje.

LEWIS, JOHN, on indian deed of Br[n] of 1670.

LEYDECKER, see Lydecker.

LEYDEN, JAN, on petition of 1664 for a canal at Red Hoek.

LEYNERSEN, SAMUEL, sold a piece of salt-meadows in G[d] to Sarah w. of Charles Bridges, who in 1678 complained to the court of sessions of James Hubbard depriving her of the use of the same.

LINDE or VAN DER LINDE, PIETER, from Belle in Flanders, paid Apl. 18, 1639, to David Pietersen and Frederick de Vries 140 Carolus gl. ($56) for passage for himself and w. to N. N., as per p. 7 of Cal. of Dutch Man. He m. 1st *Elsje Barents;* m. 2[d], July 10, 1644, in N. A., *Martha Chambers* or *Ekomberts* of Newkirk in Flanders, wid. of Jan Manje or Monnye, with whom he entered into a marriage-contract July 1, 1644, as per p. 28 of Cal. of Dutch Man. He appears to have resided at first in N. A., following his profession as a physician, and after his second marriage probably removed to Jan Manje's patent in Br[n], which he sold Jan. 23, 1652, to Barent Joosten, as per p. 55 of said Cal. Owned several pieces of property in N. A., and in 1655 was an inspector of tobacco. There is a river Linde in Friesland, a hamlet of that name in Groningen, and also in Overyssel and Gelderland. There was a Joost van der Linde in Bergen, N. J., in 1674, and members of the family abound in the vicinity of Hackensack in said State. Signed his name *"Pieter Linde."*
Roelof, m. Susanna Hendricks Brinckerhoff of Hackensack, and a mem. of the R. D. ch. of that place in 1700. He with others obtained Sept. 4, 1674, of Gov. Colve a deed for 264 A. of land on the Northwest Hoek of S. I., as per p. 55 of Vol. 1 of Land Papers.

LINTWEEVER, BART, on Stoothoff's books of 1681.

LIVINGSTON, CORNELIUS P., conveyed Nov. 23, 1693, land in Br⁰ to Jan Aersen (Middagh), as per p. 143 of Lib. 1 of Con.

LOCK, CLAES, on Stoothoff's books of 1675. There was a Claes Hendricksen Lock who m. Oct. 18, 1671, in N. Y., Cuiertje Hendricks, and had 3 chil. bp. in said city.

John Pieter and John Pices leased Apl. 8, 1643, Remmert Jansen's (Vanderbeek) plantation at the Wallabout, as per O'Callaghan's Man. Trans. of Dutch Man. Also see p. 21 of Cal. of Dutch Man.

LODEWICK, HANS, obtained a patent Nov. 3, 1645, for land in Br⁰. On absconding, an inventory of his property in Br⁰ was taken in 1648, as per p. 44 of Cal. of Dutch Man. and per p. 59 of Vol. III. of O'Callaghan's Man. Trans. of Dutch Man.

Colonel, on Stoothoff's books of 1700.

Jan, paid 2 gl. 9 st., clergyman's salary, in 1681, as per Flʰ rec.

LONDON or LONNEN, AMBROSE, (sup. English,) m. *Mary* ——; was in this country as early as 1641, as per O'Callaghan's Man. Trans. of Dutch Man., and among the first settlers of Gᵈ, where he was allotted a plantation-lot Nov. 12, 1646, as per Gᵈ rec. Mar. 26, 1653, he bought of Peter Symson, agent of Wᵐ Teller, Teller's plantation in Gᵈ. Aug. 1, 1661, he gave a note to John Ward for 200 gl. on the purchase of a house and plantation at the bay of the North River on L. I. See p. 16 of Vol. I. of Dutch Man. Made his mark to documents.

LONGSTREET or LONGESTRAET, see Langestraet.

LOOCKRMAN, GOVERT, from Turnhout in the Netherlands, emigrated in 1663 on the yacht Sᵗ Martyn as cook's mate, as per p. 432 of Vol. I. of Doc. of Col. His., and settled at first in N. A., where he was engaged in mercantile business. He m. 1ˢᵗ, Feb. 26. 1641, in Amsterdam, while on a visit there, *Ariaentje Jans;* m. 2ᵈ, July 11, 1649, *Marretje Jans;* and m. 3ᵈ *Elsje Tymens,* wid. successively of Peter Corˢ Van der Veen and of Dirck Corneliszen, as per p. 123 of Vol. VIII. of the Genealogical and Biographical Record. He d. in 1670. In 1664 he took the oath of allegiance in N. Y. to the English. His name appears among the patentees of

Fld[a] in 1667, where he at one period resided; and Mar. 22, 1674, his wid., Jacob Loockrmans, and Hans Kierstede, on the part of his heirs, sold his plantation of 200 A. in said town to Roelof Martense Schenck, as per town rec. of Fld[a]. Govert had brothers Jacob and Pieter Janse, who settled in Beverwyck (Albany). Issue:—Marretje or Maria, b. Nov. 3, 1641, and m. Balthazer Bayard; Jannetje, b. Sept. 23, 1643, and m. Dr. Hans Kierstede; (by 2[d] wife) Jacob, bp. Mar. 17, 1652, in N. Y., who was a physician in said place and m. Helena Ketin. Signed his name "*Govert Loockrman.*"

LOOSIE, CORNELIS, see Looyse.

LOOTMAN, JURRIAAN, from Kingston, of N. U. in 1684, as per Fl[h] ch. rec.

LOOYSE or LOYSE, CORNELIS, emigrated in 1651, and took the oath of allegiance in Bu[k] in 1687 ; on ass. roll of said town of 1693 and cen. of 1698. Was one of the soldiers sent to Albany in 1689, as per p. 215 of Vol. II. of Doc. His. of N. Y.
  Jacobus, on ass. roll of Bu[k] of 1693 and cen. of 1698.
  Pieter, on ass. roll of Bu[k] of 1693 and cen. of 1698.

LORAS, PIETER, bought Jan. 9, 1662, plantation-lot No. 34 in G[d], as per town rec.

LORD, ANTHONY, of G[d] Feb. 6, 1657, as per p. 181 of Cal. of Dutch Man. Made his mark to documents.

LOTT, ABRAHAM (PETERSE), m. 1st *Claesje Langestraet;* m. 2[d] *Geertje* ——. Resided in J[a]. Will da. July 1, 1760; pro. Sept. 4, 1766; rec. p. 320, Lib. 25, N. Y. surr. off. Issue:— Rem of J[a]; Hendrick; Jacob; Isaac of Bu[k]; Abraham (dec. at date of his father's will, having children, Abraham, Motye and Cornelius); John of Fld[a], bp. Apl. 25, 1696; Peter of N. Y., bp. Oct. 31, 1697; and Charity, who m. Nicholas Van Artsdalen of J[a].
  Abraham (Engelbertse) of Fl[h], b. Sept. 7, 1684; m. Nov. 15, 1709, Catharine dau. of Elbert Hegeman; d. July 29, 1754; assemblyman from 1737 to '60, as per N. Y. civil list. In early life made several voyages to the West Indies as supercargo. Owned and resided in the homestead of his father in Fl[h]. Issue:—Jacobus; Abraham of N. Y.; Cornelia, b. Apl. 20, 1714, and m. John Vanderveer of Keuter's Hoek; and Engelbert of Fl[h], b. May 7, 1719. Signed his name "*Abraham Lott.*"
  Bartel Engelbertsen from "Reynarwout" (probably *Rui-*

nerwold in Drenthe), m. Dec. 16, 1662, Harmantje Barents of the same place; d. about 1663. July 28, 1663, Edward Griffen conveyed to "Bartel Lot and Pieter Loot" bouwery No. 9 in "Midwout," next to the pastor's land, 600 rods in length and 24 in breadth, cong. 24 morgens, as per book GG in off. of Sec. of State, Albany, N. Y. Harmantje his w. joined the R. D. ch. in N. Y. in 1670. He appears to have resided at one period in Bergen, N. J., where a "Barthel Lott" took the oath of allegiance in 1665, as per p. 102 of Winfield's Hudson Co. Issue:—Engel, bp. Dec. 16, 1663, in N. A.; and Anna Maria, bp. Jan. 4, 1668, in N. Y. Signed his name *"Bartel Lot."*

Engelbert (Pieterse) of Fl[h], b. Dec. —, 1654; m. Oct. 27, 1678, Cornelia dau. of Abraham De La Noy; d. Apl. 30, 1730. Joined the R. D. ch. of N. Y. Mar. 1, 1674, and entered on the record as removed to New Castle. In his younger days resided at New Castle on the Delaware, where he owned a tract of land on Christiana Creek, as per Thompson's L. I. In 1682 he removed back to Fl[h], where he took the oath of allegiance in 1687, and in 1698 was high sheriff of the county. Issue:—Pieter, bp. Nov. 16, 1682, in N. Y.; Abraham, b. Sept. 7, 1684; Geertruy, bp. Feb. 5, 1696, in N. Y., d. young; Cornelia, bp. July 21, 1698, d. young; Johannes of Fl[h], bp. July 27, 1701, in Br[n]; Geertruy, b. Dec. 4, 1703; and Elizabeth, bp. Mar. 12, 1715, m. Jacobus Pieter Snyder. Signed his name *"Engel Bart Lott."*

Hendrick. His name appears on Do. Van Zuuren's list of ch. mem. of 1677. No further trace.

Hendrick (Pieterse), m. Catrina (sup.) De Witt, and settled in J[s], where he bought 37 A. of W[m] Creed in 1683. Took the oath of allegiance in Fl[h] in 1687. In partnership with Polhemus and Cortelyou he bought 1200 A. at Millstone, N. J., in 1701. Issue:—Dorothy, b. Dec. 14, 1686; Geertruy, b. May 4, 1688, m. Andries Onderdonk; Pieter, b. Mar. 1, 1690; Johannes, b. May 11, 1692; Maria, b. Oct. 30, 1693, (sup.) m. Johannes Schenck; and (sup.) Antie, b. Aug. 23, 1696, m. Folkert Folkertsen. Signed his name *"Hendrick Lott."*

Johannes (Pieterse), m. Antje Rapalje. Suppose he resided in Fl[h]. No further trace.

Johannes (Engelbertse), bp. July 27, 1701; m. 1st, Nov. 4, 1721, Lammetje dau. of Peter Stryker; d. 1732; resided in Fl[h]. Issue:—Engelbert, b. Sept. 23, 1722; Annetje, b. Sept. 9, 1724, and m. Cornelius Van Duyne; Peter of Fl[h], b. Aug. 14, 1726; Cornelia, b. Sept. 29, 1728; and Johannes of Fld[s], b. Sept. 2, 1730. Signed his name *"Johannes Lott."*

Johannes (Hendrickse) of Fl[h], b. May 11, 1692; m. ——

——; d. Apl. 8, 1775, in Fld⁴. Mem. of Assembly from 1727 to 1747, as per N. Y. civil list. Will da. Sept. 28, 1771; pro. May 2, 1775. Issue:—Hendrick of New J⁴, b. Nov. 7, 1715; Joris or George of N. U., b. Oct. 3, 1717; Katrina, b. Oct. 22, 1719, and m. Derick Remsen; Maria, b. Mar. 7, 1722, m. Carel Boerum; Petrus of Fld⁴, b. Nov. 20, 1723; Nicklaes, b. Apl. 30, 1728; Nieltien, b. Nov. 13, 1730, m. John Snediker; Johannes of N. L., b. Dec. 31, 1731; Folkert, b. Oct. 5, 1732; Antie, b. Mar. 19, 1737, m. Stephen Lott; Doritie, b. Nov. 10, 1740, m. John Van Leuwen; and Jeromus of Fld⁴, b. Jan. 26, 1743. Signed his name "*Johannes Lott*."

Johannes or *Jan* (Abrahamse), bp. Apl. 25, 1696; m. (sup.) Elsje dau. of Hendrick Suydam. Resided in Fld⁴, and deacon of the R. D. ch. of that place in 1722. Issue:—Geertje or Charity, b. Feb. 28, 1727, m. Johannes Van Sickelen; Hendrick of Fld⁴, b. Sept. 10, 1729; and Abraham, b. Apl. 7, 1732.

Peter, the common ancestor of the family, emigrated in 1652, and settled in Flh; m. Gertrude ——, who d. in 1704; both mem. of Flh R. D. ch. in 1677. Obtained Jan. 25, 1662, a patent for 24 morgens in Flh, which he sold Mar. 22, 1674, to Jan Cornelise Boomgaert. His name appears on Gov. Dongan's patent of Flh of 1685, of which town he was a mag. in 1656 and '73, and where he took the oath of allegiance in 1687. From a map on file in the off. of the Sec. of State at Albany, made by "Ja. Cortelyan, sworn surveyor," filed Aug. 8, 1681, of 6 farms in Flh, it appears that "Pieter Lott" owned a farm on the W. side of the "highway to the ferry" S. of Do. Polhemius's double lot and N. of that of "Klyn Dirk" (Dirk Janse Hoogland), "broad before 26 Rod 8 foot" (about $311\frac{2}{10}$ ft. English measure), "after 27 Rod" (about $325\frac{8}{10}$ ft. English), "long 600 Rod" (about 7241 ft. English). This is clearly the lot which Edward Griffen conveyed to "Bartel Lot and Peter Loot," known as No. 9, next to the pastor's (Do. Polhemius's) land, cong. 24 morgens, herein before referred to in the account of Bartel Engelbertsen Lott, and now or late the property of Sarah w. of John Ditmas and dau. of Andrew Suydam. Issue:—Engelbert of Flh, b. Dec. 1654; Catrina, m. Douwe Jansen Van Ditmarsen; Peter; Abraham; Hendrick of J⁴; and Johannes. Signed his name "*Peter Lot*" and "*Peter Lodt*."

Pieter (Engelbertse) of Flh, bp. Nov. 16, 1682, in N. Y.; m. Nishe ——; d. 1721. Settled at Hopewell, Hunterdon Co., N. J. Will 'da. Dec. 11, 1710; .pro. Apl. 17, 1721. Issue:—Theophilus; Richard of Hopewell; Hannah; Jane; Peter of South Amboy; John; and Philip.

Pieter (Hendrickse), b. Mar. 1, 1691; m. Nov. 12, 1709, (sup.) Femmetje Remsen. In 1722 he and his w. joined the R. D. ch. of N. Y. on certificate from L. I. Issue:—Hendrick of Bedford and Fld¹, b. June 28, 1716; Mouris of N. L., b. Feb. 26, 1718; Cattrina, b. Aug. 28, 1720, m. Jacob Rapalje of Hurlgate; Antje or Agnietje, b. Oct. 18, 1721, m. Isaac Lefferts; Maria, b. Mar 7, 1723, m. Johannes Cornell; Pieter (sup.) of Bushwick, b. May 7, 1725; and John, b. Sept. 2, 1730. Signed his name "*Pieter Lott.*"

Pieter (Pieterse), m. Sarah ——. No further trace.

LOURENS, CHRISTOFFEL, obtained July 3, 1643, a patent for 20 morgens in Brⁿ.

LOURESSE, see Duyts.

LOUWER, JOHANNES, one of the applicants for a canal between Red Hoek and the mainland of Brⁿ in 1664, as per p. 68 of Vol. I. of Stiles's Brⁿ. There were Louws or Lous who settled on the Raritan at an early date.

LOUWERENSE, see Duyts.

LOUWERSE, PETER, of Gᵈ in 1660. Signed his name "*Peter Louwerse.*"

LOUWSEN or LOUWEN, see Van Schoonderwoert.

LOWE, JOHN. A suit was commenced against him in the court of sessions at Gᵈ in 1671 by Thomas Lambertsen and w. for defamation of character, on which he plead guilty, and was condemned to pay the costs of court and admonished to keep a civil tongue in his head.

LOWYE, JOHN, allotted a plot in the North woods of Gᵈ in 1684, as per town rec.

LOY, CORNELIS JANSEN, on ass. roll of Buᵏ of 1683.
Jan Cornelise, on ass. roll of Buᵏ of 1683.
Pieter Jansen, on ass. roll of Buᵏ of 1683. A Pieter Loys or Loyise took the oath of allegiance in Buᵏ in 1687 as a native, who was probably this Pieter Jansen.

LOYSE, see Looyse.

13

LOZIER, PIETER JANSEN, m. Mar. 14, 1680, *Sarah Colfs.*
Issue:—Simon, bp. Jan. 30, 1681, in Br[n]. There are Losiers
residing in the vicinity of Hackensack, N. J.

LUBBERTSE, ELDERT, on ass. roll of Fl[h] of 1675.
Frederick, (or " Frerick Lubbertsen," as written by himself,)
b. 1609; m. 1st Styntje ——; m. 2[d], Aug. 17, 1657, Tryntje
Hendricks wid. of Cornelis Pietersen (Vroom). He emigrated
at an early period to this country, residing at first in N. A. as
early as 1639, where in 1641 he was one of the 12 men to whom
the trouble with the Indians was referred. May 23, 1640, he
obtained a patent for a large tract covering most of South Br[n];
Sept. 4, 1645, he obtained a patent for another plantation in
Br[n], to which place he removed; and was a mag. of said town
from 1653 to 1655, and in 1673. Issue:—Rebecca (by 1st w.),
who m. Jacob Leendertse Van der Grift; Elsje (by 2[d] w.), bp.
July 7, 1658, in N. Y., who m. Jacob Hansen Bergen; and
Aeltje, bp. July 25, 1660, who m. Cornelis Sebringh. Will da.
Nov. 22, 1679, and rec. on p. 215 of Lib. 1 (of the original) of
Con. Signed his name *"Frerick Lubbertsen."*
Gerret, allotted a farm of 27 morgens with plain and meadow
land in Fl[h] Jan. 11, 1671, in pursuance of the patent of said
town, where he resided probably as early as 1663. Resided in
the N. L. portion of the town, and on the ass. rolls of 1675 and
'83; a mem. of the R. D. ch. in 1677; on patent of 1685; and
took the oath of allegiance in said town in 1687. See p. 13 of
Lib. A of Fl[h] rec. A Gerret Lubbertse of N. Y. m. Mar. 12,
1684, Alida Evertsen of Albany, and had issue:—Grietje, bp.
Jan. 4, 1685; Grietje, bp. Aug. 15, 1686; and Rebecca, bp.
Mar. 4, 1688, as per p. 76 of Pierson's Early Settlers of Albany.
Gysbert, m. Elizabeth ——, who after his death m. Adriaan
Hendrickse Aten of Fl[h]. Issue:—Lubbert Gysbertse.
Hendrick, a representative of Br[n] in the Hempstead convention of 1665.
Lubbert (probably Westervelt), was granted Dec. 15, 1662,
on an application to the schout and schepens of Fl[h], a
building-plot on W. side of the village and S. side of the
road, as per p. 114 of Lib. B of Fl[h] rec. Bought Aug. 20,
1670, of Jan Miserol a house at "Rustenburch" (the local
name of the southerly side of the village) in Fl[h], as per p.
10 of Lib. A of Fl[h] rec. In 1678 he resided at Hackensack,
N. J., where the Westervelts are numerous. There was a
Jan, s. of Lubbert Lubbertse of N. Y., who d. at Bergen,
N. J., Aug. 23, 1674. Signed his name *"Lubbert Lubberts."*
Simon, on ass. roll of Fl[h] of 1675.
Thys from Ryp, a town in North Holland, m. Oct. 10,
1655, in N. A., Tryntje Jans from Amsterdam. In 1661 he

resided in Fl[h], where he bought a farm of 15½ morgens of "John Leek;" and in 1676 his name appears on the ass. roll of N. U., where he bought June 1, 1682, of Anthony Du Ceen a plantation on N. U. Lane lying on the S. side of land of Anthony Van Pelt. From N. U. he appears to have removed to Br[n], where he took the oath of allegiance in 1687. Issue:— —— ——, bp. Sept. 7, 1656, in N. Y.; and Pieter, bp. Dec. 26, 1657. Made his mark to documents.

William of N. U.; d. prior to Apl. 16, 1695.

LUCAS, AELBERT, paid towards the preacher's salary in Fl[h] in 1681.

LUCASSE, see Voorhees.

LUER, AUTIEN, paid towards the preacher's salary in Fl[h] in 1681.

LUINS, NATHANIEL, m. Nov. 13, 1679, at G[d], *Damris Baylies.*

LUNDE, PETER, of Br[n] Jan. 23, 1651, as per Col. Man. Probably intended for Peter Linde.

LUPARDUS, CHRISTIANUS, b. Mar. 10, 1695; m. 1st *Antye* ——; m. 2[d] *Lammetje* da. of Jan Strycker, wid. of Johannes Lott. Resided in Fl[h] in 1744. Issue:—Wilhelmus, bp. Aug. 27, 1721; (by 2[d] w.) Annetje, bp. Jan. 5, 1734-5; Christianus, bp. Aug. 27, 1737; and Antje, bp. Apl. 22, 1739. Signed his name "*Christianus Lupardus.*"

Rev. Gulielmus, m. Cornelia Van Wessel or Wesselen. Was minister of the Dutch Reformed congregations of Kings Co. from 1695 to 1702. Will da. Feb. 9, 1701-2; pro. Nov. 9, 1705; rec. p. 219, Lib. 7, N. Y. surr. off. Issue:— Anna or Johanna, b. July 29, 1694, in Dordrecht, South Holland, and m. Elbert Stoothoff; Christian, b. Mar. 10, 1695; and Adrianna, b. Dec. 29, 1697, and m. John Wyckoff. Signed his name "*W Lupardus.*"

LUQUIER or LESQUIER, ABRAHAM (Janse), of Bu[k].

Guilliam (Janse), bp. Sept. 27, 1667. Name on rec. of court of sessions of 1693.

Isaack of Bu[k], m. Mar. 29, 1711, Annetje Cortelyou of N. U.

Jan or *Jean*, the common ancestor of the family, emigrated from Paris in 1657 and settled in Bu^k, where he took the oath of allegiance in 1687. He m. Nov. 11, 1663, in N. A., Rachel Dirks, and d. in 1713. Feb. 28, 1663, he and Alexander Cochiveer petitioned each for a plantation in Bu^k (which he obtained a patent for), of which town he was a mag. in 1664 and '67; on patent of 1687 and cen. of 1698. In 1686 (John Lessurier) was commissioned ensign, as per p. 147 of Cal. of Eng. Man. Issue:—Jan or Johannes Junr; Pieter; Abraham; Isaac; Mary, who m. Dec. 5, 1693, in N. Y., John Seavenhoven from Rochelle; Rachel, b. 1679, who m. Dec. 13, 1694, in N. Y., David Sprong of Flushing, a resident of Bu^k; and Ghilliam, bp. Sept. 27, 1677.

Jan or *Johannes* Junr of Bu^k, m. Rachel ——. Their names appear on the records of the court of sessions of 1693, and his on those of 1695.

Pieter Janse of Bu^k, m. —— ——. (Sup.) Issue:—Maria, bp. Jan. 25, 1718; and Geertje, bp. June 29, 1720—both bp. in N. Y. Luquiers reside in Br^n, Queens Co., and E. N. J. An Abraham Luquier m. Maria Sebring, through whom he probably obtained the property in Br^n, on which his (Luqueer's) mill was located, and whose s. Nicholas m. Sarah da. of Jan Middagh.

Luvcasz, see Voorhies.

Luyster, Cornelis (*Pieterse*), b. 1662; m. 1st *Aaltje Willems;* m. 2^d, May 2, 1686, *Sarah Catharine Nevius*. In 1677 he and his w. Aaltje mem. of Fl^h R. D. ch., where he took the oath of allegiance in 1687 and resided as late as 1696, but finally removed to the Poor Bouwery in Newtown. By a deed recorded in Lib. 1 of Con. in 1687, his wife's name at that date appears to have been "Jannetje," from which it may be inferred that he had 3 wives. Issue:—Peter of Newtown, b. Mar. 10, 1687; Johannes of N. J., b. Mar. 22, 1691; Elbert of Fl^h, b. Mar. 21, 1693; Cornelis, who d. single; Mary, who m. Danl Rapalje; Hannah, who m. Barent Smith; Gertrude, m. Tunis Swart; Adrianna, m. Cor^s Wyckoff; Aletta, m. Joris Cowenhoven; and Sara, m. 1st Roelof Bragaw, m. 2^d Rev. Reinhart Ericksen. Made his mark to documents.

Elbert (Cornelise), b. Mar. 21, 1693, m. Oct. 6 or Sept. 27, 1720, Jacomina dau. of Gerret Cowenhoven. From Fl^h removed to the Poor Bouwery, Newtown. Issue:—Elizabeth, b. Aug. 30, 1721; Cornelius, b. Aug. 10, 1723; Gerret, b.

Dec. 24, 1725; Sarah, b. Apl. 25, 1728, m. Stephen Ryder; Jacomina, b. Sept. 4, 1730, m. John Swart; Aletta, b. May 30, 1733, m. Cor* Schenck; Jane, b. Apl. 9, 1736, m. Ab^m Rapalje; and Peter, b. Jan. 9, 1739, d. young.

Johannes (Cornelise), b. Mar. 22, 1691, in Fld*; m. Apl. 10, 1716, Lucretia Brower; d. Jan. 29, 1756. Left Fld* and settled on a farm near the village of Middletown, Monmouth Co., N. J., in 1717. Issue:—Sarah, b. Mar. 8, 1717, m. 1st Ryck Suydam, m. 2^d Wm Conover, d. Sept. 7, 1764; Peter of N. J., b. May 1, 1719, m. May 25, 1756, Anna Luyster, d. Feb. 12, 1810; Cornelius of N. J., b. Dec. 13, 1720, m. 1st Arinthe Conover, m. 2^d Marg^t Vanderbilt, d. Oct. 7, 1792; Johannes of N. J., b. May 25, 1723, m. Sarah Sweet, d. Sept. 7, 1769; Anna, b. Apl. 8, 1725, m. Oct. 17, 1744, Danl Barkeloo of Freehold; and Lucretia, b. Aug. 30, 1727, d. Mar. 26, 1792, single.

John (Pieterse), m. Wyntje dau. of Harck Siboutsen. June 1, 1697, 26 gl. were paid to the church in Fld* for a grave and the use of the pall for John Luyster, who was probably this John. Issue:—Pieter, b. Mar. 10, 1687.

Matthyas or *Tys* (Pieterse), b. in Europe, and came over with his father; m. Cornelia ——. From his being a mem. of the R. D. ch. of Br^n in 1677 and '85, hailing from Gowanus, it is evident that he resided there at that date. It is said he owned the farm in Fl^h late of John Neefus, where he probably finally resided. Issue:—Peter of Fl^h. Signed his name "*Matys Luyster.*"

Peter (Cornelise), carpenter, the ancestor of the Luyster family, emigrated in 1656 as per Riker; m. 1st Aeltje Tyssen; m. 2^d, about 1670, Jannetje dau. of Jan Snediker and wid. of Reynier Wizzelpennenk; d. 1695. Resided at first in Fld*, then in Fl^h, and afterwards in Newtown. Mag. of Fld* in 1660, '61, '62, and '64; mem. of Fl^h ch. in 1677; and on ass. roll of Fl^h of 1683. His Fl^h farm was in what is now known as N. L. Issue:—Tys or Matthias Pieterse; Gertien Pieterse, (sup.) m. Jan Monfoort; Mertien or Marretje Pieterse, m. Pieter Monfoort; John Pieterse; Cornelis Pieterse; and Wilmien Pieterse. Made his mark to documents.

Peter (s. of Cornelis Pieterse and Aaltje), b. Mar. 10, 1687; m. Apl. 30, 1712-13, Sarah dau. of Danl Rapalje; d. Dec. 17 1759. Left Fl^h and settled at the Poor Bouwery, Newtown' Issue:—Sarah, b. Jan. 31, 1714, m. Isaac Lent; Catharine' b. Aug. 7, 1716, m. Johannes De Witt; Adrianna, b. Mar. 11, 1718, m. Garret Van Nostrand; Cornelius of Fishkill, b' Aug. 26, 1720; Daniel, b. Sept. 26, 1722; Peter, b. May 6 1724; and John, b. Jan. 14, 1730.

Pieter (Matthyse), m. May 23 or 27, 1719, Anne Barkeloo
of N. U.   Resided in Fl[h], of which place he was constable
in 1724 and '25, as per Strong's Fl[h].   Issue:—Cornelia, bp.
Feb. 11, 1722; Margaret, bp. Nov. 3, 1723, m. Johannes Williamsen; Matthias of Fishkill, bp. Nov. 28, 1725; John of
Fishkill, bp. Apl. 7, 1728; Ann, bp. May 24, 1730, m. John
Nevius; Peter of Pa., bp. Oct. 29, 1732; Cornelius, bp. Mar.
9, 1735; Maria, bp. Feb. 27, 1737, m. Cor[s] Ostrander; and
Willemtje, bp. May 15, 1740, m. Peter Luyster.   Signed his
name "*Pieter Luyster.*"   Luysters reside in Queens Co., and
in Bucks Co., Pa.

LYDECKER, RYCK, m. *Claere Voorniere*, and d. prior to Nov.
28, 1666.   Was among the first settlers of Bu[k] in 1661, where
he obtained a grant of land in 1660, as per p. 54 of Cal. of
Eng. Man.   Mag. of the town in 1662, '63, and '65, and ap-.
pointed capt. of militia June 14, 1663, as per town rec.   The
muster-roll contained 40 names, including officers, who
were divided in 4 watches, of whom one fourth, or 10 men,
were on duty every night to guard against an expected attack by the Indians.   On the 22d of June of that year
Stuyvesant, the Director-Gen., visited the village and
ordered the cutting and setting of palisades to fortify the
place.   His s. Ryck appears to have settled at Hackensack,.
for in 1716 a Ryck and Elizabeth Leydecker joined the
R. D. ch. of that place, whose descendants abound in that
locality.   Suppose he had issue:—Garret, b. 1650; Ryck;
Cornelis; and Abraham.
   Gerrit, b. 1650; owned lands in Bu[k] in 1667, as per p. 54
of Cal. of Eng. Man.

LYNDELL, THOMAS, sold Aug. 2, 1693, to Richard Hawkins
of N. Y., mariner, his interest in the farm of Jan Janse
Staats at Gowanus, Br[n], as per p. 79 of Con.

MABELSON, JOHANNES, a suit commenced against by Fran-
coise De Bruynne in the court of sessions at G[d] for debt, as
per G[d] rec.

MABS, THOMAS, made an affidavit July 6, 1644, relating to
the killing of a man at the flats (Fld[s]), as per p. 89 of Cal.
of Dutch Man.

MACHIELSE or MACHIELSEN, ADAM, see Messcher.
   Hans, see Bergen.
   Johannes, took the oath of allegiance in G[d] in 1687 as a
native.

Paulus, see Vandervoort.
Richard, had a s. Lucas bp. July 14, 1678, in N. U.

MACKELYCK, JAN PIETERSE, from Amstead or Amsterdam, m. 1ˢᵗ, Feb. 10, 1664, *Styntje Jans* fromOstmarsuns or Oostmyzen in North Holland; m. 2ᵈ, Oct. 21, 1685, *Hendrica Strokles* wid. of Michiel Hainelle. Overseer of Brⁿ in 1675, as per p. 62 of Furman's Notes of Brⁿ; on ass. roll of Brⁿ in 1675, and mem. of the R. D. ch. of said place in 1677. Sept. 10, 1687, he and his wife bought of Jan Gerretse Van Cowenhoven 12 morgens of land in Brⁿ, as per p. 120 of Lib. 1 of Con. Issue:—Vintitie, bp. Oct. 30, 1667; Pieter, bp. Oct. 30, 1667; and Adriaen, bp. Mar. 20, 1681.

MAENHOUT, BOUDEWYN, see Van Crimpen.

MALET, see Marlet.

MALJEART or MALIERT, JEAN or JAN, a Frenchman, had a controversy with the magistrates of Buᵏ in 1663, as per p. 244 of Cal. of Dutch Man.; on the muster-roll of said town of that year; and in 1664 an inventory of his estate taken, as per Buᵏ rec.

MALLEMACQUE, PETER, occupied land in Brⁿ Jan. 1, 1667, as per p. 132 of Vol. 1 of Stiles's Brⁿ.

MANGUY, JONAS, was defendant in a suit of Jan Pietersen, and also of Davit Nyssen of Jan. 21, 1660, as per Lib. B of Flʰ rec.

MANJE, JAN, obtained a patent for 20 morgens in Brⁿ, Sept. 11, 1642. Mar. 11, 1664, Councillor Montague made a declaration respecting the testamentary disposition of his property as made by Jan Manje, lying wounded at Stamford, of which wounds he died, as per p. 26 of Cal. of Dutch Man. Mar. 31, 1664, Cicero Alburtus (Pieter Cæser Alburtus) receipts for his wife's (da. of Jan Manje) share of her father's estate; and Sept. 11, 1644, his wid. *Martha Chambers* m. Peter Linde or van der Linde.

MANOUT or MAENHOUT, BOUDEWYN, from Krimpen on the river Lek in South Holland, was appointed in 1662 "voorleeser" (precentor) of Buᵏ, and on the 17th of Dec. of said year, in consequence of his services proving satisfactory, the mag. of the town were sent to the authorities at the Manhattans, where an arrangement was made that in addition to his services as precentor he should keep the school and perform the duties of secretary of the town, for the sum of 400 gl. annually, and to be furnished in addition with a dwelling-house and firewood. Apl. 16, 1663, he was appointed sexton and speaker at funerals. See p. 243 of Cal. of Dutch Man. and Bu^k rec.

MARCKEN, see Van Marcken.

MARCUS or MARCUSE, JOHANNES, m. *Elsje Hendricks;* was assessed at Gowanus Feb. 7, 1657, 4 gl. towards Do. Polhe- . mius's salary; mem. of the R. D. ch. of Br^n in 1660, and on ass. roll of said town of 1675. See p. 134 of Vol. 1. of Stiles's Br^n.

MAREL, JONATHAN, m. *Judith* ——. Issue:—Jonathan, bp. Aug. 15, 1697, in Br^n.

MARIS, on ass. roll of Fl^h of 1683.

MARLET or MALET, ABRAHAM, m. *Christine Pieters.* Issue:—Margaret, bp. Mar. 31, 1678, in Fl^h; and Abraham, bp. May 16, 1680, in N. U. There was an Abraham Malet who settled on the Raritan, and had a s. Dirck bp. there Oct. 27, 1708, in which locality families of Marlets reside.
Paulus, m. Lysbeth Bunwyck, and appears to have settled on S. I. Jan. 19, 1678, he and Francis Vesselton, Hans Lawrens, Danl Stillwell, Ed. Marshall, and Peter Jansen were arrested by the constable of S. I. and imprisoned for abducting a servant-girl of Christopher Billop, and discharged from prison on bail on the 24th inst., as per p. 64 of Cal. of Eng. Man. Issue:—Jannetje, bp. May 18, 1679, in Fl^h.

MARSH, JOHN, (sup. English,) made an agreement, Aug. 19, 1698, with Pieter Corsen and Cornelis Sebringh to build a water-mill for grinding corn in Br^n, on the S.E. side of the Gowanus Kil, as per p. 105 of Lib. 1 of Con. Oct. 19, 1696, a John Marsh of Bu^k bought of John Miserole Junr the one half of the grist-mill in Bu^k, as per p. 104 of Lib. 2 of Con. Dec. 26, 1696, John Marsh of Br^n made an agreement with Elyas Stillwell of G^d to repair the running-gear of the water-mill in said town, so as to make the mill grind faster, as per G^d rec.

MARSHALL, THOMAS, (sup. English,) of G^d in 1656, as per Thompson's L. I. A Thomas Marshall, ag. 22, transported to New England in 1635, as per p. 107 of Hotten's Emigrants.

MARTEN, TONIS, on muster-roll of Bu^k militia of 1663, as per town rec.

MARTENS, PIETER, was plaintiff in a suit against Egbert Sanders Feb. 1, 1661, as per Lib. B of Fl^h rec.
Sara of the Walabocht, m. Aug. 6, 1692, in N. Y., Gerrit Burger of said city, where both resided at date of the marriage, as per N. Y. D. ch. rec.

MARTENSE, GARRET (s. of Marten Adrianse, the ancestor of the Martense family of Kings Co.), of Fl^h, b. Oct. 24, 1698; m. *Lena* or *Magdalena* da. of Leffert Pieterse; d. 1732. Will da. Mar. 21, 1732; pro. Oct. 24, 1733; rec. p. 90, Lib. 12, N. Y. surr. off. Issue:—Leffert, b. June 4, 1720, d. young; Marten of Fl^h, b. Jan. 21, 1722; Leffert, b. Jan. 16, 1725, m. May 4, 1745, Hilletje da. of Aert Vanderbilt, d. Sept. 26, 1802; and Sarah, b. Nov. 23, 1727, m. Apl. 29, 1746, John Lefferts of Fl^h, d. Dec. 30, 1762.
Jan and *Roelof*, see Schenck.
Johannes, on ass. roll of Br^n of 1675.
Joris, took the oath of allegiance in Br^n in 1687 as a native.
Rem (s. of Marten Adrianse) of Fl^h, farmer, b. Dec. 12, 1695; m. Susanna ——; d. June 14, 1760. Issue:—Joris of Fl^h, bp. May 29, 1724, O. S., in Br^n, m. 1765 Jannetje Vanderbilt, d. May 23, 1791, and was the grandfather of Margaret Caton, who m. the Hon. P. S. Crooke of Fl^h; and Rem, (sup.) m. Nov. 30, 1755, Jannetje Van Cleef. Signed his name *"Rem Martense."*
Ryer (s. of Marten Adrianse), b. at the Wallabout; m. May 22, 1696, in N. Y., Rebecca Van der Schuren, and both residents of the city of N. Y. at date of marriage.

MARTINO, DANIEL, on ass. roll of Fl^h of 1693, where he owned land in 1712.
Francis, m. Teuntje Martenooy of Fld^s. Issue:—Stephen, bp. May 25, 1679.
Stoffel, one of the arbitrators selected by Dirck Janse Hooglandt and Pieter Lott to settle a dispute about the boundary between their farms in Fl^h, who notified Gov. Andros of their decision, as per p. 53 of Lib. AA of Fl^h rec.

MARTYN, MERTYN, or MARTIN, JAN, from Harfleur, m.

Fytje Dircks. Was assessed in 1657 at Brⁿ ferry 6 gl. and at the Wallabout, where he owned land, 8 gl. towards the payment of the salary of Do. Polhemius, which in 1658 he refused to pay. Obtained Oct. 19, 1660, a patent for a lot at Brⁿ ferry. See pp. 193, 194, and 386 of Cal. of Dutch Man. Was among those of Brⁿ who in 1663 applied for leave to form a village, and for salt-meadows. Martyn's Hoek, the westernmost cape or point of the Wallabout Bay, was named after him. Issue:—Petrus, bp. Jan. 26, 1662, in Brⁿ. Signed his name *"Jan Martyn."*

Jan from Kampen, mag. of Brⁿ in 1686, as per Col. Man.

MASGROVE, WILLIAM, see Musgrove.

MASH, JOHN, (English,) on ass. roll of G^d of 1693 and cen. of 1698.

MATTHYSE, HENDRICK, mem. of R. D. ch. of Brⁿ in 1677.
Hendrick, see Van Pelt and Smock.
Loutweyns, m. Jannetje Hendricks, as per p. 224 of Lib. C of Fl^h rec.
Louwrens, of Fl^h in 1681, as per town rec. Made his mark to documents.
Peter, see Luyster.

MAURITS, WILLEM, see Willem Morris.

MAUVERYCK, CAPT. RETPERT, on Stoothoff's and Hegeman's books of 1670.

MAYERSE, LUCAS, see De Mayer.

MEDDAGH, see Middagh.

MEET, JAN (s. of Pieter Janse), from Amersfoort in the province of Utrecht, m. May 11, 1687, in N. Y., *Grietje Mandevel* of Fld^s, both residents of N. Y. at date of marriage. Feb. 25, 1692-3, he conveyed to Ruth Albertsen a house and lot in Fl^h on the E. side of the highway, and N. side of land of Pieter Strycker, as per p. 171 of Lib. A of Fl^h rec. A Jan Meet and Grietje Mandeville his w. were mem. of the R. D. ch. of Hackensack in 1700, who was probably this Jan, where they had children baptized. Signed his name *"Jan Meet."*

Peter Jansen, obtained a patent for 2 lots at Brⁿ ferry July 8, 1667. His name appears on the ass. roll of Bu^k of 1683, where he bought land of Albert Hendricksen about

1680, as per town rec. There was a Peter Meet residing at Hackensack in 1700, and a Pieter Meet who took the oath of allegiance to the English in N. Y. in 1664. Issue:—Jan; Kniertje, who m. July 5, 1676, in N. Y., Lawrence Jeuriansen from Brazil; and probably others. Signed his name "*Peter Jansen Meet.*"

MEGAPOLENSIS, DOMINIE JOANNES, b. in 1603 in Koedyk, North Holland, came to Beverwyck (Albany) in 1642 from the fatherland with his w. *Machtelt Willemse* da. of Willem Steenge, and served as clergyman of that place. Removed to N. A. in 1649, and officiated in the R. D. ch. of that place, and also assisted Do. Polhemius in Kings Co. in 1664 and '70. His name appears on the patent of Fl[h] of 1652 and '67. In 1657 he obtained a patent for 25 morgens in Fl[h] lying between the lands of Ab[m] Jorise (Brinckerhoff and those of Cor[s] Van Ruyven, and in addition plain land and salt-meadows, as per p. 29 of Lib. A of Fl[h] rec. In 1664 he and his s. Samuel took the oath of allegiance to the English in N. Y. Issue:—Hillegonde, b. 1628, m. Cornelis Van Ruyven; Derick, b. 1630; Samuel, b. 1630, who was a clergyman in N. Y. in 1664 and '68; and Jan, b. 1632, a surgeon in Albany. Signed his name "*Joannes Megapolenss*" in 1663.

MEIGES, KAREL, appointed by Capt. Scott constable of G[d] in his raid on the Dutch towns of L. I. in 1664, as per p. 401 of Vol. II. of Doc. of Col. His. of N. Y.

MEINST, PIETER, of the Walabocht. Assessed for salary of Do. Polhemius Feb. 7, 1657, as per p. 134 of Stiles's Br[n].

MELLESEN, CLAINE, see Metlaere.

MELONAER or MOLENAER, Mr. ARENT, of Fl[h] in 1665, per town rec. (See Arent Evertsen.) Signed his name "*Mr. Arent Molenaer.*"

MENJER or MINGE, SAMUEL, bought about 1651 of Pieter Ceser (Alburtus) a part of his plantation at the Walabocht. His lot at the ferry referred to in the patent of Pieter Jansen of July 8, 1667.

MENNIST, ISAAC, on ass. roll of Br[n] of 1693 and cen. of 1698.

MENTELAER, CLAES CORNELISE. His land in Br^n referred to in patent of Andries Hudden of Sept. 13, 1645. Suppose this to have been intended for Claes Cornelise Van Schouw. May 14, 1646, Capt. John Underhill obtained a patent for " Meutelaer's I." (Bergen's I. in Fld^s). Perhaps Claes Cornelise Mentelaer was the previous owner.

MERLET, see Marlet.

MERTYN, see Martyn.

MESSCHER, ADAM MACHIELSE, emigrated in 1647, and took the oath of allegiance in G^d in 1687.

MESSELAER, ABRAHAM. May 7, 1695, he and others conveyed land in Bu^k, as heirs of Pieter Janse Noorman, to Jan Cornelise Zeeuw, as per p. 81 of Lib. 2 of Con.

MESSEROLE or MESUROL, JEAN or JOHN, from Margien or Manheim in the Paltz, or from Picardy in France, emigrated Apl. 16, 1663, joined the R. D. ch. of Br^n on the 28th of Oct. of the same year with his w. *Jenne Carten*, and d. in 1695. About 1667 he bought a farm of Jan Clement in N. U., as per N. U. town rec., and resided on the same as late as 1676. Aug. 18, 1670, he sold to Lubbert Lubbertsen a house and lot in the village of Fl^h, as per p. 84 of Lib. C of Fl^h rec. He finally removed to Bu^k, where he took the oath of allegiance in 1687. His name appears on the ass. roll of N. U. of 1675, of Bu^k of 1693, and on Bu^k patent of 1687. Issue:—Jean Junr, and probably others. Signed his name " *Yean Mesurole.*"

Jean or *John* Junr, m. Nov. 24, 1682, Marretje Teunis Coevert; d. about 1712. Owned the Kijkuit (lookout) farm; and on patent of Bu^k of 1687. Issue:—John 3^d; Cornelius; Margaret, who m. —— Durje; Deborah, m. —— Van Cott; and Jane.

John 3^d of Bu^k, (sup.) had issue:—Peter, m. Saartje ——; John, m. Helen Vandervoort; Jacob, m. Oct. 5, 1745, Jannetje Stryker; Abraham, m. June 20, 1749, Maretje Simonse of Bu^k; Isaac; Sarah, m. Joost Skillman; and Marytje, m. Mar. 5, 1752, David Devoe.

METLAERE or MELLESEN, CLAINE, of Fld^s, gave a mortgage to Nicholas De Meyer, Aug. 1670, on land in Fld^s for 600 gl.

MICHAELSE, see Bergen, Parmentier, and Vandervoort.

Michil Ive, on Stoothoff's and Hegeman's books of 1670.

Michielse or Michielsen, Adam, a dealer· in whale-oil in G^d in 1670, as per Stoothoff's books; and on ass. roll of Fld^s of 1675. Sued in 1670 by Jacob Strycker for violation of a contract for threshing peas, as per p. 232 of Lib. D of Fl^h rec. Apl. 17, 1690, he bought of Reinier Van Sicklen 15 A. lot No. 30, as per G^d rec.

Johannes, m. Neeltje Harmens; paid to Fld^s ch. 8 gl. for the use of the pall in Feb. 1683. Issue:—Michael, bp. Nov. 23, 1684, in Fl^h.

John, allotted a plot on the Neck meadows of G^d in 1672, as per G^d rec. Owned a house and land in G^d prior to 1691, as per town rec. Made his mark " M " to documents.

Richard, had a s. Louis bp. July 14, 1678, at N. U. He may be the Richard Michiel of S. I. who m. Maria —— and had a dau. Annetje bp. Sept. 25, 1681, in N. U.

Middagh or Meddach, Aert, Anthonize, or Teunisen, emigrated previous to 1657 from Heikop in the province of Utrecht in the Netherlands, returned to the fatherland, and back to this country in the ship Beaver in May 1661. He m. *Breekje Hansen Bergen,* and both joined the R. D. ch. of Br^n in 1664, where he resided and owned considerable property. Issue:—Theunis, bp. Feb. 22, 1660, in N. A., d. young; Theunis, bp. Mar. 25, 1661, in N. A.; Jan Aertsen, bp. Dec. 24, 1662, in Br^n; Ann Aertsen, m. Ab^m Remsen of Newtown; Gerret Aertsen; Helena Aertsen, m. Wm Davidsz; Dirck Aertsen; Aert Aertsen; Lysbeth Aertsen, m. Pieter Staats; Matthew Aertsen; and (sup.) Willem Aertsen. See Aert Teunisen.

Aert Aertsen, m. Lysbeth or Elizabeth ——. About 1685 left Br^n and settled on the Raritan near New Brunswick, of which ch. he was an elder in 1688. Issue:—Ariaentje, bp. Sept. 17, 1699, in Br^n; Annetje, bp. Aug. 24, 1701, in Br^n; Lysbeth, bp. Apl. 18, 1704; (sup.) Helen, bp. Mar. 12, 1710, and probably others. Signed his name *"Aert Aersen."*

Aert (Janse), m. Elizabeth ——. Of Br^n in 1710, and removed from thence to the Raritan.

David (Janse) of Br^n, bp. Dec. 18, 1681; m. Heylke ——. Issue:—Willemmyntje, bp. May 14, 1702, in Br^n; Antie, bp. Nov. 3, 1703; Ariaentje, bp. Sept. 3, 1705; and Adrianna, bp. Jan. 4, 1710.

Derick (Janse), m. Katalyn Van Neşt. Left Br^n and settled on the Raritan as early as 1687. Issue:—Cornelis; Pieter, bp. Sept. 26, 1700; Derick, bp. Mar. 23, 1703; Joris, bp. Apl. 26,

1709; and Gerret, bp. Apl. 30, 1712—all of N. J., and bp. in the Raritan D. ch.

Dirck Aertsen, m. 1st Catalyntje ——; m. 2d Mary ——; d. 1710. Left Brn and settled in Flushing. Will da. Feb. 24, 1678; pro. Sept. 4, 1710; rec. p. 373 of Lib. 1, N. Y. surr. off. Issue:—Judith, bp. May 26, 1696, in N. Y.; Cornelis, bp. June 13, 1698, in N. Y.; Benjamin, (sup.) m. Annitie Stryker; Samuel, d. young; Deborah; and Samuel.

Gerridt Aertsen, b. in Brn, where he took the oath of allegiance in 1687; m. Sept. 25, 1691, Cornelia Janse Cowenhoven; d. 1710. On ass. roll of Brn of 1693 and cen. of 1698. June 2, 1688, he and Arie Rosa, Jan Glen, Jacob Kip, and Hendrick Kip obtained a patent from Gov. Dongan for a large tract on the E. side of the Hudson River, as per p. 29 of Vol. XII. of the Genealogical Record and p. 387 of Smith's His. of Dutchess Co. His will is da. Sept. 5, 1709; pro. Sept. 21, 1710; and rec. on p. 486 of Lib. 7, N. Y. surr. off. Issue:—Breckje, bp. Aug. 27, 1692, in Brn, m. —— Gleaves; Jan, bp. Aug. 13, 1693, in Brn; Dina or Diana, b. —— 1698, m. George Rapalje; and Aert of Brn, bp. Mar. 29, 1707, m. Magdalena Stryker. Signed his name "*Gerridt Middagh.*"

Jan Aertsen of the ferry, bp. Dec. 24, 1662; m. 1st Ariaentje Blyck dau. of Cornelis de Potter and wid. of Johannes Nevius; m. 2d, Jan. 4, 1690, Elizabeth Smit wid. of Peter Smit of Ja; d. previous to 1710. Owned 200 A. fronting on the East River, lying E. of Fulton Ferry and Fulton Street, late of Joshua and Comfort Sands. Constable of Brn in 1679; ferryman 1697, per rec. of court of sessions; on ass. rolls of 1676 and '83, and on cen. of 1698. Will da. Aug. 11, 1707; pro. June 6, 1709; rec. p. 368, Lib. 7, N. Y. surr. off. Issue:—Helena, m. Christopher Hoogland; Aert, m. Elizabeth —— and settled on the Raritan; David, bp. Dec. 18, 1681; (by 2d w.) Derick; Catharine; Pieter of the Raritan; Johannes, m. Elizabeth ——; Cornelis of the Raritan; and Matthew, m. Mary ——. Signed his name "*Jan Middagh.*"

Jan (*Gerretse*) of Brn, bp. Aug. 13, 1693; m. Hannah or Johanna ——. Will da. Dec. 14, 1762; Sept. 29, 1767; rec. p. 44, Lib. 26, N. Y. surr. off. Issue:—Cornelia, m. —— Gerretsen; Gerret of Brn, d. in 1771, single; Jacobus; John; Isaac; Catharine; and Mary, m. Jacob Hicks.

Matthew or *Mattheus Aertsen* of Brn, bp. Oct. 5, 1679; m. Mary or Maria —— (sup.) dau. of Johannes Nevius. Issue:— Jan, (sup.) bp. Aug. 6, 1699; Lysbeth, bp. Sept. 21, 1701, in Brn; Ariaentje, bp. Apl. 18, 1704, in Brn; Cornelis, bp. June 22, 1707, in Brn; and Matthew, bp. Mar. 15, 1710.

MILLES, CLAES, see Baes.

MILLS, RICHARD, of G^d Jan. 18, 1661, as per Col. Rec. He was schoolmaster and town-clerk of Southampton in 1651, and schoolmaster of Newtown in 1661. Members of the family are numerous in Queens Co.

MINGE or MINGER, see Menger.

MINNES or MINNEST, ALBERT (s. of Minne Johannes), from Friesland, m. Nov. 9, 1684, *Mensje Jans* of Fld'. On Gov. Andros's patent of lands in N. L. of Mar. 28, 1667. Settled in Fld', and mem. of the R. D. ch. of that place in 1677. Issue :—Rensje, bp. Oct. 30, 1692.

MINUIT, PIETER, owned land in Br^n in 1657, as per p. 132 of Vol. I. of Stiles's Br^n.

MISEROLL, see Messerole.

MITELAER or MITALERS, CLAES CORNELISE, m. *Geertjen Nanninex.* Resided in 1671 on Bergen's I., Fld', as per Hegeman's books.

MODY or MOODY, LADY DEBORAH, (dau. of Walter Dunch of England and wid. of *Sir Henry Mody*,) and her associates, to avoid persecution in Massachusetts and New England, left said locality and came to New Netherlands, settling in 1643 in G^d among the more tolerant Hollanders. In Oct. of that year she and her settlers were driven off by the Indians to Amersfoort (Fld'), where they remained to the end of the Indian war and then returned to G^d. Her name, with that of Sir Henry Mody her s., Ensign George Baxter, and Serjeant James Hubbard, appears on the patent of G^d of Dec. 10, 1645, and in 1646, on the laying out of the plantation-lots, she was allotted a bouwery. She appears to have owned and occupied a farm adjoining that of Robert Pennoyer, since of Van Brunt Magaw and late of Judge Samuel Smith, and, as near as can be ascertained, covering the farms late of Jacobus Lake and that late of Derick Stryker. Nov. 22, 1648, she let all her "broken up" (cleared) land, excepting one piece she reserved for her own use, for 3 years to "Thos. Cornewill," she furnishing him with 4 oxen and 4 cows ; he to pay 10 skipples of wheat per annum rent for the land and 60 gl. per annum for the use of the animals. A dispute having arisen between her and her tenant about the "breaking up" (clearing) a piece of land, and left to arbitrators, they decided May 5, 1650, that Cornewill should be allowed to crop the land next year, and that she should pay him 15 gl. on the surrender of the same, as per G^d rec. She

Peter, bp. 1712; Rem, bp. 1712; (by 2[d] w.) Theodore, bp. 1723; and Antie, bp. 1724.

Jan, emigrated from the Netherlands at an early period; m. Geertje Pietersen and settled at first in N. A. Dec. 8, 1630, he sold 4 ewes and lambs to the Patroon Van Rensellaer. May 29, 1641, he obtained a patent for a plantation at the Wallabout, to which he removed. In 1677 he and w. mem. of the R. D. ch. of Br[n]. In 1680 and '81 he appears to have resided in Fl[h], paying minister's salary there. Apl. 17, 1701, his brother Pieter's children, his heirs at law, sold his Wallabout farm to Gerret Cowenhoven, as per a deed, not recorded, in hands of H. C. Murphy Jun[r]. Left no issue. Signed his name "*Jan Monfoort.*"

Jan (Pieterse), bp. Feb. 23, 1648; m. 1st Geertje Pieters; m. 2[d], May 17, 1687, Ida dau. of Ab[m] Jorise Brinckerhoff of Newtown; d. 1737. Farmer in Fld[s]. Bought land in J[a] and also at Great Neck in Queens Co. He was lieut. of troop in Fld[s] in 1700; and with his w. mem. of R. D. ch. of said town in 1677. Probably removed to and d. on his Great Neck purchase. Will da. Aug. 27, 1720; pro. Oct. 24, 1745; rec. p. 380, Lib. 15, N. Y. surr. off. Issue:—Sara, b. Feb. 28, 1696, m. May 11, 1718, Peter Luyster; Aeltje or Attie, bp. Aug. 28, 1698; Peter of Redding, Hunterdon Co., N. J., b. 1700; Susanna, b. 1703, m. Nov. 9, 1720, Roelof Martense Schenck of Fld[s]; Jacob or Jacobus of Great Neck; Lammetje; and Abraham of Hempstead.

Pieter, the common ancestor of the family in this country, emigrated at an early period from the Netherlands; m. Jan. 12 or 17, 1630, Sarah de Plancken (or Blanck) at Amsterdam in Holland prior to his emigration, who after his death m. 2[d] Lambert Janse Bosch; d. Jan. 4, 1661. May 29, 1641, he obtained a patent for a plantation at the Wallabout, on which he resided, and for which he obtained a confirmatory patent Aug. 17, 1643, in which the quantity given is 25 morgens. Mag. of Br[n] in 1658, and deacon in the ch. at the time of his death. Issue:—Janica or Jannetje Pieters, bp. May 12, 1646, m. Feb. 12, 1665, W[m] Gerretse Van Cowenhoven; Jan Pieterse, bp. Feb. 23, 1648; Pieter Pieterse, bp. July 21, 1652; Sarah Pieterse, bp. Apl. 2, 1656, m. Claes Pieterse Wyckoff of Fld[s]; and (sup.) Willemtje Pieterse, m. Gerret Elbertse Stoothoff— all bp. in N. A. Made his mark to documents.

Pieter Pieterse, bp. July 21, 1652; m. Marretje Pieterse Luyster. Took the oath of allegiance in Fld[s] in 1687 as a native; mem. of the ch. in 1677; on. ass rolls of said town of 1675 and '83; and lieut. of foot in 1700, as per p. 800 of Doc. of Col. His. Bought about 104 A. at Cow Neck in Queens Co. in 1707. Issue:—Antie, b. May 1, 1677; Sara,

b. June 15, 1679, m. Isaac Remsen; Pieter, b. Feb. 16, 1681; Cornelis, b. Mar. 9, 1684, d. young; Elbert, b. Jan. 27, 1687; Cornelis, b. Apl. 25, 1694; Jacobus; Jan; and (sup.) Samuel. Signed his name *"Peter Monfoort."*

Pieter (s. of Pieter and Marretje), b. in Fld[a] Feb. 16, 1681; m. Nov. 9, 1702, Louisa ——. Settled in Somerset Co., N. J., and had issue:—Maria, b. 1705; Hendrick, b. 1710; Elbert, b. 1713; Maria, b. 1716; Sara, b. 1718; William, b. 1722; and John, b, 1726.

MONUEL or MON VEL, on Stoothoff's books of 1682.

MOODY, see Mody.

MOORE, JAN, m. Mar. 31, 1692, *Mary Paltrat* of Fl[h].

MORGAN, CHARLES or CAREL, of G[d], m. 1st, Feb. 9, 1648, in N. A., *Hannah* or *Helena Applegate;* m. 2[d], Dec. 18, 1652, in N. A., *Catlyntje Hendricks;* d. prior to 1668. At N. A. as early as 1648. Was a mag. of G[d] from 1657 to '63, as per Col. Man. There was a Charles Morgan from Newport, cadet, in the ⁄service of the West India Company, Sept. 14, 1641, as per p. 280 of Vol. 11 of O'Callaghan's Man. Trans. of Col. Doc. Issue, as per G[d] rec.:—Charles; Thomas, bp. July 17, 1650, in N. A.; John; Daniel; (by 2[d] w.) Mary or Marie, bp. Jan. 21, 1657, in N. A.; Rachel, bp. July 20, 1659, in N. A.; and Susanna. Made his mark to documents.

Charles Jun[r] of G[d]. Apl. 15, 1659, Edward Griffin and Thomas Applebee sold to Charles Morgan, for his son Charles, plantation-lot or parcel No. 14 in G[d], as per town rec. A Charles Morgan was appointed quartermaster of militia in Queens Co. in 1690, and resided in J[a] in 1680, as per p. 192 of Cal. of Eng. Man. Made his mark "M" to documents.

Daniel (s. of Charles) of G[d]. Apl. 2, 1674, Tho[s] Morgan, John Morgan of G[d], and Nich[s] Stillwell, in behalf of Dan[l] Morgan of G[d], sold to Jan Barentse (Van Driest) of Fld[a] plantation-lot No. 11 in G[d], with the improvements thereon, as per G[d] rec. Made his mark to documents.

Jan, John, or *Yan,* of G[d] in 1678, as per Col. Man. Dec. 1, 1680, he obtained a grant for 88 A. of woodland and meadows on the S. side of the Fresh Kil on S. I., as per p. 191 of Vol. 1 of Land Papers. A John Morgan obtained a grant for 300 A. on Duck Creek, Delaware, in 1676, and 600 A. on the W. side of the Delaware in 1680, as per Vol. XII. of Doc. of Col. His. of N. Y. Made his mark "I M" to documents in 1675.

Joseph of G^d, m. Oct. 14, 1696, Sarah dau. of John Emans, and settled in Freehold, N. J.

Thomas, of G^d in 1656, per Thompson's L. I., m. Jan. 24, 1672, Marretje Garretse or "Grete Garats" of N. U., as per G^d rec. Mar. 31, 1676, he appears to have obtained 94 A. at Karlis Neck, S. I., as per p. 72 of Vol. 1 of Land Papers. In 1689 he was appointed justice of the peace for Richmond Co. The descendants of Charles Morgan are numerous on S. I. and in Monmouth Co., N. J. Issue:—Adam, bp. June 27, 1680; Thomas, bp. July 14, 1686; and Margrite, bp. July 14, 1686, ag. 2 years. Made his mark to documents.

MORIS, JOHN, schout of G^d in 1653, as per p. 159 of Vol. II. of Doc. of Col. His. of N. Y., and d. in 1657.

MORRELL, THOMAS, (sup.) English, of G^d, where he was allotted a plantation-lot in 1648, as per town rec., which he sold in 1653 to Ambrose London. Mar. 29, 1659, he hired of Wm Teller plantation-lot No. 2, as per G^d rec. In 1686 a Thomas Morril Junr was among the patentees of Newtown. Made his mark to documents.

John, one of the first settlers of G^d in 1646, where he was allotted a planter's lot, as per town rec. He m. Oct. 1650 Elizabeth Cornwell wid. of Thomas Cornwell, as per G^d rec. An inventory of his estate, as made Jan. 15, 1656, and entered on the G^d rec., sums up 1928 gl. Made his mark to documents.

MORRIS or MAURITS, WILLIAM, of Br^n ferry, m. *Rebecca* ——; commissioned a justice of the peace of the county Oct. 20, 1685, as per p. 141 of Cal. of Eng. Man.; in 1687 bought of Derick Janse Woertman a house and lot at the ferry. Sold Oct. 12, 1694, to the corporation of the city of N. Y. a plot at the ferry, as per p. 102 of Furman's Br^n, the river front of which, occupying the present landing of the Fulton ferry, N. Y, continues to own. Bought Feb. 3, 1679-80, of Minne Johannes, his farm of 90 A. in N. L. on the S. side of the hills, adjoining that of Bates, as per Lib. 1 of Con. A Wm Morris emigrated to Boston in 1678, as per p. 387 of Hotten's Emigrants.

MOTT, ADAM, tailor, the common ancestor of the L. I. family, was b. in England in 1596, sailed for New England in the Defence in 1635 with his w. *Sarah,* ag. 31, and children—John, b. 1621; Adam, b. 1623; Jonathan, b. 1626; Elizabeth, b. 1629; and Mary, b. 1631—as per p. 99 of Hotten's Lists of Emigrants. In 1645 he appears to have resided in N. A., and Aug. 23, 1646, obtained a patent for 25 morgens in Bu^k on the W. side of Mespachtes Kil, as per p. 371 of Cal. of Dutch Man., which be sold to Claude Barbier and Anthony Jeroe, who sold the same Jan. 7, 1653, to Jacob Steendam, as per p. 376 of do. After this he appears to have resided in Newtown, and in 1665 in Hempstead, and has numerous descendants residing in Queens Co. See p. 37 of Vol. 2 of Thompson's L. I.

MOULJEART, JAN, among residents of Bu^k who Aug. 23, 1662, subscribed towards paying the ransom of Jacob s. of Thonis Crayen, a prisoner among the Turks.

MOURIS or MOURISON, KNOET (VAN HOSEN), d. prior to Oct. 1674. Mar. 7, 1660, the first house having been erected near the Pond in Bu^k, he and Wm Traphagen moved in the same, as per p. 343 of Prime's L. I. Mag. of Bu^k in 1663 and '64, and on muster-roll of said town.

MUFFE, GERRET, of G^d in 1653. Made his mark to documents.

MUSGROVE, WILLIAM, (sup.) English, m. *Judith* ——. Had a plantation-lot granted to him Apl. 20, 1650, in G^d, as per town rec. Made his mark to documents.

MUSSEROL, see Messerole.

NAELLER, TOMNES, of Fld* in 1665, as per town rec. Made his mark " T N " to documents.

NAGEL, BARENT (JANSE), bp. July 23, 1671, in N. Y. No further trace.
Folkert (Jurianse), bp. Dec. 27, 1697, in Br^n; resided in Bu^k. Issue:—(sup.) Philip.
Jacobus (Janse), bp. Jan. 10, 1683, in N. Y.; m. Jannetje Van Hekelen, and settled in Bucks Co., Pa.
Jacobus (Jurianse) of Bu^k, bp. Jan. 10, 1687, in N. Y.; m. Jannetje ——. Issue:—Neeltje, bp. Sept. 11, 1719.
Jan or John, m. Aug. 27, 1670, in N. Y., Rebecca Waldron. Suppose he resided in Bu^k. Issue:—Barent, bp. July 23, 1671; Jannetje, bp. Nov. 3, 1672; Jan, bp. Feb. 17, 1675; Anna Catharine, bp. Nov. 29, 1676; Barent, bp. Dec. 18, 1678; Susanna, bp. Nov. 25, 1680; Jacobus, bp. Jan. 10, 1683; Deborah, bp. Feb. 27, 1684; and Resolvert, bp. Aug. 10, 1687—all bp. in N. Y. Signed his name "*John Nagel.*"
Jan (Janse), bp. Feb. 17, 1675, in N. Y.; m. Jan. 2, 1708,

in N. Y., Magdalena Dykeman. Issue:—Jan, bp. Dec. 13, 1716.

Juriaen, m. Jan. 1, 1679, Maria Philipse Langelaar from Pymeakken in the Netherlands. Resided in Bu^k, his name appearing on the patent of said town of 1667, on ass. roll of 1693, and cen. of 1698. A Juryen Nagel in 1691 claimed pay for 22 months' service as a soldier under Capt. Leisler. Issue:—Juriaen Junr; and Folkert Juriaense, bp. Dec. 27, 1697.

Juriaen Junr of Bu^k, m. Jannetje Langelaen Philips or Klits; d. 1738. Bought land in Bu^k in 1692 of Josias Drats. Will da. Dec. 1732; pro. May 20, 1738; rec. p. 185 of Lib. 13, N. Y. surr. off. Issue:—Jan, bp. Oct. 1, 1679; Phillippus, bp. Mar. 25, 1682; Grietje or Margaret, bp. Oct. 12, 1684, m. Charles Coevert; Jacobus, bp. Jan. 12, 1687; Neeltje, m. Andrew Stockholm; Benjamin, bp. Aug. 31, 1690; and Jan or John, bp. Apl. 10, 1695—all in N. Y.

Phillipus (*Juriaense*) of Fl^h, bp. Mar. 25, 1682, in N. Y.; m. Annetje——. Issue:—Jurrie, bp. Apl. 18, 1704, in Br^n, m. Joris or George Remsen; Cornelius, bp. July 27, 1707, in Br^n; Catryna, bp. Jan. 29, 1719, in N. U.; Neeltje, bp. Sept. 30, 1722, in N. U.; (sup.) Philip of Fl^h, who owned what was late the John Lott farm, lying on the southerly side of Clarkson St., and which was probably owned by his father, for Apl. 6, 1714, Philippus Nagel and others of Fl^h authorized the selling of the common lands. Signed his name "*Philippus Nael.*"

NAZARETH, WILLEM, of Br^n in 1695; m. *Helena Adams Brouwer*. Issue:—Lysbeth, bp. Mar. 21, 1690; Anna, bp. Sept. 20, 1691; Maritje, bp. Apl. 4, 1694; and Helena, bp. Mar. 29, 1696—all bp. in N. Y. Signed his name "*Willem Nazareth*" in 1698.

NEGRO, FRANCISCO, among the early settlers of Bu^k in 1661.

NEKOERS, SOEFFEN or STEPHEN, sold Sept. 23, 1661, to Lowys Jansen a building-plot in Fl^h on the N. side of the road, as per p. 82 of Lib. B of Fl^h rec. Signed his name "*Soeffen Nekoers.*"

NELSE, JAN, m. *Hendrickje* dau. of Dirck Janse Vander Vliet of Fl^h, and had a dau. Catharine Nelse.

NEU, BLANDIN, on Hegeman's books of 1688.

NEVIUS, NEFYES, or NEEFUS, CORNELIS (s. of Johannis), of the ferry, bp. June 19, 1661, in N. A., where he was b.; m. Apl. 15, 1683, *Agatha* or *Echje Joris* of the ferry; d. prior to June 1676. Was at one period ferryman; a mem. of the D. ch. of Br[n] in 1677 ; and suppose he finally removed to Fld[s]. Issue:—Jan; Joris of S. I.; Ariaentje; Antien; Cornelius, who (sup.) was appointed ensign of militia for Richmond Co. by Gov. Leisler in 1689; and Johannis of Fld[s], bp. Feb. 17, 1684.

Johannes, the common ancestor of the family, emigrated from Solin or Solingen in Westphalia, settled at first on High (Pearl) St. in N. A.; m. Nov. 18, 1653, Ariaentje Blyck from Batavia in the East Indies, da. of Cornelis de Potter and Swantje Jans of Br[n]. After his death Ariaentje m. 2[d] Jan Arisen Middagh. In 1654 and '55 he was a schepen of N. A.; in 1657 was assessed at the ferry 15 gl. towards Do Polhemius's salary; and in 1658 was secretary of the Burgomaster's court in N. A. In 1660 he and his w. entered on the lists of mem. of the R. D. ch. of N. A. as removed to the ferry, Br[n]. In 1664 he took the oath of allegiance to the English in N. Y. In 1670 he held the position of ferryman. Issue:—Johannes, bp. Nov. 8, 1654; Sara, bp. Aug. 27, 1656; Cornelis, bp. Sept. 2, 1657; Maria, bp. Dec. 22, 1658; Cornelius, bp. June 19, 1661; Peter, bp. Feb. 4, 1663; Sara Katherine, bp. Feb. 16, 1665, m. Cornelis Pieterse Luyster; Johanna, bp. Mar. 11, 1668, m. May 10, 1684, Garret Elbertse Stoothoff—all bp. in N. A. and N. Y.; (sup.) Elizabeth, m. Jan Aersen Middagh; and Catharine, m. Garret Pieterse Wyckoff. Signed his name "*Joannes Nevius.*"

Johannes Jun[r], bp. Nov. 8, 1654. No further trace.

Joris (s. of Cornelius and Agatha of the ferry), m. Willemtje Barkeloo'and settled on S. I. Issue:—Cornelius, bp. Apl. 12, 1711; Margrietje, bp. 1715; Jan, bp. 1715; Beletje, bp. May 7, 1717; Johannis, bp. Sept. 17, 1719; Margrietje, bp. Oct. 15, 1721; Pieter, bp. Jan. 12, 1724; and Aaghje, bp. Jan. 30, 1726.

Martin (s. of Pieter and Jannetje) of Fld[s], m. Aug. 27, 1715, Willemtje Lucasse Voorhies ; settled in Monmouth Co., N. J.; and was a mem. of the Marlboro R. D. ch. in 1719. Issue:—Willemtje, bp. Sept. 4, 1720, at Freehold; and Johannes.

Pieter (s. of Johannes) of Fld[s], bp. Feb. 4, 1663; m. June 22, 1684, Jannetje Roelofse Schenck. On ass. roll. of Fld[s] of 1683 and cen. of 1698, taking the oath of allegiance there in 1687. On Do. Van Zuuren's lists he is entered as a mem. of Fld[s] ch. in 1677, and was a deacon in 1689; paid for the use of the pall of said ch. as late as Jan. 12, 1724. Issue:—

Neeltje, m. May 17, 1715, Jan Lucasse Voorhies; Peter Jun[r], bp. Oct. 30, 1695; David of Somerset Co., N. J., bp. May 14, 1702, in Br[n]; (sup.) Cornelis of S. I.; Roelof of the Raritan; Martin of Monmouth Co., N. J.; (sup.) Ariaentje, m. Peter Voorhies of Freehold, N. J.; and (sup.) Tobias of the Raritan. Signed his name *"Pieter Nevyus."*

NEWTON or NUTON, BRIAN, m. *Elsje* —— and entered the West India Company's service in 1630, coming to N. N. about 1647, in which year he was a mem. of the Council and capt. lieutenant, which office he resigned in 1661 and went to reside in Fld[s], as per p. 99 of Vol. VI. of Dutch Man. He appears to have owned a plantation in G[d], which he sold Sept. 10, 1652, to Alexander Lennsen, as per G[d] rec. In 1660 he was a freeholder of J[a]. Signed his name *"Brian Newton."*

NICHOLAS the Frenchman, of Br[n], fined Apl. 2, 1658, 12 gl. for abusing Sheriff Tonneman and refusing to pay towards Do. Polhemius's salary, as per pp. 193 and 194 of Cal. of His. Dutch Man.

NICHOLLS, WILLIAM, of G[d] in 1656, as per Thompson's L. I.

NOERTBROOK, PIETER JACOBSE, of Fl[h] in 1667, per town rec., in which year he hired of Tomas Fransen what was afterwards known as the Simon Aesen De Hart farm, and lately the farms of Simon and John S. Bergen in Gowanus. Made his mark to documents.

NOORMAN, DIRCK TEUNISEN, (or Northman,) m. *Adriaentje Walich.* Of Fl[h] May 20, 1657, as per Dutch Man.
Derick, see Derick Volkersen.
Pieter Janse. May 7, 1695, Dirck Janse Woertman, Claes Symonse, and Ab[m] Messelaer, his heirs, conveyed his farm in Bu[k] of 23 morgens to Jan Cornelisse Zieuw, as per p. 81 of Lib. 2 of Con.

NOORTBROOK, see Noertbrook and Van Noortbrook.

NORDEN, THOMAS, owned land in Gowanus, as per deed of Simon Aesen De Hart and Ann Huycken his w., of Apl. 30, 1694, to Cornelis Gerretsen Van Duyn, rec. on p. 12 of Lib. 2 of Con.

NOSTRAND or NOORTSTRANT, see Van Nostrand.

NUTON, see Newton.

NYSSEN, TEUNIS, see Tunis Denyse.
David, plaintiff in a suit against Jonas Manguy Jan. 20, 1660, as per Lib. B of Fl[h] rec.

OAKE, JAN, see Van Nuyse.

OBEE or OBE, HENDRICK HENDRICKSZEN, on lists of catechumens of Br[n] ch. in 1662. He m. 1st *Attie Claes;* m. 2[d], Jan. 3, 1692, in N. Y., *Marretje Jans*, wid. In 1664 he took the oath of allegiance in N. Y. to the English. Issue:— Lydia, bp. June 6, 1658; and Grietje, bp. Aug. 17, 1659, in N. A.

OERRETSEN, YAN, of "Midwout" (Fl[h]) in 1681, per Stoothoff's books.

OESTEROEM or OESTERSTROEM, HENDRICK JANSE, m. 1st *Tryntje Lubbertse*, who d. prior to June 1666; m. 2[d] *Gretien Jacobsz.* Mar. 3, 1661, he sold to Tomis Hellebrants (Van Duykhuys) a house-plot on the S. side of the road in Fl[h], as per p. 54 of Lib. B of Fl[h] rec. Mar. 8, 1666, he sold to Reyndert Jansen (Van Ditmarsen) a farm in Fl[h] on the W. side of the highway, on the S. side of "Pieter Lodt," and on the N. side of Gerret Lubbertse, covering from appearances the farm of Henry S. Ditmas and a part of that of John Ditmas, as per p. 56 of Lib. D of Fl[h] rec. By a deed of Jan Tuenesse to Gerret Lubbertsen of Dec. 14, 1660, he appears to have owned this farm at that date. He also appears to have owned land in Bergen, N. J. Issue:— Tryntien Hendrickse; Jan Hendrickse; and Jannetien Hendrickse, as per p. 68 of Lib. D of Fl[h] rec. Made his mark to documents.

OLIVER, WILLIAM, hired in 1651 Randell Scott's house and lot in G[d] through Rodger Scott, as per G[d] rec. Made his mark to documents.

ONDERDONK, ADRIAEN ANDRIESE*, m. *Belitje* ——. Bought land in 1672 in N. L.; on ass. roll of Fl[h] of 1675; in 1677 he and his w. mem of the D. ch. of Fl[h]; Jan. 12, 1677-8, he

---

* The name of Onderdonk is claimed to be derived from Donck, an elevation or a rising ground, signifying under or in the suburbs of Donck. There is, however, no such name as Donck in Holthrop's Dutch and English Dictionary, but it may be Swedish. There is a hamlet named "Donck" in "Noord Braband."

bought of Leffert Pieterse lot No. 41 in the new lotts of
Fl[h] for 1000 gl., as per p. 27 of Lib. AA of Fl[h] rec.; in 1680
he paid 5 gl. towards the clergyman's salary; and in 1683
was assessed for 108 A. in said town.   There was an Andries
Andriese, a Fin, from Westerover or Westeroos in Sweden,
among the Swedes on the Delaware from 1659 to '70,
who received upwards of 571 gl. from 1659 to '63 as carpenter of the galiot; his w. and house being referred to in
1662; and in 1669 was fined 50 gl. for being engaged in
the rebellion of the Long Fin, as per Vol. II. and XII. of
Doc. of Col. His.   Also an Andries Andriesen, who bought
Sept. 10, 1655, of Lieve Jansen a plantation adjoining Hellgate on L. I., and July 11, 1660, obtained a patent for a lot
on the W. side of Smith St. in N. A., as per Cal. of Dutch
Man.; and also an "Andries Andriezen," who took the oath
of allegiance to the English after the conquest of the colony
in 1664.   It is probable that the Andries Andriesen of Hellgate and of N. A. was the father of Adriaen Andries, and
there is some reason to suppose that the Andries Andriese
the Swede was the same person.   Issue:—Andries (or Andrew) Adriaense; (sup.) Adriaen Adriaense; and (sup.)
Hendrick Adriaense—the two last of Foster's Meadows.
Made his mark to documents in 1655, '78, and '84.

Andries Adriaense, m. Nov. 11, 1683, at Fl[h], Maria Van
Vliet. On the marriage registry he is entered as being a
native of New Castle (on the Delaware), and as both being
residents of Fl[h] at the date of the marriage. He d. prior
to Aug. 13, 1687, for on that date his wid. m. Jacob Janse
Vanderbilt of Manhattan I.   His name appears on the lists
of communicants of the D. ch. of Fl[h] from 1677 to '85. From
Fl[h], as per Riker's Newtown, he removed to the W. bounds
of J[a], where he was killed, it is said, by the upsetting of a
load of straw.   His sons sold his J[a] farm in 1707 and removed to Hempstead. Issue:—Adriaen, bp. Aug. 24, 1684,
at N. U., m. Sarah Snediker; and Andrew, b. June 1 and
bp. June 13, 1686, at Fl[h], m. June 2, 1706, Gertrude dau.
of Hendrick Lott. Signed his name *"Anderese Onderdonk"*
in 1685.

OP DYCK or OP TEN DYCK, GYSBERT, of N. A., emigrated
from Wesel in 1635, m. *Catharine Smith.* In 1642 was commissary of provisions for the colony. Obtained a patent
May 24, 1664, for Coney I. which was afterwards declared
void, as per p. 10 of Vol. X. of Part 1 of Dutch Man. He
afterwards undertook the making of salt on said island, in
which he was opposed by the residents of G[d], who paid La
Chair, their attorney, 8 skepels of gray peas for his legal ser-

vices in the case, but which proved a failure from other causes. Issue:—Gysbert or Gilbert, b. 1640; Elizabeth, bp. July 27, 1644; Ludowyck, bp. June 10, 1646; Sara, bp. Oct. 23, 1650; Johannes, bp. Jan. 16, 1658; and Jacob, bp. Jan. 16, 1658—all in N. A.

The présent Coney I. was, on the first settlement of this country, composed of 3 separate islands, divided from each other by inlets or guts now closed. The westernmost one was known as Coney I., the middle one as Pine I., and the easternmost one as Gisbert's or Gysbert's I., so named after Gisbert Opdyck. At a later period the easternmost one was also known as Johnson's I., from Barent and William Johnson at one period owning the tillable land (about 60 A.) on the same. About 1670 the inhabitants of G^d at a town meeting directed the division of the tillable land, which appears to have been allotted among the then residents of the town, as per G^d rec., as follows:

Tho⁹ Tilton,	No. 1.	John Tilton Junr, No.	22.
Saml Holmes,	2.	Thomas Delavall for	
John Lake,	3.	Johannes Lott,	23.
Wm Compton,	4.	Saml Spicer,	24.
Saml Spicer,	5.	Barnes Juressen,	25.
Ja⁹ Hubbard,	6.	John Griggs,	26.
John Tilton Junr,	7.	Saml Spicer,	27.
John Bowne,	8.	Ch⁹ Bridges,	28.
John Griggs,	9.	Tho⁹ Delavall for Bo-	
John Lake,	10.	man Hends,	29.
Barnes Juressen,	11.	John Lake,	30.
Obadiah Wilkins,	12.	Ann Wilkins,	31.
Saml Holmes,	13.	Wm Williamsen,	32.
Ralph Cardell,	14.	John Emans,	33.
John Bowne,	15.	Ralph Cardell,	34.
Tho⁹ Delavall,	16.	John Poland,	35.
John Tilton Senr,	17.	John Appelgate,	36.
John Cooke,	18.	Saml Holmes,	37.
Nich⁹ Stillwell,	19.	Saml Spicer,	38.
Peter Sympson,	20.	Wm Goulding,	39.
Richd Stillwell,	21.		

Nov. 4, 1693, the inhabitants of G^d petitioned the court of sessions for relief, setting forth "that whereas now lately in October last by a providence of God in a great storm our fences are taken away and covered with sand about a corne field on Gisberts island so called, Therefore met together at a town meeting," etc.

ORRETSEN, YAN, of Fl^h in 1681, as per Stoothoff's books.

OSBORNE, ALSE, on ass. roll of G^d of 1683.

William of G^d. June 29, 1683, his executors conveyed plantation-lot No. 4 in G^d, cong. 20 A., to Daniel Lake, as per p. 20 of Lib. 2 of Con. and per G^d rec. There was a Wm Osborne at New Castle on the Delaware in 1675, as per p. 524 of Vol. XII. of Doc. of Col. His., and a Wm Osborne among the patentees of Newtown in 1686. Signed his name "*William Osborne.*"

OSSTOOSTORM, HENDRIK JANSE, see Oesteroem.

OSTERLINGE, CLAES, an overseer of Fl^h in 1681.

OUKE, see Van Nuyse.

PAESSEL, JAN, on Hegeman's books of 1670. Made his mark to documents.

Thomas, on Stoothoff's and Hegeman's books of 1679.

PAINTER or PAYNTTEN, RICHARD or RICHAREN, with Catharine Cronenburgh w. of Jan Teunisse, bought Aug. 22, 1679, of Rutgert Albertse of Fld^s his house and orchard for 3000 gl., as per p. 54 of Lib. AA of Fl^h rec. Barent Jansen in his affidavit in 1664 relating to Capt. Scott's raid on the Dutch towns on L. I. states he saw "Ritsaert Panten" strike Martin Kregier's s. Martin with a rattan, as per p. 483 of Vol. II. of Doc. of Col. His. Signed his name "*Richaren Payntten.*"

PALMER, CAPT. JOHN. Jan. 20, 1683, he complained to the court of sessions of the conduct of Minne Johannes, the constable of Fl^h, as per court rec. In 1681 John Palmer of Staten I., with others, bought a large tract of the Indians in Somerset Co., N. J. A John Palmer, ag. 24, emigrated to New England in 1634, as per p. 281 of Hotten's Emigrants.

PALMETIER, see Parmentier.

PALSEN, CLAES, of G^d in 1653. Signed his name "*Claes Palsen.*"

PANSZ, LAURENS, had a s. James bp. Apl. 2, 1677, in Br^n.

PANTTER, JOHN, blacksmith, of N. Y.; m. *Sarah* dau. of John Tilton, and bought June 4, 1688, of Wm Goulding a house and garden in G^d, as per town rec. May 18, 1691,

he sold his interest in lot No. 7 in G^d cornfield to Andrew
Emans, hailing from G^d, as per town rec. In 1694 he appears to have resided at " Lewis Towne" (Lewes) on Delaware Bay, as per a deed on the G^d rec. in which he conveyed his interest in the commons on Gisbert's I. to Nicholas Stillwell Junr. Signed his name "*John Pantter.*"

PARA, PIETER, see Praa.

PARIS or PARYS, JAN, on ass. roll of Bu^k of 1675 and mus-
ter-roll of 1663.
Thomas (probably Thomas from Paris), m. Jannetie ——.
Issue:—Nicholas, bp. July 20, 1680, in Fl^h.

PARMENTIER, PALMENTIER, or DARMENTIER, MICHAEL
PIETERSE, emigrated in 1654, and took the oath of allegiance in Bu^k in 1687. He m. *Neeltje Janse Damen.* Was a
mag. of Bu^k in 1679 and '81; on ass. roll of 1683, patent of
1687, and cen. of 1698; and lieut. of foot company in 1689
and 1700, as per p. 809 of Vol. IV. of Doc. of Col. His. Issue:—Pieter Michaelse, bp. June 13, 1680, in Br^n; Jan
Michaelse, bp. Mar. 19, 1682, in N. U.; Antoinette, bp.
July 27, 1684, in N. U.; Neeltje, bp. Oct. 20, 1689, Br^n ch.
rec., Oct. 20, 1690, Fl^h ch. rec.; Damen Michaelse, bp.
Jan. 21, 1694, in Br^n; Lysbet, bp. July 16, 1699, in Br^n;
and Johanna, bp. July 5, 1702, in Kingston, N. Y. Damen
and probably the other sons of Michael Pieterse settled at
Poughkeepsie and in Dutchess Co., where in 1770 there were
several families of that name.
Pieter, mem. of the R. D. ch. of Br^n in 1663; on Indian
deed for part of Br^n of 1670, as per p. 222 of Vol. II. of
Thompson's L. I.; overseer of Br^n in 1671; on ass. roll of
Bu^k of 1675 and '76, to which town he had probably removed.
Pieter Michaelse, bp. June 13, 1680; m. Helen ——. Settled in Dutchess Co., where he was a freeholder on the
organization of the county in 1714, as per p. 100 of Smith's
His. of said co.; and also an elder of the R. D. ch. in Poughkeepsie in 1731, as per p. 352 of said His.

PARSIL, THOMAS, an appraiser of the estate of Jan Lourens in 1679, as per p. 81 of Lib. AA of Fl^h rec. There was
a Thomas Parcell among the patentees of Newtown in 1686,
and also a Thomas Possell or Persell who had a dau. Eliz-
abet bp. Mar. 23, 1703, and a son Peter bp. Oct. 25, 1704,
in the Raritan D. ch., N. J.

PASSENSEY, a servant in the employ of Gerret Elbertse Stoothoff in 1690.

PASTOOR, FRANS BARENTS, see Frans Barents.

PAULDING, WILLIAM, of G^d in 1663, as per p. 243 of Memoirs of the Stillwell Family.

PAULUSZ, CORNELIS, of N. Albany, m. Nov. 12, 1696, in N. Y., *Jannetje Andreas* of Br^n, to which place he removed. On ass. roll of Br^n of 1693 and cen. of 1698. Issue:—Annetje, bp. Dec. 26, 1697; Wyntje, bp. Aug. 20, 1699; and Andrias, bp. Mar. 30, 1701—all in Br^n.
Coenraet and *Isaac*, see Vander Beeck.
Dirck (s. of Paulus Dircksen and Geertje Willemse) of Bedford, m. 1st Echje or Aegie Teunis Coevert; m. 2^d Sarah Jeats Willems. With others petitioned May 26, 1663, for leave to found a new concentration back of the "Waalebocht," as per Stiles's Br^n. On ass. roll of Br^n of 1675, and mem. of Br^n ch. in 1677. Issue:—Johannes, bp. May 20, 1680; Wilhelmus, bp. May 23, 1680; (by 2^d w.) William, bp. Apl. 20, 1685; Dirck, bp. Aug. 29, 1686; Jannetje, bp. May 27, 1688; Thomas, bp. Apl. 6, 1690; and Jan, bp. Mar. 13, 1692.
Michael, see Vandervoort.
Paulus (s. of Paulus Dircksen and Geertje Willemse), m. Lysbeth ——. Mem. of Br^n ch. in 1677 and '85, and a resident of Bedford. Issue:—Paulus, bp. July 8, 1681.

PAYNTER, see Painter.

PEAEN, JACOB. Nov. 3, 1659, he was plaintiff in a suit against Barent Baltes, as per Lib. B of Fl^h rec.

PENEWITS, THOMAS. His name appears on a remonstrance to the Director-General and Council in 1653 against arbitrary government, as per p. 171 of Wood's L. I.

PENNOYER, ROBERT, of N. A. as early as 1642, and among the early settlers of G^d in 1643, where he obtained a patent from Gov. Kieft for 80 morgens dated Nov. 29, 1645, lying between the land of Lady Mody and that of Anthony Jansen from Salee, for which patent there was an agreement of sale dated Apl. 1, 1653, by Wm Goulding as his attorney, to Arent Van Hattem, as per p. 371 of Cal. of Dutch Man., but of which the papers do not appear to have been signed. In addition to this patent, he appears to have owned other lands in G^d (his patent being outside the original boundary of the town), for in Sept. 1647, John Ruckman and Richard Uzell bought of Roger Scott a plantation formerly of *Robert Pennoyer*, and Sept. 4, 1649, bought of the same parties a house and lot also formerly of *Pennoyer*, as per G^d rec. Nov. 1, 1665, George Baxter sold to John Tilton of G^d "a piece of land purchased of *Robert Pennoyer*, as also further confirmed unto me by Mon^r Pieter Stuyvesant late Governour," etc., containing "75 Dutch morgens," and "of ye wch James Hubbard & my selfe did bestowe on ye town of Gravesende & was hired yearly as by there Records bearing date ye 7th December 1653," etc. This abstract from the G^d rec. appears to refer to *Pennoyer's* original patent obtained from Gov. Kieft, which patent, judging from the letter of Gov. Stuyvesant to Lady Mody referred to ȯn p. 141 of the Cal. of Dutch Man., he sold prior to Sept. 3, 1654. He made his mark to documents, and probably left descendants.

PETERS, see Pieters.

PEUYKHERT, WILLIAM, m. *Annetje Andreas.* Issue:—Elizabeth, bp. Apl. 29, 1680, in Br^n.

PHILLIPS, DANIEL, of Newtown, bought Jan. 14, 1694, of Derick Janse Hoogland of Fl^h a parcel of salt-meadows in N. L., as per p. 30 of Lib. 2 of Con.
Samuel, had a dau. Maria bp. Sept. 5, 1697, in Fld^s.

PICCES, JOHN, and John Lock leased Apl. 3, 1643, of Remmert Jansen his plantation on L. I., as per Col. Man.

PICET or PIKET, MICHAEL, from Rouen in France, occupied lands granted Feb. 19, 1646, to Wm Cornelisen in Br^n, as per p. 36 of Bergen Genealogy. Banished Oct. 4, 1647, for threatening the life of the Director, as per p. 110 of Cal. of Dutch Man.

PIETERS, PIETERSEN, or PIETERSZ, ABRAM, defendant June 8, 1662, in a suit of Isaac Claesen, as per Lib. B of Fl^h rec. Had several children bp. in N. A.
Ariaen, on ass. rolls of Flds of 1675 and '83 and cen. of 1698.
Barent, Casper, and others of Br^n in 1646 petitioned for leave to form a village and for salt-meadows, as per p. 120 of Vol. II. of Stiles's Br^n.
Christian, see Duryea.

Christian, owned land in Br[n] in 1660, per Col. Rec. A Christian Pieterse, who m. Tryntje Cornelis, had several children bp. in N. A. between 1658 and 1669.

Claes, Cornelis, Gerret, and *Hendrick*, see Wyckoff.

Cornelis, see Cowenhoven and Luyster.

Diewaen, on Stoothoff's books of 1690.

Evert, occupied a portion of Coney I. about 1654, under claim of Gisbert Opdike. When of the city of N. Y., Apl. 17, 1680, he sold his interest in plantation-lot No. 16 in G[d] to W[m] Goulding, as per G[d] rec. There was an Evert Pietersen, a schoolmaster, in N. A. in 1661. Signed his name *"Evert Pietersen."*

Geertje (possibly a dau. of Pieter Monfoort) of Fld[s], m. Mar. 27, 1678, in N. Y., Jacob Cornelis Van Egmont of N. Albany, both residents of N. Y. at date of marriage.

Gerret, conveyed Feb. 8, 1694-5, to Jan Aersen (Middagh) land at Br[n] ferry, as per p. 40 of Lib. 2 of Con. There was a Gerrit Pietersen who obtained a grant of 25 morgens in Bergen, N. J., in 1654, as per p. 381 of Cal. of Dutch Man.

Gerret, a resident of Bu[k] in 1682, as per p. 332 of Vol. 2 of Stiles's Br[n].

Gilles, see Vander Gouw.

Hans, of Br[n] Jan. 28, 1655, as per Col. Man.

Hendrick, obtained a patent for 25 morgens at Fl[h] Apl. 7, 1664, as per O'Callaghan's New Netherlands. Hendrick Pietersen of Fld[s] conveyed Oct. 20, 1667, to Cornelis Hendrickse Van Eens 27 morgens in Fl[h] on the W. side of the highway, with plain and meadow land, as per p 21¼ of Lib. C of Fl[h] rec. This Hendrick may be Hendrick Pieterse Wyckoff of Fld[s]. A Hendrick Pieterse had children bp. in N. A. Signed his name *"Hendryck Pieterse."*

Jacob, see Vanderbilt and Verhulst.

Jacob, among the first settlers of N. U. in 1657, and a mag. of said town in 1663. Sold Oct. 29, 1677, his N. U. farm of 25 morgens to Jan Verkerk. A Jacob Pietersen took the oath of allegiance in N. Y. to the English in 1664, and had several children bp. in N. Y. at an early date. Signed his name *"Jacob Petersn."*

Jan, see Lott, Luyster, Makelyck, Monfoort, Staats, Van Aersdalen, Van Deventer, and Wyckoff.

Jan, obtained a patent Mar. 29, 1647, for 4 morgens in Br[n] between the land of Ryer Lambertse (Mol) and that of Claes de Noorman. Name on application for a canal at Red Hoek, Br[n], in 1664, as per p. 68 of Vol 1 of Stiles's Br[n]. A Jan Pietersen had several chil. bp. in N. A. On ass. roll of Br[n] of 1675, and mem. of Br[n] R. D. ch in 1660.

Jan and Elsie his w. mem. of R. D. ch. of Br[n] in 1677.

Jan from Deventer, and others of Br^n, in 1646 applied for leave to form a village and for salt-meadows, as per p. 120 of Vol. 1 of Stiles's Br^n.

Jean Mackenzen, emigrated in 1660, and on ass. roll of Br^n of 1675.

Jeronemus, Joris, and *John,* see Van Ness.

Johannes, see Van Blarken.

John, of G^d in 1656, as per Thompson's L. I. Nov. 5, 1656, he bought of Anneken Tomas a parcel of land and buildings in G^d, as per town rec. Made his mark to documents.

Leffert, see Lefferts.

Loras. Pieter Loras bought Jan. 9, 1662, plantation-lot No. 34 in G^d, as per town rec. By said rec. he was also called "Stinkah," and had issue:—Peter; Cate; and Johannes.

Louwrens, plaintiff in a suit against Jan Teunise Mar. 18, 1661, as per Lib. B of Fl^h rec.

Margrietje of "Gujanes," m. Nov. 8, 1695, Jacob Koning, both residents of N. Y. at date of marriage, as per N. Y. D. ch. rec.

Marten, see Wyckoff.

Mattys, see Luyster.

Michael, see Parmentier.

Nicholas, see Wyckoff.

Peter, a catechumen of the R. D. ch. of Br^n in 1662, and on ass. roll of Br^n of 1675. Among those who in 1663 asked leave to form a village back of the Wallabout.

Thys of Fl^h. Signed his name "*Thys Pietersen*" in 1689.

William, see Van Blydenstein.

Wynant, see Van Eck.

PISCHER, CRIGIER, in N. A. as early as 1645; leased land in Br^n Jan. 26, 1647, in partnership with Gerret Serdts, of Cornelis Van Tienhoven, on condition of clearing the same of trees and small stones, and of fencing it, as per p. 26 of Cal. of Dutch Man.

PLUVIER, CORNELIS JANSEN, at one period of Fl^h; b. 1626; m. 1st *Geertruyd Andries;* m. 2^d, Jan. 6, 1662, in N. Y., *Neeltje* dau. of Jacob Van Couwenhoven. He and his 1st w. were mem. of the D. ch. of N. A. in 1660. In 1664 he took the oath of allegiance in N. Y. to the English. Issue:—Hester, bp. Apl. 9, 1664; Lysbeth, bp. Jan. 27, 1666; Johannes, bp. Dec. 25, 1667; Jacob, bp. Jan. 2, 1670; Rutje, bp. Mar. 16, 1672; Peternella, bp. Dec. 24, 1673; Anna Maria, bp. Mar. 8, 1676; Jacob, bp. Jan. 23, 1678; Jacobus, bp. May 24, 1679; Cornelis, bp. Dec. 10, 1680; and Cornelis, bp. Apl. 30, 1684 —all bp. in N. Y. Signed his name "*Cornelis Pluvier.*"

15

POINGOT, FRANCIS, owner of a lot at Brooklyn ferry, referred to in patent of Dec. 12, 1653, to Adriaen Huybertse.

POLAND, see Poling.

POLHEMIUS or POLHEMUS, ABRAHAM (s. of Theodorus and
Metje), bp. Mar. 19, 1697; m. *Gertrude* da. of Ab^m and Gertrude Remsen. Suppose he resided in Br^n. Issue:—Theodorus of Bu^k; Jacob, b, 1725; and Abraham of Newtown,
b. 1727.

Cornelius (s. of Daniel of Fl^h); m. Susanna ——; d. 1741.
Will da. Aug 22, 1739; pro. July 3, 1741; rec. p. 124, Lib.
14, N. Y. surr. off. Settled in Hempstead as early as 1707.
Issue:—Matilda, who m. Folkert Rapalje; and Daniel (sup.)
of N. Y.

Daniel (s. of Do. Polhemius), m. 1st, Aug. 13, 1685, Neeltje
dau. of Cornelis Vanderveer of Fl^h; m. 2^d Cornelia ——; d.
about 1730, probably in N. Y., he and his w. Cornelia joining the R. D. ch. of that city on certificate from L. I. Previous to this he resided in Fl^h, where he took the oath of
allegiance in 1687, was on the patent of 1685, ass. roll of
1693, cornet of horse in 1690, as per p. 197 of Cal. of Eng.
Man., and capt. of militia. Dec. 19, 1702, he purchased of
the heirs of his father the homestead farm of about 104 A.
in Fl^h, as per p. 247 of Lib. 2 of Con. In 1730 his heirs
conveyed these premises to Ab^m Lott, from whom they
passed, through his son Engelbert, to his grandson the late
Jeremiah Lott. Dec. 28, 1702, he conveyed to Ryck Hen-
drickse·(Suydam) of Fl^h, for £202, 20 morgens in Fl^h,
bounded S. by the lane leading from Fl^h to N. U., N. by
Daniel Remsen's land, E. by John Damen's land, and W.
by the highway on the rear of said land leading from Roelof
Verkerk's house to N. Y.; also one fourteenth of the brew-
house in Fl^h, as per p. 255 of Lib. 2 of Con. This appears
to be the westerly and main portion of the land lying on
the S. side of what is known as the Little Lane, lately of
Tunis Bergen, Lott, and Duryea. Issue:—Johannes; Kath-
arina; Cornelius; Jacob; Daniel Junr of N. Y., bp. Dec. 10,
1695; Marya, bp. Oct. 2, 1698, in Br^n, (sup.) m. Cornelis
Evertse; Hendrick of Somerset Co., N. J., bp. Oct. 6, 1700,
in Br^n; Abram of Somerset Co., N. J.; and Margaret, bp.
Apl. 18, 1704, in Br^n, (sup.) m. Derick Amerman of Fld^s.
Signed his name "*Daniel Polmes.*"

Daniel Junr, bp. Dec. 10, 1695; m. (sup) Cornelia Sebering, residing at first in the city of N. Y., and finally settling
in East N. J.

Rev. Johannes Theodorus, the common ancestor of the family, emigrated in the employ of the West India Company from the Netherlands to Itamarca, Brazil, and thence to L. I., where he officiated in the churches of Kings Co.; m. Catharina Van Werven; and d. June 8, 1676. Obtained June 25, 1662, a patent for 25 morgens in Fl^h, and bought Mar. 6, 1674, of John Sebering an adjoining patent of 24 morgens which had been originally granted, June 25, 1662, to Cornelis Swaelwood, and sold by the latter to Sebering. Dec. 25, 1680, a confirmatory patent was granted by Gov. Andros to Catharine wid. of Do. Polhemius for all the above premises with a small addition, containing 104 A. and 360 rods. Dec. 19, 1702, the heirs of Do. Theodorus and Catharine Polhemius conveyed the same to Daniel Polhemus, as per p. 247 of Lib. 2 of Con.

From a map on file in the off. of the Sec. of State at Albany, made by "Ja. Cortelyan" and filed Aug. 8, 1681, of farms in Fl^h, it appears that "Polhemius" owned a "double lott, broad before 48 Rod 4 foot (about 583 ft. English), after 57 Rod (about 687$\frac{1}{10}$ ft. English), long 600 Rod" (about 7241 ft. English), cong. upwards of 52 morgens. These premises cover the farm of the late Jeremiah Lott on the S. side of the Little Lane in Fl^h. Issue:—Theodorus of J^a; Lammetie, who m. Johannes Willemse; Anna, who m. Cornelis Barentse Van Derwyck or Van Wyck; Daniel of Fl^h; Maragrietje, m. Wm Guilliamse Cornell; Adriana, m. John Roelofse Suebering; Elizabeth, m. Dionys Teunise of Gowanus; and (sup.) Catrina. Signed his name "*Johannes Theod. Polhemius.*"

Johannis (s. of Theodorus and Aertje), bp. July 20, 1685; m. —— ——. Issue:—Theodorus, b. 1718; Hendrick, b. 1720; and Eldert. Signed his name "*Johannis Polhemes.*"

Johannis (s. of Daniel and Neeltje), m. (sup.) Johanna Ten Eyck, and settled in N. J. Issue:—Elizabeth, bp. Aug. 13, 1710; and Cornelis, bp. Dec. 5, 1714.

Theodorus (s. of Do. Johannes), b. in Brazil; m. Oct. 14, 1677, Aertje dau. of Teunis Gysbertse Bogaert; and d. 1722. Mar. 5, 1683, he bought land of John Baylis in J^a, to which he removed from Fl^h prior to 1699. Mem. of Fl^h ch. in 1677, and mag. of said town in 1678 and '79. Will da. Feb. 14, 1721; pro. May 2, 1722; rec. p. 304, Lib. 9, N. Y. surr. off. Issue:—Tunis; Sara, bp. Oct. 18, 1680, (sup.) m. Jores Remsen of Haverstraw; Theodorus; Elizabeth, bp. Nov. 20, 1681, in N. U.; Johannis, bp. July 20, 1685, in Br^h; Elizabeth, bp. Nov. 5, 1693, in Br^n, m. Ab^m Duryea; and Abraham, bp. Mar. 19, 1697, in Br^n. Signed his name "*Theodorus Polhemius.*"

Tunis (s. of Theodorus and Aertie). Resided at first in

Fl^h and finally removed to Orange Co., N. Y.; m. Sarah
dau. of Andrew Emans; and d. 1743. Will da. Apl. 22,
1735; pro. Dec. 2, 1743; rec. p. 168, Lib. 15, N. Y. surr. off.
Issue:—Theodorus, b. 1720; Andrias, bp. Nov. 11, 1722;
Elizabeth, m. Daniel Haring of Orange Co.; Aertje, bp.
Oct. 18, 1730; Antje, bp. July 29, 1733, m. Dr. Thomas Oat-
water; Aert; and Rebecca—all bp. in N. U. Signed his
name "*Tunes Polhemels.*"

POLING or POLAND, ANTHONY, (English,) on ass. roll of
G^d of 1683 and cen. of 1698. Signed his name "*Anthony
Poland.*"

John (English) of G^d, m. Mary ——. Bought land in G^d
in 1676 of Charles Morgen, as per town rec., of which town
he was a resident as early as 1656. On ass. roll of G^d of
1683, cen. of 1698, and mag. from 1691 to '93. Mem. of
Assembly for Kings Co. from 1691 to '94. June 5, 1700,
Samuel Poling, executor of the estate of John Poland dec.,
with the approbation of Mary his wid., sold wood-lot No. 10
in G^d Neck, cong. 10 A., to "Capt. John Lake" of G^d, as
per town rec. Issue:—Mary. Signed his name "*John
Poling.*"

Samuel, allotted salt-meadows in G^d in 1700, as per town
rec. Signed his name "*Samuel Poling.*"

POPPE or POPPEN, JAN, at one period a skipper in the
West Indies, and a turner by trade, m. *Elsje Jansen*, and d.
prior to 1689. Name on ass. roll of Fld^s of 1675, and a
mem. of the R. D. ch. of said town in 1677. Removed
from Fld^s to Fl^h, and in addition to his trade was a farmer.
He and his w. made a joint will da. Aug. 21, 1684, rec. on p.
112 of Lib. 1 of Con. Issue:—Anne Janse; and Jan Janse,
who d. previous to the date of his father's will, and who
had a son named Poppe Janse. Signed his name "*Jan
Poppe.*" A Jan Janszen Poppen m. Aug. 29, 1668, in N. Y.,
Geertruydt Barents wid. of Jan Hibon.

POST or POS, WILLEM, m. May 18, 1679, in Fld^s, *Aeltje Teunis Van Couverden* of Br^n. A resident of N. Y. at the time of
his marriage, of which place his w. was a church mem.;
took the oath of allegiance in Br^n in 1687 as a native, owning land in Bedford, to which place he had removed. He
was probably a s. of Capt. Adriaen Post, an early emigrant
who finally settled in Bergen, N. J. Issue:—William, bp.
July 21, 1680, in N. Y.; Agnietje, bp. Feb. 7, 1683; Jannetje,
bp. June 12, 1695; and Elizabeth, bp. Apl. 17, 1698, in N. Y.
Signed his name "*Willem Post.*"

POULION, ISAAC, of Br[n], m. Oct. 24, 1677, *Adrianna Croseron* of Fl[h].

POULIS, CLAUS, bought Oct. 22, 1653, of Bartholemew Applegate a parcel of land in G[d], as per town rec.

POULUSSEN, DIRCK, m. *Sara Jeats Willems* of J[a]. With others in 1663 asked leave to form a new village back of the Wallabout. Issue:—William, bp. Apl. 20, 1685, in Br[n]; Sarah, bp. May 27, 1688; and Thomas, bp. Apl. 6, 1690.

PRAA or PRAT, PIETER, (or PIERRE PRAT,) a Huguenot from Dieppe in France, as per Br[n] ch. rec.; emigrated in 1659 with w. and family, residing at first in N. A. and afterwards settling in Bu[k]. He m. *Catharine* dau of Ab[m] Lothie, who after his death m. June 10, 1663, Joost Casparse Springsteen. He d. Mar. 6, 1663, at Cripplebush, Br[n]. See p. 322 of Vol. 2 of Stiles's Br[n]. Aug. 26, 1659, Derick Janse agreed to convey to "Pierre Prat" for 300 gl. a bouwery with house and barn at Gowanus, between the lands of Teunis Nyssen (Denyse) and Jan Pietersen Staats, as per p. 6 of Lib. B of Fl[h] rec. No evidence of this agreement being consummated. Issue:—Peter Jun[r]; Adam, bp. Feb. 6, 1660, in Br[n], d. Feb. 8, 1660; Abraham, bp. Mar. 5, 1662, in Br[n]; and Annatie, who m. Jan Jansen. Signed his name *"Pierre Prat."*

Pieter Jun[r] or *Capt. Peter*, b. 1655 at Leiden, and emigrated with his father; m. Mar. 15, 1684, Maria or Mary Hays wid. of Joost Adriaense, miller; d. 1740. On patent of Bu[k] of 1687, in which year he took the oath of allegiance in said town. On ass. roll of 1693, cen. of 1698, and capt. of militia in 1700, as per p. 809 of Vol. IV. of Doc of Col. His. Removed to Newtown, his name appearing on the records of said town in 1703 and 1708. Will da. Aug. 6, 1739; rec. p. 43, Lib. 13, N. Y. surr. off. Issue:—Catharina, bp. Sept. 4, 1685, in N. Y.; Maria, bp. Sept. 30, 1688, in Br[n], m. Wynant Van Zandt; Lysbeth, bp. May 13, 1691, in N. Y., m. —— Messerole; Anna, bp. Nov. 14, 1694, in N. Y., m. Daniel Boddie; and Christina, bp. May 1, 1698, in Br[n], m. David Provoost Jun[r]. Signed his name *"Pieter Praa."*

PRIENSZ, HENDRICK, of N. L., mem. of R. D. ch. of Fl[h] in 1677.

PROBASKO, ABRAHAM CHRISTOFFELSE, bp. Feb. 22, 1685; m. *Geertje Lubbertse*, and (sup.) resided in N. L.

Christoffel Jeurianse, the common ancestor of the family,

emigrated to this country in 1654, m. Ida Strycker and settled in N. L.   July 29, 1687, he and his w. made a joint will, as per p. 91 of Lib. A of Fl[h] rec.   His name appears on the ass. rolls of Fl[h] of 1675 and '83, taking the oath of allegiance there in 1687; mem. of Fl[h] ch. in 1677, and elder in 1678 and '90; mag. in 1678 and '86; justice of the peace in 1693, and on cen. of 1698.   Aug. 8, 1671, he bought a farm of 19 morgens in Fl[h] between the farms of Jan Strycker and Dirck Janse Vander Vliet, abutting against Curlaer's flats, of "Tomas Lammerse and Tunis Janse Coevers," as per p. 96 of Lib. C of Fl[h] rec.   In the body of the conveyance his name is written "Stoffel Jurianse Probaske." This farm he sold Feb. 4, 1698, to Bartel Claesen, as per p. 45 of Lib. A of Fl[h] rec.   In 1690 opposed the administration of Gov. Leisler.   Will da. Oct. 3, 1724, not recorded. Issue:—Jan; Jacob, bp. July 9, 1682; Abraham, bp. Feb. 22, 1685; Aaltje, bp. June 26, 1687; Lammetje, m. Jan Simonse Van Aersdalen; Jurryen, bp. Oct. 30, 1695; Christoffel Jun[r]; and Heyltje, m. Jeremias Remsen.   Signed his name "*Stoffel Probasko.*"

Christoffel Jun[r], m. Catalina Schenck, and settled on the Raritan in N. J.

Jacob, bp. July 9, 1682, (sup.) m. Barbara ——.   Left N. L. and settled in the vicinity of Millstone, N. J.   Issue:— Christoffel, bp. Apl. 26, 1709; Ida, bp. Nov. 2, 1711; Frederick, bp. Oct. 9, 1714; and Lisbeth, bp. May 30, 1725—all bp. at Marlboro, N. J.   Signed his name "*Jacob Probasco.*"

Jan, settled at Millstone, N. J.   Signed his name "*Jan Probasco.*"

Jurryen, m. Catelyntje ——.   Issue:—Christoffel, bp. June 13, 1649; Anne, bp. May 13, 1651.   The above certified to be a copy from the records by the Rev. Dirk Pietersen Byl, as per papers in hands of Christopher Lott, one of Jurryen's descendants.   Signed his name "*Jurryen Probasko.*"

PROBATSKIN, GEORGE, and others of Br[n] petitioned in 1663 for leave to form a village back of the Wallabout, as per Stiles's Br[n] and p. 117 of Vol. X. of Col. Man.

PROVOOST, DAVID, came to N. A. at an early period; m. *Maragretta Gillise* dau. of Gillis Jansen Verbrugge, and d. Jan. 3, 1656.   Was a trader in N. A. as early as 1639; inspector of tobacco and commissary of provisions; commissary at Fort Good Hope in 1642; notary public in 1652; scout fiscaal in 1654 of the Brooklyn district; and clerk of the court of Breuckelen, Midwout, and Amesfoort in 1665. Bought land and buildings of Thomas Greedye in G[d] in

1653. Owned land in Fl^h in 1661. Issue:—Margaret, bp. Feb. 24, 1641, m. Nov. 16, 1660, Pieter Janszen Scholt; David, bp. Sept. 30, 1645; Benjamin, bp. June 17, 1646; Elias, bp. June 17, 1646; Barbara, bp. Aug. 15, 1647, d. young; Samuel, bp. Nov. 22, 1648; Jonathan, bp. Mar. 26, 1651; Barbara, bp. Nov. 30, 1653, m. Jan Aukersz Van Nuyse; William; and Gillis, bp. Mar. 26, 1656—all bp. in N. A. Signed his name "*D Provoost.*"

Gillis, Giles, or *Jellius* (s. of David), bp. Mar. 26, 1656; m. June 9, 1680, Maria or Mary Hibon of Br^n, a resident of N. Y. His name appears on a deed of Apl. 26, 1700, for a lot at Br^n ferry, as per p. 105 of Lib. 3 of Con. Was at one period engaged in mercantile business in N. Y. His will is da. Jan. 1, 1706, and pro. July 7, 1709, in which he styles himself of Br^n, merchant. No account of any of the other children of David Provoost owning property in Kings Co., unless William was an owner.

William, of G^d in 1656, as per town rec. Signed his name "*Willem Provoost.*"

PULMAN, JAN HENDRICKSE, a mag. of Bu^k in 1664, as per town rec. See Jan Hendrickse of Bu^k.

PURDY, THOMAS. In consequence of his roaming around the country without visible means of support, he was committed July 20, 1669, by Justice William Goulding of G^d, as a vagrant, to the service of ensign Richard Stillwell, to be fed and employed until the ensuing March, as per G^d rec.

RAPALIE or RAPALJE, CORNELIS (JERONEMUSSE), b. Oct. 21, 1690; m. *Johanna* dau. of the Rev. Vincentius Antonides. Resided at first in Fl^h and afterwards in N. Y., where he joined the R. D. ch. in 1731 on certificate from Fl^h. Issue:—Jeronimus, bp. Dec. 5, 1712; Titie, bp. July 4, 1714, m. Hendrick Smith; Antie, bp. Nov. 11, 1716; Johanna, bp. Feb. 4, 1719; and Catalina, bp. Oct. 16, 1720, m. John de Graw—all bp. in N. Y.

Daniel Jorise of the Wallabout, b. Dec. 29, 1650; m. May 27, 1674, Sarah dau. of Ab^m Klock or Clock; d. Dec. 26, 1725. On ass. rolls of Br^n of 1675 and '83, where he took the oath of allegiance in 1687 as a native; ensign of Br^n company in 1673; lieut. in 1700; on cen. of 1698; and mem. of Br^n ch. in 1677. Issue:—Joris, b. Mar. 4, 1675; Mary or Marytie, b. 1677, m. Elbert Hegeman; Abraham, b. Jan. 14, 1677; Catharine, b. Feb. 7, 1679, m. Joseph Vah Cleef; Annetje, bp. Mar. 27, 1681; Sarah, bp. July 3, 1687, m. Pieter Luyster; Altie, m. Gilbert Schenck; Daniel of Newtown,

bp. Apl. 11, 1691; and (sup.) Cornelia, m. Hendrick Brinckerhoff. Signed his name *"Daniel Repreele."*

Daniel (s. of Dan¹ and Sara), bp. Apl. 11, 1691; m. Oct.
17, 1711, Altie dau. of Johannes Cornell.   Removed to Newtown. Issue:—Ann; Mary; Catharine; Lammetje, m. Jeromus Lott; Sarah, m. Isaac Brinckerhoff; Margaret, b. 1720,
m. Jacobus Lent; Alletta, m. 1ˢᵗ Johannes Lott, m. 2ᵈ Isaac
Cortelyou; Daniel of Newtown; Johannes of N. L.; and
Joris of Newtown. Signed his name *"Daniel Rapalje."*

Daniel (s. of Joris and Angenietje), b. Nov. 12, 1699; m.
1ˢᵗ Mary dau. of Cornelis Luyster; m. 2ᵈ Rensie dau. of
Marten Schenck and wid. of Peter G. Wyckoff.   Resided
at one period in Fld' where he was a deacon of the ch. in
1736, and finally settled in Newtown. Issue:—George of
N. L. and Jᵃ, b. Jan. 28, 1722; Sarah, b. Apl. 8, 1724, m.
Isaac Bogert; Agnes, b. May 28, 1729; Mary, b. Nov. 10,
1730, m. Isaac Brazier; Cornelius of Newtown, b. Jan. 16,
1732; Martin, b. May 28, 1734; Jane, b. Mar. 14, 1736, m.
Hendrick Riker; Daniel, bp. Aug. 31, 1738; Nelly, b. July
4, 1740, m. Jeremiah Remsen; and Agnes, b. May 9, 1744.
Signed his name *"Daniel Rappelje."*

George or *Joris* (s. of Daniel and Sara), b. Mar. 4, 1675;
m. Angenitje or Agnes dau. of Charles Berrien.   Removed
from Brⁿ to Newtown. Will da. Apl. 1, 1742; pro. June 17,
1743; rec. p. 64, Lib. 15, N. Y. surr. off. Issue:—Daniel of
Newtown, b. Nov. 12, 1699; Cornelius of Hellgate, bp. Oct.
26, 1702, in Brⁿ, m. Alletta dau. of Joris Brinckerhoff;
Abraham of Newtown, b. May 19, 1705, m. Anna dau. of
Joris Brinckerhoff; Jane, b. 1707, m. John Debevoise; John of
Newtown, b. June 11, 1707, m. Maria dau. of Abᵐ Lent;
Jacob of Hellgate; and Jeromus of Newtown. Signed his
name *"Joris Rappalyee."*

George Janse of Brⁿ ferry, m. Diana dau. of Garret Middagh; d. about 1747. By his will on file in the N. Y. surr.
off., da. Sept. 4, 1745, he devises his farm at the ferry, which
he inherited from his father (since of J. and C. Sands) to
his s. John, and his farm at the Wallabout to his s. Garret.
Issue:—John of the ferry, bp. Sept. 10, 1722 or '7; Garret
of N. Y.; Cornelia, m. Abᵐ Lott; and Anna or Antie, bp.
Nov. 11, 1733, in N. U., m. Gerardus Duyckinck.

George or *Joris* (s. of Teunis and Sarah) of Bedford, m.
Elizabeth dau. of Joris Remsen; d. in 1732. Will da. Dec.
20, 1731; pro. Mar. 19, 1732; rec. on p. 235 of Lib. 11, N. Y.
surr. off. Resided in Bedford. Issue:—Sarah, b. May 12,
1722, m. George Jansen; George, b. June 14, 1724, (sup.)
m. Elizabeth Vandervoort, and that, being a loyalist, after
the war of the Revolution he emigrated to Nova Scotia,

where there are numerous Rapaljes residing in the vicinity of Annapolis, some of whom may be his descendants; Tunis, b. May 27, 1726, m. Catharine Stockholm; Rem of N. Y., b. Aug. 3, 1728, m. Elenor Hardenbrook; Phebe, b. Oct. 9, 1731; and (sup.) Benjamin.

Jacob Jorise of Br^n, b. May 28, 1639; killed by the Indians.

Jacob (*Jeronimuse*), b. June 25, 1679; m. 1st Gertien ——; m. 2^d Sarah dau. of Ab^m Brinckerhoff. Left Br^n and settled near New Brunswick, N. J., prior to 1699. Issue:—Joris of N. J., b. Jan. 20, 1706; Abraham of N. J., bp. Aug. 3, 1707; Ante of N. J., b. Apl. 17, 1709; George of N. J.; Aeltie of N. J., m. Hendrick Suydam; Sara of N. J., bp. Apl. 30, 1712; and Jacob of N. J., bp. July 27, 1719.

Jan Jorise, b. Aug. 28, 1637; m. Apl. 16, 1660, Maria Fredericks of the Hague; d. Jan. 25, 1663, and was a deacon of the R. D. ch. of Br^n, where he resided at the time of his death. Issue:—Frederick, bp. Sept. 30, 1662, and d. the same year. Signed his name "*Jan Joris Rappalie.*"

Jan (*Jeronimus*) of Br^n, b. Dec. 17, 1673; m. Annatje dau. of Coert Van Voorhies; d. 1733. Owned and cultivated a large farm E. of Brooklyn ferry. In 1701 a Jan Rappelje was allotted woodland in the new lots of Fl^h, as per p. 64 of Lib. B of Fl^h rec. Will da. Sept. 8, 1732; pro. Aug. 23, 1733; rec. p. 76, Lib. 12, N. Y. surr. off. Issue:—George of Br^n ferry; Jeromus of Flushing; and John, who m. Maria Van Dyke. A Jan or Yan of Br^n signed his name in 1723 "*Yan Rapalje.*"

Jeronimus Jorise, b. June 27, 1643; m. Anna dau. of Tunis Nyssen or Denyse. Occupied and owned the ancestral farm at the Wallabout; schepen of Br^n in 1673 and '74, and justice of the peace in 1689 and '90. See p. 184 of Cal. of Eng. Man. Issue:—Joris, b. Nov. 5, 1668; Teunis, b. May 7, 1671, in N. Y.; Jan, b. Dec. 17, 1673; Femitie, b. Oct. 17, 1676, m. Jan Arianse Bennet; Jeronimus, b. Mar. 31, 1682; Cataline, b. Mar. 29, 1685, m. Peter Demond of the Raritan; Sarah, b. Nov. 4, 1687, m. Hans Bergen; and Cornelis, b. Oct. 21, 1690. Signed his name "*Jeronimus Rapalje.*"

Jeronimus of the Wallabout (s. of Jeronimus Jorise), b. Mar. 31, 1682; m. Hellitie dau. of Hendrick Van Vechten; (sup.) d. Feb. 8, 1762. Took the oath of allegiance in Br^n in 1687 as a native. Owned and occupied the homestead of his father and grandfather at the Wallabout, which he devised by will to his dau. Antie w. of Marten M. Schenck. Issue:—Annetie, b. Aug. 10, 1704, d. young; Hendrick, b. Oct. 5, 1706; Gerritie, b. May 30, 1708; Annetie or Antie, b. Aug. 19, 1710, m. Marten M. Schenck; Catalyna, b. Mar.

17, 1716, m. Johannes Alsteyn; Jannetie, b. Apl. 22, 1720, d.
young; Jeronemus of Brᵃ, b. Feb. 22, 1723, m. Jannetie dau.
of Jacobus Lefferts; Catryna, b. Sept. 29, 1726; Jannetie, b.
June 21, 1729, m. Aris Remsen; and Hilletje, b. Sept. 30,
1736. Signed his name "*Jeronimus Rapalje.*"

Jeronimus (*Teunisse*), m. Sept. 19, 1719, Altie dau. of Cor-
nelis Van Arsdalen; d. 1777. Left Bedford and settled at
New Brunswick, N. J. Issue:—(sup.) Antje, m. Ferdinand
Van Leuwen of N. J.; (sup.) Tunis of N. J., m. Chrystintje
Pietersen; (sup.) Altje, m. Hendrick Suydam of N. J.; Cor-
nelis of N. J.; Tunis of N. J., m. Antje Dorlant; and Sarah.

John (s. of Jan and Annatie), m. 1737 Maria Van Dyke.
No further trace.

Joris¹ Jansen, the common ancestor of the family, emigrated in 1623; m. Catalyntje dau. of Joris Trico of Paris;
d. about 1665. Resided at first in Albany, where his dau.
Sarah was born, and not in Brᵃ as asserted by some writers,
then in N. A. and finally on his plantation at the Wallabout
in Brᵃ of 167 morgens, for which he obtained a patent June 16,
1637. Was one of the 12 men representing the N. N. in 1641,
and mag. of Brᵃ in 1655, '56, '57, '60, and '62. Some writers
prefix a *De* to his surname so as to make it *De Rapalie*, but the
compiler has seen no conclusive evidence to justify it, nor
has he found among the public and private records of this
vicinity or elsewhere an instance where either Joris Jansen or
any of his descendants have made use of said prefix. Issue:—
Sarah Jorise, b. June 9, 1625, m. 1ˢᵗ Hans Hansen Bergen,
m. 2ᵈ Tunis Gysbertse Bogaert; Marretje Jorise, b. Mar. 16,
1627, m. Michael Paulus Vandervoort; Jannetje Jorise, b.
Aug. 18, 1629, m. Rem Jansen Vanderbeeck; Judith Jorise,
b. July 5, 1635, m. Pieter Pietersen Van Nest; Jan Jorise,
b. Aug. 28, 1637; Jacob Jorise, b. May 28, 1639; Catelyntje
Jorise, b. Mar. 28, 1641, m. Jeremias Jansen Van Westerhout; Jeronemus Jorise, b. June 27, 1643; Annetje Jorise,
b. Feb. 8, 1646, m. 1ˢᵗ Marten Reyerse, m. 2ᵈ Joost France;
Elizabeth Jorise, b. Mar. 26, 1648, m. Dirck Cornelise Hoogland; and Daniel Jorise, b. Dec. 29, 1652. Made his mark
" R " to documents.

Joris (*Jeronimuse*) of Cripplebush and Bedford, b. Nov. 5,
1668; m. July 27, 1694, Nelly dau. of John Cowenhoven; d.
1697. Issue:—Antie or Annetje, bp. Oct. 18, 1696, in Brᵃ,
m. Peter Lott of N. Y.; Jacob of N. J.; Cornelius of the
city of N. Y., m. Joanna Antonides; and Jeromus of the
Wallabout. Signed his name "*Joris Rapalie.*"

Joris (s. of Daniel), b. Mar. 4, 1675; m. Agnes or Agnietje
dau. of Corˢ Berrian; d. Jan. 19, 1741. Resided at first in
Brᵃ and afterwards in Flushing. Issue:—Daniel of New-

town, b. Nov. 12, 1699; Cornelius of Hellgate, bp. Oct. 26, 1702, in Br^n, m. Alletta Brinckerhoff; Abraham of Fish's Point, Newtown, b. May 19, 1705, m. Anna Brinckerhoff; Jane, b. 1707, m. John Debevoise; John of Newtown, b. June 11, 1711, m. Maria Lent; Jacob of Hellgate, m. Catharine Lott; and Jeromus of Newtown, m. Wyntje Lent. Signed his name "*Joris Rappalyee.*"

Joris or *George* (Teunise) of Bedford, m. Elizabeth dau. of Joris Remsen; d. 1732. Issue:—Sarah, b. May 12, 1722, m. George Jansen; George, b. June 14, 1724, (sup.) m. Elizabeth Vandervoort; Tunis of N. Y., b. May 22, 1726, m. Cath^e Stockholm; Rem of N. Y., b. Aug. 3, 1728, m. Elenor Hardenbrook; Phebe, b. Oct. 9, 1731; and Benjamin. Signed his name "*Joris Rapalie.*"

Teunis (s. of Jeronimus) of Br^n and Bu^k, bp. May 7, 1671; m. Sarah Van Vechten; d. 1723. On ass. roll of Br^n of 1693, cen. of 1698, and lieut. of militia of Br^n in 1700, as per p. 809 of Vol. IV. of N. Y. Doc. His. Issue:—Jeronimus of New Brunswick, N. J., m. Altie Van Arsdalen; George of Bedford, m. Elizabeth Remsen; Anna Maria, m. Jacob Casjouw; Derick of Somerset Co., N. J., bp. May 14, 1702, in Br^n; Tunis of Bu^k, m. Anatie Suydam; Folkert of Cripplebush, Br^n, bp. Jan. 1, 1720, m. Matilda Polhemus; Jane, m. Aris Remsen; and Sarah, m. Jacobus Van Nuyse.

Tunis of Bu^k (s. of Tunis and Sara), m. Annatie Suydam. Was a blacksmith. Will da. Apl. 29, 1734; pro. Oct. 29, 1734; rec. p. 244, Lib. 12, N. Y. surr. off. Issue:—Sarah, (sup.) m. Jacobus Van Nuyse of N. J.; Ann, m. Tunis Duryea of Bu^k; and Jane.

RASCO, SAMUEL, of Fl^h in 1680, as per Fl^h court rec.

RATEO, JOHN. A suit was brought against him Apl. 4, 1669, in the court of sessions in G^d by Richard Beach for debt, as per G^d rec.

RAWLES, JOHN, brought a suit against John Emans in the court of sessions of May 1, 1671, for the killing of one of his swine. In 1672 he was allotted a lot in the Neck or West Meadows, as per G^d rec.

REBLIANTHS, JOHN, of the city of N. Y. Sold May 4, 1691-2, to Cornelis Simons (Van Arsdalen) a half-lot in G^d Neck, as per G^d rec.

REES, JOHANNES, on ass. roll of Fl^h of 1693 and cen. of 1696.

REGGO, JOHANNES, m. *Maria* ——; on ass. roll of N. U. of 1693. Issue:—Daniel; Abraham; Adolphus; and Tuntien.

REINIERS, REYNIERSZ, or REINIERSZEN, AUKE, m. *Ida Aukes* (*Van Nuyse*); on ass. roll of Bu^k of 1693 and cen. of 1698. Issue:—Magdalen, bp. Oct. 23, 1698; and Hendrick, bp. Aug. 11, 1700. Made his mark to documents.
Arnoud, mem. of Fl^h R. D. ch. in 1677.
Garret of Fld^s, m. Maria ——. On ass. roll of Fld^s of 1675, and mem. of the ch. of that place in 1677.
Gysbert, on ass. roll of Fl^h of 1676.
Wiggert, from "Ostoriestant," joined the R. D. ch. of Br^n in 1660 on certificate from Manhattan I.

RENDENHASEN, ABEL, declared Jan. 27, 1643, that he made gloves from English duffles 3 years ago in the "bay" (Fld^s), as per p. 84 of Cal. of Dutch Man.

REMMELS, JAN. His name appears among those who paid the preacher's salary in Fl^h in 1681.

REMMERSEN or REMMERTSZ, GERRET, m. *Mary* or *Maria* ——. Both mem. of the R. D. ch. of Fld^s in 1677, where he or his heirs owned land as late as 1697, as per deed on p. 117 of Lib. 2 of Con. Jan. 6, 1684, Mary Remmersen, residing on N. Y. Island, bought of John Tilton plantation-lot No. 30 with the buildings thereon in G^d, as per town rec. Jan. 17, 1698-9, Mary Remmersen of G^d receipts for £5 to R. Van Sicklen on an agreement made by her two sons Rem and Samuel Gerretse. In 1698 Mary wid. of Gerret Remmersen of G^d conveys to Samuel Gerretse her son a house and garden-spot in G^d, and also land on Gisbert's I. bounded on the one side by the sea, as per G^d rec. Gerret Remmersen means Gerret son of Rem; and Samuel Gerretse, Samuel son of Gerret. From this Samuel Gerretse is descended the late Gerretsen family of G^d, who resided near to and owned what is known as Gerretsen's Mill, and the Gerretsen family of Br^n, of whom the late John Fletcher, Thomas, and Judge Samuel Gerretsen were members. No clue to the proper surname (if any) of this family has been found. Issue:—Rem Gerretse; and Samuel Gerretse, who m. Ida Barends. Made his mark to documents.

REMSEN, ABRAHAM, (s. of Rem Jansen and Jannetje,) b. Sept. 14, 1667; m. *Ann Aertsen Middagh;* d. Dec. 13, 1752. In 1687 took the oath of allegiance in Br^n as a native, and

on cen. of 1698. Finally settled in Newtown. Issue:—
Rem, bp. Oct. 10, 1694, in N. Y., m. Mary Letton; Aert, bp.
July 3, 1698; Jeromus, b. 1705, m. Jane Remsen; Abraham,
b. 1705; and Bregie, bp. Dec. 7, 1707, m. Ab^m Ditmars of J^a.

Aert (s. of Abraham), bp. July 3, 1698; m. Geerie ——,
and (sup.) resided in Br^n. Issue:—Abraham, b. 1719, d.
young; Margaret, b. 1722; Helena, b. 1722; and Abraham,
b. Dec. 4, 1730.

Daniel (s. of Rem) of Fl^h, b. 1665; m. Jane dau. of John
Ditmars; d. 1736. Took the oath of allegiance in Fl^h in
1687 as a native; and on ass. roll of said town of 1693 and
cen. of 1698. No male issue. Signed his name *"Daniel
Remsen."*

George, see Joris.

Isaac (s. of Rem Jansen and Jannetje) of Br^n, b. Sept. 4,
1673; m. 1st, 1699, Sarah Monfoort; m. 2^d Hendrikje ——;
d. prior to 1758. Was a farmer. Will da. July 5, 1752;
pro. May 21, 1758; rec. p. 473, Lib. 20, N. Y. surr. off.
Issue:—Rem of Br^n, bp. Sept. 17, 1699; Marytje, bp. Dec.
25, 1700; Jannetje, bp. Sept. 8, 1706, m. John Van Nostrand;
(by 2^d w.) Isaac of Oyster Bay, bp. Oct. 15, 1710—all bp. in
Br^n; John of Oyster Bay; Jacob of Br^n, bp. Feb. 13, 1719,
in N. U., m. Catharine Van Duyne; Jores of Br^n, m. Cate-
line Ditmars; Hendrikje, m. in 1753 Johannes Lott of Fld^a;
and Catrina, m. in 1744 John Boerum. Signed his name
"Isack Remsen."

Jacob (s. of Rem and Jannetje), b. Apl. 11, 1662; m. May
13, 1687, Gertrude dau. of Derick Vandervliet. In 1677
mem. of Br^n ch., and in 1687 took the oath of allegiance in
Fl^h as a native, in which town he then resided. Issue:—
Jannetje, bp. July 27, 1701, m. (sup.) Johannes Lucasse
Voorhees. Signed his name *"Jacob Remsen."*

Jacob (s. of Rem and Marretie of Fl^h) of Br^n, m. Maria
dau. of Steven Coerten Voorhies of G^d; will da. May 8,
1756, and pro. in Dec. of the same year. Issue:—Rem;
Stephen of Brooklyn ferry and of N. L., m. Catharine Ditmars; John, bp. Mar. 9, 1729; Maria or Marretje, bp. Aug.
15, 1731, m. Ab^m Montanye; Eva, (sup.) m. Lewis Fongeres;
and Anna, bp. Oct. 2, 1737—all bp. in N. U.

Jan (s. of Rem Jansen and Jannetje), b. Jan. 12, 1648; m.
Dec. 11, 1681, Martha da. of Jan Damon; d. 1696. A mag.
of Fl^h in 1682, on ass. roll of 1683, took the oath of allegiance there in 1687 as a native, and a grand-juryman in
1695. At one period resided in the city of N. Y. Will da.
May 30, 1696, and rec. on p. 17 of Lib. 3 of Con. Issue:—
Rem, bp. Oct. 6, 1682, in Fld^a, d. young; Rem Vanderbeeck,
bp. Oct. 21, 1683, in Br^n, m. Deborah Cortelyou; Sophia,

bp. Jan. 23, 1685, in Fl[h]; John, bp. Apl. 17, 1687, in Br[n]; Jane, (sup.) m. Johannes Ditmars; Martha; Cornelius; Peter of N. L.; and Elizabeth.   Signed his name "*Jan Remsen.*"

Jan or *John* (s. of Rem of Fl[h] and Marretie), m. Elizabeth ——; d. prior to 1725. Issue:—Rem of Hempstead, bp. Mar. 10, 1706; Derick of Fld[s], b. Feb. 8, 1709, m. Catharine Lott; George of Fl[h], b. 1710; Aris of J[s], b. 1712; Anna, b. 1715; and Elizabeth, b. 1715.

Jeremias (s. of Rem Jansen and Jannetje), b. Sept. 10, 1675; m. 1st, Sept. 26, 1698, Heyltje Probasco; m. 2[d] Jannetje Voorhees; d. July 3, 1757.   Occupied and owned the paternal farm at the Wallabout.   Issue:—Rem, b. Nov. 20, 1700; Ida, b. Jan. 3, 1703, m. John Van Wickelen of N. L.; Christopher of Br[n], b. Oct. 2, 1705, m. Charity ——; Jeremias, b. Aug. 22, 1708, and d. young; Jane, b. Jan. 26, 1711, m. Dec. 12, 1729, Jeromus Remsen her cousin; Jeremiah of the Wallabout, b. July 18, 1714, m. Jane dau. of Martin R. Schenck; Sarah, b. Dec. 11, 1716, m. Ab[m] Voorhees; Abraham of the Wallabout, b. Jan. 15, 1720, m. Matilda Van Duyne; and Lammatie, b. May 20, 1722, m. Luke Schenck of N. J. Signed his name "*Jeremyas Remsen.*"

Jeronimus (s. of Rem Jansen and Jannetje), b. 1664; m. 1688 Catalina dau. of Cornelis Berryan; d. 1750.   Name on ass. roll of Br[n] of 1693; cen. of 1698; took the oath of allegiance in Br[n] in 1687; and an officer of militia in said town in 1700.   Removed to N. Y., and mem. of the R. D. ch. of said city in 1722.   No male issue.

John (s. of Rem and Marretie of Fl[h]), see Jan.

Jores or *George* (s. of Rem and Marritee of Fl[h]), m. 1st Lammetje dau. of Jores Bergen; m. 2[d] Sarah dau. of Theodorus Polhemius. Left Fl[h] and settled at the Pond in Haverstraw.   Will da. Mar. 26, 1744; pro. May 12, 1748; rec. p. 276, Lib. 16, N. Y. surr. off. Issue:—Marretje, bp. Sept. 21, 1701, in Br[n]; Joris of Newtown, m. Elizabeth ——; Rem (by 2[d] w.), b. 1711; Theodorus; Ann; Ariaentje; and Lambertje, who m. —— Polhemus. Signed his name "*Jores Remsen.*"

Joris or *George* (s. of Rem Jansen and Jannetje), b. Feb. 2, 1650; m. Nov. 2, 1684, Femmetje dau. of Dirck Janse Woertman. Bought Oct. 10, 1706, his father-in-law's farm near Br[n] ferry, on Br[n] heights, to which he removed.   Previously a resident of Fl[h], where he took the oath of allegiance in 1687 as a native.   On ass. roll of Fl[h] of 1693 and cen. of 1698.   Issue:—Mary, m. Joost De Bevoise; Sarah, m. Jacobus De Bevoise; Elizabeth, bp. Mar. 5, 1699, m. George Rapalje; Antje, bp. July 28, 1701, in Br[n]; Femmetje, m. Peter Lott; Cataline, bp. Apl. 12, 1704, in N. Y., m.

Hendrick Remsen; Rem Jorise, m. Aeltie Bergen; Hilletje, bp. Jan. 12, 1705, in N. Y.; and Tunis, b. Oct. 26, 1716, m. Margrietje Valentyn.

Peter (s. of Jan and Martha of Fl[h]), resided in N. L. No further trace.

Rem[3] of Br[n] (s. of Rem and Marretje of Fl[h]), b. May 7, 1685; m. Dorothy ——; d. Mar. 5, 1752. Will da. Dec. 5, 1750; pro. Apl. 22, 1752; rec. p. 99, Lib. 17, N. Y. surr. off. Issue:—Rem, b. 1706, m. Sarah Rapalje; Hendrick, a merchant in N. Y., b. 1708, m. Catalyntje or Catharine Remsen; Marritje, b. 1710; Aris of Br[n], b. 1711, m. Jannetje Rapalje; Johannes, a baker of Br[n] and N. Y., b. 1714, d. Aug. 28, 1763, m. Dec. 11, 1737, Eliz[h] Brestede; Catharine, b. 1716, (sup.) m. John Cowenhoven; Joris of N. Y., b. 1717, m. Geertie De Hart; Jacob of Br[n], b. 1719, m. Catharine Hendricksen, d. 1784; Antie, b. 1721; Peter of N. Y., b. 1721, m. Jane De Hart; Dorothy, b. 1724, m. John Ryke; and Sarah, b. Dec. 28, 1726, d. Nov. 25, 1758. Signed his name *"Rem Remsen."*

Rem[2] (s. of Rem Jansen and Jannetje), b. Dec. 2, 1652; m. Marratie dau. of Jan Vanderbilt. Mem. of Fl[h] D. ch. in 1677, residing in N. L.; on ass. roll of 1683, and took the oath of allegiance as a native in said town in 1687. Will da. Sept. 9, 1724; rec. p. 342, Lib. 14, N. Y. surr. off. Issue:—Jores of the Pond; Annetje, bp. May, 21, 1682, in Fl[h]; Aris, bp. Jan. 13, 1684, in Fl[h], d. young; Rem, b. May 7, 1685; Jannetje, bp. Sept. 9, 1688, in Fl[h]; Jacob; John; and Peter. Signed his name *"Rem Remsen."*

Rem [1] *Jansen Vanderbeeck*, the common ancestor of the Remsen family, emigrated from Ieveren in Westphalia; by another account, from Coevorden in Drenthe in the Netherlands. His descendants dropped the family name of Vanderbeeck, and, as was the custom at the time, assumed that of Remsen, or sons of Rem. He m. Dec. 21, 1642, Jannetje dau. of Jores Jansen Rapalie; d. in 1681. Was a blacksmith by trade, residing for some time at Albany, where several of his children were born, and where he was nominated for commissaris in 1655, and sold his house and lot in 1660. He obtained a plantation at the Wallabout adjoining that of his father-in-law prior to 1643, on which he finally settled. Issue:—Annetje Remsen, bp. Mar. 12, 1645, d. young; Hillitje or Belitje Remsen, bp. Jan. 20, 1647, d. young; Jan Remsen, bp. Jan. 12, 1648; Joris Remsen, b. Feb. 2, 1650; Rem Remsen, b. Dec. 2, 1652; Hillitje Remsen, b. Sept. 16, 1653, m. Aris Janse Vanderbilt; Catalina Remsen, b. Oct. 4, 1655, m. Elbert Adrianse; Femmetje Remsen, b. Aug. 1, 1657, m. Joseph Hegeman; Anna Remsen, b.

Apl. 11, 1660, m. Jan Gerretsen Dorlandt; Jacob Remsen, b. Apl. 11, 1662; Jeronymus Remsen, b. 1664; Daniel Remsen, b. 1665; Abraham Remsen, b. Sept. 16, 1667; Sarah Remsen, b. Dec. 6, 1670, m. Martin Adrianse; Isaac Remsen, b. Sept. 4, 1673; Jeremias Remsen, b. Sept. 10, 1675; and Jannetje Remsen, m. (sup.) Gerret Hansen Van Nostrand. Signed his name *"Rem Jansen"* and *"Rem Yansen."*

Rem Jorise (s. of Joris and Femmetje of Br^n), m. Aug. 17, 1707, Aeltje Bergen; d. Jan. 1724. Suppose he resided at Br^n. Issue:—Joris or George, m. Jane Nagel; Jan or John; Femmetje, bp. May 24, 1708, in N. Y., (sup.) m. Ab^m Brinckerhoff; Sarah; and Antie.

Rem Vanderbeeck (s. of Jan and Martha of Fl^h), bp. Oct. 21, 1683; m. Deborah Cortelyou. Left Fl^h and settled on S. I., where he was a justice of the peace in 1738. His name is entered Rem Vanderbeeck on the records of the R. D. ch. of Port Richmond, where his children were bp. Issue:— Hilletje, bp. Oct. 21, 1713; Jan, bp. July 26, 1719; Rem, bp. May 28, 1721; Jaques, bp. June 2, 1723; Dorothea, bp. Jan. 21, 1727-8; and Lena, bp. June 3, 1736.

REYCKE, see Suydam.

REYERSE, REYERSEN, or RYERSEN, ADRIAEN, emigrated from Amsterdam in 1646 with his brother Marten; m. July 29, 1659, *Annetje Martense Schenck* of Fld^s; d. Nov. 24, 1710. Finally settled in Fl^h, where he was a mag. in 1677, '78, and '79; on ass. roll of 1675; obtained a patent for 24 morgens; and took the oath of allegiance in 1687. His name also appears on the ass. roll of Br^n of 1675. Issue:—Jannetje Adrianse, b. July 25, 1660, (sup.) m. Oct. 14, 1683, Jacobus Hegeman; Elbert Adrianse of Flushing, b. Aug. 14, 1663, whose descendants adopted Adrianse, as per Riker, for their surname; Marten Adrianse of Fl^h, the ancestor of the Martense family of Kings Co., b. Mar. 9, 1668, m. Sarah Remsen; Margaret or Grietje Adrianse, b. Mar. 28, 1670; Sarah Adrianse, b. June 9, 1672, d. young; Reyer Adrianse, b. May 28, 1673, d. young; Neeltje Adrianse, b. Dec. 7, 1675; Reyer Adrianse, b. Mar. 31, 1678, d. young; Abraham Adrianse, b. Nov. 21, 1680, m. Femmetje Van Cleef; Sarah Adrianse, bp. Nov. 21, 1680; Reyer Adrianse, b. May 6, 1683; and Gosen Adrianse, bp. Apl. 29, 1685 or '86, m. Femmetje Vanderbilt. Signed his name *"Adriaen Reyersen."*

Frans (s. of Marten and Annetje), bp. Aug. 2, 1685; m. 1707 (sup.) Jenneke or Jannetje dau. of Theunis Dircksen Dey. Left Br^n and settled in Bergen Co., N. J., where he d. prior to July, 1749. Issue:—Mark, bp. Mar. 10, 1708;

Theunis, bp. Mar. 13, 1709; Theunis, bp. July 15, 1711; Joris, bp. Apl. 5, 1713; Antje, bp. Nov. 10, 1714; Saartje, bp. June 24, 1716; Johannes, bp. Apl. 27, 1718; and Janneke, bp. Aug. 21, 1720—all of N. J., and all bp. in N. Y.

Jacob (sup. s. of Jacobus and Styntje) of the Wallabout, m. (sup.) Antje Voorhees. Will da. May 23, 1749. Was the ancestor of the Wallabout family of Ryersons. Issue:— Marten of the Wallabout; Geertje; Jan or John, who d. intestate about 1780; Antie or Ann; Jannetje; and Styntje.

Jacobus (s. of Marten and Annetje), bp. Dec. 26, 1677; m. Styntje ——. Resided in Fl[h], of which town he was constable in 1698. Issue:—(Sup.) Jacob of the Wallabout; Annetje, bp. July 16, 1702, in Br[n]; Geertje, bp. May 22, 1706, m. Hendrick Suydam; Jan, bp. Oct. 9, 1709; Jan, b. Dec. 11, 1715; Jannetje, bp. Feb. 29, 1721, in N. U. (sup.) m. Peter Lose or Loise; and Styntje, bp. Sept. 22, 1723, in N. U., m. Constyn Golneck.

Joris (s. of Marten and Annetje), bp. Sept. 19, 1666; m. (sup.) Aug. 11, 1691, Anneken Schouten wid. of Teunis Dircksen Dey of N. Y. Suppose he removed to Aquackanonck, N. J., a Joris Ryerson being a deacon of the R. D. ch. of that locality in 1716. Issue:—Joris, bp. Jan. 5, 1703, in N. Y.; Luykes, bp. Apl. 9, 1704; and Blandina, bp. May 8, 1706.

Marten, emigrated from Amsterdam in 1646 and settled in Br[n]; m. May 14, 1663, Annetje dau. of Joris Jansen Rapalie. On ass. rolls of Br[n] of 1675, '76, and '83; mem. of Br[n] ch. in 1677; mag. in 1679; constable in 1682, as per Furman; and name on patent of Fl[h] in 1685, to which place he may possibly have removed. Issue:—Marritje, bp. Nov. 16, 1664; Joris, bp. Sept. 19, 1666, in N. Y.; Catalyntje, bp. Jan. 3, 1671, m. Sam[l] Berry; Sara, bp. May 30, 1673; Jacobus, bp. Dec. 26, 1677; (sup.) Geertje, who m. Ab[m] Van Duyn in 1696; Helena or Lyntje, bp. Apl. 2, 1682—all bp. in N. Y.; and Frans, bp. Aug. 2, 1685. Signed his name *"Marten Reyersen."*

REVNIERSE or RYNIERSE, AARNOUD, mem. of the R. D. ch. of Fl[h] in 1677.

Aernout, a s. of Rynier Arentse of Keuter's Hoek.

Aucke, s. of Reynier Arentsz, took the oath of allegiance in Fl[h] in 1677 as a native. Bought land in Bu[k] in 1692 of Johannes Fonteyn, as per p. 157 of Lib. 2 of Con. Also bought Oct. 20, 1700, of his father Reynier Arentsz his farm with its appendages and salt-meadows located at "Keutershoek" in Fl[h] for £425, as per p. 2 of Lib. B of Fl[h] rec. At the time

16

of his death he resided in Bu^k. Made his mark to documents. See Auke Reiniers, who may be the same person.

RIBUT, JAN, of Br^n, m. Aug. 9, 1690, *Matte Beeckman* wid. of Cornelis Vanderca.

RICHARDS, PAUL or PAULUS, from Rochelle in France, m. Feb. 9, 1664, in N. Y., *Celitje Jans* wid. of Hendrick Vander Wallen, and in same year took the oath of allegiance to the English in said city. In 1674 he and Cornelis Van Borsum bought of Machtelt Megapolensus a bouwery in Fl^h, as per p. 28 of Lib. B of Fl^h rec. His name appears on Gov. Dongan's patent of Bu^k of 1687, and he bought Apl. 21, 1694, of Jacobus Vandewater a farm at Bedford, as per p. 1 of Lib. 2 of Con. Issue:—Hester, bp. Dec. 6, 1664; Paulus, bp. June 12, 1667; Stephen, bp. Jan. 23, 1670; Jacob, bp. July 9, 1673; Blandina, bp. July 9, 1673; Hester, bp. Dec. 18, 1675; and Blandina, bp. Apl. 23, 1678—all in N. Y. Signed his name *"Paul Richards."*

RICHARDSON or RICHERSON, JOHN, (English,) bought Mar. 4, 1683-4, of Anthony Wanshaer his house and lot in Fl^h, as per p. 157 of Lib. C of Fl^h rec. On ass. roll of Fl^h of 1693 and cen. of 1698. Made his mark to documents.

Richard, brought a suit in the court of sessions in G^d in 1663 against Jan Van Cleef for an ox, as per G^d rec.

William, an Englishman whose 1st w. Deliverance d. Feb. 10, 1675, on shipboard in harbor of N. Y., and was buried in G^d, as per p. 39 of Vol. VII. of the Genealogical Record. His 2^d w. Amy d. Feb. 5, 1683-4, as per p. 39 of said Vol. He is also referred to as of G^d in John Tilton's will of 1687, as per p. 108 of Lib. 1 of Con. Had, as per p. 181 of Vol. III. of the Gen. Rec., issue:—William, b. Jan. 15, 1678; Thomas, b. Sept. 10, 1680; and John, b. Dec. 10, 1683.

RICKHOUT or RICHON, JOHANNES DANIELSE, m. Apl. 21, 1694, *Mayke* da. of Jan Van Dyck of N. U. Issue:—Jan, bp. Apl. 25, 1696.

RIDER, see Ryder.

RIGHT, GEORGE (Capt.), of G^d, made an agreement Feb. 7, 1653, with Hendrick Hendricksen for the purchase of oxen and a cart, as per G^d rec.

RIKER, ABRAHAM, leased July 2, 1643, land in Bu^k, as per Col. Man.

RINIERS or RINIERSEN, see Reiniers and Van Sicklen.

RIPPLE or REPELLE, GEORGE, and Jacobus Kierstede of the city of N. Y., with consent of their wives Anna Kierstede and *Catharyn Ripple*, sold the 15 A. lot No. 17 in G^d to Capt. John Van Dyckhuysen, as per G^d rec.

RITZERSON, JAN, allotted Mar. 22, 1701, 2 wood-lots on the division of Fl^h woodlands, as per town rec. Made his mark to documents.

ROBBESON, JOSIA, m. *Margaret* ——. Issue:—Hanna, bp. Aug. 28, 1698, in Fld^a.

ROELOFSE, see Verkerk.
Dirckye, on ass. rolls of Fld^a of 1675 and '83.
John, in 1669 a grand-juryman at the court of sessions, and on ass. roll of Bu^k in 1675. Prior to 1695 he sold land in Fld^a to Pieter Guilliamse (Cornell), as per p. 38 of Lib. 1 of Con. There was a John Roelofsen who settled on the Raritan after 1683, as per p. 160 of Messler's His. Notes. Signed his name *"Yan Roelofsen"* in 1664.
Machild of the Wallabout, mem. of Br^n R. D. ch. in 1677, entered as removed to Bergen.
Pieter, among the first settlers of N. U. in 1657. Jan. 16, 1660, sold his house and building-plot to Jan Zeelan, and removed to Fld^a. He m. 1st, Feb. 1, 1653, in N. A., Willemtje Janse; m. 2^d, May 16, 1664, in N. A., Elizabeth Janse of Brazil, both residents of Fld^a. Issue:—Jacobus, bp. Oct. 14, 1667; Hendrickje, bp. Aug. 21, 1672; Abraham, bp. Apl. 21, 1675; and Susanna, bp. Mar. 23, 1678—all bp. in N. A. Signed his name *"Pieter Roelefsen."* .

ROELANTSEN, ADAM, from Dokkum in Friesland; school-master in N. A. as early as 1638; m. Lyntje Martens. His garden damaged in 1641 by cattle of Jan Damen and Jan Forbes, as per p. 17 of Cal. of Dutch Man. Sued Jan Teunissen, schout of Br^n, in 1647 for debt, as per p. 108 of said Cal.

ROEMERS, JANNETJE, bought Feb. 15, 1677-8, of Bartel Claesen (Van Ruynen) a house-lot in Fl^h on the N. side of the highway, as per p. 24 of Lib. AA of Fl^h rec.

ROMEYN, ALBERT CLAESEN, bp. May 2, 1686, at Br^n; m. Apl. 1710 *Jannetje Roelofse Westervelt*. Left Fld^a and settled in Bergen, N. J. Issue:—Nicholas, bp. 1711, m. Beletje de

Marest; Orseltje, bp. 1713, m. Isaac Albertsen Van Voorhees; Sara, bp. 1715, m. Jan Durje; Roelof, bp. 1715; Geesje, bp. 1719, m. Peter Van Voorhees; Roelof, bp. 1722, m. Lydia de Marest; Christina, bp. 1725, m. Jonathan Roos; Ariaentje, bp. 1728, m. Roelof Westervelt; and Elizabeth, bp. 1733, (sup.) m. David Simmons—all of N. J.

Claes or *Klaes Jansen*, emigrated to this country about 1653, m. May 2, 1680, Styntje Albertse Terhune. Of Fld* in 1679 and '92. Mar. 3, 1679, he bought of Wm Comton of G^d plantation-lot No. 23. Rev. Theodorus B. Romeyn, a descendant, says Claes emigrated at first from Holland to Brazil, and thence to N. N. in 1661, settling at first at New Amersfoort (Fld*), afterwards at Hackensack, N. J., and finally at Greenwich, where he died. Of this have seen no account on our local or State records. Issue:—Gerrebrechtje, bp. Dec. 18, 1681, in Fld*, m. David Ackerman; Lysbeth, bp. Aug. 12, 1683, in N. U., m. Jan Zabriskie; Lyda, m. 1st Peter Larroe, m. 2^d James Slingerlant; Albert, bp. May 2, 1686 at Br^n; Jan Claesen; Rachel, b. 1700, m. Joris Van Giesen; (sup.) Sarah, m. Hendrick Van Giesen; and Daniel—all of whom settled in Bergen Co., N. J. Signed his name "*Klas Jansen.*"

Daniel Claesen, m. Mar. 1716 Maria Jurianse Westervelt. Left Fld* and settled in the vicinity of Hackensack, N. J. Issue:—Christyntje, bp. 1720; Antie, bp. 1722, m. Rynier Berdan; Geertje, bp. 1723, m. Petrus Van Voorhees; Claes, bp. 1724; Margreta, bp. 1727, m. Nikasy Kip; and Jan, bp. 1731, (sup.) m. Catharine Kip—all of N. J.

Jacobus (Stoffelse), left G^d and settled near Freehold, N. J., where he had a s. Christoffel bp. Oct. 8, 1721.

Jan Claesen, m. May 1699 Lammetje Bougaert. Left Fld* and settled in the vicinity of Freehold, N. J., and mem. of Freehold R. D. ch. in 1711, as per p. 28 of Brick Church Memorial, on which his wife is entered as Geertje Van Dyck (doubtless a 2^d w.). Issue:—Klaes, bp. 1700, m. Elizabeth Outwater; Jan, bp. 1703, m. Catrina Outwater; Steintie, bp. 1705; Roelof, bp. 1708, m. Annetjen Freeland; (sup.)Theodorus, m. Margaret de Bane; David, bp. 1714, m. Agnietje Westervelt; Isack, bp. 1716, m. Osseltjen Casparus Westervelt; Angenietje, bp. 1718, m. Isaac Stagge; and Cristina, b. 1723, m. David Barden.

Stoffel Jansen, emigrated in 1653; m. Mar. 17, 1678, Grietje Pieterse Wyckoff; d. about 1709, judging from an entry in the Marlboro ch. rec of N. J., of Geertje wid. of Stoffel Romeyn having bought in 1709, of R. Salter, 17 A. for the use of the Freehold R. D. ch., of which church in 1711 she appears on the list of members, as per p. 24 of Brick Church

Memorial. His name appears on the ass. rolls of Fld* of 1675 and '76, and in 1677 he was a mem. of the ch. of said town. In 1687 he took the oath of allegiance in G^d. In 1693 his name appears on the ass. rolls of N. U., and in 1698 on the cen. of G^d, where he bought land of his brother Claes, and of which place he was appointed lieut. in 1689. Apl. 1, 1703, he bought of John Verkerk a farm of 100 A. in the village of N. U., of which he was assessed 98 A. in 1706, and which he sold July 20, 1708, to Andrew Emmans of G^d for £550, as per p. 339 of Lib. 2 and p. 128 of Lib. 4 of Con. Issue:—Lysbeth, bp. Feb. 16, 1679, at Fl^h; Grietje, bp. Aug. 29, 1680, at Fl^h; Annetje, bp. July 9, 1682, at Br^n; Cornelis, bp. Mar. 9, 1684, at Br^n; and Jacobus. Signed his name "*Stoffel Jansen Romeyn*" and sometimes "*Stoffel Jansen.*" Stoffel Jansen, Claes Jansen, and Symon Jansen Romeyn, all sons of Jan, as their names indicate, most probably were brothers and came to this country together.

Symon Jansen, b. in 1629, emigrated from Amsterdam probably in 1653, and m. Jan. 1, 1671, in N. Y., Sophia Jans. Settled at first in N. A., and then in Fld*, where his name appears on the ass. rolls of 1675, and where in 1664 he made an affidavit relating to Capt. Scott's raid, as per p. 482 of Vol. II. of Doc. of Col. His. He also in 1664, after the conquest of the colony, took the oath of allegiance in N. Y. to the English. In 1680 he bought lands in Bergen Co., N. J., as per p. 69 of Winfield's Land Titles of Hudson Co., to which he probably eventually removed. Mar. 1, 1680-1, he conveyed to Adriaen Van Laer a house and lot in Fld*, giving his residence as in the city of N. Y., as per p. 47 of Lib. A of Fl^h rec. Signed his name "*Symon Jansen Romeyn*" and sometimes "*Symon Jansen.*" No account of his descendants.

ROSEKRANS, JACOB DIRCKSE, took the oath of allegiance in Bu^k in 1687 as a native.

RUCKMAN, JOHN, (sup. English,) among the first settlers of G^d, where he obtained Nov. 18, 1646, a grant for a plantation-lot, which he sold shortly after to Thomas Appelgate, as per town rec. His will is d. Mar. 13, 1650, and pro. May 2 of the same year, in which he devises his property to his s. John, appointing Wm Bowne his guardian. If his s. dies a minor, he devises his property to John and James, sons of said Wm Bowne. Signed his name "*John Ruckman.*"

RUTGER, JOOSTEN, see Van Brunt.

RUTGERSZ or RUTGERSEN, JACOB, of Ulster Co. Sept.

15, 1694, Claes Teunise Clear conveyed to him a lot at the ferry in Br[n], as per p. 15 of Lib. 2 of Con.

Jan, sold Mar. 10, 1655, to Jan de Jongh 25 morgens in Fl[h] on the E. side of the highway, as per p. 366 of Vol. II. of O'Callaghan's Man. Trans. of Col. Man.

RUYTER or RUITER, CLAES JANSEN, m. *Pieterje Janse;* was in N. A. as early as 1639. Sept. 30, 1645, a patent was granted to Claes Jansen van Naerden for 21 morgens in Br[n] adjoining the lands of F. Lubbertse and J. Manje, as per p. 369 of Cal. of Dutch Man. In 1652 Peter Linde (who had m. Manje's wid.) conveyed 20 morgens on the shore of L: I. between the lands of Andries Hudde and "Claes Jansen Ruyter," as per p. 55 of said Cal. Conclude Claes Jansen Ruiter and Claes Jansen Van Naerden to be the same person, the addition of "Ruiter" to the name meaning horseman. Was Indian interpreter in 1660. Issue:—Geertruyt, bp. Dec. 4, 1644, in N. A. See Claes Jansen Van Naerden.

RYCKE, see Ryke.

RYDER, BERNARDUS, of G[d], b. Feb. 29, 1688; m. *Ariaentje* ——; d. Nov. 23, 1769. Oct. 7, 1707, "Barent Ryde" of G[d] sold Nich[s] Stillwell for £30 two 4 A. lots, as per G[d] rec. This was probably Bernardus Ryder. There is a "John Ryder" referred to in Ralph Cardell's will of June 10, 1682, as recorded on G[d] rec. This John is probably the father of Bernardus and the ancestor of the Ryder family of G[d]. Issue:—John of G[d]; Allye, who m. James Hubbard; Jacobus of G[d]; and (sup.) Phebe, b. Jan. 15, 1725. Signed his name "*Bernardus Ryder.*"

John of G[d] (s. of Bernardus), m. Altie ——. Will da. Aug. 20, 1755; pro. May 1, 1671; rec. p. 5, Lib. 23, N. Y. surr. off. Issue:—Wilhelmus of G[d], m. Geertje Van Sicklen; Bernardus of G[d], bp. Nov. 27, 1715; Stephen, m. Sarah Luyster; Johannes, bp. Nov. 24, 1717; Altje, m. Lucas Voorhies; Jannetje; Maria; Ida, b. Nov. 9, 1719, m. Ab[m] Strycker; and Hannalia.

RYERSEN, see Reyersen.

RYKE, RYKER, or RYCKEN, HENDRICK, see Suydam.

Abraham, (sup.) to have emigrated in 1638; m. Grietje dau. of Hendrick Harmensen; d. in 1689; and resided at first in N. A., where he owned a house and lot. In 1638 he obtained a deed for land near Rinnegaconck (Br[n]), and Aug.

1, 1640, a patent for a plantation, of probably the same premises, adjoining land of Gysbert Ryken, Hans Hansen (Bergen), and by another account that of Remmert Jansen (Vanderbeeck). These premises were probably in Bu^k. In 1654 he obtained a patent for a plantation in Newtown, to which he removed. Issue:—Ryck Abrahamse; Jacob, bp. Oct. 14, 1640, d. young; Jacob, bp. Oct. 18, 1643; Hendrick, bp. Feb. 17, 1647; Mary, bp. Feb. 21, 1649; John, bp. June 25, 1651; Aeltje, bp. Nov. 9, 1653; Abraham, bp. Dec. 23, 1655; and Hendrick, bp. Sept. 28, 1662—all bp. in N. A. except Ryck, and all of Newtown.

Gysbert, (sup.) emigrated in 1638. Owned land at the Wallabout adjoining that of Ab^m Rycken, as per p. 365 of Cal. of Dutch Man., which is referred to in 1640, as per p. 301 of Riker's Newtown.

Jan (s. of Abraham), b. 1651; m. 1691 Sarah Schouten wid. of Paulus Vanderbeeck. His name appears on the list of those who paid the preacher's salary in Fl^h in 1680. Issue:—Abraham, bp. Feb. 13, 1695, and settled in Essex Co., N. J.; and Helena, bp. May 24, 1696—all bp. in N. Y. Signed his name "*Jan Rycker*."

RYNDERS, AERNOUT, s. of Reyndert Arensen and Annetien Hermans, dec. His father having after the death of Annetien m. Jannetien Aukes, Seferyn Louwerens and Jan Langefelt were appointed Apl. 28, 1666, his guardians, as per p. 61 of Lib. D of Fl^h rec.

SAETLY or SATLEY, HENRY. His lands referred to in the patent of Hans Hansen (Bergen) of Mar. 30, 1647.

SALAMONS, CLEMENT, m. *Johanna* ——. Issue:—Marya, bp. July 20, 1679, in Br^n.

SALIN, ANTHONI, m. *Lysbeth Thyssen.* Issue:—Johannes, bp. Oct. 28, 1688, in Br^n.

SAMMERS, ADRIAEN, allotted a meadow-lot Apl. 21, 1667, on Fl^h meadows at Canarisie, as per Fl^h rec.

SANDERS or SANDERSEN, EGBERT, m. *Hermentje Harmens.* Owned a lot in Fl^h, which he sold in 1661 to Jan Cornelise Buys, as per p. 79 of Lib. B of Fl^h rec. May 9, 1661, he and Jan Theunisen (Van Dyckhuysen) petitioned for land to erect a saw-mill on a stream at "Gemoenepae" in Bergen Co., N. J., and move their families there, as per p. 224 of Cal. of Dutch Man. Feb. 11, 1661, Peter Martens commenced a suit against him in Fl^h, as per Lib B of Fl^h rec. Oct. 21, 1661, he and "Bertel Lot" petitioned for leave to erect a saw-mill at Bergen, N. J. Issue:—Theunis, bp. July 9, 1662, in N. A. Made his mark to documents.

Thomas, a smith, from Amsterdam; m. Sept. 16, 1640, Sarah Cornelise Van Gorcum in N. A., where he obtained a patent for a lot July 13, 1643. Of the plains in Fld^a Dec. 17, 1646, as per Col. Man. He was among the first settlers of G^d, as per town rec. Dec. 17, 1646, Thomas Spicer made a complaint against him at the sessions in G^d for keeping him out of his lands, abuse, etc., as per court rec. In 1654 he owned a house and lot at Beaverwyck (Albany), where he then resided, but afterwards returned to N. A., where he took the oath of allegiance to the English in 1664. Issue:—Robbert of Albany, bp. Nov. 10, 1641, in N. A., m. Elsje Barentse; Cornelis, bp. Nov. 25, 1643; Cornelis, bp. Nov. 17, 1644; and Thomas, bp. July 14, 1647—all bp. in N. A. Robert Sanders and Myndert Harmense obtained a grant Oct. 24, 1686, of Gov. Dongan for 12,000 A at Minnosinck in Dutchess Co. Thomas Sanders was a freeholder in said county in 1714. See pp. 100 and 334 of Smith's His. of said co.

SANSY, YAN, obtained Apl. 21, 1667, a meadow-lot on the Fl^h meadows at Canarisie, as per Fl^h town rec.

SANTFORD, ABRAHAM, had a s. Jacob bp. Nov. 10, 1689, in Br^n.

SCAMP, PIETER, of Bu^k, a soldier from "Gendt," emigrated in 1672; m. Oct. 7, 1674, in N. Y., *Jannetje Dirks* from Noortman's Kil. On ass. roll of Bu^k of 1675, Gov. Dongan's patent of 1687, and cen. of 1698, taking the oath of allegiance in said town in 1687. Issue:—Johanna, bp. Jan. 9, 1681, at Br^n; Lysbeth, bp. Aug. 10, 1684; and Pieterjen, bp. Apl. 3, 1690.

SCHAERS, JOHANNES CRISTOFFEL, of Gowanus, m. *Maria Willemse Bennet* of the same place. Maria after his death m. 2^d, Sept. 25, 1690, Hendrick Tyssen Lanen Van Pelt of Gowanus. On ass. rolls of Br^n of 1675 and '83. He bought of Thomas Verdon and Simon Aesen (De Hart) for £180 50 morgens of land in Gowanus (since of the Van Pelts), as per inventory of his estate on p. 242 of Vol. I. of Con. Issue:—Cristoffel Johannis; Alexander Johannis; Aaltje, bp. July 23, 1678, m. July 22, 1703, in N. Y., Benjamin Oldys of England; Willemtje, bp. Feb. 27, 1681, (sup.) d. prior to

1690; Saartje, bp. Sept. 9, 1683; Maria Janse or Johannes (probably the oldest child), m. Mar. 22, 1686, Wouter Tunis Lanen Van Pelt; (sup.) Cornelis Janse, m. Geertje Colfs; and (sup.) Else Janse, who m. Coenradus Vanderbeek. Signed his name "*Johannis Cristoffel.*"

Alexander Johannis, took the oath of allegiance in Brⁿ in 1687 as a native. His name does not appear on the record of the settlement of his father's estate, May 7, 1690, from which it may be inferred he was dec.

Cristoffel Johannis of Gowanus. Suppose he d. unmarried. Sept. 7, 1695, he conveyed to Woughter Van Pelt of N. U. 40 A. of land and meadows at Gowanus lying between the lands of Simon Aesen (De Hart) and those of Maria wid. of Thomas Van Dyke, dec., fronting on the bay, and bounded on the rear by the common woods, as formerly in possession of Johannis Cristoffel Schaers, dec., as per p. 74 of Vol. II. of Con. In his will—da. May 15, 1745; pro. Dec. 22, 1755; on file in the off. of the clerk of the court of appeals, Albany—he devises his Brⁿ and N. J. property to the children of Wouter Tunis Van Pelt. Made his mark to documents.

SCHAETS, CRISTOFFEL, m. *Lysbeth Jans*, who after his death m. successively Jan Claesen and Auke Jans, as per p. 85 of Lib. D of Fl^h rec. Issue:—Johannes Cristoffelse.

SCHAL, see School.

SCHENCK, ABRAHAM MARTENSE (s. of Marten Roelofse), of Fld^s, b. May 20, 1689; m. Apl. 20, 1717, *Sarah* dau. of Gysbert Tunisse Bogaert; d. prior to Nov. 1766. Left Fld^s and settled at Fresh Meadows near Flushing. Issue:—Marten of Dutchess Co., b. Apl. 18, 1718, m. Maria Rapalje; Gysbert of Fishkill, b. May 20, 1720, m. Aeltje Rapalje, and had a s. Abraham, a surveyor and State senator from Dutchess Co.; Roelof, b. June 1, 1725, d. an old man, single; Susanna, b. July 19, 1723, m. Luke Bergen of Brushville, Queens Co.: Adrianna, m. Rev. B. Mincma; and Abraham, b. Oct. 17, 1725, who probably d. a young man. The Schencks of Dutchess Co. settled about Matteawan and New Hackensack, as per p. 214 of Smith's Dutchess Co.

Garret Roelofse (s. of Roelof Martense), b. Oct. 9, 1661; m. about 1693 Neeltje Coerten Van Voorhies; d. Sept. 5, 1745. Removed from Fld^s and settled in 1696 at Pleasant Valley, Monmouth Co., N. J., selling his Fld^s farm to Stephen Coerten (Voorhies), as per p. 160 of Lib. 2 of Con. Will da. Jan. 12, 1739; pro. Oct. 7, 1745; rec. p. 376, Lib. D, in off. Sec.

State N. Y. Issue:—Antje, bp. Nov. 15, 1694, m. about 1712
Matys Lane (Van Pelt) of N. J.; Roelof of N. J., brewer,
b. Apl. 27, 1697, m. about 1718 Engeltie Van Doorn; Mary,
b. Nov. 1, 1699, m. Hendrick Smock of N. J., d. Sept. 1747;
Coert of N. J., b. 1702, m. Oct. 1724 Marike dau. of Peter
Willemse Cowenhoven, d. June 2, 1771; Aaltje, bp. May 29,
1705, m. about 1723 Tunis Vanderveer of N. J.; Neeltje, b.
about 1707, m. 1725 Hendrick Hendricksen of N. J.; Rachel,
bp. Apl. 2, 1710, m. 1ˢᵗ Gysbert Longstreet, m. 2ᵈ, Oct 17,
1763, Jacob Van Dooren; Garret, b. Aug. 30, 1712, m. Nov.
1737 Jannetje dau. of Wᵐ Kouwenhoven of Fld⁸; Margaret,
b. Apl. 17, 1715, m. 1ˢᵗ —— Cowenhoven of Penn's Neck,
N. J., m. 2ᵈ Dirck Longstreet of Princeton; Jan of Penn's
Neck, b. Apl. 19, 1721, m. 1ˢᵗ Cath⁸ dau. of Wᵐ Kouwenhoven of Fld⁸, m. 2ᵈ Angenietje dau. of Nich⁸ Van Brunt,
d. Aug. 21, 1786.

Jan Martense, emigrated in 1650 from the Netherlands,
and settled in Fld⁸; m. Jannetje Stevense Van Voorhees;
(sup.) d. in 1689.* Bought Dec. 29, 1657, of Elbert Elbertse
Stoothoff the one half of the mill and the island on which
the mill is located in Fld⁸ near Bergen's I., lately known as
Crooke's Mill, but now demolished. Aug. 20, 1660, he obtained a patent for 10 morgens in New Amersfoort (Fld⁸),
and in 1687 took the oath of allegiance in said town. Jan.
28, 1688-9, he made a will in which he devises to his s.
Marten Janse "the old land with yᵉ small Island and mill
and dependencies thereof;" to his s. Stephen Janse "the lot
in the Neck, with the meadow at hoggs Neck," etc., as per
p. 140 of Lib. 1 of Con. From this it is evident that he had
acquired, in addition to his purchase from Stoothoff, the

---

* It is claimed by some of the Schenck family that Jan and Roelof
Martense Schenck are sons of Marten Schenck of Nydack or Nydeggen,
a town about 18 miles southeast from Aix-la-Chapelle; that Marten's
father was Peter Schenck of Nydack, b. in 1547 at Goch, a small town
about 10 miles south of Cleves, m. in 1580 Johanna Scherpenzeel; and
that this Peter was a brother of the celebrated Marten Schenck, a soldier
of fortune and an officer of distinction in the wars of the Low Countries.
Without the evidence which has been gathered in Holland of the genealogy of the family, the name would imply a relationship to the soldier and
warrior, but it is singular, if this account is correct, that the name of
Peter does not appear in the family until the fourth generation, when it
is well known that it was the custom of the Netherlanders to perpetuate
the names of their ancestors, which custom prevails among many of their
descendants in this country to this day. These Schencks, according to
tradition, owned vessels which traded with the Netherlands, which often,
by way of Rockaway Inlet, came into Flatlands or Jamaica Bay to deliver or receive goods from their owners.
 There was a "Wessel Schenck" among the members of the company
chartered Oct. 11, 1614, for an exclusive trade of three years with the
New Netherlands, as per p. 149 of Vol. I. of Doc. of Col. His.

remaining one half of the mill property.* Issue:—Jannetje Janse, b. about 1673, m. May 20, 1692, Gerret Janse Dorlant; Marten Janse, b. 1675; Willemtje Janse, b. about 1677, m. Pieter Wyckoff of Monmouth Co., N. J.; Stephen Janse, b. Oct. 2, 1681, d. young; Jan or Johannes Janse, bp. Nov. 5, 1682, d. young; Neeltje Janse, bp. Nov. 23, 1683, m. Oct. 5, 1712, John Wyckoff of the Raritan; Stephen Janse, b. Jan. 22, 1686, m. Sept. 26, 1713, Antje dau. of Nicholas Wyckoff, d. Nov. 6, 1767; Aaltje or Aelken Janse; and Antje Jansen. Signed his name "*Jan Martensen Schenck.*"

Jan Roelofse, b. Mar. 1, 1670; m. about 1691 Sara dau. of Wᵐ Kouwenhoven of Fldˢ, d. Jan. 30, 1753. Took the oath of allegiance in Fldˢ in 1687 as a native. Removed from Fldˢ about 1697, and settled at Pleasant Valley, N. J. He and his w. mem. of the D. ch. of Freehold in 1709. Issue:— Roelof, b. Feb. 21, 1692, m. Geesie Hendricksen, d. July 19, 1761; Sarah, b. 1696, m. 1ˢᵗ, May 16, 1721, Johannes Voorhees of New Brunswick, m. 2ᵈ Hendrick Voorhees of Freehold; Aaltje, bp. May 25, 1705, m. Chrisyjan Van·Dooren, d. about 1801; Rachel, bp. Feb. 19, 1709, m. —— Boon of Kentucky; Maria, b. Aug. 8, 1712, m. Jacob Van Dooren; Leah, b. Dec. 24, 1714, m. Dec. 17, 1735, Peter Cowenhoven, d. Mar. 14, 1769; William, bp. Sept. 15, 1718, d. young; Jannetje, m. Bernardus Verbryck of Neshaminy, Pa.; Jan, bp. July 22, 1722, m. Jan. 25, 1750, Neeltje Bennet, d. Dec. 24, 1808; Antie, m. about 1720 Arie Van Dooren; and Peter, m. 1ˢᵗ Jannetje Hansen Van Noostrand, m. 2ᵈ, in 1747, Jannetje Hendricksen—all of N. J.

Johannes of Flʰ and Buᵏ, b. Sept. 19, 1656; m. Mary Magdalena dau. of Hendrick De Haes; d. Feb. 5, 1747-8. (Mary Magdalena was b. at Middleburg, in the Netherlands, Oct. 7, 1660, and d. Apl. 10, 1729; emigrated about 1683 from Middleburg on the I. of Walcheron in Zeeland, and is supposed to have been a relative of Roelof and Jan Martense Schenck of Fldˢ, but of this the evidence is not conclusive.) Resided at first in the city of N. Y.; then in Ulster Co.; next in Flʰ, of which town he was clerk from 1691 to '94, and from 1700 to 1712, and also schoolmaster from 1700 to 1712; and finally removed to Buᵏ, of which town he was supervisor in 1719. In 1703 he bought a tract of 640 A. on the Raritan, said to be in the boundaries of the city of New Brunswick, N. J. In 1707 he bought a plot with buildings on the W. side of the main road in the village of Flʰ, which he sold in 1712 to his son-in-

---

* The old dwelling-house of wood standing on the Mill I. according to tradition was erected by the Schencks after their purchase, and therefore is now (1881) about 224 years old.

law Johannes Janse, cooper. In 1712 he bought of Tunis
Titus a mill and plantation of 83 A. in Bu^k, to which he removed. His will is da. Jan. 4, 1745, pro. in 1748, and rec. on
p. 230 of Lib. 16, N. Y. surr. off. Issue:—Johannes, bp. Dec.
20, 1684, in N. Y., d. young; Johannes Junr, b. Apl. 30, 1691;
Susanna, m. Johannes Janse or Johnson; Margrita, m. about
1705 John Stryker of Fl^h, d. Aug. 1721; Cornelia, m. Charles
Durje of Bu^k; and Peter of Newtown. For a more full account of Johannes Schenck and his descendants, see Dr. P. L.
Schenck's Memoirs of Johannes Schenck. Signed his name
"*Johannes Schenk.*"

Johannes Junr of Bu^k, b. Apl. 30, 1691; m. Maria Lott of
Fl^h, b. 1690; he d. Apl. 1, 1729, and Maria d. May 7, 1740.
In 1713 he bought of Timothy Wood a plantation of 108 A. in
Bu^k, and also bought one in Newtown, to which place he ap-
pears to have removed. In 1728 he was supervisor of Bu^k.
His will is da. Mar. 28, 1729, and rec. on p. 111 of Lib. 11, N.
Y. surr. off. Issue:—Hendrick, b. June 17, 1714, d. young;
John or Johannes of N. J., b. Oct. 26, 1715, m. Oct. 26, 1746,
Hetty or Hellen Remsen, d. 1777; Hendrick, b. July 15, 1717,
m. Magdalena Van Lieuw, d. about Jan. 1, 1767, settled at
Marlboro, N. J.; Magdalena, b. Jan. 18, 1719, (sup.) m. Hen-
drick Suydam; Abraham (Judge) of Bu^k, of N. J., and of
Dutchess Co., b. Aug. 6, 1720, m. Elsie Vandervoort, d. 1790;
Peter, b. Mar. 27, 1722, m. Maria Vulkertse, and settled at
Millstone, N. J.; Cornelius of Bu^k, b. Jan. 27, 1724, m. Nov.
15, 1742, Abagail Lefferts, d. Nov. 15, 1744; Isaac, b. Dec. 7,
1725; and Catharine, b. Jan. 11 or 14, 1728, m. her cousin
Tunis Schenck of Bu^k, d. Apl. 9, 1793. Signed his name
"*Johannes Schenk Junior.*"

Marten Janse of Fld^s, b. 1675; m. Dec. 2, 1703, Cornelia
Van Wesell or Wesselen wid. of Do. Lupardius. Inherited by
his father's will the "old land with the small island and mill."
Issue:—John (known as Capt. John), b. Dec. 13, 1705. He m.
Nov. 15, 1728, Femmetie Hegeman, and Apl. 15, 1784, his
heirs and legatees sold the mill property, cong. about 66 A. of
upland, 6 A. of woodland, and a parcel of salt-meadows, to
Joris Martense of Fl^h for £2300. Signed his name "*Marten
Schenck.*"

Marten Roelofse of Fld^s, b. Jan. 22, 1661; m. 1st, June 20,
1686, Susanna Abrahamse Brinckerhoff; m. 2^d, Apl. 11, 1693,
Elizabeth Minne Voorhies; m. 3^d, June 24, 1704, Jannetje
Lucasse Voorhies (b. Oct. 1, 1681, d. Apl. 17, 1758); d. May
2, 1727. Inherited the homestead farm in Fld^s, where he took
the oath of allegiance in 1687 as a native. Issue:—Abraham
Martense, b. May 20, 1689; Roelof Martense, b. Dec. 24, 1694,
d. young; Roelof Martense of Cow Neck, L. I., b. Oct. 18,

1696, d. May 12, 1777; Neeltje Martense, b. (sup.) Dec. 24,
1698, m. Nov. 28, 1714, Johannes Stoothoff of N. J.; Minne
Martense of Hempstead, b. Apl. 8, 1700, m. June 3, 1737,
Maritie Monfoort, d. 1767; Rensie Martense, b. Oct. 15, 1702,
m. 1ˢᵗ, May 23, 1723, Peter G. Wyckoff of Fld⁸, m. 2ᵈ Daniel
Rapalje, d. Sept. 26, 1760; Catelina, b. May 7, 1705, m. 1ˢᵗ
Stoffel Probasco, m. 2ᵈ Jan Barentse Jansen of J⁸; Annatie, b.
Nov. 11, 1706, m. Wᵐ Boerum, d. Jan. 9, 1738; Lucas Martense, b. Oct. 11, 1708, d. young; Marten Martense of Fld⁸, b.
Oct. 9, 1710, m. Antie Rapalje, d. Oct. 30, 1761; Susanna, b.
Dec. 28, 1712, m. Apl. 10, 1731, Johannes Nevius, d. Oct. 6,
1773; Jannetie, b. June 27, 1715, m. Jeremiah Remsen; Elizabeth, b. Oct. 10, 1717, d. Dec. 17, 1732; Lucas of N. J., b.
Sept. 6, 1721, m. Lammetje Remsen, d. Jan. 1, 1784; Johannes, b. Jan. 7, 1724, d. Feb. 15, 1732; and Maria, b. Jan. 10,
1726, m. Apl. 30, 1748, Simon Boerum of Br", d. Mar. 31,
1771.

Minne (s. of Martin Roelofse) of Hempstead, b. Apl. 8, 1700;
m. June 3, 1727, Maria Monfoort; d. Mar. 3, 1767. Issue:—
Elizabeth, bp. Sept. 20, 1728, m. Peter Onderdonk; Antie, b.
Dec. 26, 1730, m. George Rapalje; Jannetie, b. Feb. 12, 1733;
Maria, b. June 2, 1736, m. Daniel Brinckerhoff of Fishkill;
Martie or Martin of Queens Co., b. Dec. 26, 1740, m. 1ˢᵗ Ag-
nietje Rapalje, m. 2ᵈ Neeltje Rapalje; and Angenietje, b. May
5, 1746.

Peter (s. of Johannis and Magdalena) of Bu^k, m. Elizabeth
——; d. 1736. Bought May 30, 1724, of his brother Johannes
his Newtown farm of 113 A. to which he removed, said farm
being located near the boundary of Bu^k and Newtown. His will
is da. July 29, 1736; pro. Dec. 12, 1738; and rec. on p. 167 of
Lib. 13, N. Y. surr. off. Issue:—Catharine, b. Aug. 29, 1721,
m. Mar. 24, 1742, Joost or George Durje or Duryea; Teunis,
b. Feb. 9 (or May 13), 1723, d. July 31, 1806, m. Sept. 14,
1749, his cousin Catharine Schenck, and was the ancestor of
Isaac and Guilliam Schenck of East New York, and of Doctors
Tunis and P. Lawrence Schenck, the latter at present (1881)
in charge of the county hospital at Fl^h; John; Madalena, m.
Adrian Bogert; Phebe; Margaret, m. Abraham Polhemus;
Cornelia, m. Jacob Duryea; and Elizabeth, b. 1736, d. young.

Roelof Martense, b. about 1630; with his brother Jan Mar-
tense emigrated in 1650; m. 1ˢᵗ, 1660, Neeltje Gerretse dau.
of Gerret Wolfertse Van Couwenhoven; m. 2ᵈ, 1675, Annatie
Pieters (sup.) dau. of Pieter Claesen Wyckoff; m. 3ᵈ, Nov. 30,
1688, Catharine Cregier of N. Y., wid. of Stoffel Hooglandt.
Jan. 29, 1661, he obtained a patent for 23 morgens at Fld⁸, and
Apl. 3, 1674, he bought of the heirs of Gerret Lookermans 200
A. in the same town, with buildings, a village lot, meadows,.

etc., as per p. 28 of Cal. of Eng. Man. In 1687 he took the
oath of allegiance in Fld[a], and Apl. 20, 1688, he bought of his
brother Jan Martense Schenck one half of the mill and island
on which the mill was located in Fld[a]. In 1662, '63, and '64 he
was a mag. of said town; in 1665 its representative in the
Hempstead convention; in 1685 sheriff of the county, as per
p. 143 of Cal. of Eng. Man; in 1689 and '92 a justice of the
peace (see pp. 132 and 185 of Cal. of Eng. Man.); in 1690
capt. of horse; and in 1701 signed an anti-Leislerian address
to the king, as per p. 938 of Vol. IV. of Doc. of Col. His. of
N. Y. Issue:—Marten Roelofse, b. June 22, 1661; Annetje
Roelofse, b. about 1663, m. June 10, 1684, Jan Albertse Terhune, d. Oct. 1685; Jannetje Roelofse, b. 1665, m. June 7,
1684, Pieter Nevius; Marike Roelofse, b. Feb. 14, 1667, m.
Feb. 15, 1687, Isaac Hegeman of Fl[h]; Jan Roelofse of N. J.,
b. Mar. 1, 1670; Gerret Roelofse of N. J., b. Oct. 27, 1671, d.
Sept. 5, 1745; Margaretta Roelofse, b. Jan. 16, 1678, m. Sept.
3, 1700, Cor[s] Cowenhoven of Pleasant Valley; Neeltje Roel-
ofse, b. Jan. 3, 1682, m. Oct. 2, 1701, Albert Cowenhoven of
N. J., d. May 7, 1751; Mayken Roelofse, b. Jan. 14, 1684, m.
Mar. 5, 1704, Jan Luycase Van Voorhees, d. Nov. 25, 1736;
and Sarah Roelofse, b. Dec. 18, 1685, m. Nov. 12, 1705, Jacob
Cowenhoven of Middletown, N. J. Signed his name "*Roelof
Martensen.*"

Roelof Martense 2[d] (s. of Marten Roelofse and Susanna), b.
Oct. 18, 1696; m. Nov. 9, 1727, Susanna dau. of Pieter Monfort. Resided in Fld[a], and at one period in Cow Neck in
Hempstead. Will da. May 20, 1775, and pro. May 18, 1785.
Issue:—Marten Roelofse of Hempstead, b. Nov. 14, 1728,
m. Phebe Prince; Ida Roelofse, b. Apl. 14, 1731, m. 1764
George or Isaac Rapalje; Lammetje Roelofse, b. Oct. 25,
1734, d. Sept. 30, 1742; Neeltje Roelofse, b. Oct. 24, 1736,
m. 1766 George Debevois; Sara Roelofse, b. Mar. 6, 1738, d.
Sept. 1738; John Roelofse, known as Judge Schenck of Hempstead, b. Apl. 16, 1740, m. Elizabeth Layton, d. 1832; Abra-
ham Roelofse of Great Neck, b. Aug. 1, 1742, m. Cataline
Hoogland; Sara Roelofse, b. Mar. 25, 1745; and Pieter
Roelofse, b. Dec. 5, 1746. Signed his name "*Roelof Schenck.*"

Roelof (s. of Jan Roelofse and Sara), b. Feb. 21, 1692; m.
Geesie Hendricksen; d. July 19, 1761. Left Fld[a] with his
father and settled near the Brick Ch. at Marlborough, Monmouth Co., N. J. Issue:—Sara, b. May 22, 1715, m. Dec. 1,
1734, Joseph Van Mater, d. Dec. 1, 1748; Katrintje, bp. Mar.
19, 1717, d. young; Katrya, bp. Dec. 21, 1718, m. 1st Simon
De Hart 3[d] of Gowanus, m. 2[d] Peter Cowenhoven of N. J.;
Jan, b. Jan. 22, 1721, m. Nov. 26, 1741, Jacomyntje Cowen-

hoven, d. Jan. 27, 1749; Daniel, bp. May 26, 1723, d. Sept
20, 1747; Nelke or Neeltje, b. Sept. 10, 1724, (sup.) m. Oct.
13, 1744, Gerret Cowenhoven, d. Mar. 25, 1800; Engeltie, bp.
Apl. 28, 1732; and Hendrick, b. July 9, 1731, m. Caty Holmes,
d. Aug. 4, 1766—all of N. J.*

Roelof (s. of Gerret Roelofse and Neeltje), b. Apl. 7, 1697;
m. about 1718 Engeltie Van Dooren; d. Aug. 22, 1765. Re-
moved with his father from Fld⁴ to N. J., and was a brewer in
Pleasant Valley, Monmouth Co. Issue:—Gerret of Amwell,
Hunterdon Co., b. May 23, 1719, m. 1ˢᵗ, Dec. 23, 1747, Maria
Van Sicklen, m. 2ᵈ, Aug. 3, 1778, Mary Van Mater, m. 3ᵈ,
Sept. ——, 1780, Anne Ten Eyck; Marike, b. June 3, 1720, m.
Nov. 12, 1741, Jacob Sutphen of Amwell, d. about 1755; William of Amwell, b. 1721, m. Mary Winters, d. Dec. 13, 1806;
Nelkie, bp. Jan. 17, 1724, m. Feb. 18, 1743, Derick Sutphen of
Peacock; Antie, bp. May 1, 1726, m. 1748 John Tice, d. Sept.
1772; Jacob of Penn's Neck, bp. May 1, 1726, m. Mary Con-
over, d. Dec. 19, 1786; Catryna, bp. May 22, 1730, m. about
1755 Oert or Aert Van Dyke of Ohio; Margaret, b. about
1732, m. —— Emmans; Angenietje, bp. May 5, 1734, m. 1ˢᵗ,
about 1756, John Van Doorn, m. 2ᵈ Hans Voorhees; Roelof ot
Amwell, b. Apl. 5, 1737, m. 1ˢᵗ Ann Hoogland, m. 2ᵈ Rebecca
Hoogland, d. Oct. 22, 1803; and Jan of Penn's Neck, bp. Feb.
3, 1740, m. Mary or Maria Van Doorn—all of N. J.

Stephen Janse (s. of Jan Martense), b. Jan 22, 1686, by one
account, and Feb. 2, 1685, by another; m. Sept. 16, 1713,
Antie dau. of Nicholas Wyckoff; d. Nov. 6, 1767. A farmer
in Fld⁴. Will da. June 7, 1758; pro. Feb. 25, 1768; rec. p.
160, Lib. 26, N. Y. surr. off. Issue:—Yannetie, b. Sept. 17,
1714, m. Folkert Sprong, d. Mar. 19, 1778; Jan of Oyster Bay,
b. May 23, 1718, m. Mary Hegeman, d. Dec. 15, 1775; Sara,
b. Nov. 12, 1720, m. Nov. 5, 1743, Abᵐ Emans, d. Dec. 3, 1797;
Antie, b. Apl. 26, 1723, m. Abᵐ Duryea, d. Aug. 1, 1805; Wil-
lemtie, b. Oct. 4, 1726, m. Nov. 3, 1753, Peter Amerman, d.
Dec. 18, 1802; Neeltie, b. Apl. 17, 1730, m. Jan Willemse, d.
Oct. 9, 1780; Nicklaes of Fld⁴ (the ancestor of the Canarisie
branch of the family), b. Sept. 4, 1732, m. Oct. 11, 1757, Willemtje Wyckoff, d. Apl. 3, 1810; Margrita, b. Jan. 17, 1736, m.
Peter Monfoort of Fishkill, d. Sept. 20, 1814; and Marya, b.
Mar. 17, 1739, m. Nov. 27, 1768, Samuel Stryker of Gᵈ, d.
May 13, 1813.

SCHOENMAKER, ARYIAN, farmer. His name appears in
1677 and '81 on the Stoothoff papers.

Hendrick, probably a shoemaker, in 1678 and '81 on the
Stoothoff papers.

Jan, a tobacco dealer in 1678, as per Stoothoff papers.

Willem, a shoemaker in 1675, '77, '79, '81, and '82, as per Stoothoff papers.

SCHOOL, SCHOL, or SCHAL, PETER JANSE, of Br^n, m. Grietje Provoost. Nov. 27, 1668, he sold to Gerret Jansen Van Campen a house and lot in Fl^h, as per p. 45 of Lib. C of Fl^h rec. His name appears on a deed of Aug. 27, 1677, on p. 179 of Lib. 2 of Con. Issue:—Annetje, bp. July 16, 1662; Grietje, bp. Sept. 24, 1664; Johannes, bp. Oct. 15, 1666; and David, bp. Aug. 13, 1671—all bp. in N. A. There was a Pieter Schol who had a dau. Margriet bp. Apl. 3, 1717, in the Raritan D. ch. Signed his name "*Pieter Janse Schal.*"

SCHOT, WILLEM, on Stoothoff's books of 1686.

SCHOTDELT, WILLEM, on Stoothoff's books of 1676.

SCOTT, RANDELL, (sup.) English, leased his house and land in G^d in 1651 for one year to Rodger Scott, the latter sub-letting the same to Wm Oliver, as per G^d rec. Made his mark to documents.

Rodger, among the first settlers of G^d in 1646, where he was allotted a plantation-lot, as per town rec. Suppose he m. Abigal dau. of John Tilton of G^d. Made his mark to documents.

William of G^d, bought May 31, 1660, of Nich^s Stillwell a house and garden in G^d, as per town rec. Signed his name "*William Scot.*"

SCHROECH, MARY. It appears from a dispute between her and Christian Jacobsen Wolfe before the court of sessions, Feb. 29, '1663, that she owned a house and land in G^d, as per town rec.

SCHUT, CORNELIS, in 1657 sold a farm in G^d to Jan Tomasse, as per Col. Man.

SCHUYLER, AARON or ARENT, of Albany, N. Y., Fld^s, and N. J., a s. of Col. Philip Pieterse Schuyler of Albany, b. June 25, 1662; m. 1st, Nov. 2, 1684, *Janneke Teller;* m. 2^d, prior to 1699, *Swantje* dau. of John Van Duyckhuysen and granddau. of Elbert Elbertse Stoothoff, and was a party in 1702 on the division of the estate of his father-in-law Van Duyckhuysen, as per p. 249 of Lib. 2 of Con. As a trader he was admitted to the freedom of the city of N. Y. in 1695. In 1710 he bought a tract of land in Bergen, N. J., of Edmond Kingsland, to which he removed, and on which a copper-mine at one period was worked. Issue:—Margareta, bp. Sept. 27, 1685; Phillippus, bp. Sept. 11, 1687; Maria, bp. Oct. 6, 1689; Judik, bp. Mar. 13, 1692—all bp. in Albany; Casparus, bp. May 5, 1695, in N. Y.; and Wilhelmus, bp. June 2, 1700, in N. Y., all as per p. 98 of Pearson's Early Settlers of Albany; also John and Arent, as per pp. 327 and 328 of Winfield's Land Titles of Hudson Co., N. J.

Arent Schuyler Jun[r] is said to have been the discoverer of the copper-mines, and his youngest son, Gen. Philip Schuyler, who d. in 1762 at the age of 52 years, was the commander of the provincial troops in several campaigns against the French in Canada, ranking high as a military man, as per p. 237 of Vol. 1 of Raum's N. J.

Cornelis Janse, among those of Br[n] who in 1663 applied for leave to form a new village and for salt meadows.

SCUDDER, JOHN, English, owned as early as 1668 the mill-pond in Bu[k] on which Schenck's mill was erected, which at that date was supposed to be the cause of the fever and ague prevailing in the vicinity, and as a preventive its dam was ordered by the court to be cut to let out the water. See p. 79 of Riker's Newtown and p. 15 of the Memoir of Johannes Schenck. John Scudder was b. in 1619, emigrated from London to New England in 1636, and thence to Mespat Kils, as per p. 94 of Riker's Newtown.

SEBRING, see Seubring.

SEEN, JAN CORNELISE, of G[d]; made his mark to documents in Kings Co. at an early date.

Hendrick Jansen, m. Jannetje Duurkop; among those of Br[n] who in 1663 applied for leave to form a new village and for salt-meadows. Sold Sept. 12, 1670, to Hendrick Jansen Oestertroam a farm of 29 morgens on the W. side of the highway in Fl[h] between the farms of Gerret Lubbertse and Jan Cornelise Boomgaert, with plain and meadow land, as per p. 85 of Lib. C of Fl[h] rec. Issue:—Jan, bp. Dec. 3, 1662, in Br[n]. Signed his name *"Heyndyck Jansen Seen."*

SEERJERSY, GERRET, laborer. His name appears in 1670 on Fl[h] ch rec.

SEERS, SERDTS, or LEERS, GERRET, and Cregier Pischer, leased Jan. 26, 1647, of —— Van Tienhoven a plot in Br[n], as per O'Callaghan's Man. Trans. of Dutch Man.

17

SEGERSE, GERRITT, in 1677 allotted a plot in N. U., which he sold to Thomas Sparse, as per town rec. May 4, 1662, was plaintiff in a suit against Jan Janse, as per Lib. B of Fl[h] rec. There was a Gerrit Segerse at Albany in 1757, whose surname was probably Van Voorhoudt.

SELOVER, ISAAC, schoolmaster and chorister of Fld[s] in 1695, m. 1st *Hester Leenda;* m 2[d], Jan. 23, 1695, in N. Y., *Janneken Van Wilkenhof* wid. of Jan Thyssen, as per N. Y. D. ch. rec. Issue:—Jacquemyntje, bp. Mar. 27, 1696; Abraham, bp. Aug. 29, 1697; Jannetje, bp. Aug. 20, 1699; Daniel, bp. Aug. 14, 1700, settled in Somerset Co., N. J., where he has numerous descendants; Maria, bp. Aug. 31, 1701; Anna, bp. July 21, 1703, m. Dec. 1, 1723, Bragon Coevert—all bp. in N. Y.; and Isaac, m. Jan. 1, 1700, Judith Waldron. Signed his name "*Isaac Seloover.*" One of his descendants in 1770 signed " Isaac Selover."

SELY or ZEELEN, JAN, was among the first settlers of N. U. in 1657. Bought Jan. 1660 of Pieter Roelofse a plantation in said town located along the hills, and also owned a village-plot in 1665, as per town rec.

SELYNS, REV. HENDRICUS, b. in Amsterdam in 1636; m. 1st, July 9, 1662, *Machteld* da. of Herman Specht; m. 2[d], Oct. 20, 1686, *Margaretta de Riemer* wid. of Cornelis Steenwyck. Officiated in the R. D. ch of Br[n] in 1660 and '64. Returned to the Netherlands, and in 1682 came back to N. Y., where he officiated in the R. D. ch. until his death in 1701. Issue:— Agneta, bp. July 1, 1663, in N. A. Signed his name "*Hendricus Selyns.*"

SERDTS or LEERS, GERRET, see Seers.

SEUBRING, SEBRING, or SEBERING, CORNELIS, m. Sept. 3, 1682, *Altie Fredericks* da. of Frederick Lubbertse of Br[n]; d. (sup.) about 1723. Resided in Fl[h] at the date of his marriage and afterwards at Br[n], where his wife inherited from her father in what is known as South Br[n] a large farm, and where he took the oath of allegiance in 1687 as a native. On ass. rolls of Br[n] of 1676 and '83, and member of Assembly for Kings Co. from 1695 to 1726. Will da. May 23, 1721; pro. Mar. 25, 1723; and rec. p. 371, Lib. 9, N. Y. surr. off. Issue:—Ariaentje or Adriana, bp. July 22, 1683, in Fl[h], m. Thomas Fardon; Frederick of N. Y., m. Dec. 7, 1711, in N. Y., Maria Provoost; Johannes of N. Y.; Catharine, m.

John Bon or Hibon; Isaac of Br^n, bp. May 14, 1693, in Br^n; Cornelia, bp. Oct. 20, 1695, in Br^n, (sup.) m. Daniel Polhemius; Jakob, bp. Nov. 5, 1697, in Br^n; Elizabeth, bp. Nov. 12, 1699, in Br^n; Abraham; and Maria, bp. July 19, 1702, in N. Y., (sup.) m. Ab^m Marshalk. Signed his name "*Cornelis Sebering.*"

Daniel (Roelofse). A Daniel Seubering on the Raritan in 1699, supposed to be this Daniel.

Frederick (Cornelise), m. Dec. 7 or 11, 1711, Maria da. of Jonathan Provoost. Left Br^n and settled in N. Y., where he was appointed a gauger in 1713. Issue:—Catharina, bp. Oct. 4, 1713, in N. Y., (sup.) m. Gerardus Smith; Aaltje, bp. Oct. 5, 1715, in N. Y., (sup.) m. Nicholas Kermer; Maria, bp. Dec. 29, 1717, in N. Y., (sup.) m. Stephen Terhune; Cornelia, bp. Apl. 17, 1720, in N. Y., (sup.) m. Isaac Van Hook; Cornelius, bp. Mar. 25, 1722; Margareta, bp. Oct. 25, 1724; Elizabeth, bp. Mar. 15 or 29, 1729, (sup.) m. Louis Andre Gautier; Frederick, bp. Feb. 14, 1730, d. young; Frederick, bp. Feb. 19, 1731; and Elizabeth, bp. Mar. 18, 1733.

Isaac (Cornelise) of Br^n, bp. May 14, 1693; m. Catharine ——; d. prior to 1785. Will da. Sept. 14, 1771; pro. May 3, 1784; rec. p. 443, Lib. 36, N. Y. surr. off. Owned what was lately known as Cornell's tide-mill in South Br^n. Issue:— Cornelius of Br^n, who inherited the homestead and mill, m. (sup.) Maria Howard; Altie, m. Cornelis Sebering; Katharine, (sup.) m. Gerardus Smith; Elizabeth; and Margreta, bp. Apl. 30, 1717. Signed his name "*Isaac Sebring.*"

Jacob (Roelofse). A Jacob Sebering, supposed to be this Jacob, resided on the Raritan about 1685. Signed his name "*J R Sueberingh.*"

Jakob (Cornelise), bp. Nov. 5, 1697; m. Femmetje Vanderveer, and resided in Br^n, his will being da. Feb. 11, 1776; pro. July 29, 1782; and rec. p. 337, Lib. 33 N. Y. surr. off. Issue:—Cornelius J., a merchant in N. Y.; Femmetje, bp. Mar. 20, 1737, in Br^n; m. Rinier Suydam; Jan, bp. Oct. 15, 1738, in Br^n; Jacob, m. Jannetie da. of Nicholas Lefferts; Margaret, b. 1746; Isaac, (sup.) m. Cath^e Van Wyck; Catharine; and Altie, m. —— Suydam.

Jan Roelofse, b. 1631; m. 1st Adrianna Polhemus; m. 2^d Aeltye ——. Emigrated from the province of Drenthe in the Netherlands; resided in Fl^h in 1675 and '88, of which place he was a mem. of the R. D. ch. in 1677, and constable in the same year. From Fl^h he removed to Bergen, N. J Sold May 17, 1681-2, to Roelof Verkerk of N. U. his cultivated land in Fl^h, lying N. of the land of Jacob Hendrickse (of Michael Vanderveer in 1767, and late of heirs of Jacob

Duryea), E. of the public highway from the village of Fl[h] to N. U., S. of the church-lots, and W. of the land of W[m] Gerardus Beekman (late of John C. Bergen), as per p. 157 of Lib. AA of Fl[h] rec. Issue:—Cornelis Janse, m. Maria Williams; Daniel Janse of the Raritan, bp. July 2, 1682, at Fl[h]; Elizabeth Janse, bp. May 8, 1687, in Br[n]; and (sup.) Roelof Janse of the Raritan. Signed his name "*Jan Suebering.*"

Johannes (Cornelise), m. 1st (sup.) Aeltje ——; m. 2[d] Rachel Bona Hibon. Resided in Fl[h] in 1701, carried on a bakery in Br[n] in 1715, '16, and '17, and appears to have removed to N. Y., where he and his w. joined the R. D. ch. on certificate from L. I. He finally settled on the Raritan, N. J. Issue:—Johannes, bp. Aug. 10, 1700, in Br[n], d. young; Aer Jaentien, bp. Mar. 23, 1703; Lefkes or Leffert, bp. Aug. 28, 1704; Annetje or Jannetje, bp. Apl. 28, 1708—all bp. in the Raritan D. ch.; Geertruy, bp. Feb. 4, 1711, in N. Y., (sup.) m. Cornelis Van Ranst; Barent, bp. July 13, 1718, in N. Y.; Johannes, bp. Mar. 5, 1726, in N. J.; and Elizabeth, bp. May 28, 1732, in N. J. Made his mark to documents.

Lucas, m. Apl. 25, 1690, Marretje Dorlant. Was mem. of the R. D. ch. of Fl[h] in 1677, entered on the ch. rec. as removed. No further trace.

Roelof. No account except his name and that of his children, and have seen no positive evidence of his having been in this country. Issue:—Jan Roelofse, b. 1631; Willemtje Roelofse, b. in Drenthe, m. Stephen Coerten Van Voorhees of Fld[s], of which place they were both mem. of the ch. in 1677; (sup.) Jacob Roelof; and Daniel of the Raritan.

SEUW, JAN CORNELISE, see Zeuw.

SEVENHOVEN, JAN, a resident of N. U. Dec. 5, 1693, when he m. in N. Y. Mary Lequier of Bu[k], to which place he appears to have removed. On census of Bu[k] of 1698.

SHAREX, THOMAS, owned land in Gowanus in 1695 near that of the Van Pelts, as per deed from Bennet to Van Dyck on p. 72 of Lib. 2 of Con.

SHARPE, JOHN, (sup.) English, banished from N. N.; returning in 1674 without leave, was banished by Gov. Colve and Council for 10 years, as per p. 709 of Vol. 2 of Doc. of Col. His. of N. Y. Brought a suit against Nathaniel Brittaine June 15, 1675, in the sessions of G[d], as per p. 36 of Cal. of Eng. Man. Signed his name to documents in Fl[h] in 1678, from which it is evident he returned on the restoration of the province to the English.

SHARSE, THOMAS, bought a plot in N. U. allotted in 1677 to Gerret Segerse. He may be the same person entered as Thomas Sharex.

SHUTTER, JOHN, owned land in N. L. in 1683, as per deed of Floris Willemse (Krom) oh p. 160 of Lib. C of Fl^h rec.

SICKELLS or SICKELEN, LAMBERT. A "Lambert Sickles" of Br^n ferry had a slave named Minck convicted of riot in Fl^h by the sessions in 1700, and sentenced to be whipped, as per court rec. in off. of the clerk of Kings Co. A "Lambert Sickells" of Fl^h bought May 4, 1695, of Jan Harmense the one half of a building-plot in the village of Fl^h, as per p. 211 of Lib. A of Fl^h rec.; also Apl. 29, 1700, of Barbara Lucas wid. of Theunis Janse Coevert a farm at Bedford known as "Markier" plantation, as per p. 233 of Lib. 2 of Con. There was a Lambert Sickels, s. of Zacherias of Albany, who had children bp. in N. Y.:—Johannes, Dec. 18, 1692; and Alida, May 3, 1703.

SIGHALSZ, LAMBERT, on ass. roll of G^d of 1693 and on cen. of Fl^h of 1698. July 9, 1695, he bought of Jan Harmense a garden-plot and orchard in Fl^h. Suppose this to be the same person as the Lambert Sickells of Fl^h who bought a farm of Barbara Lucas.

SIMMONS, JOHN, (English,) on ass. roll of Fl^h of 1693 and cen. of G^d of 1698.

SIMONS, CLAES, took the oath of allegiance in Br^n in 1687 as a native. He was one of the heirs of Pieter Janse Norman, as per p. 81 of Lib. 2 of Con.

SIMONSE, SYMONSE, or SIMONSEN, AERT, took the oath of allegiance as a native in Br^n in 1687.
Arnetas, paid a marriage-fee to Fld* ch. in 1691, as per ch. rec.
Claes or *Klaes* (sup. Van Arsdalen), m. Hilletje Jans. Took the oath of allegiance in Br^n in 1687. In 1693 he was accused at the Court of Sessions of refusing to obey the orders of a justice of the peace, as per court rec. Sold a house, lot, and orchard in Br^n to Dirck Janse Woertman. Issue:—Symen, bp. Apl. 2, 1692, in Br^n.
Cornelis, see Van Arsdalen.

Cornelis, owned lots Nos. 1 and 29 in G^d Neck in 1688, as per G^d rec. A Cornelis Simonse was a grand-juryman at the court of sessions in 1695. The said Cornelis was probably Cornelis Simonse Van Arsdalen of Fld^s. Signed his name *"Cornelis Symons"* and *"Cornelis Symonsen."*

Elyas, see De Hart.

Frederick, see Van Nostrand.

Frederick of Fl^h, m. Aug. 13, 1687, Lea Fonteyn. On ass. roll of Bu^k of 1693 and cen. of 1698. Issue:—Carel, bp. Apl. 25, 1688; and Christyntje, bp. June 30, 1692, both in N. Y. Signed his name *"Frederick Symonse."*

James, on ass. roll of Fl^h of 1693.

Johannes, on cen. of Fl^h of 1698, where he owned land in 1696, as per deed on p. 95 of Lib. 2 of Con.; and also bought a house and lot of Gysbert Jansen Dec. 12, 1696, as per p. 219 of Lib. A of Fl^h rec. Signed his name *"Johannes Symonsens,"* and also *"Yohannes Symense"* in 1713.

John or *Jan*, of G^d in 1698, where he was allotted salt-meadows in 1700, as per town rec. Sept. 2, 1700, he sold to Barent Joosten and Albert Coerten (Voorhees) 6 A. on the S. side of the 12 morgens, as per p. 261 of Lib. 2 of Con. Signed his name *"Jan Symonsen"* in 1698. This possibly may be John Simonse Van Arsdalen.

Joost, on list of catechumens of Br^n ch. in 1662, as per ch. rec.

Klaes, see Claes Simonse.

Nicholas of Bu^k, in 1695 conveyed land, as per p. 97 of Lib. 2 of Con.

Peter, took the oath of allegiance in Br^n in 1687 as a native.

Peter, m. Aug. 2, 1650, Greten ——. Owned a plantation in G^d Mar. 4, 1650, and also of G^d in 1656, as per town rec. May 2, 1687, he sold his G^d lands to Reynier Van Sicklen, as per p. 88 of Lib. 2 of Con.

Symon, see Van Arsdalen.

SIMPSON, SIMSON, or SYMPSON, ALEXANDER, m. Feb. 29, 1690, *Jonica* or *Jannetje Stevense* (Van Voorhees); m. 2^d, Sept. 10, 1709, *Metthe Lee*, from London, wid. of Thomas Radjes. Was a grand-juryman in 1692, as per rec. of the sessions. May 8, 1697, he with others conveyed 26 A. in Fld^s to Gerret Coerte (Voorhees). On cen. of Fld^s of 1698, and a resident of said town in 1710. (Sup.) issue:—Jannetje, bp. Jan. 28, 1719, in N. Y. Made his mark to documents.

James, (English,) m. Martha ——; constable of Fl^h in 1690, on cen. of 1698, and keeper of the court-house and jail in 1700.

Peter, granted a plantation-lot Mar. 4, 1650, in G^d, as per town rec. He m. Aug. 2, 1650, Grietje ——; d. prior to Dec. 20, 1696. Bought Apl. 26, 1657, or was allotted by the town authorities, plantation-lot No. 27 in G^d, with the improvements. Name on ass. roll of said town of 1683, and May 7, 1687, he sold land there to Reinier Van Sicklen of Fld^a for £75. In 1696 Grietje his w. resided in G^d. Issue:—Robert. Made his mark to documents.

Peter, bought Mar. 17, 1676, of Albert Cornelise Wantenaer a house, lot, and garden in Br^n, as per p.'68 of Vol. 1 of Land Papers.

Sɪʀᴇx or Sʏʀᴀᴄʜs, Tɪᴛᴜs, see De Vries.

Sᴋᴇɴɴɪs, Cᴀʀʙʀo. His name appears on a deed of freeholders of Br^n to Adriaen Bennet of 1696-7.

Sᴋɪʟʟᴍᴀɴ, Tʜoᴍᴀs. Was in this country as early as 1671, and by tradition emigrated in 1664. Suppose he resided in Br^n. Issue:—Thomas Junr; and Elsje.

Thomas Junr, m. Annatie ——. Suppose he resided in Br^n. Issue:—Peter, bp. Mar. 4, 1694, in Br^n; Elizabeth (twin with Peter), bp. Mar. 4, 1694, in Br^n; John; Ann; Mercy, bp. Feb. 2, 1701, in Br^n; Mary; Abraham, bp. Apl. 18, 1704, in Br^n, m. Margaret Fine and resided at Dutch Kils; Isaac, sold his farm in 1727 and (sup.) settled in N. J.; Jacob, m. Jane Van Alst and resided south of Newtown; Benjamin, m. Margaret Coe and (sup.) settled in N. J.; and Joseph, m. Sarah Messerole and settled in Bu^k.

Sʟᴇᴄʜᴛ, Aʙʀᴀʜᴀᴍ Hᴇɴᴅʀɪᴄᴋsᴇ, of Br^n in 1705; m. *Jannetje* ——. Issue:—Hendrick, bp. May 7, 1704, in N. Y.; Elsje, bp. May 29, 1705; and Cornelis, bp. Feb. 22, 1708.

Barent Hendrickse, wheelwright, took the oath of allegiance in Br^n in 1687 as a native; m. May 1, 1692, Hilletje Jans of Br^n; and on ass. roll of Br^n of 1693 Issue:—Christopher, bp. Jan. 11, 1693; Hendrick, bp. Mar. 27, 1696; and Yan, bp. Oct. 30, 1698.

Cornelis Barentse. In 1661 he was a mag. at Wiltwyck or Esopus, where in 1663 he was granted a lot for a brewery and bakery, as per p. 256 of Cal. of Dutch Man. Apl. 12, 1669, he bought of "Titus Syrachs" (De Vries) a house and lot in Fl^h, as per p. 53 of Lib. C of Fl^h rec. Made his mark to documents.

Cornelis Hendrickse, m. Apl. 11, 1696, Johanna Vandewater. On ass. roll. of Br^n of 1693 and cen of 1698. Issue:—Engeltie, bp. Nov. 12, 1699; and Hendrick, bp. May 14, 1702.

Hendrick Cornelise, emigrated in 1652; m. Elsje Barens Lieveling; d. prior to May 1705. Mem. of the R. D. ch. of Brⁿ in 1677, and precentor of said ch. in 1685, as per Fld' papers. Bought a house-plot in Fl^h in 1672, and on ass. roll of Brⁿ of 1683, where he took the oath of allegiance in 1687. Will da. Sept. 23, 1690; rec. p. 156 of Lib. A of Fl^h rec. Issue:—Barent Hendrickse; Cornelis Hendrickse; Anna Catharine, bp. July 12, 1685, in N. Y., m. Jurje Hefts or Haf of N. U.; Abram Hendricks; and Johannes Hendricks. Signed his name *"Hendrick Cornelisse Slecht."*

Johannes Hendrickse, m. Catharine Jacobse Bergen. On ass. roll of Brⁿ of 1693 and cen of 1698. Removed to N. Y. Issue:—Elsje, bp. May 3, 1704; Hendrick, bp. Sept. 15, 1706; Jacob, bp. Sept. 15, 1708; Johannes, bp. May 1, 1711—all bp. in N. Y.; Cornelis, bp. Apl. 17, 1720; and Catharine (twin), bp. Apl. 17, 1720.

SLODT pr SLOT, JAN PIETERSEN, from Holsteyn, sold Jan. 20, 1662, to Derick Jansen, cooper, a house and lot in Fl^h. between the school-lot and land of Jan Strycker, as per p. 18 of Lib. C of Fl^h rec. There was a Jan Slot in N. Y. who had children bp. about 1700.

SLOOVER, see Selover.

SMACK or SMOCK, HENDRICK MATTHYSE, emigrated in 1654; m. *Geertje Harmens;* d. after June 1708. Settled in N. U., where he bought of Jacques Cortelyou, Jan. 16, 1665, plantation-lot No. 10, cong. 30 morgens, as per town rec., and where he took the oath of allegiance in 1687. Was a mag. of said town in 1669, '73, '76, '79, '82, and '89; on ass. rolls of 1675 and '83; and on patent of 1686. His descendants reside principally in E. N. J. Issue:—Matys Hendrickse of N. U. and N. J.; Johannes Hendrickse; Leonard or Leendert Hendrickse; Marretje or Marike Hendrickse, m. Oct. 4, 1685, Jaques Cortelyou Jun'; Sarah Hendrickse, m. Adrian Boerum; Martyntje Hendrickse, m. Adrian Laning (Van Pelt); Aertje or Aerlee Hendrickse; Rebecca Hendrickse, bp. Feb. 27, 1681, in N. U., m. Johannis Swart, and a mem. of Middletown, N. J., ch. in 1731. Signed his name *"Henderick Matysen Smock."*

Johannis Hendrickse, m. Femmetje or Catharine Barents. Left N. U. and in 1712 settled in Monmouth Co., N. J.; d. Dec. 14, 1756. Issue:—Hendrick, b. Oct. 16, 1698, m. 1721 Mary Schenck, d. May 30, 1747; Barnes, m. Hanna Luyster; Ann, m. John Tunisen; Matye, m. Cornelius Van De Veer; and Femmeke, bp. June 13, 1718, at Marlboro.

Leendert or *Leonard Hendrickse*, left N. U. and settled in Piscataway, N. J.; (sup.) m. Sara Van Sant. Will da. Oct. 11, 1738; pro. Apl. 12, 1739. There was a Leendert Smack in Somerset Co., N. J., in 1717. Issue:—Leendert, bp. Feb. 11, 1716; John; Sytie, m. —— Boice; Sarah, m. —— Clasen; and Neeltje, m. —— Tunisen.

Matthyse Hendrickse, m. Sept. 12, 1701, in N. Y., Elizabeth Stevens, wid. On ass. roll of N. U. of 1693 and cen. of 1698; lieut. of militia in 1700. Sold his N. U. farm of 48 A. and about 1718 removed to Piscataway, N. J. In his will, da. Oct. 2, 1721, pro. May 30, 1727, his wife is named Elizabeth Smalle. Issue:—Hendrick; John; Elizabeth, bp. Mar. 26, 1704, in N. Y.; Lucas; Mathias; Jacob; Gastie; and Mary. Made his mark to documents.

SMITH, SMIDT, or SMIT, ANNEKEN, of Bu^k, m. May 13, 1697, Justus Bosch of N. Y., as per N. Y. D. ch. rec. A resident of N. Y. at date of her marriage. ·

Bernardus of Bu^k, m. Oct. 30, 1698, in N. Y., Elsje Meyer of said city, as per N. Y. D. ch. rec., where he had 9 children bp., as per p. 818 of Valentine's Manual of 1864. A resident of N. Y. at date of marriage.

Claes Claesen, from Amersfoort in the Netherlands, m. Sept. 11, 1653, Geertruyd Willekens of Hamburg. He was among the first settlers of N. U. in 1657, and obtained July 29, 1664, a patent for plot No. 11 of 24 morgens in N. U., which he sold to Balthazer Vosch, and Vosch sold in 1677 to Tunis Janse Van Pelt. Apl. 6, 1674, he sold to Jan Cornelise Damen of Norman's Kil a farm at "Kyckuyt" for 3000 gl., as per p. 114 of Lib. C of Fl^h rec. Issue:—(sup.) Neeltje, bp. Mar. 21, 1655, in N. A. Made his mark to documents.

Claes Cornelise, owned land in Br^n as early as 1639, as per deed from Thomas Bescher to Cornelis Lambertse Cool on p. 56 of Vol. 1 of Stiles's Br^n.

Hendrick Barentse, m. Geertje Willemse; d. prior to 1693. Jan. 5, 1663, he was required to build on his plot in Bu^k and reside in the village. On ass. roll of Bu^k of 1675 and '83, and schepen in 1673 and '74. In 1678 he applied to the court of sessions for leave to set up gates on the highway which passed through his farm, which was granted; he also complained of his neighbors cutting the best timber in his woodland for bark, allowing the trunk and limbs to lie and encumber the ground, and asked that they be compelled to remove or burn the same. He and his w. made a joint will Oct. 24, 1687, as per p. 336 of Lib. 1 of Con. Issue:—Willemtje; Aeltje; Johanna; Coenradus; and Annatie. Signed his name "*Hendryck Barentsz Smidt.*"

Herreman, on ass. roll of N. U. of 1683.

Jan or *John,* bought Mar. 17, 1680, of Isaac Deschamps of N. Y. a house and lot of 2 A. and a farm of 40 A. at Bedford, Br^n, lying between the farms of Thomas Jansen and that of Peter Parmentier, as per p. 47 of Lib. 2 of Con. On ass. roll of Br^n of 1683, in which year it is supposed he died.

Jan Cornelise, of Br^n July 11, 1651, as per p. 54 of Cal. of Dutch Man.

John, bought Feb. 13, 1660, of Derick Cornelisen·(Hoogland) plantation No. 35 in G^d, and Jan. 1, 1661, he sold the same to Wm Goulder, his father-in-law, as per G^d rec. Made his mark to documents.

John, m. Anna ——; sold Oct. 9, 1689, land and buildings at Br^n ferry to Henry Filkins, as per p. 188 of Lib. 1 of Con. He probably kept a tavern at the ferry in 1693, for in that year the court of sessions met at his house, as per court rec.

Klaes, of Fld^s in 1675, as per town rec.

Peter, of Br^n in 1678, was clerk of Kings Co. in 1682 and '83. Signed his name "*Peter Smith.*"

Thomas of J^s, bought Mar. 20, 1694-5, of Isaac Deschamps of N. Y. a house and lot at Bedford, as per p. 49 of Lib. 2 of Con. Oct. 23, 1696, Thomas Smith and Jasper Smith, late of Bedford, sold to John Bibout of Bedford a 2 A. house-plot and 40 A. farm at Bedford. See p. 106 of Lib. 2 of Con. In 1642 a Thomas Smith of N. A. contracted to marry Nanne wid. of Thomas Beets, as per p. 15 of Cal. of Dutch Man.

Tomas, m. Sept. 29, 1692, in Br^n, Sarah Adamse Brouwer wid. of Tunis Jansen.

William, of G^d in 1656, as per Thompson's L. I. Nov. 9, 1658, sold plantation-lot No. 1 in G^d to Water Wall. Removed to Hempstead. See p. 13 of Vol. X. of Gen. Rec. Made his mark to documents.

SMOCK, see Smack.

SMYT, HERREMAN, a resident of N. U. as early as 1683, and probably same as Herreman Smith.

SNEDEKER, ABRAHAM (s. of Gerret Janse), bp. Sept. 16, 1677. Suppose he resided in N. L. Issue:—Abraham (sup.) of Haverstraw; Johannes; Gerret; Theodorus; Elizabeth, m. —— Smith; Altie, m. —— Cortie; and Sarah, m. Peter Vandervoort. Signed his name *"Abram Snedeker."*

Christiaen (Gerretse), m. Apl. 25, 1689, Pieterje Ariaense. Took the oath of allegiance in Fl^h in 1687 as a native. Removed to J^a, and an elder in the R. D. ch. in said town in 1709. Issue:—Willemtje, bp. Mar. 4, 1691, in N. Y.; and Adriana, bp. May 22, 1698.

Gerret (Gerretse), m. Marya ——. Issue:—Elsje, bp. June 27, 1731; and Catharine, bp. Dec. 25, 1739.

Gerret Janse of N. L., farmer, bp. Mar. 25, 1660; m. 1st Willemtje Vooks or Vookes; m. 2^d Elsje Tunis dau. of Tunis Nyssen (Denyse); d. 1694. Obtained Jan. 24, 1662, a patent for 27 morgens on the W. side in Fl^h, which he sold Mar. 6, 1680-1, to Pieter Guilliamse (Cornell), as per p. 151 of Lib. AA of Fl^h rec. On ass. rolls of 1675 and '83; mem. of Fl^h ch. in 1677; mag. in 1679; and took the oath of allegiance in said town in 1687. Joint will with Elsje da. Oct. 10, 1680, at about date of marriage, and recorded on p. 118 of Lib. A of Fl^h rec. Issue:—Jan of J^a; Margaret, m. Jan Jacobse of Noortwyck, N. Y.; Christiaen of J^a; Abraham (by 2^d w.), bp. Sept. 16, 1677, in Fl^h; Isaac of N. L., bp. Jan. 16, 1681; Sara, bp. Oct. 14, 1683, in Fl^h, (sup.) m. Adriaen Onderdonk; Gerret; and Elsje, m. Charles Boerum. Signed his name *"Gerret Snedeker."*

Isaac (Gerretse) of N. L., bp. June 16, 1680; m. Catalyna or Catryntje Janse; d. prior to Oct. 31, 1758. Will da. Dec. 19, 1750; pro. Oct. 31, 1758; rec. p. 115, Lib. 21, N. Y. surr. off. Issue:—Gerret; Abraham, bp. Jan. 15, 1710; Antie, m. Benjamin Emmans; Sara, m. Aert Van Pelt; Isaac; Catryntje, bp. Apl. 2, 1721, m. Douwe Ditmars; Jacob of N. L., (sup.) m. Emmetje Blom; Femmetje, m. Johannes Eldert of N. L.; and Elsje, bp. June 27, 1731, in N. U., m. Ruluf Van Brunt of N. U. Signed his name *"Isaac Snedeker."*

Jan, the common ancestor of the family, came to this country as early as 1642; was a shoemaker by trade; m. 1st Annetje Buys of Rys or Ryssen, a town in the province of Overyssel; m. 2^d Egbertje or Lybertje Jans wid. of Herman Hendrickse; d. in 1679. Settled at first in N. A., where he kept a taphouse or tavern, and was afterwards among the first settlers of Fl^h, where he was a mag. from 1654 to 1664; a mem. of the R. D. ch. in 1677; and on the patent of said town of 1652, as per p. 13 of Strong's Fl^h, and that of the new lotts of 1667.* Will da. Dec. 12, 1670, in which he

---

* The present town of Flatbush was originally known by the name of Midwout or Midwoud, from "Midwoud," a village in the province of

devised his lands to his s. Gerret. Issue:—Anna, (sup.) d. single; Jannetje, m. 1st Reynier Wizzelpenning, m. 2^d Pieter Cornelise Luyster; Gerret Janse; Styntje; and Tryntje, bp. Feb. 23, 1642, in N. A. Signed his name "*Jan Snedeker.*"

Jan Gerretse, m. 1st, Aug. 5. 1692, Helena Hensha; (sup.) m. 2^d Catharine ——. Left N. L. and settled in J^a, where he bought land prior to 1692, as per p. 191 of Lib. A of Queens Co. Con. Will da. May 31, 1740; pro. Aug. 26, 1749; rec. p. 3, Lib. 17, N. Y. surr. off. Issue:—Gerret; Johannes; Jacobus, bp. Oct. 26, 1702, in N. U.; Willemtje; and Margaret, m. Ab^m Lent. Signed his name "*Jan Snedeker.*"

SNYSKEN, TONIS, of Br^n, among those who in 1663 applied for leave to form a village, and for salt-meadows, as per Stiles's Br^n.

SOISSEN, MARCUS, from Leiden, m. *Lysbeth Rossillon*, and joined the Br^n ch. in 1660 on certificate from the Manhattans.

SOLDAEL, JACOB. May 25, 1688, made an agreement with Gerret Sprung relating to land in Bu^k, as per p. 130 of Lib. 2 of Con.

North Holland in the Netherlands; and New Lotts as "Oostwoud," from a village of that name near "Midwoud." The other towns in Kings Co. (except Bushwick) being named by the first settlers after the localities in the fatherland from which some of them came, the inference appears to be a fair one that it was also the case with Flatbush, especially since at least one of its early settlers came from Hauwert or Hoogwoud, a village in the vicinity of "Midwoud" and "Oostwoud." The earliest document on which Flatbush is designated as Midwout, which has come to the notice of the compiler, is on a grant of land to Jacob Corlaer of Oct. 7, 1652, on p. 129 of Cal. of Dutch His. Man. The name on the early colonial and town records is generally written "Midwout." The principal exceptions, caused by the peculiar methods of spelling of different town-clerks and others, are that from 1660 to 1680 it appears on the town records as "Midewout," "Midwoudt," "Middewout," "Middwout," "Middelwoudt," "Middlewout," and "Midelwout;" from 1700 to 1712 as "Midwoud;" afterwards as "Midwout" (with the exception of 1760, in which year at least in one case Jeremias Vanderbilt, the town-clerk, wrote it "Midderwout"). See pp. 30 and 71 of Lib. A of Fl^h town rec.; pp. 4, 8½, 17, 19, 30, 31, 42, 43, 45, 49, and 79 of Lib. B; and p. 115 of Lib. AA of do. From about the period of the Revolutionary war the town has been known as "Flatbush," the former name having been dropped. The name "Flatbush" was, however, occasionally used at an early date; as an instance, it appears on a deed of Nov. 24, 1654, of Dirck Jansen to Cor^s Van Ruyven, of premises "in Flatbush, otherwise called Midwout," as per p. 58 of said Cal. of Dutch Man. The name of "Vlachte Bos" and "Flackebos," the Dutch for flat woods or level woods, was also occasionally used.

SOUSO, ANTHONY, emigrated in 1682, and took the oath of allegiance in Br[n] in 1687.

SOUTHARD or SOUTHART, THOMAS, of G[d], (sup.) English, m. *Annica* da. of Anthony Jansen from Salee. Bought Dec. 20, 1650, of Thomas Applegate the one half of the lot Applegate bought of Randell Hunt, as per G[d] rec. Owned plantation-lot No. 11 in G[d] in 1653. He quarrelled with his father-in-law Anthony Jansen about the ownership of cattle, on which Anthony was imprisoned by the local court of G[d], but released by the higher one of the colony, as per p. 136 of Calendar of Dutch Man. He appears to have removed to Hempstead, where he resided in 1670, having sons Thomas Jun[r] and John, whose descendants reside in that locality. He was also probably the ancestor of the Southards of N. J. Abraham, son of Thomas Jun[r], settled in Bernardstown, N. J., whose grandson, the Hon. Samuel L. Southard, represented N. J. as Senator in the Congress of 1821, in 1823 was Secretary of the Navy, in 1841 chosen president of the Senate, and on the death of Harrison, in April of that year, acting Vice-President, as per p. 47 of Vol 2 of Thompson's L. I. Made his mark to documents.

SPARSE or SPARARE, THOMAS. His house in N. U. referred to, as situated adjoining the boundary line of Br[n], on p. 232 of Lib. 2 of Con., being probably a tenant on the Van Dyck property. .

SPICER, JACOB, of Fld[s] in 1648, and of G[d] in 1656, as per Thompson's L. I. The Spicers removed to N. J., where a Jacob Spicer was a member of the Provincial Assembly in 1709, and where a Jacob Spicer was born in Cape May Co. in 1716, who was a merchant and surveyor and held important offices.

Abraham, d. July 26, 1679, as per p. 39 of Vol. VII. of Gen. Rec.

Michall, Michael, or *Mactel,* sold his house and lot in G[d] to Carston Johnson, who sold the same Feb. 17, 1697, to Jacobus Emans. Nov. 25, 1665, for 125 gl. wampum value Elbert Elbertse Stoothoff bought of "Mactel (Michael) Spicer" "Meautelaer's," now known as Bergen's, Island in Fld[s], as per p. 247 of the Bergen Genealogy. Michall was probably a s. of Thomas Spicer. Made his mark to documents.

Samuel, a Quaker of G[d] in 1656, of which town he was a mag. in 1673. He m. Esther da. of John Tilton of G[d]. Mar. 3, 1663, he bought of Ralph Cardell plantation-lot No. 6 of

said town, as per G[d] rec. He sold to Bartel Claessen (Van
Ruynen) at vendue 10 morgens located on the plains in
Fld[s], as per deed of said Claessen to Aucke Jans Van Nuyse
of Oct. 15, 1681, on p. 142 of Lib. AA of Fl[h] rec. He was
also interested with his neighbors in the tract they purchased in Monmouth Co., N. J., to which he probably removed. Had issue, as per p. 186 of Vol. III. of the Gen.
Rec.:—Abraham, b. Oct. 27, 1666; Jacob, b. Mar. 29, 1668;
Mary, b. Oct. 20, 1671; Sarah, b. June 14, 1674; Martha, b.
Jan. 27, 1676; Sarah, b. Feb. 20, 1677; and Abigal, b. Mar.
26, 1683. Signed his name "*Samuell Spicer*."

Thomas, resided at first on Manhattan I.; was one of the
first settlers of G[d] in 1643, and as a patentee allotted a plantation-lot Feb. 20, 1646, as per town rec. He resided on
the plains in Fld[s] Dec. 17, 1646, while driven from G[d] by
the Indians, as per Col. Rec.; and d. in 1658, in which year
he was one of the mag. of G[d]. His will is da. Sept. 30,
1658; pro. Nov. 4, 1658; and recorded on the G[d] rec., in
which he devises his real estate to his wife and sons, subject to legacies to his daughters. Issue:—Michael; Samuel;
Ann, m. John Lake ; and Susanna, m. 1st Willem Wathens,
m. 2[d] Henry Bresier. Signed his name "*Thomas Spicer*."

SPIEGELAER, JAN, emigrated in 1662, and m. *Geertje* ——.
Was a mem. of the R. D. ch. of Fl[h] in 1677, where he owned
land, which he sold to Catharine Bayard, and where in 1687
he took the oath of allegiance. Jan. 17, 1696, his wid. was
about to marry Peter Bijhou or Biljou of S. I. Signed his
name "*Jan Spiegelaer*."

SPRAT, JAN, a merchant in 1691, as per Stoothoff
papers.

SPRINGSTEEN, CASPER (sup. s. of Joost), m. 1st *Maria* da.
of Derick Storm; m. 2[d], Aug. 9, 1693, in N. Y., *Wyntie Jurex*
of Albany; m. 3[d], July 28, 1695, in N. Y., *Jannetje Jacobs;*
d. May 21, 1729. Resided at first in Bu[k], from which place
he removed to Westchester Co. or the Highlands, and in
1700 to Newtown. Issue:—Joost; Derick, who settled in
Kent Co. on the Delaware; Abraham, m. Abigal Betts;
David, m. Mary Alburtus; Gertrude, m. W[m] Miller; and
Melie, bp. Jan. 31, 1694, in N. Y.

Johannes Casparse, emigrated in 1652 with his mother
Geertje Jans and brother Joost Casparse, and among the
first settlers of Bu[k] in 1661. He m. Maria Johannes or
Maria Theunis; took the oath of allegiance in Br[n] in 1687,

residing at one period at the Cripplebush in said town. Will da. Apl. 4, 1676, as per p. 3 of Lib. 2 of Con. Issue:—Barbara; Jannetje, bp. Jan. 5, 1667; and Anna Maria, bp. Oct. 4, 1676—all bp. in N. Y.

Joost Casparse, emigrated in 1652 with his mother and brother from Groningen, and in 1661 among the first settlers of Bu^k. He m. 1st, June 10, 1663, Catharine da. of Ab^m Lothie and wid. of Pieter Praa; m.2^d Magdalena Jans or Joosten; living as late as 1687, in which year he took the oath of allegiance in Bu^k. Owned land in Br^n in 1678; bought Feb. 17, 1677-8, of Minne Johannes wood-lot No. 8 in the New Lotts of Fl^h, as per p. 25 of Lib. AA of Fl^h rec., which he sold Oct. 30, 1684, to Jan Dircksen Vander Vliet, as per p. 176 of Lib. C of Fl^h rec. There was a Casper Springsteen, miller, of Schenectady in 1707, whose descendants reside jn that vicinity and in that of Albany. Issue:—(sup.) Casper; Johannes, bp. Mar. 16, 1679, in Fl^h; Catharine, bp. Feb. 6, 1681, and d. young; Catharine, who m. Oct. 5, 1700, in N. Y., Johannes Texsel; and Jannetje, bp. Apl. 6, 1684—all bp. in Br^n. Made his mark "K" to documents. There was a Mellen and a Jury Springsteen among the freeholders of Dutchess Co. in 1714, as per p. 100 of Smith's His. of said co.

SPRONG or SPRUNGH, COERT (s. of Jan or Johannes), conveyed May 8, 1697, with others 26 A. in Fld^s, as per p. 134 of Lib. 2 of Con.

David (Janse), m. Dec. 13, 1694, in N. Y., Rachel Luquier of Bu^k, he being a resident of Flushing at date of marriage, as per rec. of R. D. ch. of N. Y. By another account he also m. Rachel Onderdonk. Settled in Bu^k, and on ass. roll of said town of 1683 and cen. of 1698. Will da. Oct. 23, 1731; pro. May 16, 1739; rec. p. 203 of Lib. 13 of N. Y. surr. off. Issue:—Antje, bp. Mar. 29, 1696, in Br^n, m. Cor^s Van Cott; John, b. Feb. 6, 1697; David Junr, b. Oct. 29, 1700; Ragel or Rachel, b. Dec. 12, 1702; Gerret, b. Mar. 13, 1705; Crystine, bp. Oct. 26, 1707, in Br^n; Gabriel, b. Aug. 21, 1711; Catrina, b. Oct. 15, 1713, (sup.) m. Johannes Van Kats or Cott; Marya, b. Oct. 15, 1713; and Folkert of Fld^s, bp. Jan. 18, 1718, m. Yannetje Schenck.

David Junr, b. Oct. 29, 1700, m. Nov. 10, 1742, Sytie da. of Jacobus Van Deventer. Resided in Fld^s. Issue:—Phebe, b. 1746, m. John Suydam; Femmetje, bp. July 5, 1747; Elizabeth, bp. Oct. 25, 1749; Barent, bp. July 19, 1752; and Jacobus, bp. July 11, 1756.

Gabriel (Janse) of Bu^k, m. May 28, 1692, Geertruy Dirckse

Woertman.   On ass. roll of Bu^k of 1693 and cen. of 1698.
Issue:—Annetje, bp. May 5, 1695, m. Simon Duryea of Bu^k;
Eightje, bp. Dec. 13, 1696; Yan, bp. Nov. 27, 1698, m. Sara
Hansen; Lucas, bp. June 27, 1701; Marytje, bp. Aug. 7, 1705
—all bp. in Br^n; and Gabriel.

Gerret (Janse) of Br^n, bp. Sept. 2, 1663; m. Apl. 16, 1687,
Anneke or Annatje Teunissen (Coevert) of Bedford.   On
ass. roll of Br^n of 1693 and cen. of 1698.   Issue:—Barbara,
bp. Oct. 11, 1689; Jan, bp. Nov. 27, 1692, m. Elizabeth Dykeman; Tunis, bp. July 29, 1694; Mouris, bp. Dec. 25, 1698;
and Echje, bp. June 8, 1701—all in Br^n.

Jan or *Johannes*, the common ancestor of the family, a
soldier from Bon in the Province of Drenthe, m. Oct. 23,
1660, Anna or Johanna Sodelaers from Connex in Bergen,
Norway, and d. prior to Sept. 15, 1694, for at that date his
wid. was m. to Claes Tunisse Clear.   Was a smith by trade,
residing at first in N. A. and afterwards at Flushing, and
while a resident of the latter place he bought May 29, 1679,
of Catharine Van Werven wid. of Do. Polhemius for 3300
gl. a house and outbuildings with 5 house-lots in the village
of Fl^h, as per p. 63 of Lib. AA of Fl^h rec., to which he
probably removed and joined the R. D. ch. of said town.
In 1689 he bought a lot of Derick Woertman at the ferry,
as per p. 137 of Lib. 1 of Con.   He finally removed to Bu^k.
Issue:—Barbara, bp. July 27, 1661, in N. A., m. Lucas Tunis Coevers; Gerret, bp. Apl. 2, 1663, in N. A.; Coert; Gabriel; Catharine, m. Tunis Dircksen Woertman; John or
Johannes, bp. Feb. 16, 1667, in N. Y.; David; Abraham, bp.
July 18, 1668, in N. Y.; and Lucas.   Signed his name "*Johannis Sprungh.*"

Lucas (s. of Jan or Johannes), conveyed May 8, 1697, with
John Sprungh, Albert Stevense, John Kiersted, Barne
Vrianse, Alexander Sympson, and Albert Terhune, 26 A. in
Fld^s to Gerret Coerten (Voorhees).

STAATS, JAN JANSE, of Gowanus, m. 1st *Catharine Corsen;*
m. 2^d, June 11, 1682, *Jonica* or *Annatie Janse,* or *Annatie
Pieters* wid. of Andries Janse Juriansz, and previously wid.
of Jan Evertse Bout.   Took the oath of allegiance in Br^n in
1687 as a native.   Issue:—Jan Janse Junr of Gowanus;
Pieter Janse of Gowanus; and (sup.) Ann Janse.   Made
his mark to documents.   An Abraham Staats, surgeon,
came to Rensellaerwick in 1642, who has numerous descendants residing in that vicinity, but have seen no evidence of their connection with the Gowanus family.

Jan Pieterse of Gowanus, the common ancestor of the
Gowanus family, known as old Jan Pieterse, m. 1st, May 16,

1652, Grietje Jans; m. 2^d, Nov. 15, 1663, the wid. of Frederick Jansen, ship-carpenter; d. about 1714. Owned and occupied the farm at Gowanus late of Adriance Van Brunt. On ass. rolls of Br^n of 1675 and '83 and cen. of 1698. Issue:—Pieter Jansen; Jan Jansen; Neeltje Jansen; and Sarah Jansen.

Johannes Pieterse (s. of Pieter Janse), m. Annetje ——·. There was a Jan Pieterse and Geertruy his w., of Yellow Hoek, on a deed of Feb. 2, 1708-9. Issue:—Mary, bp. Feb. 3, 1689, in Br^n.

Pieter Janse of Gowanus, m. 1st Annatie Pieterse Praa; m. 2^d Antie Janse Van Dyck. In 1673 he petitioned Gov. Colve for a piece of land on Staten I. opposite Amboy, the matter being postponed until the Gov. could obtain knowledge of the premises. Oct. 20, 1674, he and his sons Jan and Peter Petersen obtained a patent for the land applied for, as per p. 31 of Cal. of Eng. Man. In 1694 he sold his Gowanus farm of 30 morgens, located· between land of Gerbrand Claasen and that of Cor^a Van Duyn, to his s. Pieter Pieterse for £200, as per p. 37 of Lib. 2 of Con. Took the oath of allegiance in Br^n in 1687 as a native. Issue (by 2^d w.):—Geesje, bp. Dec. 18, 1661, in Br^n; Pieter Pieterse, bp. July 8, 1663, in Br^n; Annetje Pieterse, m. Cornelis Jorise of the ferry; Neeltje Pieterse, m. Harmen Jorisen; and Johannes Pieterse. Made his mark to documents.

Pieter Pieterse, bp. July 8, 1663; m. Lysbeth Aersen Middagh. Moved from Gowanus and resided in Richmond Co. in 1694. Issue:—Pieter, bp. Feb. 16, 1690, in Fl^h; and John. Made his mark to documents.

Pieter (s. of Pieter Pieterse and Lysbeth), bp. Feb. 16, 1690; m. 1st, Aug. 29, 1712, Lammetje Veghte; m. 2^d (sup.) Rebecca Ditmas. Resided at Gowanus. Will da. Oct. 4, 1760; pro. Sept. 2, 1761; rec. p. 118, Lib. 23, N. Y. surr. off. Issue:—Pieter, bp. May 21, 1721, in N. U., (sup.) m. Jannetje dau. of Johannes Ditmas; and (sup.) John. Signed his name *"Piter Staats."*

STANSON or STAUSIE, HENDRICK CORNELISE, of G^d, sold land in Fld^s in 1676 to Jan Janse ver Rhyn, as per Stoothoff papers. Made his mark to documents.

STEALMAN, JOHN, (English). See Jan Hendrick Stelman.

STEENDAM, JACOB, emigrated about 1650; m. *Sara de Bosjou.* Obtained a patent Nov. 12, 1652, for a plantation in Fld^s, which he sold June 17, 1660, to Albert Albertsen

18

Terhune. Bought Jan. 7, 1658, of Claude Barbier and Anthony Jeroe a tract in Bu[k] on the W. side of Mespath Kil, originally granted to Adam Mott, as per p. 367 of Cal. of Dutch Man.   Issue:—Dredegind, bp. Apl. 4, 1655; Samuel, bp. Nov. 18, 1657; and Jacob, bp. Dec. 4, 1658—all bp. in N. A.

STEENHUYS or STEENHUYSEN, ENGELBERT, tailor, emigrated in 1659 from Soest in Westphalia, and resided at first in N. A.; d. about 1678. Obtained a farm in Fl[h], which he sold Feb. 19, 1661, to Derick Jansen, cooper, with the plain and meadow land thereto belonging, and a house and village-plot, as per p. 52 of Lib. B of Fl[h] rec.   July 22, 1670, he obtained a patent of Gov. Carteret of N. J. for 7 tracts in Bergen, N. J., to which he removed shortly after the sale of his Fl[h] property, and of which place he was licensed to teach school by Gov. Stuyvesant in 1662. Issue:— Stephen; Joost; and Pieter, as per p. 91 of Winfield's Land Titles of Hudson Co., N. J. Signed his name *"Engelbert Steenhuys."*

STEINMETS.   Members of this family at an early period resided in and owned land in G[d] and meadow-lots on Coney I.   The ancestor of the family was Casper Stymats or Steinmets, who settled in Hudson Co., N. J., and had 9 children bp. in N. A., as per p. 812 of Valentine's Manual of 1863. See p. 78 of Winfield's Land Titles of Hudson Co.

STEGGELLER, JEAN, paid 2 gl. 9 st., minister's salary, in Fl[h] in 1680, as per town rec.

STELMAN, JAN HENDRICKSE, (English,) in 1651 rented Herry Breser's plantation in Br[n].   Mar. 7, 1652, he bought of Frederick Lubbertse 15 morgens in Br[n], as per Col. Man. Of Bu[k] in 1665, as per town rec.; in 1665 represented said town in the Hempstead Convention, and in 1668 a mag.

STEPHENS or STEPHENSE ABRAHAM, ALBERT, COURT, JAN, and LUCAS, see Vorhees.

Egbert, on ass. roll of Br[n] of 1675.

Jan, bought Oct. 21, 1681, of Jan Aucke Van Nuyse the farm which Van Nuyse bought Oct. 15, 1681, of Bartel Claesen and Claesen bought Feb. 15 of that year of Stoffel Probasco, located in Fl[h] and bounded on the S. side by land of Jan Strycker, N. side by land of Dirck Janse Vander Vliet, W. side by the common highway, and on the E. side by Coerlars Flats, as per p. 38 of Lib. A and pp. 122 and 123 of Lib. AA of Fl^h rec.

Oloffe of city of N. Y., where he took the oath of allegiance to the English in 1664, sold Apl. 9, 1670, to Wm Goulding all his right in plantation-lot No. 16 in G^d, as per town rec. This is probably Oliffe Stephense Van Cortland. Signed his name *"Oloffe Stevense"* in 1674.

Thomas, in 1651 in partnership with J. H. Stelman rented Breser's plantation in Br^n. See p. 130 of Cal. of Dutch Man. He afterwards removed to Middleburgh (Newtown, L. I.), as per p. 148 of said Cal. A Thomas Stephensen m. Aug. 15, 1645, in N. A., Maria Bernards, wid.

Thomas, b. 1615. Resided in 1653 in Bu^k on the plantation of David Jochems, late of Jan Messerole Senr.

STEPPER, HARMEN, m. *Neltye Jansen.* Assessed Jan. 13, 1666, in Bu^k for payment of the clergyman's salary, as per town rec.; a mag. in 1667.

STIGER, DANIEL, and Hans Jongh obtained Aug. 25, 1657, a patent for a lot at Br^n ferry.

STILLE, CORNELIS JACOBSE, sometimes written "Cornelis Jacobse alias Stille" (or the silent), of N. A. in 1639, m. 1st *Claesje Theunis;* m. 2^d, July 28, 1669, in N. A., *Tryntje Walings* of Amsterdam. Occupied the plantation in Bu^k, afterwards in Williamsburgh, adjoining that of Hans Hansen Bergen in Br^n, which he sold July 29, 1641, to Lambert Huybertsen Moll, as per p. 16 of Cal. of Dutch Man. Mar. 10, 1661, with others petitioned for a piece of woodland in Bedford lying in the rear of Rapalje's plantation. In 1664 he took the oath of allegiance in N. Y. to the English. Issue:— Jacob Cornelisen, m. Mar. 11, 1671, in N. Y., Aeltje Fredericks from Brazil; Aefje, bp. Apl. 2, 1646; Neeltje, bp. Dec. 13, 1649; Waling, bp. Oct. 6, 1660; Tymen, bp. Aug. 21, 1672; Frederick, bp. Jan. 24, 1680; Frans, bp. July 14, 1689; and Rachel, bp. Apl. 17, 1692—all bp. in N. A. and N. Y. Made his mark to documents.

STILLWELL, DAVID (s. of Nicholas the emigrant), bp. Nov. 13, 1653, in N. A.; m. *Maria* or *Mary* dau. of Adam Mott; d. about 1720. Left G^d about 1664 and removed to S. I., where he obtained grants for about 279 A. of land, and from there removed to Middlesex Co., N. J. Issue:— Nicholas 5th of N. J., b. 1678; Samuel of Freehold, b. 1680, d. 1753; Daniel of N. J., b. Dec. 10, 1687, m. Catharine

Larzelere, d. 1766; and Richard,,a physician of Monmouth Co., N. J., d. 1756.*

Elias (s. of Nicholas the emigrant) of G^d. Name on ass. roll of G^d of 1683 and cen. of 1698. Owned a tide-mill in G^d in 1696,. as per G^d rec. Jan. 13, 1698-9, he sold his dwelling-house and two garden-plots in G^d, one of which he had purchased of his brother Richard, to John Poling, as per G^d rec. Mar. 12, 1698, he sold lot No. 13 on Gisbert's I. of 2 A. to Reynier Van Sicklen. Signed his name in 1697 "*Elias Stilwill*." No account of his issue.

Elias (s. of Nicholas 2^d), b. Dec. 13, 1685; m. Anne Burbank of S. I. Settled on S. I. Issue:—Thomas, bp. June 30, 1726, m. Deborah Martling; Daniel, bp. Mar. 24, 1728; and John, bp. Mar. 17, 1730, m. Helen Van Name—all of S. I.

Jeremiah (s. of Nicholas the emigrant), bp. Jan. 13, 1663, in N. A.; m. Maria ——; d. about 1720. On ass. roll of G^d of 1683 and cen. of 1698; owned several plots of land in said town, as per G^d rec. Removed from G^d to S. I., and finally joined the Quakers and settled in Phila. Issue:— Thomas, b. 1701, m. Sarah Van Name; Nicholas of Whitehouse, Hunterdon Co., N. J., b. 1705, d. 1780; and Sophia, m. Abednego Thomas of Phila. Signed his name "*Jeremiah Stillwell*."

Jeremiah (s. of Richard 1st and Mary Holmes), b. Oct. 26, 1678; d. about 1750; m. —— ——. Removed from G^d to Aquackanonck, N. J., and from thence to Hancock, Md. Issue:—Richard, b. 1712 and settled at Mecklenburg, N. C.; William, b. 1715; John, b. 1718; and Jeremiah, b. 1725 and settled at Montgomery, Va.—all as per p. 282 of Memoirs of the Stillwell Family.

John (s. of Richard 1st and Mary Holmes), b. May 18, 1660; m. 1st Elizabeth ——, whose name appears on the G^d rec. in 1693 as his w.; m. 2^d Rebecca Throckmorton; d. 1724. Left G^d, settled on S. I., was sheriff of Richmond Co. in 1693, as per p. 27 of Vol. IV. of Doc. of Col. His.; member of the Colonial Assembly from 1702 to 1716, as per p. 111 of N. Y. civil list; and in 1701 an opponent of the Leislerian faction. Will da. Aug. 29, 1724; pro. Jan. 1725-6; rec. p. 140, Lib. 10, N. Y. surr. off. Issue:—Richard of N. Y., who d. 1748; John of Middlesex Co., N. J.; Joseph of Porrassye or Norrophyd; Thomas, d. 1760; Rebecca, b. 1693, m. Ebenezer Salters; Mary, b. 1696, m. Danl Seabrook; Abagail, b. 1706; and Daniel of Rhode Island,

---

* The compiler is indebted for some of the information relating to the Stillwell family to B. M. Stillwell's "Memoirs of the Stillwell Family," published in 1878; and to Dr. J. E. Stillwell of the city of N. Y.

b. May 10, 1720, d. May 20, 1770. Signed his name "*John Stillwell*."

Nicholas, the emigrant and ancestor of the Stillwells of this vicinity (English), came to this country about 1638 from Holland, and settled at first on Manhattan I. He m. 1st Abagail dau. of Robert Hopton; m. 2d Ann Van Dyke of Holland; d. Dec. 22, 1671, at Dover, S. I. His wid. m. 2d Wm Wilkins. In 1639 he located a tobacco plantation on Manhattan I., and in 1643 purchased a house and lot on the present Beaver St. in N. A. When the Lady Mody in 1643, accompanied by several Englishmen from Massachusetts, undertook the settlement of Gd ("Graoenzande"), he with other Englishmen who had previously settled on Manhattan I. joined her and took up lots in the new settlement. In the Indian war which took place shortly after the commencement of the settlement, and caused its temporary abandonment, as Lieut. Stillwell he defended the place, and afterwards appears to have returned to N. A. In 1648 he bought of Richard Dunn the village lot in Gd which Dunn had bought of Ralph Cardell, this being the first account of his owning land in said town after its abandonment during the Indian war, his name not appearing among the associates who in 1646, '47, and '48 were allotted plantation-lots of 50 A. Oct. 6, 1649, he bought of George Homes, for his s. Richard, Homes's plantation-lot, for which he agreed to pay 900 lb. of good merchantable tobacco. This plantation he agreed Oct. 10, 1650, to sell to Richard Cluffe for the use of Thomas Doxsey. By O'Callaghan's Register he was a mag. of Gd in 1650 and '51, a mag. of Fld in 1654 and '55, where he probably resided at that date, and a mag. of Gd in 1657 and '64. Dec. 27, 1657, he sold to John Bowne 12 A. lying on the "Cellers Neck" (Sellers Neck), being part of plantation-lot No. 40, which lot No. 40 he bought Aug. 25, 1654, of the agent of William Hallet. Aug. 29, 1659, he sold John Wilson a part of plantation-lot No. 40—all as per Gd rec. Feb. 9, 1660, he bought of Anthony Jansen from Salee his patent of 100 morgens. Apl. 2, 1660, he sold to Richard Aste 12 A. of the E. end of the plantation he bought of Anthony Johnson, as per Gd rec. Jan. 15, 1663, he sold to Mr. Francoys de Bruynne, for 700 gl. in wampum, the balance of said plantation; reasonable satisfaction to be made by said Francoys to "my son in law Nathaniell Brittanie at or upon the 25th of March next for the house and housing which hee the said Nathaniell built upon said land." All the above Gd and N. U. purchases copied from the Gd town rec., on which numerous other purchases and sales of Nicholas are entered. Nicholas

Stillwell is entitled to credit for, never swerving from his
allegiance to the Dutch government, which is more than
can be said of many of his English neighbors, who, on what
they supposed to be the first favorable opportunity, proved
themselves to be traitors to the colony to which they fled
from persecution, and to which they were indebted for pro-
tection and the enjoyment of religious liberty. In 1663 he
was an ensign in the Esopus expedition against the Indians, and the same year commissioned as lieut., as per Col.
Man. He finally removed to Dover, S. I., where he d. Dec.
22, 1671, his will being da. Dec. 22, 1671; pro. June 17, 1672;
and rec. p. 161, Lib. 1, N. Y. surr. off. His wid., Ann Stillwell of Dover, bought June 21, 1672, of Jan Jansen Ver
Rhyn plantation-lot No. 18, with the buildings in G^d, as per
town rec. Issue by 1st w., as per Memoirs of Stillwell
Family:—Richard, b. 1634; Nicholas 2^d, b. 1636; (by 2^d w.)
Anne, b. 1643, m. 1660 Nathaniel Brittan; Ales or Abagail,
b. 1645, m. Oct. 26, 1665, Samuel Holmes; William, bp. May
11, 1648; Thomas, bp. July 9, 1651; Daniel, bp. Nov. 1,
1653, in N. A.; Jeremiah, bp. Jan. 13, 1663, in N. A.; and
Elias. Made his mark to manuscripts with a bungling
reversed "N," in no manner resembling that which would
be made by a scholar with his left hand, who had had the
misfortune of losing his right one as has been claimed.
Dr. J. E. Stillwell of N. Y., in behalf of the claim that
Nicholas made his mark in consequence of the loss of his
right arm, has exhibited to the compiler of this work an
original and genuine document (stating that he had seen
another) on which his name was subscribed in full in a good
and legible hand. Against this evidence are documents of
a prior date, with numerous ones later, with the bungling
mark, from which it may fairly be inferred that the name
on the document exhibited had been written by some other
person at Nicholas's request, as is occasionally done at the
present day.

Nicholas 2^d (s. of Nicholas the emigrant), came over with
his father in 1638 from Holland; b. 1636; m. 1st, Nov. 6,
1671, by Justice James Hubbard, Catharine wid. of Charles
Morgan of G^d, who was living as late as 1693; m. 2^d, in
1703, Elizabeth Corwin or Cornell; d. in G^d in 1715. By
occupation a farmer; a justice of the peace in 1685, '88, '89,
and '93; from 1691 to '94 a member of the Colonial Assembly for Kings Co., as per N. Y. civil list; and capt. of the
militia of G^d in 1689, as per p. 190 of Cal. of Eng. Man. In
1693, as capt. of the Kings Co. contingent of 50 men, he
accompanied Gov. Fletcher's expedition against the French
and Indians, as per p. 15 of Vol. IV. of Doc. of Col. His.

On ass. roll of G^d of 1683 and cen. of 1698. Jan. 2, 1670, he commenced a suit in the sessions against Wm Compton for trespass done by his hogs in his cornfield on "Sellers Neck," as per G^d rec., from which it is evident that the Stillwells at this date owned at least a part if not the whole of said neck. Will da. Jan. 19, 1715; pro. Mar. 5, 1715; rec. p. 394, Lib. 8, N. Y. surr. off. Issue:—Nicholas 3^d, b. Apl. 25, 1673; Rebecca, b. 1675, m. Oct. 20, 1693, Ab^m Emans of G^d; Richard, b. May 11, 1677; John, of whom no further trace; Anna Catharine, b. May 15, 1681, m. 1720 Barent Christopher of S. I.; Mary, b. 1683, m. Hendrick Johnson of Br^n; Elias, b. Dec. 13, 1685; and Thomas 3^d, b. May 16, 1688. Signed his name "*Nicolaes Stillwell*" in 1662.

Nicholas 3^d (s. of Nicholas 2^d and Cath^e Morgan), b. Apl. 25, 1673; m. 1703 Elizabeth dau. of Richard Cornell of Flushing; d. prior to 1735. Settled at J^a, L. I., on land his father bought Mar. 6, 1681, of John Skidmore. Issue:— Marian, m. Charles Marsh; Esther, m. John Sayres; Mary, m. Samuel Southward of Hempstead, as per p. 283 of Memoirs of the Stillwell family; Elizabeth, m. James Millard; and probably others, from whom are descended the Queens Co. branch of the family. Signed his name "*Nicholas Stillwell Jun*" in 1692.

Nicholas 4th (s. of Richard 1st and Mary), b. June 11, 1664; m. Mary dau. of Gersham Moore of Br^n; d. 1725. Left G^d and settled on S. I. Issue:—Gersham, b. Aug. 17, 1685, d. June 24, 1752; Richard, b. Sept. 16, 1688; John, b. May 9, 1690, d. Aug. 9, 1750; Mary; and Elizabeth. Signed his name "*Nick: Stilwell*" in 1692.

Nicholas 5th (s. of Daniel and Mary Mott), b. in G^d in 1678, and settled at Shrewsbury, N. J., where he d. in 1759. Will pro. May 15, 1769; rec. p. 193, Lib. G, sec. off. Trenton. Issue:—Obadiah; Elias; William; Joseph; Martha; Mary; Rebecca; Lydia; and Priscilla—as per p. 288 of Memoirs of Stillwell Family.

Capt. Richard 1st (s. of Nicholas the emigrant), emigrated with his father, and b. in 1634 in Holland; m. 1st, May 1655 Mary dau. of Obadiah Holmes; m. 2^d Freelove or Mary dau. of John Cooke; d. about 1688 at Dover, S. I., intestate. Nov. 9, 1663, he bought of Wm Lawrence plantation-lot No. 4. Resided on a plantation in G^d, of which town he was a mag. in 1670, '73, and '74, and capt. of militia in 1673, as per p. 646 of Vol. II. of Doc. of Col. His. Sold Mar. 31, 1681, to Wm Osborne plantation-lot No. 4 of G^d, at which date he resided on S. I., as per G^d rec., and where he obtained grants for about 237 A. of land, and in Jan. 1683 was appointed justice of the peace, as per Cal. of Eng. Man. Oct.

29, 1691, Wilhelmus de Meyer applied for letters of administration on his estate, as per p. 219 of Cal. of Eng. Man. Issue:—John, b. May 18, 1660; Nicholas 4th, b. Jan. 11, 1664; Thomas, b. Dec. 4, 1666; Mary, b. July 13, 1668, m. 1st Nathaniel Brittan Jun[r] of S. I., m. 2[d], Feb. 1703-4, Valentine Dushan, d. about 1703; Richard 2[d], b. June 25, 1671; and Jeremiah, b. Oct. 26, 1678. Signed his name *"Richard Stillwell."*

Richard 2[d] (s. of Richard 1st and Mary), b. June 25, 1671; m. 1st, Sept. 3, 1705, Deborah Reed or Cowne of N. J.; m. 2[d], —— 1722, Mercy or Mary Sands; d. Apl. 16, 1743, at Shrewsbury, N. J. Removed from G[d] to the city of N. Y. and engaged in mercantile business, and from thence to Shrewsbury. Will da. Nov. 17, 1742; pro. Mar. 31, 1747; rec. p. 89, Lib. 16, N. Y. surr. off. Of Shrewsbury, N. J., at date of will. In 1747 the plantation of Mary his wid. at Shrewsbury, between the Neversink and Shrewsbury rivers, as lately bought, was offered for sale by Catharine and Elizabeth Stillwell, her executors. Issue:—Richard; Mary, m. Col. Thomas Clark of the British army; Deborah, m. Lieut. Richard Smith of the British army; Catharine, m. Rev. Richard Pemberton; Ann, m. 1st Theodosius Bartow of Shrewsbury, 2[d] Pierre de Vismes; Samuel, m. Hannah Van Pelt; Elizabeth, m. 1st Peter Wrexall, 2[d] Maj.-Gen. Maunsell of the British army; and Lydia, m. Dr. John Watkins of N. Y., as per p. 281 of Memoirs of the Stillwell Family.

Richard 3[d] of G[d] (s. of Nicholas 2[d] and Catharine Morgan, and the ancestor of the Stillwell family of G[d]), b. May 11, 1677; m. 1st Maria ——; m. 2[d], Oct. 22, 1733, Altie Ditmars; d. Feb. 11, 1758. Suppose he resided on and owned the Sellers Neck farm, late of his descendant Richard Stillwell, and now (1880) of Cornelius Stryker, his descendant on the female side. In 1702 he was high sheriff of the county, as per p. 298 of Cal. of Eng. Man.; in 1715 col. of the militia; and in 1725 and '27 mem. of the Colonial Assembly, as per p. 111 of N. Y. civil list. Issue:—Daniel of S. I., b. July 7, 1702, m. Oct. 14, 1736, Catharine Johnson, d. May 19, 1760; Katharine, b. Feb. 16, 1703, m. Apl. 22, 1727, Jeronemus Rapalje, d. Jan. 14, 1732; Nicholas of G[d], b. Dec. 2, 1709, m. Dec. 22, 1733, Altie Van Brunt, d. Oct. 1, 1776; Mary, b. June 10, 1712, m. 1st, Sept. 11, 1731, W[m] Van Voorhies, m. 2[d], Feb. 2, 1734, Jacobus Debevoise, d. Sept. 22, 1768; and Richard of G[d], b. Oct. 3, 1720, m. Jan. 14, 1760, Ann Cortelyou, and owned and resided on the Sellers Neck farm. Signed his name *"Richard Stillwell."*

Richard 4th (s. of William and Hanna), removed with his

father to Cape May, N. J., and d. in 1793. Issue:—Elijah; Phebe; Zeniah, m. Richard Stiles; Elizabeth; and Mary, m. Daniel Foster. Signed his name "*Rich⁴ Stillwell*."

Samuel (s. of Daniel and Mary), b. 1680; d. 1753. Suppose removed with his father from G⁴ to S. I., and finally settled at Upper Freehold, N. J. A Samuel Stillwell appears to have been engaged in mercantile business in N. Y. in 1751, per p. 653 of Cal. of Eng. Man. Issue:—Daniel of N. J., b. Jan. 8, 1747.

Thomas 1ˢᵗ (s. of Nicholas the emigrant), bp. July 9, 1651; m. June 8, 1670, by Justice James Hubbard, as per G⁴ rec., Martha Baleiu of S. I., of which place he was also a resident at date of marriage. Martha after his death m. 2⁴ the Rev. David Du Vonrepos. Left G⁴ and settled on S. I., and in 1686 was high sheriff of Richmond Co. He appears, however, to have retained an interest in G⁴ lands, for May 16, 1671, Matthew Force on his behalf recorded on the town-book an earmark for his cattle. Oct. 28, 1677, he obtained a grant for 73 A. under the hills on the S.E. side of S. I.; and Apl. 4, 1685, one for 145 A. at the old town on said island, as per p. 144 of Vol. I. and p. 45 of Vol. II. of Land Papers in off. of Sec. of State at Albany. Will da. May 21, 1704; pro. May 9, 1705; rec. p. 148, Lib. 7, N. Y. surr. off. Issue:—Thomas Junʳ of S. I., b. 1671; Nicholas of S. I.; John of S. I.; Ann. of S. I., b. 1675, m. Jacobus Billop of S. I.; Rachel of S. I. b. 1677, m. Wᵐ Brittan; and Frances, bp. Aug. 31, 1679, m. Nicholas Brittan of S. I. Signed his name "*Thomas Stillwell*."

Thomas 2⁴ (s. of Richard 1ˢᵗ and Mary), b. Dec. 4, 1666; (sup.) m. 1ˢᵗ Ann Hubbard; (sup.) m. 2⁴, 1703, Alice Throckmorton. Left G⁴ and settled on S. I., where he held the office of capt. of militia, and represented Richmond Co. from 1691 to 1698 in the Assembly, as per N. Y. civil list. Among those who in 1701 petitioned King William III. for relief from the power and influence of the friends of the dec. Gov. Leisler, as per p. 942 of Vol. IV. of Doc. of Col. His. Issue:—Daniel of S. I., b. 1696, m. Mary Poillion; John, b. 1709; Thomas; and Elizabeth, bp. May 23, 1718. (There may be errors in this issue.) Signed his name "*Thomas Stillwell*."

Thomas 3⁴ (s. of Nicholas 2⁴ and Catharine), b. May 16, 1688; m. Catharine Day. Owned a farm at Yellow Hoek (Bay Ridge) covering the premises (1880) of T. G. Bergen, J. R. Bennett, Wᵐ H. and Samˡ Thomas, and those of B. C. Townsend, on which he obtained a grant about 1739 from Gov. Clarke (see p. 537 of Cal. of Eng. Man.) for a ferry to S. I., at that period one of the routes of travel from the city of N. Y. to Philadelphia. In 1715 was capt. of G⁴ militia,

as per p. 184 of Vol. III. of Doc. His. of N. Y. This Thomas
is supposed to be the ancestor of the N. U. branch of the
family. Resided in 1753 in Fld'. Issue:—John, b. 1709, d.
1794; Thomas; Nicholas; and Christopher or Stoffel of N. U.,
b. Jan. 17, 1716, d. Apl. 15, 1780—as per p. 284 of Memoirs of
the Stillwell Family. Signed his name *"Thomus Stilwell."*

Thomas 4th (s. of Thomas 1st and Martha), b. 1671; m.
Martha dau. of Jaques Poillion; d. 1703, intestate. Left Gd
and settled on S. I., and was among the opponents of the
Leisler faction in 1701. In 1686 he was commissioned
sheriff of Richmond Co., as per p. 147 of Cal. of Eng. Man.;
and 1700 capt. of militia in said county, as per p. 809 of
Lib. 4 of Doc. of Col. His. Issue:—Nicholas of S. I., m.
Mary ——, d. 1756; Mary, m. John Hopper; and Anne of
S. I., m. 1st Paul Michard, and 2d Saml Van Pelt, both of
the same place, as per p. 287 of Stillwell Memoirs.

William (s. of Nicholas the emigrant), bp. May 11, 1648,
in Gd; m. 1st Hannah ——; m. 2d Mary ——, who was living
in 1694; d. about 1720. On ass. roll of Gd of 1883 and cen.
of 1698. Left Gd and removed to S. I., where he obtained
Oct. 28, 1677, a grant for 75 A. of upland on the hills and
salt-meadows, as per p. 145 of Vol. I. of Land Papers.
From S. I. he removed in 1691 to the vicinity of Cape May,
N. J., as per p. 276 of Memoirs of the Stillwell Family.
Issue:—William Junr of S. I., b. May 11, 1678 or '79; John of
Gd and Cape May, b. 1681, m. Elizabeth Perrine; Nicholas
of Cape May; Richard of Cape May; Daniel of Cape May,
who d. 1793; and Mary, who m. Feb. 20, 1698, Dr. Thomas
Walton of N. Y. Made his mark to documents.

William Junr, b. May 11, 1678 or '79; m. Sarah Perrine of
S. I.; d. 1719. Suppose he removed with his father from
Gd to S. I. Issue:—William, bp. Sept. 6, 1719, on S. I.; and
Daniel (twin), bp. Sept. 6, 1719, on S. I.

STOCK, STOOK, or HOOCK, HUBERT JANSEN, cooper, among
the first settlers of N. U. in 1657, and on ass. rolls of said
town of 1675 and '76. His name also appears on the ass.
roll of Fld' of 1675.

STOCKHOLM, ARENT, m. *Magdalena* ——, and resided in
Buk, where he died. Will da. Oct. 27, 1727; pro. Apl. 1,
1736; rec. p. 449, Lib. 12, N. Y. surr. off. Issue:—Andrew;
Magdaline; Mary; Catrin; Hanna; Aleida; and John.

Andrew or *Anderies* (s. of Arent) of Buk, m. 1st Aeltje Nagel; (sup.) m. 2d Margrietje ——. Issue:—(sup.) Jannetje,
m. Jan Bragaw of Newtown; (sup.) Lena or Magdalena,
m. Jacob Cassouw; (sup.) Aaron, m. Dec. 14, 1746, Heiltje

Van Alst; (sup.) Margrietje, m. Magiel Vandervoort of Bedford; and Martin, bp. May 18, 1729, in N. U. Signed his name "*Anderies Stockholm.*"

STOFFELSZ, DERICK, see Langestraet.

Gerret, emigrated in 1651, and took the oath of allegiance in N. U. in 1687; m. 1ˢᵗ Lysbeth Gerrets; m. 2ᵈ Lysbeth Cornelis. Aug. 18, 1678, he sold 25 morgens of land in Brⁿ to Barent Egbertse. In 1685 he occupied as a tenant Rutger Joesten Van Brunt's farm at Yellow Hoek (Bay Ridge), now (1880) of Rulef and Danˡ Van Brunt. Bought Feb. 1, 1691-2, of Denys Teunissen (Denyse) for 4300 gl., 2 lots at Yellow Hoek, lying S.W. of the lane and land of the wid. of Swaen Janse, and N.E. of that of Dirk Janse Zutven, to whom July 31, 1695, he sold his purchase, as per town rec. These 2 lots cover a considerable tract, extending from the Bay to 3ᵈ Ave., lying on the S. side of Bay Ridge Ave. His name appears on the ass. rolls of N. U. of 1683 and '93, Dongan's patent of 1686, and as a mag. of said town in 1691. Issue (by 1ˢᵗ w.):—Herman Gerretse, bp. June 10, 1674, in N. Y.; Josias Gerretse, bp. Oct. 29, 1676, in N. Y.; Albert Gerretse; (by 2ᵈ w.) Jacobus Gerretse, bp. Jan. 15, 1685; Jores Gerretse, bp. Apl. 24, 1687; Tryntje Gerretse, bp. Oct. 20, 1689; and Josyntje Gerretse, bp. Oct. 20, 1690. Signed his name "*Gert. Stoffelsen.*"

Jacob, b. 1601; m. in 1639 the wid. of Cornelis Van Voorst; d. 1677. He came over from Zierikzee in Zeeland at an early period. In 1645 he was a member of the Council, and held land in Brⁿ, as per patent of Jan Evertse Bout of July 18, 1645. In 1656 he hired the Company's bouwery at Ahasimus, and in 1663 he was commissary of stores and overseer of the West India Company's negroes. For a further account see pp. 46 and 426 of Winfield's Hudson Co., N. J.

Pieter, of Fldˢ in 1688, as per town rec. Made his mark to documents.

STOLL, ROBERT, of Boston, sold Feb. 3, 1654, to Wᵐ Bell, through John Tilton, plantation-lot No. 21 in Gᵈ, as per town rec.

STOMMATIE, alias WILLEM BRUYNE, see Wᵐ Bruyne.

STOOTHOFF, CORNELIUS (Gerretse), b. 1698; m. —— ——; d. Mar. 1781. Left Fldˢ and settled in Six Mile Run, Somerset Co., N. J. Issue:—Annetje or Johanna, m. Abᵐ Demarest of North Bend; Cornelius, m. —— Cornell; Altie;

(sup.) Maria; and probably others. Signed his name "*Cornelius Stoothof*" in 1765.

Elbert Elbertse, the common ancestor of the family, b. 1620; m. 1st, Aug. 27, 1645, Altje Cornelise Cool wid. of Gerret Wolfersen Van Couwenhoven; m. 2d, July 21, 1683, Sarah Roelofse wid. of Cornelis Van Rossum of N. Y.; d. about 1688. Emigrated from Nieuw Kercken in Zeeland, or Nieuw Kerken in North Brabant, about 1637. At first in the employment of Gov. Van Twiller and the Patroon Van Rensselaer, and finally settled in Fld, where he took the oath of allegiance in 1687, of which town he was for many years a mag. and largest land-holder, having purchased Van Twiller's and Van Cowenhoven's interests in their patent for the flats or plains; was a member of committees appointed by the colonists to vindicate and protect their rights, and one of the representatives in the Hempstead convention of 1665. On the conquest of the colony by the Dutch in 1673, he was appointed by Gov. Colve capt. of militia.[*] Among the premises he owned was Bergen's Island, which he bought in 1665 of Martel or Michael Spicer, and Bearen, now Barren Island, which he bought of Spicer and Tilton. He also owned what was lately known as Crooke's Mill in said town, which mill was in operation as early as 1674. His will, not recorded, is da. Dec. 18, 1686, in which he devised Bergen's Island to his s. Gerret and

---

[*] The following is a copy, from p. 269 of Lib. D of Fl rec., of the oath taken by the military appointees of Kings Co. at "Middlewout" on the 30th of October, 1673, in presence of the schout, Jacob Strycker, and Francois De Bruynne, secretary:

"We promise and swear in the presence of Almighty God to be bound and true to their High Mightynesses, the Lords States General of the United Netherlands and his Highness the Lord Prince of Orange, and his Governor already here placed, or who may be hereafter placed, our companies in good order to maintain, and to perform the duties of our respective offices, in truth of which so help us God.

For Amesfoort:
Capt. Elbert Elbertse,
Lieut. Roelof Martense,
Ensign Derick Janse.

For Breuchelen:
Capt. Jores Rapalje,
Lieut. Michal Hanse,
Ensign Daniel Rapalje.

For Middlewout:
Capt. Jan Strycker,
Lieut. Titus Sirix,
Ensign Pieter Gilyamse.

For N. Uytrecht and Boswyck:
Capt. Jacob Cortelyou,
Lieut. Joost Kockout,
Ensign Cryn Janse.

For Grouesandt:
Capt. Richard Stillwell,
Lieut. —— ——,
Ensign Wil. Goldingh."

entailed it to his descendants. Issue:—Gerret Elbertse;
Elbert Elbertse, bp. Jan. 26, 1648, and d. young; Helen or
Heiltie Elbertse, m. Thomas Willet of Flushing; and Achye
or Aegge Elbertse, m. Jan Van Duyckhuys. Signed his
name "*Elbert Elbertsen.*"

Elbert Gerretse of Fld⁸, m. Mar. 28. 1714, Johanna or Annatje Lupardius of Dortrecht; d. Sept. 19, 1756. Removed
to N. J. and resided in Somerset Co. from 1717 to 1730, and
then returned to Fld⁸. Issue:—Gerret Elbertse of Fld⁸, b.
Aug. 13, 1715, O. S., m. 1739 Lammetje Stryker, d. Aug. 1,
1746, O. S.; and Wilhelmus of Fld⁸, m. Nov. 9, 1728, Altie
Coerten Voorhies, d. Feb. 14, 1783.

Gerret Elbertse of Fld⁸, m. 1ˢᵗ Willemtje Pieterse Monfoort; m. 2ᵈ, Aug. 10, 1684, Johanna Nevius; d. Mar. 30,
1730. Commissioned major by Gov. Slaughter; was a
mem. of the D. ch. in 1677; took the oath of allegiance in
Fld⁸ in 1687; on ass. roll of Fld⁸ of 1683 and cen. of 1698,
and signed an anti-Leislerian petition to the king in 1701.
Will da. Feb. 25, 1729, but not recorded. Issue:—Elbert
Gerretse; Arinthe or Adrianna, b. Aug. 6, 1686, d. prior to
1735; Altie; Johannis Gerritse of New Brunswick, N. J.;
Sara, m. Mar. 29, 1711, Laurens Williamsen of Fld⁸; Petrus
Gerretse of Somerset Co., N. J., m. Margaret ——, d. 1728;
Helena, m. Apl. 26, 1714, Ruluf Lucasse Van Voorhies;
Cornelius Gerretse of Somerset Co., b. 1698, d. 1781; Ger-
ret Gerretse of Somerset Co.; and Wilhelmus Gerretse of
Somerset Co., b. May 30, 1705, m. Sara ——, d. Feb. 14,
1783. Signed his name "*Gerret Stoothoff.*"

Gerret Gerretse, m. Catharine Roelofsen, left Fld⁸, settled
on the Raritan, and living as late as 1763. No further
trace.

Johannes Gerretse, m. Mar. 28, 1714, Neeltje Schenck; d.
about 1730. Left Fld⁸ and settled at New Brunswick,
N. J. Issue:—Elizabeth, bp. Aug. 14, 1717, d. young;
Elizabeth, bp. 1720, at Six Mile Run; Gerret; Johanna; and
Neeltje.

Petrus Gerretse, m. Margaret ——; d. 1728. Left Fld⁸
and settled in Somerset Co., N. J. Will da. Apl. 20, 1727;
pro. Mar. 30, 1728; rec. p. 109, Lib. B, in off. of Sec. State
of N. J. Issue:—Sarah; and Johannes.

STORM, DIRCK, emigrated in 1662 from the "Maiery of Bos"
with his w. *Maria Pieters* and 3 children, settling at first in
N. Y., where in 1665 he kept a taphouse. Was appointed by
the court of sessions Dec. 15, 1669, town-clerk or secretary
of Brⁿ, which office he held for several years. On ass. rolls
of Brⁿ of 1675 and '76; mem. of Flʰ ch., and residing in N. L.

in 1677; schoolmaster of N. L. in 1680 and '81; town-clerk of Fl^h in 1681; and a resident of Bedford in 1694. Issue:— Pieternella, bp. June 1, 1673; Aaltje, bp. Oct. 20, 1678, d. young; Aaltje, bp. Oct. 31, 1680—all bp. at Br^n; Joris; and Maria, m. Casper Springsteen. Signed his name "*Dirck Storm.*" There was a Dirck Storm clerk of Orange Co. in 1691, as per p. 43 of Ruttenber's Orange Co.; and there was an Isaac Storm in Dutchess Co. prior to 1716, as per p. 207 of Smith's Dutchess Co.

Joris (Dirckse) of N. L., m. Engeltje Thomas. Issue:— Derick, bp. Oct. 20, 1695.

STORY, ROBERT, d. Dec. 28, 1683, as per p. 39 of Vol. VII, of the Genealogical Record. He bought Dec. 5, 1677, of John Jaffers a farm of 26 morgens with plain and meadow land in Fl^h, as per p. 29 of Lib. C of Fl^h rec. June 22, 1683, he petitioned for license to purchase any parcel or tract of unsold land on or near the Hudson River, as per p. 19 of Vol. II. of Land Papers. There was a Robert Story, a trader in 1676, who bought 2 houses and lots in Albany in said year, as per Pearson's First Settlers of Albany. Story sold his Fl^h farm Aug. 24, 1668, to Balthazer De Hart, as per p. 39 of said Lib. C. In 1676 he was taxed £6 5 sh. for a house in N. Y. Issue:—Robbert, bp. July 4, 1657, in N. A., m. Patience ——, and had children Mary and Enoch. Signed his name "*Robert Story.*"

STOUT or STOUCE, RICHARD, one of the first settlers of G^d in 1643, and allotted plantation-lot No. 18 in 1646, as per town rec.; d. about 1688. He also bought Apl. 5, 1661, plantation-lot No. 26 of Edward Griffen. With a number of his neighbors he left G^d and settled at Middletown, Monmouth Co., N. J., of which place he was one of the patentees or original purchasers of the Indians, as per p. 73 of Vol. I. of Raum's N. J. There is a story, founded on tradition, on p. 76, etc., of said Vol., of the shipwreck of a Dutch ship on Sandy Hook; of the crew and passengers leaving a sick young Dutchman and his wife there while they went for relief; of the Indians tomahawking the man, mangling the wife and leaving her for dead; of her recovering and crawling into a hollow log and subsisting for several days on berries, and then being discovered and taken prisoner and her life preserved by an old Indian, ransomed by the Dutch of N. Y., where she married *Richard Stout*, being at the time in her 22^d year and he in his 40th. They settled at Middletown, where the old Indian often visited her, and on one occasion, by informing her of a plot to massacre the whites, put them on their guard and saved the settlement from destruction. This woman, whose maiden name was *Penelope Van Prince*, lived to the age of 110 years, her posterity numbering 502 at the time of her death. The compiler gives this tradition as he finds it, having little faith therein. Issue (per Rev. G. C. Schenck):—John; Richard; Jonathan; Peter; James; Benjamin; David; Deliverance; Sarah; and Penelope, whose descendants are numerous in N. J. Made his mark to documents.

STRAETMAN, TEUNTJE, bought land of Claes Bartel in Fl[h] prior to 1660, as per Br[n] D. ch. rec.

STROCKLES, Madam HENDRICKA, and Dirck Janse Woertman conveyed Sept. 20, 1686, to Jeronemus Rapalje land and meadows at the Wallabout, as per p. 75 of Lib A. of Fl[h] rec. Signed her name *"Hendrica Strockels."*

STRYKER or STRYCKER, BARENT or BARNT (Pieterse), b. Sept. 14, 1690; m. Feb. 16, 1717, *Libertje Hegeman;* d. June 1758. Left Fl[h] and settled on the Raritan, N. J. Issue:— Peter; John, m. Grietje Van Liew; Jacob; and Barent, m. Elizabeth Bennet—all of N. J. Signed his name *"Barnt Stryker"* in 1712.

Cornelis (Gerretse) of G[d], b. 1691; m. Rebecca Hubbard; d. Oct. 23, 1769. Owned and occupied the farm his father bought of W[m] Goulding, which is yet held by his descendants. Will da. Feb. 21, 1769; pro. Apl. 12, 1781; rec. p. 145, Lib. 34, N. Y. surr. off. Issue:—Gerret of Fld[s], b. Mar. 27, 1729, m. Ida Van Deventer; Hanna, b. Feb. 13, 1733, m. Michael Stryker of Fl[h]; Samuel of G[d], b. Oct. 22, 1737, m. Marretje Schenck, and owned and occupied a part of the homestead farm; Cornelius of G[d], b. May 2, 1739, m. Maria Lake, and owned and occupied the balance of the homestead farm devised to him and his brother Samuel by his father's will; and Elizabeth, b. Sept. 28, 1741, who probably d. young. Signed his name *"Corneles Stryker."*

Gerrit[2](*Jacobse*) of Fld[s], m. Dec. 1673 Wyntje Cornelise Boomgard; d. in 1694 or 1700. On ass. rolls of Fld[s] of 1675 and '83, and mem. of the R. D. ch. of said town in 1677. Mar. 17, 1691-2, he bought of Reinier Van Sickelen 15 A. "lot No. 7" in G[d], and on the same date he bought a 4 A. lot of John Barentse (Van Driest), as per G[d] rec. Jan. 21, 1692-3, he bought of William Goulding of G[d] his house with all the lands and meadows he owned in G[d] for £297 10 sh., as per G[d] rec., the main farm cong. 108¾ A., as surveyed by Roger Strong in 1788, on which his s. Cornelis

settled. His will is da. May 24, 1693; rec. p. 351, Lib. 7,
N. Y. surr. off. Issue:—Eyda; Gezina, bp. Dec. 9, 1677, in
Fl^h, (sup.) d. young; Jannetje, bp. Dec. 26, 1679, in Fl^h,
(sup.) m. Thomas Lake of S. I.; Jacob, bp. Aug. 27, 1682, in
Fl^h; Gerrit, b. Nov. 23, 1684, (sup.) d. young; Geesje, bp.
Jan. 11, 1685, in Fld^s; Maria; Catharine; Cornelis; and
Gerretje, bp. Nov. 14, 1694, (sup.) m. Jan Wyckoff. Signed
his name "*Gerrit Strycker.*"

Gerrit (*Janse*) of Fl^h, emigrated with his father in 1652;
m. Dec. 25, 1683, Styntje Gerretse Dorland. Mem. of R. D.
ch. of Fl^h in 1677, where he took the oath of allegiance in
1687; on ass. roll of said town of 1683 and cen. of 1698.
High sheriff of Kings Co. in 1686, as per p. 148 of Cal. of
Eng. Man. Issue:—Lammetje, bp. Nov. 23, 1684, in Fl^h, m.
1st John Wyckoff of Six Mile Run, N. J., m. 2^d Minne Van
Voorhees of New Brunswick; John of N. J., m. Grietje or
Margaret Van Liew; Aulche; and Gaertje. Signed his
name "*Gerrit Strycker.*"

Hendrick (Janse), m. Feb. 16, 1687, Catharine Hys of Fl^h.
Mem. of the R. D. ch. of Fl^h in 1677;. on patent for the land
in N. L. of 1673; and on ass. roll of Fl^h of 1675. He sold
June 12, 1680, to Jan Van der Vliet wood-lot No. 7 in the
N. L. for 1000 gl., as per p. 125 of Lib. AA of Fl^h rec. Oct.
7, 1686, he bought of Cornelis Janse Berrien 2 lots of land,
Nos. 46 and 47, in the N. L. of "Midwout," they being the
2 outside numbers on the Fresh Kil or Shoemaker's Bridge,
as per p. 78 of Lib. A of Fl^h rec. From his will, da. Jan. 23,
1684, on p. 155 of Lib. C of Fl^h rec., it is inferred that he
had no children. Signed his name "*Hendrick Strycker.*"

Jacob '*Gerritse*, the common ancestor of one branch of the
family, emigrated in 1651, and settled in N. A. He m. Ida
Huybrechts; and d. Oct. 1687. Was a tailor by trade, and
schepen of N. A. from 1665 to 1674, and with his w. a mem. of
the D. ch. of that place. Removed to Fld^s, where he took
the oath of allegiance in 1687, but may have resided in Fl^h
previous to his removal to Fld^s, for on p. 3 of Lib. A of Fl^h
rec. he is entered as having obtained a patent for 25 morgens in said town lying on the E. side of the highway, S.
of Jan Strycker, and N. of Symon Hansen (Van Noostrand),
stretching W. and so southerly, in breadth 25 rods and
length 600 rods. Was schout fiscaal of the Br^n district in
1673, and mem. of the R. D. ch. of Fld^s in 1677. Issue:—
Gerrit of Fld^s; and Ida, who m. Christoffel Probasco of
Fl^h. Signed his name "*Jacob Strycker.*"

Jacobus (s. of Gerrit and Wyntje), bp. Aug. 27, 1682; m.
Martha ——. Resided in G^d until 1722, when he removed
to the Raritans, N. J., and joined the R. D. ch. of that lo-

cality. Issue:—Wyntje, bp. July 13, 1718, in G[d]. Signed his name "*Jacobus Strycker*" in 1763.

Jacob (Pieterse), b. Aug. 24, 1688; (sup.) m. Dec. 17, 1710. Annetje Vanderbeeck, and settled in Somerset Co. on the Raritan.

Jan,[1] the common ancestor of the Fl[h] branch of the family, and supposed to be a brother of Jacob Gerritse, emigrated in 1652 from Ruinen in the province of Drenthe in the Netherlands, settled in Fl[h] as early as 1654, having probably previously resided in N. A.; was b. in 1615; m. 1st Lambertje Seubering, by whom all his children; m. 2[d], Apl. 30, 1679, Swantje Jans wid. of Cornelis de Potter of Br[n]; m. 3[d], Mar. 31, 1687, in N. Y., Teuntje Teunis of Fl[h], wid. of Jacob Hellekers, alias Swart or Swartcop, of N. Y.; d. prior to 1697. On a declaration he made in 1679 he is styled "armorer," as per p. 80 of Cal. of Eng. Man. Mag. of Fl[h] for several years; one of its representatives in the Hempstead convention of 1665; name on its town patents, and took the oath of allegiance there in 1687. Issue:— Altje, b. in the Netherlands, m. Ab[m] Jorise Brinckerhoff; Jannetje, also b. in the Netherlands, m. Cor[s] Janse Berrian; Gerrit Janse; Angenietje, m. 1st Claas Tysen, m. 2[d] Jan Cornelise Boomgaert or Bougaert; Eytie or Ida, m. Stoffel Probasco of N. L.; Pieter of Fl[h], b. Nov. 1, 1653; Sara, m. Joris Hansen Bergen; and Hendrick. Signed his name "*Jan Strycker*."

Jan (Pieterse) of Fl[h], b. Aug. 6, 1684; m. 1st, 1705, Maragrita Schenck; m. 2[d], Feb. 17, 1722, Sara dau. of Michael Hansen Bergen; d. Aug. 17, 1770. Will da. Oct. 4, 1768; pro. Sept. 15, 1770; rec. p. 314, Lib. 27, N. Y. surr. off. Issue:—Pieter of the Raritan, b. Sept. 14, 1705, m. Antie Deremer; Johannes of the Raritan, b. Feb. 12, 1707; Annetje, b. Dec. 20, 1708, m. Roelof Cowenhoven of N. J.; Madalena, b. Dec. 19, 1710, m. Aert Middagh of Br[n]; Maragreta, b. May 24, 1713, d. young; Abraham of the Raritan, b. Aug. 4, 1715, m. Ida Ryder and Catrina Cornell; Lammetje, b. Feb. 11, 1716, m. Gerret Stoothoff, and Jan Amerman; Jacobus of the Raritan, b. Sept. 29, 1718, m. Geestie Duryee and Jannetje ——; Maragrita, b. Dec. 9, 1719, m. Jacobus Cornell; Mighiel or Michiel of Fl[h], b. Mar. 4, 1723, m. Hanna Stryker; Femmetje, b. June 19, 1725, m. Jacobus Vanderveer; Barent, b. Nov. 13, 1728; and Sara, b. June 15, 1731. Signed his name "*Jan Strycker*."

Pieter[2] (Janse) of Fl[h], b. Nov. 1, 1653; m. May 29, 1681, Annetje Barends or Joosten; d. June 11, 1741; took the oath of allegiance in Fl[h] in 1687 as a native; on ass. roll of said town of 1683 and cen. of 1698; on patent of 1685; and

19

capt. of militia in 1689, as per p. 190 of Cal. of Eng. Man.
Will da. Apl. 13, 1729; pro. May 27, 1742; rec. p. 251, Lib.
14, N. Y. surr. off. Issue:—Lammetje, b. Mar. 20, 1682, d.
young; Lammetje, b. Feb. 16, 1683, d. young; John of Fl[h],
b. Aug. 6, 1684; Barent, b. Sept. 3, 1686, d. young; Jacob of
the Raritan, b. Aug. 24, 1688; Barent of the Raritan, b.
Sept. 14, 1690; Hendrick, b. Dec. 3, 1692, d. young; Pieter
of Fl[h], b. Feb. 12, 1697; Hendrick of Fl[h] and Br[n], b. Feb.
18, 1699; and Lammetje, b. Dec. 21, 1700, m. 1st Johannes
Lott, m. 2[d] Christiaens Lupardus. Signed his name
"Pieter Strycker."

Pieter (Pieterse) of Fl[h], b. Feb. 12, 1697; m. May 18, 1720,
Jannetje Martense dau. of Marten Adrianse; d. Dec. 24,
1766. Sheriff of Kings Co. in 1736. Will da. June 9, 1773;
pro. May 27, 1784; rec. p. 24, Lib. 37, N. Y. surr. off.
Issue:—Annetje, b. Mar. 20, 1721, d. young; Sara, b. July
3, 1722, (sup.) m. Dec. 10, 1743, Cornelis Cornell; Antje, b.
Oct. 5, 1724, d. young; Jannetje, b. Oct. 5, 1724, m. Jacob
Mizorel or Messerole; Pieter of Fl[h], b. Dec. 22, 1730, m.
successively Jannetje Verkerk and Femmetje Schenck;
Gerrit, b. Oct. 13, 1733; and Jan, b. Feb. 15, 1738-9. Signed
his name *"Pieter Stryker."*

William, m. Annetje —— of Fld[t]. Was a mem. of Do.
Van Zuuren's ch. in 1677 and '85, and entered as removed
to Br[n]. Have seen no account of this William's relationship to the families of Jan or Jacob Gerritse Strycker the
emigrant.

STUYVESANT, COERT, mem. of Assembly for Kings Co. in
1693 and '94, as per N. Y. civil list of 1861.

Petrus, director-general of the New Netherlands, who
owned a boᴜwery in Fld[t], which he leased with the stock
Aug. 28, 1655, to Jacobus Van Dalen, as per Col. Man.
Had sons Balthazar Lazarus and Nicolaes Willem bp. in
N. A. Signed his name *"Petrus Stuyvesant."*

STYSSEN, JACOB, see Stille.

SUEBERING, see Seuberingh.

SULLIVAN, PETER, an early settler who was buried in G[d],
as per p. 171 of Vol. II. of Thompson's L. I.

SURTELL, JAMES, sold Apl. 5, 1659, to Henry Brazier a
house and a half-acre of plantation-lot No. 28 in G[d], as per
town rec. Made his mark to documents.

SUTPHEN, ABRAHAM (Dirckse), bp. Sept. 26, 1696; m. *Maria Maritje* or *Mayke Barkeloo*. Left N. U. and removed to S. I., where he remained until about 1720, when he settled at Freehold, N. J. Issue:—Grietje, bp. Oct. 29, 1721, at Freehold; Elizabeth, bp. Nov. 25, 1723; Abraham, bp. July 19, 1726; Maria, bp. June 4, 1727; Antje, bp. Oct. 26, 1729, d. young; Jannetje, bp. Oct. 24, 1731; Abraham, bp. Feb. 20, 1737; Jacob, bp. June 17, 1739; Cornelius, bp. Aug. 10, 1741; and Antje, bp. May 6, 1744.

Derick Janse (Van Sutphen), the common ancestor of the family, emigrated from Zutphen or Sutphen in Gelderland in 1651, settling at first probably in N. A., and afterwards in Flᵇ. He m. Lysbeth Janse Van Nuyse, and d. about 1706 or '7. He sold June 21, 1681, his Flᵇ farm to "Denyse Theunise," receiving in payment 4 lots of woodland lying together at Yellow Hoek (Bay Ridge), N. U., on the N. side of land of Rutger Joesten (Van Brunt), subject to a lease of 3½ of the lots to Gerret Stoffelse, to which premises he probably finally removed. Denyse, in addition to the land, agreed to build for Sutphen a boat 18 ft. long, wood measure, and a barn and barrack on the lots, as per p. 155 of Lib. AA of Flᵇ rec. He took the oath of allegiance in N. U. in 1687, and his name appears on the patent of said town of 1686. In 1706 he was assessed for 164 A. in N. U. The 4 Yellow Hoek lots, known as Nos. 7, 8, 9, and 10, now (1879) cover the premises of J. R Bennet, T. G. Bergen, W. H. and Samuel Thomas, B. C. Townsend, and perhaps a part of the farm of the late J. I. Bennet. Will da. Sept. 4, 1702; pro. Oct. 29, 1707; rec. p. 319, Lib. 7, N. Y. surr. off. Issue:—Hendrikje or Hank, bp. Dec. 18, 1681, at Fldˢ, m. 1ˢᵗ Pieter Turckse, m. 2ᵈ Benjᵃ Van Cleef; Jacob bp. Jan. 20, 1684, at Flᵇ; Jan, bp. Dec. 18, 1685, in Flᵇ, d. young; Jan, bp. Feb. 6, 1687, in Flᵇ; Geertie, bp. Mar. 3, 1689, in Flᵇ; Dirk; Guisbert or Gilbert, b. Oct. 14, 1693; Abraham, bp. Sept. 25, 1696; Isaac; Elsje, m. Herman Gerretse; and Elizabeth, b. Apl. 6, 1699, m. Danˡ Lake of Gᵈ. Signed his name *"D. Js. Sutphen."*

Derick (Derickse), m. Grietje or Margaret dau. of Aert Teunisse Van Pelt of N. U. After his marriage he left N. U. and settled at Freehold, N. J., where he was a mem. of the D. ch. in 1713 and '31. Issue:—Dirck of N. J., bp. Apl. 6, 1712 (sup.) m. Jannetje Voorhees; Aert of N. J., bp. May 11, 1716, m. Maria Schenck; Jan, bp. Jan. 20, 1721, (sup.) m. Neeltje Van Pelt; Petrus, bp. Aug. 21, 1726; and Abram, bp. July 16, 1733—all bp. at Freehold. Made his mark to documents.

Gilbert or *Guisbert* (Dirckse), b. Oct. 14, 1693, at N. U.;

m. Geertruy dau. of Aert Tunisz Lanen Van Pelt of N. U.;
d. Aug. 18, 1763.   Left N. U. and settled in Monmouth Co.,
N. J., probably as early as 1713.   Issue:—Derick, bp. Apl. 8,
1716, m. Maria Longstreet; Aert of N. J., bp. Apl. 13, 1718,
m. Jannetje Van Meteren; Guisbert of N. J., b. Aug. 23, 1720,
m. Ariaentje Van Pelt; Pieter; Margaret, bp. Mar. 17, 1723;
Neeltje, bp. May 22, 1730; John of N. J., b. 1732, m. Johanna
Nevius; and Maria, bp. June 5, 1737, m. Cryn Janse Van
Meteren of N. J.—most of whom were bp. at Freehold,
N. J.

Isaac (Derickse), of N. U. in 1698, but no further trace.

Jacob (Derickse), bp. Jan. 20, 1684; m. Antie or Nelke
Bennet.   Left N. U. and settled near Freehold, N. J., about
1717, and mem. of the D. ch. of that locality in 1721.   Issue:—Jan, bp. Jan. 20, 1717, d. young; Jan, bp. Oct. 18,
1722, m. Maritie Cowenhoven; and Isaac, bp. May 22, 1730,
m. Jannetie Barkeloo—all bp. at Freehold.   Signed his
name "*Jacob Van Zutvin*" and "*Jacob Sutvin.*"

Jan (Derickse), bp. Feb. 6, 1687; m. Engeltie Bennet.
Left N. U. and settled near Freehold, N. J., about 1709, in
which year he was a mem. of the D. ch. of that locality.
Issue:—Jan, bp. Nov. 18, 1711, m. Catryntje Langestraat;
Agnietje, m. Johannes Wilmsze or Philipse; Anneke, bp.
Apl. 2, 1713, m. (sup.) Andrias Voorhees; Isaac, bp. Dec. 5,
1714; Elizabeth, bp. Apl. 15, 1722, m. (sup.) Mattheus Laen
or Lane; and Benjamin, bp. Aug. 17, 1732, m. Eyda Van
Meteren—all bp. at Freehold.

SUTTON, AMBROSE, (sup.) English, of Gᵈ.   On his will being
proved the court of sessions admitted Obadiah Holmes to
act as administrator, as per court rec.

SUYDAM, ABRAHAM (Hendrickse), bp. Mar. 12, 1684.   No
further trace.

Hendrick Reycke, emigrated in 1663 from Zutphen in the
Netherlands; m. Ida Jacobs; d. 1701.   Was a blacksmith,
residing at first in N. A.   Feb. 5, 1677-8, he bought of Simon
Hansen (Van Nostrand) for 3300 gl. his bouwery in "Midwout," except a village building-plot 12½ rods in breadth,
having on its N. side that of Rem Janse Van Coeverden, on
its S. side that of Dirck Janse Van der Vliet, as per p. 21 of
Vol. AA of Flᵇ rec., to which he removed.   Was a mem. of
Flᵇ ch. in 1678; on ass. roll of 1683; cen. of 1698; and took
the oath of allegiance there in 1687.   Will da. Dec. 13, 1689;
pro. June 26, 1701; rec. p. 129, Lib. 2, N. Y. surr. off.   Issue:—Ryck, bp. Oct. 10, 1666, (sup.) d. young; Jacob, b.
(per Riker) in 1666; (sup.) Cornelius; Hendrick of Bedford;

Ryck, bp. Oct. 10, 1675; Ida, bp. Apl. 6, 1678, in N. U., m.
Jan Aertsen or Arison; Jannetje, bp. June 27, 1680, in N. U.,
d. young; Jannetje, bp. Sept. 23, 1683, in Br\ d. young;
Abraham, bp. Mar. 12, 1684; Jannetie, bp. June 23, 1685, m.
Tunis Rapalje of Bu\; and Gertrude, bp. Mar. 20, 1692.
Signed his name "*Heyndryck Reycke*" and also "*Heyndryck
Reycke van Zutphen.*"

Hendrick (Hendrickse), m. Bennetie ——; d. about 1730.
Owned a farm at Bedford, Br\. Will da. Aug. 28, 1730.
Issue:—Hendrickje, bp. Jan. 1697; Lambert of Bedford;
Elsje, bp. Apl. 18, 1704, in Br\, m. John Lott of Fld\; Eytie;
and Hendrick of Bedford, b. Dec. 2, 1706, m. Geertje Ryerson, who occupied and to whom was devised the homestead farm.

Hendrick (Jacobse) of Fl\, b. Feb. 28, 1696; m. Apl. 24,
1719, Geertje dau. of Evert Van Wickelen of N. L.; d. about
1774. Will da. Aug. 13, 1769; pro. Oct. 17, 1774; rec. p.
207 of Lib. 29, N. Y. surr. off. Issue:—Evert of N. U., b.
Mar. 24, 1720, m. Maria Bogert; Jacob of Fld\, b. Nov. 18,
1722, d. Nov. 15, 1801, single; Seytie, b. Sept. 28, 1725, m.
Evert Hegeman; Mette, b. Sept. 4, 1727, m. Samuel Gerretsen; Geertie, b. Dec. 31, 1729; Hendrick, of Fl\, b. Feb. 9,
1731, m. Maria Amerman; Pieter Nelletie, b. Feb. 15, 1734,
m. Jacobus Vanderveer; Jan, of Newtown, b. Feb. 10,
1737, m. Femmetje Hegeman; and Cornelius, b. Feb. 19,
1739.

Jacob (Hendrickse), b. 1666; m. Sytje Jacobse; d. 1738.
Was a blacksmith by trade, and for a short period plied his
occupation in N. U. On an indenture in 1695, in which
Jonathan Mills of J\ binds his son Jonathan to him to learn
the smith's trade, in the body of the instrument he is called
"Jacob Hendrickse van Zuyt-dam," signing the same
"Jacob Henderse van Suydt-dam;" hence the family surname of Suydam, derived from a hamlet of that name in
the Netherlands, or from having resided south of a dam.
Will da. Oct. 12, 1737; pro. June 23, 1738; rec. p. 177, Lib.
13, N. Y. surr. off. Issue:—Jacob, bp. Mar. 29, 1696; Hendrick of Fl\, bp. Mar. 29, 1696; Johannes of Flushing; Jan;
Ryck of N. J., b. 1703; Cornelius of Oyster Bay, m. Margaret Van Sicklen; Jannetie, bp. Aug. 7, 1705, in Br\, m.
Thomas Van Dyck; Adriaentje; Geertie or Gertrude; Isabella or Belitie; Ada or Eytie, m. Peter Lefferts of Fl\;
Seytie; and Dow of Newtown, b. 1707, m. Sarah Vanderveer. In addition to signing his name "*Jacob Henderse
van Suydt-dam,*" he at times signed his name "*Jacob Suy-
daem.*"

Jacob (Jacobse), bp. Mar. 29, 1696; m. Mar. 21, 1737, Ante

Luquier. Issue:—Jan. bp. July 2, 1738, in N. U., and d. young. No account of any other children.

Johannes (Jacobse), m. Cornelia ——; d. 1791. Settled at Bayside, Flushing. Issue:—Seytie, m. —— Aersen; Jane, m. —— Eldert; Ida, m. Jacob Thorne of Flushing; and Jacob.

Lambert (s. of Hendrick and Bennetie of Bedford), m. Abagail dau. of Jacob Lefferts; d. in 1797. Resided in Bedford, and will da. Nov. 10, 1766, pro. Mar. 30, 1767. Issue:— Hendrick of Bedford; Bennetie, b. 1736; Jane, m. Gilliam Cornell of Bucks Co., Pa.; Ida, m. Martin Schenck; Jacobus, bp. Oct. 15, 1752, d. young; Jacobus of Bedford and Newtown, bp. Dec. 4, 1758, m. Adrianna Rapalje; and Adrianna, b. Apl. 16, 1766. Signed his name "*Lamberth Suydam.*"

Ryck (Hendrickse) of Flds, b. Oct. 10, 1675; m. 1ˢᵗ Jannetje ——; m. 2ᵈ Dorritie ——; d. 1741. On ass. roll of Fld° of 1693; and lieut. of troop in 1715. Feb. 2, 1697, his father Hendrick Rycken conveyed to him 52 morgens in Bedford, bounded on the S. side by land of Thomas Lambertse and that of the wid. Jorise, on the N. side by land of Jacobus Vandewater, and on the E. and W. sides by the common woods, as per p. 149 of Lib. 2 of Con. Will da. Feb. 25, 1740-1; pro. Feb. 9, 1742. Issue:—Hendrick of Monmouth Co., N. J., bp. Feb. 2, 1701, in Brᵑ, (sup.) m. Marytie Van Sicklen; John; Ryck of Monmouth Co., N. J., m. Sarah Luyster; Ida or Eitie, m. (sup.) Jan Van Mater of N. J.; Anna or Antie; Gertrude or Geertie, m. William Bennet; Jane or Jannetie, m. (sup.) Abraham Bennet; Christina or Styntie, m. Johannis Bennet of Bucks Co., Pa.; and Mary or Marytie, m. Benjamin Carson of Bucks Co., Pa. Signed his name "*Ryck Suydam*" in 1725.

SWAEN the negro, of N. U., see Swaen Janse Van Luane.

SWART or SWAERTWOUT, CORNELIS (possibly a s. of Jacob), was plaintiff in a suit against Glonde La Metre July 7, 1659, as per p. 105 of Lib. B. of Flʰ rec. Jan. 25, 1662, he obtained a patent from Gov. Stuyvesant, under the name of "Cornelus Swaertwout," for 24 morgens in Flʰ on the W. side of the road, S. of Do. Polhemius and to the N. of "Jan Sebringh," with plain and meadow land in addition, which premises Jan Sebringh, as his attorney, sold Mar. 6, 1674, to Do. Polhemius, as per p. 29 of Lib. A of Flʰ rec. and p. 247 of Lib. 2 of Con. July 24, 1664, he obtained another patent for 29 morgens in Flʰ. A Cornelis Swartwout was a mem. of the D. ch. of N. A. prior to 1660.

Jacob (alias Hellakers), emigrated to this country from Amsterdam as early as 1634; was b. in 1612; m. 1st, in Europe, —— ——, by whom he had 3 children; m. 2d, in this country, *Truytje Teunisse*, sometimes called *Truytje Jacobs*, wid. of the father of Teunis Idesse. Truytje m. after the death of Jacob, Jan Strycker of Flh. There was a Jacob Swart in N. A. in 1638, a soldier, who July 28, 1639, was found guilty of mutiny, as one of the ringleaders in refusing to work on the fort, and was banished. It is possible that this may have been another Jacob. Jacob Swart was a master-carpenter, residing in N. A., who in 1652 sued Wm De Kay for 48 beavers for building a saw-mill in the Virginias. In 1657 he appears to have resided in Gd, and was entered on the records of said town as having 17 A. under cultivation, from whence in that year he removed to N. U., where he was among the first settlers, and in which place he built the first house. Apl. 21, 1661, he obtained from Gov. Stuyvesant a patent for 24 morgens in N. U., lying between the lands patented to Claes Claesen (Smit) and those patented to Jaques Cortelyou. This patent is to "Jacob Swart," but in the body of the instrument his name is entered as "Jacob Swarwout." He was a mag. of N. U. in 1661 and '64, and on the patent of 1668. In 1679 he appears to have resided in N. Y., and is referred to by the "De Labadiests" on p. 286 of Vol. 1 of the Memoirs of the L. I. His. Soc. Issue (by 1st w., and as per p. 287 of the above Vol. 1):—Jacomynchy, who m. Gerret Cornelise Van Duyn; a dau. who in 1679 resided in Amsterdam in the Netherlands; a s., a carpenter, in 1679 in the East Indies; (by 2d w.) William, who is probably the Willem Hallakers who joined the R. D. ch. of N. Y. in 1681. Signed his name "*Jacob Hellakers.*"

Johannes, m. Femmetje ——. Was among the first settlers of N. U. in 1657; on ass. roll of said town of 1693 and cen. of 1698; constable in 1700; assessed for 26 A. in 1706; and a church officer in 1711. Was a freeholder of Gd in 1680. Issue:—Jan; Barent; Jacobus; and Lysbet—all b. prior to 1704, and whose descendants are supposed to reside in Monmouth Co., N. J. Made his mark to documents.

Thomas, m. Hendrickje Barents and obtained Mar. 7, 1661, a patent for 58 morgens in Flh, of which town he was a mag. in 1655. At one period, prior to 1660, he and his w. were mem. of the D. ch. in N. A. Mar. 15, 1677, he sold the one half of his patent to Jan Snediker, as per pp. 11 and 13 of Lib. C of Flh rec. A Johannes Swartwout was the first settler of the village of Johnsville in Dutchess Co., and the first settler near Johnsville was "Rodolphus Swartwout from L'. I.," as per pp. 182 and 183 of Smith's Dutchess Co.

SWEERS, HENDRICK, a soldier in 1656, whose name appears on the application of Mar. 10, 1661, to the Director-Gen. and Council for a parcel of land at Bedford; also on the ch. rec. of June 17, 1665, relating to Do. Polhemius's salary.

SWEET, PIETER. On the patent in 1677 of Gov. Stuyvesant to Do. Johannes Megapolensis of a plantation in Fl[h], with meadows and plain land thereto appertaining. The two pieces of salt-meadows are described to be held in common by said Megapolensis and "*Pitter Sweet*," as per p. 29 of Lib. A of Fl[h] rec.

SWELLINANT, CORNELIUS, one of the first settlers of G[d], was allotted in 1646 a plantation-lot, as per G[d] rec.

SWIRREL, HENDRICK, a shoemaker in 1678, as per Stoothoff's books.

SWOL, JAN, m. *Grietje* ——, and had a dau. Geertruy bp Oct. 30, 1695, in Fl[h].

SYMONSE, see Simonse.

SYMPSON or SYMSON, see Simson.

SYN, JAN JANSZ, and *Hester Syn*, both mem. of Fl[h] ch.; from N. L. in 1677, entered on the ch. rec. as removed.

TADENS or TATES, MICHIL, m. 1st *Annetje Eduwarts;* m. 2[d], June 17, 1668, in N. A., *Tryntje Jacobs* wid. of Jacob Stoffles. Settled at first on Manhattan I. as early as 1644, from which he was banished in 1656 for selling spirituous liquors to the Indians, with leave to reside on L. I. (See p. 172 of Cal. of Dutch Man.) In 1657 he appears to have owned a yacht which traded on the Delaware. Bought Mar. 13, 1660, of Claes Janse Van Naerden his patent of Sept. 30, 1645, of about 21 morgens on the East River, Br[n], which he sold Apl. 3, 1664, to Michael Hainelle. In 1657 he was assessed at the ferry 10 gl. towards Do. Polhemius's salary. In 1664 he took in N. Y. the oath of allegiance to the English, and in 1663 he was licensed to keep a taphouse in N. Y.

Issue:—Catryntje, bp. Dec. 18, 1650; Tades Michaëlse, bp. Sept. 29, 1654, who owned land in N. J. in 1686; Eduart Michaëlse, bp. Aug. 4, 1660, d. young; and Eduart Michaëlse, bp. Dec. 18, 1661—all bp. in N. A.

. TAYLOR, STEVEN, (sup.) English, owned land in G^d at an early date, as per map of the village on file in the town-clerk's office.

TELLER, WILLEM, emigrated in 1638; b. 1610; m. 1st *Margaret Donchesen;* m. 2^d, Apl. 9, 1664, in N. A., *Mary* or *Maria Verleth* wid. of Paulus Schreck; d. in 1701.   Resided mainly in Albany as a trader until 1692 (where in 1684 he was appointed a justice of the peace), when he removed to N. Y. and was engaged (as per Stoothoff books) in the dry-goods trade.   Was one of the early proprietors of Schenectady.   Obtained a farm in G^d, which he leased Aug. 26, 1653, to Thomas Morrell for 4 years.   May 7, 1659, he bought of Peter Symson plantation-lot No. 27 in G^d for the use of his s. Andrew Teller, as per G^d rec.   Will da. Mar. 19, 1669; pro. 1701, as per p. 108 of Pearson's Early Settlers of Albany.   Issue, as per do.:—Andrew or Andries, b. 1642; Helena, b. 1645, m. 1st Cornelis Bogardus, m. 2^d Francis Rombouts; Maria, b. 1648, m. 1st Pieter Van Alen, m. 2^d —— Loockermans, d. prior to 1700; Elizabeth, b. 1652, m. 1st Ab^m Van Tricht, m. 2^d Melgert Wynantse Van der Poel; Jacob, b. 1655, m. Oct. 24, 1683, in N. Y., Christina Wessells, d. prior to 1700; Willem, b. 1657, resided in Albany, and m. Dec. 15, 1686, in N. Y., Rachel Kierstede; Johannes, b. 1659; Casper, d. prior to 1700; and Jannetje, m. Arent Philipse Schuyler.   Signed his name "*Willem Teller.*"

Andrew or *Andries* (s. of Willem), b. 1642; m. May 6, 1671, in N. Y., Sophia dau. of Oloff Stevense Van Cortlandt. For many years a merchant and magistrate of Albany. About 1671 removed to N. Y.   Owned a farm in G^d which his father bought in 1659.   Will da. Dec. 16, 1702.   Issue:— Andries, (sup.) m. Sept. 15, 1722, in N. Y., Catharine Vandewater; Margarita; and Oliver Stephen, (sup.) m. Oct. 12, 1712, in N. Y., Cornelia De Peyster.

TEN EYCK, DERICK (s. of Coenraed), bp. Jan. 26, 1653, in N. A.; m. Mar. 14, 1675, in N. Y., *Aefje Boelen* from Amsterdam, both of N. Y. at date of marriage.   Owned land in Bu^k in 1697, as per deed of Charles Fountain on p. 147 of Lib. 2 of Con.   Issue:—Andries, bp. July 22, 1676; Jacob, bp. Nov. 14, 1678; Andries, bp. May 4, 1681; Coenraedt, bp.

June 15, 1684; Mayken, bp. Dec. 12, 1686; Abraham, bp.
June 15, 1691; Dirck, bp. Dec. 25, 1694—all bp. in N. Y.

Tobias (s. of Coenraed), bp. Jan. 26, 1653, in N. A.; m. 1st,
in N. A., Aeltje Duycking; m. 2^d, Sept. 17, 1684, Elizabeth
Hegeman of Fl^h. Was allotted lot No. 11 in the first division of Fl^h woodlands. Joined the D. ch. of N. Y. in 1672.
Will da. Nov. 29, 1699, and rec. on a loose sheet in Lib. A
of Fl^h rec. The Ten Eycks are numerous on the Hudson
River, as per Pearson's Albany, and are also to be found in
Monmouth and Somerset counties, N. J. Issue:—Coenraedt, bp. Nov. 20, 1678; Maria, bp. Apl. 3, 1680; Hendrickje,
bp. July 1, 1682; Johannes, bp. May 10, 1685; Coenraedt,
bp. Mar. 4, 1687; Adriaen, bp. Jan. 30, 1690; Catharina, bp.
May 4, 1692; and Jacob, bp. July 1, 1696—all bp. in N. Y.
Signed his name "*Tobyas ten Eyck.*"

TENES, JAN, paid 2 gl. 9 st. towards the clergyman's salary in Fl^h in 1681.

TER HART, see De Hart.

TERHUNE, ALBERT ALBERTSE Senr, or Albert the "Lient-
wever" (ribbon weaver), m. *Geertje* ——; d. 1685. Resided at first in N. A., and then, in 1657, on the Nyack tract
in N. U. where in Jan. 1662 he obtained a patent for a farm,
which he sold Apl. 3, 1664, to Nathaniel Brittan. In 1660
and '65 he bought land of —— Van Cowenhoven in Fld^s, and
also in 1665, in said town, of Elbert Elbertse Stoothoff, to
which he removed after 1663. Albert Albertse (Terhune),
Jaques Cortelyou, and others obtained a patent for 5000 A.
on the Passaic River, N. J., as per p. 118 of the Record of
the Gov. and Council of E. N. J. Issue:—Jan Albertse of
Fld^s; Albert Albertse Junr of Hackensack; Heyltje Albertse,
b. Jan. 12, 1650, in N. A.: (sup.) Annetje Albertse, bp. Mar. 3,
1653, in N. A.; Styntje Albertse, m. Claes Janse Romeyn;
and Sarah Albertse, m. Volkert Hanse Van Noortstrant.
Signed his name "*Albert Albertse.*"

Albert Albertse Junr, bp. (sup.) Aug. 13, 1651; m. 1st Hendrickje Stevense Van Voorhees; m. 2^d Wyntje Brickers. Resided at first in Fld^s, where his name appears on the ass. rolls
of 1675 and '76, and then removed to Hackensack, of which
place he was a mem. of the D. R. ch. in 1689, and in 1696 a
mem. of the E. N. J. Legislature. Will da. Feb. 3, 1704, and
rec. on p. 15 of Lib. 3, off. surr. of N. Y. Issue:—Willemtje,
bp. Apl. 2, 1677, d. young; Albert 3^d of Hackensack, m. Maratie de Graves; Jan Albertse, m. Elizabeth Bertholf; Anneke
or Antie Albertse, m. Jacob Zabriskie; Gerbringer or Gerre-

brecht Albertse, m. Ab^m Houseman; Willemtje Albertse, m.·
Jacobus Bougaert; Stephen Albertse of Hackensack, m. Lidia
de Maree; Maratie or Magtie Albertse, bp. Oct. 11, 1686, m.
Hendrick Bertholf; Geertruyd Albertse; and Rachel Albertse,
bp. Apl. 21, 1690, m. Jan Hendrickse Hoppe—all of N. J.

Albert 3^d (s. of Albert Albertse Junr and Hendrikje), m.
1st, ——; m. 2^d, Sept. 1705 Maratie de Graves wid. of Andries
Tiebout. Will da. Feb. 16, 1707-8; pro. Sept. 9, 1709; rec.
p. 273, Lib. 9, N. Y. surr. off. Issue:—Geertruy, b. 1694, m.
Hendrick Hendrickse Banta of N. J.; Alburtus, b. 1695, m.
Anna Maria Ackerman of Hackensack; Johannes of Hackensack, b. 1700, m. Geesje R. Westervelt; Annell; Steven; Gerbrecht; Willemtje; Marretje; and Rachel.

Albert (Janse) of Fld^t, bp. Apl. 13, 1684; m. Oct. 17, 1708,
Aaltje Voorhees. Will da. Apl. 11, 1721; pro. Dec. 18, 1721;
rec. p. 273, Lib. 9, N. Y. surr. off. Issue:—John of Fld^t, m.
Nelly Duryee; Gerret; Ann, (sup.) m. Cornelius Bulsen; Willemtje, m. Joost Duryee; and Sarah.

Jan Albertse of Fld^t, m. 1st, July 1, 1683, Annetje Roelofse
Schenck; m. 2^d, June 6, 1691, Margrietje Van Syschellen or
Sichlen of Fld^t; (sup.) d. in 1705. Took the oath of allegiance in Fld^t in 1687 as a native, where he owned and occupied the paternal farm, of which place his name appears on the
ass. roll of 1683, and cen. of 1698; was lieut. of militia in 1691,
and capt. in 1700. In 1690 he and others obtained a tract of land
near Duck Creek at St. Jones's on the Delaware, as per p. 666
of Vol. XII. of Doc. of Col. His. Issue:—Roelof of Fld^t; Albert of Fld^t, bp. Apl. 13, 1684, at Fld^t; and Aucke. Signed
his name "*Jan Albertsen Ter Hunen*" and "*Jan ter hunen.*"

John (s. of Albert and Aaltje) of Fld^t, inherited his father's
farm; m. Nelly Duryee. No further trace.

Roelof (Janse) of Fld^t, m. May 5, 1706, Maryke or Marretje
Gerretse dau. of Gerret Pieterse Wyckoff. Elder in the D. ch.
of Fld^t in 1748. Issue:—Gerret, (sup.) m. Alice dau. of Steven
Coerte Voorhees; Albert of G^d, m. Antie or Annatie Van
Dyck, and was the father of the late Ab^m and John Terhune;
Willemtje; Marya; Hyntie; Aeltie; and Margrietje, (sup.) m.
Jacobus Van Dyck. Signed his name "*Roelof Terhune.*"

TERNEUR, DANIEL. His land referred to in the patent of
Gov. Petrus Stuyvesant to Cornelis Janse Berrien of 26 mor-
gens in Fl^h, da. Mar. 12, 1661, on p. 25 of Lib. A of Fl^h rec.
Joined the D. ch. of N. Y. in 1672. A Daniel Terneur m. Ja-
comina —— and had children, Maria, bp. Mar. 4, 1654, and
Marretje, bp. Sept. 1, 1661, in N. A.

TERRAGON, PETER, and 5 or 6 other Frenchmen of Br^n were

refused leave Mar. 29, 1661, during the Indian troubles, to remain and reside on their farms, as per p. 222 of Cal. of Dutch His. Man.

TERRIN, THOMAS, mem. of R. D. ch. of Br^n in 1663.

TEUNISE, TEUNISZ, THEUNISE, or TUNISE, AERT, see Middagh.

Aert, on list of residents of the Wallabout who in 1657 were assessed for Do. Polhemius's salary. This is possibly Aert Anthonize or Teunize Middagh.

Adriaen, Cornelis, and *Gysbert,* see Bogaert.

Anthony, Aert, Hendrick, Jan, and *Wouter,* see Van Pelt.

Claes, m. Feb. 12, 1692, Anna or Annetje wid. of John Sprung of Bu^k.

Claes, from Appledoorn or Appeltern in Gelderland, m. Dec. 26, 1662, Metje Bastiaens of Br^n. A Claes Teunisen made his mark to documents in 1662.

Claes, see Cleer.

Cornelis and Harmtje Dircks of Br^n ferry, mem. of Br^n R. D. ch. in 1677.

Cornelis, of N. A. in 1645. July 3, 1647, he bought of Willem Gerretse (Van Cowenhoven) 32 morgens on the N. end of the plains in Fl'd^s. Jan. 1, 1657, he obtained a patent for 25 morgens in Fl'd^s. There was a Cornelis Teunisen who had children bp. in N. A. in 1647 and '50. Signed his name "*Cornelse Teunyse.*"

Denyse, Jaques, Jan, Joris, and *Teunis,* see Denyse.

Dirck, owned land in Br^n in 1660, as per Col. Man., and in 1680 his name appears on the Stoothoff books.

Dirck (Noorman) of Fl^h, m. Adriaenje Walich, a wid. Was accused of crime, as per p. 181 of Cal. of Dutch Man.

Dirck, see Woertman.

Gysbert, made his mark to documents in Fl^h in 1670. A Gysbert Teunisen of Katskill in 1657.

Hans, Johannes, Lucas, and *Maurits,* see Coevert.

Hans and Marretje Teunis of Bu^k, mem. of Br^n R. D. ch. in 1677.

Hendrick, on ass. roll of N. U. of 1663.

Henricus of Br^n in 1663, with others, petitioned for salt-meadows and leave to found a village. Resided at Bedford, and mem. of R. D. ch. of Br^n in 1677.

Jacob, employed by Anthony Jansen from Salee on his bouwery in N. U. and G^d, and in 1656 commenced a suit against him for wages.

Jan, on list of catechumens of Br^n ch. in 1662, and on ass. roll of Br^n of 1683.

Jan, from Leerdam, on the river Linge, in South Holland,· resided in Fl^h May 9, 1661, as per Col. Man.

Jan, carpenter, m. Catharine Cronensburgh. Dec. 12, 1660, he sold to Gerret Lubbertse his plantation in Fl^h, lying on the W. side of the road, containing 27 morgens, with plain and meadow land thereto appertaining, as per p. 41 of Lib. B of Fl^h rec. Aug. 22, 1679, his w. bought of Rutgert Albertse his house and orchard in Fl^h for 200 gl., as per p. 54 of Lib. AA of Fl^h rec. Signed his name "*Jan Teunesse.*"

Jan, see Van Dyckhuys.

John, brought a suit against John Whitlock Oct. 2, 1671, at the sessions in G^d for taking away his canoe, as per G^d rec.

John, and Peter Hendricksen, carpenters, built a windmill in 1684 for Michiel Hainelle in Br^n, as per p. 24 of Lib. 1 of Con.

Rebecca of N. U., m. Feb. 27, 1689, at N. Y., Abraham de La Montagnie of Haerlem. At date of marriage she resided at Haerlem and he at "Bloemdale," as per N. Y. D. ch. rec.

Theymese Hendrick, on ass. roll of Br^n of 1675.

THOMAS, ARMAH (alias Smith), of the Manhattans, bought Sept. 4, 1654, of George Jewell his plantation and buildings in G^d for 360 gl., as per G^d rec.

Gilbert, of Bu^k, as per p. 332 of Vol. II. of Stiles's Br^n.

Gysbert, on a deed of the freeholders of Br^n of Jan. 2, 1696-7, to Adriaen Bennet to perfect the title of his Gowanus lands.

John, bought Oct. 26, 1649, of Richard Stoute of G^d his crop of tobacco for 210 gl. Jan. 27, 1650, he agreed with the inhabitants of G^d to attend to their cows and calves as herder for 8 months for 300 gl. June 27, 1650, a plantation-lot was assigned to him in said town. Dec. 6, 1657, he bought of John Peeters plantation-lot No. 4 in G^d, which he sold Sept. 2, 1664, to Wm Lawrence—all as per G^d rec. Made his mark to documents.

THOMASSEN, TOMASSEN, or TOMASE, AERT, owned land in Fl^h in 1655, as per O'Callaghan's Man. Trans. of Col. Man.

Claes or *Nicholas, Hendrick, Isaac,* and *Tjerck,* see Van Dycks.

William, sold Jan. 24, 1643, to Cornelis Dircksen (Hoogland) his farm of about 17 morgens at Br^n ferry for 2300 gl. in cash, as per Vol. II., p. 144, of Col. Man.

THORNE, WILLIAM, one of the first settlers of G^d in 1646, and granted a plantation-lot, as per town rec. This is probably the William Thorne who with other Englishmen (as per p. 68 of Vol. 2 of Thompson's L. I.) arrived from Vlissengen in the Netherlands at N. A., and finally located at Flushing, where there was a Joseph Thorn in 1680.

THUL, PIETER, (see Tul,) mem. of Fl[h] ch. in 1677.

THYSZ or MATTHYSZ, ANTHONY, ADRIAEN, GYSBERT, HEN-DRICK, JACOB, JAN, and PETER, see Van Pelt.
   Barend, m. Magdalena Janse. Issue:—Matthyas, bp. July 14, 1678, in N. U.; and Johannes, bp. Jan. 27, 1680, in N. U.
   Derick (Tyssen), on ass. roll of Br[n] of 1693 and cen. of 1698. He m. Annetje ——, and had issue:—Thys, bp. Mar. 28, 1699, in Br[n]. Made his mark to documents.
   Pieter of N. U., m. Barbara Jones. On Gov. Dongan's patent of N. U. of 1686. Owned 30 morgens on the E. side of the road from N. U. to Fl[h], between the lands of Gerret Cornelise Van Duyn and those of Ab[m] Willemse Van Westervelt, prior to 1700, as per p. 236 of Lib. 2 of Con. Issue:—Catryn Pieterse, bp. Mar. 25, 1699, in Br[n]. Made his mark "P M" to documents. There was a Pieter Thysz in Monmouth Co., N. J., in 1712, and there is a probability of this Pieter Thysz being the same person as Pieter Thysz Van Pelt.

TIBOUT, JAN, m. 1st *Sarah Van der Vlucht* or *Ulmst;* m. 2[d], Nov. 6, 1687, at Haerlem, *Hester Dubois* wid. of Claude Lemaistre, both residents of Haerlem, as per N. Y. D. ch. rec. Was schoolmaster of Fl[h] and precentor of the ch. from 1681 to '82, as per p. 109 of Strong's Fl[h]. In Jan. 1669 (as per p. 157 of Lib. D. of Fl[h] rec.) he appears to have been in possession of the school-lot and premises of that town, for on that date he complained to the magistrates of Abram Joorise (Brinckerhoff) encroaching on the premises. There being an agreement entered into Dec. 25, 1666, N. S., with a schoolmaster and precentor for Fl[h] (but no name given), as per p. 87 of said Lib. D, it appears probable that this agreement was made with Tiebout, and that he commenced his services at Christmas 1666, continuing them until about Nov. 1, 1670, O. S., when Jacob Joosten commenced, and was succeeded by Jan Gerretse Van Marcken, who was discharged Mar. 2, 1681. Nov. 4, 1681, Jan Tiebout or "Thiebald" appears to have been again employed, continuing until July 30, 1682, when he was discharged, and removed to N. Y. There was a Jan Tibout on the Delaware in 1656, and a Jan Tiebout, court-messenger in Bergen, N. J., in 1661, as per p. 85 of Winfield's Hudson Co., who was probably this John. In Jan. 1660 he and his w. "Sarah Van der Ulmst" joined the R. D. ch. of N. A., and are entered on the ch. rec. as removed to "Midwout." Issue, bp. in N. A. and N. Y.:—Dirck, bp. May 4, 1661, d. young; Theunis, bp. Sept.

30, 1663, m. Apl. 11, 1690, Maryhen Vandewater; Jacomyntie, bp. June 4, 1666, m. Apl. 15, 1685, at Haerlem, Reyer Michilszen from Schoonderwoerd in South Holland; (sup.) Jannetje, m. in 1692 Hendrick Oblinus; Magdalena, bp. Feb. 20, 1674, d. young; Dirck, bp. Mar. 10, 1675; Magdaleentje, bp. May 3, 1676; Henricus, bp. Sept. 19, 1677; and Jacobus, bp. May 22, 1681. Tunis Tiebout (a grandson of Jan Tibout), b. Jan. 18, 1722, O. S., d. Apl. 13, 1823, m. Garetta dau. of Nicholas Vechte of Gowanus, whose dau. Mary m. 1ˢᵗ Tunis Johnson and 2ᵈ Theodorus Polhemus. Signed his name "*Jan Tibout.*"

TIERCKSEN or TERCKSE, THOMAS, emigrated in 1652; m. *Engeltie* ——. In 1677 he bought of Jan Gysbertse Van Meteren 24 morgens in·N. U., where he appears to have settled. Oct. 7, 1679, he sold to Anthoni dén Ryck wood-lot No. 4 in N. U., as per p. 64 of Lib. AA of Flʰ rec. On patent of N. U. of 1686, took the oath of allegianee there in 1687, and a resident in 1707. Issue:—Tyerk; Pieter; Hendrick; and Teuntje. Signed his name "*Tomas Tereckse.*"

TIETUS, ARAYS. His name appears on the Flʰ rec. in· 1693, and was probably a s. of Tietus Syrachs De Vries. Signed his name "*Arays Tietus.*"

TILJE or LE TELIER, JAN, Frenchman. Among the first settlers of Buᵏ in 1661, and a mag. in 1661 and '62, as per Prime's L. I. and p. 143 of Cal. of Dutch Man. Appointed ensign of militia in 1663.

TILTON, JOHN, said to have come over with Lady Mody, was among the early settlers of Gᵈ in 1646, in which year he was granted plantation-lot No. 18, as per town rec. He m. *Mary* ——, who d. May 23, 1683, at Gᵈ, and he d. in 1688. Town-clerk in 1650, '51, '52, '53, mag. in 1674, and on ass. roll of 1683. Nov. 1, 1665, as per town rec., he bought of Gov. Baxter plantation-lot No. 19, formerly of Thoˢ Greedy; also "a piece of land purchased of Robert Penyer (Pennoyer) as also further confirmed unto me by Monnʳ Pieter Stuyvesant late Governor," etc., containing 75 Dutch morgens, "and of ye wᶜʰ James Hubbard & my selfe did bestow on ye town of Gravesend & was hired yearly as by these Records bearing date ye 7th December 1653. And the moyitie of ye other third pt. I doe now grant sell & make over by these presents unto ye said John Tilton," etc. Mar. 8, 1691-2, he sold to Coert Stevense (Voorhees) of Fldˢ all his remaining real-estate in Gᵈ for £295, reserving the use of the same for 12 months unless he sooner removed from the town, as per G^d rec. This purchase is the commencement of the numerous ownerships of land of the Voorhees family in G^d. In his will of Jan. 15, 1687, he devises lands in G^d for a burial-ground "for all persons in ye Everlasting truthe of ye gospel as occasion surves for ever to have and to hold, and make use of to bury their dead there," which probably covers at least a part of the present burial-ground in the village of G^d, the only one known to have been used in said town by Europeans since its first settlement. By said will he had issue:—John; Peter; Thomas; Sarah, who m. John Pantter or Painter; Abagail, m. Rodger Scott; Ester, m. May 21, 1663, at Oyster Bay, Samuel Speier; and Mary or Maria, m. Henry Boman. By p. 184 of Vol. III. of the Genealogical Record he had issue:—John, b. June 4, 1640; Peter, b. Jan. 1642; Sarah, b. May 4, 1644; Abagail, b. 1650; Thomas, b. Mar. 1, 1652; and Mary, b. June 1654. His children settled in Monmouth Co., N. J., where their descendants are to be found. Signed his name "*John Tilton Sen*."

John Junr, b. June 4, 1640; m. 1st, Oct. 10, 1670, at Oyster Bay, Mary Coats; m. 2^d, May 12, 1674, at Flushing, Rebekkah Terry. Resided in G^d. Issue, as per p. 187 of Vol. III. of Genealogical Record:—John, b. Apl. 14, 1675; Abraham, b. Jan. 14, 1676; Samuel, b. Mar. 1, 1678; Sarah, b. Nov. 14, 1680; Daniel, b. Dec. 27, 1682; Thomas, b. Dec. 20, 1684; Mary, b. Oct. 21, 1686; and Hester, b. Apl. 2, 1689. Signed his name "*John Tilton Jun*" in 1681.

Joseph, of G^d in 1649, as per Thompson's L. I. He may have been a brother of John Tilton Senr.

Peter (s. of John), b. Jan. 1642, a devisee in Thomas Grady's will, and a justice of the peace for Shrewsbury, N. J., in 1683, as per p. 42 of Rec. of Gov. and Council of E. N. J.

Thomas of G^d (s. of John), b. Mar. 1, 1652. Signed his name "*Thomas Tilton*" as a witness to a deed in 1678, as per G^d rec.

TIMONSZ, HENDRICK, of Bedford, a mem. of R. D. ch. of Br^n in 1677. A "Hendrick Tymens" of Bu^k paid Oct. 28, 1666, a marriage-fee to Fl^h ch.

TINUS, JOST, of the Manhattans, bought Aug. 28, 1652, of Richard Gibbins his plantation and buildings in G^d for 400 gl., as per G^d rec.

TITUS, FRANCIS, a s. of Titus Sirach De Vries, m. 1st *Antie Fonteyn* wid. of Maurits Coevert; m. 2^d *Elizabeth* ——;

d. about 1760. Owned the farm in Bu^k patented Aug. 14, 1664, to Paulus Richards. Issue:—Francis; John; Charles; Titus; Antie; Helen; Elizabeth; Aentje; Jannetje; and Christina, m. Ab^m Polhemus.

Syrach (s. of Titus Sirach), bp. Dec. 28, 1679, in Br^n, m. Aeltje —— and settled in Newtown.

Teunis (s. of Titus Sirach). May 14, 1695, he and his mother Jannetje conveyed to Johannes Van Ekelen a piece of land in Fl^h located on the N. of land of Leffert Pieterse, and on the E. of the highway, cong. about 5 morgens. In 1703 he appears to have resided in Newtown, and removed from thence to Mansfield, N. J. See Lib. A of Fl^h rec. and p. 133 of Riker's Newtown. Signed his name "*Teunis Titus.*"

TOBIASSEN, TEUNIS, was a dealer in whalebone in 1678, as per Stoothoff papers; of Fl^h in 1685, where he took the oath of allegiance in 1687, and about this date he and Pieter Pieterse Staats sold to Leffert Pieterse 80 A. of woodland, as per p. 183 of Lib. C of Fl^h rec. Made his mark to documents.

TOLIER, JAN JAKOBSEN, from "Keruer in Walslant," m. Aug. 25, 1677, in Br^n, *Mathaleen Louwrens* of South River.

TOMASSE or TOMASSEN, see Van Dyck.

Aert, owned land in Fl^h in 1655, as per the description in deed of Jan de Jongh to Jan Hendricksen on p. 366 of Vol. II. of O'Callaghan's Man. Trans. of Col. Man. Have been unable to decide whether this is Aert Teunissen of the Wallabout or Aert Teunissen Middagh.

William, bought Jan. 20, 1643, of Cornelis Dircksen (Hoogland) a house and 16 or 17 morgens of land with the ferry at Br^n, as per p. 21 of Cal. of Dutch Man.

TONNEMAN, PIETER, appointed schout (sheriff) and clerk of Br^n district Jan. 25, 1656, and held the position until 1660, when he was appointed schout of N. A. Was a member of the Council in 1657, '58, and '59. (See pp. 150, 174, and 292 of Cal. of Dutch Man.) July 2, 1659, he obtained a patent for a double building-plot on the N. side of the road in Fl^h, as per p. 4 of Lib. B of Fl^h rec. In 1664 he took the oath of allegiance to the English in N. Y., and in Oct. of that year sailed for Holland.

TOURNEURS, MAGDALEENTJE, from ("Midwout") Fl^h, m. June 25, 1673, in N. A., Jan Dyckman from Benthem.

20

TRAPHAGEN, WILLEM JANSEN, a Frenchman from Lemgo, m. 1st *Justje Claes Groenvis ;* m. 2d, June 1, 1658, in N. A., *Aeltje Dirck* from Steenwyck in Overyssel; and m. 3d, Jan. 15, 1661, *Joosje Willems* wid. of Jan Verkinderen. Mar. 7, 1660, he moved with his family into the first house erected near the Pond in Buk, and at the same time Knoert Mourisen came to dwell there, as per Buk town rec. May 12, 1664, he was sentenced to banishment for abusing the magistrates of the town, as per p. 265 of Cal. of Dutch Man. Oct. 2, 1676, Gov. Andros conveyed to him 20 A. at Esopus (Kingston), as per p. 90 of Vol. I. of Land Papers. Issue:—Rebecca, bp. June 19, 1662, in Brn; and probably other children. There are families of Traphagens residing in Bergen, N. J., and also on the Raritan, where a Hendrick resided in 1713. Signed his name *"Wilmen Jansen Traphagen."*

TRIMBEL, PETER JANSEN, of Norman's Kil, Buk, May 25, 1662, on which date he obtained permission to make a concentration or hamlet of 4 families on his land, as per p. 237 of Cal. of Dutch Man.

TUL, PIETER PIETERSE, emigrated in 1657; was a weaver and trader in oil and whalebone in 1678, as per Stoothoff's books; mem. of Fldª ch. in 1677; on ass. roll of said town of 1683, where he took the oath of allegiance in 1687; and a pauper in said town in 1690.

TUNISSEN, see Teunissen.

TURCK, SYMON, plaintiff in a suit against Pieter Jansen Feb. 17, 1662, as per Lib. B of Flh rec.

TYMENS, HENDRICK, of Buk, paid Oct. 28, 1666, 5 gl. 12 st. as a marriage-fee to Flh R. D. ch., as per Flh book of minutes of town meetings, etc.

TYN, JOHANNES, had a s. Jan bp. May 28, 1699, in Brn.

TYSSE, JAN, among the soldiers sent from Kings Co. to Albany in 1689, as per p. 216 of Vol. II. of Doc. His. of N. Y.

TYSSEN, see Van Pelt.

UNDERHILL, JOHN, d. Sept. 21, 1672. Jan. 16, 1642, leased

for 2 years of Andrus Hudden "his present house and plantation situated on the Flatland and Kiskachqueren" for the annual rent of 500 lbs. well-cured tobacco, as per O'Callaghan's Man. Trans. of Dutch Col. Man. May 14, 1646, he obtained a patent for Meutelaer's or Bergen's I. of 50 morgens in Fld[s], as per p. 247 of Bergen Genealogy. In 1648 he was schout of Flushing, and 1653 rebelled against the Dutch Government. Signed his name "*John Under-hill.*"

URIN, BARN, schepen of G[d] in 1673, as per p. 577 of Vol. II. of Doc. of Col. His. This name may be intended for Richard Uzell.

USIELLE, see Uzielle.

UYTHUYSEN, CLAES SIMONS, of the ferry. On a deed in 1695 of Joris Jacobs, conveying for £113 a lot between the ferry and the village of Br[n], as per p. 59 of Lib. 2 of Con.
Jan Simons of the ferry, on a deed in 1695, as per p. 59 of Lib. 2 of Con.

UZELL or USILL, RICHARD, among the first settlers of G[d] in 1646, in which year he was allotted a plantation-lot in said locality, as per G[d] rec. Jan. 10, 1654, he sold to Johannes Van Beek plantation-lot No. 30 in G[d], probably the premises allotted to him in 1646. Made his mark "R" to documents.

UZIELLE, UZIE, or USIELLE, PIETER, of Maynhem, m. Apl. 6, 1686, in N. Y., *Cornelia Damen* of Fl[h], a resident of the Walabocht, and he of S. I. at date of marriage. On ass. roll of Bu[k] of 1693 and cen. of 1698. Feb. 12, 1693-4, he sold to Pieter Willemse of Fl[h] 2 lots of land in Bu[k], as per p. 193 of Lib. A of Fl[h] rec. He appears to have finally settled in Esopus (Kingston). Issue:—Jan, bp. Sept. 28, 1688; Sophia, bp. May 3, 1691, m. Feb. 24, 1712, Storm Bradt; Cornelia, bp. Apl. 2, 1693, m. Oct. 15, 1714, Johannes Becker of Albany; Helena, bp. Mar. 27, 1696, m. Nov. 9, 1716, Willem Hooghteling; Peter, bp. Feb. 5, 1699, m. June 4, 1724, Anna Ackerson; Lysbet, bp. May 1, 1701; David, bp. Feb. 1, 1708, m. Engeltie Vroman; and Maria, m. Jonar Larua (Le Roy)—all as per the Rev. R. Randell Hoes of New Rochelle, and the bp. mainly in Kingston. Signed his name "*Pieter Uzielle.*"

VAN AARNHEM, HENDRICK, probably from Arnhem in

Gelderland, owned land in Br^n, as per an Indian deed of May 14, 1670. See p. 16 of Furman's Notes of Br^n. Families of this name reside in the vicinity of Albany.

VAN AELOKMAN, CORNELIS JANSEN, bought Mar. 1, 1668, of Jan Gouwenberg a farm of 23 morgens on the W. side of the road in Fl^h, with plain and meadow lands, as per p. 33 of Lib. C of Fl^b rec.

VAN AELTEMAER or AELOKMAER, CORNELIS JANSEN, allotted a lot on the division, Aug. 6, 1668, of the Fl^h salt-meadows at Canarisie, as per Fl^h town rec.

VAN AMACK, THEUNIS JANSE, see Amack.

VAN AMERSFOORT, JAN HARMENSEN, or from Amersfoort in Utrecht in the Netherlands, emigrated in 1658, and took the oath of allegiance in Fl^h in 1687.

VAN AMSTERDAM, JAN PIETERSEN, probably intended for Jan Pietersen from Amsterdam in the Netherlands, obtained Mar. 26, 1647, a patent for 4 morgens in Bu^k between land of Roger Lambertsen and that of Claes Carstensen or Claes de Noorman.

VAN ARSDALEN, CORNELIS SIMONSE, of Fld^s, where he took the oath of allegiance in 1687 as a native; m. 1st *Tjelletje Reiniers Wizzelpenning;* m. 2^d, Mar. 16, 1687, *Aeltje Willemse Kouwenhoven* of Fld^s; m. 3^d, May 2, 1691, *Mary* or *Marretje Dirckse.* May 7, 1700, he bought of his father a farm in G^d, as per G^d rec. Will dа. Apl. 25, 1738; pro. Apl. 19, 1745; rec. p. 380, Lib. 15, N. Y. surr. off. Issue:—Dirck; John; Symon of Pa., b. Aug. 16, 1697; Philip, m. Jannetje dau. of Hendrick Van Dyck; Abraham; Jacobus, (sup.) b. 1676, m. Alida dau. of Jacob Hoogland of N. J.; Jannetje, m. Dirk Barkeloo of Freehold, N. J.; Aeltje, m. Jeronemus Rapalje; Peternella; and Maria. Signed his name "*Cornelis Symens.*"

John or *Jan Simonse* of Fld^s, m. 1st, Oct. 22, 1719, Jannetje Dorlant of New Jamaica; m. 2^d Lammetje dau. of Christoffel Probasko; m. 3^d, Apl. 3, 1743, Sarah Van Voorhees; (sup.) m. 4th, Apl. 2, 1751, Libertje Newberrie, a wid., of Fl^h. May 10, 1700, he bought of his brother Cornelis the farm in G^d Cornelis bought of his father. Issue:— Christopher of N. J.; and John. Signed his name "*Jan Van Aersdalen.*"

Symon Janse, emigrated in 1656, settled in Fld⁸, and m. Pieterje Claesen Wyckoff. Mag. of Fld⁸ in 1661 and '86; mem. of Flᵇ ch. in 1677; deacon in 1686; took the oath of allegiance there in 1687; and on cen. of 1698. Issue:— Geertje Simonse, m. Cornelis Pieterse Wyckoff; Cornelis Simonse of Fld⁸; Jannetje Simonse, m. 1ˢᵗ John ——, m. 2ᵈ, Apl. 16, 1689, Gysbert Teunisse Bogaert; John Simonse of Fld⁸; (sup.) Symon Symonse of N. J.; (sup.) Marretje Simonse, m. Jan Barendsz; and Matty Simonse, m. Evert Jansen Van Marklen of Flᵇ. Signed his name "*Symon Jansen Van Arsdalen.*"

Symon (s. of Cornelis), b. Aug. 16, 1697; m. Oct. 30, 1716, Yannetje Romeyn. Left Fld⁸ and settled in Bucks Co., Pa., where he was an elder in the R. D. ch. Issue:—John, b. June 27, 1718, m. Elizabeth Kroesen; Lammetje, b. Aug. 11, 1720; Stoffel, b. Apl. 15, 1722, m. Elizabeth Kroesen; Symon, b. Apl. 18, 1726, m. Elsie Kroesen; Margaret, b. Jan. 12, 1729, m. Derrick Kroesen; Jacobus, b. Jan. 25, 1732; Nicholas, b. July 14, 1736; and Peter, b. Mar. 2, 1739—all of Pa.

VAN AS, EVERT DIRX, or from As or Asch in Gelderland. Feb. 10, 1661, he and others requested permission to build a block-house in the vicinity of the Wallabout for their defence, as per p. 114 of Vol. 1 of Stiles's Brⁿ. He owned land in Bedford in 1689, as per p. 148 of Lib. 1 of Con., which was probably the proposed locality of the block-house.

VAN BAES, CLAES MELLES, bought Aug. 10, 1664, of Jan Cornelise Damen 26 morgens on the W. side of the road in Flᵇ, with plain and meadow land, as per p. 7 of Lib. D of Flᵇ rec. Also bought Nov. 19, 1677, of Cornelis Hendricx Van Eens 27 morgens on the W. side of the road in Flᵇ, as per p. 25 of Lib. C of Flᵇ rec. Had a child buried in Flᵇ ch. Feb. 20, 1666. Signed his name "*Claes Melles Van Baes.*"

VAN BARKELOO, see Barkelo.

VAN BEECK, JOHANNES, probably from Beek in Gelderland. Desiring in Feb. 1654 to marry *Maria Verleth* in Gᵈ, and being opposed by Gov. Stuyvesant, he and Maria ran off to New England and were married at Greenwich, Conn. He d. prior to Mar. 1656. Jan 10, 1654, he bought of Richard Usill plantation-lot No. 30 in Gᵈ, as per town rec. After his death his wid. m. Wᵐ Teller of Albany. Issue:— Judith. Signed his name "*Johannes Van Beeck.*"

Van Blarken, Johannes Jansen, m. June 11, 1693, at Fl[h], *Mattye Symonsen* of Br[n].

Van Blydenstein, Willem Pietersz, of Fl[h], m. Mar. 20, 1684, *Styntje Hendricks.* Removed to Hempstead.
Harmen Pietersz, m. July 20, 1682, Cornelia Cornelise Van Oosten of Fl[h].

Van Boerum, see Boerum.

Van Borcum, Evert Duyckingh, see Duycking.

Van Borsum, Borssum, or Bossum, Cornelis, of Amsterdam (brother of Egbert), m. Sept. 1, 1668, in N. Y., *Sara Roelofs* wid. of Hans Kierstede, residing at Br[n] ferry at the date of his m.; (sup.) he also m. *Geertje Gysbertse.* Allotted Aug. 6, 1668, a meadow-lot on the Fl[h] meadows at Canarisie, as per Fl[h] town rec. July 5, 1654, he and Poulus Richard bought a farm in Fl[h] of Machtelt Megapolensis, as per p. 28 of Lib. A of Fl[h] rec. A Saartie or Sara Van Borsum was a celebrated Indian interpreter.
Egbert from Amsterdam (brother of Cornelis), skipper of the ship Prince William in 1664, m. Anneken Hendricks; obtained July 15, 1654, a patent for 2 lots at Br[n] ferry; and Mar. 12, 1666, a patent for a lot at the ferry. Leased the ferry June 1, 1654, and in 1657 was assessed among the residents of Br[n] located at the ferry 10 gl. towards the salary of Do. Polhemius. Prior to 1660 he was a mem. of the R. D. ch. of N. A., and in 1664 took the oath of allegiance to the English in N. Y. In 1670 he appears to have resided in Fld[s]. Issue:—(sup.) Hermanus, bp. Sept. 7, 1640; Cornelis, bp. Oct. 5, 1642; Hendrick, bp. Apl. 26, 1648; Tymon, bp. Sept. 17, 1651; Janneken, bp. Nov. 23, 1653; and Annetje, bp. Apl. 30, 1656—all bp. in N. A. Made his mark to documents in 1639.

Van Bosch, Jan Wouterse, emigrated in 1659; probably from Bosch—Capelle in Zeeland, and took the oath of allegiance in Fl[h] in 1687, where he appears to have resided.

Van Breuckelen, Martin Jansen, or from Br[n], was a mag. of Amersfoort or Fld[s] in 1656, '57, and '58.

Van Brevoort, see Brevort.

Van Brunt, Adriaen (s. of Cor[s] Rutgersz), m. *Jannetje*

Hendricks and resided in N. U. Issue:—Jannetje, b. Oct. 3, 1726, m. her cousin Albert Van Brunt; and Cornelius, living and an adult in 1650, but no further trace. Signed his name "*Adriaen Van Brunt.*"

Cornelis Rutgersz of N. U., farmer; m. Nov. 23, 1685, Tryntje dau. of Adriaen Willemse Bennet; d. about 1748. Apl. 18, 1718, for £365 he bought of James Hubbard of Monmouth Co., N. J., the Pennoyer patent in G[d]. From 1698 to 1717 he was a mem. of the N. Y. Colonial Assembly. He was a large landholder in N. U., assessed for 144 A. in 1706, residing in the village in a house he bought in 1714 of Johannes Swart, taking the oath of allegiance there in 1687. This house is probably the one lately sold by the heirs of Rutgert A. Van Brunt to T. G. Bergen, and is yet in good condition. Issue:—Rutgert of N. U.; Nicholas of N. J.; William; Adriaen of N. U.; Angenietje, bp. June 30, 1689; Maria or Marrytie, bp. Dec. 10, 1694, m. James Spencer of N. Y.; Tryntje, m. 1st Jacob Van Dyck of S. I., m. 2[d] Louis Dubois of S. I.; Gretien or Margaret, m. Thomas Pollock of N. U.; and Neeltie, m. Derick Pieters or Pietersen. Signed his name "*Cornelis Van Brunt.*"

Joost Rutgersz of N. U., farmer; m. 1st —— ——, who was buried in Fld[s] about 1686; m. 2[d], Apl. 16, 1687, Altie dau. of Steven Coerte Van Voorhees; d. about 1746. Held the office of supervisor nearly if not all the time from 1703 to 1743 inclusive, except in 1721, in which year Peter Cortelyou was elected. Also that of ensign, capt., lieut.-col., and col. of militia. He was a large landholder, assessed for 120 A. in 1706, and took the oath of allegiance in 1687 as a native. Issue:—Rutgert; and (sup.) Altie, m. Joseph Ditmars of Fl[h]. Signed his name "*Joost Rutgerse Van Brunt.*"

Nicholas Rutgersz, farmer, of N. U., m. Aug. 19, 1683, Helena dau. of Jacques Cortelyou of N. U.; d. about 1684, his father surviving him. Helena his w. m. 2[d] Deonyse Teunisse (Denyse), and m. 3[d] Hendrick Hendricksen. Issue:— Nicholas or Claes, bp. Aug. 31, 1684.

Nicholas or *Claes* (s. of Nicholas Rutgersz of N. U.), bp. Aug. 31, 1684; m. Maria or Mayken dau. of Roeloffe Janse Verkerk; d. about Mar. 1713-14. His w. after his death m. 2[d] Samuel Gronendyck. Was assessed in 1706 for 80 A. Will da. Feb. 18, 1713-14, and pro. Mar. 22, 1713-14; rec. on p. 264 of Lib. 8, N. Y. surr. off. Issue:—Nicholas, (sup.) d. young; Roelof; and Jaques, (sup.) d. young. Signed his name "*Nicholas Van Brunt.*"

Nicholas (s. of Cornelis Rutgersz), m. Geesje, Geertje or Geassey (sup.) dau. of Hendrick Hendrickse of the Narrows, N. U., by his first w. He removed to Monmouth Co.,

N. J., as early as 1731, for in that year he and Geertje Hendricksen his w. were members of the Freehold R. D. ch., as per p. 86 of the Marlboro Brick Ch. Memorial. He finally settled on a tract of 600 A. at Tinton Falls near Red Bank, N. J., which he bought of Robert Hunter Morris by conveyances of May 1, 1750, and May 21, 1752, for £2770. Will da. Apl. 12, 1760; pro. Feb. 1, 1782; rec. p. 101, Lib. 24, off. of Sec. of State N. J. Issue:—Hendrick, m. Nelly or Neeltje Schenck; Nicholas; Cornelius, m. (sup.) Ellen ——; Catharine; Jannetje; Anne, m. Cornelius Wynantze; Engeltie, bp. Apl. 28, 1732, at Freehold; Agnes or Angenietje, bp. Feb. 9, 1734-5, at Freehold, m. Albert Schenck of Monmouth Co.; and Geesie, bp. Oct. 23, 1737, at Freehold. Signed his name "*Nicolaes Van Brunt.*"

Rutger Joesten, the common ancestor of the family, emigrated from the Netherlands in 1653, and was one of the first settlers in N. U. in 1657. He m. 1st Tryntje Claes or Claesen wid. of Stoffel Harmensen; m. 2d Gretien ——; d. prior to 1713 intestate, leaving his grandson Nicholas, s. of Nicholas Rutgersz, his heir at law. Was a mag. of N. U. in 1661, from 1678 to '81, and in 1685; on Dongan's patent of 1686; took the oath of allegiance in 1687; and was assessed in 1693 for 100 A. of land. Jan. 18, 1662, he obtained a patent for a double lot of 48 morgens in N. U.; also was allotted two half-lots by the "fontein" (Yellow Hoek or Bay Ridge) numbered 11 and 12, "stretching on the one side of the lot of Arie Willemse (Bennet), on the other of that of Luykes Mayers," which premises are at present (1880) owned and occupied by Rulaf and Daniel Van Brunt, his descendants. He also owned other large plots in N. U. Mar. 29, 1674, Rutger Joesten bought at public auction of Nicholas Bayard, curator or trustee of Nicasius De Sille, and Tryntje Croegers his w., De Sille's house and grounds in the village (the old stone house with a tile roof east of the church, torn down in 1850 by Barent Wyckoff, its last occupant), with other premises. Issue:—Nicholas Rutgersz; Cornelis Rutgersz; and Joost Rutgersz. Signed his name "*Rutger Joesten.*"

Rutgert (s. of Cornelis Rutgersz) of N. U., farmer, m. Nov. 3, 1714, Elizabeth dau. of Albert Coerten Van Voorhies of Fld*; d. Apl. 7, 1760. Was deacon in the R. D. ch. of N. U. from 1717 to 1723, and elder from 1726 to 1729; in 1722 capt. and in 1740 col. of militia. In addition to large tracts in N. U. he owned the Pennoyer patent in G*, being assessed in 1716 for 104 A. and in 1734-5 for 303 A. in N. U. Will da. Apl. 4, 1760; pro. May 9, 1760; rec. p. 67, Lib. 22, N. Y. surr. off. He devised to his s. Wilhelmus the

De Sille house with a farm adjoining it and about 90 A. on the E. side of the road leading from the village of N. U. to Nyack (Fort Hamilton); to his s. Rutgert the Pennoyer patent in G[d]; and to his s. Adriaen 120 A. extending from the main road in the village to the bay, including the present Bath House property, all subject to legacies to his other children. Issue:—Cornelis of N. U., b. Mar. 6, 1716, m. Helletje or Magdalena Finton; Sartie or Sarah, b. May 4, 1718, m. Aris or Jeremiah Vanderbilt; Albert of N. U., b. Nov. 14, 1720, m. Jannetje Van Brunt; Wilhelmus or William of N. U., b. July 26, 1723, m. Jannetje Van Voorhees; Catryntje, b. Feb. 14, 1726, d. young; Rutgert, b. Sept. 13, 1728, d. in 1732; Joost or George of N. U., b. Mar. 4, 1731, m. 1st Lydia Griggs, m. 2[d] Elizabeth Duryea; Rutgert of G[d], b. Jan. 16,1733, m. Altie Cortelyou; Adrian of N. U., b. Nov. 5, 1735, m. Engeltie Rapalje; Catryntje, b. Jan. 29, 1738, m. Daniel Hendricksen of Middletown, N. J.; and Elizabeth, b. Nov. 28, 1740, m. Hendrick Jansen of Middletown, N. J. Signed his name "*Rutgert Van Brunt.*"

Rutgert (s. of Joost Rutgersz), commonly known as "Ryke Bood," or rich brother, m. Jannetje dau. of Jan Janz Van Dyck of N. U.; d. July 5, 1758. Suppose he resided on his N. U. Lane farm. From 1744 to '59 was supervisor of N. U., and also held the office of ensign and capt. of militia. Was a large landholder, and conveyed · May 1, 1752, to Joris Lott, his son-in-law, for £2200 a tract of about 246 A. in N. U., comprising what was lately the farms of John and Leffert Lefferts. Will da. July 17, 1752; pro. Aug. 3, 1758; and rec. p. 71, Lib. 21, N. Y. surr. off. Issue:— John, m. Sarah Bergen, d. about 1751, prior to the death of his father; Altie, b. Apl. 22, 1712, m. Dec. 22, 1733, Nicholas Stillwell of G[d]; Teuntje, m. Denyse Denyse of the Narrows; Tryntje, m. John Rapalje of Br[n]; and Maria, m. Joris Lott. Signed his name "*Rutgert Van Brunt.*"

William (s. of Cornelis Rutgersz). No further trace than the name, and from an entry in the church books of a grave of a s. of Cornelis Rutgersz in 1732 he probably d. in that year.

VAN BURSUM, HARMANUS, m. July 30, 1769, *Wybrecht Hendricks*, and had a dau. Femmetje bp. Mar. 20, 1681, at Br[n].

VAN CAMPEN, GERRET JANSEN, bought Dec. 27, 1668, of Peter Jansen Schol a house and lot in Fl[h], as per p. 27 of Lib. C of Fl[h] rec. Made his mark to documents.

VAN CASSANT, ISAAC, emigrated in 1652, and took the oath of allegiance in Fl[h] in 1687.

Van Cleef, Benjamin (Janse), bp. Nov. 25, 1683; m. 1ˢᵗ *Hank* or *Hendrickje Sutphen;* m. 2ᵈ —— ——. Left N. U. and settled in Monmouth Co., N. J., as early as 1707. Issue:—Lysbeth, bp. May 19, 1705, m. William Cowenhoven of N. J.; Johannes of N. J., bp. June 3, 1711, m. successively Maria Koffert and Sarah Cowenhoven; Derick of N. J., bp. May 3, 1713; Marike, bp. Oct. 6, 1715, m. Jan Berkan; Derk of N. J., bp. Dec. 21, 1718, m. Elizabeth Leek; Benjamin of N. J., bp. Dec. 3, 1721, m. Helen Cowenhoven —all bp. at Freehold; Nelke; Laurens of N. J., m. Jannetie Laan; Helena, m. John Brower of N. J.; (sup.) Joseph of N. J., m. Sytie Van Sicklen; (sup.) Elsje, m. Wᵐ Beyrt of N. J.; and (sup.) Antje, m. —— Wilson of N. J.

Cornelis (Janse) of N. U., where he took the oath of allegiance in 1687 as a native; m. Femmetje Vandeventer. Mar. 10, 1704-5, sold a house and village-plot in N. U. to Anthony Holsart or Hulst, as per Lib. 4 of Con. Apl. 30, 1706, he sold (hailing from Gᵈ) to Jacques Cortelyou his interest in the tract on Gᵈ or N. U. Bay, lying E. of Cortelyou's lane, commonly known as the gun-field from a block-house being located in it in the last war with Great Britain, and known on a map on file in the office of the register of Kings County as Brighton or La Grange, as per an unrecorded deed among the Isaac Cortelyou papers. In 1706 he was assessed for 18 A. Aug. 10, 1708, he sold to Joost Van Brunt the plot of 21 A. in the road from the village of N. U. to the Narrows, commonly known as the Island, as per an unrecorded deed among the Leffert papers. Sept. 26, 1713, he sold to Cornelis Van Brunt a tract of 28 A. fronting on Gᵈ and N. U. Bay, E. of the gun-field and W. of De Bruynne's Lane, covering the land at present occupied by the Bath Hotel and adjoining premises, as per deed among Rutger A. Van Brunt papers. His name appears on the N. U. ass. roll of 1693 and Gᵈ cen. of 1698. Issue:—John of Gᵈ, who m. Catharine ——; Laurens, bp. Apl. 25, 1696, of N. J.; and (sup.) Maria or Maritje. Made his mark to documents.

Isbrant Janse, m. Janneke Aertse Vanderbilt of Flʰ. Was a grand-juror at the sessions in 1699. Left N. U. and settled in Monmouth Co., N. J. Issue:—Marretje, bp. Jan 25, 1716, in N. Y.; Janneke, bp. Mar. 8, 1720, at Freehold; (sup.) Benjamin, bp. Jan. 7, 1724, at Freehold, m. successively Rachel and Sara Cowenhoven.

Jan, the ancestor of the family, emigrated in 1653; b. in 1628; m. Engeltie Louwerens dau. of Louwerens Pieterse, prior to Mar. 10, 1681. He probably came from Cleef in the Netherlands. Farmer in Gᵈ in 1656, as per Thompson's

L. I., residing in N. U. as early as 1659. Dec. 23, 1662, he bought of Albert Albertse (Terhune) his patent of 24 morgens in N. U., which premises he conveyed to Balthazer de Vos and De Vos conveyed Apl. 6, 1669, to Hans Harmense Van Barkeloo, as per N. Y. town rec. Dec. 27, 1677, he bought of Arie Willemse (Bennet) a pasture-lot in N. U., for which in exchange Arie conveyed to him lots Nos. 6 and 7 at Yellow Hoek (Bay Ridge), where he also owned lots Nos. 13 and 14. In 1677 he was a mem. of the N. U. ch., in 1678 constable of said town, on Dongan's patent of 1686, and took the oath of allegiance there in 1687. There was a Jan Van Cleef of Bu^k in 1664, as per p. 339 of Vol. II. of Stiles's Br^n. Issue:—Catharine, bp. Oct. 23, 1681; Benjamin of N. J., bp. Nov. 25, 1683; Joseph, bp. Nov. 25, 1683; Angelica, m. John Emans of G^d; Ceytie, bp. May 13, 1688; Isbrant of N. J.; Nelke, m. Jan Van Meteren of N. J.; Cornelius of N. U.; and Rebecca, m. Andrew Emans of G^d. Made his mark to documents.

Joseph of N. U., bp. Nov. 25, 1683; m. Catharine dau. of Daniel Rapalje. Issue:—Sarah, bp. Sept. 25, 1709. Made his mark to documents.

VAN CORLER, see Van Curler.

VAN CORTLAND, STEPHANUS, m. Sept. 10, 1671, Gertrude Schuyler. Bought Aug. 10, 1695, Red Hoek of the authorities of Br^n, cong. 50 A., which his heirs sold May 23, 1712, to Matthyas Van Dyck. In 1693 he was col. of the militia of Kings Co., as per p. 29 of Vol. IV. of Col. His. He appears to have resided mainly in N. Y. For an account of the family, see p. 212 of O'Callaghan's New Netherlands.

VAN COSSANT, ISAAC, emigrated in 1652, and took the oath of allegiance in Fl^h in 1687.

VAN COTT or VAN CAT, CLAES CORNELISE, emigrated in 1652, and took the oath of allegiance in Bu^k in 1687, where he settled, and where his name appears on the ass. roll of 1683. He d. prior to Aug. 21, 1694. There was a Cornelis Van Cott of Flushing who m. Mar. 11, 1710, Antie Sprung, who may have been his s.

Cornelis, on Dongan's patent of Bu^k of 1687.

VAN COVERDE or COVERDEN, REM JANSEN, bought Mar. 22, 1676-7, of Cornelis Janse Boomgart lot No. 23 in the N. L. of Fl^h with a parcel of salt-meadows for 1300 gl., as per p. 12 of Lib. AA of Fl[h] rec. He also bought Mar. 27, 1680, of Jacob Strycker a farm in Fl[h], as per p. 37 of Lib. A of Fl[h] rec. Signed his name *"Rem Jansen."*

Aeltje Theunis of Br[n], m. May 18, 1679, at Fld[s], Willem Pos (Post) of N. Y., as per N. Y. D. ch. rec.

VAN COWENHOVEN, see Cowenhoven.

VAN CURLER, JACOBUS, b. about 1611; m. Aug. 1652 *Elizabeth Van Hoochvelt* or *Hoogvelt* in N. A. In 1633 was commissary of cargoes for the colony. Obtained June 16, 1636, a patent for the little plains, the middlemost of the three flats in Fld[s], known as Corlers Flats and Castuteauw. In 1638 he taught a school in N. A.; Oct. 2. 1652, obtained a patent for a plantation in Fl[h], as per Col. Man.; in 1655 he appears to have resided in G[d]; in 1657 was among the first settlers of N. U.; in 1660 resided on his plantation in said town, of which he was a mag. in 1659 and '60, and clerk in 1662. Mar. 20, 1662, he bought plantation-lot No. 18 in G[d] of "Eman Benam." In 1672 he appears to have been a bankrupt. Signed his name *"J. V. Curler."*

VAN DALEN, JACOBUS, alias HERPERT CLUNSEN, probably from Dalen in Emberland, leased for 6 years, commencing Oct. 1, 1656 and ending in 1662, of Petrus Stuyvesant his bouwery at Amersfoort with the buildings, as per p. 384 of Vol. III. of O'Callaghan's Man. Trans. of Col. Man.

VANDEGRIFT, FREDERICK, (supposed s. of Jacob Leendertsen, the surname being probably derived from the river Grift in Gelderland,) of Bu[k], and Joost Duryee or "Derjee," guardians of the orphan children of Hendrick Barentse Smith, conveyed Smith's real estate at Bu[k] to the 3 orphan children, viz. Willemtje Smith, Aeltje Smith, and Johannes Smith, 16 morgens each, as per p. 176 of Lib. A of Fl[h] rec. Frederick was bp. Dec. 19, 1655, in N. A.; m. Nov. 3, 1678, Styntje Elswarts of N. Y.; was an elder in the R. D. ch. of Bensalem, Bucks Co., Pa., in 1710, to which place he appears to have removed. Issue:—Christoffel, bp. Aug. 6, 1681, in N.Y.; and Abram, bp. Dec. 18, 1691. Signed his name *"Frederick Vandegrift."*

Jacob Leendertsen, m. July 19, 1648, in N. A., Rebecca Frederickse dau. of Frederick Lubbertse of Br[n]; mem. of the R. D. ch. of Br[n] in 1664. Removed to N. Y. and elected schepen in 1673; and one of the patentees of Newtown in 1686. Issue:—Marretje Jacobse, bp. Aug. 29, 1649, m. Mar. 11, 1666, in N. Y., Cornelis Corsz Vroom; Christine Jacobse, bp. Feb. 26, 1651, m. 1ˢᵗ, Sept. 22, 1678, Cornelis Jacobse Schippen, m. 2ᵈ, Mar. 20, 1681, Daniel Van Vos; Anne Jacobse, bp. Mar. 16, 1653, m. Aug. 26, 1674, Jacob Claesen; Leendert Jacobse, bp. Dec. 19, 1655, m. Nov. 3, 1678, Styntje Elswaerts; (sup.) Frederick Jacobse; Nicholas Jacobse, bp. May 5, 1658; Rebecca Jacobse, bp. May 22, 1661; Rachel Jacobse, bp. Aug. 20, 1664, m. 1689 Barend Verkerk; and Johannes Jacobse, bp. June 26, 1667—all bp. in N. A. and N. Y. Signed his name "*Jacob Leendertsen Vandergrift.*"

Johannes Jacobse, bp. June 26, 1667; (sup.) m. Sept. 23, 1692, Neeltje Volkers wid. of Cornelis Cortelyou of N. U. Resided in N. U. and removed from thence to Bensalem, Bucks Co., Pa., where he was an elder in the R. D. ch. in 1724. Issue:—Hester, bp. Jan. 21, 1710, in Bucks Co., Pa., and probably others.

Nicholase Jacobs, m. Aug. 24, 1684, at N. U., Barendje Janse Verkerken or Ker Kerke. Took the oath of allegiance in N. U. in 1687; bought Feb. 24, 1690-1, of Anthony Du Ceen a farm in N. U. Lane, which he sold Apl. 5, 1697, to Abᵐ Willemse (Van Westervelt), at which date he resided at Bensalem, Bucks Co., Pa., as per p. 132 of Lib. 2 of Con., and at which place he was an elder in the R. D. ch. in 1710. Issue:—Jan, bp. Jan. 1, 1691, in N. Y. Signed his name "*Nichloes Vandergrift.*"

Paulus Leendertse, m. Jannetje Gerretse; was a property-holder in N. A. as early as 1644; skipper of the Neptune in 1645, and of the Great Gerrit in 1646; a mag. of said city most of the time from 1653 to 1665, and in 1647, '48, and '49 a member of the Council. After the conquest he took the oath of allegiance to the English in 1664. He obtained a patent in 1668 for 25 morgens of land in Brⁿ, which he bought Jan. 22, 1654, of Wᵐ Cornelise, which premises had been previously held by Michael Picet, as per p. 82 of Vol. 1 of Stiles's Brⁿ. In 1671 he sold his property (on which there is no account of his having resided), and returned to Europe, as per p. 43 of Vol. II. of Col. His. Issue:—Margriet or Grietje, bp. May 22, 1649, m. Jacob Mauritzen; Gerret, bp. Apl. 30, 1651; Marritie, bp. Apl. 29, 1653, m. Gerrit Van Tricht; and Johannes, bp. Jan. 27, 1655—all bp. in N. A. Signed his name "*P. L. Van de grift.*"

VANDER BEEK, ABRAHAM (COENRADUSE), bp. Apl. 1, 1682; m. Oct 22, 1702, *Moltje Woodert;* d. prior to 1706. Left Brⁿ and settled in N. J. Issue:—Elsje, bp. Sept. 1, 1704.

Coenradus Coenraet (Pouluse), bp. Sept. 1; 1647; m. 1ˢᵗ Elsje or Eesje Janse (sup.) Schaers; m. 2ᵈ, Oct. 20, 1702, Catharine Cook, wid. Resided in Gowanus, mem. of Brⁿ D. ch.

in 1677, and on ass. rolls of Brⁿ of 1675 and '76. Removed to N. Y., and a measurer there in 1699. Will da. July 17, 1706; pro. Jan. 9, 1709; rec. p. 280, Lib. 7, N. Y. surr. off. Issue:—Anna Margaret; Paulus; John, m. June 23, 1699, in N. Y., Lysbet Woeder; Marie, bp. May 10, 1679; Abraham, bp. Apl. 1, 1682; Isaac, bp. June 3, 1685; Jacob, bp. Mar. 2, 1688, d. young; Coenradus, bp. Nov. 5, 1693 (sup.) m. Oct. 12, 1712, in N. Y., Ariaentje De Vou—all bp. in N. Y.; Mary or Maria, bp. May 10, 1699, m. Hendrick Bosch Junr; Burger; and Jacob—the last 2 by 2^d wife.

Coenradus (*Coenraduse*), bp. Nov. 5, 1693; m. 1st, Oct. 12, 1702, Adriaantje De Vou; m. 2^d, May —, 1717, (sup.) Angenietje Westervelt of Hackensack. On ass. rolls of Brⁿ of 1675 and '76. Dec. 30, 1699, he sold to Cornelis Gerretse Van Duyn the one half of the Bredenbent farm at Gowanus. Left Brⁿ and settled in Hackensack, N. J. Issue:— Burger, bp. Aug. 4, 1703; Jacobus, bp. Dec. 9, 1705, m. Antje Vreeland; Paulus, bp. 1718, m. Annetje Amerman; Geesje, bp. 1721, m. Cornelis de Groot; Jannetje, bp. 1723, m. David Akerman; Cornelia, bp. 1725, m. Hendrick Sturm; Juryan, bp. 1730; and Abraham, bp. 1732.

Isaac (*Pouluse*), bp. Nov. 5, 1656; m. —— ——. Issue:— Arent, bp. Apl. 20, 1690.

Isaac (*Coenraduse*), bp. June 3, 1685; m. June —, 1736, Annetje de Boog. Left Brⁿ and settled at Hackensack. Issue:—Poulus, bp. 1737, m. Sara Berdan; Barent, bp. 1739; Jannetje, bp. 1741; Isaac, bp. 1743; Jacob, bp. 1746, m. Margrietje Berdan; Salamon, bp. 1749, m. Geesje Terhune; Ragel, bp. 1752, m. Salamon Kalugs; Abram, bp. 1756; and Hendrick, bp. 1759—all bp. in Hackensack.

Jacob (*Coenraduse*), m. Femmetje Van Voorhees. Left Brⁿ and settled in Hackensack. Issue:—Paulus, bp. 1725; Jan, bp. 1727; and Abram, bp. 1735—all bp. in Hackensack.

Paulus, the common ancestor of the family, emigrated from Bremen; m. Oct. 9, 1644, Maria or Mary Thomas or Baddie, successively wid. of Thomas Farden and Willem Arianse Bennet of Gowanus; d. 1680. Of Brⁿ in 1655, as per Col. Man.; in 1660 a butcher in N. A.; in 1661 farmer of the excise of L. I.; in 1662 ferry-master; Oct. 24, 1663, bought plantation-lot No. 17 in G^d of Jan Jansen Ver Rhyn, as per G^d rec.; on ass. roll of Brⁿ of 1675 and patent of 1677. Aug. 6, 1679, he sold to Willem Huyken the one half of a farm in Gowanus formerly of Willem Bradenbent for 3000 gl. He resided on the farm in Gowanus late of Garret Bergen. Issue:—Coenradus, bp. Sept. 1, 1647; Aaltje, bp. May 30, 1649, m. Dirck Janse Amerman; Poulus Junr, bp. Nov. 17,

1650; Hester, bp. Dec. 15, 1652, m. Juriaen Blanck Jun';
Isaac, bp. Nov. 6, 1656—all bp. in N. A.; and Catharine, m.
1ˢᵗ Daniel Richauco, m. 2ᵈ Pieter Corsz Vroom. Signed
his name *"Mʳ Poulus Van der bek."*

Poulus Jun', bp. Nov. 17, 1650; m. June 13, 1677, Sara
Schouten; d. about 1690. Resided at Gowanus, and mem.
of R. D. ch. of Brⁿ in 1677 and '85. Issue:—Sara, bp. Feb.
10, 1678, d. young; Maria, bp. Mar. 15, 1679, m. (sup.) Cornelis Christiansen of Hackensack; Poulus, bp. Nov. 6, 1681;
Sara, bp. Oct. 6, 1683, m. Hendrick Pieters from Amsterdam; Lucas, bp. Mar. 6, 1687; and Janneken, bp. Oct. 14,
1688—all bp. in N. Y.

Poulus (*Coenraduse*), m. 1ˢᵗ, Nov. 18, 1695, Jannetie Johannes wid. of Jacob Colve; m. 2ᵈ, June 1703, Catryn Martens
wid. of Samuel Berry. Left Gowanus, Brⁿ, prior to his
marriages and resided in N. Y., from whence he removed to
N. J. Issue:—Coenradus of N. J., bp. July 15, 1696; Jacob
of N. J., bp. Jan. 1, 1699; Elsie, bp. Dec. 29, 1700, (sup.) m.
Mar. 5, 1720, Pieter Kip; Poulus of N. J., bp. Apl. 7, 1703;
and Catharine, bp. Feb. 6, 1706—all bp. in N. Y.

Poulus (s. of Poulus Jun'), bp. Nov. 6, 1681; (sup.) m. Jannetje Springsteen. Left Gowanus and settled at Hackensack. Issue:—Abram, bp. 1708; and Isaac, bp. 1712 in
Hackensack.

Rem and *Rem Janse*, see Remsen.

VANDER BILT or BILD, ARIS JANSE, of Flᵸ, m. Oct. 6, 1677,
Hildègonde or *Hilletje Remsen* dau. of Rem Janse Vanderbeek; d. after 1711. On ass. rolls of Flᵸ of 1675 and '83,
took the oath of allegiance there as a native in 1687, on
patent of 1685, cen. of 1698, and capt. of infantry in 1700, as
per p. 809 of Vol. IV. of Doc. of Col. His. He appears to
have removed to Bergen, N. J., before he died. Issue:—
Jan Aertse, bp. Aug. 11, 1678, in N. U.; Jannetje or Annetje Aertse, bp. Jan. 9, 1681, in Brⁿ, d. young; Jannetje Aertse,
bp. Sept. 17, 1682, in N. U., m. Eyzebrand Van Kloof or
Isbrant Van Cleef; Femmetje Aertse, bp. Sept. 14, 1684, in
N. U., m. Gosen Adrianse Ryerson; Rem Aertse, bp. Aug. 29,
1686, in Brⁿ; Aert Aertse, bp. June 11, 1693, in Brⁿ; Jeremyas
Aertse, bp. Oct. 19, 1695, in Brⁿ; Cornelius Aertse, b. Jan.
11, 1697; Hendrick Aertse of N. J.; (sup.) Jacob Aertse;
and (sup.) Catharine Aertse, b. Mar. 1, 1713, m. Jacobus
Lefferts of Flᵸ. Signed his name *"Aris Janse Vandebielt."*

Aert Aertse of Flᵸ, b. June 11, 1693; m. Mar. 14, 1717,
Seytie Strycker. Will da. Dec. 9, 1754; pro. Nov. 27, 1762;
rec. p. 332, Lib. 23, N. Y. surr. off. Issue:—Antie, m. Leffert Lefferts; Lammetje, b. May 25, 1720, m. John Lefferts;
Hilletje, b. Apl. 19, 1721, m. Leffert Martense; Margrietje,

m. Ab^m Bogert; Scytie, bp. Dec. 20, 1730, m. Douwe Van Duyn; Aris of Fl^h, bp. Feb. 29, 1736, m. Annetje Nagel; Jannetje, (sup.) m. Joris Martense; and Peter of N. U., m. Jannetje Willemse. Signed his name *"Art Van der Belt."*

Cornelius Aertse, b. June 11, 1697; m. Jannetje Wyckoff; d. Jan. 22, 1782. Left Fl^h and settled at Sommerville, N. J. Issue:—Cornelia, bp. Oct. 15, 1738, at Sommerville; and probably other children.

Hendrick Aertse, m. Neeltje Van Cleef. Left Fl^h and settled near Freehold, N. J., and on ass. roll of Franklin township in 1735. Issue:—Benjamin of N. J., bp. Aug. 29, 1731; Hendrick of Middletown, N. J., bp. June 10, 1733, m. Catharine Snyder; Aris of N. J., bp. June 22, 1735, (sup.) m. Ann Dorset; Eyda, bp. May 8, 1737; Derick of N. J., bp. Sept. 9, 1739; Neeltje, bp. July 12, 1741, m. Piter Van Pelt; Maria, bp. July 24, 1744, m. Samuel Dennis; and Elsje, bp. Dec. 25, 1749—all bp. in N. J.

Jacob Janse of Fl^h, m. Aug. 13, 1687, Marretje dau. of Derick Janse Van Der Vliet and wid. of Andries Onderdonk. On ass. rolls of Fl^h of 1675, '76, and '83, and took the oath of allegiance there in 1687. Issue:—Jacob Junr of S. I., b. 1692; Derick, bp. Apl. 25, 1696; Antje, m. Isaac Symonse of S. I.; (sup.) John of Hempstead; and Femmetje, m. Gozen Adriaans of S. I. Made his mark to documents.

Jacob Junr of S. I., b. 1692; m. Neeltje Denyse; d. Dec. 14, 1760. Bought a farm on S. I. in 1718, to which he removed from Fl^h, and was a mem. of the Moravian ch. of that place in 1756. Will da. May 10, 1759; pro. Feb. 9, 1761; rec. p. 345, Lib. 42, N. Y. surr. off. Issue:—Aris, b. Feb. 2, 1716; Dennis or Denyse, bp. Sept. 22, 1717, in G^d, settled on the Raritan; Hilletje, bp. Mar. 27, 1720, on S. I., where the remainder of his children were bp.; Jacob of S. I. (the grandfather of Commodore Cornelius Vanderbilt of N. Y. Central R. R. memory), bp. Feb. 3, 1723, m. Mary Hoogland; Helena or Magdalena, bp. Dec. 25, 1725, m. Cornelius Ellis of S. I.; John or Johannes of S. I., bp. Dec. 25, 1731; Cornelius of S. I., farmer, bp. Dec. 25, 1731, m. Elenor Van Tile; Ann or Antje, bp. Feb. 24, 1734; Phebe, b. Apl. 27, 1737, m. Christopher Gerretsen of S. I.; Anthea, b. Jan. 3, 1739; Neeltje, bp. Sept. 13, 1742; and Adrian of S. I. Signed his name *"Jacob Vanderbilt."*

Jacob Aertse (sup.) of Fl^h, m. Altie or Neltie dau. of Jacobus Lefferts of Fl^h. Issue:—Jacob.

Jan Aertsen, the common ancestor of the Vanderbilt family of this vicinity, or Jan s. of Aert from "the Bilt," a village in the province of Utrecht, (Bilt or Bylt means hill,) came to this country as early as 1650; m. 1st, Feb. 6, 1650,

Anneken Hendricks from Bergen in Norway; m. 2ᵈ Dierber Cornelis; m. 3ᵈ, Dec. 16, 1681, Magdalena Hanse wid. of Hendrick Jansen Spier of Bergen, N. J.; d. Feb. 2, 1705, at Bergen, N. J. Resided in N. A. as early as 1663, after which he settled in Flʰ, where Feb. 5, 1667, he gave a mortgage on his bouwery to Nicholas de Meyer. From Flʰ he removed to Bergen, N. J., where he owned land in 1694, as per Winfield's Hudson Co. Land Titles, and probably at an earlier date. Issue:—Aris Janse; Geertje or Gerretje Janse, m. Jan Spiegelaer; Jacob Janse; Marretje Janse, m. Rem Remsen of N. L.; and Jan Jansen Junʳ, by last wife. His mark to documents resembles a window-sash with 4 panes of glass.

Jan (sup. s. of Jacob and Marretje), m. Margaret ——. Owned and occupied a farm in Fldᵃ, late the southerly side of the Emmans farm, which he sold and then removed to Hempstead. Will da. Apl. 30, 1761; pro. Apl. 30, 1768; rec. p. 280, Lib. 26, of N. Y. surr. off. Issue:—Jacob; Gerret; William; Hendrick; Mary, m. and d. prior to Apl. 1761; Margaret, m. —— Dodge; and Geertruy, m. —— Remsen.

Jan Janse (s. of Jan Aertse) of Flʰ, m. about 1733 Helena or Magdalena Lefferts dau. of Leffert Pieterse and wid. of Gerret Martense. On ass. rolls of Flʰ of 1675 and '76, and on Gov. Andros's patent for the New Lotts of Flʰ of 1677. About 1680 he removed to Bergen, N. J. No account of his children.

Jan Aertse (s. of Aris Janse), bp. Aug. 11, 1678; m. (sup.) Hilletje Remsen and resided in Flʰ. Issue:—(sup.) Auries or Aris of N. J.; (sup.) Jeremiah of Flʰ, Brⁿ, and Hempstead. Signed his name "*Jan Van Der bilt.*"

Jeremyas Aertse (s. of Aris Janse) of Flʰ, bp. Oct. 19, 1695; m. Nov. 11, 1715, Peternella dau. of Cornelis Pieterse Wyckoff. Issue:—George, bp. Dec. 19, 1718; Hilletje, bp. Feb. 29, 1721, m. Leffert Martense of Flʰ; Pieternella, bp. Mar. 5, 1727—all bp. in N. U.; and Jeremias of Flʰ, the ancestor of the Flʰ branch of the family, m. Sarah Van Brunt. Signed his name "*Jerimyas van Der Bilt*" in 1727.

Rem Aertse (s. of Aris Janse) of Flʰ, bp. Aug. 29, 1686; m. Margreta ——. Issue:—Jan; Rem. b. 1712; and Hilletje, bp. Oct. 21, 1713, on S. I. Signed his name "*Rem Vander bilt.*"

VAN DER BOSCH, JAN WOUTERSZ, and *Wyntje* his w., mem. of Flʰ R. D. ch. in 1677.

VAN DER BREETS, JURIAN HENDRICKSE, took the oath of

21

allegiance in Brⁿ in 1687 as a native. Had land conveyed to him Oct. 19, 1687, in Brⁿ, by Sophia Van Loedsteyn as per p. 116 of Vol. 1 of Con.

Volkert, took the oath of allegiance in Brⁿ in 1687 as a native.

VAN DER BURCH, CORNELIS, probably from Burch in Zeeland, was a resident of N. U. in 1682, as per town rec. Signed his name "*Cornelis Vander Burch.*"

VAN DER EYCK, ANTHONY, on ass. rolls of N. U. of 1675 and '76.

VAN DER GOUW, GILLES PIETERSEN, a carpenter, probably from Gouda in South Holland, testified Mar. 22, 1639, to the building among others of the house of Wolfert Gerretse (Van Couwenhoven) standing at the Bay (Flatlands), erected by the Company's carpenter, as per O'Callaghan's Man. Trans. of Dutch Col. Man. He appears to have been engaged during Van Twiller's administration on many buildings.

VAN DER GRIFT or VANDER GRIST, see Vandegrift.

VAN DER HARD, SIMON AERDSZ, of Gowanus, m. *Geertje Cornelis*. Issue:—Dorothea, bp. Aug. 1, 1680, at Fl^h; Gerritje, bp. Aug. 20, 1682, in N. U.; Simon, bp. Mar. 30, 1684, in N. U., and d. young; and Simon, bp. May 3, 1685, in N. U. From his having a sister Lysbeth Aards who hailed from Nieuwkoop in South Holland, it may be inferred he emigrated from the same place.

VAN DER HOVE or HOVEN, CORNELIS, probably from Hoven, a village in Gelderland, settled in Bedford, m. *Matye* dau. of Marten Beekman; d. in 1705. His wid. after his death m. John Bibon of Bedford. There was a Cornelis Cornelise Van der Hoeven in Albany, who sold Mar. 4, 1677-8, a house and lot at that place to Wm Loveridge, hatter; and a Cornelis Van Der Hoeven at Albany who d. in 1690, as per Pearson's First Settlers in Albany. Issue:— Cornelis Junr; Alke; Nellye, m. Johannes Van Duyn; Martha; Jonica; Martin; Susan; and Johannes—all bp. in Albany; and Christine, m. Ruluf Duryee. Signed his name "*C Vanderhoeven.*"

Cornelis Junr, m. Lysbeth ——. Resided in Bedford, was one of the justices of Brⁿ in 1673, and on cen. of 1698.

Issue:—Cornelis, bp. Nov. 27, 1698, in Br^a; Metje, bp. Dec. 1, 1700, in Br^a; and Michiel, bp. Sept. 17, 1730, in N. U.

Martin, left Bedford and settled near New Brunswick, N. J., prior to 1699, as per p. 35 of Messler's Somerset Co.

VANDERICK, RICK JANSEN, on Stoothoff's books of 1676.

VANDERING, TILEMAN, emigrated in 1674, and in 1687 took the oath of allegiance in N. U.

VAN DER LINDE, see Linde.

VAN DER LIPHORST, LUYKAS, bought Dec. 17, 1653, of Arent Van Hattem Junr plantation-lot No. 23 in G^d, as per town rec.

VAN DER MEYER, TILEMAN JACOBSZ, from Kamerik, a village in Utrecht in the Netherlands, m. Aug. 11, 1678, *Tryntje* wid. of Jan Thomasse Van Dyck, and resided in Br^a.

VANDER NEXTER, JAN, on ass. roll of N. U. of 1683.

VAN DER VEEN, POULUS JANSEN, probably from Veen, a village in North Braband, owned land in Canarisie June 10, 1661, as per Col. Man.

VANDERVEER, CORNELIS JANSE (from the ferry), the common ancestor of the family, emigrated in 1659 from Alkmaar in North Holland; m. *Tryntje Gillis de Mandeville.* Bought Feb. 24, 1678-9, of Jan Janse Fyn for 2600 gl. a farm in Fl^h lying S. of the purchaser's farm, as per p. 57 of Lib. AA of Fl^h rec., from which it is evident that he was a resident of Fl^h at this date. The *purchaser's farm* referred to in the above description was probably a tract of 26 morgens in Fl^h, patented Mar. 12, 1661, by Gov. Stuyvesant to "Cornelis Janse," lying on the N. side of the land of Jan Snediker. His name appears as a mag. of Fl^h in 1678 and '80, and on the patent of said town of 1685. Issue:—Cornelis Junr; Neeltje Cornelise, m. Daniel Polhemus; Dominicus Cornelise, bp. Nov. 16, 1679, in Fld^a; Jan Cornelise; (sup.) Jacobus Cornelise; Micheal Cornelise; Maria Cornelise, bp. July 30, 1682, in Fl^h; Hendrikje Cornelise, bp. May 17, 1684, (sup.) m. Johannes Wyckoff; Jakoba Cornelise, bp. Apl. 29, 1686, in Br^a, (sup.) m. John Cowenhoven of N. J.; and Pieter Cornelise. Signed his name *"Cornelis Janse Vande Veer."*

Cornelis Jun[r] of Fl[h], m. Jannetje (sup.) Van Norstrand.
On ass. roll of Fl[h] of 1683 and cen. of 1698; sheriff of the
county in 1731. Will da. June 7, 1775; pro. Apl. 8, 1782;
rec. p. 483 of Lib. 34 of N. Y. surr. off. Issue:—John;
Catrina, b. May 30, 1722, m. (sup.) Jacobus Lefferts; Cornelius of Fl[h] (father of the late John C. and grandfather of
the present (1880) John Vanderveer of Fl[h]), b. Dec. 5, 1731,
m. Leah Ver Kerk; and Petrus, b. June 5, 1735.

Dominicus (*Cornelise*) of Fl[h], bp. Nov. 16, 1679; m. 1st Jannetje ——; (sup.) m. 2[d], Feb. 7, 1702-3, Maria Margreta
Nortlyck or Van Orteck. His name appears on the Fl[h]
rec. in 1704, '27, and '49, in relation to salt-meadows and
church funds. Was sheriff of Kings Co. in 1736. Issue:—
Dominicus of Fl[h], m. Elizabeth Laquire; Catlyntje, bp. July
25, 1715; Jannetje, bp. June 21, 1719; Jacobus of the Raritan, N. J., bp. Dec. 10, 1721, m. Femmetje Strycker; (sup.)
Tunis of Freehold, m. Aeltje Schenck; Neeltje, bp. July 9,
1727, m. Peter Lott of N. L.; Jeremias of N. L., bp. Mar.
30, 1729, m. Elizabeth Ditmas; Antje, bp. Oct. 17, 1731;
Jan of Fl[h], bp. Aug. 19, 1733—all bp. in N. U.; (sup.) Cornelia; (sup.) Cornelius of Shrewsbury, m. Matje or Marytje
Schenck; and (sup.) Hendrick of Monmouth Co., N. J., m.
Neeltje Van Cleef. Signed his name "*Dominicus Van der
veer.*"

Jacobus (*Cornelise*), bp. Oct. 29, 1686; m. Catharine ——;
d. 1726. Left Fl[h] and removed to Penn's Hoek, Salem Co.,
N. J. Will da. Aug. 15, 1726; pro. Dec. 17, 1726; rec. p. 2,
Lib. 38 of Sec. off. of N. J. Issue:—Helena, bp. Mar. 4,
1698, in N. Y., m. Andrew Tossaway; Jacob of Redington,
N. J.; William of N. J.; and Henry of Penn's Neck, N. J.

Jan (*Cornelise*) of Fl[h], m. Jan. 6, 1695, Femmetje dau. of
Michael Hansen Bergen. Took the oath of allegiance in
Fl[h] in 1687, of which town he was supervisor from 1708 to
1714. Jan. 1, 1696, he bought of Daniel Polhemius the one
half of a corn-mill with its appurtenances, with the one
half of the dwelling-house and of the ground thereto belonging, for 4000 gl., as per p. 221 of Lib. A of Fl[h] rec.
Jan. 19, 1698, he bought of D. Polhemius the remaining one
half of the corn-mill with the ground thereto belonging, as
granted by the town, located on the "Varse Kil" (Fresh
Kil), as per p. 233 of said Lib. A. This is clearly the mill
in N. L. at present known as Vanderveer's mill. Issue:—
Katryna, bp. Mar. 29, 1696, in Br[n]; Femmetje,.m. Jacob
Sebring ; and Jan of Keuter's Hoek, Fl[h], b. July 7, 1706, m.
Cornelia dau. of Ab[m] Lott. Signed his name "*Jan Van
Der Veer.*"

John (s. of Cornelis Jun[r]) of Fl[h], m. —— ——; d. prior to

1782. Issue:—Gerrit; John; Peter; Hendrick; Jannetje; and Belitje.

Michael or *Macchiel* (*Cornelise*) of N. U., m. Belitje ——; d. prior to 1770.. Deacon in D. ch. of N. U. in 1726. Issue:—Michael, m. Margaret Stockholm; Scytie, bp. Mar. 17, 1723; Eytje, bp. Dec. 6, 1724; Jan, bp. Nov. 6, 1726; Catharine, bp. Oct. 13, 1728, d. young; Jacobus, bp. Jan. 18, 1730; Catharine, b. Aug. 11, 1732, m. Pieter Antonides of Fl^h; Cornelius, bp. Feb. 16, 1735—all bp. in N. U.; and Hendrick of Fl^h, the father of the late Abraham Vanderveer, for many years clerk of the County of Kings, m. Maria Voorhees. Signed his name *"Macchiel Vander Veer."*

Pieter Cornelise. Oct. 15, 1653, Gerrit Lookermans conveyed to Pieter Cornelise Vanderveer of N. A. a house and lot on the present Pearl St. of N. Y., as per Lib. GG of patents in off. of Sec. of State, Albany; and May 2, 1658, he obtained a patent for a lot in said city. From these dates conclude that this Pieter Cornelise is not a son of Cornelis Janse.

VAN DER VLIET, VLIDT, or VLIT, CORNELIS BARENTSE, probably from Vliet, a village in South Holland, was allotted Aug. 6, 1668, a meadow-lot on the division of the Fl^h meadows at Canarisie, as per Fl^h town rec.

Dirck Janse, the common ancestor of the family, emigrated from the Waal in the Netherlands in 1660: b. about 1612; m. 1st, in Europe, Lyntje Aertse; m. 2^d, in Europe, Geertje Gerretse. Settled in Fl^h, where he obtained Nov. 24, 1654, a patent for 25 morgens, as per Col. Man. On ass. rolls of Fl^h of 1675, '76, and '83; mag. in 1679, '80 and '81; mem. of the R. D. ch. in 1677 and deacon in 1680; on Gov. Andros's patent for the New Lotts of 1677; and took the oath of allegiance in said town in 1687. Jan. 15, 1679-80, he and his w. Geertje made a joint will, which is recorded on p. 95 of Lib. AA of Fl^h rec. Issue:—Hendrikje Dirckse, m. Jan Nelsie; Jan Dirckse; Hendrick Dirckse; Mary or Margaret Dirckse; Geertruyd Dirckse; and Gerret Dirckse. Signed his name *"Dirck Jansen Van der Vliet."*

Gerret Dirckse of Fl^h, probably the oldest son of Derck Janse. Settled on the Raritan prior to 1699, as per p. 35 of Messler's Somerset Co. There was a Garret Van Vliet among the Freeholders of Dutchess Co. in 1714, as per p. 100 of Smith's Dutchess Co.

Hendrick Dirckse of Fl^h. Jan. 15, 1679-80, he and his brother Jan bought of their father Dirck Janse, wood-lot No. 9 in the new division (New Lotts) of Fl^h, lying between the lots of Jan Snediker and that of Pieter Lott, as per p. 93 of Lib. AA of Fl[h] rec. Name on cen. of Fl[h] of 1698. Signed his name *"Hendrick Dircksen Vander Vlit."*

Jan Dirckse of Fl[h], b. in the Waal of the Netherlands; m. Dec. 2, 1683, Geertje Verkerk from Buurmalzen in Gelderland, dau. of Jan Janse Verkerk. Resided in N. L., taking the oath of allegiance in Fl[h] in 1687, being at the time a mem. of the R. D. ch. of the same place. On ass. rolls of Fl[h] of 1683 and '93, and patent of 1685. Oct. 30, 1684, he bought of Joost Casparse lot No. 8 in the new lotts of Fl[h], as per p. 176 of Lib. C of Fl[h] rec. Issue:—Jan Janse of Six Mile Run, bp. Oct. 3, 1684, in Br[n]; Geertje, (twin) bp. Oct. 3, 1684; Rebecca, m. Adriaen ten Eck of Newtown; Sarah, bp. Nov. 14, 1694, m. Joseph Hegeman of Fl[h]; and Elsje, bp. May 19, 1702. Signed his name *"Jan Dircksen Vander Vlidt."*

Jan Janse, bp. Oct. 3, 1684. Left Fl[h] and settled at Six Mile Run in Somerset Co., N. J. Issue:—Grietje, m. Simon Wyckoff of N. J.; John, m. Gerite Wyckoff; Derick, d. young; Sarah; Rebecca, (sup.) m. Folkert Van Nostrant; and Maria, m. Adriaen Hegeman of Fl[h].

Pieter Janse, among the first settlers of Bu[k] in 1661, as per Thompson's L. I. Of Bu[k] in 1665, per town rec. Van Vliets or Vanfliets are found among the residents of Orange and Dutchess Cos., N. Y.

VAN DER VOORT, CORNELIS or CORNELIS JANSE, was an overseer of Fl[h] in 1680, as per town rec. Conveyed land in Fl[h] in 1680 to Cornelis Berrian, as per p. 41 of Lib. A of Fl[h] rec.

Hendrick Machielse of Br[n], bp. Aug. 22, 1655. No further trace.

Jan Machielse of Br[n], bp. Dec. 11, 1650. Signed his name *"Yan Van Dervoort"* in 1723. No further trace.

Michael Paulusen, the common ancestor of the family, emigrated from Dermonde in Flanders and settled in Br[n]. He m. Nov. 18, 1640, Maria dau. of Joris Jansen Rapalie. On ass. roll of Br[n] of 1675. Issue:—Michael Michealse, bp. Jan. 19, 1642; Josyntie, bp. Dec. 20, 1643, d. young; Josyntie, bp. June 2, 1647; Paulus Michaelse, bp. Jan. 3, 1649; Jan, bp. Dec. 11, 1650; Maria, bp. July 27, 1653; Hendrick, bp. Aug. 22, 1655; Joris, bp. Oct. 18, 1656; Claertje, bp. Oct. 27, 1658—all bp. in N. A.; (sup.) Aeltje, m. Derick Janse; and (sup.) Elizabeth Paulus, m. Volckert Hendricksen. Signed his name *"Maghial Paulusen"* in 1658.

Michael Michaelse of Br[n], bp. Jan. 19, 1642; m. Styntje or

Christine ——. Issue:—Lysbeth, bp. July 16, 1699, in Br^n; and Jannetje, bp. Apl. 18, 1704, in Br^n.

Paulus Michaelse of Br^n, bp. Jan. 3, 1649; m. Lysbeth or Elizabeth ——; d. June 2, 1681. An inventory of his estate taken Apl. 24, 1685. His wid. m. 2^d Claes Barentse Blom. His name appears on the ass. rolls of Br^n of 1675 and '76. Issue:—Paulus, bp. July 8, 1681, in Fl^h.

Paulus or *Pouwel* (s. of Paulus Michaelse), bp. July 8, 1681; m. 1st Neeltje ——; m. 2^d Jannetje ——. Resided at Bedford, Br^n. Issue:—Elizabeth, bp. Feb. 10, 1706, in Br^n; and Helena (by 2^d w.), bp. Apl. 9, 1727, at N. U. Signed his name "*Pouwel Van Dervoort*" in 1729.

VANDER WEEN, JAN, m. *Maatje Corneliss;* both mem. of the R. D. ch. of N. U. in 1682.

VANDER WYCK, see Van Wyck.

VANDE SPIEGEL, LAUWERENS, on petition of May 1664 for a canal at Red Hoek, as per p. 68 of Vol. I. of Stiles's Br^n.

VAN DEVENTER, BARENT (Jacobse), of Fl^h in 1719, and of Fld^s in 1775; m. *Geertje* ——. Issue:—Barent, bp. Dec. 25, 1720; Seytie, bp. Aug. 15, 1725, m. David Sprung; Jacobus of Fl^h, bp. May 20, 1732, m. Abagail Lefferts; Ida, b. Nov. 18, 1734, m. Gerret Strycker of G^d; and Marya, bp. Apl. 21, 1737—all bp. in N. U. Signed his name "*Barent Van Deventer.*"

Cornelis Jansen, m. Sept. 1, 1695, Maria ——. Took the oath of allegiance in N. U. in 1687 as a native. Issue:—Jan, bp. June 13, 1697; Geertruyt, bp. Aug. 25, 1700; and Annetje, bp. Nov. 4, 1705—all in N. Y. and (sup.) to be his children.

Dirck Jansen, alias *Smith*, m. Oct. 7, 1660, in N. Y., Marrytje Dircks from Hoorn. He was a ship-carpenter, residing on High St. in N. Y. in 1665, and d. in 1686, as per Valentine's Manual. He was fined in 1674 25 Beavers for insulting Lieut. Quirynsen, as per 692 of vol. II. of pp. 686 and Doc. of Col. His. Possibly not a s. of Jan Pietersen.

Jacobus Janse, m. Femmetje Barends. On a deed of 1698 his w. is called Engeltie, who may have been his second one. Oct. 12, 1696, he bought of Lambert Durland of S. I. and Harmpie his w. a farm of 40 A. in Br^n, where he at the time resided, and of which place in 1697 he was one of the commissioners appointed to divide the common lands.

Suppose that at one period he resided in N. U. Issue:—
Jan, bp. July 26, 1688; and Barent of Fl[h] in 1719.

Jan Pietersen, the ancestor of the family, emigrated
in 1662 from the "Steght" in the Netherlands, and may
at one period have resided at Deventer in Overyssel. He
was b. in 1629; m. 1st Maria ——; m. 2[d] Engel Teunis.
Settled at first in Br[n], and from thence removed to N. U.,
of which place he was appointed schepen by Gov. Colve in
1673, where his name appears on the ass. roll of 1675, and
where he and his w. were mem. of the R. D. ch. in 1677.
Owned plot No. 5 at Yellow Hoek (Bay Ridge) as early as
1677, which he sold Nov. 17, 1680, to Hendrick Mattyse Van
Pelt. Bought May 14, 1682, of Claes Claesen Smith his
farm in N. U., as per p. 132 of Lib. 2 of Con., and which he
sold Sept. 1694 to his s. Pieter Janse for 6000 gl. In 1687
he took the oath of allegiance in N. U. Issue:—Pieter
Jansen; Jacobus Jansen; Henry Jansen; Cornelis Jansen;
Dirck Jansen; and Femmetje Jansen, m. 1st Cornelis Van
Cleef, and m. 2[d] William Hansen.

Pieter Jansen, emigrated with his father Jan Pietersen,
and m. Mar. 22, 1686, Mayke or Maria Christiaan of Yellow
Hoek, N. U. In 1677 mem. and in 1697 a deacon of the
R. D. ch. of N. U.; in 1686 resided at Marteman's Neck; in
1698 and 1709 in N. Y., and on ass. roll of G[d] in 1693.
Issue:—Cristiaen, bp. Mar. 29, 1687, in Fl[h]; Maria; Abraham, bp. Sept. 5, 1697, and settled in Monmouth Co., N. J.,
m. Neeltje Cowenhoven; and Isaac (twin), bp. Sept. 5, 1697,
m. Saartje Cowenhoven, and also settled in Monmouth Co.

VAN DE WATER, BENJAMIN (Jacobse), of Bedford, Br[n], bp.
Feb. 17, 1669; m. *Engeltie Harmense;* and took the oath of
allegiance in Br[n] in 1687 as a native. Was sheriff of Kings
Co., his term expiring in 1702, as per p. 298 of Cal. of Eng.
Man. Issue:—Harman, bp. June 9, 1695; Engeltie, bp. Aug.
11, 1700, in Br[n]; and Bernhardus, bp. Jan. 15, 1710. Signed
his name *"Ben Vandewater."*

Cornelis Jacobse of Br[n], bp. Nov. 9, 1673; m. Dorothea
——. On cen. of Br[n] of 1698. Issue:—Engeltie, bp. Mar.
20, 1709.

Hendrick of Br[n] in 1662. A Hendrick Van de Water from
Amsterdam m. Apl. 21, 1662, in N. A. Margariet Van der
Meulen from Rotterdam, and took the oath of allegiance in
N. Y. to the English in 1664. Signed his name *"Hendrick
Van de Water."*

Jacobus, emigrated from the Netherlands in 1658; m.
Engeltie Juriaans ; d. Jan. 1730-31. In 1674 appointed town
major of N. A. by Gov. Colve. Left N. Y. after 1677 and

settled in Bedford, and in 1689 was appointed clerk of Kings Co., as per p. 188 of Cal. of Eng. Man., which office he held until 1704, taking the oath of allegiance in Br^n in 1687. Issue:—Lysbeth, bp. July 20, 1667; Benjamin, bp. Feb. 17, 1669; Cornelis, bp. Nov. 19, 1673; Jacobus, bp. May 3, 1676, m. Helena ——; (all bp. in N. Y.;) Elizabeth, bp. July 20, 1677, m. 1st, July 4, 1695, in N. Y., Johannes Pauluzen of Esopus, m. 2^d John Quitans, m. 3^d, July 29, 1715, Patrick Heas of Ireland; Johanna, bp. Aug. 7, 1678, in N. Y., m. Cornelis Hendricks Sleght; Alburtus, m. Heyltie ——; Jurriaan, bp. Nov. 30, 1684, in Br^n; (sup.) Johannis of N. Y., m. Baefje Jans; (sup.) Jannetje, m. Derick Benson of Haerlem; (sup.) Ariaentje, m. Willem Willemse Bennet of Gowanus; (sup.) Femmetje, m. Cornelis Van Cleef of N. U. There also emigrated from Amsterdam a Hendrick and Pieter Van de Water, who resided in the city of N. Y. and left descendants.

VAN DE WERVE or WERFT, CATHARINE, wid. of Do. Polhemius, bought Aug. 11, 1680, of Titus Syrachs de Vries a lot in Fl^h first owned by Peter Jacobse, as per p. 44 of Lib.· A of Fl^h rec. May 6, 1682, she sold to Jacob Lazilier woodlots Nos. 13 and 14 in the N. L. of Fl^h, as per p. 159 of Lib. AA of Fl^h rec.

VAN DITMARSEN, see Ditmars.

VAN DOESBURGH, ADRIAEN HENDRICKS, probably from Doesborgh in Gelderland, m. *Lysbeth Thomas.* There was a Hendrick Andriese Van Doesburgh in Beverwyck as early as 1654, who m. Maritie Damon, as per Pearson's First Settlers of Albany. Issue:—Marytje, bp. Mar. 31, 1678, in Fl^h.

VAN DRIEST, JAN BARENTSE, from Sutphen in Gelderland, emigrated in 1658 and was a carpenter by trade. He m. May 18, 1679, *Jannetje* dau. of Willem Jansen Van Barkeloo; d. prior to 1697. Jannetje after the death of her husband m. 2^d Elias Hubbard. Resided in 1672 and '74 in Fld^s and afterwards removed to G^d, where he bought land June 26, 1666. Apl. 9, 1674, he bought of the estate of Daniel Morgen, dec., plantation-lot No. 11, with the buildings and improvements, as per G^d rec., to which he probably removed. Issue:—Barent Janse of G^d, bp. Dec. 18, 1681; Cornelis Janse, bp. June 29, 1684, no further trace; Margrietje Janse,. bp. Dec. 10, 1695; William Janse, a merchant in N. Y., who d. single in G^d; and (sup.) Jan Jansen. His descendants dropped " Van Driest " and adopted " Johnson " as their family name, and constitute the present Johnson family in G^d, the descendants of Gen. Jeremiah Johnson of Brⁿ and others. For a further account of his descendants, see "Johnson." Signed his name "*Jan Barense*" as near as it can be made out, and on some occasions made his mark "I. B."

VAN DUYCKHUYSEN, see Van Dyckhuysen.

VAN DUYN, ABRAHAM GERRETSE, emigrated from Zwolle in Overyssel with his father; m. Apl. 3, 1696, *Geertje Martens* of the Wallabout, being a resident of N. U. at the date of his marriage. In 1698 his name appears on the cen. of Brⁿ, after which he resided at Maspeth Kils, then on the Raritan, N. J., and in 1714 in Cecil Co., Md. Issue:—Marten, bp. July 31, 1698; Abram, bp. Oct. 30, 1699; Isaac, bp. Apl. 3, 1706, in N. J.; and Geertje, bp. Nov. 10, 1710, at Neshaminy, Pa.

Cornelis Gerretse, bp. July 16, 1664; m. 1st, Jan. 4, 1691, Matilda dau. of Willem Huyken of Gowanus; m. 2^d, June 14, 1714, Christina Gerbrands. In 1687 he took the oath of allegiance in N. U. as a native; commissioned as justice of the peace of the county in 1689, and on ass. roll of N. U. of 1693. Apl. 30, 1699, he bought of Simon Aesen De Hart and w., executors of Wm Huyken or Heocken, dec., for £262 10 sh. a farm at Gowanus 400 rods in length and 78½ rods in breadth. Dec. 30, 1699, he bought of Conrades Vanderbeek a farm in Gowanus, as per p. 210 of Lib. 2 of Con. Suppose these purchases, or at all events the one of the Huyken's, to be the farm late of Peter Wyckoff and since the farms of his sons Peter and John Wyckoff as shown on Butt's map of Brⁿ. Apl. 16, 1705, as per town rec., his father Gerret Cornelise conveyed to him the farms in N. U. now (1880) occupied by Ab^m Duryee and Peter Cowenhoven on behalf of their wives, descendants of said Cornelis Gerritse. In 1706 he was assessed in N. U. for 102 A. With others, about 1710, he bought the Harlington tract in Somerset Co., N. J. Will da. Mar. 3, 1752; pro. Oct. 26, 1752; rec. p. 145, Lib. 19, N. Y. surr. off. Issue:—Gerret, b. Sept. 6, 1691; Machiltie, m. Hendrick Staats; Christina ; Stynthe or Seytie, m. Gerret Nostrand; William, b. Mar. 26, 1693; Annetje, bp. Nov. 15, 1694, m. Folkert Rapalje; Jackomyntje, bp. Jan. 14, 1700, m. Reinier Veghte; Cornelis, bp. Nov. 14, 1704, d. young; Cornelia (twin), b. Feb. 12, 1709, m. Nicholas Veghte; and Cornelis, b. Feb. 12, 1709, m. Femmetje or Phebe ——, d. Sept. 1779, owned the Peter Wyckoff and Richard Berry farms in Gowanus, and with his w. was buried in the graveyard on said P. Wyckoff farm located within the boundaries of what is now Hamilton Ave., and whose bones, with those of the other tenants of said graveyard, were removed by the Wyckoff family to Greenwood Cemetery. Signed his name *"Cornelis Van Duyn."*

Denys or *Dionys Gerretse,* m. ·Feb. 4, 1691, Maria or Marretje Heocken or Huyken; d. 1729. Left Fl[h] and removed to Three Mile Run, Somerset Co., N. J., where he resided as late as 1723. Returned to Fl[h] and resided on the farm conveyed to him by his father, as per p. 174 of Lib. 2 of Con., adjoining to and partly in N. U., now (1880) of the heirs of George Martense, dec. Took the oath of allegiance in Fl[h] in 1687 as a native; on cen. of 1698, and in 1707 a deacon in Fl[h] ch. Assessed in 1706 in N. U. for 35 A. Issue:—William of N. J., bp. Mar. 4, 1695, m. Sybrech Verkerk; Denyse of N. J.; Gerret, m. Seytie Verkerk; Jacobus; and David. Signed his name *"Denys Van Duyn."*

Denyse (s. of Denys Gerretse), m. Antje ——. Settled in Middlebush, Somerset Co., N. J. Issue:—Adriaentje, bp. Feb. 23, 1733, d. young; Maria, bp. June 22, 1735; Jan of Flushing, bp. Aug. 7, 1737, m. Magdalena Van Nuyse; and Adriaentje, bp. Jan. 29, 1740.

(Sup.) *Dirck Gerretse,* m. Gerten Hoppe; d. 1686. Obtained a patent from Philip Cartaret for land at Bergen, N. J., and in 1662 a patent from the Dutch Director-gen. for the same premises, as per p. 101 of Winfield's Land Titles of Hudson Co. His children wrote their names " Van Dien." Issue:—Gerret of Hackensack, who m. in 1696 Vroutie Verway; and Geertien, m. in 1714 Hendrick Kip of Hackensack.

Gerret Cornelise, the common ancestor of the family, emigrated in 1649 from Nieuwkerk in Zeeland; m. Oct. 1663 Jacomina or Jacomynchy Jacobs Swarts of N. A.; d. in 1706. Was a carpenter and wheelwright by trade, and Apl. 9, 1658, while a resident of Br[n] was fined for refusing to pay towards Do. Polhemius's salary. Aug. 10, 1670, he obtained permission from the director-gen. to return to Holland, and with his wife kept house at Zwolle in Overyssel, but not prospering he returned in 1679 in the ship The Charles, the vessel in which were embarked Pieter Sluyter and Jasper Dankers, De Labidists, whose interesting journal was procured and has been translated by the Hon. H. C. Murphey and published by the L. I. His. Society. He finally settled on a farm partly in N. U. and Fl[h], conveyed to him by Jacques Cortelyou, his brother-in-law, as per p. 231 of Lib. 1 of Con., which farm he conveyed to his s. Denyse. He also bought tracts of land on the S. side of the main road from the village of N. U. to Fl[h], which he conveyed to his s. Cornelis Gerretse. His name appears on the patent of N. U. of 1686, and in 1687 he took the oath of allegiance in said town, of which place he was a mag. in 1687 and '88, and justice of the peace in 1689 and '90. From this it is evident that the old Van Duyn house, in which it is supposed he resided and which was demolished a few years ago, was at this period considered to be located within the boundaries of N. U., although as the line is now fixed it would have been in Fl[h]. Will da. June 30, 1705; pro. June 14, 1706; rec. p. 250, Lib. 7, N. Y. surr. off. Issue:— Cornelis Gerretse, b. July 16, 1664; Gerret Gerretse; Denys or Dionys Gerretse; Willem Gerretse; (sup.) Dirck Gerretse of N. J.; Cornelia Gerretse, m. Cornelis Bogaert; Abraham Gerretse; Aeltie Gerretse, m. 1st Jan Thysen Lanen Van Pelt, m. 2[d] Peter Cornell of Newtown; and Jackomyntie Gerretse, m. George Anderzy or Anderse of N. Y. Signed his name *"Gerret Cornellissen Van Duyn"* and at times *"Gerret Cornellissen."*

Gerret Gerretse, referred to in papers of 1704, but no further trace, and possibly the reference may be to some other Gerret.

Gerret Cornelise (s. of Cornelis Gerretse and Matilda), b. Sept. 6, 1691; m. Altie Van Nostrand; d. Aug. 7, 1777. Resided in N. U. Will da. May 3, 1773; pro. Oct. 16, 1784; rec. p. 33, Lib. 38, N. Y. surr. off. Issue:—Cornelius of Fl[h], bp. Sept. 27, 1724, m. Sarah Verkerk; Altie or Alletta, b. Oct. 22, 1729, m. Anthony Hulst of Gowanus; Mageltie or Matilda, b. Aug. 23, 1732, m. W[m] Brouwer of Fishkill; Jacomyntje, b. Aug. 22, 1737, d. in 1746; and John of N. U., b. Mar. 14, 1743, m. successively Nelly Martense and Nela Vander Hoven. From Cornelius and John are descended the Fl[h] and N. U. branches of the family. Signed his name *"Gerret Van Duyn."*

Gerret (Denyse), m. Seytie dau. of John Verkerk. Owned and occupied the homestead of his father partly in Fl[h] and N. U., now of the heirs of George Martense, dec. Issue:— Adriaantje, bp. Feb. 23, 1733, d. young; Maria, bp. June 22, 1735; Jan of Flushing, bp. Aug. 7, 1737, m. Magdalena Van Nuyse; and Adriaantje, bp. Jan. 29, 1740. Signed his name *"Gerret Van Duyn."*

(Sup.) *William Gerretse.* A William Van Duyn, supposed to be this William, resided at Three Mile Run, N. J., in 1703, and was a mem. of the Raritan D. ch. in 1723. Signed his name *"Willem Van Duyn."*

William Cornelise, b. Mar. 26, 1793; m. Adrianna dau. of Dowe Ditmars; d. Feb. 20, 1769. Resided in Newtown as early as 1731. Will da. Dec. 1. 1768; pro. Feb. 23, 1769; rec. p. 41, Lib. 27, N. Y. surr. off. Issue:—Catharine, b. 1721, m. Jacob Remsen; Cornelius, b. 1724, m. Ann dau. of Dominicus Vanderveer; Matilda, b. 1726, m. Abraham Remsen; Dowe of Newtown, b. 1730, m. 1ˢᵗ Sytie Vanderbilt, m. 2ᵈ the wid. of Gerret Springsteen; and Arriaentie.

William (Denyse), bp. May 4, 1695; m. Sybrech dau. of Roelof Verkerk. Settled in Middlebush, Somerset Co., N. J., and joined the R. D. ch. of New Brunswick in 1753. Issue:— Denyse of N. J., bp. Sept. 13, 1724; Cornelius of N. J., m. Jannetje Williamsen; William of N. J., bp. Oct. 3, 1733, m. Lena Voorhees; and (sup.) Jacobus of N. J.

VAN DYCK (sup.) ABRAHAM JANSE of N. U., m. *Elizabeth* ——. Aug. 25, 1705, he and w. of Yellow Hoek (Bay Ridge), N. U., conveyed to Pieter Tyssen (sup. Van Pelt) a house and lot of 30 A. at Yellow Hoek. These premises were conveyed Sept. 10, 1709, by said Pieter Tyssen to Derick Tyssen, and by Derick Tyssen to John Pieterse of Brⁿ in 1709, as per pp. 188 and 191 of Lib. 1 of conveyances, and appear to have been located on the bay at Bay Ridge, on the S. side of Bay Ridge Ave.

Achias, Agyas or *Haggiaus Janse,* emigrated in 1651; m. 1ˢᵗ Jannetje Lamberts or Lammers; m. 2ᵈ, Dec. 1693 Magdalena Henderse or Hendrica wid. of Minne Johannes. He bought Nov. 30, 1695, of Adriaen Bennet Senʳ land in Gowanus, Brⁿ, bounded by and between lands of Thomas Shirox, Tunis the fisher (Tunis Van Pelt), and Gertie Haddam fronting on the bay and cong. 60 A., as per p. 72 of Lib. 2 of Con. This farm which he occupied adjoined or was near the N. U. boundary, and his heirs sold the same in 1708 to Tjerck Van Dyck. Mem. of D. ch. of Brⁿ in 1677; on ass. roll of Brⁿ of 1676 and cen. of 1698, and took the oath of allegiance there in 1687. Issue:—Lambert bp. Sept. 16, 1677, in Brⁿ; Susanna, bp. May 18, 1679, in Fldˢ; Tryntje, bp. Oct. 17, 1680, in N. U., m. Hendrick Hendricksen; Barber or Barbara, b. Dec. 20, 1682, m. Johannes Coerte Van Voorhees; Barent, bp. May 20, 1685, in N. Y.; Thomas, bp. Apl. 17, 1687, in N. U.; Jacob; and Janneke. Made his mark to documents.

*Carel,*¹*Karel* or *Charles Jansen,* emigrated from Amsterdam in 1652; m. June 27, 1680, Lysbeth Aards Vander Hard; d. in 1734. On ass. rolls of N. U. of 1675 and '83; mag. in 1683 and '84; on Dongan's patent of 1686; and took the oath of allegiance there in 1687. Assessed in N. U. in 1706 for 80 A. From N. U. he removed to Shrewsbury, N. J., where he died. Will da. Dec. 1, 1732; pro. Mar. 11, 1734; rec. p.

12 of Lib. C, off. Sec. of State, Trenton, N. J. No Thomas, Peter or Elizabeth named in the will, consequently doubts of their being his children. Issue:—Geertje, bp. May 8, 1681, in Fl^h, (sup.) m. 1st Jan Romeyn of N. J., m. 2^d (sup.) Jan Bennem of N. J.; Jan of Shrewsbury, bp. Nov. 19, 1682, in Fl^h; Engeltie, bp. Aug. 17, 1684, m. Hendrick Varwie or Verwie of N. J.; (sup.) Nelke, m. Daniel Hendricksen of N. J.; Aert, bp. May 6, 1688, in Br^n, d. prior to 1732; (sup.) Thomas of N. J., m. Mayke Wyckoff of N. J.; (sup.) Pieter of N. J., m. Adriaentje Neefus; and (sup.) Elizabeth, m. Thomas Heyer of N. J. Made his mark to documents. There was a Van Dyck in 1687 and '90, who signed his name "*Carel Van Dyck.*"

Claes or *Nicholas Thomasse*, m. 1st, Apl. 20, 1689, Tryntje Rinerse or Remmerse dau. of Rinier Arends of Fl^h; m. 2^d, June 4, 1692, Fransyntie Hendricks of Fl^h. Resided in Gowanus, Br^n, owning the farm late of Theodorus and Leffert Bergen, where he took the oath of allegiance in 1687. On ass. roll of 1693 and cen. of 1698. In 1683 and 1702 a Nicholas Van Dyck (who may have been this Nicholas) resided on the Raritan in N. J. Apl. 6, 1724, Claes Van Dyck and Fransyntie his w. sold his Br^n farm of 200 A. to Joseph Hegeman Junr, as per p. 6 of Lib. 5 of Con., and removed to George's Hundreds, New Castle Co., Delaware. Issue:—Tryntje, bp. Aug. 24, 1690, in Br^n; Thomas, b. Apl. 11. 1693; Geesje, (by 2^d w.) b. Oct. 4, 1694, (sup.) m. Ojen Caerty of "Midwout;" Maria, b. July 3, 1696; Henricus, b. May 3, 1698; Johannes, b. Mar. 22, 1700; Abraham, b. Jan. 22, 1702, m. Elizabeth ———; Antje, b. July 5, 1704; Nicholas of New Castle, the ancestor of the Delaware branch of the family, b. Jan. 6, 1706, m. Rachel De Allee wid. of Capt. Tybout; Hendrick or Hendricus of the Raritan, b. Feb. 10, 1709, (sup.) m. Margrietje Terhune; Margrietje, b. Jan. 11, 1711; Daniel, b. Nov. 3, 1713; and (sup.) Neeltje Claessen, who m. Daniel Lake of G^d. Made his mark to documents.

Derick Janse from Amsterdam, m. Apl. 25, 1674, in N. Y., Urseltje Jans of the same place. No trace of issue.

Hendrick Janse, b. July 2, 1653; m. Feb. 29, 1680, Jannetje or Femmetje Hermans dau. of Herman Janse Van Borkuloo, both residents of N. U. at date of marriage, where he was assessed in 1676. He finally removed to S. I. and was among those who Dec. 30, 1701, petitioned King William III. to be relieved from the influence of the Leislerian faction, as per p. 942 of Vol. IV. of Doc. of Col. His. of N. Y. There was a Hendrick Van Dyck and w. mem. of Bensalem D. ch. in Bucks Co., Pa., in 1710, who may have been this Hendrick. Issue:—Willemtje, bp. July 8, 1681, in Fl^h, (sup.)

m. Christian Van Hoorn of Bensalem, Pa.; Annetje or Jannetje, bp. 1698, on S. I., (sup.) m. Jan Van Vleck of Bensalem, Pa.; Jacob of Six Mile Run, N. J.; and (sup.) Frederick of Bensalem, Pa., m. (sup.) Jannetje Harense or Havende. Made his mark to documents.

There was a Hendrick Van Dyck who emigrated from Utrecht in the Netherlands in 1645, was schout-fiscall under Stuyvesant, and left descendants in this country, but he was of a different family from the Long Island Van Dycks.

Hendrick (Tierckse) of Br^n, m. Engeltie or Jonica ——; d. 1751. Assessed in N. U. in 1706 for 16 A. Bought in 1708 of the heirs of Achias Van Dyck his farm on the Bay at Gowanus, as per N. U. town rec. Apl. 3, 1701, for £300, he bought of David Stout of Monmouth Co., N. J., a large tract at Rowoms Creek, which he sold in 1705 to Hendrick Hendricksen, as per p. 366 of Lib. 1 of Con., in off. of Sec. of State of N. J. Will da. Mar. 1, 1751; pro. Oct. 30, 1751; rec. p. 31, Lib. 18, N. Y. surr. off. Issue:—Peter; Hendrick of N. J., m. Margeritje Terhune; John of Br^n, who inherited his father's farm; Gerretje, m. James Robinson; Jannetje, m. Phillp Van Arsdalen; Teuntje, m. Teunis Denyse; and Maria, (sup.) m. 1st Johannes Rapalje of N. L., m. 2^d Gerret Boerum; and Pieternella. Signed his name *"Henderick Van Dyk."*

Hendrick ^{2}*Thomasse* of Br^n, m. Sept. 7, 1679, Neeltje Adriaens wid. of Jan Lauwrensz of N. U., both being residents of Yellow Hoek in said town at the time. Dec. 2, 1685, he mortgaged his farm of 12 morgens at Yellow Hoek to John Knight, as per p. 15 of Lib. 1 of Con. Suppose he removed to Six Mile Run, N. J., a Hendrick Van Dyck being a resident of that place in 1717. No account of his issue. Signed his name *"Hendrick Tomisson."*

Isaac (s. of Thomas Janse) of Br^n, bp. Sept. 11, 1681, in Br^n; (sup.) m. Barbara ——. Settled on the Raritan and mem. and elder of the R. D. ch. of New Brunswick in 1703, 1717, etc. Will. da. Mar. 31, 1727; pro. May 15, 1727; rec. in off. of Sec. of State of N. J. Issue:—Thomas; Mary; and Isaac—all of N. J.

Jacob (s. of Achias), m. Catharine Van Brunt. Left Br^n and settled on S. I., and in 1710 with others bought the Harlington tract in Somerset Co., N. J. Issue:—Catharine, bp. Feb. 8, 1721, on S. I., d. young; Catharine, bp. Feb. 30, 1730, on do.; and Zacheus, bp. Jan. 16, 1732, on do.

Jan 'Janss of Amsterdam, emigrated in 1652; m. May 9, 1673, in N. Y, Teuntje Tyssen Van Pelt; d. 1736. Owned and resided on the farm late of Wynant I. Bennet of N. U., adjoining the Br^n line. On ass. rolls of N. U. of 1675 and

'83; mem. of D. ch. in 1677; mag. in 1679; on Dongan's
patent of 1686; and took the oath of allegiance there in
1687. Assessed in N. U. in 1706 for 126 A. Will da. May
16, 1735; pro. Nov. 9, 1736; rec. p. 35, Lib. 13, N. Y. surr.
off. Issue:—Catalyntje, bp. Nov. 13, 1681, in Brⁿ, m. Gerret Ketteltas; John; Thys or Matthys of Red Hoek, Brⁿ,
bp. Nov. 4, 1683, in Brⁿ; Tryntje, m. Daniel Hendricksen;
Angenietje, bp. Apl. 29, 1686, m. Simon De Hart Jun'; and
Jannetje, m. Rutgert Van Brunt of N. U. Made his mark
to documents.

Jan² Thomasse, emigrated from Amsterdam in 1652 and
settled in N. U.; (sup.) m. 1ˢᵗ ——— ———, by whom Thomas,
Carel, Derick, and Pieter; m. 2ᵈ Tryntje Agias, Achias, or
Hagen, who after his death m. 2ᵈ Tileman Jacobsz Vander
Meyer. In 1673 he was appointed one of the schepens of
N. U. by Gov. Colve. Jan. 25, 1675, his old farm in the village of N. U. was sold at auction to "Rut Joosten" (Van
Brunt) for 2500 gl.; his new farm was at the same date sold
to Cryn Janse (Van Meteren) for 2000 gl.; and his 2 house-
plots in the village to Hendrick Janse Van Dyck for 750 gl.,
as per town rec. There was a Jan Tomassen on the Delaware in 1659, as per p. 286 of Vol. XII. of Doc. of Col. His.
of N. Y., who possibly may have been this Thomas. Issue:—
Thomas Jansz; Derick Jansz; Carel or Charles Jansz; Pieter Jansz; Achias or Agyas Jansz; Hendrick Jansz, bp. July
2, 1653, in N. A.; Jan Jansz; Antje Jansz, m. Pieter Staats
of Brⁿ; Angenietje or Annetje Jansz, m. Adriaen Willemse
Bennet; Mayke or Marretje Jansz, m. Johannis Daniels
Rinckerhoudt; (sup.) Tryntje Jansz; and (sup.) Lambert
Jansz.

Jan'(s. of Carel Janse and Lysbeth), bp. Nov. 19, 1682;
m. 1ˢᵗ, June 6, 1706, Ann or Annetje Verkerk; m. 2ᵈ (sup.)
Rebecca ———. Left N. U. and settled at Shrewsbury, N. J.
Issue:—Teuntje, b. July 18, 1707; John, b. Nov. 6, 1709;
Ruloff, b. May 18, 1711; Matthias, b. Aug. 28, 1714; Abraham, b. Oct. 3, 1716; Simon, b. Aug. 12, 1718; Abraham, b.
1719; Isaac, b. June 28, 1721; Jacob. b. Nov. 12, 1723; Anna,
b. 1728, m. James Emmans—all of N. J.

John²(s. of Jan Jansz and Teuntje Tyssen), m. Martha
dau. of John Griggs of Gᵈ. Owned and occupied the farm
of his father at Bay Ridge, late of W. I. Bennet. His w.
after his decease m. 2ᵈ Adolph Benson. Will da. Oct. 11,
1754. In 1700 was capt. of the militia of N. U., as per p.
809 of Vol. IV. of Doc. of Col. His. Issue:—Hendrick, bp.
Sept. 28. 1740, of whom no further trace; John of N. U. (m.
Martha dau. of Coert Johnson), who owned the homestead
of his father, which he devised by will of Apl. 8, 1772, to his

only child Engeltie, who m. Jacobus Bennet, father of Winant I., who at his death owned said homestead farm; Engeltie; William G. of G^d, b. Jan. 17, 1755, (the ancestor of the G^d Van Dycks) m. Jannetje Denyse; and Jannetje. Signed his name "*Jan Van Dyck.*"

(Sup.) *Lambert* or *Lammert Jansz*, m. Fytje Barents. Suppose he resided in N. U., his first 4 children being bp. there. Issue:—Ida, bp. Dec. 25, 1677; Styntje, bp. Feb. 12, 1682; Barend, bp. Nov. 12, 1683; Feyteye, bp. June 15, 1685; Jacob, bp. Mar. 24, 1687, in Fl^h; and Jan, bp. Apl. 21, 1689, in Fl^h.

Lambert (s. of Achias), bp. Sept. 16, 1677; m. Mayke or Maryke Hooglant. Left Brⁿ and in 1712 he and his w. mem. of Six Mile Run D. ch. in N. J. In 1721 he appears to have resided on S. I. Issue:—Janneke, bp. Dec. 16, 1705, in N. Y.; Dirk, bp. Oct. 1, 1707, in N. Y.; Achias, bp. Oct. 26, 1709, at Raritan; Jenneke, bp. Oct. 24, 1711, in N. Y.; Adrian, bp. Nov. 18, 1713, in N. Y.; Achias, bp. Sept. 7, 1715, in N. Y., m. Ann Andrewart; Johannes, bp. Jan. 8, 1718, in N. Y.; Johannes, bp. Mar. 4, 1719, in N. Y.; Henricus, bp. June 11, 1721, on S. I.; and Elizabeth, bp. Apl. 1723, on S. I.

Nicholas, see Claes Van Dyck.

Pieter Jansz, of N. U. in 1720; m. Annetje Jansz. Issue:— Agneta, bp. July 25, 1680, in Brⁿ; Isaac, bp. June 30, 1682, in Fl^h; and Jacob of N. Y., bp. Oct. 4, 1685, in Fl^h. Signed his name "*Pieter Van Dyck.*"

Thomas (s. of Achias), bp. Apl. 17, 1687; m. 1st Annetje ——; m. 2^d —— ——. Suppose he owned and occupied the farms N. of Bay Ridge Ave. in Bay Ridge, formerly of John and Wynant Bennet, now (1880) of H. C. Murphy, Sedgwicks, Kent, and others. A justice of the peace in N. U. in 1751. Issue:—Jannetje, bp. Mar. 5, 1732, in N. U. Made his mark " T " to documents.

Thomas Janse of Amsterdam, the ancestor of the Kings Co. Van Dycks, m. Sytie Dirks. A Thomas Jansz of N. Y. and Sytie Dirks from Amsterdam admitted a mem. of the R. D. ch. of Brⁿ in 1661, supposed to be this Thomas. Issue:—Jan Thomasse; Claes or Nicholas Thomasse; and Hendrick Thomasse.

Thomas³ Janse (s. of Jan Thomasse and Tryntje), m. Maritje Andriesen; d. prior to Sept. 1695. Obtained a patent for 24 morgens in N. U. Dec. 26, 1661, which he sold Oct. 28, 1677, to Rutger Joesten (Van Brunt). A mag. (schepen) of N. U. in 1673; on ass. rolls of Brⁿ of 1675 and '76, where he owned a farm on the Bay or River, lying on the southerly side of the premises Stoffel Johannes Schaers sold Sept. 17,

22

1695, to Woughter Van Pelt. Issue:—Tjerck of N. U.;
John of Middlesex, N. J.; Andries of New Castle, Delaware,
bp. Aug. 11, 1675, in N. Y.; and Isaac of Middlesex, N. J.
Signed his name "*Tomas Yansen.*"

Thys or *Matthyas* (s. of Jan Jansz) of Red Hoek, bp. Nov.
4, 1683; m. Angenietje ——; d. Mar. 1749. Bought May
23, 1712, of the Van Cortlands, Red Hoek, Brⁿ. Will da.
Mar. 8, 1749; pro. Apl. 10, 1749. Issue:—Jan, who owned
and occupied the Red Hoek homestead, m. Margaretta
Folkers; Catharine, m. (sup.) Hendrick Van Borre; Teuntje,
m. Folkert Van Hosen; Jannetje; Maria, (sup.) m. William
Bennet; Maghee; Engeltie; and Margrietje. Signed his
name "*Matthias Van Dike.*"

Tjerck or *Tierck Thomasse* of N. U., m. Pieternella ——.
Resided at Yellow Hoek (Bay Ridge), where he owned a
house and 48 A., for which he was assessed in 1706, and
which he sold to Cornelis Van Brunt. In his will, da. May
1, 1749, pro. Feb. 6, 1750, he directs his lands in N. U. to be
equally divided among his children. Issue:—Thomas, (sup.)
m. Jannetje Suydam; Peter; Hendrick of Yellow Hoek, m.
Engeltie or Jonica ——; Gerrit; Ariaentje; and Engeltie.
Made his mark to documents.

Van Dyckhuys, Tomis Hillebrants, probably from
Dykhuizen, a village in Utrecht, bought Mar. 3, 1661, of
Hendrick Janse Oesterstroem a building-plot on the S.
side of the road in Flᵇ, as per p. 54 of Lib. B of Flᵇ rec.,
which premises he appears to have sold Mar. 31, 1661, to
Derick Huysen and Rynier Bastiaensen Van Giesen, as per
p. 58 of Lib. B of said rec. Jan. 6, 1663, he sold to Dirck
Janse Vander Vliet a farm with plain and meadow land in
Flᵇ, as per p. 118 of said Lib. B. Mar. 15, 1667, he bought
of Tomas Swartwout 23 morgens in Flᵇ, with plain and
meadow land, as per p. 11 of Lib. C of Flᵇ rec. In 1666 he
resided in Fldˢ. Signed his name "*Tomis Hillebrants.*"

. Van Dyckhuysen, Jan Tuenessen, (probably from Dykhuizen, a village in the province of Utrecht in the Netherlands, where he may have at one period resided,) a carpenter
by trade, emigrated from Leerdam in South Holland in
1643; m. *Agatha* or *Achia* dau. of Elbert Elbertse Stoothoff;
and d. about 1699. At first he appears to have resided in
N. A., where he plied his trade, and to have removed to Brⁿ,
of which place he was schout fiscal in 1646. Mar. 17, 1662,
he obtained a patent for 17 morgens in Flᵇ. After his marriage he appears to have removed to Fldˢ, where he took
the oath of allegiance in 1687, his name appearing on the

ass. rolls of said town of 1675 and '83, patent of 1685, cen. of 1698, and was justice of the peace in 1693. He was also a mem. of the D. ch. of said town in 1677 and a deacon in 1681; and appointed lieut. of militia in 1689. After his marriage he appears to have visited Holland, his fatherland, and returned from thence to this country in 1679 in the same vessel with Dankers and Sluyter, De Labidists, as per the Hon. H. C. Murphy's trans. of their journal. His will (not recorded) is da. June 22, 1699, in which his dau. Auke, Swaentje, and Alida are named and his w. Achia. On the settlement of his estate in 1702, as per p. 244 of Lib. 2 of Con., it appears he owned in addition to his Fld' lands considerable land in G^d. Issue:—Auke, bp. Apl. 7, 1677, m. John Lucassen Van Voorhees; Aeltje (twin with Auke), bp. Apl. 7, 1677, d. prior to the death of her father; Swantje, bp. July 18, 1680, in Fld', m. Aaron Schuyler of Fld'; and Alida, bp. Oct. 12, 1684, in Fld', single in 1702. Signed his name "*Jan Tuenessen Van Dyckhuysen.*"

VAN ECK, PIETER WINANTSE or WYNANTSE, bp. Sept. 9, 1663, and b. at Bedford, Br^n; m. *Anna Maria* ——. Took the oath of allegiance in 1687 in Br^n as a native. Issue:— Winant Pieterse.

Winant Pieterse, from Betuwe in Gelderland, b. 1632; m. Dec. 4, 1661, at Br^n, Anneken Auckes (Van Nuyse). Feb. 10, 1661, he and others asked permission to build a block-house in the vicinity of the Wallabout for their defence, from which it is evident he was then residing in that vicinity. In 1664, as a resident of the ferry, he made an affidavit relating to Capt. Scott's raid on the Dutch towns of the county. On ass. roll of Br^n of 1675. Sept. 30, 1678, he obtained a patent for Red Hoek, as per p. 103 of Vol. I. of Land Papers. Nov. 1695 he conveyed 24 A. at Red Hoek to Stephanus Van Cortland, as per p. 60 of Vol. I. of Stiles's Br^n. Issue:—Pieter Winantse, bp. Sept. 9, 1663; Ariaentje Winantse, m. June 4, 1693, in N. Y., Teuriaen Van der Berg; and Altje Winantse, m. Jan Willemse Bennet of Gowanus.

VAN EKELEN, JOHANNES, from Beverwyck (Albany) in 1657 and '67, from which place he came to Fl^h; m. Sept. 9, 1683, *Tryntje Titus* of Br^n. Schoolmaster and clerk of Fl^h from 1682 to 1706, as per Strong's Fl^h; on ass. roll of 1693 and cen. of 1698, residing at the time in N. L. Mem. of Assembly from 1693 to '98, and appointed clerk of the county in 1698, as per rec. of court of sessions. Will da. Jan. 9, 1696-7, as per Fl^h rec. Issue:—Johannes; Johanna;

Geesje; Jannetje, bp. Oct. 11, 1689, in Br^n, d. young: Jan-netje, bp. July 28, 1691, in Br^n; Anna; and Helena. Signed his name "*Johannes Van Ekelen.*"

Albert, brother of Johannes, bound Oct. 24, 1684, to John Poppen to learn the turner's trade, as per p. 175 of Lib. C of Fl^h rec.

VAN ELFLAND or ESLAND, CLAES, owned Nov. 7, 1651, about 2 morgens at Br^n ferry, as per deed of Cornelis Dircksen to Cornelis de Potter. In 1655 he was surveyor-gen. of the colony; in 1664 he took the oath of allegiance to the English in N. Y.; and in 1677 he resided in Albany. Had a s. Claes who was court messenger at N. A. in 1656.

VAN ENGEN, WILLEM WILLEMSE, among the first settlers of N. U. in 1657, and allotted a plantation which he sold May 9, 1661, to Rutger Joesten Van Brunt. Van Engen signifies from England, and it is probable he was the same person as Willem Willemse Bennet, a brother of Arie Wil-lemse Bennet, also one of the first settlers of N. U.

VAN ENS or EENS, CORNELIS HENDRICKSEN, and Reydert Aertsen, bought Feb. 12, 1661, of Hendrick Pieterse (Wyckoff) of Fld^s a bouwery in Midwout of 27 morgens, with plain and meadow land in addition, as per p. 50 of Lib. B of Fl^h rec., which bouwery Van Ens sold Aug. 21, 1663, to Jan Damen, as per p. 143 of Lib. B of Fl^h rec.   Oct. 27, 1677, Hendrick Pieterse (Wyckoff) appears again to convey the same bouwery to "Cornelis Hendrickx Van Eeens," as per p. 21¾ of Lib. C of Fl^h rec., and Nov. 19, 1677, Van Eeens to convey the same to Claes Milles Baes, as per p. 25 of Lib. C of Fl^h rec. Signed his name "*Cornelis Hendrickse Van Ens.*"

VAN ESLAND, see Van Elfland.

VAN FLAESBEECK, FEMMETJE, of Bu^k, m. July 12, 1682, in N. Y., *Henricus de Foreest*, both residents of N. Y.

VAN FRURDE, HENDRICK JANSE, on petition of May 1664 for a canal at Red Hoek, as per Stiles's Br^n.

VAN GEESCHER, JAN WILLEMSE, m. *Harmtje Harmse.* Was born in Deventer in Overyssel; they emigrated to this country with their s. Wilhelmus, and on Jan Willemse and his w. dying Wilhelmus was left the only survivor and heir. The above ap-pears from an affidavit made by Gerrit Gerritse and Geesje his

w. before Justice Joseph Hegeman at Fl[h] on the Oct. 26, 1696, as per p. 227 of Lib. A of Fl[h] rec.

VAN GIESEN, REYNIER BASTIAENSEN, probably from Giessen, a village in North Braband, m. Dirckje Cornelis, and entered into an agreement June 6, 1660, with the magistrates of Fl[h] and the consistory of the R. D. ch. of said place to teach school, perform the duties of court messenger, to ring the bell, keep the church in order, perform the duties of precentor, attend to the burial of the dead, and all that was necessary and proper in the premises, for an annual salary of 200 florens exclusive of perquisites. This agreement was signed by Adriaen Hegeman, Willem Jacobse Van Boerum, Elbert Elbertsen, Jan Snediker, Jan Strycker, and Pieter Cornelise, probably as mag. of Fl[h] and Fld[s], and by Johannes Theodorus Polhemius, Jan Snediker, Jan Strycker, and Willem Jacobse Van Boerum, as the consistory of the church, on the one part, and by Reinier Van Giesen (omitting the "Bastiaensen" which is inserted in the body of the instrument), of the other part, for which see p. 24 of Lib. B of Fl[h] rec. Strong on p. 109 of his History of Fl[h] places Adriaen Hegeman as the first schoolmaster of the town, and as serving from 1659 to '71, omitting Van Giesen from his list. The above agreement shows this to be an error; and that Van Giesen was probably the first schoolmaster. Jan. 6, 1663, he sold to Jan Strycker a house and lot in Fl[h], styling himself in the deed "court attendant," as per p. 117 of Lib. B of Fl[h] rec. He probably finally removed to Bergen, N. J., for on p. 66 of Winfield's Land Titles of Hudson Co. is found a Rynier Michealsé prior to 1713, and who was probably a s. of the schoolmaster. Issue:—Jacob, bp. Jan. 16, 1670; and Gysbertje, bp. Apl. 30, 1673 — both in N. Y. There was also a Rynier Van Giese, who m. 1st Dirckje Van Greenland, m. 2[d], Sept. 1699, at Hackensack, Hendrickje Buys wid. of Cornelis Verwey, as per Hackensack D. ch. rec.; and an Isaac, Abraham, and Bastiaen Van Giesen, of Acquackannonck in 1700, in which localities their descendants are to be found. Signed his name "*Reynier Van Giesen.*"

VAN GOEDE, see Jochem Wouterse.

VAN GUNST, JAN HENDRICKSE, m. *Helena Pieterse.* Bought Mar. 10, 1655, of Jan Jansen de Jongh (or Junier) 25 morgens in Fl[h] for 800 carolus gl., for which he obtained a patent May 22, 1655. These premises were located on the easterly side of the village, adjoining on their S. side the land of Rutger Jansen, on the W. side Aert Tunisen, on the E. the highway, and on the N. the hills, and with the buildings thereon were bought by Jan Jansen of Jan Rutgersen. Aug. 22, 1658, a sale of land in Fl^h by him to Willem Douklis was confirmed, as per p. 949 of Vol. VIII. of Dutch Man. in off. of Sec. of State, Albany.

VAN HAMBURGH, JAN, or Jan from Hamburgh, was a jury-man May 9, 1698, on a coroner's inquest on a body lying on the shore between Red Hoek and Bomtje's Hoek.

VAN HASYMES, CORNELIS KLAESSEN, m. *Antje Teunis.* Issue:—Sara, bp. Jan. 17, 1687, in Br^n.

VAN HATTEM, AERNT, probably from Hattem, a village in Gelderland, was a burgomaster in N. A., and obtained June 4, 1654, a patent for a plantation in Fl^h, of which place, as per Hon. H. C. Murphy, he was among the earliest proprietors. Bought Apl. 1, 1653, of Wm Golder, attorney of Robert Pennoyer, a tract in G^d, as per Col. Doc. Signed his name *"Aernt Van Hattem."*

VAN HEEMST, ALBERT JANSE, (probably from Heemstede, a village in North Holland, after which place Hempstead on L. I. was probably named,) sold Sept. 12, 1661, a house and lot at the ferry to Jacob Kip, as per p. 322 of Br^n Manual of 1863.

VAN HENDEEN, WILLEM. His name appears as a resident on an agreement for settling the boundaries of the common lands of N. U. of Jan. 31, 1671-2, as per town rec.

VAN HEYNNIGHE, CLAES JANSEN, m. *Jannetje Kiersen,* who joined the R. D. ch. of N. Y. in 1672. He was guardian of the minor children of Gerrit Snediker and Willemtje Vookes, as per p. 180 of Lib. D of Fl^h rec. Issue:—Hillegond, bp. Nov. 14, 1686; Cornelia, bp. Aug. 30, 1689; Cornelis, bp. Nov. 15, 1693; and Sara, bp. June 28, 1695—all in N. Y. Signed his name *"Claes Jansen Van Heynnighe."*

VAN HOESEN, KNOET MOURIS, see Koert Mouris.

VAN HOOCHTEN, FRANS JANSEN, a carpenter, sued Oct. 6, 1662, Wolfert Gerritsen Van Couwenhoven for lands in Amersfoort (Fld^t), as per p. 230 of Cal. of Dutch Man. In 1664 he took the oath of allegiance to the English. He m. *Marretje Gerrits,* and had a dau. Marritie bp. Dec. 13, 1665, in N. Y.

VAN HOUGEM OR HOUWEGEM, CORNELIS, m. *Maria Winter-*

slick; d. prior to 1697; made his will Mar. 5, 1689-90, as per p. 150 of Lib. A of Fl[h] rec., in which he names his s. Cornelis. Signed his name *"Cornelis Van Hougem."*

Cornelis (s. of Cornelis and Maria), on ass. roll of Fld[e] of 1693. June 19, 1697, he bought of Reynier Arentsen a house and lot on the N. side of the highway and back of the church in Fl[h], as per p. 231 of Lib. A of Fl[h] rec., and was allotted 2 lots on the division of the Fl[h] woodlands in 1701, in which year he appears to have resided in Newtown. Signed his name *"Cornelis Van Houwegem"* and at times *"Cornelis Van Hougem."*

VAN HUYNN, see Idesse.

VAN ISELSTEYN, JAN WILLEMSE, called Jan of Leiden, m. *Willemtje Willems.* May 12, 1664, while a resident of Bu[k], he was sentenced to be punished and banished for abusing the magistrates of that place. Issue:—Willem, bp. Feb. 20, 1658; Jacomyntje, bp. Nov. 30, 1661; and Cornelis, bp. June 24, 1669—all bp. in N. A.

VAN KERK, see Verkerk.

VAN LAER, ARYAN or ADRIAN, m. 1st *Abagail* dau. of Abram Isaacsen Plank or Verplancken, the owner at one period of Poulus Hoek (Jersey city); m. 2[d], Apl. 28, 1672, *Luytie Schonen,* wid. In 1664 he took the oath of allegiance to the English in N. Y. Apl. 1666 he bought of Isaac Claesen two double building-plots in Fld[t], as per p. 58 of Lib. D of Fl[h] rec. Owned property in N. Y. in 1672. Mar. 1, 1680-81, he bought of Simon Romeyn a house and lot in Fl[h], as per p. 47 of Lib. A of Fl[h] rec. His name appears on the ass. roll of Br[n] of 1683. Issue:—Gerret, bp. Nov. 27, 1669, in N. Y. Signed his name *"Aryan Vanlaer."*

VAN LIEW or LIEUWEN, JAN FREDERICKS, emigrated in 1652, as per his marriage record, from Utrecht, having been probably at one period a resident of Leuwen, a village in Gelderland, on the Waal, in the Netherlands; m. *Aeltje Jans* dau. of Jan Jansen. On ass. rolls of Br[n] of 1675, '76, '83, and '93; deacon in the R. D. ch. in 1683; and took the oath of allegiance in Br[n] in 1687. Issue:—Jan, bp. Dec. 9, 1677; Margriet, bp. Mar. 14, 1680; Abraham, bp. July 9, 1682; Grietje, bp. Apl. 20, 1685; Dina, bp. Mar. 25, 1687; Esje, bp. Nov. 10, 1689; Hendrick, bp. Apl. 30, 1694; and Elizabeth, bp. Dec. 13, 1697—all in the Kings Co. churches. There was a Frederick Van Liew of J[a], L. I., who emigrated from Utrecht and had 9 children, many of whose descendants are to be found in Somerset Co., N. J., and whose s. Hendrick, bp. Oct. 14, 1683, m. 1ˢᵗ, Apl. 18, 1713, Geertje Cortelyou of N. U. (at which place he probably at one period resided), m. 2ᵈ Marya ——, and had a s. Jeurien (by 2ᵈ w.) bp. Aug. 26, 1721, in N. U.

VAN LODESTEYN, SOPHIA, sold Oct. 19, 1687, to Jurian Hendricks Vander Breets a house and lot in Brⁿ, bounded on the one side by the house of Jorias Drets and land of Joris Hansen (Bergen), and on the other "the laning of the town before the highway," as per p. 118 of Lib. 1 of Con.

VAN LOPHORST, LURUS. On a "list of what land every man hath in tillage ter yeare in Gravesend" in 1657, as filed in the town-clerk's office, he is entered for 8 morgens. The other residents of the town are entered as follows:

	Morgens.		Morgens.
Wᵐ Goulder Junʳ,	8	Thoˢ Whitlocke,	5
Jacob Swart,	7	John Ruckman,	7
Water Wall,	7½	Thoˢ Greedy,	8
Charles Morgan,	9	Richᵈ Gibbons,	10
Peter Symson,	13	Richᵈ Stoute,	17
John Cooke,	10	James Hubbard,	15
John Hans,	11	The Lady Mody,	16
Lorence Johnson,	12	Ed. Browse,	8
John Vaughan,	18	John Thomas,	8
Wᵐ Wilkins,	13	John Bowne,	6
John Tilton,	14	John Pieters,	5
John Van Cleeve,	14	John Applegate,	9
Thomas Spicer,	9	Symon Lane,	8
Ralph Cardell,	12	Thomas Morrell,	9
James Grover,	6	James Curler,	6
Lizabet Appelgate,	11	Bartʷ Applegate,	8
Carson Johnson,	8		
Wᵐ Bowne,	12		356½
Lieut. Stillwell,	7		

VAN LUANE or LOWAANEN, SWAEN JANSE, (Van Luane may be intended for "from Sierra Leone"on the coast of Africa,) a free negro, emigrated or came to this country in 1654; m. 1ˢᵗ *Cristine Maniel;* m. 2ᵈ, Dec. 18, 1685, *Sᴂsanna Pieters;* d. previous to 1696. Bought Apl. 13, 1680, for 2000 gl. of Teunis Janse Van Pelt lot No. 4 at Yellow Hoek, N. U., a farm on the N. side of the present Bay Ridge Ave. fronting on the Bay, as per p. 117 of Lib. AA of Flʰ rec. This farm covers what was a few years ago, at least a part if not the whole of the premises owned by Winant and John Bennet, now of Murphy, Sedgwick, Kent, Brown, and others. Swaen took the oath of allegiance in N. U. in 1687, and in 1680 he and his w. were mem. of the R. D. ch. of said town. There was a "Swaen Janse" assessed in Fld* in 1675, who was probably the above Swaen. Issue :—Philip, bp. July 6, 1669, in N. Y. Made his mark to documents.

Teuntje of Br⁰, m. Jan. 20, 1705, in N. Y., Antony Byvank of N. Albany.

VAN LYDEN, JOHN, (probably John from Leiden,) of Buᵏ, per Thompson's L. I. He was sentenced to be banished for libel, as per court rec.

VAN MARCKEN, JAN GERRITSE, probably from Marken, an island in the Zuider Zee in the Netherlands, came over in the ship St. Jacob in 1654, m. *Geestje Huybertse* in Europe; was a free merchant and resident of New Amstel on the Delaware in 1657 and '61; farmer of the excise at Fort Orange (Albany) in 1661 and '62; schout or sheriff of Schenectady in 1673; and from 1679 to '82 clerk and schoolmaster of Flʰ, where he owned land. Issue:—(sup.) Catharine, who m. 1ˢᵗ, July 2, 1682, Nieuw Amstel Hoop of Amsterdam, and m. 2ᵈ, May 18, 1684, Barend Barendsz of Amsterdam—both residents of Flʰ. Signed his name "*J G Van Marcken.*"

VAN MECKELEN, EVERT JANSE, probably from Mechelen, a village in Limburg, m. Feb. 7, 1690, *Metje Simonse Van Aersdalen*, residing at the time in Flʰ.

VAN METEREN or VAN MATER, JAN GYSBERTSEN, from Bommel in South Holland in 1663. On ass. rolls of N. U. of 1675, '76, and '83, and cen. of 1698; mag. in 1673, and deacon of the D. ch. in 1683. He removed to Middletown, N. J., and has numerous descendants in Monmouth Co. Issue:—Kryn Jansen. Signed his name "*Jan Gysbertsen Metrn.*"

Jan (s. of Kryn Jansen), bp. Apl. 24, 1687, in N. U., m. 1ˢᵗ Nelke Van Cleef; m. 2ᵈ Ida Suydam. Left N. U. and settled in Monmouth Co., N. J.; mem. of Freehold D. ch. in 1713, and deacon in 1729. Issue:—Kryn Janse (by 1ˢᵗ w.), bp. Sept. 28, 1718, at Middletown; Ryck (by 2ᵈ w.), bp. June 19, 1720, in N. U.; (sup.) Elizabeth, who m. Wᵐ Bennet; Maria, bp. Mar. 1731 at Marlboro, m. Daniel Polhemus; Ida, bp. Mar. 4, 1733, · m. Benjamin Sutphen; Cornelius, bp. July 25, 1737; Annie, bp. Oct. 14, 1739; and Geertje, bp. Mar. 29, 1763, m. Aert Vanderbilt.

Kryn Jansen, emigrated with his father in 1663, and settled at first in N. U.; m. Sept. 9, 1683, Neeltje Van Cleef of N. U. On ass. rolls of N. U. from 1675 to 1709; mem. of the D. ch. in 1677, and deacon in 1699; on Dongan's patent of 1686; and took the oath of allegiance in said town in 1687. Assessed for 46 A. in N. U. in 1701. In 1709 he removed to Middletown, Monmouth Co., N. J. Issue:—Jan, bp. Apl. 24, 1687; Engeltie; Gysbert of N. J., m. Mayke Hendricksen; Kryn Janse of N. J., m. Mayke Verkerk; Benjamin of N. J., m. Elizabeth Laan; Eyda or Eyke, m. Jan Bennet of N. J.; Joseph, bp. Aug. 30, 1710, in Middletown, m. Sarah Schenck; Cyrenius, m. 1st Elizabeth Laan, m. 2d Abagail Lefferts; and (sup.) Jannetje, m. Aart Sutphen. Signed his name "*Kryn Jansen Van Meteren*" and at times "*Kryn Van Meteren.*"

VAN NAERDEN, CLAES JANSE, probably from Naarden, a town in North Holland, petitioned the Director and Council for 21 morgens in Br^n, for which he obtained a patent Sept. 30, 1645, as per p. 369 of Cal. of Dutch Man. There was a Pieter Van Naerden who had children bp. in N. A. from 1654 to '62, as per the R. D. ch. rec. of that place. See Claes Jansen Ruyter.

VAN NAS, GERRIT DIRCKSE, with others petitioned Feb. 10, 1661, for leave to build a block-house on a point of Rapalie's land at the Wallabout for defence.

VAN NEF, EVERT DERCKSEN, owned land at the Wallabout in 1661, as per Notarial Register of Solomon La Chaire. Signed his name "*Evert Dercksen.*"

VAN NES, CORNELIS, probably from Nes, a village in Friesland, obtained a patent May 23, 1659, for 50 morgens at Flds adjoining land of Wolfert Gerritse Van Couwenhoven. There was a Cornelis Hendrickse Van Nes in Beverwyck in 1642, as per Pearson's First Settlers of Albany.

VAN NESS or NEST, JERONEMUS or HIERONEMUS PIETERSE, of Br^n, m. Aug. 22, 1691, *Neeltje Hewerse*, both of Br^n, and mem. of D. ch. of said town in 1677 and '85. Left Br^n and settled on the Raritan, N. J., about 1683. Issue:—Hendrick, bp. Mar. 21, 1696, in N. U.; Judith, b. Mar. 8, 1699; Catalyntje, bp. June 11, 1701; Margrietje, bp. Apl. 20, 1704; Jeronemus, bp. Apl. 14, 1706; William, bp. Apl. 26, 1709—all of N. J. and all bp. in the Raritan D. R. ch.

(Sup.) *John Pieterse* of Br^n. Settled on the Raritan.

Joris Pieterse of Br^n, bp. July 19, 1676, in N. Y.; m. Maria ——. Mem. of D. ch. of Br^n in 1677, and finally settled on the Raritan. Issue:—Maria, bp. July 16, 1699; Pieter, bp. Oct. 6, 1700; Jantien, bp. Oct. 27, 1702; Joris, bp. Oct. 25, 1704; Reynier, bp. Oct. 30, 1706; Abraham, bp. Apl. 26, 1709; Judith, bp. Aug. 17, 1711; Abraham, bp. Oct. 27, 1713; Hendrick, bp. Apl. 12, 1716; and Jacob, bp. Oct. 14, 1719—all of N. J. and bp. in the Raritan ch.

Pieter Pietersen, the common ancestor of the family, emigrated from the Netherlands in 1647 and settled in Br^n; m. Judith dau. of Joris Jansen Rapalie. On ass. rolls of Br^n of 1675, '76, and '83; entered as of the Wallabout on Do. Van Zuuren's lists of ch. mem. of 1677; and took the oath of allegiance in Br^n in 1687. There was an Abraham Van Nas on the Delaware in 1659, a notary public, etc. Issue:— Pieter Pieterse Junr; Catalyn Pieterse, bp. Mar. 3, 1672, in N. Y., m. Derick Middagh; Jeronemus or Hieronemus Pieterse; Lysbeth Pieterse; Joris Pieterse, bp. July 19, 1676, in N. Y.; Marretje Pieterse, bp. June 4, 1678, in N. Y.; Josina Pieterse, bp. Sept. 10, 1680, in N. Y., m. Hendrick Corsz Vroom of N. J.; Jakemyntje Pieterse, b. in N. Y., m. Klaes Arendsz Tours of Amsterdam, a resident of Bergen, N. J.; Judith Pieterse, bp. Sept. 30, 1685, in N. Y.; and (sup.) John Pieterse. Signed his name "*Pieter Pietersen Van Nest.*"

Pieter Pieterse Junr, b. in N. A., and resided with his father at the Wallabout in Br^n, and a mem. of the R. D. ch. of said town in 1677; m. Apl. 13, 1684, Margaret Crocheron of S. I. Finally settled on the Raritan near Sommerville, and was a member of the Assembly of E. N. J. in 1699, as per p. 221 of Rec. of Gov. and Council of E. N. J. Issue:— Jeronimus, bp. May 2, 1697, in N. Y.; Jaquemina, bp. Mar. 8, 1699; Joris, bp. June 20, 1703; Annatien, bp. Nov. 14, 1705; Bernardus, bp. Apl. 18, 1708; Jan, bp. Mar. 11, 1719; and Jacob, murdered by his negro slave—all of N. J.

VAN NESTUS, JOORES, may be intended for Joris Van Ness. He with John Rapalie, Joris Danielse Rapalie, Isaac Remsen, Jacob Reyerse, Aert Aersen (Middagh), Theunis Buys, Gerrit Cowenhoven, Gabriel Sprong, Urian Andriese, Jan Willemse Bennet, Jacob Bennet, and John Messerole Junr, were fined 10 sh. each for defacing the king's arms in the county court-house on the evening of Sept. 14, 1697, as per court rec. From this it may be inferred that these residents of Br^n failed to have that respect for their "dreade Sovereign" which loyal subjects were expected to entertain.

VAN NEW KERK, GARRET CORNELISE, same as Gerrit Cornelise Van Duyn.

VAN NOORT BROOK, PIETER JACOBSE, probably from "Noordbroeck," a village in Groningen, leased Feb. 7, 1667, of Tomas Fransen his plantation at Gowanus, lying on the S. side of that of W. Poules Vander Beeck, with house, barn, and barrack thereon, for 3 years commencing May 1, 1667, on condition that the lessor during said term clear 3 morgens of land and enclose the same in a post and 5-rail fence, for which the lessor is to do the carting; the lessee with his neighbor to fence in the meadows at the cost of the lessor; the lessor to furnish and let to the lessee 2 milch-cows, of which he is to be entitled to one half of the increase and 16 lbs. of butter annually for each cow; also 10 sheep, of which he is to be entitled to one half of the increase and wool, following the custom of the country. If after the lessee has been a year on the land he finds it necessary to have a pair of draught oxen, the lessor to furnish them, for which a reasonable compensation to be given. If the lessee in the last year of the term sows any of the land with winter grain, the lessor to allow what is reasonable for the same. In addition the lessor to furnish the lessee with 2 sows, for which he is to be annually entitled to one half of the increase. The lessor sells to the lessee a canoe, for which he is to deliver to the lessor on the shores of Manhattan I. 2000 pieces of wood in the month of June of this year. The lessor must also, on the edge of the land of Mr. Poulus, where there. stands a 3-rail fence, change it to a 5-rail one, an increase of about 50 rails. It is also expressly understood that such firewood as the lessee may cut to sell at the Manhattans the lessor shall have the privilege to purchase at the market price in preference to his selling to others. If it occurs that the lessor during the continuance of the lease from any cause should conclude to build and reside on the premises, if not damaging to the lessee, the lessor to be entitled so to do. The above is a translation of the main part of the record in Dutch of this lease, as recorded on p. 91 of Lib. D of Fl^h rec., and is given as a specimen of an ancient lease showing the customs of the times. The plantation referred to is the one occupied by Simon De Hart when visited in 1679 by the De Labidists, as set forth in Vol. 1 of the Transactions of the L. I. His. Soc., late the farms of Simon and John S. Bergen at Gowanus. The adjoining plantation of Vander Beeck is the one lately occupied by Garret Bergen. He made his mark to documents.

VAN NORT, PIETER PIETERSE, emigrated from the Netherlands in 1647 and settled in Brⁿ.

VAN NORTWYCK, PIETER JACOBSE, probably from " Noord-
wyck," a village in Groningen. Having m. Oct. 1662 *Femmetje Hermans* wid. of Pieter Janse, at her request, on the
15th of Oct. of said year, " Pieter Lodt and Jan Seuberen"
were appointed guardians of " Leffert Pieterse" (the ancestor of the Lefferts family) and " Pieter Pieterse" (the ancestor of the Hagewout or Houghwout family of S. I.), her
children by her first husband, as per p. 108 of Lib. B of Fl^h
rec.

VAN NOSTRAND, NOOSTRAND, or NOORSTRANT, AREN,
bought Mar. 7, 1695-6, of Gerardus Beekman 2 house-plots,
with house, barn, and orchard, in Fl^h on the S. side of the
highway leading to " East Midwout," as per p. 223 of Lib.
A of Fl^h rec. Issue:—(sup.) Jacob, bp. July 31, 1692; and
Albert, bp. Feb. 12, 1696—both bp. in N. Y. Signed his
name "*Aren Van Noostrand.*"

Albert Volkertse of Fl^h, bp. Feb. 22, 1687. No further
trace.

Frederick Symonsen of Fl^h, m. Aug. 13, 1687, Lea Fonteyn.
Issue:—Frederick, bp. Feb. 12, 1699, in Brⁿ.

Gerret Hansen, m. Apl. 20, 1685, Jannetje Remsen. Was
a farmer in Fld^s, mem. of the D. ch. in 1677, and took the
oath of allegiance there in 1687. Will pro. Feb. 22, 1742,
and rec. on p. 15 of Lib. 15 in off. of surr. of N. Y. Issue:—
Jannetje, (sup.) m. Cornelis Vanderveer; Aeltje, m. Gerrit
Van Duyn; Hans Gerretse; Joris Gerretse, bp. Dec. 9, 1694,
at Brⁿ; John Gerretse; Gerret Gerretse, bp. Apl. 10, 1699;
Rem Gerretse, m. Antie dau. of Steven Coerte Voorhees;
Peter Gerretse of J^a; and Daniel Gerretse. Signed his
name "*Gerret Hansen.*"

Gerret Gerretse, bp. Apl. 10, 1699; m. Seytie or Christina
Van Duyn. Issue:—Johannes, bp. Mar. 14, 1755; and Cornelis, bp. Jan. 12, 1757, in N. Y.

Hans Hansen or *Jansen*, the common ancestor of the
family, emigrated in 1639 from Noordstraat or Noord-
strandt in Holstein (there is also a Noordstraat in Zeeland); m. 1st, Nov. 29, 1652, Janneken Gerrits Van Loon;
m. 2^d —— ——; d. about 1679. Was a farmer, and settled
on the New Lotts of Fl^h. Will da. Aug. 20, 1679 ; rec. on
p. 195 of Lib. 4 in surr. off. of N. Y. Oct. 18, 1690, Peter
Gerrit and Jan Hansen (Van Noostrand) were required to
show cause for selling the estate of Hans Hansen (Van
Noostrand), dec., without administering thereon, as per p.

199 of Cal. of Eng. Man. Issue:—Gerret Hansen of Fld[a];
Pieter Hansen of Fld[a]; Jannetje Hansen, m. Pieter Schenck
of N. J.; Symar Hansen of Fl[h]; Jan Hansen; Volkert
Hansen; and Catharine Hansen, m. 1st Lucas Stevense
(Van Voorhees), (sup.) m. 2[d] Pieter Lourense Van Boskerk.
Made his mark "H" to documents.

Hans Gerrise of Fld[a], bp. June 26, 1687; (sup.) m. May 22,
1714, Reinsche Lucase Van Voorhies. Issue:—Gerrit.

Hans Volkertse of Fld[a], b. 1687 and settled at Hackensack,
N. J.

Jan Hansen, emigrated in 1639 with his father, b. 1637;
m. 1st Marretje ——; m. 2[d] Willemtje Van Boxum. Resided in Fld[a], Bu[k], and N. U. Dec. 10, 1675, he and Barent
Joosten of Bu[k] bought of Francois De Bruynne the main
part of the Anthony Jansen from Salee patent lying partly
in N. U. and partly in G[d], which they sold Dec. 11, 1693, to
Albert Coerten Van Voorhees. On ass. rolls of N. U. of
1675 and '83; deacon of the ch. in 1677; on Dongan's patent
of 1686; took the oath of allegiance in said town in 1687;
and capt. of militia in 1689. After selling his N. U. property
it is supposed he removed to Hackensack, N. J. Issue:—
Hans (by 2[d] marriage), bp. Oct. 30, 1695; Hendrick, bp.
Apl. 18, 1704, in Br[n]; and Marytje, bp. Dec. 25, 1709.
Signed his name "*Jan Hansen.*"

John or *Jan Gerritse* of Fld[a], m. Marya ——. Issue:—
Gerrit Janse, bp. Mar. 29, 1719, in Br[n]; Albert Janse, bp.
Oct. 8, 1721, in Br[n], (sup.) m. Sophia dau. of Joost De Be-
voise; and Mary Janse, bp. Aug. 19, 1733, in Br[n].

Pieter Gerritse of Fld[a], m. Elizabeth ——; d. 1746. Settled in J[a]. Will da. Aug. 22, and pro. Sept. 30, 1746; rec.
p. 8, Lib. 16, N. Y. surr. off. Issue:—Mary; Aram; Jacobus; and Peter.

Pieter Hansen of Fld[a], m. Hilletje Andriese dau. of Andries Janse of Fl[h]. Owned 10 morgens in Fld[a]. Will da.
Nov. 17, 1691; pro. May 26, 1692. From it is inferred
he had no issue. He and his brother Gerrit inherited his
father's farm.

Symon Hansen, emigrated in 1639; m. Oct. 24, 1663, Maria
Fredericks wid. of Jan Jorise Symons. On the marriage
record he is entered as from Amsterd or Amsterdam, which
raises the question whether he was a s. of Hans Hansen
Van Noostrand. Resided in Fl[h]; mem. of the D. ch. of
said town in 1677; and took the oath of allegiance there in
1687. Jan. 20, 1662, he bought 19 morgens in Fl[h] of Jan
Pieterse, which he sold Feb. 7, 1677-8, to Hendrick Ryke
for 3300 gl., as per p. 21 of Lib. AA of Fl[h] rec. He was allotted plots Nos 30 and 31 in the New Lotts of Fl[h], which he

sold to Cornelis Pieterse Wyckoff. Issue:—Frederick Symonsen; Riemerick Symonsen, m. Mar. 23, 1689, Johannes Fonteyn of Buᵏ; and Sara Symonsen, bp. Nov. 6, 1681. Signed his name "*Symen Hanssen.*"

Volkert Hansen, m. Apl. 3, 1681, Sarah Albertse Terhune of "Najack," N. U. Mem. of D. ch. of Fldᵃ in 1677, where he resided in 1685; removed to Hackensack in 1687, and at Middlebush, Somerset Co., N. J., in 1703. Issue:—Janneke Volkertse, bp. Nov. 13, 1681, at Fldᵃ; Albert Volkertse, bp. Feb. 22, 1685, in Flʰ, and entered on the record as of Hackensack; and Hans Volkertse, bp. ——, 1687, at Hackensack.

VAN NUKERK, GERRIT CORNELISE, probably from "Nykerk," a town in Gelderland, or "Nieuwerkerk," a town in Zeeland, sold Mar. 10, 1665, to Arent Evertse, molenaer (miller), a farm on the E. side of the road in Flʰ of 18 morgens, abutting against Corlaer's Flats, as per p. 20 of Lib. D of Flʰ rec. Made his mark to documents.

VAN NUYSE, AUCKE JANSEN, the common ancestor of the Van Nuyse family, emigrated in 1651 from Amsterdam (there is a village named Nuis in Groningen), commonly writing his name and known as Aucke Janse; m. 1ˢᵗ *Magdalena Pieterse;* m. 2ᵈ, about Dec. 1666, *Elizabeth Janse* wid successively of Christopher Schaets and of Jan Claesen; m 3ᵈ *Geertje Gysbrechts* wid. of Jan Jacobse. Was a carpenter, residing at first in N. A., where May 6, 1653, he sold his house and lot to Hendrick Hendricksen. In 1661 he resided at Brⁿ ferry; in Fldᵃ in 1665; in Flʰ in 1669, where he built the church in 1654 and '60, was appointed schepen in 1673 under Gov. Colve, and took the oath of allegiance in 1687; and in N. U. in 1675, where his name appears on the ass. roll of that year. Oct. 15, 1681, he bought of Bartel Claesen his house and farm in Flʰ of 19 morgens; also Claesen's share of the land lying at the Paerde Gat, patented by Gov. Andros Mar. 17, 1677, to said Claesen and Louis Janse; also 10 morgens on the plains of "Amersfoort," which Claesen bought of Samuel Spicer; and also 2 morgens on the "Midwoutse" plains known as No. 10, with salt-meadows, as per p. 142 of Lib. AA of Flʰ rec. Will da. May 15, 1694; pro. ——, 1698; rec. p. 303, Lib. 5, N. Y. surr. off. Issue:—Annetie or Anneken Auckersz, m. 1ˢᵗ Winant Pieterse Van Eck, m. 2ᵈ Derick Janse Woertman; Geertruyd Auckersz, m. Frans Joosten; Janneke Auckersz, m. Reinier Arendsz; Jan Auckersz; Abagail Auckersz, m. Leffert Pieterse of Flʰ; Pieter Auckersz, of whom no further trace;

Jacobus Auckersz; Femitie Auckersz, m. Jan Stevense Voorhees; and (sup.) Yda Auckersz, m. Aucke Rynierse. Signed his name "*Aucke Jansen.*"

Aucke Janse (s. of Jan Auckersz) of Fld⁸, m. Catryntje——; deacon in Fld⁸ ch. in 1725. Removed to the Raritan in N. J. Issue:—Barbara, bp. Nov. 18, 1701, d. young; Barbara, bp. Apl. 21, 1702; Her Jantien, bp. Apl. 20, 1704; Jan, bp. Apl. 3, 1706; William, bp. Aug. 4, 1708; Aucke, bp. Oct. 25, 1710; Ida, bp. Aug. 25, 1715; and Abraham, bp. Mar. 23, 1718—all of N. J., and bp. in the Raritan D. ch.

Aucke Jacobusz, m. Dec. 1, 1715, Altie dau. of Dirck Janse Amerman. Resided in N. U. in 1703, '15, etc., and assessed in said town for 55 A. in 1706. Issue:—Catrina, bp. June 23, 1721, in N. U.; Isaac, bp. Jan. 16, 1732, in N. Y.; and (sup.) Elizabeth Griggs.

Isaac Jacobusz of N. U., bp. Oct. 20, 1695; m. Catrina ——. Settled at Millestone, N. J., about 1727. Issue:— John of N. J., b. 1720, m. Martha Van Aersdalen; Isaac of Millstone, m. —— Quick and finally settled in Kentucky; Jacobus of N. J., m. Maria or Mary Hoogland; Cornelius, bp. July 13, 1735, settled in Kentucky; and Mary Ouke (sup.) m. Abᵐ Heyer of N. J.

Jacobus Aucker or *Ouke*, m. Apl. 26, 1685, Mary or Maria Willemse Cornel of Flʰ; d. about 1710. Resided in Flʰ in 1688, '96, and 1704. Left Flʰ and settled near New Brunswick, N. J., about 1699, and afterwards in N. U. Will rec. on p. 2 of Lib. 5 of Con., which gives the names of his children as William of N. U.; Johannes or Jan; Isaac; Magdalena; Margarite; Elizabeth; Maria; and Jacobus of N. J. Signed his name "*Yacobes Auckes.*"

Jan Auckes or *Ouke*, b. in Amsterdam and emigrated with his father in 1651, and was a carpenter by trade; m. 1ˢᵗ, July 29, 1673, Barbara Provoost of N. Y.; m. 2ᵈ, Apl. 4, 1680, Eva Janse dau. of Jan Jacobse of Brⁿ, where he resided at the date of his marriage. In 1678, in partnership with Ruth (Rutgert) Albertse, built by contract a parsonage in Flʰ, at which place he took the oath of allegiance in 1687. In 1691 he bought land in Jˢ, where he resided in 1699 and 1710. Issue:—Aucke Janse of N. J.; William, of Buᵏ in 1715, bp. Sept. 28, 1679, in N. U.; Jan Janse Junʳ of N. J., bp. July 17, 1681, in Brⁿ; Geertje Janse, bp. Nov. 19, 1682, in Flʰ; Barbara Janse, bp. Apl. 12, 1685, in N. U.; Maria Janse, bp. July 31, 1687, in N. U.; Isaac Janse, bp. Oct. 20, 1695, in Brⁿ, m. Maria ——; William Janse, bp. Feb. 5, 1699; and Abram Janse (twin) of Somerset Co., N. J., bp. Feb. 5, 1699, m. 1ˢᵗ Antie ——, m. 2ᵈ Henne ——, and had children

Abraham and Maria. Signed his name "*Jan Aukes Van Nuys*" and sometimes "*Jan Aukes.*"

Jan Janse Jun[r], bp. July 17, 1681; m. Lena or Helena (sup.) Duryea. Resided in Fld[s], and deacon of the D. ch. of said place in 1721. A Jan Van Nuyse of Fld[s] bought Apl. 28, 1722, of Enoch Freeland 100 A., now within the bounds of New Brunswick, N. J., on which it is supposed he settled. Issue:—Isaac, bp. Mar. 9, 1708, in Br[n]; Jacobus, bp. Oct. 17, 1725, in N. U.; and James—all of N. J.

Jan Jacobse of N. U. and N. J., m. Mar. 17, 1716, Adriaentje Wyckoff. Removed to New Brunswick, N. J., where he bought a farm about 1727. Will da. Sept. 29, 1747; pro. Nov. 3, 1747; rec. p. 192 of Lib. E in off. of Sec. of State of N. J. Issue:—Jacobus; Margrietje, bp. Apl. 23, 1725, in N. U.; Lena; Elizabeth; and Anne—all of N. J.

Pieter Auckerss, bp. Oct. 27, 1652. A suit was commenced against him Feb. 4, 1680-81, in Fl[h], by Cornelis Verway for 20 gl., the price of a gun, as per Fl[h] rec. No further trace.

William Jacobse of N. U., m. Magdalena ——; d. Sept. 16, 1771. Issue:—William of N. U., m. Anna dau. of Jan Verkerk and owned and resided on the farm in N. U. Lane late of James Arlington Bennet; Maria, m. Ferdinand Van Sicklen; George or Joost of Fld[s], bp. Sept. 16, 1716, m. Elizabeth Emmans; and Jacobus of N. U., m. Sarah dau. of Tunis Rapalje. The Van Nuyse family of Kings Co., whose farms are or were located mainly in Fld[s] and N. U., are descendants of this William Jacobse.

William Janse, bp. Feb. 5, 1699, and resided in Bu[k] in 1715.　⌐

VAN OOSTEN, CORNELIS, m. *Josyna Verhagen*, who after his death m. 2[d], about 1689, Rut Albertse. Issue:—Jakobus Cornelise; Elizabeth Cornelise; and Cornelia Cornelise of Fl[h], who m. July 20, 1682, Harmen Pieterse Van Blydenstein.

VAN OSTRAND, AARON, on ass. roll of Fl[h] of 1693 and cen. of 1698. This Aaron was probably same as Aeren Van Nostrand.

VAN PELT, AERT TEUNISZ, of N. U., (Van Pelt probably meaning "from 'Peel'" or "from the morass,") m. Sept. 10, 1686, *Neeltie Janse Van Tuil* of N. Y.; d. after 1639. Took the oath of allegiance in N. U. in 1687 as a native; on ass. roll of said town of 1693; cen. of 1698; mag. in 1698; lieut. of militia in 1705; and assessed in 1706 for 80 A. Bought

23

land at Millstone, N. J., in 1702. Issue:—Petrus Aertse of
N. U.; Jan Aertse, bp. Dec. 25, 1696, in Brⁿ; Neeltje Aertse,
m. Peter Cortelyou; Grietje or Margaret Aertse, m. Dirk
Van Sutphen; Geertruy Aertse, b. Oct. 10, 1693, m. Gysbert
Sutphen; Catlyn Aertse, bp. Nov. 9, 1695, in Brⁿ; Lysbet
Aertse; and (sup.) Aert Aertse, m. Annetje Voorhies. Made
his mark "A V P" to documents.

Aert Janse of N. U., m. Christyntje Emmit or Immit.
Resided at one period on S. I. and afterwards at Hackensack. Issue:—Maria, bp. Dec. 10, 1721; Jan, bp. 1723;
Marytje, bp. 1731; Abraham, bp. 1733; and Hendrick, bp.
1739. Signed his name "*Art Van Pelt.*"

Anthony Teunisse, emigrated from Liege in 1663 with his
father and settled in N. U.; m. Magdalena or Helena
Joosten; d. Feb. 2, 1720-21. On ass. rolls of N. U. of 1675,
'76, and '83; Dongan's patent of 1696; cen. of 1698; took the
oath of allegiance there in 1687; and assessed in 1706 for 98
A. In Nov. 1674 he petitioned the Gov. for a grant of land
on S. I. Issue:—Joost of S. I.; Teunis of S. I., m. Maria
Degreau; John of N. U. and S. I., m. Susanna La Tourette;
Maria, bp. Oct. 14, 1681, in Fld^s, m. Ary Schouten; Adriaentje, bp. Feb. 3, 1684, in N. U., d. young; Adriaentje, bp.
May 25, 1690, in Brⁿ, m. —— Taylor; Helena, bp. May 29,
1695, in Brⁿ, m. Teunis Stoutenburg; Grietje, m. —— Bond;
and Saartje, m. Cor^s Dorlant. Made his mark to documents.

Anthony Thyssen, b. 1646, and emigrated with his father in
1663. Resided in N. U. in 1693. No further trace.

Arie or *Adriaen Thyssen Lanen* or *Lane* of N. U., m. Marrytje or Martyntje Smack. On ass. roll of N. U. of 1693
and cen. of 1698. Of Middletown, Monmouth Co., N. J.,
in 1700, at which date, and as a resident of which place, he
conveyed land in N. U. to Gysbert Tysson (Van Pelt). At
one period of G^d. Issue:—Jannetje; Geertruy; and Hendrick, bp. 1707, in N. Y. Signed his name "*Adriaen Lane.*"

Cornelis Gysbrechtse, bp. Apl. 3, 1685, in Brⁿ. Removed
with his father to Monmouth Co., N. J. Issue:—Catryntje,
bp. Nov. 26, 1710; and Cornelis, bp. May 7, 1714, at Marlboro.

Derick Thyssen (sup. s. of Matthys Janse Van Pelt), m.
Antie ——. Resided in N. U. in 1709, and made his mark
to documents.

Gysbrecht Thyssen Lanen, b. in 1652, and emigrated with
his father in 1663; m. Jannetje Ariens or Adriaens. Mem.
of the N. U. ch. in 1677 and deacon in 1683. On Dongan's
patent of 1686, cen. of 1698, and in 1706 assessed for 83 A.
In 1709 he appears to have resided near Freehold, N. J. It

is probable that many of the numerous individuals in E. N. J. whose surnames are Laan or Lane are his descendants or those of his brother Adriaen, having dropped the *Van Pelt.* Will da. Nov. 7, 1720; pro. May 17, 1727; rec. p. 66 of Lib. B in off. Sec. State of N. J. Issue:—Jannetje; Wilhelmyntje, bp. Sept. 16, 1677, in Fl^h, m. Wm Hendricksen; Matthys, bp. Aug. 23, 1679, in Br^n, d. young; Catalina, bp. Apl. 24, 1681, in Fl^h, m. (sup.) Elias De Hart; Thys of N. J., bp. Mar. 30, 1683, in Br^n; Cornelis of N. J., bp. Apl. 3, 1685, in Fld^s; Mary, bp. Mar. 3, 1689, in Fl^h, m. (sup.) Ferdinand Van Sicklen; Joost of N. J.; and Maicken, m. Stoffel Langestraet. Made his mark to documents.

Hendrick Thyssen Lanen of Br^n; b. 1650; emigrated in 1663 with his father; m. 1st, Sept. 28, 1679, Annatie Tileman Vander Meyer; m. 2^d, Apl. 25, 1690, Marritje Bennet wid. of Johannes Christoffel Schaers of Gowanus; d. about 1693. Mem. of R. D. ch. of Br^n in 1677; on ass. roll of Br^n of 1673; on ass. roll of N. U. of 1683; patent of 1686; and took the oath of allegiance there in 1687. Issue:—Tileman, bp. Dec. 12, 1680, in N. U.; Thys, bp. May 13, 1683, in Br^n; and (by 2^d w.) Mayke, bp. Apl. 23, 1693, in Br^n. Made his mark to documents.

Hendrick Janse, left Kings Co. and settled on S. I.; m. 1st (sup.) Titje Anderis; m. 2^d Maritje De Hart. Issue:— Antje, bp. May 5, 1696; Aeltje, bp. Mar. 25, 1701; Jan, bp. Aug. 15, 1705, in N. Y.; Annetje, bp. 1706; Catlyntje, bp. May 12, 1719; and Hendrick, bp. Jan. 1, 1720-21—all except Jan on S. I.

Hendrick Teunise of N. U., m. Annitie Minders. On ass. roll of Br^n of 1676, of N. U. of 1683, and patent of N. U. of 1686. Issue:—Pieter, bp. Jan. 23, 1681, in Fld^s; Meindert or Meinherd, bp. Mar. 30, 1684, in N. U., d. young; Grietje, bp. May 7, 1685, in Fl^h; Myndert, bp. Jan. 9, 1687, in Fl^h; and (sup.) Hendrick of S. I. Made his mark to documents.

Jacob Janse, left L. I. and settled on S. I.; m. (sup.) Aeltje Hagewout. Issue:—Jan, bp. Apl. 17, 1711; Derekje, bp. in 1715, m. John Lawrence; Marytje, bp. 1715; Pieter, bp. Apl. 16, 1717; Jan, bp. Oct. 15, 1721; and Catlyntje, bp. Sept. 27, 1724—all on S. I.

Jacob Thyssen Lanen, was a minor in 1683, and took the oath of allegiance in N. U. in 1687 as a native. Suppose he had a s. John Lane or Lanen, who owned the farm N. of Bay Ridge Ave. at Bay Ridge, m. Ida ——, and d. in 1766. This John made a will da. Mar. 18, 1766; pro. July 29, 1766; rec. p. 273, Lib. 25, N. Y. surr. off. There was a Jacob Lane and Elizabeth Barkeloo his w. mem. of the R. D. ch. of Freehold, N. J., in 1709.

Jan Thyssen Lanen, a minor in 1683; m. Aeltie dau. of
Gerrit Cornelise Van Duyn, and took the oath of allegiance
in 1687 as a native. At one period resided in Newtown.
Issue:—Gerrit, bp. Oct. 30, 1695, in Br", d. young; Thys,
bp. Sept. 19, 1708; and Jackamintje.

Jan Teunise of N. U., m. Maria·Pieterse; d. after 1720.
Settled on S. I., where he obtained Oct. 10, 1674, a patent
for a tract of land, and where he also bought land in 1683.
Appointed lieut of infantry for Richmond Co. in 1689, and
mem. of Assembly in 1692. Was among those who Dec. 30,
1701, petitioned King William III. to be delivered from the
power of the Leislerian faction, as per p. 942 of Vol. IV. of
Doc. of Col. His. of N. Y. Will da. Dec. 11, 1719; pro. Dec.
11, 1734; rec. p. 253 of Lib. 12, N. Y. surr. off. Issue:—
Teunis Jansen; Pieter Jansen; John, Hannis, or Johannes
Jansen; Hendrick Jansen; Jacob Jansen; Daniel Dehart
Jansen; Anna Jansen; Margaret Jansen; and Aert Jansen.
Signed his name "*Jan Tonissen Van Pelt*" and "*Jan Tenissen
Pelt.*"

Jan (s. of Jan Teunisse), settled on S. I. and (sup.) m.
Aeltje Hoogland. Issue:—Marytje, bp. Oct. 22, 1710; Jan,
bp. July 6, 1712; Marrytje, bp. Feb. 9, 1715; Theunis, bp.
Apl. 1, 1716; Elizabeth, bp. June 15, 1718; Daniel, bp. Dec.
25, 1719; Catlyntie, bp. Oct. 16, 1720; Sara, bp. Jan. 25,
1718-19, m. Simon Simonse; and Catryntje, bp. Nov. 8, 1719
—the three last on S. I.

Jan Aertse of N. U., bp. Dec. 25, 1696; m. Feb. 8, 1716,
Catharine Hegeman. In 1742 Jan Van Pelt and Catharine
his w. conveyed land in N. U. to Joris Lott. Issue:—Adriaentje, b. Jan 11, 1720, m. Guysbert Sutphen, her cousin;
Catharine, bp. May 9, 1731; Teunis, bp. May 5, 1734; and
Jan, bp. Apl. 17, 1737—all bp. in N. U. Made his mark to
documents.

Jan or *John Janse*, m. —— ——. In 1732, '33, and '34 a
Jan Van Pelt was capt. of a sloop which sailed from N. Y.
to N. C. Issue:—Marytje, bp. Oct. 22, 1710; Jan, bp. July
6, 1712; Marytje, bp. Feb. 9, 1715; Theunis, bp. Apl. 1, 1716;
Elizabeth, bp. June 15, 1718; and Daniel, bp. Dec. 25, 1719
—all bp. in N. Y.

Johannis or *Hannis* (s. of Jan Teunise), settled on S. I., m.
1st Sarah Le Roy; m. 2^d Sophia Sloger. Will da. Oct. 1,
1748; pro. Sept. 18, 1750; rec. p. 214 of Lib. 17 in surr. off. in
N.Y. Issue:—Blandina, bp. Apl. 23, 1707, m. Titus Tetus;
Simon, bp. Apl. 20, 1708, d. young; Catalyna, bp. ——,. 1710;
Symon, bp. Apl. 15, 1715; Petrus, bp. Apl. 16, 1717; Johannis, bp. June 7, 1719; Sara, bp. Jan. 1, 1720-21—all bp.
in S. I.; and Anne, m. Hannis Simonse.

Johannes Wouterse, bp. May 8, 1687; m. Maria ——.
Owned and resided on the farm at Gowanus, afterwards of
Peter Bergen. Removed to Six Mile Run in N. J., and there
in 1748. Will da. Feb. 5, 1787; pro. Sept. 3, 1790; rec. p.
290 of Lib. 31, N. Y. surr. off. Issue:—Johannes of N. J.;
Sarah or Maria, m. Johannes Cray; and Annatye, who m.
—— Sutphen—all of N. J.

Matthys or *Thys Gysbrechtse*, bp. Mar. 30, 1683, in Brⁿ; m.
Ann or Auke Schenck, and removed with his father to
Monmouth Co., N. J. His will is da. June 27 and pro. Aug.
18, 1729, and rec. on p. 215 of Lib. B in off. of Sec. of State,
Trenton. Issue:—Gilbert, m. Jan. 7, 1741, Nellie Schenck;
Gerret, bp. Nov. 3, 1716, at Marlboro, m. Mayke Sutphen;
Aaron of the Raritan, m. Sara Cowenhoven at Marlboro;
Matthys, bp. Feb. 26, 1723, m. Elizabeth Sutphen; Cor-
nelius, m. Maria Warnsly; Ralph; and Nelly or Helena,
(sup.) m. Tunis Amak.

Matthys or *Thys Janse Lanen*, emigrated with his brother
Teunis Janse from the land of "Luyck" (Liege) in 1663 with
his w., who d. on the passage, and 4 children. He m. 2ᵈ
Adriaentje Hendricks, who after his death m. Cornelis
Wynhard. Settled in N. U., and his name appears on the
ass. rolls of 1675 and '76. Issue:—Anthoine or Anthony
Thyssen, b. 1646; Teuntje or Tryntje Thyssen, b. 1648, m.
Jan Janse Van Dyck; Hendrick Thyssen Lanen, (sup.) b.
1650; Gysbrecht Thyssen Lanen, (sup.) b. 1652; Annetje
Thyssen, m. Jurian Lootman of Esopus; Jan Thyssen La-
nen; Jacob Thyssen Lanen; (sup.) Adriaen Thyssen Lane;
(sup.) Pieter Thyssen; (sup.) Jannetje Thyssen, m. Tunis
Idense; and (sup.) Lysbeth Thyssen, m. Anthoni Juchum
of Buᵏ. Signed his name *"Thys Jansen Van Pelt."*

Peter Thyssen (s. of Thys Janse) of N. U., where he took
the oath of allegiance in 1687 as a native, m. Barbara Houl-
ten. Was assessed in N. U. in 1706 for 49 A. Issue:—
Teunis; Matys; Maria; Catryna; and Rebecca. Made his
mark to documents.

Peter Wouterse of Gowanus, Brⁿ. No evidence of his
marriage or having issue. By his will of Apl. 22, 1756, pro.
Mar. 2, 1773, he devises his real estate to his brothers Alexander, Teunis, and Johannes. This will being recorded on
p. 157 of Lib. L of wills in off. of Sec. of State of N. J.,
shows that at the time of his death he was a resident of
N. J., or at least that he owned land in that State. Signed
his name *"Peiter Van Pelt."*

Petrus Aertse of N. U., m. Oct. 19, 1734, Antje Dorland; d.
Sept. 6, 1781. Was capt. of the N. U. company of militia in
1758. Issue:—Neeltje, b. July 27, 1735, m. Nicasius Cowen-

hoven of N. U.; Rem of N. U., b. Apl. 17, 1738, the grandfather of the present (1880) John L. Van Pelt of N. U., m. Ida
dau. of Jacobus Lefferts; Elizabeth, bp. Aug. 2, 1745, m. Johannes Cowenhoven of N. U.; Aert of N. U., b. Oct. 20, 1748,
m. Femmetje Stellenwerf; Sarah, b. Dec. 20, 1750, m. Abraham Duryee of N. U.; Anna (twin), b. Dec. 20, 1750; John of
N. U., b. Oct. 20, 1754, m. Femmetje Duryee; and Peter
(twin) of N. U. and Pompton, b. Oct. 20, 1754, m. Maria Van
Nuyse.

Teunis (s. of Jan Teunise and Maria), m. Elsje Hendrix.
Issue:—Fransyntje, bp. Aug. 1, 1700; Samuel, bp. Dec. 13,
1704; Jacob, bp. Nov. 20, 1706; Theunis, bp. Sept. 2, 1709;
and Samuel, bp. July 31, 1715—all bp. in N. Y.

Teunis (s. of Anthony Teunise of N. Y.), m. Maria Dregeau
and settled on S. I. Will da. June 25, 1765; pro. Mar. 25,
1776; rec. on p. 210 of Lib. 25 in off. of surr. of N. Y. He
bought land on S. I. as early as 1727. Issue:—Anthony,
bp. Oct. 9, 1726, m. Jenneke Simonse; John, bp. Feb. 14,
1731, m. Mary Tonge; Maria or Mary, bp. June 3, 1734, m.
John Foy; Peter; Joseph; Joost, bp. May 10, 1737; Tunis,
bp. Nov. 19, 1738; Jacob; and Benjamin—all of S. I.

Teunis Jansen or "*Tonis Jansen Lanen Van Peelt*," as
written by himself, from the land of "Luyck"
(Liege), emigrated in 1663 with w. and 6 children.
He m. 1st (sup.) Grietje Jans; m. 2d, Aug. 6, 1696,
Gertrude Jans wid. of John Otter. Bought Apl. 7, 1670, of
David Jochems of N. Y. land near to "Rechawyck" (Brn),
previously granted to Ryer Lambertse, cong. 57 morgens,
located in Buk. Suppose he sold these premises to Jan
Messerole. Bought land in N. U. in 1675, '78, and '80; on
Dongan's patent of 1686; took the oath of allegiance there
in 1687; and was known as Tunis the fisher, that being
probably his principal occupation. Issue:—Jan Teunise;
Anthony Teunise; Elizabeth Teunise; Magdalena Teunise
or Jackemyntje, by a deed of 1700 m. Joachim Gulick; Aert
Teunise Lanen; Wouter Teunise; Hendrick Teunise;
Teuntje Teunise, m. Harmanus Van Gelder; and Rebecca
Teunise, m. Abm de La Montange. Signed his name "*Tonis
Jansen Lanen Van Peelt.*"

Teunis Wouterse of Gowanus, Brn, bp. Oct. 30, 1695; m.
Apl. 26, 1718, Greetje or Geertruy dau. of Willem Willemse
Bennet of Gowanus; d. about 1779. Bought land in Monmouth Co., N. J., where he resided at one period, but returned to Gowanus, where he d. By his will, da. Feb. 28,
1774, and pro. Dec. 17, 1779, he devised his N. J. lands to
his sons Peter and Christopher, and his Gowanus lands to
his son Winant. Issue:—Wouter, bp. Apl. 12, 1719, in

N. U., d. young; John of Br⁰ and of Monmouth Co., N. J., m. Jannetje Heyer; Peter of N. J., bp. June 22, 1735, at Freehold, (sup.) m. Neeltje Vanderbilt; Winant of Gowanus, (sup.) m. Mary Heyer; Marritie or Maria, bp. Sept. 9, 1739, at Freehold, m. Wᵐ Holland; Christopher of N. J., m. Aaltie Bennet; Johannes or Hannes of Monmouth Co., N. J., m. Anne Heyer; Alexander or Sander of Monmouth Co., N. J., m. Jannetje Heyer; and Aeltje, m. Peter Heyer of N. J.

Thys, see Matthys.

Wouter Theunise Lanen of Gowanus, Br⁰, emigrated with his father in 1663; m. Mar. 22, 1686, Maryte Janse dau. of Johannes Christoffelse Schaers of Gowanus. Sept. 15, 1695, he bought of Stoffel Johannes Schaers 40 A. at Gowanus lying between the lands of Simon Aersen (De Hart) and those of Maritie wid. of Thomas Van Dyck, fronting on the Bay, formerly of Johannes Christoffelse Schaers, dec., as per p. 74 of Lib. 2 of Con. On the date of this purchase he hailed from N. U., where he took the oath of allegiance in 1687. In 1702 he bought lands at Millstone, and about 1710 with others the Harlington tract in Somerset Co., N. J. Will da. May 10. 1728; pro. Sept. 29, 1744; rec. on p. 291 of Lib. 15, off. surr. of N. Y. Issue:—Jakemyntie or Jemina, m. Samuel Berrie; Maria, m. Arian or Adriaen Bennet; Johannes, bp. May 8, 1687; Tunis, bp. Mar. 16, 1690, d. young; Tunis of Gowanus, bp. Oct. 30, 1695; Lysbeth or Elizabeth, bp. Mar. 10, 1716, (sup.) m. Petrus Wyckoff of Fld'; Alexander of N. J.; and Peter of Gowanus. Made his mark "W" to documents.

Van Purmarent, Claes Jansen (from Purmarent, a town in North Holland), m. 1ˢᵗ *Pietersje,* dau. of Altien Brackhoengie of Gowanus; m. 2ᵈ, Nov. 11, 1656, in N. A., *Annetje Van Vorst.* He obtained a patent Jan. 1, 1662, for a tract of land near Horsimus or Ahasymus, near Jersey City, in Hudson Co., N. J., on which he resided. Through his first w. he inherited land at Gowanus. He was sometimes known as Jan Pottagie, and in his latter days as "Kuyper," probably from being a cooper by trade. See p. 42 of Winfield's Land Titles of Hudson Co., N. J.

Van Rossem, Huych Aerts, or from the village of "Rossem" in Gelderland, m. 1ˢᵗ *Annetje Teunis;* m. 2ᵈ, June 14, 1643, *Tryntje Harders Van Tuningen* wid. of Hendrick Holst. In 1646 he was a mag. of Br⁰, and Feb. 22, 1646, he obtained a patent for 29 morgens in Br⁰, which passed to Albert Cornelisen Wantenaer who m. his wid., and sold the same

Mar. 2, 1674, to Michael Hansen Bergen. Signed his name *"Huych Aerts Van Rossem."*

VAN ROTTERDAM, JAN CORNELISE, or from Rotterdam, occupied land at Gowanus May 17, 1639, as per Col. Man. Suppose he m. *Marretje Gerrits,* and had issue:—Jan, bp. Sept. 30, 1640; Cornelis, bp. Aug. 3, 1642; Abraham, bp. Jan. 24, 1655; Gerrit, bp. Feb. 15, 1660; and Jannetje, bp. Dec. 8, 1666—all bp. in N. A.

VAN RUYNEN, see Bartel Claesen.

VAN RUYVEN, CORNELIS, probably from the manor of Ruyven in South Holland, m. June 25, 1654, *Hillegond Megapolensis.* Sept. 6, 1658, he bought of Evert Duyckingh Van Borchem his patent of 26 morgens in Fl[h], lying on the E. side of the road, which he sold June 5, 1674, to Pieter Balyou or Billou, as per p. 37 of Lib. A of Fl[h] rec. He also appears to have obtained a patent about 1662 for 25 morgens in Fl[h], N. of Cor[s] Janse, along Longest Hill, and by land of Cor[s] Janse Bougart, as per p. 35 of Lib. A of Fl[h] rec. Van Ruyven was at one period sec. of the colony and a justice of the peace in the County of Kings. Issue:— Johannes, bp. Apl. 4, 1655, in N. A. Signed his name *"Cornelis Van Ruyven."*

George, owned a plantation in "Midwoud" (Fl[h]) July 12, 1655, as per Col. Man.

VAN RYDEN, BAREND. His name appears on a deed of the freeholders of G[d] dated Apl. 26, 1680, to Jacobus Oke (Van Nuyse) for 5 or 6 A of land, as per G[d] rec.

VAN SALEE, see Anthony Jansen.

VAN SANT, see Claes Carsten.

VAN SAXWSOELL, ISAAC, of Br[n]. His name appears on a deed of Aug. 20, 1667, per p. 179 of Lib. 2 of Con.

VAN SCHOONDERVOOERT, JAN or JOHN LOUWEN or LOWSEN (probably from Schoonderwoerd in South Holland), was an overseer of Br[n] in 1670, as per deed of Willem Bredenbent to W[m] Willemse Bennet. Owned land in Bedford in 1689, as per deed on p. 148 of Lib. 1 of Con.; also in 1700, as per deed of Lambertsen to Vanderhove, on p. 694 of Lib. 9 of Con. Pearson, in his First Settlers of Albany, states that 2 brothers, Teunis Jacobse and Rutger Jacobse Van Schoenderwoert, came to Fort Orange about 1640, the descendants of the former remaining in Albany, assuming the name of Van Woert, and those of the latter removing to N. Y. and taking the name of Rutgers.

VAN SCHOUW, CLAES CORNELISE, probably from the island of "Schouwen" in Zeeland, obtained Nov. 14, 1642, a patent for 16 morgens in Brⁿ, located between the ferry and the lands of, Andries Hudde. See Claes Cornelise Mentelaer.

VAN SECHTEN, FRANS JANSE, was plaintiff in a suit against Albest Albertse (Terhune) Aug. 18, 1660, as per Lib. B of Fl^h court rec. There was a Frans Janse, a carpenter, in Fld^s in 1660.

VAN SUTPHEN, see Sutphen.
Jan Barentse, see Van Driest.

VAN SYCKLEN or SICKLEN, CORNELIS REINIERSE, of G^d, m. *Maria* ——. Left G^d and settled at Amentien, Hunterdon Co., N. J., as early as 1717. Issue:—Neeltje, bp. July 29, 1718, in N. J.; Marytje, bp. Sept. 23, 1722, in N. J., m. Gerrit Schenck; (sup.) Gerrit, m. Margrita Van Leuwen; and (sup.) Andrew, who m. Mary ——. Made his mark to documents.

Ferdinando, a farmer, emigrated in 1652 and settled at first in N. A. and then in Fld^s. He m. Eva Antonise dau. of Anthony Jansen from Salee. Was a mem. of Fld^s D. ch. in 1677, and took the oath of allegiance in said town in 1687. Dec. 6, 1669, he bought of Anthony Jansen, his father-in-law, plantation-lot No. 29, with the buildings thereon, in G^d, as per town rec., to which he probably removed. May 11, 1682, he bought of Louies Janse a parcel of land at "Paerde Gat" in Fl^h, as per Fl^h rec. Issue:—Reinier; Eva, m. Jan Bordet or Boudet of Hackensack; Johannes; Margrietje or Grietje, 'm. Jan Albertse Terhune; Fernandes Junr; Susanna, bp. May 1, 1681, in N. U.; Cornelia, m. Jan Cornelise Banta of Hackensack; and (sup.) Jannetie, m. Adriaen Laen or Laan. Signed his name *"Ferdinando Van Sycklen."*

Fernandes Junr, m. Geertje ——. On ass. rolls of Fld^s of 1676 and '83 and cen. of 1698. Issue:—Eva, m. Hendrick Janse of N. U.; Margrietje, m. Cornelis Suydam of Oyster Bay; Fernandes, (sup.) m. Mary or Maria Van Nuyse; and Minne, m. —— Emans. Signed his name *"Fernandes Van Sychllen."*

Fernandus Reinierse of G^d and N. J., m. Mary or Maria (sup.) Laan; d. prior to 1767. Inherited the homestead in

G^d from his father. In 1736 he bought 200 A. of Lawrence Haff on Holland Creek in Hunterdon Co., N. J. In 1718 he resided at Arenten, Hunterdon Co., N. J. Will da. Apl. 28, 1749, and not recorded. Issue:—Mary, b. Nov. 14, 1709, (sup.) m. Samuel Linnington; Jannetje, b. Mar. 3, 1711, (sup.) m. Jan Suydam; Eva, b. July 14, 1714, m. Hendrick Johnson; Reinier, b. Sept. 8, 1716, (sup.) m. Mary ——; Gysbert of Fl^h, b. Oct. 8, 1718, m. Annetje Ryder; Johannes, the ancestor of the N. L. branch of the family, b. Nov. 22, 1722, m. Geertje Lott; Cornelius, the ancestor of the G^d branch of the family, m. 1st Femmetje Vanderveer, m. 2^d Catharine Johnson; and Catharine, b. Oct. 21, 1727, m. Hendrick Lott of Bedford.

(Sup.) *Jan Reinierse* of Fld^a, bp. June 19, 1695, in N. Y.; m. Lena ——, and settled on the Raritan, N. J. Issue:— Andries, bp. July 29, 1718, in N. Y.; Johannes, bp. Oct. 30, 1720, m. Christine or Styntje Sebring; Abraham, bp. Mar. 3, 1723, m. Antje or Saertje Ross; (sup.) Reinier; and (sup.) Marytie—all of N. J.

Johannes Ferdinanse of Fld^a, (sup.) m. Jannetje ——. Resided in G^d in 1694 and in 1699 on the Raritan. Issue:— Reinier, bp. Apl. 12, 1716, in N. J.; and Johanna, bp. May 29, 1726, in N. J.

Reinier Ferdinandese of G^d, m. Mar. 26, 1687, Jannetje Van Hooren or Horne of N. Y. wid. of Joseph Hegeman. Of Fld^a in 1667; of G^d in 1687, where he took the oath of allegiance as a native. Apl. 15, 1698, he bought of Wm Wilkins for £185 20 A. and some smaller plots in G^d. He also bought of Jochem Gulick, John Griggs, and Saml Gerritsen of G^d for £198 all their right in the mill standing on the Storm or Stroom Kil at Hugh Gerretsens so-called with the dam and all the property and right belonging to said mill, of which he conveyed Feb. 12, 1703-4, to his w. the one third part, as per G^d rec. Will da. Nov. 18, 1703; pro. Jan. 21, 1707; rec. on p. 336 of Lib. 4 in N. Y. surr. off. Issue:—Ferdinandus Reinierse of G^d; Cornelius; (sup.) Jan Reinierse, bp. Jan. 19, 1695, in N. Y.; and (sup.) Reinier. Signed his name "*Reinier Van Sichlen.*"

VAN TESSEL, JAN CORNELISE, was allotted in pursuance of the patent of Fl^h 23 morgens in said town on the S. side of the bouwery of Bartel Claesen, with plain land and salt-meadows, which he sold Jan. 20, 1670-1, to Aucke Janse Van Nuyse, as per p. 15 of Lib. A of Fl^h rec. Also allotted Mar. 14, 1670-1, a building-plot in Fl^h, as per p. 17 of said Lib. A. Signed his name "*Jan Cornelise*" and "*Jan Cornelisse Van Tessel.*"

VAN TIENHOVEN, CORNELIS (probably from "Tienhoven," a village in South Holland), of N. A. He obtained Mar. 15, 1647, a patent for a plantation in Br^n. Held offices and had several children baptized in N. A., as per p. 827 of Valentine's Manual of 1863. His will is da. Mar. 30, 1724; pro. July 27, 1737; and rec. on p. 88 of Lib. 13, N. Y. surr. off. Signed his name "*Cornelis Van Tienhoven.*"

Nicholas of Fl^h, m. Dec. 27, 1693, in N. Y., to which place he had removed, Maria Abrahamse from Amsterdam, a resident of N. Y.

VAN TILLBURGH, BARENT, (probably from the town of Tilburg in North Braband) m. Maria or Marritje dau. of Adam Brouwer of Gowanus, his name appearing on a Brouwer deed of 1698. Members of the family reside in Somerset Co., N. J. Made his mark to documents.

VAN TWILLER, WOUTER, director-gen. of New Netherlands, obtained a patent June 22, 1643, for Red Hoek, Br^n, which was forfeited; also a patent July 16, 1638, for one of the flats (prairies) in Fld^a known as Kaskutensuhane.

VAN UYTHUYSEN, SIMON, of Br^n (probably an emigrant from the village of Uithuyzen in Groeningen), m. ——— ——. Issue:—Elizabeth, who m. Mar. 17, 1685, Ditmars Jansen of Bergen, N. J.

VAN VARACK, see Varick.

VAN VECHT, VECHTE, or VECHTEN, KLAES ARENTSE (probably at one period from Vechten, a hamlet in Utrecht, or the river Vecht in the Netherlands), emigrated from Norg in the province of Drenthe with w. Lammetshe and 3 children in 1660 and settled in Br^n, where he owned a farm in Gowanus as early as 1672, on which he resided and on which the old stone and brick house near Fifth Ave., erected in 1699, now (1880) about disappearing, was probably built by him. On ass. rolls of Br^n of 1675 and '83; took the oath of allegiance there in 1687; on cen. of 1698; member in 1677, and an elder in the R. D. ch. of Br^n in 1681. There was a Teunis Dirkse Van Vechten who emigrated in 1638 and settled at Greenbush opposite Albany, whose descendants are to be found in the vicinity of Albany, Catskill, etc., but have seen no evidence of his relationship to Claes Arentse. Issue:—Hendrick Claesen; Gerrit Claesen; and (sup.) Michael Claesen. Signed his name "*Klaes Arents Vecht.*"

Gerrit Claesen, of Br[n] and S. I., emigrated with his father in 1660; m. 1st, Sept. 25, 1682, Jannetje Crocheron from "Walsh Vlanderin" and of S. I.; m. 2[d], Mar. 20, 1693, Magdalena Jans wid. of Jan Homs. Was a mem. of Br[n] ch. in 1677. Left Gowanus and removed to S. I. on a tract of 120 A. on Kil Van Kull, which his father obtained of Gov. Andros, and which he conveyed Jan. 17, 1689, to him. Member of the Colonial Assembly from Richmond Co. from 1699 to 1702. Will pro. Mar. 9, 1722-3, and rec. on p. 256 of Lib. 12, N. Y. surr. off. Issue:—Gerret of S. I., bp. Apl. 4, 1694; Lammetje, m. Ab[m] Lacheman; and John of S. I.

Hendrick Claesen of Br[n], emigrated with his father in 1660; m. Dec. 10, 1680, Gerritje Reiniers Wizzelpenning; d. Dec. 8, 1716. Mem. of D. ch. of Br[n], in 1677, took the oath of allegiance there in 1687, and on cen. of 1698. Owned the homestead in Gowanus of his father. Bought land at Millstone, N. J., in 1702, and in 1710 with others bought the Harlington tract in Somerset Co.. N. J. Issue:—Hilletje, bp. May 9, 1684, m. Hieronemus Rapalie; Famitje, bp. Jan. 30, 1687; Lammetje, bp. Apl. 23, 1693, m. Pieter Staats of Gowanus; Gerritje, bp. Oct. 19, 1696; Jannetje, bp. June 12, 1701, m. Pieter Dumont of the Raritan, N. J.; Claes or Nicholas, bp. Sept. 9, 1704, m. 1st Cornelia Van Duyne, m. 2[d] Abagail Lefferts, resided on and owned the homestead farm in Gowanus; and Reinier, bp. Oct. 13, 1706, m. Jacomyntje dau. of Cornelis Gerritse Van Duyn, and settled at Millstone, N. J.

(Sup.) *Michael Claesen*, settled on the Raritan, N. J., about 1683, and in 1710 a mem. of the North Branch R. D. ch. Issue:—(sup.) Derick of N. J., b. 1697, m. Rebecca Antonides Wickhant; and (sup.) Michael of N. J.

VAN VEN, RENYS, paid Apl. 2, 1664, towards the repairs of the roof of Fl[h] ch., as per town rec.

VAN VLECK or VLEECK, ISAAC, b. 1645; m. 1st *Cornelia Beekman;* m. 2[d], Mar. 5, 1680, *Catalyntje de Lanoy.* Was a dealer in beaver-skins in 1674 and '76, as per Stoothoff's Papers. Made an affidavit June 11, 1690, relating to the troubles under the administrations of Gov. Leisler. Had several children bp. in N. Y., as per p. 827 of Valentine's Manuel of 1863.

Tielman, an attorney for the heirs of Barent Baltus in a suit against Eaggeryn Balthus wid. of said Barent, of Apl. 7, 1660, as per Lib. B of Fl[h] court rec. Tielman Van Vleck was originally from Bremen, practised as a notary in N. A., and obtained a patent for sundry parcels of land in Bergen,

N. J., in 1770, to which he removed and of which place he was the first schout, as per p. 114 of Winfield's Land Titles of Hudson Co. No account of his having resided in Kings Co., although he appears to have practised there in his profession. Signed his name "*Tielman Van Vleeck.*"

VAN VLIET, see Vander Vlidt.

VAN VLIERDEN, JEREMIAS (probably from "Vlierden," a village in North Braband), of N. Y., bought Dec. 10, 1700, of John Marsh, the one fourth of a mill in Bu[k], which he sold Feb. 23, 1701-2, to John Messerole, as per p. 237 of Lib. 2 of Con.

VAN WERCKHOVEN, CORNELIS, a member of the West India Company, emigrated from Utrecht (probably from "Werckhoven," a village in the province of Utrecht), about 1652. Previous to his emigration his agent Augustus Heermans had, among other large tracts, purchased for him from the Indians what is known as the Nyack or Najeck tract in N. U. for 6 shirts, 2 pairs of shoes, 6 pairs of stockings, 6 adzes, 6 axes, 6 knives, 2 scissors, and 6 combs, described as "land lying East of the North River in the *Hoofden* (Heights), so as said land previous to this to the Noble Company was sold and once more paid for; said land extending in the rear of M[r] Paulus land (the late Garret Bergen and Schemerhorn farms at Gowanus) named Gewanus, or obliquely through the hills to Meghevamenek (probably Merackawick, the Indian name for Br[n],) said land lying on the Southwest side of Amersfoort (Fld[s]), and from thence along Gravesend to the sea, as by many trees is marked out," etc., and for which Van Werckhoven procured the Indian deed on Nov. 22, 1652. This description appears to cover at least the whole of the present town of N. U., with other lands. Shortly after his purchase Van Werckhoven commenced a settlement on his Nyack lands, on which he built a residence and secure retreat, returning to Holland in 1654 for the purpose of obtaining the requisite number of settlers to entitle him to full feudal privileges on his purchase, which number he failed to furnish, leaving Jacques Cortelyou, the private tutor of his children, to manage his colony and affairs during his absence. He died in Holland in 1655, leaving surviving a wid. and minor children, Peter and Cornelis Jansen Van Werckhoven, who after his death claimed from Cortelyou an account of his stewardship. Among the merchants trading to N. A. in 1677 who petitioned for a reduction of duties appears the name of

" Pieter Van Werckhoven," as per p. 752 of Vol. II. of Doc. of Col. His. of N. Y.

VAN WESTERHOUT, JEREMIAS JANSZEN (on the marriage rec. of the D. ch. of N. Y. "Jeremias Janszen from Wester-hout, young man out of the Hage"), m. Aug. 16, 1664, *Catelyna* dau. of Joris Jansen Rapalie. He came over in the ship Rosetree, but no further trace.

VAN WESTERVELT, ABRAHAM WILLEMSE, a weaver, m. *Margaret* ——. Bought a farm in N. U. Lane Apl. 5, 1697, of Nicholas Vander Grift of Bucks Co., Pa., as per p. 132 of Lib. 2 of Con., to which he probably removed, and in which town he was assessed for 38 A. in 1700. This farm he sold Nov. 12, 1705, for £352 to Anthony Holsart of Fld⁸. Mar. 31, 1694, with consent of *Dirkje* or "*Dirkyen*" his mother, he sold to Reinier Van Sicklen his interest in a house and lot in Fld⁸, a 70 A. plot in said town next to land of Pieter Monfoort, and 10 A. on the plains next to Jan Damon, as per Van Sicklen Papers. His will is da. Apl. 22, 1697, and rec. on p. 297 of Lib. 2 of Con. His descendants, known as Westervelts, abound in Bergen and Hudson counties, N. J. Made his mark to documents.

Jeremias Jansen, paid Jan. 1664 a marriage-fee of 4 gl. 12 st. to Flᵇ ch., as per town rec.

William of N. U., m. Dirkyen or Dirkje ——. In his will. rec. on p. 10 of Lib. 3 of Con., he devises all his property to his s. Abraham Willemse; and Dirkje in her will, da. Sept. 1, 1697, and pro. Aug. 22, 1704, devises all her property to said Abraham Willemse.

VAN WETMONT, BARENT JOOSTEN, see Barent Joosten.

VAN WICKELEN, EVERT JANSE, the common ancestor of the family, a carpenter, emigrated in 1664, probably from Wykel or Wykeler, a village in Friesland; (sup.) m. *Elizabeth* dau. of Frederick Van Liew; bought land in N. L. in 1686 to which he removed; and took the oath of allegiance in Flᵇ in 1687. About 1700 he bought 800 A. on the Raritan of Wᵐ Dockwra, as per p. 21 of Corwin's His. Discourse. May 29, 1703, he with Gerardus Beekman and Leffert Pieterse bought of Thomas Cardal of Jˢ 450 A. on the Raritan River for £200. Issue:—Jan of N. L.; Zytie or Eytie, m. Hans Bergen of Brⁿ; Coevert, m. Mattje ——; Pieternel-letje, m. Rem Hegeman of Flᵇ; Symon; Gerrit; and Geertje, m. Hendrick Suydam of Flᵇ.

Gerrit (sup.) of N. L., m. Tryntje ——. Issue:—Evert, bp. Mar. 5, 1699, in Fl[h].

Jan of N. L., m. Jan. 3, 1723, Ida dau. of Jeremias Remsen. Will da. Jan. 17, 1731; pro. June 8, 1732. Issue:—Hyltie, bp. Sept. 22, 1723, at N. U., (sup.) m. Steven Williamson; and Mettje or Meltie, bp. Jan. 17, 1725, at Fl[h].

Symon, m. Gerradine Kouwenhoven and settled on the Raritan, N. J., as early as 1735. Issue:—Elsje, bp. June 9, 1723, at Fl[h], and probably other children.

VAN WYCK or VANDER WYCK, CORNELIS BAREND, probably from "Wyk" a village in North Braband, emigrated in 1660; m. 1st *Anna* dau. of the Rev. Theodorus Polhemius; m. 2[d], 1684, *Jannetje* ——. Settled in Fl[h], where he owned a farm as early as 1661, of which place he was a mem. of the D. ch. in 1677, and took the oath of allegiance in 1687. Mar. 7, 1684, about the time of his marriage with Jannetje, they made a joint will to settle their property, rec. p. 169 of Lib. C of Fl[h] rec. Issue:—Johannes, bp. Jan. 17, 1677, in N. Y.; Aaltje, bp. Oct. 5, 1679; Anna, bp. July 9, 1682; Elizabeth, bp. Jan. 16, 1685, m. Adriaen Hegeman of Fl[h]; Adriaentje, bp. Sept. 9, 1688, m. Joseph Hegeman of Fl[h]; Marretje, m. Hendrick Wiltze of Newtown; and Theodorus. Signed his name "*Cornelis Barend V Wyck.*"

Cornelis. Signed his name "*Cornelis Van Wick*" at Fl[h] in 1712, probably a grandson of Cornelis Barend.

Theodorus, m. Margrietje ——, and took the oath of allegiance in Fl[h] in 1687 as a native. In 1712 there was a Theodorus Van Wyck of Hempstead, a farmer. About 1715 Theodorus Van Wyck was one of the first settlers of Fishkill, as per p. 180 of Smith's His. of Dutchess Co. Issue:—Cornelis, bp. Apl. 30, 1694. There was an Anthoni Vander Wyck who had a dau. Jannetje bp. Apl. 2, 1676, on which occasion Abraham Vander Wyck and Jannetje his w. were witnesses. Signed his name "*Theodorus Van Wyck.*"

VAN ZUTPHEN, see Sutphen.

VAN ZUUREN, CASPARUS (Rev.), emigrated to this country in 1677; m. Apl. 20, 1677, *Louise Hellenias*; settled as pastor of the R. D. churches of Kings Co.; resigned his charge and returned to Gouderach, Holland, in 1685, where he d. It appears that Jan. 1, 1685, previous to his resignation, he agreed with Claes Arentse Vechte to purchase the bouwery in Fl[h] in the possession of Titus Sirachs, which on Apl. 11 of said year Vechte took back and sold to Aucke Janse Van Nuyse, as per pp. 178 and 181 of Lib. C of Fl[h] rec. Issue:—

Johanna Hellenius, b. 1678; Altie, b. 1679; Jacobus, b. 1681; and Samuel, b. 1683. Signed his name *"C Van Zuuren."*

VANE, J., on lists of residents of G^d in 1650, as per town rec.

VARDON or VERDEN, see Ferdon.

VARICK, RUDOLPHUS (Rev.), probably from "Varick," a village in Gelderland, emigrated to this country in 1685, and was pastor of the R. D. churches of Kings Co. until 1694, in Aug. of which year he died. He m. *Margaret Visboom* and had issue:—Joanna; Marinus; Rudolphus; and Cornelia. Signed his name *"Rudolphus Varick."*

VAUGHAN or VAUHAN, JOHN, bought Dec. 28, 1651, Cornelis the ferrymans plantation in G^d. Jan. 1, 1658, he and Elizabeth his w. conveyed to John Hawse plantaion-lot No. 18 in G^d, all as per town rec. Made his mark to documents.

VECHTE or VECHTEN, see Van Vechten.

VEDDER, HARMAN, occupied a portion of Coney I. about 1654 under claim of Gysbert Updike. The children of Harmen Albertse Vedder (who was an early trader in Albany), and who is probably the same person, as per Pearson's Genealogies of the First Settlers of Albany, settled in Schenectady, where he bought a bouwery in 1672.

VEERMAN, DIRK JANSE, see Hoogland.

VENNAGER, JAN, conveyed about 2 morgens in Fld', through Jan Hansen (Bergen), to Claes Pieterse (Wyckoff), as per p. 91 of Bergen Genealogy.

VELTHUYSEN, GYSBERT PHILIPSE, a serjeant, of "Midwoud," as per letter of Gov. Stuyvesant of Oct. 12, 1655, on p. 99 of Vol. IV. of Dutch Man. He afterwards resided at Esopus, and about 1659 was murdered by the Indians, as per p. 199 of Pearson's Early Rec. of Albany.

VERDEN, see Ferdon.

VERDONCK, THOMAS, probably from "Donk," a hamlet in North Braband, a mag. of Brⁿ in 1663 and '64. This name may be intended for Thomas Verdon. A "Tomas

Verdonck's" name appears on the request in 1664 to the authorities to send an embassy to States-General for assistance, as per p. 375 of Vol. 2 of Doc. of Col. His.

VERHAGEN, JOSYNA, conveyed Feb. 20, 1692-3, to Jan Teunisse Coevers, a house and building-plot in Fl[h] lying on the W. side of the highway and the N. side of land of Peter Strycker, as per p. 172 of Lib. A of Fl[h] rec.

VERHOVEN, CORNELIS, probably from " Haven," a village in Gelderland, was constable of Br[a] in 1700, as per p. 65 of Furman's Notes and court rec.

VERHULST, JACOB, probably from " Hulst," a town in Zeeland, where he may at one period have resided, emigrated from Vlissingen in said province of Zeeland, and m. Apl. 19, 1679, in N. Y., *Maria Willemse Bennet* of Gowanus. Issue:—Cornelis, bp. Dec. 3, 1681; Lysbeth, bp. July 29, 1687; Abraham, bp. Apl. 20, 1690; Isaac, bp. Apl. 20, 1690—all bp. in N. Y.

Jacob Pietersen from Lubeck, m. Sept. 20, 1676, in N. Y., Mary or Marretje Adams Brouwers of Gowanus.

VERITIE, PIETER, mem. of N. U. ch. in 1677, and removed to S. I.

VERKERK or VERKERKEN, AERD or AERT JANSE, of N. U., b. 1655; m. *Gratioser* ——. In 1695 he resided in Lewis Co. on the South River or Delaware. His descendants are to be found in E. N. J. Issue:—Jan of N. J., bp. Nov. 12, 1682, at N. U.; (sup.) Mayke, m. Jan Lambertse of N. J.; (sup.) Hendrick of N. J.; Gerrit of N. J.; and Syke or Seytie, m. Johannes Truwexs. Made his mark "A" to documents.

Barend Janse of N. U. and Pa., m. 1689 Rachel Vander Grift and settled in Bensalem, Bucks Co., Pa., as early as 1695. Took the oath of allegiance in N. U. in 1687 as a native. Mem. of D. ch. of Bensalem in 1710, and of Neshaminy D. ch. in said county in 1719. Issue:—Johannes, bp. Apl. 2, 1695, in N. Y. Made his mark to documents.

Cornelis Janse, b. 1661, and emigrated in 1663 with his father from Buren. Suppose he d. prior to 1689.

Hendrick Janse, m. Geertje ——. Mem. of D. ch. of N. U. in 1682. No further trace.

(Sup.) *Hendrick* (s. of Aerd or Aert), left N. U. and settled in N. J.; m. Dorothy Morgan. Issue:—Jan, bp. Nov. 1, 1724, at Freehold, N. J.

24

Jan Janse, the common ancestor of the family, emigrated in 1663 from Buren in Gelderland, as per Riker's Newtown, with w. and 5 children; from Buurmelzen (a town on the river Linge near Buren), as per rec. of the m. of his dau. Geertje, and settled in N. U., where he owned large tracts of land; m. Mayke Gisberts; d. 1688. On ass. rolls of N. U. of 1675, '76, '83, and '93; mag: in 1679 and '84; on Dongan's patent of 1686; cen. of 1698; and took the oath of allegiance there in 1687. Will da. Nov. 10, 1688. Issue:—Roelof Janse, b. 1654; Aerd or Aert Janse, b. 1655; Geartie, emigrated with her father in 1663, m. 1ˢᵗ Hendrick Janse, m. 2ᵈ Jan Dirkse Van Vliet; Barendje, emigrated in 1663, m. Nicholas Vander Grift; Cornelis Janse emigrated in 1663, d. prior to 1698; Jan Janse Junʳ; Barend Janse of Pa.; and (sup.) Hendrick Janse. Made his mark to documents.

Jan Janse Junʳ of N. U.; m. Gertie ——; d. after 1709, and took the oath of allegiance in N. U. in 1687 as a native. Issue:—(sup.) Jannetje, m. Peter Strycker of Flʰ; and (sup.) Rebecca, m. Hendrick Lott. Made his mark to documents.

Jan Roelofse of Flʰ and N. U., m. 1ˢᵗ Elsie or Alsie ——; m. 2ᵈ, after 1704, Anne or Annetje dau. of Andries Emmans. Was a surveyor employed on L. I. and its vicinity, and owned and occupied the homestead of his father on N. U. Lane. Issue:—Sytje, bp. May 29, 1705, at Brⁿ, (sup.) m. Gerrit Van Duyn of N. U.; (by 2ᵈ w.) Roelof, bp. Feb. 8, 1723, d. young; Sara, b. Sept. 10, 1727, m. Cornelis Van Duyn of N. U.; Annetje, bp. Mar. 12, 1732, m. William Van Nuyse of N. U.; Mayke, bp. Aug. 25, 1734, m. Jacob Van Dyke of E. N. J.; Elizabeth, b. Jan. 20, 1736, d. in 1765, single; and Lea, bp. Feb. 1, 1741, m. Cornelius Vanderveer Junʳ of Flʰ—all bp. in N. U. Signed his name *"John Verkerk."*

Jan (s. of Aerd or Aert), bp. Nov. 12, 1682; m. 1ˢᵗ Alice ——; (sup.) m. 2ᵈ Cornelia Brakel or Van Brakele. Left Kings Co. and settled in Monmouth Co., N. J. Issue:— William, bp. Feb. 5, 1710; Sara, bp. Dec. 14, 1712; Alica, bp. June 21, 1716; Aert, bp. Nov. 9, 1718; (by 2ᵈ w.) Jan, bp. Apl. 10, 1726; Enelya, bp. Jan. 20, 1731; Martenus, bp. Jan. 20, 1731; Maria, bp. Apl. 3, 1737; Jacobus, bp. Aug. 12, 1739. Sara, bp. Feb. 28, 1742; and Stephanus, bp. Aug. 18, 1745—all bp. at Marlboro D. ch.

Roelof Janse, emigrated in 1663 with his father, b. 1654; m. Aug. 7, 1681, Catharine Simons of Brⁿ; living in 1718. Occupied the old stone house lately torn down, on the main road leading from the village of N. U. to Flʰ, on the Flʰ side of the present boundary line between the towns, and on the farm late of Cornelius Bennet. At the date of his m. he

hailed from N. U.; in Oct. 1681 on lists of mem. of N. U. ch.;
and in 1698 on cen. of said town. Took the oath of allegiance in 1687 in Fl^h, where he bought May 3 of that year
lands of Hendrick Ryke adjoining N. U. In 1688 he bought
land in Fl^h of Cornelis Barendse (Van Wyck) on the N. side
of the main road leading from N. U. to Fl^h and E. of the
Fl^h ch. lands. In 1706 assessed for 110 A. in N. U. Issue:—
Annetje, bp. Oct. 29, 1682, d. young; Annetje, bp. Jan. 13,
1684, m. Jan Van Dyck of Shrewsbury, N. J.; Sybrech, bp.
May 4, 1695, m. Wm Van Duyne of Somerset Co., N. J.;
Jan; Mary or Mayke, m. 1st Nicholas Van Brunt of N. U.,
m. 2^d Samuel Groenendyck; Jannetje, m. Hendrick Claesen
Kuypers of N. J.; and Sara, m. Hendrick Emans of N. J.
Signed his name "*Roelof Ver Kerck.*"

VER RYN, ABRAHAM JANSE, of G^d in 1659, per town rec.
  Jan Janse, m. —— ——; bought Mar. 7, 1659, of Peter
Ebell plantation-lot No. 27, with the improvements there-
on, in G^d, which he sold Mar. 4, 1663, to Nicholas Stillwell. May 11, 1659, he bought of Henry Mody a double
plantation-lot, Nos. 9 and 10, in G^d, (for which his mother
Lady Mody had obtained a patent,) for the use of his s.
Ab^m Janse Ver Ryn, which double-lot he sold Mar. 20,
1663, to Ralph Cardell. Feb. 10, 1660, he bought of Nicholas Stillwell plantation-lot No. 18 in G^d, which he sold
June 21, 1672, to Ann Stillwell of Dover, S. I., wid. of said
Nicholas. Oct. 24, 1663, he sold to Paulus Vanderbeeck
plantation-lot No. 17 in G^d. Apl. 4, 1665, he bought of
Francois de Bruynne "a certain parcell of Land Lying
and being ye Northern parte of my Bouwerye beginning at a certain marked tree standing by a valley at y^e
South West, so going along ye South West side from y^e
valley to a Chopped Oake tree, fallen down and Lying on
ye ffence, and from there uppon a rite line to ye North East
to that land which was formerlie Jacob Bakers" (Backers),
etc. etc.; "the corner Land uppon ye said Land at present
shall be onlie to and for ye use of mee ye said ffrancis
Browne, but the house and Barn thereon which sometime
belonged to one Nathaniel Brittan," etc., "shall be the said
Jan Jansens," etc. All the above purchases and sales, per
G^d rec. In 1679 Jan Janse sold a part of this purchase,
located on De Bruynne's Lane or the old Bath road, to
Myndert Korten for 770 gl., as appears by the rec. of the
court of sessions of that year relating to a dispute between
the parties to the sale. From the above it is evident
that Jan Janse prior to his purchase of De Bruynne was
a resident of G^d, and that after that date removing to

said purchase, a resident of N. U., of which town in 1673 he was ensign of the militia company, and had disputes with the residents about his fences, as per p. 665 of Vol. II. of Doc. of Col. His. In 1675 and '76 his name appears on the ass. rolls of said town. Issue:—Abraham Janse, and probably other children. Signed his name *"Jan Jansen Ver Ryn."*

VER SCHIEUR or VOORSCHEUR, WOUTER GYSBERTSE or GYSBRECHTSE, emigrated in 1649; m. 1st *Dorothea Callen;* m. 2d *Margrietje* ——. Settled in Bu[k]; on muster-roll of said town of 1663; mag. in 1679; and took the oath of allegiance there in 1687. Issue:—Magdalena, bp. Apl. 22, 1662; (sup.) Hendrick; and Jochem. His w. signed her name *"Margrietje Voorscheur."* See Wouter Guysbertse, who is probably the same individual as this Wouter.

Hendrick, took the oath of allegiance in Bu[k] in 1687 as a native. On cen. of Bu[k] of 1698 and ensign of militia of said town in 1700, as per p. 809 of Vol. IV. of Doc. of Col. His.

VERSCHURSON, VEUTER, on Dongan's patent of Bu[k] of 1687. The name is probably a corruption of Wouter Ver Scheur.

VERSTRAALEN, JOOST, with others of Br[n], petitioned in 1663 for leave to found a village and for salt meadows, as per p. 120 of Vol. I. of Stiles's Br[n].

VERTEIN, JAN WILLEMSE, among the first settlers of Bu[k] in 1661, as per Thompson's L. I.

VER VEELEN, DANIEL, of N. U., m. *Alletta* or *Alida Schaats.* He appears to have resided at first in Albany, where he sold his real estate in 1661. Joined the R. D. ch. of N. A. in 1661, and entered on the record as removed to N. U., of the D. ch. of which town he was a mem. in 1677, an elder in 1678, and entered on the ch. rec. as removed to G[d]. In 1664 he took the oath of allegiance to the English in N. Y. Oct. 16, 1678, he bought a house-plot in the village of N. U. of Jacques Cortelyou. In 1687 he resided on the Spuyten Devil Creek, where he held a ferry grant. Issue:—Anna Maria, bp. Apl. 21, 1663, d. young; Anna Maria, bp. Jan. 10, 1666—both bp. in N. Y.

VERWAY, CORNELIS, m. 1st *Annetie Cornelis;* m. 2d *Hendrikje Jans.* Was engaged in a law-suit with Cornelis Berrian in 1681, as per Fl[h] rec. Issue:—Margrietje, bp. Sept.

23, 1674, in N. Y.; Neeltje, bp. June 31, 1678, in Brⁿ; and Annetje, bp. Nov. 21, 1683, in N. Y. There was a Hendrick Verway and Engeltie Van Dyck of Monmouth Co. who had children, Hendrick, bp. Feb. 16, 1713-4; Kasel, bp. Jan. 1, 1715-16; Elizabeth, bp. Apl. 12, 1719; and Jacob, bp. Nov. 6, 1720—all at Marlboro. There were Verways at Albany known as Van Wies.

VIELE, AERNOUT, on ass. roll of Fl^h of 1693. There was an Arnout Cornelise Viele, an Indian interpreter, who m. Gerretje Gerritse from Amsterdam in 1677, was carried away from Schenectady by the French and Indians in 1690, and absent 3 years before his return, as per Pearson's First Settlers of Albany.

VIENS, MINSTER, a dealer in dry-goods, as per Stoothoff's books of 1682.

VIL, MON, a dealer in merchandise in 1677, as per Stoot-hoff books.

VILLET, CLAES GANGELOFFE, one of the curators of the estate of Nicholas Volthuysen of Fl^h, sold to Anthony Jansen (Westbrook), as per p. 109 of Lib. A of Fl^h rec.

VIS, WILLEM JACOBSE. His name appears on a deed of Mar. 28, 1689, conveying land in Fl^h to Theodorus Polhemus, on p. 128 of Lib. A of Fl^h rec.

VLASBECK, see Barent Gerritse.

VLECK, ISAAC, on Stoothoff's books of 1674 and '76.

VLIET, see Vander Vliet.

VOGEL, CORNELIS HERMANSE, on ass. roll of Bu^k of 1676. *Arie Cornelise*, on ass. roll of Bu^k of 1675.

VOLKERTSE, DERICK, a Noorman or Norwegian and a carpenter, m. —— ——; obtained a patent Apl. 3, 1645, for 25 morgens on the East River and Mespath Kil, which he sold Sept. 9, 1653, to Jacob Hay, as per p. 278 of Cal. of Dutch Man., and which was patented May 1, 1679, to David Jochems, who m. Christina Cappeoens wid. of said Hay, as per p. 321 of Vol. II. of Stiles's Brⁿ. Volkertse continued to reside in Bu^k after its organization as a town, was assessed there in 1675, and a mag. in 1681. In 1689 he was appointed ensign of the militia of Bu^k. Issue:—(sup.) Derick Junr; Rachel, bp. Sept. 8, 1641; Volkert, bp. Nov. 15, 1643; Ariaentje, bp. Aug. 21, 1650; and Janneken, bp. Dec. 7, 1653—all in N. A.   Made his mark to documents.

Derick Junr of Bu^k, m. Sept. 25, 1694, Maria Dewitt. Was ensign of militia of Bu^k in 1689, and prior to 1699 removed to the vicinity of New Brunswick, N. J., where he appears to have resided, as per p. 35 of Messler's Somerset Co. About 1710 he with others purchased the Harlington tract in said county.

Philip, on ass. roll of Bu^k of 1676.

Volkert, bought land of Derick Volkertse in Bu^k in 1670, as per town rec.

VOLKERTSEN, see Folkertsen.

VOLMAN, BARENT, on ass. roll of Fl^h of 1693 and cen. of 1698.

VOLTHUYSEN, NICHOLAS, owned 18 morgens of land on the E. side of the road in Fl^h (sold in 1661 to Anthony Jansen [Westerbrook] by the curators of his estate), and also a mill-house standing on his village building-plot, as per p. 109 of Lib. A of Fl^h rec.

VONCK, ALLIDY or ALIDA, owned land in Fl^h in 1696, as per p. 95 of Lib. 2 of Con.; also allotted woodland on the division of the Fl^h woods in 1701.

Cornelis, m. Magdalena Rixe or Hendrixc, who m. 2^d Minne Johannis. Issue:—Ida, bp. Nov. 4, 1681, in Fl^h.

VOOKIC, AMMODOER, made his mark to documents in Fl^h in 1670.

VOORESLIN, DANIEL, a farmer in Kings Co. in 1677, as per Stoothoff's books.

VOORHIES, VOORHEES, VORIS, or VAN VOORHIES, ABRAHAM STEPHENSE, of Fld^s, m. *Aeltie Stryker*. Suppose he had a s. John who resided in Fl^h, and whose descendants reside in the vicinity of Princeton, N. J.

Albert Stephense, emigrated with his father in 1660, and resided at first in Fld^s; m. 1st Barentje Willemse; m. 2^d, Apl. 24, 1681, Tjelletje Wizzel-penning; m. 3^d Elina Vander Schure.   On ass. roll of 1683, and about 1685 he removed to Hackensack, N. J., where his descendants principally reside.   Issue:—Cornelia Albertse, bp. Oct. 14, 1681, at Fl^h,

m. Juriaen Lubbertse Westervelt; Stephen Albertse, bp. Oct. 28, 1683, at Fld⁸, d. young; Stephen Albertse, bp. Apl. 12, 1685, in N. U., m. Jannetje Allica or Alje; Jannetje Albertse, m. Gerrit Abramse Ackerman; Margrietje Albertse, m. Pieter Alice or Alje; Lucas Albertse, bp. ——, 1699, at Hackensack, m. Annetje Kip; Rachel Albertse, m. Gellyn Ackerman; Femmetje Albertsen, m. Jacob Vanderbeeck; Albert Albertse, bp. 1704, m. Cornelia Van Giesen: (sup.) William Albertse, m. 1ˢᵗ Susanna Laroe, m. 2ᵈ Maria Van Gelden; Petrus Albertse, bp. 1706, m. Geesjean Romaine; Isaac Albertse, bp. 1708, m. Urseltje Romeyn; Wilmetje Albertse, m. Cornelis Bougaert; Jan Albertsen, m. Elizabeth Adamson; and Jacobus Albertsen, m. Jannetje Ackerman—all of Hackensack, N. J.

Albert Coerte, m'. 1ˢᵗ Sara Willemse Cornel of Fl'ʰ; m. 2ᵈ, May 15, 1743, Willemtje Suydam. Took the oath of allegiance in Fld⁸ in 1687 as a native, and was ensign of militia of said town in 1691 and 1700. In 1699 he bought of his brother Gerrit Coerte his interest in the Anthony Jansen's patent, and Feb. 12, 1702-3, the interest of Barent Joosten, thus becoming the sole owner, as per Lib. 2 of Con. On ass. roll of N. U. of 1723. Aug. 6, 1718, he obtained liberty from the freeholders and inhabitants of Gᵈ to erect a mill on a creek known as De Bruynne's Creek, which mill, afterwards known as Voorees's mill, was used for many years in grinding the grists of the surrounding farms, afterwards bought by Mr. Patridge and changed to grinding paints, and finally swept out of existence by fire. Will da. May 14, 1747; pro. Apl. 14, 1748; rec. p. 251, Lib. 16, N. Y. surr. off. Issue:—Coert Albertse; Elizabeth, bp. Dec. 10, 1695, in Brⁿ, m. Rutgert Van Brunt; Mary or Maria, m. John Nostrand; Margaret, m. 1ˢᵗ Petrus Stoothoff, m. 2ᵈ David Nevius; Altie, m. Wilhelmus Stoothoff; Neltje, m. Christopher Hoogland; and Ann, m. Hendrick Cortelyou. Signed his name "*Albert Coerten.*"

Albert Lucasse of Fld⁸, b. May 10, 1698; m. 1ˢᵗ, May 10, 1720, Arrejeantje Ditmarse; m. 2ᵈ, 1722, Catryntje Cornell. Removed to the vicinity of New Brunswick, N. J., about 1720, in which year he and his w. were received as mem. of the D. ch. of that locality on certificate. Will da. Jan. 22, 1730; pro. Dec. 2, 1734; rec. p. 3 of Lib. C in off. of Sec. of State of N. J. Issue:—Arryaen of Fl'ʰ, b. Apl. 14, 1721, m. Phebe Ryder; Cornelius, b. Sept. 6, 1725, m. Elizabeth Johnson; Albert of New Brunswick, N. J., b. Apl. 6, 1727, m. Adrianna Vandervont; Jannetje, b. Apl. 2, 1729, (sup.) m. Jacobus Cornel; Johannis, b. Aug. 11, 1731, m. Antie Schenck; and Minnie, b. Jan. 13, 1734.

Coert or *Coort Albertse* of G^d, m. Annatie Van Dyck; d.
May 31, 1757. Bought May 9, 1747, of his father Albert
Coerte, Bruynnesburg or Anthony Jansen's patent, which
he conveyed Oct. 5, 1656, to his sons Court and Bernardus.
Issue:—Court of N. U., m. Sarah Van Brunt; Albert Coerte
of G^d, N. U., and N. J., b. Aug. 1, 1716, m. 1st Katrina
Doremus, m. 2^d Nelly Van Nostrand; Antje or Annatie, b.
1698, m. John Rapalje; Altie, b. May 3, 1709, m. Wilhelmus
Stoothoff; Zacheus of N. J.; Bernardus of N. U., b. Mar. 1,
1725, m. Femmetje Latter; and Jannetje, b. Sept. 7, 1728,
m. Wilhelmus Van Brunt. Signed his name *"Coort Van
Voorhies."*

Coert or *Koert* (Gerritse) of G^d, m. Apl. 13, 1716, Neeltje
Hegeman; d. prior to Apl. 1750. Will da. Jan. 3, 1746;
pro. July 24, 1750; rec. p. 191, Lib. 17, N. Y. surr. off.
Issue:—Roelof of Somerset Co., N. J.; Johannis of do.;
Geertje, m. Gerrit Van Arsdalen of do.; Eva, bp. Jan. 29,
1719, in N. U., m. Charles Debevoise of Bu^k; Stephen of
Fishkill, m. (sup.) Maria Lake; Gerrit; Adriaen of G^d, m.
Altie Cowenhoven; Antje, bp. Feb. 11, 1722, d. young;
Antje, bp. Sept. 13, 1724, in N. U., m. Johannes Derje of
N. Y.; Maria, m. Dirk Lake of G^d; Lucretia; Catharine, m.
Simon Van Arsdalen of Somerset Co., N. J.; Neeltje, bp.
May 23, 1734, in N. U., m. Daniel Lake of G^d; Sarah, bp.
July 5, 1737; and Isaac.

Coert or *Koert Stevensen* of Fld^s, emigrated with his father
in 1660; b. 1637; m. prior to 1666, Marretje Gerritse Van
Couwenhoven. On ass. rolls of Fld^s of 1675 and '83; mem.
of D. ch. and deacon in 1677; mag. in 1664 and '73; took
the oath of allegiance there in 1687; and capt. of militia in
1689. Mar. 8, 1691-2, he bought of John Tilton all his real
estate in G^d (reserving the use thereof for 12 months unless
he sooner removed from the town) for £295. Tilton's
property was mainly located in G^d Neck, and much of it is
yet held by the Voorhees family, this purchase being the
first of any amount by said family in G^d. June 20, 1699, he
conveyed this property for £295 to his s. Albert Coerte, as
per G^d rec. Issue:—Steven Coerte; (sup.) Neeltje Coerte,
b. June 30, 1676, m. Gerrit R. Schenck of Monmouth Co.,
N. J.; (sup.) Marretje Coerte; Albert Coerte; Gerrit Coerte;
Altie Coerte, m. 1st Johannes Willemse, m. 2^d Rutgert Van
Brunt; Cornelis Coerte, bp. Jan. 23, 1678; Annatie Coerte,
bp. Dec. 5, 1680, in Fld^s, (sup.) m. John Rapalje of Br^n; and
Johannes Coerte, b. Apl. 20, 1683. Signed his name *"Koert
Stevensen,"* and at times *"Koert Stevensen Van Ruinen."*

Coert (s. of Steven Coerte and Agatha Jans), bp. Nov. 15,
1694; (sup.) m. Peternelletje ——. Issue:—Antie, (sup.) b.

June 27, 1721, m. Jan Ryersen; Cornelis, bp. Oct. 17, 1731, d. young; and Cornelis, bp. Aug. 12, 1733.

Coert of N. U. (s. of Coert and Annatie Van Dyck), m. Sarah Van Brunt, who m. 2^d Aert Van Pelt of N. J. and Fld². Will da. Sept. 17, 1761; pro. Mar. 11, 1762; rec. p. 263, Lib. 23, N. Y. surr. off. Issue:—Annatie, b. May 16, 1761, m. Apl. 1780, William Bernard Gifford, d. May 13, 1790. W. B. Gifford m. 2^d Frances Nickoll and d. in 1814 on S. I. Annatie had 5 children one of whom d. young.

Cornelis Coerte or *Koerte* of Fld², bp. Jan. 23, 1678; (sup.) m. Antie ——. Ensign of militia of Fld² in 1700, as per p. 809 of Vol. IV. of Doc. of Col. His. Issue:—Abraham of Fld²; Daniel of Oyster Bay; Cornelius of Fld², m. Marretje dau. of Dowe Ditmars; and Heiltje, b. Aug. 27, 1746, m. Wm Stoothoff. Signed his name *"Cornelis Koerte."*

Cornelius of Fld² (s. of Cornelis Coerte and Antie); m. Marritje dau. of Dowe Ditmars. Will da. Apl. 1, 1718; pro. Feb. 13, 1769; rec. p. 545, Lib. 26, N. Y. surr. off. Issue:— Catryna, bp. Sept. 26, 1712; Sarah, (sup.) m. John Blom of Fl^h; and (sup.) Cornelis. Signed his name *"Cornelius Voorhies"* in 1755.

Eldert Lucase of Fld² and Fl^h, m. Styntje Hendricks dau. of Hendrick Hermanse. May 4, 1674, he leased for 4 years of Cornelis Janse Boomgart his bouwery in Fl^h, as per p. 110 of Lib. C of Fl^h rec. Bought May 19, 1692, of Wm Creed, 40 A. in J², on the Br^n and J² turnpike and Eldert's Lane, as per p. 61 of Lib. A of Con. in off. of clerk of Queens Co., on which he settled, having previously in 1684 purchased a house and lot in the village of J². On ass. roll of Fld² of 1676. His descendants dropped the surname of Voorhees and adopted and used that of Eldert, and are numerous in Queens Co. Will da. Feb. 23, 1714; pro. Apl. 17, 1722; rec. p. 291, Lib. 9, N. Y. surr. off. Issue:—Lucas Eldertse, bp. Dec. 25, 1677, in Fl^h; Rachel Eldertse, m. Adam Smith; Hendrikje Eldertse, bp. Apl. 4, 1680, at Fl^h; Johannes Eldertse, bp. Dec. 26, 1681, in Fl^h; Annatje Eldertse, bp. Feb. 24, 1684, in Fld², m. Hans Bergen of J²; Egbertje Eldertse, m. Ab^m Coevert; and Hendrick Eldertse, bp. Mar. 4, 1691. Made his mark to documents.

Gerret Koerten of Fld², m. 1st Mensje Janse; m. 2^d Willemtje Pieters; d. about 1703. Mem. of Fld² D. ch. in 1677. Took the oath of allegiance in Fld² in 1687 as a native, and on cen. of said town of 1698. Dec. 11, 1693, he bought of Jan Hansen (Van Noorstrand) and Barent Joosten, Bruynnesburg or Anthony Janse's (from Salee) patent for 38,750 gl., and in 1699 he conveyed his interest in the same to his brother Albert Coerte. Will da. Oct. 1, 1702; pro. Sept. 23, 1704; rec. p.

175, Lib. 7, N. Y. surr. off. Issue:—Koert (Gerretse) of G^d; Altie, bp. Oct. 4, 1685, in Fld^s, m. Johannes Willemse; Peter (Gerretse), bp. Dec. 10, 1694, in Br^n; Hendrick (Gerretse); Stephen (Gerretse); Gertie or Greetje, m. Gerret Van Aersdalen; and Marike, m. Jan Remsen. Signed his name "*Gerret Koerten.*"

Hans Lucasse of Fld^s, bp. Sept. 7, 1679; (sup.) m. May 17, 1715, Neeltje Nevius. There was a Jan Voorhees and Neeltje his w. of New Brunswick who may have been this Hans. No further trace.

Hendrick Gerretse of Fld^s, m. 1st, May 3, 1717, Jannetje Andreas dau. of Andreas Jansen of Fl^h; m. 2^d Jannetje Van Aersdalen; m. 3^d (sup.) Sarah Schenck. Removed from Fld^s and settled near Freehold, N. J., joining the D. ch. of that locality in 1719. Issue:—Garret, bp. Mar. 18, 1720; Willempie, bp. Feb. 8, 1722, m. Peter Albertse Cowenhoven of N. J.; Garret, bp. Nov. 24, 1723; Peter, bp. July 8, 1733; William, bp. May 22, 1738; Hendrick, bp. June 15, 1740; Roelof, bp. Sept. 19, 1742; Albert, bp. June 2, 1745; Garret, bp. June 30, 1748—all at Freehold; (sup.) Sara, m. Garret Albertse Cowenhoven; and (sup.) Catharine, m. Jan Albertse Cowenhoven—all of N. J.

Jan Stevense of Fld^s, emigrated with his father in 1660; b. 1652; m. 1st, Mar. 17, 1678, Cornelia Rinierse Wizzel-penning; m. 2^d, Oct. 8, 1680, Femmetje Aukes Van Nuyse. On ass. rolls of Fld^s of 1675 and '83, and took the oath of allegiance there in 1687. Oct. 2, 1681, he bought of Auke Janse Van Nuys for 300 gl. the land at "Pardegat," which Auke Janse bought Oct. 15, 1681, of Bartel Claesen, as per p. 144 of Lib. AA of Fl^h rec. Issue:—Stephen Janse of J^a, bp. Dec. 20, 1679, at Fld^s; Auke Janse of Fld^s, bp. May 21, 1682, at Fld^s; Willemtje Janse, bp. Feb. 24, 1684, at Fld^s; Jan Janse of S. I., bp. May 2, 1686, at Br^n; Jacobus Janse, bp. Mar. 24, 1696; (sup.) Roelof Janse of S. I.; (sup.) Albert Janse of Fld^s; (sup.) Abraham Janse of Fld^s; and (sup.) Lucas Janse of Fl^h. Signed his nane "*Jan Stevens*" in 1700.

Jan Lucasse of Fld^s, b. Feb. 19, 1675; m. 1st, Oct. 10, 1699, Ann Van Duyckhuysen; m. 2^d, Mar. 5, 1704, Mayke or Sara R. Schenck. In 1717 he appears to have resided near Six Mile Run, N. J. Issue:—Johannes Lucasse, b. July 19, 1700, m. Jannetje Remsen and settled at Piscataway, N. J.; Lucas of Fld^s, b. Sept. 15, 1705, m. 1st Altje Ryder, m. 2^d Catrina Staat; Roelof of Fld^s, b. Aug. 19, 1707; Stephen of Fld^s, b. Oct. 23, 1753, m. Maria Leak; Antie; Petrus; Marten; Isaac, bp. Mar. 21, 1716, m. Sara ——; Catlyntje, b. June 8, 1718, (sup.) m. Simon Van Arsdalen; Garret of N. J., b. Sept. 6, 1720, (sup.) m. Johanna Van Harlington; Abraham of Fld^s,

b. June 8, 1724, m. Adrianna Lefferts, and was the ancestor of the present Voorhees family of Fld⁸; Sarah, b. Oct. 18, 1727; and Maria, b. Apl. 5, 1731.

Johannes Coerten of Fld⁸ and Dutchess Co., b. Apl. 20, 1683; m. 1ˢᵗ, Nov. 19, 1703, Barbara dau. of Achias Van Dyck, b. Dec. 20, 1683, d. Apl. 18, 1743; m. 2ᵈ, May 22, 1744, Sarah Van Vliet, b. Nov. 7, 1694. Will da. Aug. 15, 1755; pro. Feb. 25, 1658; rec. p. 19, Lib. 21, N. Y. surr. off. Resided in 1709 and '11 at Freehold, N. J., at which dates he and his w. Barbara were mem of the Marlboro D. ch., as per p. 84 of the Brick Church Memorial. June 20, 1730, he bought of Philip Verplanck of the manor of Cortland 2790 A. on the Hudson River near Fishkill for £670. (See p. 107 of Vol. IV. of the Doc. His. of N. Y.) Settled on his lands at Rombout in said county, his name appearing on the books of the D. ch. at Fishkill in 1734. Issue:—Jannetje, b. Sept. 15, 1704, m. Mar. 12, 1725, John Brinckerhoff of Dutchess Co.; Court of Dutchess Co., b. Apl. 5, 1706, m. June 16, 1717, Catharine dau. of Henry Filkin of Flʰ, will da. Sept. 16, 1782, and had 10 children; Johannes Junʳ of Bombout, b. Aug. 6, 1708, m. Sept. 30, 1731, Gerritje dau. of Elias Van Benschouten, will pro. Apl. 5, 1751, and had 8 children; Zacharias of Dutchess Co., b. Dec. 10, 1710, d. Apl. 1784, without issue; Gerrit, b. Mar. 13, 1713; Maria, b. Sept. 16, 1716, m. June 12, 1749, Elias Dubois of Dutchess Co.; Hendrick, b. Mar. 20, 1719, drowned Nov. 4, 1745; and Jacobus of Dutchess Co., b. Oct. 14, 1723, d. Oct. 27, 1750. Signed his name "*Johannes Coerten Van Voorhes*" and sometimes "*Johannes Van Voorhes.*"

Lucas Stevense, emigrated with his father in 1660; b. 1650; m. 1ˢᵗ Catharine Hansen (Van Noostrand); m. 2ᵈ Jan. 26, 1689, Jannetje Minnes dau. of Minne Johannis; (sup.) m. 3ᵈ, in 1703, Catharine Van Dyck; d. 1713. Mem. of Fld⁸ ch. in 1677; on ass. roll of said town in 1675; and in 1680 a mag. From the bp. rec. of Hackensack it appears he resided in that place in 1685, but in 1687 he took the oath of allegiance in Fld⁸. Issue:—Eldert Lucasse; Jan Lucasse, bp. Feb. 19, 1675; Stephen Lucasse, bp. Sept. 6 or 16, 1677; Hans Lucasse, bp. Sept. 7, 1679; Jannetje Lucasse, bp. Dec. 25, 1681, m. Martin R. Schenck; Willemtje Lucasse, bp. Nov. 19, 1683, d. young; Anna Lucasse, b. Apl. 25, 1686, m. Wᵐ Kouwenhoven of Fld⁸; Catryntje Lucasse, m. Roelof Nevius of N. J.; Elsje Lucasse; Reinsche Lucasse, m. Johannes Nostrand; Willemtje Lucasse, m. Martin Nevius; Albert Lucasse of N. J., b. May 10, 1698; Roelof Lucasse of N. J.; Minne Lucasse of N. J.; and Abraham Lucasse of N. J. Signed his name "*Luichas Stevensen.*"

Minne Lucasse of Fld⁸, m. 1ˢᵗ, Apl. 25, 1717, Antje dau. of ➤

Gerrit Pieterse Wyckoff; (sup.) m. 2[d] Lammetje dau. of
Gerrit Stryker of Six Mile Run, N. J.; d. 1733. Removed
to the vicinity of New Brunswick, where in 1720 he owned
a large tract of land on the S. side of the Raritan. Will da.
Sept. 20, 1733; pro. Nov. 15, 1733; rec. on p. 494, of Lib. B,
in off. of Sec. of State of N. J. Issue:—Elizabeth Minne,
m. Martin Roelofse Schenck; Lucas of New Brunswick,
m. Neeltje Vanderbilt; Garret of Middlebush, b. May 13,
1720, m. Neeltje Nevius and Sarah Stoothoff; Minne of
Hillsborough, m. Mary ——; John of N. J.; Abraham of
Reading, m. Maria or Mary Van Dorn; and Catharine—all
of N. J., whose descendants reside mainly in Somerset Co.,
N. J., in Ohio, and other Western States.

Roelof Lucasse of Fld[s], m. 1st, Apl. 26, 1714, Helen dau. of
Gerret Stoothoff; m. 2[d] Margreta Cortelyou; d. 1751. Re-
moved to Three Mile Run, N. J., about 1684, and mem. of
D. ch. of New Brunswick in 1703. In 1737 he appears to
have resided on S. I. Will da. Aug. 16, 1750; pro. Apl. 5,
1751; rec. on p. 518, of Lib. E, in off. Sec. State, N. J.
Issue:—Johannes; Luke; Garret, m. Deborah —— ——; Roelof;
Janetie; Maria, bp. Oct. 23, 1737, on S. I.; Helena; and
Catlyna. Signed his name *"Roelof Voorhees"* in 1715.

~ *Stephen ¹Coerte*, the common ancestor of the Voorhees
family in this country, emigrated in 1660 with wife and 7
children from Ruinen in Drenthe, and from in front of the
hamlet of Hees near said locality, hence the name, and settled in Fld[s]; b. 1600; m. 1st, in Europe, —— ——; m. 2[d], in
1677, Willempie Roelofse Seubering; d. about Feb. 16,
1684. Bought Nov. 29, 1660, of Cornelis Dircksen Hoogland 9 morgens of corn-land, 7 of wood-land, 10 of plain-
land, and 5 of salt-meadows, making in all 31 morgens, in
Fld[s] for 3000 gl.; also the house and house-plot lying in
the village of *"Amesfoort en bergen,"* with the brewery and
all the brewing apparatus, kettle-house, and casks, with the
appurtenances, as per p. 37 of Lib. B of Fl[b] rec. His name
appears on the ass. roll of Fld[s] of 1675 and '83; as a .mag.
in 1664; and on patent of 1667. Issue:—Hendrickjen Stevense of Holland, m. Jan Kiers; Mergin Stevense of Holland, m. 1st —— Roelefse, m. 2[d] Remmelt Willemse; Coert
Stevense of Fld[s], b. 1637; ¬Lucas Stevense, b. 1650; Jan
Stevense, b. 1652; Albert Stevense; Aaltje Stevense, m.
Barent Juriaansz; Jannetje Stevense, m. 1st Jan Martense
Schenck, m. 2[d] Alexander Sympson; Hendrickje Stevense,
m. 1st Jan Kiestede, m. 2[d] Albert Albertse Terhunen; and
Abraham Voorhees. Signed his name *"Steven Koerten"* and
at times *"Steven Koerts."*

Steven Coerte (s. of Coert Stevense) of G[d], m. Agatha or

Egge Janse; d. Feb. 16, 1723-4. Of Fld^a in 1699 and G^d in 1723. In 1693 he bought 40 A. of Wesevel Pieterson in J^a. Will da Feb. 5, 1723-4; pro. Aug. 23, 1754; rec. p. 388, Lib. 29, N. Y. surr. off. Issue:—John Stevense, known as John Coerte Voorhees; Coert Stevense of G^d; (sup.) Antie; Lu-cresy, m. Nicholas Williamson of G^d; Allie, Alice, or Aeltje, m. Albert Terhune; Sara, m. Jacobus Gerrisen; and Maria, m. Jacob Remsen. Signed his name "*Steven Koerten.*" The G^d Voorhies are mainly descendants of this *Steven Coerte.*

Stephen Janse (s. of Jan Stephense), bp. Dec. 20, 1679; m. Sarah ——. Left Fld^a and settled at J^a. Will da. Nov. 12, 1757; pro. Sept. 18, 1759; rec. p. 413, of Lib. 21, N. Y. surr. off. Issue:—Cornelia, m. Lawrence Haft; Jan or John Stephense, m. Geertje ——; Stephen Stephense, m. Maria ——; Cornelius Stephense, m. Femmetje ——; Roelof Stephense of Hempstead, m. Cornelia ——; Lucas Ste-phense; and Annetje Stephense, m. Jonathan Pratt of Oyster Bay.

VOORVELEN, DANIEL, see Vervalen.

VORHAGEN, GESIAS, mem. of Fl^h D. ch. from N. L. in 1677.

VOS or VOSCH, BALTHAZER Junr, sometimes written Jonck-er de Vosch (young de Vosch), emigrated from Utrecht in 1662; bought in July of that year 2 farms in Fl^h, as per pp. 103 and 105 of Lib. B of Fl^h rec.; and settled in N. U., of which town he was a mag. in 1663, '64, and '65. In 1665 he and Jacques Cortelyou represented N. U. in what is com-monly known as the Duke's Convention or Assembly of the Colony, which met at Hempstead, and in which was enacted what is known as the Duke's laws. Singularly by Thomp-son and nearly all of our historians, he is designated as "Younger Hope," the "Younger" being probably derived from "Joncker," which means young mister or junior, but how "Vosch" or "de Vosch" became transformed into "Hope" is not so easily explained, especially when the English of the Dutch word "Vos" is "Fox." Jan. 16, 1665, he bought of Claes Claesen (Smit) a plantation in N. U., be-tween that of Jacob Swart and that of Albert Albertse (Ter-hune). He removed from N. U. to Fld^a, where he resided Dec. 6, 1669, at which date he bought of Ferdinandus Van Sicke-len a parcel of land with the improvements in G^d, as per G^d rec. From Fld^a he appears to have returned to the Nether-lands in embarrassed circumstances, a farm which he

owned in Fl[b] being sold after his departure to pay his debts.
Signed his name "*B Vosch.*"

Hans, on Stoothoff's and Hegeman's books of 1670. There
was a Hans Vos in Albany in 1642 and '61, as per Pearson's
early rec. of that place; and a Hans de Vos who m. Geertje
Seltens and had a dau. Mary bp. Sept. 24, 1659, in N. A.
Made his mark to documents.

VREDERICKSZ or VREDENKSZ, JAN, a mem. of the consistory of one of the Kings Co. churches in 1685. Made his
mark to documents.

VRIANSE, BARNE, with others conveyed May 1, 1697, to
Gerrit Coerte (Voorhees) 26 A. in Fld[s], as per p. 134 of Lib.
2 of Con.

VROOM, CORNELIS PIETERSE (sup. of Br[n]), m. *Tryntje Hen-
dricks,* who after his death m. 2[d], Aug. 17, 1657, Frederick
Lubbertse of Br[n]; d. prior to 1657.   Resided at one period
in N. A., where his children were all bp.   Issue:—Cornelis
Corsen, bp. 1645; Pieter Corsen, bp. Mar. 5, 1651; Hendrick
Corsen, bp. Nov. 30, 1653—all in N. A.; and Catherine Cor-
sen, m. Jan Stats or Stals.   A Catharine Corsen Vroom m.
Jan. 4, 1700-1, in N. Y., Johan Boutier.

Cornelis Corssen of Br[n], bp. Apl. 23, 1645, in N. A.; m. Mar.
11, 1666, Marretje Jacobse Vander Grift of Br[n]; d. 1693.   On
ass. rolls of Br[n] of 1675 and '76; constable 1677, and mem.
of the R. D. ch. hailing from the Walabocht.   Left Br[n] and
removed to S. I., where he obtained title to 352 A. to the W.
of Miles Creek on the 24th of Dec., 1680; and also for 180
A. on said island on the 28th of said month.   In 1684 he was
appointed a justice of the peace for Richmond Co., as per
p. 132 of Cal. of English Man.; Apl. 2, 1685, he was appointed capt. of militia for Br[n], as per p. 137 of do.   In 1689 he
held the office of capt. of militia and justice of the peace on
S. I.   In 1681 he purchased land on the Raritan, N. J., at 3
cts. per A., as per p. 122 of 2[d] Edition of Whitehead's
E. N. J., and p. 103 of the Records of the Gov. and Council
of. E. N. J.   Will da. Dec. 9, 1692, and pro. Aug. 13, 1693.
Issue:—Jacob Corsen of S. I., m. Elizabeth ——; Cornelia
Corsen of S. I., bp. Aug. 13, 1681, m. Jannetje dau. of Peter
Van Boskerk; Christian Corsen of S. I.; Cornelius Corssen; and Daniel Corssen of S. I., bp. Nov. 28, 1690, in N. Y,
His descendants appear to have adopted Corssen or Corsen
as their family name, many of whom reside on S. I.   Signed
his name "*Cornelis Corssen.*"

Hendrick Corson of Br[n], bp. Nov. 30, 1653, in N. A.; m. 1st Josina Pieterse Van Nest of Br[n]; m. 2[d] Judith Rapalie. Mem. of R. D. ch. of Br[n] in 1677, hailing from the Wallabout, and on ass. rolls of Br[n] of 1683 and '93. Finally settled on the Raritan in the vicinity of New Brunswick, N. J., and is the ancestor of Gov. Vroom of said State. Issue:—Corson or Cornelius Vroom of the Raritan, bp. June 27, 1677, in N. Y.; Judith Vroom, bp. Mar. 16, 1679; (sup.) Rachel Vroom, m. Christoffel Van Zandt; Hendrick Vroom of the Raritan, bp. May 7 or 13, 1683, m. 1st Jannetje Bergen, m. 2[d] Dartie Demond; (sup.) Alfred Vroom; and Katryna Vroom, bp. Apl. 6, 1690—all of N. J.

Peter Corson of Br[n], bp. Mar. 5, 1651; m. Oct. 19, 1679, Katharine Vander Beek wid. of Daniel Richauco. Mem. of the R. D. ch. of Br[n] in 1677 and '85, hailing from the Wallabout. Resided at one period on S. I. County-clerk of Kings Co. in 1739, and removed to the city of N. Y. His father-in-law, Frederick Lubbertse, devised to him in his will a part of his South Br[n] farm, a part of which he sold Oct. 10, 1689, to Thomas Lambertse, administrator, as per p. 180 of Lib. 1 of Con., and the balance of 100 A. to Cor[s] Sebring, as per p. 162 of Lib. 2 of Con. Issue:—(sup.) Jacob, who had children Hester bp. Mar. 25, 1701, Jacob, bp. 1707, and Benjamin, bp. Apl. 1, 1709—all on S. I. Signed his name *"Peter Corson."*

VROOMAN, ADAM HENRDICKSE, of Schenectady, as attorney of his father, Oct. 21, 1677, bound his brother Bartholemew Vrooman, aged 18, to W[m] Huycken, tailor, of Gowanus, for 5 years to learn the tailor's trade, as per p. 15 of Lib. AA of Fl[h] rec. For an account of the Vroomans see Pearson's Early Settlers of Albany.

WAERNER, RAEFF or RALPH, with others petitioned Feb. 22, 1675, for a grant of land in Br[n] formerly of Charles Gabrie, as per p. 121 of Vol. 23 of English Man. Was a town officer of Br[n] in 1672, as per p. 8 of Cal. of Eng. Man.

WALDRON, DANIEL, (sup.) s. of Resolvert, emigrated in 1652 from Amsterdam; m. Oct. 11, 1673, *Sara Rutgers* from Wesop; joined the R. D. ch. of N. Y. in that year, and took the oath of allegiance in Br[n] in 1687, to which place he had removed. Issue:—Joseph, bp. July 29, 1674; Judith, bp. Dec. 22, 1675; Rutger, bp. Oct. 24, 1677; Annetje, bp. July 7, 1680; Sara, bp. May 5, 1683; Jan, bp. Jan. 20, 1685; Maria, bp. July 25, 1686; Cornelia, bp. Feb. 1, 1688; and Catharine, bp. Sept. 29, 1689—all in N. Y.

WALL, WATER or WALTER (sup. English), among the
early settlers of G^d, where he was granted a plantation-lot
Aug. 10, 1645, as per G^d rec. Sept. 22, 1654, he bought of
"Enum Benum" plantation-lot No. 14; and Nov. 9, 1658,
he bought of Wm Smith of Hempstead plantation-lot No. 1
in said town, all as per G^d rec. A Mary Wall, either his
dau. or sister, appears to have been in service with Nathaniel Brittan, who in an agreement with Water promised to
give said Mary at the end of her term of service 2 suits of
clothes and a cow calfe, as per G^d rec. Removed to E. N. J.,
where his descendants reside, one of whom, Garret D. Wall,
was Governor of the State. Issue:—Rutgert, bp. July 25,
1651, in N. A., aged 4 years; and Maria, bp. at the same
time, aged three fourths of a year. Made his mark to documents. A Walter Wall, aged 16, was transported to St.
Christopher's in 1635, as per p. 126 of Hotten's Lists of Emigrants.

WANDEL, CORNELIS, plaintiff in a suit against Jan Cornelise, Jan. 21, 1660, as per Lib. B of Fl^h court rec.

WANSHAER, ANTONY, cooper, m. June 8, 1681, *Maritje
Herberts* or *Hubbard* of Fld^s; mem. of Fld^s D. ch. in
1677. Aug. 16, 1680, he bought of Jan Woutersz a lot and
orchard in Fl^h, as per p. 131 of Lib. AA of Fl^h rec. Mar. 4,
1683-4, he sold to "John Ritcherson" his house and lot in
Fl^h, as per p. 157 of Lib. C of Fl^h rec. In 1698 he sold lands
in Fld^s to Stoffel Langestraet and others, as per p. 180 of
Lib. 2 of Con. Issue:—Catharine, bp. Apl. 22, 1682; Jan,
bp. Nov. 11, 1684, at N. U.; and Abraham, bp. Apl. 1, 1696,
in N. Y. Signed his name *"Antony Wanshaer."*

WANTENAER, ALBERT CORNELYSEN, of Br^n, (or Albert Cornelise, the glovemaker,) emigrated from Vechten in the
province of Utrecht in 1642, residing at first in N. A., where
he learned the trade of a wheel-wright. He m. *Tryntje
Harders* wid. of Huyck Aertsen Van Rossum, and finally
settled in Br^n, of which place he was a mag. in 1654, '55,
'56, '57, '63, and '64, and on the patent of said place of 1667.
June 21, 1677, he obtained in his own name a confirmatory
patent for Van Rossum's farm in Br^n, a few years ago
known as the Powers farm, which he occupied and afterwards sold to Michael Hansen Bergen. Signed his name
"Albert Cornelysen Wantenaer."

WARTONN or NEWTOUN, THOMAS, on petition of May

1664, for a canal at Red Hoek, Br^a, as per p. 68 of Vol. 1 of Stiles's Br^a.

WASHBURNE, WILLIAM, of Br^a, Oct. 16, 1646, as per Col. Man.

WATERMAN, RAEF, on Stoothoff's and Hegeman's books of 1670.

WATSON, NATHANIEL (sup. English), on lists of inhabitants of G^d in 1650, as per town rec., where he appears to have owned salt-meadows. Apl. 21, 1651, he bought of Edmond Audley his house and plantation in said town, as per town rec. Made his mark " W " to documents.

WEBBER, WOLFERT, brought a suit Feb. 16, 1654, against Albert Albertsen (Terhune) for services of his son hired by Albert for 2 years. Was a carman in N. A. in 1673, and a mag. of Haerlem in 1674. There was a Wolfert Webber Junr on the Delaware in 1662, as per p. 381 of Vol. XII. of Doc. His. of N. Y.; and a Wolfert Webber who had 9 childred bp. in N. Y. from 1698 to 1717, as per p. 834 of Valentine's Manual of 1864.

WEEKS, FRANCIS (sup. English), among the early settlers of G^d and granted a plantation-lot there Aug. 10, 1648, as per town rec. At the same date the town offered a reward of 3 gl. for every wolf, and 2 gl. for every fox killed within its bounds. Jan 1, 1655, *Elisabeth* his w., as his attorney, sold plantation-lot No. 12 to John Applegate, as per G^d rec. Made his mark " W " to documents.

WEERMAN, ARADUS, a surgeon or physician in 1687, as per Fl^h rec.

WENTWORTH, see Windtwordt.

WERTZE, JAN, one of the soldiers sent from Kings Co. to Albany in 1689, as per p. 216 of Vol. II. of Doc. His. of N. Y.

WESH, JAN, of Fld^s in 1700, as per town rec., in which year he signed his name "*Jan Wesh.*"

WESSELL, LAURENS, of G^d in 1656, as per Thompson's L. I.

25

WESSELS, ABRAHAM, see Westervelt.

Cornelis, farmer of excise of Kings Co. Dec. 10, 1654.

Warnaer, farmer of excise (as per p. 58 of Cal. of N. Y.
Dutch Man.) on wine and beer retailed in N. A., Brⁿ, Fl^h,
and· Fld^s, Dec. 1, 1654 and '55.   In 1665 was licensed to keep
a taphouse in N. Y.   He m. Anna Elizabeth Maskop or
Masschop.   Issue:—Gerardus, bp. Apl. 8, 1657; Geertruy,
bp. Mar. 31, 1659; Maria, bp. Oct. 24, 1660; and Christina,
bp. Mar. 5, 1662—all bp. in N. A.   Signed his name "*Warnaer Wessels.*"   There was a Dirck Wesselse among the
early settlers of Dutchess Co.

WEST, JOHN, a lawyer, emigrated from England; m. *Ann
Rudyard.* Clerk of Kings Co. from 1671 to '82, and at one
period clerk of the city of N. Y.   Appointed sheriff for the
East Riding of L. I. in 1681, as per p. 96 of Cal. of Eng.
Man.   Returned to England in disgrace in 1690.   His wid.
after his death m. Robert Wharton.

William, (English,) on ass. roll of Bu^k of 1693, cen. of 1698,
and constable in 1697, as per court rec.

WESTERBROOK, ANTHONY JANSEN, bought Oct. 27, 1661, of
Tielman Van Vleeck and Claes Gangeloff Villet, orphan-
master of N. A., in charge of the estate of Nicholas Volthuysen, a parcel of land in Fl^h on the E. side of the road,
cong. 18 morgens, with plain and meadow land abutting on
Canarisie flats or plains, with 2 small house-plots, as per p.
109 of Lib. A of Fl^h rec.   The name in the deed is simply
Anthony Jansen, by which name he is generally designated
on the Fl^h rec.   This land he conveyed Mar. 20, 1670, to
Wil and Thomas Willets, and by them was conveyed in
1677 to Cornelis Janse Vanderveer.   Signed his name "*Anthony Jansen.*"

WESTERHOUT, JEREMIAH JANSEN, see Van Westerhout.

WESTERVELT, see Van Westervelt.

WHITE, THOMAS, of Brⁿ, and *Elizabeth* his w. mortgaged
a lot in said town between the lot of Randolph Evans and
that of Hendrick Steght, as per p. 26 of Lib. 1 of Con.

William of G^d, m. Aug. 28, 1669, by Justice Hubbard,
to Katharine Downs of Maryland.

WHITEHEAD, see Whyteheade.

WHITLOCK or WITLOCK, THOMAS, of G^d, (sup. English,) where he bought of Nicholas Stillwell plantation-lot No. 29. Aug. 26, 1655, *Mary* his w., as his attorney, sold George Balden a parcel of land with buildings in G^d, as per town rec. He removed to Monmouth Co., N. J., where he obtained 200 A. in Middletown in 1684, as per p. 111 of Rec. of Gov. and Council of E. N. J., and where he was appointed ensign by Gov. Colve in 1673, as per p. 608 of Vol. II. of Doc. of Col. His. of N. Y. Made his mark " T W " to documents. A Thomas Whitlock of Shoal Harbor, N. J., made a will, da. Nov. 1, 1700, and had children William, John, Susanna, Sarah, Abagail, and Rebecca. A Wm Whitlock, ag. 31, transported to Barbadoes in 1635, as per p. 50 of Hotten's Emigrants.

WHITMAN, NATHAN, (sup. English,) tailor, of G^d in 1677, in Aug. of which year he sold to Bartholemew Appelgate plantation-lot No. 62, as per G^d rec. Signed his name *"Nathan Whitman."*

WHYTHEADE or WHITEHEAD, DANIEL, (sup. English,) d. about 1603; bought June 2, 1653, of Jan Hayes a house and lot at Br^a ferry, which he sold Oct. 18, 1683, to Cornelis Dircksen (Hoogland), as per pp. 378 and 379 of Cal. of Dutch Man. Was among the freeholders of Hempstead in 1647, and a mag. in 1652, as per p. 6 of Vol. II. of Thompson's L. I. and per p. 14 of Vol X. of Gen. and Bio. Rec Sept. 16, 1685, he was commissioned to be ranger-general on L. I., as per p. 140 of Cal. of Eng. Man.
David of G^d, where he made his mark to documents in 1685, as per G^d rec.

WIKLEY, EVERT, on ass. roll of Fl^h of 1693.

WILCOCK, referred to in Hans Hansen (Bergen's) patent of 1647. There was a Jan Wilcox in N. A. as early as 1644 as per p. 29 of Cal. of Dutch Man.

WILLEKES, WILLEKINS, or WILKESSEN, CLAES, emigrated in 1662, and took the oath of allegiance in Fl^h in 1687; on ass. roll of 1675; and Mar. 23, 1677-8, he let land in said town to Cornelis Berrian, as per p. 26 of Lib. AA of Fl^h rec.

WILLETT, THOMAS, of Flushing, (sup. English,) m. *Helen* or *Heiltie* dau. of Elbert Elbertse Stoothoff of Fld^s. He appears to have been on the Delaware in 1669, as per p. 469,

of Vol. XII. of Doc. of Col. His. of N. Y.   In 1688 a Thomas
Willet was high sheriff of Queens Co.   His name appears in
1695 as a grantor on several deeds disposing of his father-
in-law's property, as per p. 32 of Lib. 2 of Con.; also as the
owner of several tracts of land in G^d, as per town rec.   He
was probably a s. of Thomas Willet, the first mayor of the
city of N. Y., and an anti-Leislerian.   Issue:—Helena, bp.
May 27, 1681, in Fld^s; William; Thomas; Charles; Cornelis; Abraham; John; Sarah; Elizabeth; and (sup.) Elbert.
Signed his name "*Thomas Willett.*"

Wil or *William.*   Mar. 28, 1670, Anthony Jansen (Westerbrook) conveyed to him and Maj. Thomas Willett a farm
of 18 morgens, with plain and meadow land, in Fl^b, as per
p. 109 of Lib. A of Fl^b rec.

WILLIAMSE, WILLEMSE, or WILLIAMS, ABRAHAM, see Van
Westervelt.

Abraham, emigrated in 1662, and mem. of Fl^b D. ch. in
1677, where he took the oath of allegiance in 1687.   Made
his mark to documents.

Arie or *Adriaen,* see Bennet.

Claes, on ass. roll of Fl^b of 1676.   Hired himself Mar. 25,
1677-8, to Cornelis Berrian to perform all kinds of farm
labor for a year, for 540 gl., as per p. 26 of Lib. AA of Fl^b
rec.   Made his mark to documents.

Coenrad, see Barkeloo.

Cornelis and *Christiaan,* see Bennet.

Cornelis, on ass. roll of Fl^b of 1693, and a deacon of Fl^b
D. ch. in 1707.   Signed his name "*Cornelis Willemse.*"

Cornelis, bought Oct. 9, 1685, of Saml Spicer of G^d Nos.
30, 31, and 32 of the 15 A. allotments of G^d, with the right
of commonage on the beach and on Coney I., which premises he sold Mar. 23, 1686, to Symon Jansen (Van Aersdalen)
of the Little Flats, as per G^d rec.   Oct. 13, 1693, he was
chosen a fence-viewer of said town.

Daniel and *Dirk,* see Barkeloo.

Floris or *Floor,* see Krom.

Garret, see Cowenhoven.

Gerardus, see Beekman.

Guilliam or *William,* see Cornell.

Hendrick, see Bennet and Boerum.

Hendrick of Br^n, on petition of May 1664 for a canal at
Red Hoek, as per p. 68 of Vol. 1 of Stiles's Br^n.

Hendrick of Fl^b, m. Apl. 1667 Maria Adriaensz.   Bought
Dec. 1672 of Jan Jansen or Hansen, farmer, of N. U., a farm
in Fl^b.   On ass. roll of said town of 1675, and mem. of D.
ch. of Fl^b in 1677.   Made his mark to documents.

Isaac, see Bennet.

Jacob, a mem. of Fl[h] R. D. ch. in 1677, hailing from N. L. Suppose this to be Jacob Willemse Van Boerum.

Jacob or *Jacobus*, see Beekman, Bennet, and Boerum.

Jan, see Barkeloo, Bennet, Van Iselsteyn, and Vertien.

Jan, of Fl[h] in 1663. Made his mark to documents.

John, exchanged salt-meadows with Bartholemew Appelgate Mar. 31, 1661, as per G[d] rec.

Johannes, see Bennet.

Johannes, on ass. roll of Fl[h] of 1693 and cen. of 1698; also mem. of Fl[h] D. ch. in 1677. Signed his name "*Johannes Willemsen.*"

Johannes of Fld[s], m. Aug. 20, 1687, Magdalena Winants.

Johannes, emigrated in 1662; m. Aeltje Coerten (Voorhees); mem. of Fld[s] ch. in 1677. This is probably Johannes Willemse Cornel.

Johannes of G[d], had a s. Harman bp. May 14, 1681, in N. U.

Joores, on ass. roll of Fl[h] of 1693.

Nicholas (s. of W[m] Willemse and Mayke Pieterse Wyckoff) of G[d], b. 1680; m. Ida dau. of Jeremias Remsen. Issue:— Jeremias, bp. May 13, 1733, in N. U.; Nicholas, bp. May 13, 1733, in N. U.; Johannes, bp. Nov. 17, 1734, in N. U.; Rem of G[d], the ancestor of the present G[d] Williamsens, b. Apl. 18, 1738, m. Susan Basset; Cornelius, bp. July 15, 1739, in N. U.; (sup.) Stephen, m. Heiltje Van Wickkelen, and is probably the ancestor of the Fl[h] branch of the family; and (sup.) Antje, m. Joost Stillwell of G[d]. Made his mark to documents.

Pieter, on ass. roll of Bu[k] of 1693 and cen. of 1698.

Pieter, see Cornel.

Pieter, m. Catharine Kip. Issue:—William, bp. Sept. 10, 1697, in Br[n].

Pieter (s. of W[m] Willemse and Mayke Pieterse Wyckoff), of G[d], bp. Apl. 16, 1682; (sup.) m. Cornelia ——. Issue:— William, bp. June 5, 1717-18, in G[d]; Johannes, bp. July 13, 1718, in G[d], d. young; and Johannes, b. Jan. 1, 1721, who assumed the surname of Wyckoff to inherit the property of his great-uncle Hendrick Pieterse Wyckoff, and from whom is descended the Gowanus branch of the Wyckoff family and a portion of the G[d] and Fld[s] Wyckoffs. Signed his name "*Pyeter Willemsen.*"

Roelof from Beverwyck (Albany), m. Willemtien ——, and mem. of Br[n] D. ch. in 1663.

Roelof, m. Willemtje Tyson after 1663, who m. 2[d] Jan Cornelise Buys. Roelof d. prior to 1686. Issue:—Roelof; and Machteltje Roelofse.

Willem, emigrated in 1657, and took the oath of allegiance in G^d in 1687, where he settled. He m. Mayke Pieterse Wyckoff. On ass. roll of G^d of 1683 and cen. of 1698. Sold his G^d lands to his s. Nicholas for £600. Will da. (sup.) Dec. 1, 1721; pro. Sept. 19, 1722; rec. p. 288 of Lib. 9, N. Y. surr. off. Issue:—Nicholas of G^d, b. 1680; Peter, bp. Apl. 16, 1682; Willem Junr; Jacobus; Cornelis; Mary or Marretje, bp. Apl. 12, 1685, m. Ab^m Emans of G^d; and Anne, bp. May 29, 1695, m. John Griggs Junr of G^d. Signed his name "*Willem Willemsen*." It is probable that this William is the ancestor of the G^d, Fld^s, Fl^h, and N. L. Williamsens.

Willem Junr of G^d, (sup.) m. Catelyntje Gulick. Issue:— (sup.) Forem or Forme, bp. Sept. 18, 1709, in Fl^h. Signed his name "*Willem Willemsen*."

₁₂ *Willem*, of Fl^h in 1663; m. Jannetje Juriaansen (sup.) Probasco. Issue:—Jurrie or Juriaen, bp. Dec. 20, 1685; Cbarbar, bp. Jan. 9, 1687; Elsje, bp. Sept. 9, 1688—all in Fl^h; and Jan, bp. May 4, 1695. Signed his name "*Willem Willemsen*."

Willem of G^d, m. Nov. 9, 1678, by Justice Stillwell, Jane Nearson.

Willem, see Barkeloo, Bennet, Cowenhoven, and Van Engen.

WILLKINS, OBADIAH (s. of William), of G^d, (sup. English,) m. *Martha Wilkins*. In 1684 his children were allotted a plot in the N. woods of G^d, as per town rec. Apl. 13, 1698, William his s. and heir' confirmed a sale made by his dec. father to John Emans of plantation-lot No. 13, as per G^d rec. Signed his name "*Obadiah Willkins*."

William of G^d, of which place he was among the early settlers in 1646, where he was allotted a plantation-lot. He m. Dec. 29, 1672, Annetje dau. of Nicholas Stillwell, a wid. In 1698 his w. signed her name "*Alse Wilkins*," who may have been a 2^d w. He held in partnership with Bartholemew Appelgate a mill in G^d which, in consequence of their disputes, being allowed to get in disorder, the town was directed by the court of sessions to repair and use the same until the costs of the repairs were reimbursed, as per G^d rec. Suppose this mill to have been located on what was known as Hubbard's Creek. Was a mag. of G^d from 1650 to '65, as per town rec. Issue:—Obadiah. Made his mark "W" to documents.

WILSEE, TEUNIS, m. *Diertie* ——. Issue:—Geertruy, bp. Apl. 25, 1698, in Fl^h.

WILSON or WILLSON, GEORGE, a Quaker preacher in G^d in 1661, who probably afterwards settled in Middletown, N. J.

John, bought Jan. 20, 1659, of Wm Compton plantation-lot No. 25 in G^d; also Aug. 29, 1659, of Nich^s Stillwell plantation-lot No. 40, as per G^d rec. Made his mark to documents.

Willem, bought Nov. 20, 1676, of Ralph Cardell a house and plantation in G^d, as per town rec. Signed his name "*Willem Willson.*"

WINANTSE, see Wynantse.

WINDERWODT or WENTWORTH, JOHN, (English,) was shot in 1664 at the flats or plains in Amersfoort (Fld^s) by Thomas Mabs, a soldier, as per Col. Man.

WINTER, JACKSON, on ass. roll of Fl^h of 1675.

WITT, VOLKERT, took the oath of allegiance in Bu^k in 1687.

Peter Jansen, see De Witt.

WIZZELPENNING or WISSELPENNINGH, REYNIER, m. *Jannetje Snediker* of Fl^h, who m. after his death Pieter Cornelise Luyster; d. prior to 1670. In Jan. 1662 he and his w. joined the R. D. ch. of N. A. There was a Reynier Wisselpenningh, a carpenter, of Beverwyck (Albany) in 1654 and '61, who m. the wid. of Simon Root, said wid. dying prior to 1654, as per Pearson's First Settlers of Albany. These Reyniers were probably the same individual. (See p. 185 of Lib. D of Fl^h rec.) Issue:—Cornelia Reyniers, m. Jan Stevense Van Voorhees; Tjellitien Reyniers, m. Albert Stevense Van Voorhees; Geertje^L Reyniers, m. Hendrick Claesz Vechten; (sup.) Marytie Reyniers; (sup.) Gerritje^L Reyniers; (sup.) Teunis Reyniers, m. Margrietjen ——; (sup.) Auke Reyniers, m. Ida ——; (sup.) Mayke or Lientje Reyniers, m. Charles Fonteyn of Bu^k.

WODE or WOOD, JOHN, (sup. English.) Apl. 5, 1667, the constable and overseer of G^d on behalf of the inhabitants of said town entered into an agreement with him to attend as herder of their milch-cows and working oxen for 7 months for the sum of 350 gl., as per G^d rec.

WODT or WOOD, JOHN or JOHANNES, (sup. English,) hired Mar. 1640 Thomas Bescher's farm at Gowanus, and in 1641

sold to Ambrose Lonnen or London for 2000 gl. a plantation on the Bay of the North River on L. I., as per O'Callaghan's Trans. of Dutch Man. This may be a sale of his
lease of Bescher's farm.

WOERTMAN, DIRCK JANSE, emigrated from Amsterdam in
1647; m. 1st *Marretje Teunise Denyse;* m. 2d *Annetje Aukes,*
wid. of Winant Pieterse and dau. of Auke Janse Van Nuyse.
Settled in Brⁿ; mem. of the R. D. ch. of that town in 1661;
was a town officer in 1673; took the oath of allegiance there
in 1687; on ass. roll of 1693 and cen. of 1698. Oct. 10, 1706,
sold his Brⁿ lands, which covered several patents on the
East River S. of Fulton Ferry, to Jores Remsen his son-in-
law. Will da. Apl. 10, 1694. Issue:—Harmtje Dircksen,
bp. June 6, 1661, m. Thomas Coeck; Femmetje Dircksen,
m. Jores Remsen; Jan Dircksen; Geertruy Dircksen, m.
Gabriel Sprong; Tunis Dircksen; Paulus Dircksen; Denys
Dircksen, bp. July 28, 1678; Lysbeth Dircksen, bp. Apl. 4,
1681; Annetje Dircksen, bp. June 15, 1684; Marretje Dircksen, bp. Nov. 21, 1686; Peter Dircksen; Ludewick Dircksen;
Barentje Dircksen; and (sup.) Andrias Dircksen, who settled at New Brunswick, N. J., prior to 1699, as per Messler's
Somerset Co. Signed his name "*Dierck Janssen Woertman.*"

Denyse Dircksen, bp. July 28, 1678; m. May 24, 1702, in
N. Y., Margaret Beekman of said city. Probably left Brⁿ
and settled in N. Y. Issue:—Maritie, bp. Feb. 10, 1703;
Antje, bp. Oct. 10, 1708; Samuel, bp. Sept. 30, 1711; and
Maria, bp. Jan. 4, 1718—all bp. in N. Y.

Jan Dircksen, m. Jan. 17, 1690, Anna Maria Andreas. On
ass. roll of Brⁿ of 1693 and cen. of 1698. Probably left Brⁿ
and settled on the Raritan, for there appears to have been
a John Woertman there in 1699, as per p. 34 of Messler's
Somerset Co. Issue:—Andreas, bp. Nov. 22, 1691; Dirck,
bp. Nov. 26, 1693; Jan Albertse Bout, bp. May 10, 1695; and
Peter, bp. Sept. 30, 1698—probably all of N. J. and all bp.
in Brⁿ.

Paulus Dircksen, emigrated in 1651, and took the oath of
allegiance in Brⁿ in 1687. He m. Rachel ——. Issue:—
Tammas, bp. Aug. 11, 1700, in Brⁿ. No further trace.

Tunis Dircksen of Buᵏ, farmer; m. Dec. 28, 1694, Cath-
arine Sprung. Resided on Noorman's Kil; on ass. roll of
Buᵏ of 1693 and cen. of 1698. In 1689 he was one of the
soldiers sent to Albany, as per p. 216 of Vol. II. of Doc. His.
of N. Y. Issue:—Marretje, bp. Dec. 17, 1697; Anneke, bp.
Sept. 7, 1698, in N. Y.; Lysbeth, bp. Mar. 10, 1700; and
Catryntje, bp. Apl. 18, 1704—all except Anneke bp. in
Brⁿ.

WOLF, CLAES, on muster-roll of Bu^k militia of 1663, and a mag. in 1664, as per Bu^k rec.

WOLF or WOLFMAN, DERICK, see De Wolf.

WOLFE, CHRISTIAN JACOBSEN, bought May 21, 1666, of Wm Jansen (Van Barkeloo) plantation-lot No. 34 in G^d, as per town rec. Made his mark to documents.

WOLFERSEN or WOLPHERSEN, see Cowenhoven.

WOLSPENDER, NICHOLAS, was paid for 25 plank used in the repairs of Fl^h D. ch. Oct. 27, 1666, as per book of minutes of town meetings, etc., of Fl^h.

WOLSY, JORIS, came to N. A. in 1647; m. Dec. 9, 1647, in N. A., *Rebecca Cornell.* Issue:—Sara, bp. Aug. 7, 1650; Joris, bp. Oct. 18, 1652; Rebecca, bp. Apl. 4, 1659; Johannes, bp. Jan. 16, 1661; Marritje, bp. Mar. 19, 1664—all at N. A.; and William and Marritje, bp. June 30, 1678, at Br^n, by which it may be inferred he resided there at that date. There was, as per p. 128 of Vol. IV. of the Genealogical Record, a George Woolsey, an English boy, b. in 1610, who had resided with his parents in Rotterdam, came over in a Dutch vessel with emigrants in 1623 and went to Plymouth, Mass., and in 1647 made his appearance in N. A. In 1648 he was a fire-warden in said city. In 1661 there was a George Woolsey among the freeholders of J^a, and in the beginning of the 18th century there were Woolseys, probably descendants of Joris or George, residing in Fld^a. Signed his name "*Joris Wolsy.*"

WOLWESEN, JACOB JANSE, on Hegeman's books of 1680.

WOOD, GEORGE, of Newtown, of which place he was among the patentees of 1686; bought May 9, 1695, of Derick Janse-Hoogland of Fl^h his interest in a parcel of land in Fl^h, as per p. 166 of Lib. 2 of Con.
*Johannes.*and *John,* see Wode or Wodt.

WOUTERS, JAN, of Fl^h, a master-shoemaker, b. 1638. Owned salt-meadows in Fl^h in 1667. July 2, 1678, he hired out his s. Ruth (Rutgert) Janse, ag. 8 years, to his brother-in-law Lourens Jurianse for 8 years to do all kinds of service proper for a lad; Jurianse to board, clothe, and send to evening school said lad, and at the end of the term to fur-

nish him with a good Sunday and every-day suit of gar-
ments of linen and woollen and also a milch-cow, as per p. 30
of Lib. AA of Fl[h] rec. Aug. 16, 1680, he sold to Anthony
Wansair a lot and orchard in Fl[h], as per p. 131 of Lib. AA
of Fl[h] rec. Mar. 1, 1694-5, Jan Wouters of N. Y., shoemaker, to which place he appears to have removed, sold to
Lammert Zichels, smith, a house and lot in Fl[h] on the E.
side of the highway, as per p. 204 of Lib. A of Fl[h] rec.
Signed his name "*Jan Wouters.*"

WOUTERSE, see Van Bosch and Van Pelt.
Jochem (Van Goede), b. 1637. Allotted a lot of salt-
meadows at Canarisie in 1666, as per Fl[h] rec. Resided in
the village of Fl[h] in 1670, and Nov. 13, 1683, sold a house
and lot in Fl[h] to Jan Aucke (Van Nuyse), as per p. 151 of
Lib. C of Fl[h] rec. Guardian of the minor children of Gerrit Snediker and Willemtje Vooks in 1669, as per p. 180 of
Lib. D of Fl[h] rec. Made his mark to documents.
Piere and others of Br[n] in 1663 applied for leave to form
a new village and for a grant of salt-meadows, as per p. 120
of Vol. I. of Stiles's Br[n].

WREW, KORNELIS, paid preacher's salary in 1680 in Fl[h],
as per town rec.

WYCKOFF, CLAES[z] or NICHOLAS PIETERSE, of Fld[s], m. *Sarah*
dau. of Pieter Monfoort ; elder in Fld[s] D. ch. in 1677 ; on ass.
rolls of said town of 1675, '76, '83, and '93 ; cen. of 1698 ; and
took the oath of allegiance there in 1687. Issue:—Nicholas,
bp. Feb. 16, 1679 ; Sara, bp. Feb. 27, 1681 ; Cornelius Claesen,
bp. Aug. 5, 1683, in Fld[s] ; (sup.) Antje, b. Aug. or Sept. 1, 1693,
m. Stephen Janse Schenck ; and Pieter Claesen, b. Mar. 28,
1704. Made his mark to documents.
Corneles[3]Claesen of N. J., bp. Aug. 5, 1683 ; m. May 13, 1708,
Adriaentje dau. of Cornelis Luyster of Newtown. Left Fld[s]
and settled at Middlebush, N. J., about 1715. Bought a tract
of 600 A. at Middlebush and one of 600 A. at Three Mile Run,
N. J. Was a deacon in Freehold D. ch. in 1715, and an elder
in 1719, '23, and '27. Issue—John ; Cornelis, who m. Catryntje
——— ; Peter ; Hendrick ; and Jacob—all of N. J. Signed his
name "*Corneles Wycof.*"
Cornelis Cornelise (s. of Cornelis Pieterse and Gertrude), bp.
Dec. 19, 1694, in N. Y. ; m. Sarah Duryea ; d. 1757. Left
N. L. and settled near Millstone, N. J. Will da. Sept. 11,
1756 ; pro. May 16, 1757 ; rec. on p. 425 of Lib. F in off. of
Sec. of State of N. J. Issue :—Peter, b. May 11, 1742, m. 1st
Sytie Cornell, m. 2[d] Jemima Veghte ; Catharine, b. Dec. 25,

1743; Jacobus, b. Aug. 4, 1748; and Willempie, b. Jan. 11, 1751, m. Sam[l] Terhune—all of N. J.

Cornelis [2]*Pieterse* of N. L., m. Oct. 13, 1678, Gertrude Simonse dau. of Simon Van Aersdalen; d. in 1706. Resided on and owned a farm in "Oostwoud" or New Lotts of 195 A., comprising wood-lots Nos. 30 and 31, with other lands, which he bought Mar. 15, 1678-9, of Symon Hansen (Van Noostrand) for 3600 gl., as per p. 69 of Lib. AA of Fl[h] rec. Mem. of Fl[h] D. ch. in 1677; on ass. rolls of Fl[h] of 1683 and '93 and cen. of 1698. In 1703 bought 1200 A. in Middlebush, Somerset Co., N. J., which he conveyed to his sons John, Peter, Jacob, and Simon. Will da. Apl. 4, 1736; pro. May 10, 1746; rec. p. 539, Lib. 15, N. Y. surr. off. Issue:—Peter Cornelise of N. J., bp. Sept. 14, 1679, in Br[n]; Mary or Maria, bp. Dec. 11, 1681, in Br[n], d. young; Simon Cornelise of N. J., bp. Nov. 23, 1683, in Fld[a]; Nicholas Cornelise of N. L.; Jacob Cornelise of N. J.; Hendrick Cornelise of N. L.; Charles Cornelise, of whom no further trace; John Cornelise of N. J.; Petronella, m. Jeremias Vanderbilt of Fl[b]; Margaret, m. Jonathan Forman of N. J.; Hannah; Cornelis Cornelise of Millstone, N. J., bp. Dec. 19, 1694; Marretje or Mary, bp. May 16, 1701; and Martin Cornelise of Redington, N. J. Signed his name *"Corneles Wycof."*

Garret [2]*Pieterse* of Fld[a], m. Catharine dau. of Johannes Nevius; d. prior to 1708. On ass. rolls of Fld[a] of 1675 and '93; cen. of 1698; and took the oath of allegiance there in 1687. Will da. Oct. 9, 1704; pro. June 12, 1707. Issue:—Peter G. of Fld[a], m. Rensie dau. of Martin Schenck; Gretie, m. Coert Van Voorhees; Adrianna, m. John Van Nuyse; Antje, (sup.) b. Sept. 1, 1693, m. Minne Lucasse Voorhees; Maryke, m. Roelof Terhune; Jonica; and Garret G. of N. J.

Garret G. of N. J., m. Aeltie Gerretse. Left Fld[a] and settled in N. J., and in 1731 was a mem. of Freehold D. ch. Issue :— Samuel, bp. Oct. 19, 1732; Petrus, bp. Mar. 31, 1734; and Garret, who m. Patience Williamson—all of N. J.

Hendrick [3]*Cornelise* of N. L., m. Annatie ——; d. in 1747. Owned and occupied what is known as the Sheriff John Wyckoff farm in N. L. Will da. Oct. 31, 1746; pro. Apl. 3, 1747; rec. p. 94, Lib. 16, N. Y. surr. off. Issue:—John, a merchant of N. Y., m. Mary Nostrand; Femitie, bp. Jan. 5 or 11, 1728, m. her cousin Cornelius Wyckoff; Geertje, bp. Nov. 7, 1730, m. Derick Brinckerhoff; Antie, bp. Feb. 3, 1733-4, d. young; and Hendrick, b. Jan. 18, 1736. Signed his name *"Henderick Wickof."*

Hendrick [2]*Pieterse* of Fld[a], m. 1st Geertie ——; m. 2[d] Helena ——; d. Dec. 6, 1744. On ass. rolls of Fld[a] of 1675, '76, and '93; mem. of the R. D. ch. of said town in 1677; on cen. of

1698; and took the oath of allegiance there in 1687. Had no issue. By his will (da. July 25, 1741; pro. Dec. 29, 1744; rec. p. 312, Lib. 15, N. Y. surr. off.) he devised his property in Fld⁸ to Johannes Willemse (a grandson of his sister Mayke or Maria, who m. Willem Willemse of G^d), on condition that he assumed the surname of Wyckoff, which condition he complied with. Signed his name "*Heyndrick Pitters*."

Jacob²Cornelise of N. L. and N. J., m. Oct. 16, 1706, Lammetje or Willemtje Johnse Stryker. Settled on the Raritan about 1707; was a mem. of Freehold D. ch. at its organization in 1709, and a mem. of the R. D. ch. of Six Mile Run in 1720. Will. da Sept. 18, 1719; pro. May 2, 1720; rec. p. 169 of Lib. A in off. of Sec. of State of N. J. Issue:—Styntje, bp. Sept. 14, 1707; Nicholas of Reading; Sara, bp. Mar. 4, 1711, (sup.) m. Carel Eckman of Freehold; Femmetje, bp. June 14, 1713, (sup.) m. Joseph Van Dorn; Jacobus, bp. Nov. 6, 1715, m. Frances ——; and Peter, bp. Feb. 9, 1719—all of N. J.

Jan Cornelise of N. L. and N. J., m. 1ˢᵗ, Oct. 11, 1709, Geertje Stryker of Fld⁸; m. 2^d, Oct. 25, 1712, Neeltje Schenck of Fld⁸; m. 3^d, in 1726, Adrianna dau. of Dominie Lupardus. Said to have bought 300 A. of his father's N. J. lands at Middlebush, on which he settled. There was a John Wyckoff in N. J. as early as 1707 and elder in Freehold D. ch. in 1709, as per p. 19 of the Brick Church Memorial of Marlborough. Will da. Feb. 22, 1746; pro. Sept. 25, 1746; rec. p. 376 of Lib. D in off. of Sec. of State of N. J. Issue:—Cornelius, said to be the first child of European parentage born in Middlebush, m. Catalintje ——; John; Pieter, d. young; Jacob, m. Jannetje ——; Geertje; Neeltie; and Johanna—all of N. J.

Jan²Pieterse of Fld⁸ and N. J., b. Feb. 16, 1665; m. Neeltje dau. of Wm Kouwenhoven of Fld⁸. Mem. of D. ch. of Fld⁸ in 1677; deacon in 1693; on cen. of 1698; and took the oath of allegiance there in 1687. Removed to Monmouth Co., N. J., about 1702, selling his farm in Fld⁸ May 14 of that year to Cornelis Coerte (Voorhees), as per Lib. 2 of Kings Co. reg. off. Mem. of Freehold D. ch. in 1709. Issue:—Pieter, bp. June 5, 1695, d. young; Pieter of Fld⁸, bp. Apl. 23, 1704, in N. Y., the ancestor of the Newtown branch of the family; (sup.) Cornelius, bp. Apl. 4, 1711, in N. Y.; Johannes of N. J., bp. Dec. 16, 1711, at Freehold, N. J., m. Aeltie Barkeloo; and (sup.) William of Freehold, N. J., m. Angenietje dau. of Jacob Van Doorn.

Marten²Pieterse of G^d, m. 1ˢᵗ Femmetje Aukes (Van Nuyse); m. 2^d, May 17 or 27, 1683, Hannah Willemse of Fld⁸; (sup.) m. 3^d Jannetje ——; d. about 1699. Mem. of Fld⁸ D. ch. in 1677. Bought Aug. 13, 1683, of John Tilton Senr of G^d plantation-lot No. 19, with the buildings thereon, in G^d, as per town rec., being at the time a resident of Fld⁴, and on the ass. roll of that town of 1683. He probably removed to those premises, and took the oath of allegiance in G⁴ in 1687 as a native. Will da. Sept. 27, 1690; pro. Feb. 6, 1707; rec. p. 340, Lib. 7, N. Y. surr. off. Issue:—Grietje, bp. Mar. 30, 1684, m. Sam¹ Poling of G⁴; Marytie or Marritee, bp. Dec. 20, 1685, in Flᵇ, (sup.) m. Garret Garretse of N. J.; Anne or Hanna, bp. June 8, 1688, m. Sam¹ Hubbard of G⁴; Sarah, bp. Sept. 22, 1689, m. Dan¹ Tilton of Middletown, N. J.; Mayken, (sup.) m. Thomas Van Dyck of N. J.; Jannetie, m. Wᵐ Johnson of G⁴; Pieter, bp. May 29, 1695, in Brⁿ, d. young; and William, who also d. young. Signed his name "*Marten Pieterse.*"

Nicholas²Claese of Fld⁴ and N. J., bp. Feb. 16, 1679. On ass. roll of Fld⁴ of 1693. Settled on the Raritan near Three Mile Run as early as 1702. No further trace.

Nicholas³Cornelise of N. L., (sup.) m. Mattie Howard. Owned and occupied what is known as the Linnington farm in N. L. Issue:—John, b. Nov. 1, 1720, m. Nelly Wyckoff; Cornelius of N. L., b. May 10, 1722, m. Phebe Wyckoff; Nicholas of N. L. (the father of Sheriff John Wyckoff), b. Apl. 26, 1725, m. 1ˢᵗ Catharine Lefferts, m. 2ᵈ Aeltie Lefferts; Jacob of N. L.; and Hendrick of N. L., b. Apl. 14, 1733. Made his mark to documents.

Pieter¹Claess, the common ancestor of the Wyckoff family, emigrated from the Netherlands in 1636, and finally settled in Fld⁴; m. Grietje dau. of Hendrick Van Ness. Cultivated the bouwery of Director Petrus Stuyvesant in Fld⁴ in 1655, having previously in 1653 bought of Wolfert Gerritse Van Couwenhoven 29 morgens in said town, and in 1656 another tract of said Wolfert. Was a mag. of Fld⁴ in 1655, '62, and '63, on patents of 1667 and '86, and a mem. of Fld⁴ D. ch. in 1677. Issue:—Annetje Pieterse, (sup.) bp. Nov. 27, 1650, in N. A., (sup.) m. Roelif Martense Schenck; Mayken or Maria Pieterse, (sup.) bp. Oct. 17, 1653, in N. A., m. Willem Willemse of G⁴; Geertje Pieterse, m. Christoffel Janse Romeyn; Margrietje Pieterse, m. Matthias Adamse Brouwer; Claes or Nicholas Pieterse of Fld⁴; Cornelis Pieterse of N. L.; Hendrick Pieterse of Fld⁴; Garret Pieterse of Fld⁴; Martin Pieterse of G⁴; Pieter Pieterse of N. J.; Jan Pieterse of Fld⁴; and (sup.) Willemtje Pieterse. Made his mark to documents.

Pieter²Cornelise of N. L. and N. J., bp. Sept. 14, 1679; m. 1ˢᵗ, Sept. 5, 1719, Elizabeth dau. of Aert Van Pelt of N. U.; m. 2ᵈ Gertrude Romeyn; d. in the war of the Revolution. May 20, 1701, he bought of John Gysbertsen for £300 a tract of 104 A., called Strawberry Field, in Monmouth Co., N. J., as per p. 44 of Lib. I. of Con. in off. of Sec. of State

of N. J., to which he probably removed. He also bought a
farm at Middletown in said county, and was an elder in
Freehold D. ch. in 1709. Will da. Nov. 16, 1776; pro. Mar.
3, 1777. Issue:—Cornelius of New Brunswick; Nelly, m.
John Wyckoff of N. J.; Aert or Arthur, b. 1717, m. Elenor
or Nelly Cruser; Peter Junr; Elizabeth; Maria, m. Jacobus
Suydam; Gertrude, m. Frederick Van Liew; John C. of
Cranbury; Simon, b. 1738, m. Alche Van Dooren; Jacob,
m. Lena Crusen; and Jane—all of N. J.

Pieter G. (s. of Garret Pieterse) of Fld^s, m. May 23, 1723,
Rensie dau. of Martin Schenck, who after his death m.
Daniel Rapalje; d. Mar. 7, 1731. Will da. Mar. 7, 1731;
pro. Sept. 6, 1732; rec. p. 80, Lib. 12, N. Y. surr. off. Issue:—
Garret of Fld^s, b. Oct. 15, 1725, whose descendants reside
mainly in Fld^s; Martin, b. Apl. 12, 1729, d. young; and
Elizabeth, b. Aug. 15, 1731, m. Andrew Riker.

Pieter [2] *Pieterse* of Fld^s and N. J., m. Willemtje Schenck.
On ass. roll of Fld^s of 1693 and cen. of 1698. Removed to
Monmouth Co., N. J., about 1702; was a mem. of Free-
hold D. ch. at its organization in 1709, and an elder in 1713.
Issue:—Anna, bp. Feb. 18, 1711, m. Claes Johnson of N. J.;
and Cornelis, bp. Sept. 11, 1716—all at Freehold, N. J.
Signed his name *"Pieter Wychof."*

Symon [3] *Cornelise* of N. L. and N. J., bp. Nov. 23, 1683; m.
Elizabeth ——; d. Apl. 4, 1796. Purchased 2 large tracts
in Somerset Co. at Three Mile Run, to which he removed
previous to 1699. Elder in the R. D. ch. of New Brunswick
in 1734. Issue:—Gretie, m. 1st John Vliet Junr, m. 2^d John
Van Cleef Senr; Ghaerty, m. Ab^m Van Cleef; George, m.
Rebecca dau. of John Van Cleef Senr; Cornelia; Corne-
lius, m. Sophia Ten Eyck; Simon, (sup.) m. Grietje Vander
Vliet; and Denyse—all of N. J. Signed his name *"Symon
Wyckof."*

WYNANTSE or WINANTSE, WYNANT and PIETER, see Van
Eck.

WYNHARD, CORNELIS, emigrated in 1657 from Groningen
in the Netherlands; m. 1st *Catharine Pella;* m. 2^d, May 20,
1683, *Adriaentje Hendricks* wid. of Tys Jansen Van Pelt.
Mar. 15, 1674, Jan Spiegelaer was prosecuted by the fiscaal
for tapping rum contrary to law for Pieter Janse, drummer,
Dirck Jansen and "Cornelis Wynhardt," soldiers, when
fuddled. It was also charged that defendant's wife bit off
half of "Cornelis Wynhardt's" finger and cut 2 holes in his
head. Jan was found guilty, and sentenced not to allow
any strong liquor to be sold in his house for one year and

six weeks, and to pay costs of suit, as per p. 698 of Vol. II. of
Doc. of Col. His. Resided in N. U. in 1682, in which year he
was a mem. of the R. D. ch. of that place. On ass. roll of
N. U. of 1683; on Dongan's patent of 1686; and in 1687
took the oath of allegiance in Bu^k. Jan. 12, 1686-7, he sold
to Laurents Jansen the rear half of his land in N. U. adjoining land of Gysbert Tyson (Van Pelt) and that of said
Laurents Jansen. Issue:—Ann, who removed to Hackensack,
as per ch. rec.

WYNHOUTS, ARIAENTJE, of the Walebocht, m. May 12,
1693, in N. Y., *Jeuriaen Van den Berg*, both residents of
N. Y., as per N. Y. D. ch. rec.

YDESSE, TEUNIS, see Idesse.

YOLCX, ANNETJE HENDRICX, of Br^n, m. Oct. 9, 1692, at
S. I., *Mangel Janssen Noll* of N. Albany; the 1st a resident
of S. I. and the 2^d of N. Y., as per N. Y. D. ch. rec.

YOUNG, HANS, see Jongh.

YSEESTEIN, YSTEIN, or YSSELSTEIN, JAN WILLEMSE, among
the first settlers of Bu^k in 1661, and on muster-roll of the
militia of said town in 1663, as per Bu^k town rec.

ZEELAN, JAN, see Sely.

ZEEWIS, JOHN HORN, among the first settlers of Bu^k in
1661, as per Thompson's L. I.

ZEUW or SEUW, see De Seen.

ZWAAN, the negro, and Christine his w., of N. U. R. D.
ch. in 1680 (see Swaen Janse Van Luane).

INDEX.

INDEX.

CPSIA information can be obtained
at www.ICGtesting.com
Printed in the USA
BVHW040311110419
545246BV00008B/161/P